opulation, Area and Land Use

YO-ABD-865

ITY (per sq. mile)	AREA (in sq. miles) b	Arable & orchard	Permanent meadow & pasture	Forest & woodland	Waste, city areas etc.
3	42,000	13.5	5.3	44.4	36.8
1.1	35,000	—	0.6	95.0	4.4
0	95,000	n.a.	n.a.	4.3	n.a.
8.9	83,000	0.9	11.8	84.3	3.0
6	11,000	13.4	18.0	25.2	43.4
3	43,000	7.3	30.5	26.9	35.3
3	8,900	1.4	0.7	45.8	52.1
0	400	12.6	—	9.7	77.7
6	36,000	60.7	14.0	15.3	10.0
5.0	40,000	—	22.1	—	77.9
5	1,263,000	49.6	4.3	17.1	29.0
3	736,000	9.3	*	63.8	26.9
4	628,000	7.0	4.1	7.3	81.6
	172,000	16.7	9.5	4.3	69.5
3	27,000	18.0	49.0	2.8	30.2
	8,000	19.9	33.9	4.6	41.6
	116,000	50.8	17.1	20.2	11.9
	124,000	6.4	n.a.	74.4	n.a.
	4,400	21.1	23.4	19.2	36.3
	143,000	16.2	2.6	68.7	12.5
	37,000	11.6	2.2	0.7	85.5
	220,000	2.9	6.7	2.9	85.5
	47,000	15.7	n.a.	74.4	n.a.
	38,000	22.9	0.2	67.1	9.8
	5,800	—	—	n.a.	n.a.
	90,000	3.4	3.4	59.3	33.9
	3,400	28.5	1.0	9.1	61.4
	418	43.0	12.0	13.0	32.0
	12,000	11.7	82.2	—	6.1
	43,000	34.5	2.2	32.5	30.8
.8	679,000	1.9	8.0	0.2	89.9
	62	12.5	43.7	25.0	18.8
	1,000	26.7	24.7	33.2	15.4
	230,000	4.9	52.0	21.7	21.4
	37,000	10.7	3.4	8.8	77.1
	128,000	18.9	n.a.	65.7	n.a.
	115	n.a.	n.a.	n.a.	n.a.
5	465,000	1	n.a.	3.8	n.a.
	121	50.0	—	—	50.0
	420	29.1	18.2	24.5	28.2
.7	419,000	0.2	36.2	13.9	79.7
	720	50.6	16.1	21.5	11.8
	760,000	12.1	40.1	22.1	25.7
0	604,000	2.3	n.a.	16.3	n.a.
	171,000	17.7	17.2	12.0	53.1
	298,000	3.4	56.2	24.8	15.6
	54,000	13.0	14.2	32.2	40.6
	13,000	28.8	38.3	8.6	24.3
3	7,330	4.3	21.4	14.5	59.8
5	184,000	0.6	—	n.a.	n.a.
	104,000	3.0	47.8	23.2	26.0
	57,000	6.2	6.6	46.2	41.1
5	459,000	11.8	2.3	12.3	73.6
	357,000	23.6	n.a.	34.2	n.a.
	125,000	2.6	0.5	21.7	75.2
9	82,000	n.a.	n.a.	n.a.	n.a.
4	310,403	17.6		1.6	78.5

COUNTRIES	POPULATION (to nearest thousand) a	DENSITY (per sq. mile) a÷b	AREA (in sq. miles) b	Arable & orchard	Permanent meadow & pasture	Forest & woodland	Waste, city areas etc.
Panama	1,417,000	49	29,000	7.5	11.0	80.5	1.0
Paraguay	2,303,000	14.6	157,000	2.2	24.3	51.0	22.5
Peru	13,172,000	27	496,000	2.0	21.7	67.7	8.6
Philippines	37,158,000	520	116,000	26.4	11.0	41.2	21.4
Poland	32,555,000	274	120,000	50.3	13.7	25.8	10.2
Portugal	9,560,000	281	34,000	49.2	6.0	28.1	16.7
Portuguese Guinea	530,000	37	14,000	7.3	n.a.	6.3	n.a.
Puerto Rico (U.S.)	2,754,000	800	3,400	30.4	35.3	13.3	21.0
Qatar	100,000	250	4,000	n.a.	n.a.	—	n.a.
Réunion (Fr.)	436,000	448	970	24.7	8.0	38.2	29.1
Rhodesia	5,090,000	33	150,000	4.7	12.5	60.0	22.8
Romania	20,101,000	218	92,000	44.1	18.2	26.8	10.9
Rwanda	3,500,000	350	10,000	37.8	33.0	5.9	23.3
São Tomé and Principe (Port.)	66,000	186	372	31.3	n.a.	—	n.a.
Sa'udi Arabia	7,200,000	7.8	927,000	0.2	37.7	0.8	61.3
Senegal	3,780,000	49	76,000	28.0	n.a.	27.1	n.a.
Seychelles (Br.)	51,000	318	160	42.1	1.0	12.4	44.5
Sierre Leone	2,512,000	87	28,000	51.1	30.7	4.2	14.0
Singapore	2,017,000	9,000	244	22.4	—	20.7	56.9
Somali Rep.	2,730,000	11	246,000	1.5	32.3	22.6	43.6
South Africa	19,618,000	41	472,000	9.9	74.0	1.3	14.8
South-West Africa	615,000	1.9	318,000	0.8	64.2	6.4	28.6
Spain	32,949,000	167	195,000	40.8	28.1	23.0	8.1
Spanish North Africa	164,000	13,666	12	n.a.	n.a.	n.a.	n.a.
Spanish Sahara	63,000	0.6	105,000	n.a.	7.5	n.a.	n.a.
Sudan	15,186,000	15	967,000	2.8	9.6	36.5	51.1
Surinam (Neth.)	389,000	7.1	55,000	0.3	—	45.0	19.9
Swaziland	410,000	61	6,700	14.5	73.4	7.4	4.7
Sweden	7,978,000	46	173,260	7.1	1.2	50.0	41.7
Switzerland	6,230,000	389	16,000	16.2	42.2	23.8	23.8
Syria	5,866,000	81	72,000	35.9	33.0	2.4	28.7
Taiwan	13,800,000	985	14,000	24.7	n.a.	70.9	n.a.
Tanzania	12,926,000	32	362,000	12.7	36.9	37.6	12.8
Thailand	34,738,000	175	198,000	21.9	—	52.8	25.3
Togo	1,815,000	86	21,000	38.2	3.5	9.4	48.9
Trinidad and Tobago	1,040,000	515	1,980	34.1	1.0	45.0	19.9
Trucial States	135,000	4.2	32,000	n.a.	n.a.	n.a.	n.a.
Tunisia	5,027,000	79	63,362	34.6	45.2	6.7	13.5
Turkey	34,375,000	114	296,000	33.5	36.2	13.5	16.8
Uganda	9,500,000	102	93,981	16.0	n.a.	7.0	n.a.
Union of Soviet Socialist Republics	240,000,000	27	8,648,000	10.3	16.6	40.6	32.5
United Kingdom	55,534,000	620	89,736	30.7	49.7	7.4	12.2
United States of America	203,216,000	57	3,554,000	19.8	27.4	32.2	20.6
Upper Volta	5,278,000	49	106,000	17.9	n.a.	7.3	n.a.
Uruguay	2,852,000	37	72,000	12.0	74.1	3.2	10.7
Venezuela	10,035,000	28	352,000	5.7	18.3	52.6	23.4
Viet-Nam, North	21,340,000	340	63,000	12.7	n.a.	49.8	n.a.
Viet-Nam, South	17,867,000	272	66,000	17.2	16.8	32.8	33.2
Windward Is.	384,000	464	826	33.9	3.0	36.2	26.9
Yemen A. R.	5,000,000	67	75,000	n.a.	n.a.	0.8	n.a.
Yemen, P. D. R.	1,220,000	20	62,000	6.9	31.3	8.9	58.9
Yugoslavia	20,000,000	204	99,000	32.5	25.2	34.4	7.9
Zaire (Kinshasa)	17,100,000	18	906,000	20.9	1.0	42.7	35.4
Zambia	4,208,000	14	290,000	2.6	43.8	50.0	3.6

centages are calculated from figures given in the *FAO Year Book*.   They do not necessarily total 100 per cent.   Water is included as waste land.

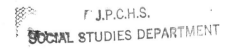
J.P.C.H.S.
SOCIAL STUDIES DEPARTMENT

The Canadian Oxford School Atlas

Third Edition

Oxford University Press
70 Wynford Drive
Don Mills (Toronto), Ontario

First Edition 1957
Second Edition 1963
Third Edition 1972

23456789101112 – 98765432

Printed in Canada by
The Bryant Press Limited

ISBN 0-19-540195-6

Prepared by
The Cartographic Department
of the Clarendon Press

Advisory Editor
E. G. Pleva
Professor of Geography
University of Western Ontario

Assisted by
Spencer Inch
Associate Professor of Geography
University of Western Ontario

Geography Consultant for
Oxford University Press (Canadian Branch)
Quentin Stanford

© Oxford University Press (Canadian Branch) 1972

Contents

COUNTRIES OF THE WORLD
Statistics on Population, Area, & Land Use   Front endpapers

CANADA
Statistics on Population, Production, & Trade   v

EXPLORERS   xxiv

Title	Representative fraction (R/f) (approx.)	Miles per inch (approx.)	Page
The Arctic	1:25,000,000	400	1

Canada

Title	Representative fraction (R/f) (approx.)	Miles per inch (approx.)	Page
Canada	1:19,000,000	300	2-3
Canada–Population	1:24,000,000	375	4
Canada–Communications	"	375	5
Canada–Vegetation	"	375	6
Canada–Climatic Regions	"	375	7
Canada–Soils	"	375	8
Canada–Agriculture & Forestry	"	375	9
Canada–Geology	"	375	10
Inset: Physiographic Regions			
Canada–Minerals & Industry	"	375	11
Eastern Canada*	1:8,000,000	125	12-13
Atlantic Provinces*	1:5,000,000	80	14-15
Inset: N.S., P.E.I., South N.B.	1:3,150,000	50	
Ontario*	1:8,000,000	125	16-17
Central Canada	1:3,150,000	50	18-19
Lake Ontario & Upper St. Lawrence	1:1,500,000	24	20-1
Insets: Land use–Toronto, Montreal	1:380,160	6	
Western Provinces*	1:8,000,000	125	22-3
Prairie Provinces*	1:5,000,000	80	24-5
British Columbia (South)*	1:5,000,000	80	26-7
Insets: Southwestern B.C.	1:2,500,000	40	
Environs Vancouver	1:1,000,000	16	
Northwest Territories & Yukon*	1:8,000,000	125	28-9
Environs: Calgary, Edmonton, Regina, Winnipeg, Ottawa, Québec, Halifax, St. John's	1:1,000,000	16	30

North & South America

Title	Representative fraction (R/f) (approx.)	Miles per inch (approx.)	Page
Environs: Detroit, Boston, New York, Chicago, Houston	1:1,000,000	16	31
Physical	1:44,000,000	700	32-3
Inset: Build			
Vegetation	1:44,000,000	700	34-5
Inset: Annual Rainfall			
Population & Communications	1:44,000,000	700	36-7
Inset: Agriculture			
United States & Central America	1:19,000,000	300	38-9
Inset: Panama Canal	1:1,500,000	24	

*These maps include panels with area, communications, population, and production statistics for each province and for the Territories.

Title	Representative fraction (R/f) (approx.)	Miles per inch (approx.)	Page
Eastern United States	1:8,000,000	125	40-
Western United States	1:8,000,000	125	42-
N.E. United States	1:1,900,000	30	44-
California	1:6,300,000	100	4
Insets: Environs–San Francisco, Los Angeles	1:1,000,000	16	
The Caribbean	1:12,500,000	200	4
South America	1:25,000,000	400	48-
Central South America	1:8,000,000	125	5
Insets: Environs–Rio de Janeiro, Buenos Aires	1:1,000,000	16	
The Antarctic	1:25,000,000	400	5
The Atlantic Ocean	1:63,000,000	1,000	5

British Isles

Title	Representative fraction (R/f) (approx.)	Miles per inch (approx.)	Page
General	1:4,750,000	75	5
Insets: Power, Population			
Great Britain	1:2,200,000	35	54
Insets: Central Scotland, North-East England	1:1,000,000	16	
Ireland	1:2,217,000	35	5
North & Central England; Thames Valley	1:1,000,000	16	5

Europe

Title	Representative fraction (R/f) (approx.)	Miles per inch (approx.)	Page
Physical	1:19,000,000	300	58
Insets: Build, Political			
Climate	1:19,000,000	300	
Population	1:19,000,000	300	
Europe & the Mediterranean	1:12,500,000	200	62
Western Europe	1:6,300,000	100	64
Inset: Environs–Paris	1:1,000,000	16	
Eastern Europe	1:6,300,000	100	66
Inset: Environs–Rome	1:1,000,000	16	
Scandinavia	1:6,300,000	100	68
Inset: Iceland	1:6,300,000	100	
France	1:3,150,000	50	70
Germany & the Alps	1:3,150,000	50	72

Asia

Title	Representative fraction (R/f) (approx.)	Miles per inch (approx.)	Page
Physical	1:44,000,000	700	7
Inset: Build			
Vegetation	1:44,000,000	700	7
Inset: Rainfall			
Population & Communications	1:44,000,000	700	7
Inset: Agriculture			
U.S.S.R.	1:25,000,000	400	8
Western U.S.S.R.	1:12,500,000	200	8
Inset: Environs–Moscow	1:1,000,000	16	
Middle East	1:12,500,000	200	8
Insets: Cairo to Beirut	1:4,000,000	64	
Environs–Cairo	1:1,000,000	16	
Middle East, Pakistan & India	1:19,000,000	300	8
India & Pakistan	1:12,500,000	200	
Inset: Monsoon Rainfall			
China	1:12,500,000	200	
Far East	1:19,000,000	300	9
Insets: Environs–Peking, Shanghai, Canton	1:1,000,000	16	
Japan	1:6,300,000	100	

Title	Representative fraction (R/f) (approx.)	Miles per inch (approx.)	Page
Australasia			
New Zealand	1:6,300,000	100	93
Australia & the Far East–Population & Communications	1:44,000,000	700	94
Inset: Australia & New Zealand–Agriculture			
Australia & New Zealand–Vegetation	1:44,000,000	700	95
Inset: Annual Rainfall			
Australia & New Zealand	1:44,000,000	700	
Inset: Build			
Australasia	1:22,000,000	350	96-7
Eastern Australia	1:6,300,000	100	98-9
Inset: South-West Australia			
The Pacific Ocean	1:63,000,000	1,000	100-1
Africa			
Physical	1:44,000,000	700	102-3
Insets: Build, Annual Rainfall			
Population & Communications	1:44,000,000	700	104
Inset: Agriculture			
Vegetation	1:44,000,000	700	105
Inset: Tsetse Fly			
North Africa	1:19,000,000	300	106-7
Southern Africa	1:19,000,000	300	108
South Africa	1:12,500,000	200	109
World			
Physical	1:100,000,000		110

Title	Representative fraction (R/f) (approx.)	Miles per inch (approx.)	Page
Build	1:100,000,000		111
Climatic Regions	1:100,000,000		112
Rainfall	1:100,000,000		113
Rainfall, Temperature, Pressure & Winds			114-15
Soils	1:100,000,000		116
Vegetation	1:100,000,000		117
Agriculture	1:100,000,000		118
Wheat; Maize; Rice	1:150,000,000		119
Cattle; Pigs, Sheep	1:150,000,000		120
Apples, Bananas; Citrus Fruits, Dates	1:150,000,000		121
Petroleum; Coal	1:150,000,000		122
Thermal Electricity; Hydro-Electricity	1:150,000,000		123
Iron Ore; Steel	1:150,000,000		124
Copper, Tin, Bauxite; Zinc, Lead	1:150,000,000		125
Shipbuilding; Motor Vehicles	1:150,000,000		126
Cotton; Wool	1:150,000,000		127
Population	1:65,000,000		128
ABBREVIATIONS			129
GAZETTEER OF CANADA			129
GAZETTEER OF THE WORLD			141

Metric Conversion Tables

Millimetres	Inches	Metres	Feet	Kilometres	Miles	Square Kilometres	Square Miles
1	0.04	1	3.28	1	0.62	1	0.39
2	0.08	2	6.56	2	1.24	2	0.77
3	0.12	3	9.84	3	1.86	3	1.16
4	0.16	4	13.12	4	2.49	4	1.54
5	0.2	5	16.4	5	3.11	5	1.93
6	0.24	6	19.69	6	3.73	6	2.32
7	0.28	7	22.97	7	4.35	7	2.7
8	0.32	8	26.25	8	4.97	8	3.09
9	0.35	9	29.53	9	5.59	9	3.48
10	0.39	10	32.81	10	6.21	10	3.86
100	3.94	100	328.08	100	62.14	100	38.61
1,000	39.37	1,000	3,280.8	1,000	621.37	1,000	386.1

Temperature Conversions

To convert degrees Fahrenheit (°F) to degrees Centigrade (or Celsius) (°C), subtract 32 from the degree Fahrenheit, multiply by 5, and divide by 9.

To convert degrees Centigrade (or Celsius) to degrees Fahrenheit, multiply the degree Centigrade by 9, divide by 5, and add 32.

Canada: Statistics on Population, Production & Trade

List of Tables

1. Land Area and Density of Population, 1951, 1956, 1961, 1966, and Estimate of April 1970 — vi
2. Distribution of the Population by Principal Ethnic Groups, 1941 and 1961 — vi
3. Country of Birth of the Population in 1941 and 1961 — vii
4. Population of Metropolitan Areas, 1966, and Estimate of June 1970 — vii
5. Percentage of Population in Urban Areas, 1851 to 1966 — vii
6. Factors in the Growth of Population, 1961 to 1966, and Vital Statistics Rates, 1930 to 1967 — viii
7. Average Size of Census-farms, 1931, 1941, 1951, 1961 and 1966 — ix
8. Census-farms – Population, Number, Use of Land, and Capital Value, 1931, 1951, 1961 and 1966 — ix
9. Acreages, Production, and Values of Field Crops by Province, 1945 to 1949 and 1963 to 1967 Averages — x
10. Number and Proportion of Commercial Farms Classified by Type of Farm, 1966 — xiii
11. Livestock on Farms, 1959 and 1969 — xiv
12. Value of Production of Principal Minerals, 1969 — xv
13. Quantity and Value of Sea and Inland Fish Landed, 1962 to 1968, and Persons Employed, 1968 — xvi
14. Lumber Production and Shipments and Value of all Shipments of the Sawmill and Planing Industry, 1968 — xvi
15. Pulp Production, 1964 and 1968 — xvii
16. Pulp Production: Exports and Imports by Leading Countries, 1967 — xvii
17. Estimated World Newsprint Production and Exports by Leading Countries, 1966 and 1968 — xvii
18. Electric Energy Generated, by Type of Station by Province, 1969 — xvii
The St. Lawrence Seaway (Note) — xviii
19. St. Lawrence Seaway: Type of Traffic, 1969 — xix
20. St. Lawrence Seaway Traffic Classified by Type of Cargo, 1966 and 1969 — xix
21. Principal Commodities in Water-Borne Cargo Loaded and Unloaded at Ports Handling the Largest Tonnages in 1968 — xx
22. Summary Statistics of the Twenty-five Leading Industries, 1968 — xxi
23. Value of Shipments of Goods of Own Manufacture, 1961 and 1968, and Employees in Manufacturing, 1968 — xxii
24. Exports by Commodities Valued over 100 Million Dollars, 1968 and 1970 — xxii
25. Imports by Commodities Valued over 100 Million Dollars, 1968 and 1970 — xxiii
26. Exports: Principal Nations — xxiii
27. Imports: Principal Nations — xxiii

1. Land Area and Density of Population, 1951, 1956, 1961, 1966, and Estimate of April 1970

PROVINCE OR TERRITORY	LAND AREA (sq. miles)	POPULATION 1951		POPULATION 1956		POPULATION 1961		POPULATION 1966		POPULATION ESTIMATE 1970	
		TOTAL	PER SQ. MILE	TOTAL	PER SQ. MILE	TOTAL	PER SQ. MILE	TOTAL	PER SQ. MILE	TOTAL ('000)	PER SQ. MILE
NEWFOUNDLAND (incl. Labrador)	143,045	361,416	2.53	415,074	2.90	457,853	3.20	493,396	3.45	517	3.6
PRINCE EDWARD ISLAND	2,184	98,429	45.07	99,285	45.46	104,629	47.91	108,535	49.70	109	49.9
NOVA SCOTIA	20,402	642,584	31.50	694,717	34.05	737,007	36.12	756,039	37.06	765	37.5
NEW BRUNSWICK	27,835	515,697	18.53	554,616	19.93	597,936	21.48	616,788	22.16	623	22.4
QUÉBEC	523,860	4,055,681	7.74	4,628,378	8.84	5,259,211	10.04	5,780,845	11.04	6,005	11.5
ONTARIO	344,092	4,597,542	13.36	5,404,933	15.71	6,236,092	18.12	6,960,870	20.23	7,611	22.1
MANITOBA	211,775	776,541	3.67	850,040	4.01	921,686	4.35	963,066	4.55	981	4.6
SASKATCHEWAN	220,182	831,728	3.78	880,665	4.00	925,181	4.20	955,344	4.34	943	4.3
ALBERTA	248,800	939,501	3.78	1,123,116	4.51	1,331,944	5.35	1,463,203	5.88	1,593	6.4
BRITISH COLUMBIA	359,279	1,165,210	3.24	1,398,464	3.89	1,629,082	4.53	1,873,674	5.22	2,128	5.9
YUKON TERRITORY	205,346	9,096	0.04	12,190	0.06	14,628	0.07	14,382	0.07	16	0.08
NORTHWEST TERRITORIES	1,253,438	16,004	0.01	19,313	0.02	22,998	0.02	28,738	0.02	33	0.03
CANADA	3,560,238	14,009,429	3.93	16,080,791	4.52	18,238,247	5.12	20,014,880	5.62	21,324	6.00

Source: *Canada Year Book 1970-71*, Dominion Bureau of Statistics, Ottawa, and *DBS Daily*, Thursday, June 3, 1971, Dominion Bureau of Statistics.

2. Distribution of the Population by Principal Ethnic Groups, 1941 and 1961

ETHNIC GROUP	1941[1]	1961	
British Isles	5,715,904	7,996,669	43.8
English	2,968,402	4,195,175	23.0
Irish	1,267,702	1,753,351	9.6
Scottish	1,403,974	1,902,302	10.4
Other	75,826	145,841	0.8
Other European	5,526,964	9,657,195	53.0
Austrian	37,715	106,535	0.6
Czech and Slovak	42,912	73,061	0.4
Danish	37,439	85,473	0.5
French	3,483,038	5,540,346	30.4
German	464,682	1,049,599	5.8
Hungarian	54,598	126,220	0.7
Italian	112,625	450,351	2.5
Jewish	170,241	173,344	1.0
Netherlands	212,863	429,679	2.4

ETHNIC GROUP	1941[1]	1961	
Norwegian	100,718	148,681	0.8
Polish	167,485	323,517	1.8
Russian	83,708	119,168	0.7
Swedish	85,396	121,757	0.7
Ukrainian	305,929	473,337	2.6
Yugoslavic	21,214	68,587	0.4
Other	136,614	279,350	2.0
Asiatic	74,064	121,753	0.7
Chinese	34,627	58,197	0.3
Japanese	23,149	29,157	0.2
Other	16,288	34,399	0.2
Other Origin	189,723	462,630	2.5
Native Indian and Eskimo	125,521	220,121	1.2
Other and not stated	64,202	242,509	1.4

[1]Excludes Newfoundland.

Source: *Canada Year Book 1970-71*, Dominion Bureau of Statistics, Ottawa.

3. Country of Birth of the Population in 1941 and 1961

COUNTRY	1941[1]	1961	
Canada	9,487,808	15,393,984	84.4
British Isles	960,125[2]	969,715	5.3
Other Commonwealth	43,644	47,887	0.3
Europe	653,705	1,468,058	8.0
Austria	50,713	70,192	0.4
Czechoslovakia	25,564	35,743	0.2
France	13,795	36,103	0.2
Germany	28,479	189,131	1.0
Greece	5,871	38,017	0.2
Hungary	31,813	72,900	0.4
Italy	40,432	258,071	1.4
Netherlands	9,923	135,033	0.7
Poland	155,400	171,467	0.9
Scandinavian countries[3]	72,473	74,616	0.4
U.S.S.R.	124,402	186,653	1.0
Yugoslavia	17,416	50,826	0.3
Other European	77,424	149,306	0.8
Asia	44,443	57,761	0.3
China	29,095	36,724	0.2
Other Asian	15,348	21,037	0.1
United States	312,473	283,908	1.6
Other Countries	3,512	16,934	0.1
Totals	11,506,656[4]	18,238,247	100.0

[1]Excludes Newfoundland. [2]Includes the Republic of Ireland.
[3]Includes Denmark, Iceland, Norway and Sweden.
[4]Includes persons whose birthplace was not stated.

Source: *Canada Year Book 1970-71*, Dominion Bureau of Statistics, Ottawa.

4. Population of Metropolitan Areas, 1966, and Estimate of June 1970

	1966	ESTIMATE 1970	% INCREASE[1] 1969-70
	(Thousands)		
CALGARY	331	387	3.2
EDMONTON	401	449	2.7
HALIFAX	198	204	0.0
HAMILTON	449	484	1.0
KITCHENER	192	210	2.4
LONDON	207	228	1.8
MONTRÉAL	2,437	2,570	0.7
OTTAWA	495	536	1.7
QUÉBEC	413	436	1.4
REGINA	131	141	0.7
SAINT JOHN	101	101	0.0
ST. JOHN'S	101	111	0.9
SASKATOON	116	128	− 0.8
SUDBURY	117	124	1.6
TORONTO	2,158	2,366	2.2
VANCOUVER	892	1,012	3.3
VICTORIA	173	189	2.7
WINDSOR	212	226	1.3
WINNIPEG	509	545	2.1
19 METROPOLITAN AREAS (total)	9,633	10,447	1.7
CANADA	20,015	21,377	1.5
% OF ALL CANADA	48.1	48.9	

[1]Based on rounded figures shown.

Source: *DBS Daily*, Thursday, June 3, 1971, Dominion Bureau of Statistics.

5. Percentage of Population in Urban Areas, 1851 to 1966[1]

PROVINCE	1851	1871	1891	1911	1931	1951	1961	1966
NEWFOUNDLAND	—	—	—	—	—	43.3	50.7	54.1
PRINCE EDWARD ISLAND	—	9.4	13.1	16.0	19.5	25.1	32.4	36.6
NOVA SCOTIA	7.5	8.3	19.4	36.7	46.6	54.5	54.3	58.1
NEW BRUNSWICK	14.0	17.6	19.9	26.7	35.4	42.8	46.5	50.6
QUÉBEC	14.9	19.9	28.6	44.5	59.5	66.8	74.3	78.3
ONTARIO	14.0	20.6	35.0	49.5	63.1	72.5	77.3	80.4
MANITOBA	—	—	23.3	39.3	45.2	56.0	63.9	67.1
SASKATCHEWAN	—	—	—	16.1	20.3	30.4	43.0	49.0
ALBERTA	—	—	—	29.4	31.8	47.6	63.3	68.8
BRITISH COLUMBIA	—	9.0	42.6	50.9	62.3	68.6	72.6	75.3
CANADA	13.1	18.3	29.8	41.8	52.5	62.4	69.7	73.6

[1] The 1966 percentage of the population classified as urban, rural farm, and rural non-farm is shown on the various provincial maps in the *Atlas*.

Source: *Urban Development in Canada* by Leroy O. Stone, 1961 Census Monograph, Table 2.2.

6. Factors in the Growth of Population, 1961 to 1966, and Vital Statistics Rates, 1930 to 1968

PROVINCE OR TERRITORY	POPULATION 1961	BIRTHS	DEATHS	NATURAL INCREASE	IMMI-GRATION	ACTUAL INCREASE	NET MIGRATION	POPULATION 1966
NEWFOUNDLAND............	457,853	75,251	15,674	59,577	2,256	35,543	−24,034	493,396
PRINCE EDWARD ISLAND.....................	104,629	13,577	5,071	8,506	466	3,906	−4,600	108,535
NOVA SCOTIA...............	737,007	91,138	31,612	59,526	6,241	19,032	−40,494	756,039
NEW BRUNSWICK...........	597,936	76,943	23,714	53,229	4,460	18,852	−34,377	616,788
QUÉBEC....................	5,259,211	646,621	188,904	457,717	122,897	521,634	+63,917	5,780,845
ONTARIO...................	6,236,092	752,511	264,659	487,852	287,054	724,778	+236,926	6,960,870
MANITOBA.................	921,686	108,858	38,518	70,340	15,433	41,380	−28,960	963,066
SASKATCHEWAN............	925,181	112,249	36,558	75,691	8,988	30,163	−45,528	955,344
ALBERTA..................	1,331,944	181,753	47,146	134,607	29,394	131,259	−3,348	1,463,203
BRITISH COLUMBIA.........	1,629,082	181,467	77,364	104,103	60,822	244,592	+140,489	1,873,674
YUKON & NORTHWEST TERRITORIES...	37,626	8,394	1,649	6,745	544	5,494	−1,251	43,120
CANADA..................	18,238,247	2,248,762	730,869	1,517,893	538,555	1,776,633	+258,740	20,014,880

Source: *Canada Year Book 1970–71*, Dominion Bureau of Statistics Ottawa.

Vital Statistics Rates, 1930 to 1968

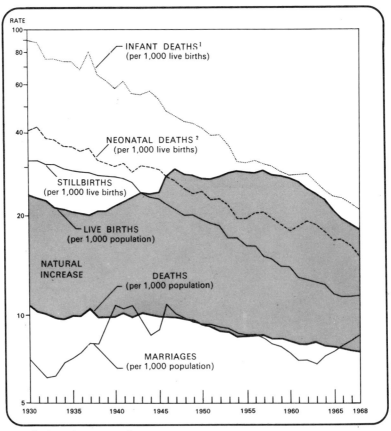

[1] Deaths under one year of age.

[2] Deaths within the first four weeks of birth.

7. Average Size of Census-farms[1] 1931, 1941, 1951, 1961 and 1966

PROVINCE OR TERRITORY	1931	1941	1951	1961	1966	PERCENTAGE CHANGE	
			Acres			1951–61	1961–6
NEWFOUNDLAND......	n.a.	n.a.	23	31	29	+34.8	− 6.5
PRINCE EDWARD ISLAND.................	93	96	108	131	146	+21.3	+11.4
NOVA SCOTIA.........	109	116	135	178	192	+31.9	+ 7.9
NEW BRUNSWICK......	122	124	131	187	208	+42.7	+11.2
QUÉBEC...............	127	117	125	148	160	+18.4	+ 8.1
ONTARIO..............	119	126	139	153	162	+10.1	+ 5.9
MANITOBA............	279	291	338	420	480	+24.3	+14.3
SASKATCHEWAN.......	408	432	550	686	763	+24.7	+11.2
ALBERTA..............	400	434	527	645	706	+22.4	+ 9.5
BRITISH COLUMBIA ...	136	153	178	226	277	+27.0	+22.6
YUKON & NORTHWEST TERRITORIES..........	127	107	108	330	225	+205.0	−31.8
CANADA[2]............	—	—	**279**	**359**	**404**	**+28.7**	**+12.5**

[1] A census-farm is defined in the 1966 Census as an agricultural holding of one or more acres with sales of $50 or more of agricultural products in the year prior to the census.

[2] Includes data for Yukon and Northwest Territories.

Source: *Agricultural Trends in Canada, Census of Canada, 1966*, Special Bulletin S-403, September 1969 and *Selected Statistical Information on Agriculture in Canada*, Economics Branch, Canadian Department of Agriculture, October 1969.

8. Census-farms[1] – Population, Number, Use of Land, and Capital Value, 1931, 1951, 1961 and 1966

	Unit	1931	1951	1961	1966
POPULATION ON CENSUS-FARMS.....	no.	3,289,140	2,911,996	2,128,400	1,960,365
Percentage living on census-farms........	%	31.7	20.8	11.7	9.8
NUMBER OF CENSUS-FARMS.........	no.	728,623	623,091	480,903	430,522
AREA IN CENSUS-FARMS.............	ac.	163,114,034	174,046,654	172,551,051	174,124,828
Percentage of total land area in census-farms...........................	%	7.5	7.7	7.6	7.6
USE OF AGRICULTURAL LAND:					
Improved land..........................	ac.	85,732,172	96,852,826	103,403,426	108,154,377
Under crops...........................	ac.	58,339,948	62,212,148	62,435,534	69,053,004
Pasture...............................	ac.	8,011,716	10,005,126	10,247,896	10,941,740
Summer fallow.......................	ac.	17,007,278	22,032,062	28,243,386	25,631,683
Other improved land..................	ac.	2,373,230	2,603,490	2,476,610	2,527,950
Unimproved land.......................	ac.	77,381,862	77,193,828	69,147,625	65,970,451
Woodland............................	ac.	26,645,281	22,779,944	17,247,389	14,183,924
Other unimproved land	ac.	50,736,581	54,413,884	51,900,236	51,786,527
Total capital value......................	$	5,247,753,468	9,470,876,372	13,171,221,700	19,075,320,600
Land and buildings......................	$	4,053,282,300	5,527,207,155	8,622,641,300	13,173,964,200
Machinery and equipment...............	$	650,664,000	1,933,312,262	2,568,631,500	3,552,411,400
Livestock and poultry...................	$	543,807,168	2,010,356,955	1,979,948,900	2,348,945,000

[1] A census-farm is defined in the 1966 Census as an agricultural holding of one or more acres with sales of $50 or more of agricultural products in the year prior to the census.

Source: *Census of Canada, 1966*, Vol. III (3-1), June 1968.

9. Acreages, Production, and Values of Field Crops by Province,[1] 1945 to 1949 and 1963 to 1967 Averages[2]

FIELD CROP AND PROVINCE	AREA		TOTAL PRODUCTION		GROSS FARM VALUE	
	Average 1945–9	Average 1963–7	Average 1945–9	Average 1963–7	Average 1945–9	Average 1963–7
	'000 acres	'000 acres	'000 bu.	'000 bu.	$'000	$'000
Wheat...............	**24,558**	**29,076**	**362,774**	**678,779**	**587,412**	**1,145,512**
Prince Edward Island...............	2	3	54	82	84	141
Nova Scotia...........	1	1	23	36	34	62
New Brunswick.......	2	3	46	95	77	164
Québec..............	12	23	206	599	313	1,024
Ontario:						
Winter..............	621	397	18,100	15,923	28,358	27,547
Spring..............	40	20	810	529	1,287	915
Manitoba............	2,420	3,311	48,000	78,800	79,827	132,286
Saskatchewan........	14,438	18,937	185,000	423,400	301,085	719,844
Alberta..............	6,915	6,273	108,000	156,600	171,983	259,464
British Columbia......	106	109	2,615	2,714	4,365	4,064
Oats................	**11,513**	**8,209**	**326,437**	**374,344**	**219,370**	**261,224**
Prince Edward Island...............	110	88	4,073	4,369	3,113	3,559
Nova Scotia..........	64	28	2,221	1,270	1,891	1,138
New Brunswick.......	178	80	6,136	3,462	4,799	2,891
Québec..............	1,377	1,074	32,961	42,431	26,716	36,992
Ontario..............	1,503	1,368	56,770	72,485	42,078	56,534
Manitoba............	1,460	1,582	49,000	67,800	31,402	45,526
Saskatchewan........	4,084	1,795	96,000	81,600	60,134	51,872
Alberta..............	2,645	2,123	75,000	97,600	46,148	60,542
British Columbia......	93	71	4,535	3,327	3,088	2,169
Barley..............	**6,569**	**6,674**	**141,171**	**231,579**	**133,431**	**226,867**
Prince Edward Island...............	6	13	169	541	172	585
Nova Scotia..........	6	3	153	120	172	149
New Brunswick.......	11	5	312	187	346	228
Québec..............	84	16	1,869	575	2,006	688
Ontario..............	234	197	7,477	8,966	7,148	10,391
Manitoba............	1,766	705	42,000	23,000	40,907	23,118
Saskatchewan........	2,354	1,937	43,000	67,200	39,813	66,146
Alberta..............	2,088	3,656	45,000	126,800	42,121	121,832
British Columbia......	21	142	731	4,191	746	3,730
Rye................	**1,192**	**721**	**13,182**	**14,628**	**24,362**	**15,942**
Québec..............	4	4	59	95	77	106
Ontario..............	86	53	1,771	1,372	2,900	1,559
Manitoba............	50	121	813	2,593	1,395	2,831
Saskatchewan........	723	358	6,240	6,760	11,916	7,330
Alberta..............	328	183	4,269	3,736	8,024	4,040
British Columbia......	2	2	29	72	50	76

Table 9 continued

FIELD CROP AND PROVINCE	AREA		TOTAL PRODUCTION		GROSS FARM VALUE	
	Average 1945–9	Average 1963–7	Average 1945–9	Average 1963–7	Average 1945–9	Average 1963–7
	'000 acres	'000 acres	'000 bu.	'000 bu.	$'000	$'000
Soybeans...........	**73**	**259**	**1,492**	**7,422**	**3,492**	**20,886**
Ontario..............	73	259	1,492	7,422	3,492	20,886
Mixed Grains........	**1,226**	**1,615**	**44,046**	**76,112**	**36,988**	**68,250**
P.E.I.	48	48	1,878	2,466	1,590	2,269
Nova Scotia..........	4	10	139	437	135	473
New Brunswick.......	3	9	97	384	79	397
Québec..............	189	100	4,921	3,976	4,852	4,590
Ontario..............	916	800	35,438	44,006	29,194	39,415
Manitoba.............	18	152	496	5.669	364	4,943
Saskatchewan........	13	122	255	4,534	192	3,652
Alberta..............	33	370	736	14,439	512	12,286
British Columbia......	2	4	86	200	70	225
Flaxseed	**1,164**	**1,783**	**9,502**	**20,399**	**37,188**	**57,799**
Québec..............	—	26	—	377	—	1,111
Ontario..............	39	18	463	286	1,879	787
Manitoba.............	449	992	4,267	10,360	16,732	29,182
Saskatchewan........	526	442	3,360	5,340	12,872	15,170
Alberta..............	146	304	1,373	4,020	5,555	11,501
British Columbia......	4	2	39	17	149	47
Shelled Corn........	**244**	**727**	**11,038**	**57,787**	**14,056**	**77,233**
Ontario..............	231	715	10,734	57,080	13,726	76,198
Manitoba.............	13	5	304	172	330	233
			'000 lb.	'000 lb.		
Rapeseed............	**40**	**1,170**	**29,663**	**18,938**	**1,746**	**44,595**
Manitoba.............	—	118	—	1,806	—	4,262
Saskatchewan........	40	480	29,663	8,588	1,746	20,252
Alberta..............	—	572	—	8,544	—	20,082
Mustard Seed	—	**156**	—	**119,040**	—	**5,495**
Manitoba.............	—	26	—	18,060	—	927
Saskatchewan........	—	60	—	47,470	—	2,139
Alberta..............	—	70	—	53,510	—	2,429
			000 cwt.	'000 cwt.		
Potatoes...........	**417**	**296**	**39,704**	**48,120**	**72,522**	**100,208**
P.E.I.	46	46	5,993	8,879	7,746	16,071
Nova Scotia..........	16	6	1,767	825	3,436	1,787
New Brunswick.......	61	58	8,730	12,151	13,241	20,944
Québec..............	118	72	8,956	8,585	17,485	18,153
Ontario..............	92	51	8,004	9,413	16,877	20,957
Manitoba.............	21	23	1,405	2,632	2,371	5,571

Continued overleaf

Table 9 continued

FIELD CROP AND PROVINCE	AREA		TOTAL PRODUCTION		GROSS FARM VALUE	
	Average 1945–9	Average 1963–7	Average 1945–9	Average 1963–7	Average 1945–9	Average 1963–7
	'000 acres	'000 acres	'000 cwt.	'000 cwt.	$'000	$'000
Saskatchewan........	24	9	1,230	702	2,570	1,909
Alberta.............	23	23	1,679	3,007	3,706	8,495
British Columbia......	16	10	1,940	1,927	5,089	6,321
			'000 tons	'000 tons		
Tame Hay.........	**10,535**	**12,802**	**16,729**	**23,554**	**250,847**	**430,464**
Prince Edward Island................	221	179	333	327	4,620	4,410
Nova Scotia..........	403	224	699	473	11,773	7,668
New Brunswick.......	534	251	748	474	11,849	7,305
Québec.............	3,959	3,363	5,526	6,057	87,681	109,928
Ontario.............	3,371	3,385	6,128	7,386	86,292	146,814
Manitoba............	324	1,017	556	1,732	6,021	28,198
Saskatchewan.........	481	1,162	681	1,741	9,029	28,077
Alberta.............	940	2,786	1,370	4,353	19,053	75,507
British Columbia......	302	434	688	1,011	14,530	22,558
Fodder Corn........	**404**	**531**	**3,509**	**6,166**	**17,951**	**38,877**
Québec.............	71	66	605	777	4,172	5,506
Ontario.............	308	415	2,790	5,047	12,910	30,828
Manitoba............	16	39	58	235	422	1,599
Saskatchewan........	5	6	14	22	137	266
British Columbia......	4	5	42	85	309	677
Sugar Beets........	**66**	**89**	**690**	**1,195**	**9,080**	**19,784**
Québec.............	3	10	27	137	344	2,397
Ontario.............	22	15	219	260	2,950	3,942
Manitoba............	11	27	90	273	1,113	4,494
Alberta.............	30	38	354	524	4,672	8,951

[1] Excluding Newfoundland.

[2] Because of rounding and some minor omissions, columns may not always add up to the totals indicated.

Source: *Canada Year Book 1961* and *1970–71*.

10. Number and Proportion of Commercial Farms[1] Classified by Type of Farm, 1966

PROVINCE	TOTAL, COMMER-CIAL FARMS	TYPE OF FARM									
		Dairy	Cattle, hogs, sheep	Poultry	Wheat	Small grains	Other field crops	Fruits and vege-tables	Forestry	Miscel-laneous specialty	Mixed combina-tions
		Number of Commercial Farms									
NEWFOUNDLAND........	301	75	41	72	—	—	70	6	2	21	14
PRINCE EDWARD ISLAND.................	3,328	388	752	33	—	8	1,226	44	6	9	862
NOVA SCOTIA...........	2,867	1,290	553	238	—	—	63	290	100	82	251
NEW BRUNSWICK........	2,938	957	475	150	—	7	842	85	76	33	313
QUÉBEC.................	41,961	26,609	5,945	1,714	2	156	1,449	1,313	180	470	4,123
ONTARIO...............	70,724	21,159	28,809	2,179	137	4,862	4,488	3,920	118	1,399	3,653
MANITOBA..............	27,372	1,240	5,488	542	8,198	8,307	340	66	4	218	2,969
SASKATCHEWAN.........	69,962	592	6,605	173	51,650	7,746	63	3	2	133	2,995
ALBERTA...............	48,971	2,089	20,418	402	11,238	8,250	897	39	10	341	5,287
BRITISH COLUMBIA......	8,407	2,061	1,850	796	188	406	358	1,726	131	602	289
CANADA[2]................	276,835	56,460	70,936	6,299	71,413	29,742	9,798	7,492	629	3,309	20,757
		Percentage Distribution									
NEWFOUNDLAND.........	100.0	24.9	13.6	23.9	—	—	23.2	2.0	0.7	7.0	4.7
PRINCE EDWARD ISLAND.................	100.0	11.7	22.6	1.0	—	0.2	36.8	1.3	0.2	0.3	25.9
NOVA SCOTIA...........	100.0	45.0	19.3	8.3	—	—	2.2	10.1	3.5	2.9	8.7
NEW BRUNSWICK........	100.0	32.6	16.2	5.1	—	0.2	28.6	2.9	2.6	1.1	10.7
QUÉBEC.................	100.0	63.4	14.2	4.1	—	0.4	3.5	3.1	0.4	1.1	9.8
ONTARIO...............	100.0	29.9	40.7	3.1	0.2	6.9	6.3	5.5	0.2	2.0	5.2
MANITOBA..............	100.0	4.5	20.0	2.0	30.0	30.3	1.2	0.2	—	0.8	10.8
SASKATCHEWAN.........	100.0	0.8	9.4	0.2	73.8	11.1	0.1	—	—	0.2	4.3
ALBERTA...............	100.0	4.3	41.7	0.8	22.9	16.8	1.8	0.1	—	0.7	10.8
BRITISH COLUMBIA......	100.0	24.5	22.0	9.5	2.2	4.8	4.3	20.5	1.6	7.2	3.4
CANADA................	100.0	20.4	25.6	2.3	25.9	10.7	3.5	2.7	0.2	1.2	7.5

[1] A commercial farm is defined in the 1966 Census as an agricultural holding of one or more acres with sales of $2,500 or more of agricultural products in the year prior to the Census.

[2] Includes data for Yukon and Northwest Territories.

Source: *Agricultural Trends in Canada, Census of Canada, 1966*, Special Bulletin S-403, September 1969.

11. Livestock on Farms, 1959 and 1969

PROVINCE AND ITEM	1959	1969	PROVINCE AND ITEM	1959	1969
	'000	'000		'000	'000
Prince Edward Island			**Manitoba**		
Horses..................	10.6	4.0	Horses..................	60.0	36.0
Milk cows...............	40.8	36.0	Milk cows..............	214.0	123.0
Other cattle.............	68.2	81.0	Other cattle.............	669.0	896.0
Sheep..................	34.0	11.0	Sheep..................	78.0	41.0
Swine..................	63.0	94.0	Swine..................	505.0	612.0
Nova Scotia			**Saskatchewan**		
Horses..................	14.0	4.8	Horses..................	132.0	62.0
Milk cows...............	69.0	47.0	Milk cows..............	248.0	117.0
Other cattle.............	88.0	94.0	Other cattle.............	1,602.0	2,063.0
Sheep..................	78.0	41.0	Sheep..................	187.0	126.0
Swine..................	51.0	71.0	Swine..................	845.0	580.0
New Brunswick			**Alberta**		
Horses..................	14.5	5.0	Horses..................	120.0	84.0
Milk cows...............	75.0	45.0	Milk cows..............	272.0	200.0
Other cattle.............	86.0	83.0	Other cattle.............	2,298.0	3,061.0
Sheep..................	65.0	25.0	Sheep..................	530.0	218.0
Swine..................	70.0	52.0	Swine..................	1,780.0	1,220.0
Québec			**British Columbia**		
Horses..................	138.0	49.0	Horses..................	23.0	26.5
Milk cows...............	1,083.0	1,023.0	Milk cows..............	91.0	78.0
Other cattle.............	917.0	852.0	Other cattle.............	329.0	444.0
Sheep..................	290.0	101.0	Sheep..................	97.0	58.0
Swine..................	1,290.0	1,115.0	Swine..................	68.0	38.0
Ontario			**TOTALS**		
Horses..................	102.0	70.0	**Horses**..............	614.1	341.3
Milk cows...............	1,015.0	895.0	**Milk cows**............	3,107.8	2,584.0
Other cattle.............	1,955.0	2,309.0	**Other cattle**...........	8,012.2	9,883.0
Sheep..................	402.0	262.0	**Sheep**................	1,761.0	883.0
Swine..................	2,200.0	2,010.0	**Swine**................	6,872.0	5,792.0

Source : *Canada Year Book 1961* and *1970-71.*

12. Value of Production of Principal Minerals, 1969[1]

Metals	NEWF.	N.S.	N.B.	QUÉ.	ONT.	MAN.	SASK.	ALTA.	B.C.	Y.T. & N.W.T.	CANADA
					(Thousands of dollars)						
CADMIUM....................	—	—	395	1,077	8,453	811	290	—	3,740	244	15,010
COBALT......................	—	—	—	—	5,431	1,491	—	—	—	—	6,922
COPPER.....................	19,944	84	7,264	162,477	235,492	38,101	18,526	—	83,670	8,635	574,193
GOLD.......................	280	—	59	27,806	45,470	1,105	1,427	4	4,253	13,927	94,332
IRON ORE...................	178,993	—	—	109,405	126,081	—	—	—	17,451	—	431,930
IRON, remelt...............	—	—	—	23,475	—	—	—	—	—	—	23,475
LEAD.......................	6,387	789	16,999	425	3,859	179	—	—	31,052	35,700	95,392
MAGNESIUM.................	—	—	—	—	7,094	—	—	—	—	—	7,094
MOLYBDENUM...............	—	—	—	5,499	—	—	—	—	47,124	—	52,623
NICKEL.....................	—	—	—	622	330,967	147,714	—	—	3,110	—	482,413
PLATINUM GROUP............	—	—	—	—	26,449	—	—	—	—	—	26,449
SILVER.....................	1,859	477	8,052	7,920	42,524	944	1,229	—	10,482	9,682	83,169
URANIUM (U_3O_8)..........	—	—	—	—	38,751	—	10,915	—	—	—	49,666
ZINC.......................	10,328	37	48,188	59,678	106,430	14,898	7,500	—	45,120	72,213	364,390
Total—All Metals..............	**217,791**	**1,388**	**81,334**	**407,221**	**979,135**	**205,766**	**40,204**	**4**	**247,704**	**140,401**	**2,320,948**
Non-metallics											
ASBESTOS...................	10,100	—	—	154,410	4,224	—	—	—	15,324	12,701	196,759
GYPSUM....................	1,176	9,215	237	—	1,539	488	—	—	778	—	13,433
NEPHELINE SYENITE..........	—	—	—	—	5,882	—	—	—	—	—	5,882
PEAT MOSS.................	—	383	2,495	3,343	487	353	10	232	1,414	—	8,717
POTASH (K_2O).............	—	—	—	—	—	—	67,120	—	—	—	67,120
QUARTZ....................	—	110	—	3,919	469	1,034	167	—	155	—	5,854
SALT.......................	—	4,615	—	—	19,618	900	1,829	2,462	—	—	29,424
SODIUM SULPHATE...........	—	—	—	—	—	—	8,389	—	—	—	8,389
SULPHUR, in smelter gas........	—	—	445	1,100	3,629	—	—	—	3,048	—	8,222
SULPHUR, elemental...........	—	—	—	—	40	174	905	60,716	1,151	—	62,986
TITANIUM DIOXIDE, &c........	—	—	—	29,067	—	—	—	—	—	—	29,067
Total—All Non-metallics	**14,862**	**15,423**	**3,178**	**197,449**	**36,297**	**2,948**	**78,420**	**63,410**	**22,400**	**12,701**	**447,089**
Fuels											
COAL.......................	—	21,584	5,832	—	—	—	3,618	13,896	7,110	—	52,039
NATURAL GAS................	—	—	93	20	4,382	—	7,210	218,791	33,048	21	263,565
NATURAL GAS BY-PRODUCTS.	—	—	—	—	—	—	2,557	129,845	3,164	—	135,566
PETROLEUM, CRUDE..........	—	—	12	—	3,239	15,511	201,546	731,121	57,811	988	1,010,230
Total—All Fuels..............	—	**21,584**	**5,937**	**20**	**7,621**	**15,511**	**214,930**	**1,093,654**	**101,133**	**1,010**	**1,461,400**
Structural Materials											
CLAY PRODUCTS	145	1,568	620	7,415	31,213	449	1,629	3,840	4,116	—	50,995
CEMENT....................	1,960	4,164	2,170	47,378	59,337	11,262	7,970	19,139	17,878	—	171,258
LIME.......................	—	—	—	4,760	12,788	825	—	1,736	—	—	20,108
SAND AND GRAVEL..........	3,400	7,700	1,650	18,000	55,500	6,000	4,500	10,800	22,200	—	130,650
STONE......................	935	2,348	3,505	37,825	32,565	2,835	—	697	7,334	—	88,195
Total—All Structural Materials.	**6,440**	**15,780**	**7,945**	**115,377**	**191,404**	**21,370**	**14,099**	**36,212**	**51,529**	—	**461,206**
Grand Totals 1969............	**239,094**	**54,175**	**98,394**	**720,067**	**1,214,457**	**245,596**	**347,652**	**1,193,280**	**422,766**	**154,112**	**4,690,642**
Grand Totals 1968............	**309,712**	**56,928**	**88,451**	**728,784**	**1,355,629**	**209,626**	**357,174**	**1,091,749**	**389,311**	**137,002**	**4,725,341**

[1] Based on rounded figures shown.

Source : *Preliminary Report of Mineral Production 1969*, Dominion Bureau of Statistics, Ottawa.

13. Quantity and Value of Sea and Inland Fish Landed, 1962 to 1968, and Persons Employed, 1968

PROVINCE OR TERRITORY	QUANTITY		VALUE		PERSONS EMPLOYED 1968
	1962	1968	1962	1968	
	'000 lb.	'000 lb.	$'000	$'000	
NEWFOUNDLAND.......	549,341	961,350	17,222	28,007	19,355
PRINCE EDWARD ISLAND.................	37,630	46,995	4,361	7,399	3,301
NOVA SCOTIA...........	435,903	795,421	30,928	52,250	13,108
NEW BRUNSWICK.......	204,511	545,104	9,182	15,581	5,942
QUÉBEC................	133,443	204,522	5,534	8,544	4,945
ONTARIO...............	63,780	55,707	5,341	5,968	2,044
MANITOBA.............	36,105	25,734	4,229	3,276	4,018
SASKATCHEWAN........	14,999	10,972	1,478	1,382	2,348
ALBERTA...............	9,025	11,883	714	917	4,758
BRITISH COLUMBIA.....	686,918	267,239	49,067	57,274	12,133
YUKON & NORTHWEST TERRITORIES...........	6,544	4,296	859	781	401
Totals..................	2,178,199	2,929,223	128,915	181,379	72,353
Sea Fish................	2,041 168	2,814,071	115,570	168,422	
Inland Fish.............	137,031	115,152	13,345	12,957	

Source: *Canada Year Book 1969* and *1970-71*.

14. Lumber Production and Shipments and Value of all Shipments of the Sawmill and Planing Industry, 1968

PROVINCE OR TERRITORY	LUMBER			Value of Shipments of Goods of Own Manufacture
	Production	Quantity Shipped	Value of Shipments	
	M ft. b.m.[1]	M ft. b.m.	$'000	$'000
NEWFOUNDLAND...........	7,338	10,688	931	1,106
PRINCE EDWARD ISLAND......................	2,782	977	73	n.a.
NOVA SCOTIA..............	216,742	186,414	15,572	19,305
NEW BRUNSWICK...........	266,199	281,284	24,886	35,518
QUÉBEC....................	1,611,553	1,539,348	135,075	167,536
ONTARIO...................	841,642	736,302	76,824	98,258
MANITOBA..................	33,866	28,849	1,849	2,210
SASKATCHEWAN............	84,436	106,656	8,767	10,355
ALBERTA...................	341,626	385,520	29,950	35,389
BRITISH COLUMBIA.........	7,341,007	7,703,089	707,896	809,175
YUKON & NORTHWEST TERRITORIES...............	7,332	7,904	584	n.a.
CANADA....................	10,754,523	10,987,031	1,002,407	1,179,573

[1] Thousand-feet board measure.

Source: *Canada Year Book 1970–71*, Dominion Bureau of Statistics, Ottawa

15. Pulp Production, 1964 and 1968

	1964	1968
	'000 tons	'000 tons
Total pulp production....	13,742	16,762
Québec.................	5,204	5,918
Ontario.................	3,317	3,644
British Columbia	2,827	4,378
Other provinces	2,393	2,822

Source: *Canada Year Book 1970-71.*

16. Pulp Production: Exports and Imports by Leading Countries, 1967

COUNTRY	PRODUC-TION	EXPORTS	IMPORTS
	'000 tons	'000 tons	'000 tons
CANADA............	15,767	4,268	36
UNITED STATES......	35,478	1,720	3,141
FINLAND............	6,302	2,341	8
NORWAY...........	1,984	940	1,135
SWEDEN............	7,548	3,893	6

Source: *FAO Year Book of Forest Products Statistics.*

17. Estimated World Newsprint Production and Exports by Leading Countries, 1966 and 1968

COUNTRY	1966		1968	
	Production	Exports	Production	Exports
	'000 tons	'000 tons	'000 tons	'000 tons
CANADA.............	8,419	7,764	8,031	7,422
UNITED STATES.......	2,408	99	2,935	129
JAPAN...............	1,301	26	1,622	6
FINLAND.............	1,330	1,210	1,227	1,131
BRITAIN	825	3	811	2
U.S.S.R................	972	197	1,120	241
SWEDEN.............	760	474	844	555

Source: Newsprint Association of Canada.

18. Electric Energy Generated, by Type of Station by Province, 1969

PROVINCE OR TERRITORY	GENERATED BY				Total
	WATER POWER		THERMAL POWER		
	'000 kwh.	%	'000 kwh.	%	'000 kwh.
NEWFOUNDLAND......	3,975,000	96.6	138,000	3.4	4,113,000
PRINCE EDWARD ISLAND.................	—	—	218,000	100.00	218,000
NOVA SCOTIA..........	634,000	20.4	2,476,000	79.6	3,110,000
NEW BRUNSWICK......	2,527,000	53.9	2,160,000	46.1	4,687,000
QUÉBEC...............	65,125,000	94.5	3,769,000	5.5	68,894,000
ONTARIO..............	40,089,000	66.1	20,604,000	33.9	60,693,000
MANITOBA.............	7,279,000	98.9	78,000	1.1	7,357,000
SASKATCHEWAN.......	3,123,000	56.8	2,376,000	43.2	5,499,000
ALBERTA..............	1,376,000	15.7	7,407,000	84.3	8,783,000
BRITISH COLUMBIA....	23,447,000	89.1	2,877,000	10.9	26,324,000
YUKON & NORTHWEST TERRITORIES..........	347,000	83.6	68,000	16.4	415,000
CANADA.............	147,922,000		42,171,000		190,093,000

Source: *Canada Year Book 1970-71.*

The St. Lawrence Seaway

(See pages 16 and 17.)

The St. Lawrence Seaway project, officially opened in 1959, provides 27-foot navigation from Montréal to the head of the Great Lakes, a distance of over 2,000 miles. That part of the Seaway on the St. Lawrence River above Montréal divides naturally into five sections, in three of which major works were necessary to make substantial improvements in navigational facilities and also to increase the river's production of hydro-electric power.

I. In the International Rapids section, the main power works include an upper control dam near Iroquois, Ont., the Long Sault dam, the Saunders and Moses power-houses near Cornwall, and channel enlargements to reduce current velocities in some stretches. Two short side canals, one at each of the dams, provide 27-foot navigation past these obstacles. The Long Sault dam near Cornwall, which raised the water level by 24 feet to inundate the Long Sault Rapids, Rapide Plat, and Galop Rapids, created Lake St. Lawrence. The town of Iroquois, railways, and highways all had to be relocated on the shoreline of the new lake, which extends 26 miles upstream.

II. In the Soulanges section, short access channels and entry locks enable the Seaway to use the previously existing 27-foot navigational channel along one side of the present canal of the Beauharnois power development, which was built by Québec in 1932.

III. The Lachine Rapids were bypassed by a 10-mile canal, considerable channel enlargement, and necessary control locks.

IV. Lake St. Francis and the Thousand Islands: minor dredging is necessary here to maintain Seaway standards.

In the International Rapids section, where the river marks the boundary between Canada and the United States, a total of 2,200,000 horsepower is divided equally between the Ontario Hydro-Electric Power Commission and the Power Authority of the State of New York. In the Soulanges section, the Beauharnois power development of the Québec Hydro-Electric Commission harnesses 1,300,000 horsepower and will be extended eventually to 2,000,000 horsepower. A third possible site for power development is in the Lachine section, where a capacity of 1,200,000 horsepower could be developed. The Soulanges and Lachine sites are entirely within Canadian territory and power development is at the discretion of the Province of Québec.

In the Great Lakes area proper, the channels of the Welland Ship Canal were deepened from 25 to 27 feet; the existing locks were completed to Seaway specifications in 1932. A new bypass of 8.3 miles will be opened in April 1973 to take the Welland Canal around rather than through the City of Welland. The elimination of 6 lift bridges will improve road traffic in the city and speed up ship traffic on the canal.

The maintenance of Seaway standards requires considerable dredging in the important connecting channels between Lakes Huron and Erie and in the St. Marys River between Lakes Superior and Huron (see p. 18).

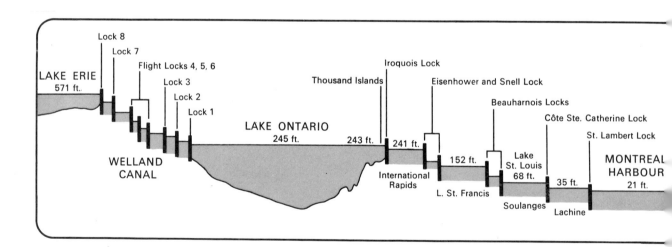

19. St. Lawrence Seaway: Type of Traffic, 1969

	UPBOUND		DOWNBOUND				UPBOUND		DOWNBOUND	
	No. of Transits	Cargo Tons	No. of Transits	Cargo Tons			No. of Transits	Cargo Tons	No. of Transits	Cargo Tons
Domestic					**Foreign**					
CANADA TO CANADA...............	1,455	5,980,119	1,628	8,902,123	CANADA	Import....	266	1,023,764	—	—
CANADA TO UNITED STATES.......	1,494	12,364,839	16	3,617		Export....	—	—	292	740,254
UNITED STATES TO CANADA.......	18	104,799	1,304	17,856,575	UNITED STATES	Import....	935	5,567,196	—	—
UNITED STATES TO UNITED STATES	368	273,757	391	584,762		Export....	—	—	927	7,414,187

Source: *Canada Year Book 1970-71.*

20. St. Lawrence Seaway Traffic[1] Classified by Type of Cargo, 1966 and 1969 [2]

COMMODITY	1966		1969		COMMODITY	1966		1969	
	Cargo Tons	% of Total	Cargo Tons	% of Total		Cargo Tons	% of Total	Cargo Tons	% of Total
Agricultural Products.......	**22,092,223**	**33.0**	**14,236,468**	**23.4**	**Forest Products ....**	**402,707**	**0.6**	**355,346**	**0.6**
Wheat.........................	12,172,173	18.2	5,568,614	9.2	Pulpwood	288,962	0.4	199,958	0.3
Corn..........................	3,669,283	5.5	3,608,498	5.9	Other forest products............	113,745	0.2	155,388	0.3
Oats..........................	808,648	1.2	268,477	0.4					
Barley........................	1,482,556	2.2	964,413	1.6	**Manufactures and Misc........**	**11,245,380**	**16.9**	**14,659,404**	**24.1**
Flour, wheat..................	164,850	0.2	137,590	0.2	Gasoline......................	374,377	0.6	762,923	1.3
Flour, edible, other............	18,218	—	8,682	—	Fuel oil.........................	2,814,311	4.4	3,358,422	5.6
Soybeans.....................	1,666,589	2.5	2,129,722	3.5	Lubricating oils and greases.......	232,151	0.3	126,210	0.2
Soybean oil, cake and meal	408,258	0.6	213,747	0.4	Rubber, crude, natural and synthetic	145,865	0.2	170,349	0.3
Beans and peas...............	204,864	0.3	96,758	0.2	Chemicals......................	366,534	0.6	406,075	0.7
Flaxseed......................	545,300	0.8	435,952	0.7	Sodium products.................	136,824	0.2	170,396	0.3
Other agricultural products.....	589,982	0.9	651,526	1.1	Tar, pitch and creosote...........	148,918	0.2	176,060	0.3
Animal Products............	**388,769**	**0.6**	**347,422**	**0.6**	Pig iron.........................	356,656	0.6	248,936	0.4
Hides, skins and pelts.........	88,203	0.1	100,768	0.2	Iron and steel, nails, wire.........	139,510	0.2	138,745	0.2
Other animal products.........	202,590	0.3	167,498	0.3	Iron and steel, manufactured......	2,836,517	4.4	4,268,408	7.0
Mineral Products...........	**31,911,611**	**47.6**	**30,367,581**	**49.9**	Machinery and machines..........	105,422	0.2	96,471	0.2
Bituminous coal...............	8,525,793	12.6	11,043,334	18.2	Cement.........................	138,218	0.2	146,027	0.2
Coke.........................	239,209	0.4	392,780	0.6	Newsprint.......................	595,235	0.9	322,080	0.5
Iron ore......................	19,624,222	29.3	15,300,264	25.2	Syrup and molasses.............	122,150	0.2	131,314	0.2
Aluminum ore and concentrates.	122,550	0.2	142,408	0.2	Sugar..........................	197,588	0.3	206,815	0.3
Clay and bentonite............	193,790	0.3	245,489	0.4	Food products..................	192,642	0.3	309,287	0.5
Gravel and sand..............	152,045	0.2	105,904	0.2	Scrap iron and steel.............	177,169	0.3	1,353,857	2.2
Stone, ground or crushed.......	1,422,164	2.1	1,321,273	2.2	Other manufactures and miscellaneous...................	1,791,030	2.2	2,082,149	3.4
Stone, rough..................	5,135	—	3,530	—	**Package Freight.............**	**899,747**	**1.3**	**849,771**	**1.4**
Petroleum, crude..............	41,641	0.1	102,130	0.2	Package freight – domestic.......	869,454	1.3	827,125	1.4
Salt..........................	771,110	1.1	821,358	1.3	Package freight – foreign..........	30,293	—	22,646	—
Sulphur.......................	50	—	—	—	**Totals.....................**	**66,940,437**	**100.00**	**60,815,992**	**100.00**
Other mineral products........	831,902	1.3	889,111	1.4					

[1] Combined traffic of Montréal – Lake Ontario Section and the Welland Canal, with duplications eliminated.

[2] Bold figures represent total tonnages and percentages and include commodities not listed.

Source: *Canada Year Book 1969* and *1970-71.*

21. Principal Commodities in Water-Borne Cargo Loaded and Unloaded at Ports Handling the Largest Tonnages in 1968[1]

PORT & COMMODITY	INTERNATIONAL Loaded	INTERNATIONAL Unloaded	COASTWISE Loaded	COASTWISE Unloaded	TOTAL
	tons	tons	tons	tons	tons
Montréal	**3,418,268**	**5,777,673**	**5,202,313**	**2,975,479**	**17,373,733**
Wheat	1,121,593	30,039	—	1,642,917	2,794,549
Fuel oil	126,604	1,734,863	3,012,714	65,412	4,939,593
Gasoline	—	285,022	1,401,777	—	1,686,799
Crude petroleum	—	689,759	—	—	689,759
Salt	26	105,079	5,840	350,189	461,134
Coal, bituminous	55	369,521	10	—	369,586
Corn	34,133	304,293	3,743	3,798	345,967
Gypsum	77	—	21	312,258	312,35
Raw sugar	154	306,221	—	—	306,375
Vancouver	**12,955,584**	**2,400,032**	**5,483,821**	**4,951,621**	**25,791,058**
Wheat	4,343,192	112	22,635	—	4,365,939
Pulpwood	286,159	—	2,343,285	413,113	3,042,557
Sand and gravel	14,500	463,360	28,265	1,835,455	2,341,580
Lumber and timber	1,281,188	19,432	153,960	177,465	1,632,045
Potash	1,617,685	197	852	310	1,619,044
Logs	156,048	4,374	150,988	1,193,962	1,505,372
Fuel oil	95,336	176,977	1,018,977	33	1,291,323
Coal, bituminous	1,091,869	5	142	—	1,092,016
Sulphur in ores	1,037,518	—	21,907	—	1,059,425
Pulp	506,786	36	5,000	343,837	855,659
Hogged fuel	52,900	—	694,520	11,100	758,520
Barley	542,890	—	1	—	542,891
Sept Îles-Pointe Noire	**20,782,138**	**692,422**	**3,878,515**	**593,913**	**25,946,988**
Iron ore and concentrates	20,777,996	—	3,719,866	—	24,497,862
Fuel oil	—	485,505	2,829	205,580	693,914
Thunder Bay	**3,726,301**	**241,131**	**8,457,580**	**1,037,939**	**13,462,951**
Wheat	263,819	—	5,429,740	—	5,693,559
Iron ore and concentrates	2,655,972	—	1,687,204	—	4,343,176
Barley	150,657	—	576,255	—	726,912
Oats	17,772	—	328,102	—	345,874
Port Cartier	**10,990,733**	**742,168**	**30,712**	**844,271**	**12,607,884**
Iron ore concentrates	9,620,879	—	29,792	—	9,650,671
Wheat	1,162,461	414,157	—	811,040	2,387,658
Hamilton	**257,812**	**7,150,808**	**489,091**	**4,100,713**	**11,998,424**
Iron ore concentrates	—	2,371,395	—	3,538,441	5,909,836
Coal, bituminous	—	4,143,500	—	—	4,143,500
Fuel oil	—	218,256	—	302,246	520,502
Halifax	**2,191,929**	**4,934,386**	**2,049,174**	**475,194**	**9,650,683**
Crude petroleum	—	3,146,052	—	—	3,146,052
Fuel oil	37,001	1,404,075	1,419,034	113,627	2,973,737
Gypsum	1,542,409	—	6,831	—	1,549,240
Gasoline	368	25,327	586,149	107,069	718,913
Québec	**2,003,512**	**1,545,529**	**136,311**	**2,979,595**	**6,664,947**
Fuel oil	—	874,597	88,372	622,193	1,585,162
Wheat	598,275	121,895	—	521,520	1,241,690
Pulpwood	6,719	—	—	903,178	909,897
Gasoline	—	94,307	20,146	594,993	709,446
Zinc ore concentrates	482,297	—	—	—	482,297
Toronto	**205,657**	**3,305,040**	**154,419**	**2,044 936**	**5,710,052**
Coal, bituminous	153	2,018,590	—	602,145	2,620,888
Fuel oil	36	137,734	80,492	454,829	673,091
Cement	54	670	—	360,517	361,241
Saint John	**1,068,114**	**3,076,595**	**931,012**	**400,172**	**5,475,893**
Crude petroleum	—	2,047,603	—	—	2,047,603
Fuel oil	21,730	540,785	630,566	203,682	1,396,763
Gasoline	—	—	261,529	147,366	408,895
Sault Ste. Marie	**263,349**	**3,095,638**	**187,475**	**1,698,826**	**5,245,288**
Coal, bituminous	—	2,453,438	—	—	2,453,438
Iron ore and concentrates	—	122,342	—	1,252,471	1,374,813
Limestone	—	487,964	—	—	487,964
Baie Comeau	**2,137,075**	**1,147,720**	**208,608**	**1,212,663**	**4,706,066**
Wheat	1,121,681	295,849	765	903,819	2,322,114
Corn	366,334	417,556	—	—	783,890

[1] Bold figures represent total tonnage and include commodities not listed.

Source : *Canada Year Book 1970–71*, Dominion Bureau of Statistics, Ottawa.

22. Summary Statistics of the Twenty-five Leading Industries, 1968[1]

| | | | MANUFACTURING ACTIVITY | | | | | | | TOTAL ACTIVITY | | |
| | | | Production and Related Workers | | | Cost of Fuel and Elec- tricity | Cost of Materials and Supplies Used | Value of Ship- ments of Goods of Own Manu- facture | Value Added | Total Employees | | Total Value Added |
RANK	INDUSTRY	ESTAB- LISH- MENTS	Number	Man- Hours Paid	Wages					Number	Salaries and Wages	
		No.		'000	$'000	$'000	$'000	$'000	$'000		$'000	$'000
1	Motor vehicle manufacturers.	21	26,965	62,014	231,001	11,472	2,195,259	3,002,279	827,182	39,112	349,489	1,053,754
2	Pulp and paper mills.......	137	60,296	131,653	437,135	181,194	1,183,007	2,446,874	1,080,941	73,498	552,162	1,089,986
3	Slaughtering and meat processors..............	433	22,294	47,025	132,210	10,799	1,448,562	1,772,506	310,009	30,540	190,975	321,653
4	Petroleum refining.........	41	6,284	14,363	53,064	15,950	1,315,863	1,621,887	307,298	9,091	80,010	314,425
5	Iron and steel mills........	43	36,324	76,124	250,865	52,870	630,974	1,367,087	684,684	44,634	323,573	692,767
6	Motor vehicle parts and accessories manufacturers...	179	31,720	69,684	212,769	13,863	667,993	1,193,805	512,418	39,454	280,666	521,489
7	Dairy factories...........	1,037	13,406	29,455	65,210	21,436	874,202	1,184,638	290,529	29,841	160,943	316,635
8	Sawmills and planing mills..	1,894	42,820	92,314	226,359	22,197	634,164	1,179,572	542,206	47,987	264,281	545,183
9	Miscellaneous machinery and equipment manufacturers....	609	30,407	65,225	184,858	7,600	484,022	1,008,012	519,247	47,813	313,711	566,205
10	Smelting and refining......	24	25,572	51,904	172,282	72,387	382,435	932,585	477,763	34,710	250,948	493,024
11	Manufacturers of industrial chemicals................	139	12,963	28,066	93,566	70,284	342,555	846,952	431,211	20,335	157,016	451,764
12	Metal stamping, pressing and coating industry......	734	22,358	48,255	127,357	8,431	418,699	771,326	348,960	29,560	185,161	360,619
13	Miscellaneous food industries................	275	10,056	21,645	49,732	7,481	384,480	676,825	286,353	15,882	91,598	301,100
14	Communications equipment manufacturers.............	192	27,820	59,239	144,700	3,542	285,718	674,467	386,452	43,117	248,880	402,275
15	Aircraft and parts manufacturers.............	85	22,247	46,413	146,881	4,114	293,962	653,899	355,823	35,143	257,734	367,078
16	Commercial printing.......	2,088	27,293	55,894	154,329	4,580	244,987	624,142	377,281	38,437	239,714	384,319
17	Publishing and printing.....	684	16,046	31,799	102,671	4,189	131,713	537,863	402,009	34,113	219,774	401,817
18	Feed manufacturers........	872	5,237	11,899	25,480	7,382	397,698	513,287	108,377	9,256	48,412	130,987
19	Fruit and vegetable canners and preservers.............	295	14,738	30,621	57,883	6,318	302,015	509,986	208,009	19,343	90,073	214,799
20	Bakeries.................	2,135	17,932	38,632	79,281	12,533	214,663	484,135	257,068	32,342	153,634	269,425
21	Women's clothing factories..	642	27,075	53,836	97,401	1,106	264,313	476,722	215,047	31,054	126,768	216,668
22	Synthetic textile mills......	81	15,700	33,854	75,496	9,345	238,917	454,183	204,164	20,293	108,357	206,848
23	Men's clothing factories....	483	28,925	58,168	99,557	1,527	241,788	441,194	200,848	33,201	131,162	202,128
24	Manufacturers of electrical industrial equipment.......	157	14,716	30,850	84,137	3,672	185,678	433,399	244,040	22,634	145,865	249,383
25	Miscellaneous metal fabricating industries.......	487	15,352	31,864	82,238	5,925	204,430	421,543	213,663	20,825	121,923	222,828
	Totals— All Manufacturing Industries..............	32,643	1,160,226	2,458,791	6,278,429	808,764	23,090,970	42,061,554	18,332,204	1,641,559	9,896,397	19,494,039

[1] Ranked according to value of shipments of goods of own manufacture.

Source: *Canada Year Book 1970-71.*

23. Value of Shipments of Goods of Own Manufacture, 1961 and 1968, and Employees in Manufacturing, 1968

PROVINCE OR TERRITORY	1961	1968	EMPLOYEES 1968	PROVINCE OR TERRITORY	1961	1968	EMPLOYEES 1968
	$'000,000	$'000,000	'000		$'000,000	$'000,000	'000
NEWFOUNDLAND.........	135.9	197.5	11.9	MANITOBA...............	716.7	1,118.8	48.1
PRINCE EDWARD ISLAND...................	30.6	51.7	2.3	SASKATCHEWAN.........	331.9	489.2	15.7
NOVA SCOTIA............	381.4	663.3	32.9	ALBERTA................	935.5	1,667.0	49.8
NEW BRUNSWICK........	390.6	633.6	28.1	BRITISH COLUMBIA......	1,927.0	3,550.4	121.5
QUÉBEC...................	7,022.2	11,742.9	520.4	YUKON & NORTHWEST TERRITORIES.............	3.4	4.5	0.2
ONTARIO................	11,563.7	21,942.6	810.8	CANADA.................	23,439.5	42,061.6	1,641.6

Source: *Canada Year Book 1970-71.*

24. Exports by Commodities Valued over 100 Million Dollars, 1968 and 1970

		1968	1970			1968	1970
		Thousands of dollars				Thousands of dollars	
1	Passenger automobiles and chassis.......	1,235,189	1,555,387	16	Communication and related equipment....	188,869	224,354
2	Newsprint paper.......................	902,860	1,014,013	17	Asbestos, unmanufactured...............	175,439	207,234
3	Motor vehicle parts, except engines......	527,653	756,364	18	Fertilizers and fertilizer materials.........	152,017	206,663
4	Wood pulp and similar pulp.............	577,390	715,351	19	Natural gas............................	139,466	186,246
5	Wheat................................	639,452	636,957	20	Aircraft parts, except engines...........	199,718	182,792
6	Lumber, softwood.....................	565,358	592,792	21	Other motor vehicles...................	73,300	162,799
7	Crude petroleum......................	409,060	590,577	22	Whisky...............................	140,220	162,462
8	Trucks, truck tractors and chassis........	347,640	505,329	23	Metal fabricated basic products..........	67,470	130,899
9	Iron ores and concentrates.............	416,024	449,212	24	Aircraft, engines and parts..............	131,147	123,043
10	Copper and alloys.....................	358,016	442,476	25	Office machines and equipment..........	54,550	118,604
11	Aluminum, including alloys..............	399,464	428,076	26	Barley................................	38,455	117,094
12	Nickel and alloys......................	245,390	425,218	27	Plate, sheet and strip, steel.............	101,495	114,626
13	Nickel in ores, concentrates and scrap....	238,343	348,048	28	Zinc in ores, concentrates and scrap......	88,495	111,066
14	Motor vehicle engines and parts.........	228,986	307,884		Total—All Exports..................	12,368,677	15,473 686
15	Copper in ores, concentrates and scrap...	214,822	242,907				

Source: *Summary of Exports*, November 1970, Dominion Bureau of Statistics.

25. Imports by Commodities Valued over 100 Million Dollars, 1968 and 1970

	1968	1970			1968	1970
	Thousands of dollars				Thousands of dollars	
1 Motor vehicle parts, except engines......	1,342,300	1,653,049	12 Inorganic chemicals....................		67,710	140,322
2 Sedans, new.........................	940,986	781,531	13 Office machines and equipment.........		91,447	137,711
3 Crude petroleum.......................	372,586	415,161	14 Organic chemicals....................		129,036	133,543
4 Telecommunication and related equipment.	313,262	378,572	15 Plate, sheet and strip, steel.............		103,175	128,875
5 Motor vehicle engines and parts.........	354,311	374,252	16 Machine tools, metalworking...........		82,008	127,760
6 Trucks, truck tractors and chassis........	167,501	232,574	17 Books and pamphlets..................		105,392	126,078
7 Aircraft, complete with engines..........	233,704	205,883	18 Fuel oil...............................		142,497	122,225
8 Electronic computers...................	108,606	176,290	19 Plastics materials, not shaped...........		99,433	112,190
9 Photographic goods...................	133,311	165,914	20 Aircraft parts, except engines...........		115,944	1 02,830
10 Miscellaneous equipment and tools......	143,697	162,458	21 Other motor vehicles..................		72,465	101,683
11 Coal.................................	160,390	150,832	**Total**................................		**12,357,982**	**13,939,371**

Source : *Summary of Imports*, December 1970, Dominion Bureau of Statistics.

26. Exports: Principal Nations

	1968	1970
	Thousands of dollars	
1 United States...........................	8,366,172	10,044,575
2 United Kingdom........................	1,120,404	1,375,737
3 Japan.................................	543,481	731,317
4 West Germany.........................	211,951	348,097
5 Netherlands............................	165,038	262,060
6 Australia...............................	178,694	189,090
7 Belgium & Luxembourg.................	118,520	180,625
8 Italy...................................	122,835	168,621

Source : *Summary of Exports*, November 1970, Dominion Bureau of Statistics.

27. Imports: Principal Nations

	1968	1970
	Thousands of dollars	
1 United States...........................	9,048,372	9,905,110
2 United Kingdom........................	696,085	738,261
3 Japan.................................	360,180	581,715
4 West Germany.........................	298,869	370,934
5 Venezuela.............................	357,862	339,212
6 France................................	121,647	158,358
7 Australia...............................	75,990	146,148
8 Italy...................................	114,492	144,973

Source : *Summary of Imports*, December 1970, Dominion Bureau of Statistics.

Explorers
The routes followed by the explorers are shown in this *Atlas* on the pages indicated in parentheses.

Before the Fifteenth Century

Vikings Leif Ericsson (c.1000) and Thorfinn Karlsefni (c.1010) probably reached the North American coast between Labrador and Cape Cod by way of Iceland and Greenland. (p. 32)

Marco Polo 1271-95: Travelled overland from Acre in present-day Israel to Peking. He lived in China for seventeen years before returning to Venice by sea around India. (p. 75)

Fifteenth and Sixteenth Centuries

Christopher Columbus 1492-3: Made the first voyage across the Atlantic, leading to the opening-up of North America. After his return to Spain he made three subsequent voyages to the Caribbean. (p. 32)

John Cabot 1497: Sailing from Bristol, he landed in North America, probably on the southwest corner of Newfoundland or the northern tip of Cape Breton Island. (p. 32)

Vasco da Gama 1497-9: Followed up Bartholomew Dias's discovery of Cape of Good Hope by sailing up the east coast of Africa and across the Indian Ocean to pioneer the sea-route to India. (pp. 102-103)

Ferdinand Magellan 1519-22: First circumnavigation of the world. Magellan was killed in the Philippines in 1521 and Sebastián del Cano assumed command and brought the *Victoria* back to Spain. (p. 33)

Francisco Pizarro 1531-3: Commanded the Spanish conquest and exploration of the Inca empire, which constituted most of modern Peru and Ecuador. (p. 33)

Jacques Cartier 1534: Sailed around Gulf of St. Lawrence, claiming the land for France somewhere on the tip of the Gaspé Peninsula. 1535: Sailed from St. Malo and explored the St. Lawrence River as far as the Lachine Rapids. (p. 32)

Francisco de Orellana 1540-1: Starting from Peru, he travelled down the Amazon River by boat to the sea. (p. 33)

Hugh Willoughby 1553: Attempting to find the Northeast Passage, rounded Norway and may have reached Novaya Zemlya before dying in Lapland. (p. 74)

Francis Drake 1577-80: Made the first English circumnavigation of the world. (pp. 100-101)

Seventeenth Century

Willem Janszoon 1606: Partially explored the Gulf of Carpentaria and was likely the discoverer of Australia. (p. 95)

Henry Hudson 1610-11: In search of the Northwest Passage, he entered Hudson Bay and wintered in James Bay. His crew mutinied and he was set adrift in an open boat to die. (p. 32)

Abel Tasman 1642-3: Starting from Batavia (Djakarta), he sailed in a great circle round Australia without seeing it, but discovered Tasmania and New Zealand. (p. 95)

Robert de La Salle 1681: Travelled down the Illinois and Mississippi Rivers to the Gulf of Mexico and took possession of the whole valley for France, naming the region Louisiana in honour of Louis XIV. (p. 32)

Eighteenth Century

James Bruce 1768: Entering Abyssinia from the Red Sea, Bruce discovered the source of the Blue Nile. (p. 103)

James Cook 1768-71: On his first great voyage Cook proved that New Zealand was two islands and discovered the existence of Torres Strait between New Guinea and Australia. (p. 95) 1772-5: On his second voyage Cook searched the South Pacific for a supposed southern continent, *Terra Australis Incognita*, and successfully destroyed any hope of its existence. (p. 101) 1776-80: After exploring the Bering Strait region, he was killed in Hawaii. (pp. 32, 100-101)

Alexander Mackenzie 1789: Traced the course of the Mackenzie River from Great Slave Lake to the Arctic Ocean. (p. 32) 1793: Mackenzie left the forks of the Peace and Smoky Rivers, crossed the Continental Divide, and followed a route along or near the Fraser, Backwater, and Bella Coola Rivers to a tidal inlet of the Pacific, having completed the first overland journey across North America north of Mexico. (p. 32)

George Vancouver 1791-5: Carried out an accurate survey of the northwest Pacific coast of North America. (p. 32)

Nineteenth Century

Mungo Park 1805-6: After reaching the Niger River in 1796, Park returned as head of an expedition to trace the river to its mouth. He sailed down the Niger as far as the Bussa Rapids, where the party was attacked by natives and Park was drowned. (p. 102)

E. J. Eyre 1839-41: Made the first crossing of South Australia from Spencer Gulf to Albany. (p. 95)

John Franklin 1845-8: In search of the Northwest Passage he discovered the correct route but his ships were caught in impenetrable ice. Franklin died in 1847 and the rest of the expedition perished trying to march overland to safety. (p. 32)

David Livingstone 1849: Crossed the Kalahari Desert and reached Lake Ngami. 1851: Discovered the Zambezi River (pp. 102-103) 1853: Crossed Angola to Luanda on the west coast. 1856: Followed the Zambezi River to discover Victoria Falls and reach the sea. (pp. 102-103) 1858-61: Explored the Zambezi region from the river's mouth, discovering Lake Nyasa. (pp. 102-103) 1866-72: Seeking the source of the Nile, he discovered Lakes Mweru and Bangweulu and the Lualaba River. Stanley found him at Ujiji on Lake Tanganyika in 1871, and the two men explored the lake. (pp. 102-103)

J. H. Speke and J. A. Grant 1861: Proved that Lake Victoria was the main source of the Nile. (p. 103)

J. M. Stuart 1860-2: After two attempts, Stuart finally crossed Australia from south to north. (p. 95)

H. M. Stanley 1871: Sent out to search for Livingstone, he found him at Ujiji but was unable to persuade him to return. In a later expedition (1874-7) he crossed Africa from east to west sailing round Lake Victoria and Lake Tanganyika and down the Congo River to sea. (pp. 102-103)

A. E. Nordenskjöld 1878-9: Made the first successful navigation of the Northeast Passage. (p. 74)

J. B. Marchand 1898: Made a trans-continental journey from the Congo to the Gulf of Aden. (pp. 102-103)

Twentieth Century

Roald Amundsen 1903-6: Made the first successful navigation of the Northwest Passage. (p. 32) 1911: Reached the South Pole for the first time on December 14th, beating Scott's expedition by a few weeks. (p. 51)

Robert Peary 1909: After repeated attempts, he became the first man to reach the North Pole. (p. 74)

Robert Scott 1911-12: With four companions he reached the South Pole on January 17th, 1912, to find that Roald Amundsen had preceded him by a few weeks. All five perished on the return journey. (p. 51)

Kon-Tiki Expedition 1947: A spectacular drift across the Pacific on a balsa-wood raft, undertaken to provide evidence for the theory of Inca colonization of the Pacific islands. (p. 101)

Everest Expedition 1953: First ascent of Everest (Hillary and Tensing) by British expedition under Sir John Hunt. (p. 75)

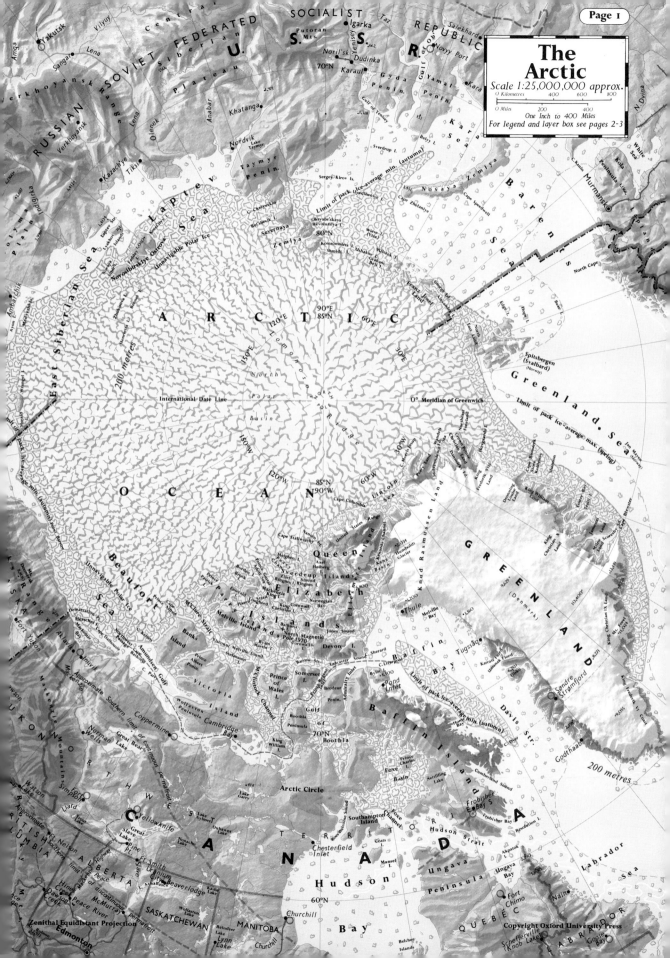

The Arctic
Scale 1:25,000,000 approx.

0 Kilometres 400 600 800
0 Miles 200 400
One Inch to 400 Miles
For legend and layer box see pages 2-3

SOCIALIST REPUBLIC

U.S.S.R.

Central Siberian Plateau

RUSSIAN SOVIET FEDERATED

ARCTIC

OCEAN

North Polar Basin

International Date Line

0° Meridian of Greenwich

90°E 85°N

Limit of pack ice-average min. (autumn)

Barents Sea

Kara Sea

Laptev Sea

East Siberian Sea

Beaufort Sea

Greenland Sea

GREENLAND (Denmark)

Baffin Bay

Davis Str.

Spitsbergen (Svalbard) (Norway)

Jan Mayen (Norway)

Limit of pack ice-average max. (spring)

Queen Elizabeth Islands

Sverdrup Islands

Parry Islands

Melville Island

Banks Island

Victoria Island

Baffin Island

Hudson Bay

Foxe Basin

CANADA

NORTH WEST TERRITORIES

ALBERTA

SASKATCHEWAN

MANITOBA

QUEBEC

LABRADOR

YUKON

BRITISH COLUMBIA

ALASKA

200 metres

Arctic Circle

Hudson Strait

Ungava Peninsula

Ungava Bay

Labrador Sea

Zenithal Equidistant Projection

Copyright Oxford University Press

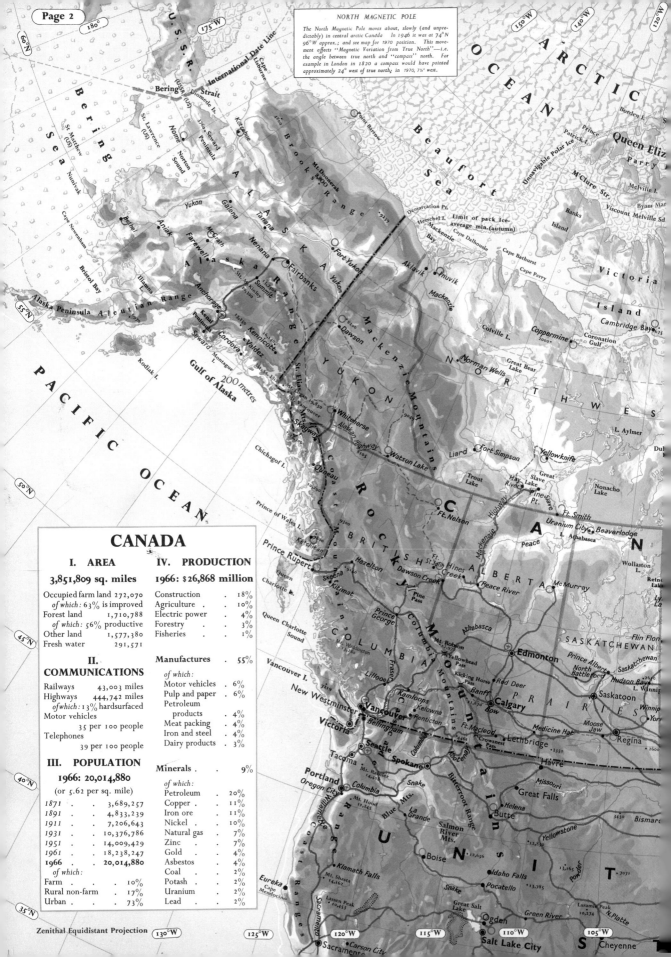

NORTH MAGNETIC POLE

The North Magnetic Pole moves about, slowly (and unpredictably) in central arctic Canada. In 1946 it was at 74°N 96°W approx.; and see map for 1970 position. This movement affects "Magnetic Variation from True North" — i.e. the angle between true north and "compass" north. For example in London in 1820 a compass would have pointed approximately 24° west of true north; in 1970, 7½° west.

CANADA

I. AREA

3,851,809 sq. miles

Occupied farm land	272,070
of which: 63% is improved	
Forest land	1,710,788
of which: 56% productive	
Other land	1,577,380
Fresh water	291,571

II. COMMUNICATIONS

Railways	43,003 miles
Highways	444,742 miles
of which: 13% hardsurfaced	
Motor vehicles	35 per 100 people
Telephones	39 per 100 people

III. POPULATION

1966: 20,014,880

(or 5.62 per sq. mile)

1871	3,689,257
1891	4,833,239
1911	7,206,643
1931	10,376,786
1951	14,009,429
1961	18,238,247
1966	20,014,880

of which:

Farm	10%
Rural non-farm	17%
Urban	73%

IV. PRODUCTION

1966: $26,868 million

Construction	18%
Agriculture	10%
Electric power	4%
Forestry	3%
Fisheries	1%

Manufactures	55%

of which:

Motor vehicles	6%
Pulp and paper	6%
Petroleum products	4%
Meat packing	4%
Iron and steel	4%
Dairy products	3%

Minerals	9%

of which:

Petroleum	20%
Copper	11%
Iron ore	11%
Nickel	10%
Natural gas	7%
Zinc	7%
Gold	4%
Asbestos	4%
Coal	2%
Potash	2%
Uranium	2%
Lead	2%

Zenithal Equidistant Projection

CANADA
Scale 1:19,000,000 approx.

0 Kilometres   300   450   600
0 Miles   150   300   450
One Inch to 300 Miles

Towns over 1 million people
" over 100,000 people
Boundaries international
- provincial etc
Railways   Major
projected   Highway
Airports   Canal
Sand desert   Marsh
Salt pan   Ice cap

GREENLAND
(Denmark)

ICELAND

Cape Columbia
Alert
United States Range
Humboldt Glacier
Axel Heiberg
Ellesmere Island
Cape Morris Jesup
Thule
Melville Bay
Tugssaq
Sondre Stromfjord
Arctic Circle
Mt. Forel
Godthaab
Cape Farewell

Jones Sound
Devon I.
Cornwallis I.
Barrow Str.
Somerset I.
Boothia Penin.
Lancaster Sound
Pond Inlet
Bylot I.
Baffin Bay
Disko
Davis Strait
Baffin Island
Ice-bound Dec.-Apr.
Limit of pack ice - average min. (autumn)
Cumberland Sound
Frobisher Bay
Resolution I.
Limit of pack ice - average max. (spring)

Arctic Circle
TERRITORIES
Southampton Island
Chesterfield Inlet
Hudson Strait
Ungava Peninsula
Ungava Bay
Foxe Basin

Hudson Bay
Churchill
James Bay
MANITOBA
Fort Chimo
Nain
Schefferville (Knob Lake)
Churchill Falls
Goose Bay
Happy Valley
Battle Harbour
Strait of Belle Isle
LABRADOR
NEWFOUNDLAND

Fort Albany
Moosonee
Ashuanipi L.
Gagnon
Allard L.
Anticosti I.
Corner Brook
Grand Falls
Gander
Wabana
St. John's
C. Race
Grand Banks
Placentia Bay

ONTARIO
Lake Nipigon
Fort William
Thunder Bay
Lake Superior
Sault Ste Marie
Sudbury
North Bay
Georgian Bay
Midland
Lake Huron
Kapuskasing
L. Abitibi
Timmins
Kirkland Lake
Cobalt
S. Porcupine
Noranda
Rouyn
Val d'Or
Gouin Reservoir
Chibougamau
Lake Mistassini
Port Cartier
Sept Iles
QUEBEC
Trois-Rivieres
Quebec
Montreal
Ottawa
Gaspe Peninsula
Rimouski
Gaspe
Saguenay
Chicoutimi
Dolbeau
St. John
Edmundston
NEW BRUNSWICK
Fredericton
Saint John
St. Lawrence
Gulf of St. Lawrence
Cabot Strait
Port aux Basques
St. Pierre & Miquelon (Fr.)
Sydney
Cape Breton I.
Glace Bay
Canso
Charlottetown
PRINCE EDWARD I.
Moncton
Pictou
Truro
NOVA SCOTIA
Halifax
Bay of Fundy
Yarmouth
Cape Sable

Duluth
St. Paul
Minneapolis
Sioux Falls
Madison
Milwaukee
Chicago
Des Moines
Omaha
Peoria
Detroit
Toledo
Cleveland
Fort Wayne
Columbus
Pittsburgh
Toronto
Kitchener
Hamilton
London
Windsor
Sarnia
Grand Rapids
Flint
Lake Michigan
Lake Erie
Lake Ontario
Niagara Falls
Buffalo
Peterborough
Kingston
Albany
Hartford
Providence
Boston
Fall River
Manchester
Portland
Scranton
Trenton
New Haven
Jersey City
New York
Philadelphia
Wilmington
Baltimore
Washington
UNITED STATES

ATLANTIC OCEAN

SPOT HEIGHTS IN FEET

Ft.	M.
16,000	4,800
10,000	3,000
6,000	1,800
3,000	900
1,500	450
1,000	300
600	180
300	90
Sea Level	
Land Depression	

200 metres

© Oxford University Press

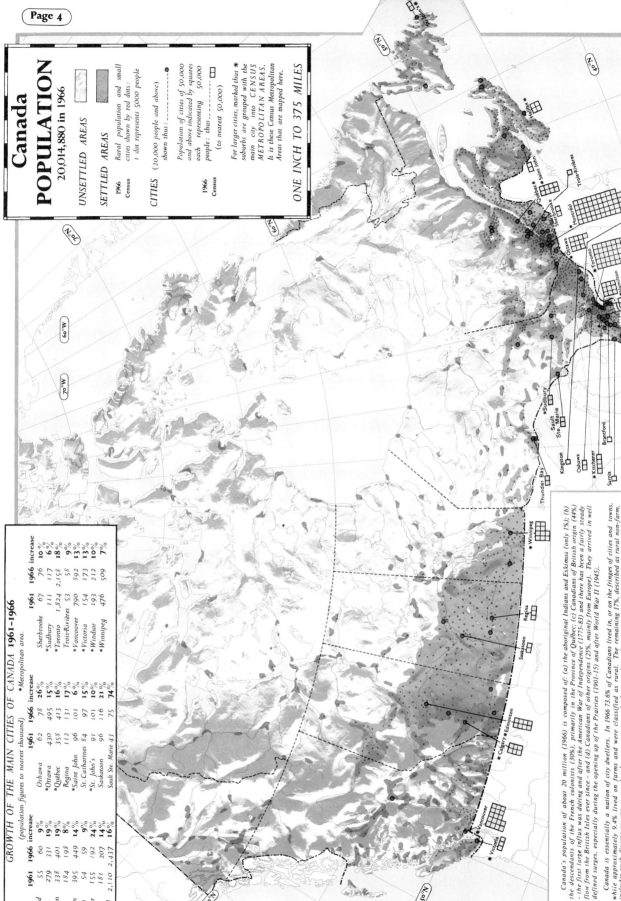

Canada
POPULATION
20,014,880 in 1966

UNSETTLED AREAS
1966 Census

SETTLED AREAS
1966 Census

CITIES (20,000 people and above)

Rural population and small cities shown by red dots:
1 dot represents 5000 people

Population of cities of 50,000 and above indicated by squares each representing 50,000 people: thus:
(to nearest 50,000)

For larger cities, marked thus * their suburbs are grouped with the main city into CENSUS METROPOLITAN AREAS. It is these Census Metropolitan Areas that are mapped here.

ONE INCH TO 375 MILES

GROWTH OF THE MAIN CITIES OF CANADA 1961-1966
(population figures to nearest thousand) *Metropolitan area.

	1961	1966	increase		1961	1966	increase		1961	1966	increase
Branford	55	60	9%	Oshawa	62	78	26%	Sherbrooke	67	76	10%
*Calgary	279	331	19%	*Ottawa	430	495	15%	*Sudbury	111	117	6%
*Edmonton	338	401	19%	*Québec	358	413	16%	*Toronto	1,824	2,158	18%
Halifax	184	198	8%	Regina	112	131	17%	Trois-Rivières	53	58	9%
*Hamilton	395	449	14%	*Saint John	96	101	6%	*Vancouver	790	892	13%
Kingston	54	59	9%	St. Catharines	84	97	15%	*Victoria	154	173	13%
*Kitchener	155	192	24%	*St. John's	91	101	10%	*Windsor	193	212	10%
*London	181	207	14%	Saskatoon	96	116	21%	*Winnipeg	476	509	7%
*Montréal	2,110	2,437	16%	Sault Ste. Marie	43	75	74%				

Canada's population of about 20 million (1966) is composed of: (a) the aboriginal Indians and Eskimos (only 1%); (b) the descendants of the French colonists (30%), primarily in the Province of Quebec; (c) Canadians of British origin (44%) - the first large influx was during and after the American War of Independence (1775-83) and there has been a fairly steady flow from the British Isles ever since - and (d) Canadians of other origins (25%, mainly from Europe). They arrived in well defined surges, especially during the opening up of the Prairies (1901-15) and after World War II (1945).

Canada is essentially a nation of city dwellers. In 1966 73.6% of Canadians lived in, or on the fringes of cities and towns, while approximately 9.4% lived on farms and were classified as rural. The remaining 17%, described as rural non-farm, includes such diverse groups as people who commute to work-places within urban centres, miners, forest workers, fishermen, etc. The urban proportion of the population has been steadily increasing (from approximately 69.5% in 1961) and will likely continue to do so, as most of the future increase in Canada's population will occur in urban areas, particularly in the larger cities. Much of the land of Canada cannot support a large population: important industries like forestry, mining and the

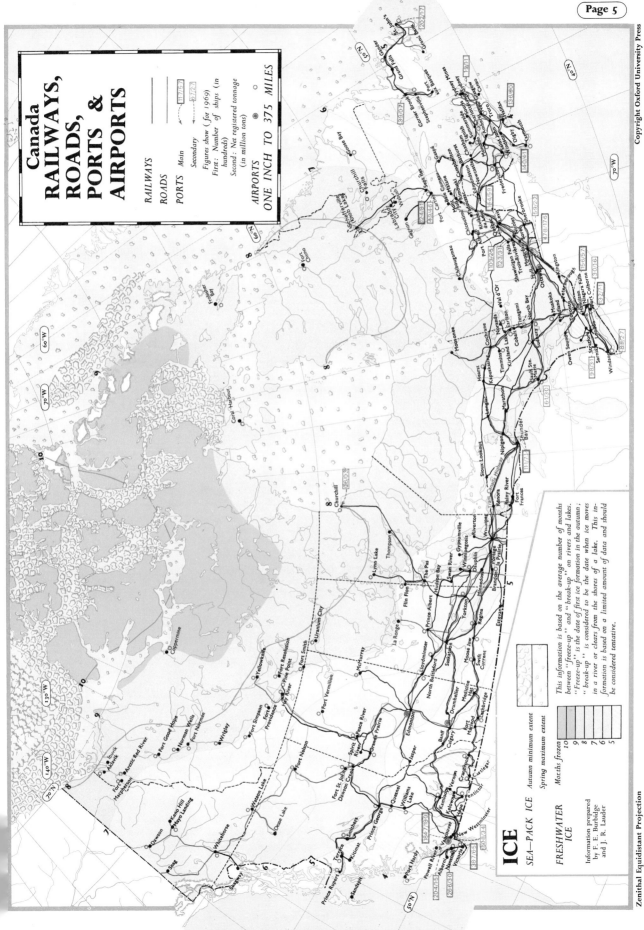

Canada
RAILWAYS, ROADS, PORTS & AIRPORTS

RAILWAYS
ROADS

PORTS   Main
         Secondary
    Figures show (for 1969)
    First: Number of ships (in hundreds)
    Second: Net registered tonnage (in million tons)

AIRPORTS

ONE INCH TO 375 MILES

ICE

SEA-PACK ICE   Autumn minimum extent
                Spring maximum extent

FRESHWATER ICE   Months frozen
    10
    9
    8
    7
    6
    5

Information prepared by F. E. Burbidge and J. R. Lauder

This information is based on the average number of months between "freeze-up" and "break-up" on rivers and lakes. "Freeze-up" is the date of first ice formation in the autumn; "break-up" is considered to be the date when ice moves in a river or clears from the shores of a lake. This information is based on a limited amount of data and should be considered tentative.

Zenithal Equidistant Projection

Copyright Oxford University Press

Canada VEGETATION

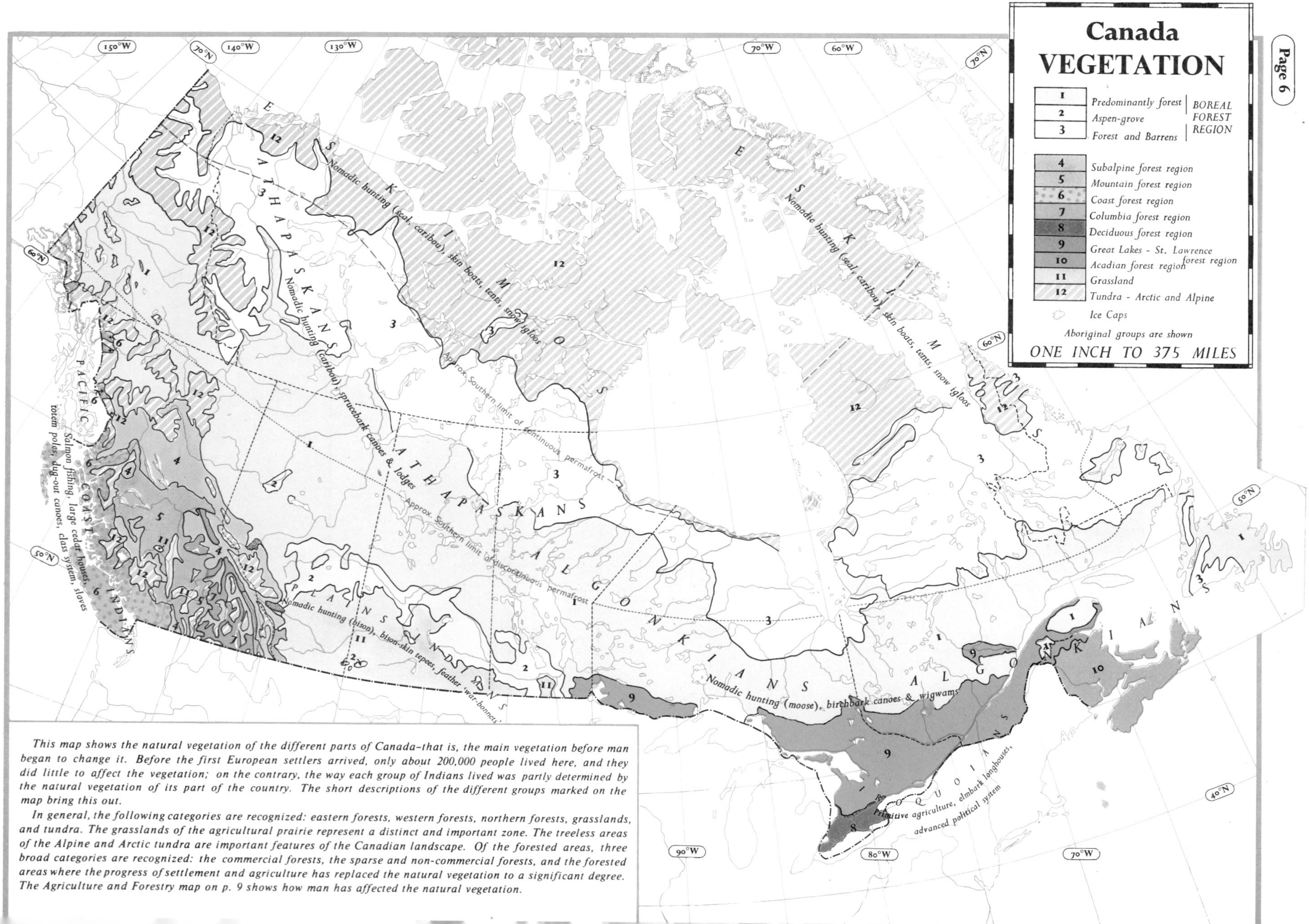

BOREAL FOREST REGION

1 Predominantly forest
2 Aspen-grove
3 Forest and Barrens

4 Subalpine forest region
5 Mountain forest region
6 Coast forest region
7 Columbia forest region
8 Deciduous forest region
9 Great Lakes – St. Lawrence forest region
10 Acadian forest region
11 Grassland
12 Tundra – Arctic and Alpine

Ice Caps

Aboriginal groups are shown

ONE INCH TO 375 MILES

This map shows the natural vegetation of the different parts of Canada—that is, the main vegetation before man began to change it. Before the first European settlers arrived, only about 200,000 people lived here, and they did little to affect the vegetation; on the contrary, the way each group of Indians lived was partly determined by the natural vegetation of its part of the country. The short descriptions of the different groups marked on the map bring this out.

In general, the following categories are recognized: eastern forests, western forests, northern forests, grasslands, and tundra. The grasslands of the agricultural prairie represent a distinct and important zone. The treeless areas of the Alpine and Arctic tundra are important features of the Canadian landscape. Of the forested areas, three broad categories are recognized: the commercial forests, the sparse and non-commercial forests, and the forested areas where the progress of settlement and agriculture has replaced the natural vegetation to a significant degree. The Agriculture and Forestry map on p. 9 shows how man has affected the natural vegetation.

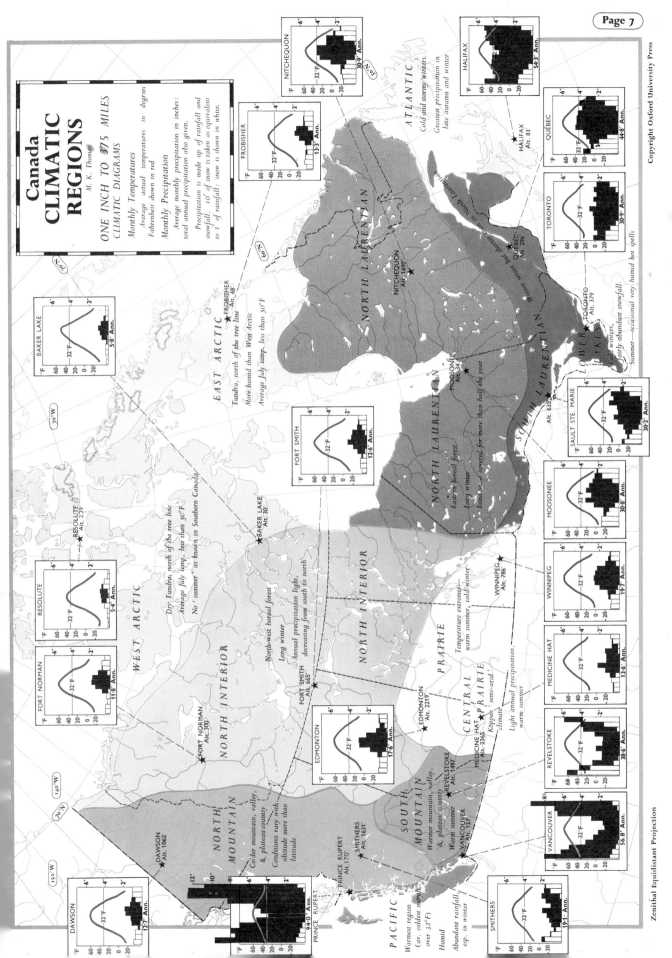

Canada
CLIMATIC REGIONS

M. K. Thomas

ONE INCH TO 375 MILES
CLIMATIC DIAGRAMS

Monthly Temperatures

Average actual temperatures in degrees Fahrenheit shown in red

Monthly Precipitation

Average monthly precipitation in inches: total annual precipitation also given.

Precipitation is made up of rainfall and snowfall. 10″ of snow is taken as equivalent to 1″ of rainfall: snow is shown in white.

EAST ARCTIC
Tundra, north of the tree line
More humid than West Arctic
Average July temp. less than 50°F

WEST ARCTIC
Dry Tundra, north of the tree line
Average July temp. less than 50°F
No 'summer' as known in Southern Canada

NORTH INTERIOR
North-west boreal forest
Long winter
Annual precipitation light, decreasing from south to north

NORTH LAURENTIAN
Eastern boreal forest
Long winter
Land snow covered for more than half the year

NORTH MOUNTAIN
Colder mountain, valley, & plateau country
Conditions vary with altitude more than latitude

SOUTH MOUNTAIN
Warmer mountain, valley & plateau country
Warm summer

PACIFIC
Warmest region (av. coldest month over 32°F)
Humid
Abundant rainfall, esp. in winter

PRAIRIE
Temperature extremes, warm summer, cold winter

CENTRAL PRAIRIE
Köppen semi-arid 'climate'
Light annual precipitation, warm summer

SOUTH LAURENTIAN
Cold winters, early abundant snowfall.
Summer—occasional very humid hot spells

LOWER LAKES
Cold winters.
Early abundant snowfall.
Summer—occasional very humid hot spells

ATLANTIC
Cold and stormy winters.
Greatest precipitation in late autumn and winter

Winter storms move north up Laurentian

Copyright Oxford University Press

Zenithal Equidistant Projection

Climatic diagrams (with altitude and annual precipitation):
NITCHEQUON Alt. 1690 — 30·9″ Ann.
FROBISHER Alt. 68 — 13·3″ Ann.
HALIFAX Alt. 83 — 54·3″ Ann.
QUÉBEC Alt. 296 — 44·8″ Ann.
TORONTO Alt. 379 — 30·9″ Ann.
BAKER LAKE Alt. 30 — 5·8″ Ann.
FORT SMITH Alt. 665 — 12·6″ Ann.
SAULT STE. MARIE Alt. 635 — 30·2″ Ann.
MOOSONEE Alt. 34 — 30·8″ Ann.
RESOLUTE Alt. 229 — 5·4″ Ann.
FORT NORMAN Alt. 300 — 11·8″ Ann.
WINNIPEG Alt. 786 — 19·7″ Ann.
EDMONTON Alt. 2219 — 17·6″ Ann.
MEDICINE HAT Alt. 2365 — 13·6″ Ann.
REVELSTOKE Alt. 1497 — 38·6″ Ann.
VANCOUVER Alt. 127 — 56·8″ Ann.
DAWSON Alt. 1062 — 12·7″ Ann.
PRINCE RUPERT Alt. 170 — 94·0″ Ann.
SMITHERS Alt. 1631 — 19·1″ Ann.

60° N
60° W
70° W
90° W
140° W
150° W
70° N

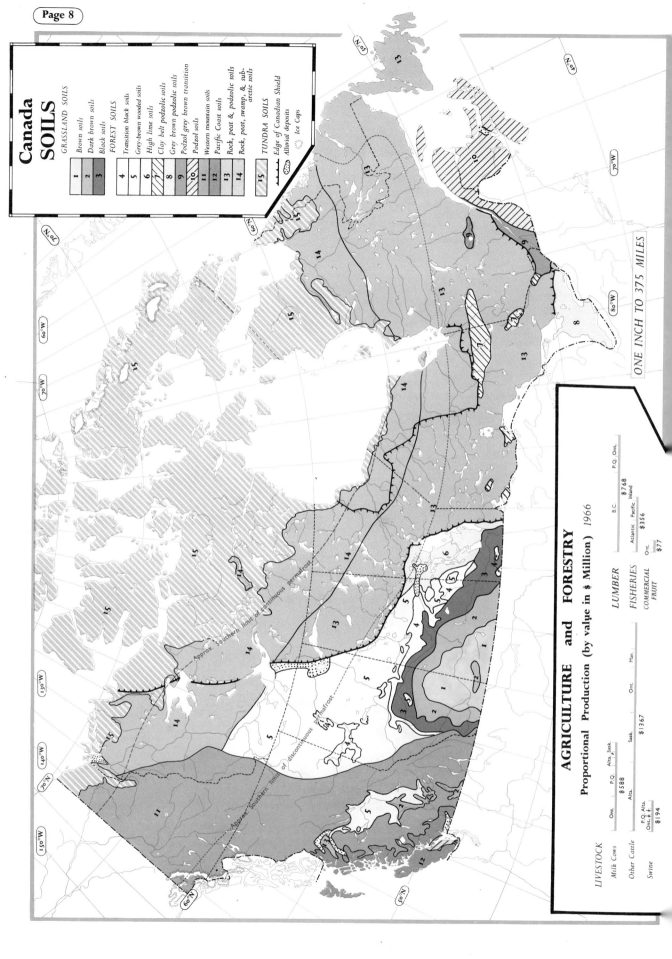

Canada
SOILS

GRASSLAND SOILS

1	Brown soils
2	Dark brown soils
3	Black soils

FOREST SOILS

4	Transition black soils
5	Grey-brown wooded soils
6	High lime soils
7	Clay belt podzolic soils
8	Grey brown podzolic soils
9	Podzol grey brown transition
10	Podzol soils
11	Western mountain soils
12	Pacific Coast soils
13	Rock, peat & podzolic soils
14	Rock, peat, swamp, & sub-arctic soils

TUNDRA SOILS

15	

⎯ Edge of Canadian Shield
Alluvial deposits
Ice Caps

ONE INCH TO 375 MILES

Approx. Southern limit of continuous permafrost

Approx. Southern limit of discontinuous permafrost

AGRICULTURE and FORESTRY
Proportional Production (by value in $ Million) 1966

LIVESTOCK

Milk Cows

Ont.	P.Q.	Alta., Sask.
	$588	

Other Cattle

Alta.	Sask.	Ont.	Man.		$1367

Swine

P.Q. Alta. Ont.		$194

LUMBER

	B.C.	
	$768	

Atlantic	Pacific	Inland	P.Q.	Ont.

Ont.	$356

FISHERIES

COMMERCIAL FRUIT

$77

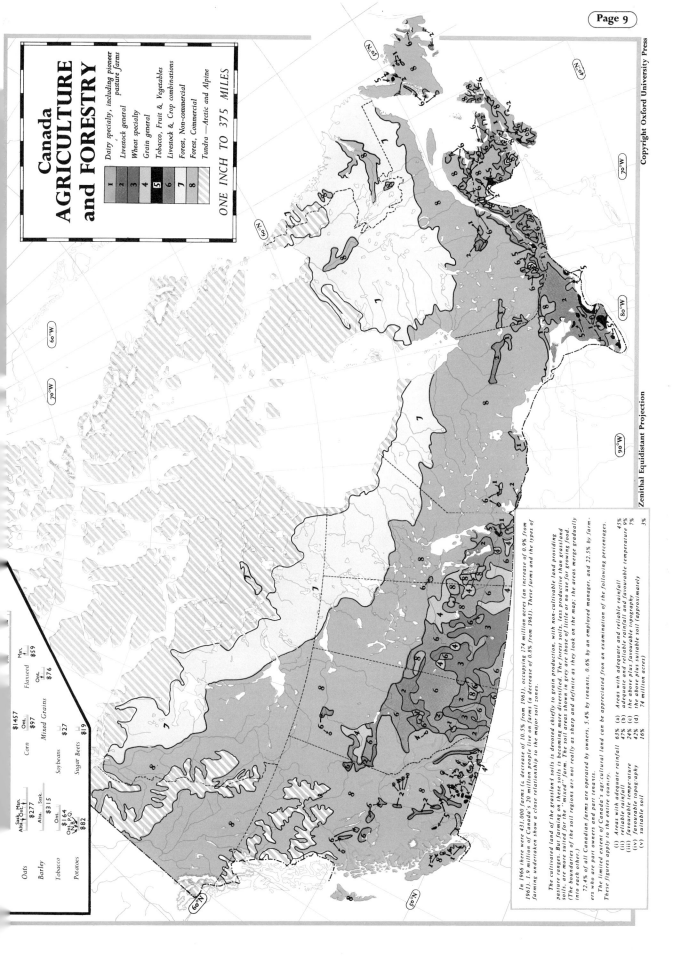

Copyright Oxford University Press

Canada
AGRICULTURE and FORESTRY

1	Dairy specialty, including pioneer pasture farms
2	Livestock general
3	Wheat specialty
4	Grain general
5	Tobacco, Fruit & Vegetables
6	Livestock & Crop combinations
7	Forest, Non-commercial
8	Forest, Commercial
	Tundra — Arctic and Alpine

ONE INCH TO 375 MILES

Zenithal Equidistant Projection

In 1966 there were 431,000 farms (a decrease of 10.5% from 1961), occupying 174 million acres (an increase of 0.9% from 1961). 1.9 million of Canada's 20 million people live on farms (a decrease of 0.8% from 1961). These farms and the types of farming undertaken show a close relationship to the major soil zones.

The cultivated land of the grassland soils is devoted chiefly to grain production, with non-cultivable land providing pasture ranges. But farming on these soils is becoming more diversified. The forest soils, less productive than grassland soils, are more suited for the "mixed" farm. The soil areas shown in grey are those of little or no use for growing food. (The boundaries of the soil regions are not really as sharp and definite as they look on the map; the areas merge gradually into each other.)

72.4% of all Canadian farms are operated by owners, 5.4% by tenants, 0.6% by an employed manager, and 22.5% by farmers who are part owners and part tenants.

The limited extent of Canada's agricultural land can be appreciated from an examination of the following percentages. These figures apply to the entire country.

(i) Areas with adequate rainfall 63% (a) Areas with adequate and reliable rainfall 45%
(ii) reliable rainfall 24% (b) adequate and reliable rainfall and favourable temperature 9%
(iii) favourable temperature 24% (c) the above plus favourable topography 7%
(iv) favourable topography 42% (d) the above plus suitable soil (approximately)
(v) suitable soil 16% 74 million acres) 3%

Oats	Sask. Man. Alta. Ont.	$1457 Ont. $97
Barley	Alta. Sask. $277 $315	Corn
Tobacco	Ont. $164	Mixed Grains
Potatoes	Ont. N.B. $82	Soybeans $27
	Flaxseed	Sugar Beets $19
	Sask. $76 Man. $59	

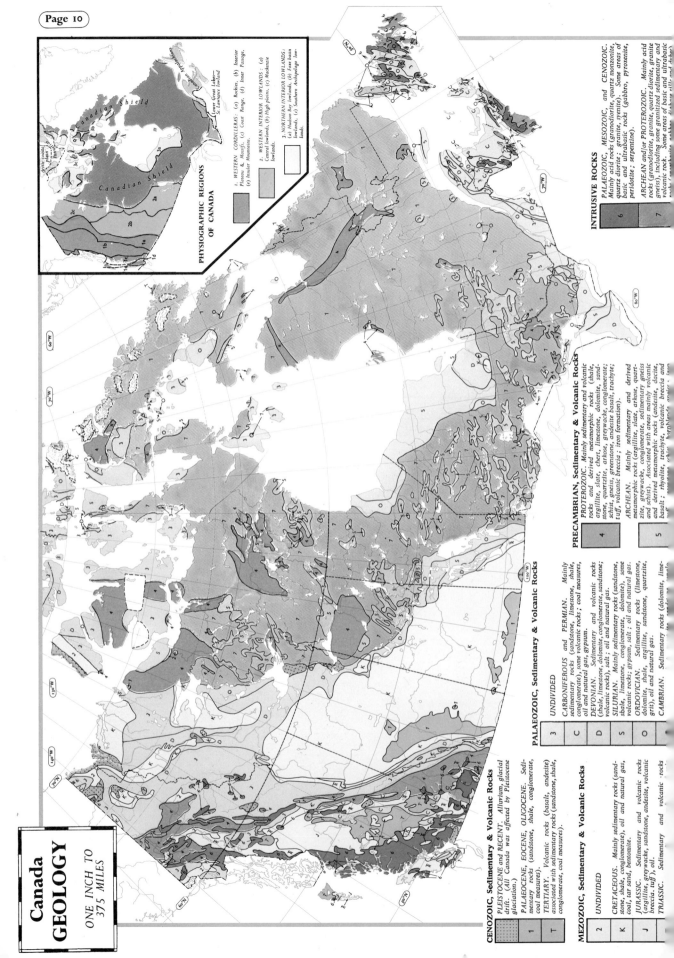

Canada GEOLOGY

ONE INCH TO 375 MILES

PHYSIOGRAPHIC REGIONS OF CANADA

1, WESTERN CORDILLERAS: (a) Rockies, (b) Interior Plateau & Massif, (c) Coast Range, (d) Inner Passage, (e) Insular Mountains.

2, WESTERN INTERIOR LOWLANDS: (a) Central lowlands, (b) High plains, (c) Mackenzie lowlands.

3, NORTHERN INTERIOR LOWLANDS: (a) Hudson Bay lowlands, (b) Foxe basin lowlands, (c) Southern Archipelago lowlands.

Canadian Shield

Lower Great Lakes—St. Lawrence lowland

CENOZOIC, Sedimentary & Volcanic Rocks

1 PLEISTOCENE and RECENT. Alluvium, glacial drift. (All Canada was affected by Pleistocene glaciation.)

PALAEOCENE, EOCENE, OLIGOCENE. Sedimentary rocks (sandstone, shale, conglomerate, coal measures).

T TERTIARY. Volcanic rocks (basalt, andesite) associated with sedimentary rocks (sandstone, shale, conglomerate, coal measures).

MESOZOIC, Sedimentary & Volcanic Rocks

2 UNDIVIDED

K CRETACEOUS. Mainly sedimentary rocks (sandstone, shale, conglomerate), oil and natural gas, coal, tar sand, bentonite.

J JURASSIC. Sedimentary and volcanic rocks (argillite, greywacke, sandstone, andesite, volcanic breccia, tuff), oil.

TRIASSIC. Sedimentary and volcanic rocks

PALAEOZOIC, Sedimentary & Volcanic Rocks

3 UNDIVIDED

C CARBONIFEROUS and PERMIAN. Mainly sedimentary rocks (sandstone, limestone, shale, conglomerate), some volcanic rocks; coal measures, oil and natural gas, gypsum.

D DEVONIAN. Sedimentary and volcanic rocks (shale, limestone, dolomite, conglomerate, sandstone, quartzite, slate, chert, limestone, dolomite, greywacke, conglomerate; volcanic rocks), salt; oil and natural gas.

S SILURIAN. Mainly sedimentary rocks (sandstone, shale, limestone, conglomerate, dolomite), some volcanic rocks; gypsum, salt; oil and natural gas.

O ORDOVICIAN. Sedimentary rocks (limestone, dolomite, shale, argillite, sandstone, quartzite, grit), oil and natural gas.

CAMBRIAN. Sedimentary rocks (dolomite, lime-

PRECAMBRIAN, Sedimentary & Volcanic Rocks

4 PROTEROZOIC. Mainly sedimentary and volcanic rocks and derived metamorphic rocks (shale, argillite, slate, chert, limestone, dolomite, sandstone, quartzite, arkose, greywacke, conglomerate; schist, gneiss, greenstone, andesite basalt, trachyte; tuff, volcanic breccia; iron formation).

5 ARCHEAN. Mainly sedimentary and derived metamorphic rocks (argillite, slate, arkose, quartzite, greywacke, conglomerate, sedimentary gneiss and schist). Associated with areas mainly volcanic and derived metamorphic rocks (andesite, dacite, basalt; rhyolite, trachyte, volcanic breccia and

INTRUSIVE ROCKS

6 PALAEOZOIC, MESOZOIC, and CENOZOIC. Mainly acid rocks (granodiorite, quartz monzonite, quartz diorite; granite, syenite). Some areas of basic and ultrabasic rocks (gabbro, pyroxenite, peridotite; serpentine).

7 ARCHEAN and/or PROTEROZOIC. Mainly acid rocks (granodiorite, granite, quartz diorite, granite gneiss including granitized sedimentary and volcanic rock. Some areas of basic and ultrabasic

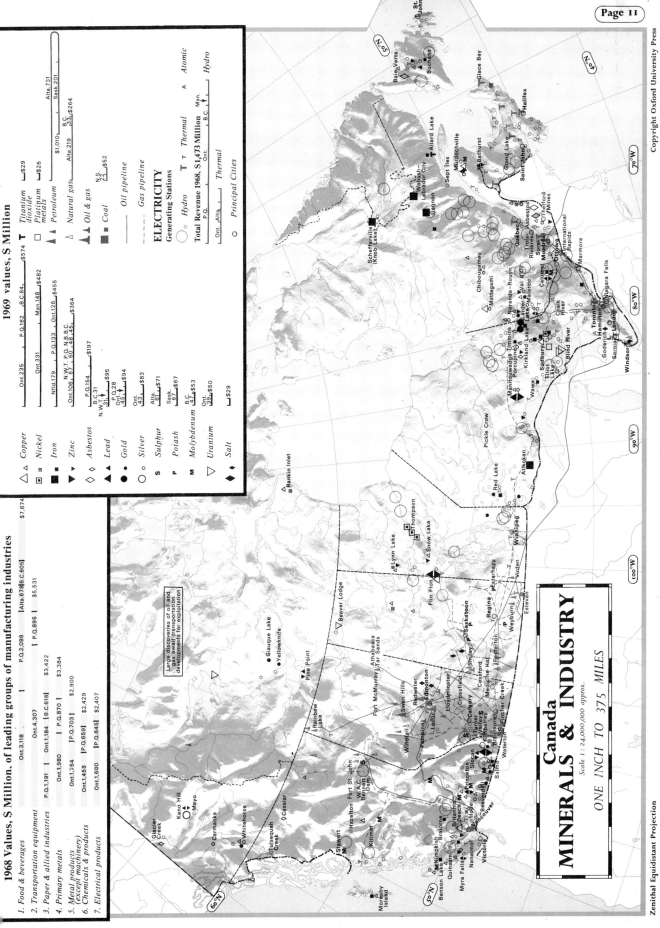

Canada
MINERALS & INDUSTRY

Scale 1 : 24,000,000 approx.

ONE INCH TO 375 MILES

Zenithal Equidistant Projection

Copyright Oxford University Press

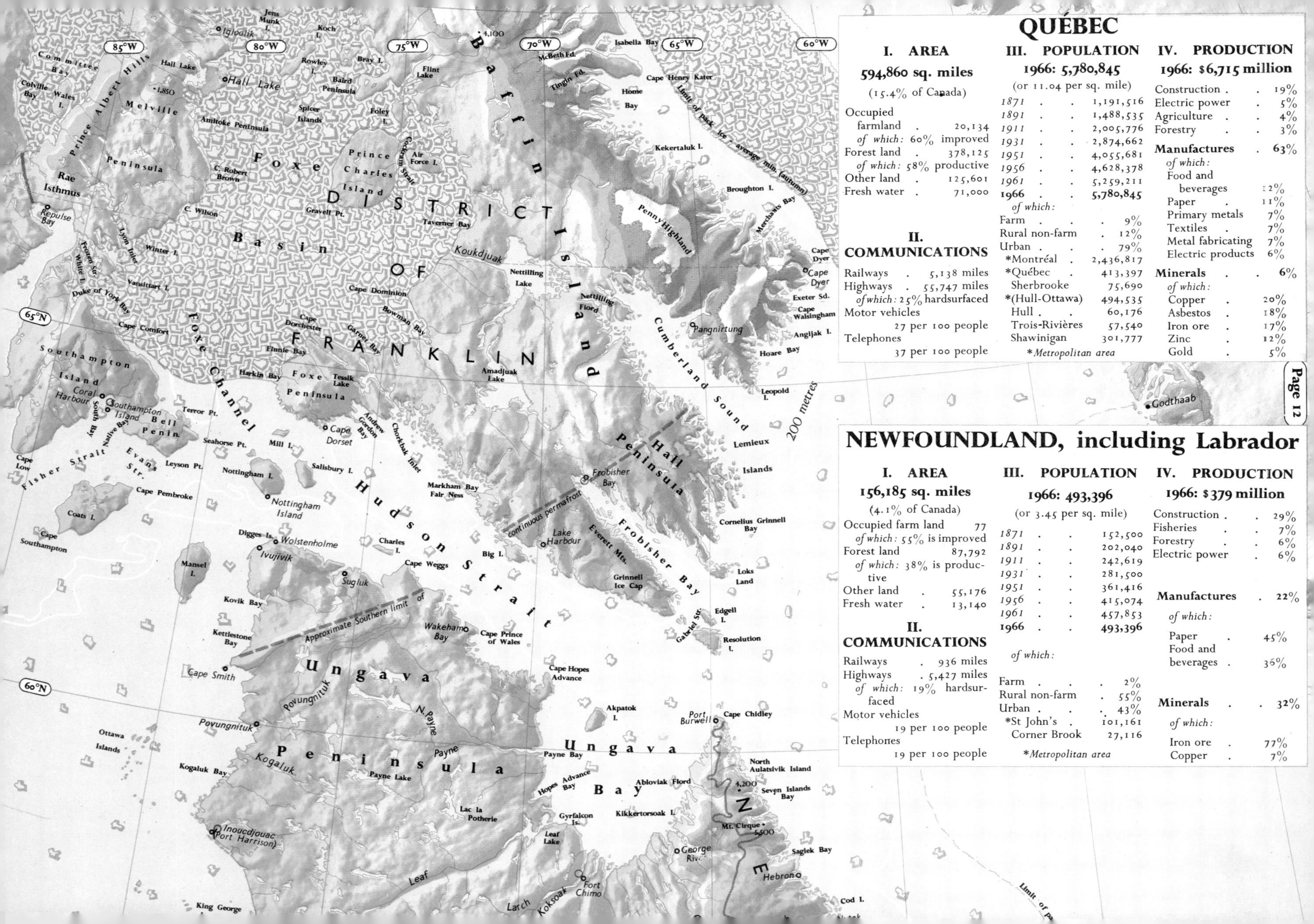

QUÉBEC

I. AREA

594,860 sq. miles

(15.4% of Canada)

Occupied farmland	.	20,134
of which: 60% improved		
Forest land	.	378,125
of which: 58% productive		
Other land	.	125,601
Fresh water	.	71,000

II. COMMUNICATIONS

Railways	.	5,138 miles
Highways	.	55,747 miles
of which: 25% hardsurfaced		
Motor vehicles		27 per 100 people
Telephones		37 per 100 people

III. POPULATION

1966: 5,780,845

(or 11.04 per sq. mile)

1871	.	1,191,516
1891	.	1,488,535
1911	.	2,005,776
1931	.	2,874,662
1951	.	4,055,681
1956	.	4,628,378
1961	.	5,259,211
1966	.	5,780,845

of which:

Farm	.	9%
Rural non-farm	.	12%
Urban	.	79%
		2,436,817
*Montréal	.	413,397
*Québec	.	75,690
*(Hull-Ottawa)	.	494,535
Hull	.	60,176
Trois-Rivières	.	57,540
Shawinigan	.	31,777

Metropolitan area

IV. PRODUCTION

1966: $6,715 million

Construction	.	19%
Electric power	.	5%
Agriculture	.	4%
Forestry	.	3%
Manufactures		**63%**
of which:		
Food and beverages		12%
Paper		11%
Primary metals		7%
Textiles		7%
Metal fabricating		7%
Electric products		6%
Minerals		**6%**
of which:		
Copper		20%
Asbestos		18%
Iron ore		17%
Zinc		7%
Gold		5%

NEWFOUNDLAND, including Labrador

I. AREA

156,185 sq. miles

(4.1% of Canada)

Occupied farm land	.	77
of which: 55% is improved		
Forest land	.	87,792
of which: 38% is productive		
Other land	.	55,176
Fresh water	.	13,140

II. COMMUNICATIONS

Railways	.	936 miles
Highways	.	5,427 miles
of which: 19% hardsurfaced		
Motor vehicles		19 per 100 people
Telephones		19 per 100 people

III. POPULATION

1966: 493,396

(or 3.45 per sq. mile)

1871	.	152,500
1891	.	202,040
1911	.	242,619
1931	.	281,500
1951	.	361,416
1956	.	415,074
1961	.	457,853
1966		493,396

of which:

Farm	.	2%
Rural non-farm	.	55%
Urban	.	43%
*St John's	.	101,161
Corner Brook	.	27,116

Metropolitan area

IV. PRODUCTION

1966: $379 million

Construction	.	29%
Fisheries	.	7%
Forestry	.	6%
Electric power	.	6%
Manufactures		**22%**
of which:		
Paper		45%
Food and beverages		36%
Minerals		**32%**
of which:		
Iron ore		77%
Copper		7%

Scale 1:8,000,000 approx.
One Inch to 125 Miles
For legend & layer box see pages 16/17
Conical Orthomorphic Projection

© Copyright Oxford University Press

200 metres

N E W F O U N D L A N D

L A B R A D O R

Q U É B E C

N E W   B R U N S W I C K

M A I N E

NOVA   SCOTIA

PRINCE EDWARD ISLAND

Gulf of St. Lawrence

James Bay

NEW HAMPSHIRE

VERMONT

NEW YORK

St. Lawrence

Jacques Cartier Passage

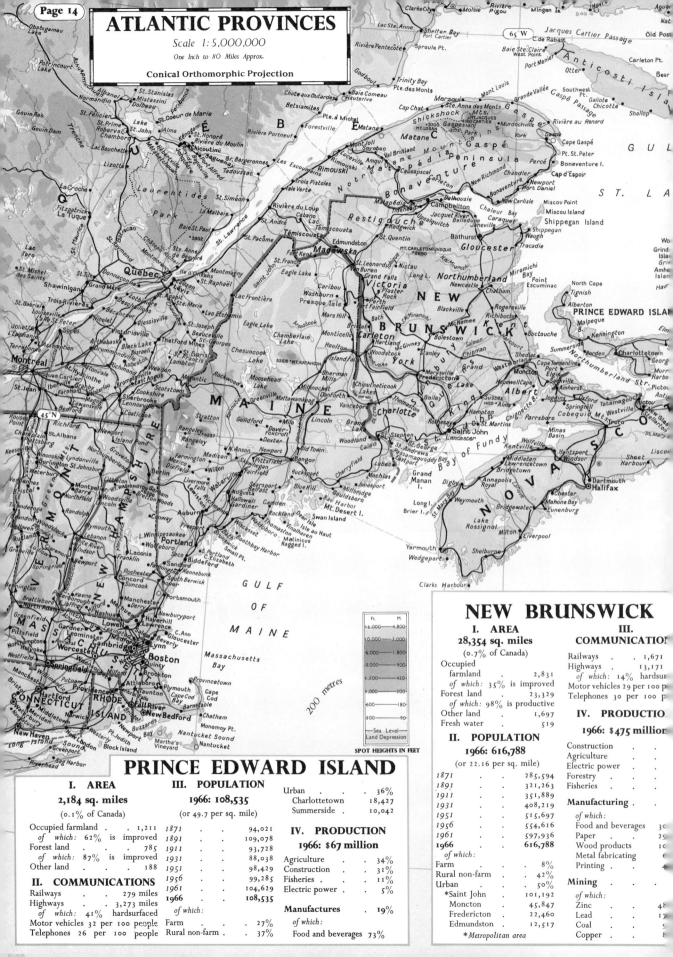

ATLANTIC PROVINCES

Scale 1 : 5,000,000

One Inch to 80 Miles Approx.

Conical Orthomorphic Projection

Ft.	M.
16,000	4,800
10,000	3,000
6,000	1,800
3,000	900
1,500	450
600	180
300	90
Sea Level	
Land Depression	

SPOT HEIGHTS IN FEET

200 metres

NEW BRUNSWICK

I. AREA

28,354 sq. miles

(0.7% of Canada)

Occupied farmland	2,831
of which: 35% is improved	
Forest land	23,329
of which: 98% is productive	
Other land	1,697
Fresh water	519

II. POPULATION

1966: 616,788

(or 22.16 per sq. mile)

1871	.	285,594
1891	.	321,263
1911	.	351,889
1931	.	408,219
1951	.	515,697
1956	.	554,616
1961	.	597,936
1966		**616,788**

of which:

Farm	.	8%
Rural non-farm	.	42%
Urban	.	50%
*Saint John	101,192	
Moncton	45,847	
Fredericton	22,460	
Edmundston	12,517	

*Metropolitan area

III. COMMUNICATION

Railways	.	1,671
Highways	.	13,171
of which: 14% hardsur		
Motor vehicles 29 per 100 p		
Telephones 30 per 100 p		

IV. PRODUCTIO

1966: $475 million

Construction	.
Agriculture	.
Electric power	.
Forestry	.
Fisheries	.

Manufacturing

of which:

Food and beverages	30
Paper	29
Wood products	10
Metal fabricating	
Printing	4

Mining

of which:

Zinc	48
Lead	17
Coal	
Copper	

PRINCE EDWARD ISLAND

I. AREA

2,184 sq. miles

(0.1% of Canada)

Occupied farmland	1,211
of which: 62% is improved	
Forest land	785
of which: 87% is improved	
Other land	188

II. COMMUNICATIONS

Railways	279 miles
Highways	3,273 miles
of which: 41% hardsurfaced	
Motor vehicles 32 per 100 people	
Telephones 26 per 100 people	

III. POPULATION

1966: 108,535

(or 49.7 per sq. mile)

1871	.	94,021
1891	.	109,078
1911	.	93,728
1931	.	88,038
1951	.	98,429
1956	.	99,285
1961	.	104,629
1966		**108,535**

of which:

Farm	.	27%
Rural non-farm	.	37%
Urban	.	36%
Charlottetown	18,427	
Summerside	10,042	

IV. PRODUCTION

1966: $67 million

Agriculture	34%
Construction	31%
Fisheries	11%
Electric power	5%

Manufactures	19%

of which:

Food and beverages	73%

Scale 1:3,150,000 approx.
One Inch to 50 Miles

Copyright Oxford University Press

Legend:
Boundaries—international
—provincial, etc.
—county
Limited access highways
Other main roads
Secondary roads
Railways
Airports
Ferries
Marsh

NOVA SCOTIA

III. POPULATION
1966: 756,039
(or 37.06 per sq. mile)

1871	. .	387,800
1891	. .	459,396
1911	. .	492,338
1931	. .	512,846
1951	. .	642,584
1956	. .	694,717
1961	. .	737,007
1966		**756,039**

of which:

Farm	.	6%
Rural non-farm	.	37%
Urban	.	57%
*Halifax	.	198,193
Sydney	.	32,767
Glace Bay	.	23,516
Truro	.	13,007
New Glasgow	.	10,489
New Waterford	.	9,725

*Metropolitan area

I. AREA
21,425 sq. miles
(0.6% of Canada)

Occupied farmland	2,893	
of which: 26% is improved		
Forest land	15,274	
of which: 93% is improved		
Other land	2,235	
Fresh water	1,023	

II. COMMUNICATIONS

Railways	.	1,313 miles
Highways	.	15,510 miles
of which: 26% is hardsurfaced		
Motor vehicles		30 per 100 people
Telephones		31 per 100 people

IV. PRODUCTION
1966: $524 million

Construction	.	25%
Fisheries	.	10%
Agriculture	.	6%
Electric power	.	6%
Forestry	.	2%
Manufactures	.	**42%**

of which:

Food and beverages	28%
Transportation equipment	14%
Paper	10%
Metal fabricating	6%
Wood products	5%

Mining	.	**9%**

of which:

Coal	61%
Gypsum	10%
Salt	6%

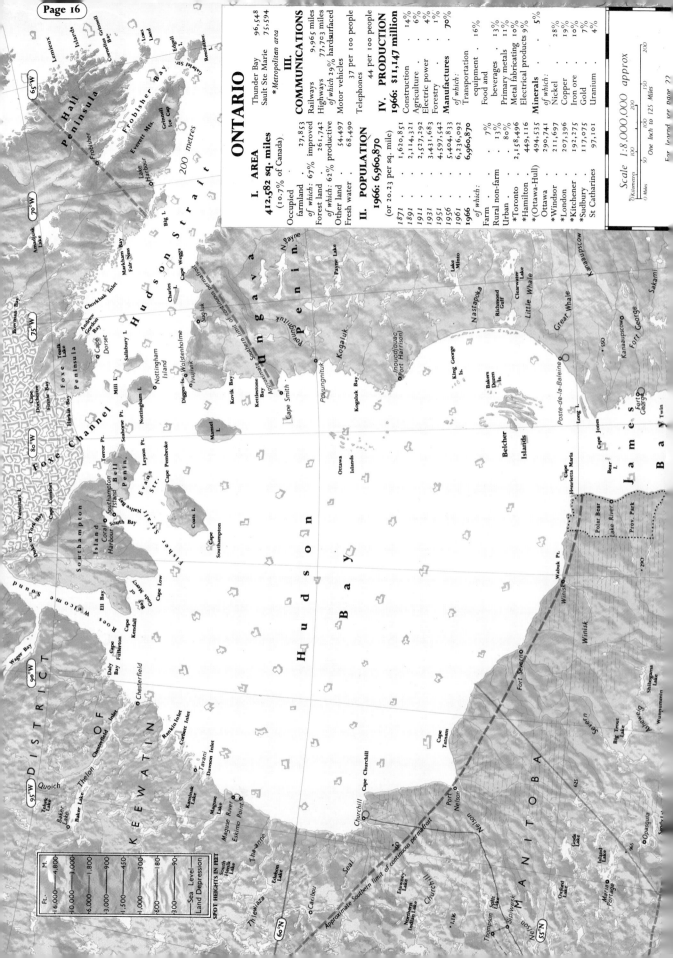

ONTARIO

I. AREA
412,582 sq. miles
(10.7% of Canada)

Occupied farmland	27,853
of which: 67% improved	
Forest land	261,742
of which: 62% productive	
Other land	54,497
Fresh water	68,490

II. POPULATION
1966: 6,960,870
(or 20.23 per sq. mile)

1871	1,620,851
1891	2,114,321
1911	2,527,292
1931	3,431,683
1951	4,597,542
1956	5,404,833
1961	6,236,092
1966	**6,960,870**

of which:

Farm	7%
Rural non-farm	13%
Urban	80%
*Toronto	2,158,496
*Hamilton	449,116
*(Ottawa-Hull)	494,535
Ottawa	290,741
*Windsor	211,697
*London	207,396
*Kitchener	192,275
*Sudbury	117,075
St Catharines	97,101
Thunder Bay	96,548
Sault Ste Marie	75,594

*Metropolitan area

III. COMMUNICATIONS

Railways	9,965 miles
Highways	77,703 miles
of which 29% hardsurfaced	
Motor vehicles	
Telephones	37 per 100 people
	44 per 100 people

IV. PRODUCTION
1966: $11,147 million

Manufactures	**70%**
Construction	14%
Agriculture	6%
Electric power	4%
Forestry	1%
of which:	
Transportation equipment	16%
Food and beverages	13%
Primary metals	11%
Metal fabricating	10%
Electrical products	9%
Minerals	**5%**
of which:	
Nickel	28%
Copper	19%
Iron ore	10%
Gold	7%
Uranium	4%

Scale 1:8,000,000 approx

One Inch to 125 Miles

For legend see page 22

SPOT HEIGHTS IN FEET

Ft.	M
16,000	4,800
10,000	3,000
6,000	1,800
3,000	900
1,500	450
1,000	300
600	180
300	90
Sea Level	
Land Depression	

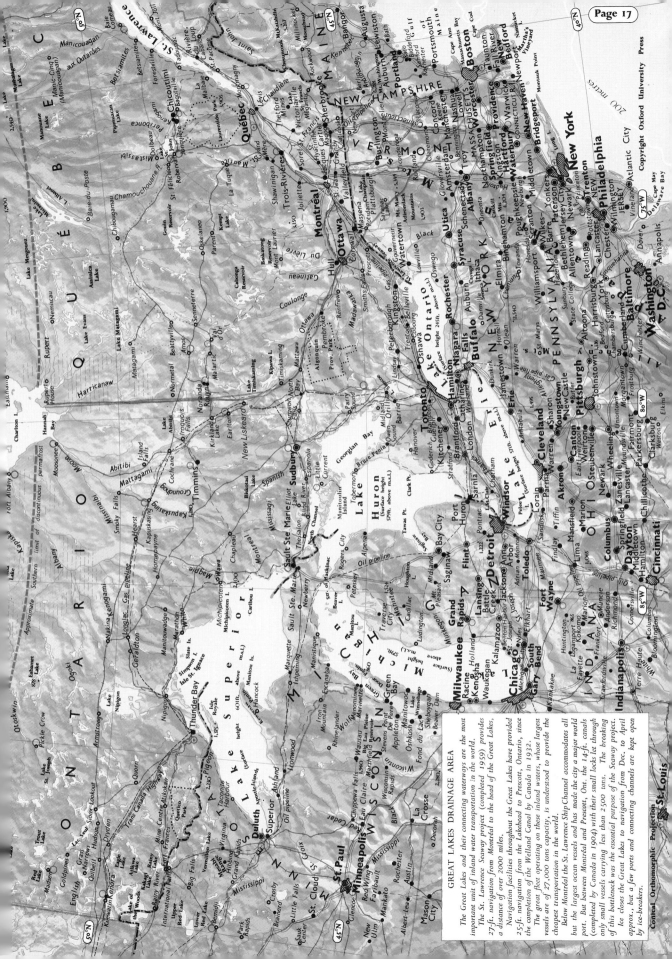

GREAT LAKES DRAINAGE AREA

The Great Lakes and their connecting waterways are the most important unit of inland water transportation in the world.

The St. Lawrence Seaway project (completed 1959) provides 27-ft. navigation from Montréal to the head of the Great Lakes, a distance of over 2000 miles.

Navigation facilities throughout the Great Lakes have provided 25-ft. navigation from the Lakehead to Prescott, Ontario, since the completion of the Welland Canal by Canada in 1932.

The great fleet operating on these inland waters, whose largest vessels are of 27,000 tons capacity, is understood to provide the cheapest transportation in the world.

Below Montréal the St. Lawrence Ship Channel accommodates all but the largest ocean vessels and has made the city a major world port. But between Montréal and Prescott, Ont. the 14-ft. canals (completed by Canada in 1904) with their small locks let through only small vessels carrying less than 2500 tons. The breaking of this bottleneck was the essential purpose of the Seaway project. Ice closes the Great Lakes to navigation from Dec. to April approx., but a few ports and connecting channels are kept open by ice-breakers.

Conical Orthomorphic Projection

Copyright Oxford University Press

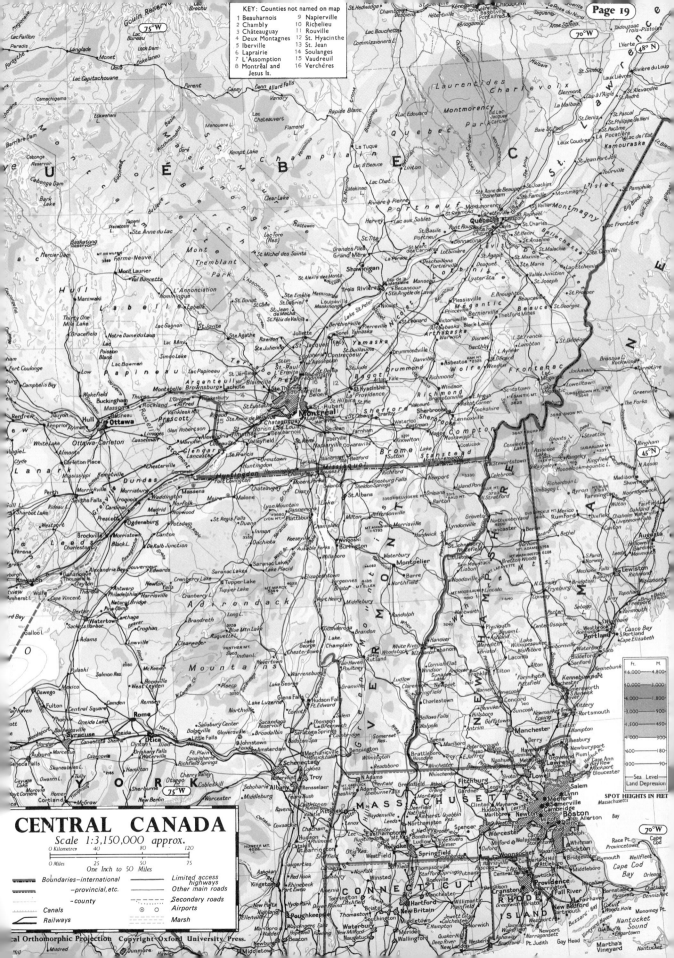

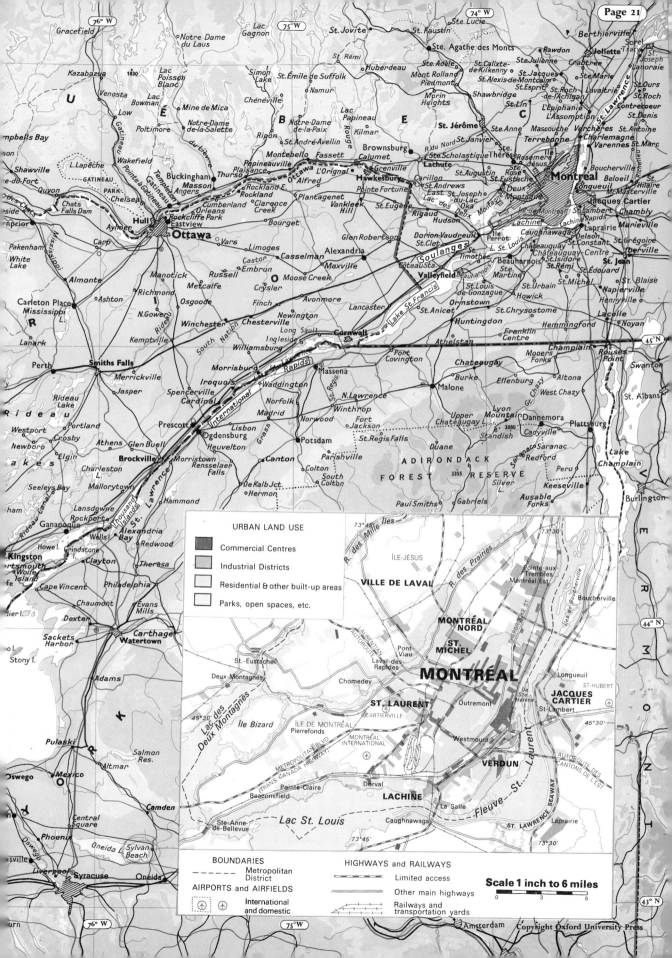

76° W   75° W   74° W

Gracefield   Lac Gagnon   St. Jovite   Ste. Lucie   Berthierville   Joliette   Sorel

Notre Dame du Laus   St. Faustin   Rawdon   Crabtree   Lanaraie

Kazabazua   1830   Lac Poisson Blanc   Simon Lake   St. Rémi   Ste. Agathe des Monts   Ste. Julienne   St. Marie   St. Ours   St. Roch

Venosta   Lac Bowman   Mine de Mica   Chénéville   St. Émile de Suffolk   Huberdeau   Ste. Adèle   Mont Rolland   St. Calixte-de-Kilkenny   St. Alexis-de-Montcalm   L'Épiphanie   Lavaltrie   Contrecoeur

Low   Poltimore   Notre-Dame de-la-Salette   Ripon   Namur   Notre-Dame de-la-Paix   Lac Papineau   Lac Rouge   Piedmont   St. Jacques   St. Esprit   L'Assomption   St. Denis

Campbells Bay   Wakefield   Pointe à Gatineau   Templeton   St. André-Avellin   Kilmar   Morin Heights   Shawbridge   St. Lin   Terrebonne   Mascouche   Charlemagne   St. Antoine

Shawville   Buckingham   Masson   Thurso   Montebello   Fassett   Calumet   Brownsburg   St. Jérôme   St. Janvier   Ste. Thérèse   Rosemère   Varennes   St. Marc

Quyon   Chats Falls Dam   Angers   Orleans   Plaisance   Papineauville   Ottawa   L'Orignal   Grenville   Lachute   Ste. Scholastique   St. Augustin   St. Eustache   Deux   Montréal   Boucherville   Beloeil

Chelsea   Rockcliffe Park   Cumberland   Rockland   Alfred   Hawkesbury   Carillon   St. Andrews   Oka   Lac des Deux   Île de Montréal   Montréal   Longueuil   St. Hilaire   McMasterville

Aylmer   Hull   Eastview   Ottawa   Clarence Creek   Plantagenet   Rockland E.   Pointe Fortune   East St. Joseph-du-Lac   Île Perrot   Lachine   Lachine Rapids   St. Lambert   Jacques Cartier   Chambly

Carp   Vars   Bourget   Vankleek Hill   St. Eugene   Rigaud   Hudson   Dorion Vaudreuil   St. Clet   L. St. Louis   Caughnawaga   Laprairie   Marieville

Pakenham   Almonte   Manotick   Limoges   Alexandria   Glen Robertson   St. Timothée   Côte Ste A.   Chateauguay   St. Constant   St. Grégoire   iberville

White Lake   Carleton Place   Richmond   Castor   Casselman   Maxville   Soulanges   Valleyfield   Beauharnois   Ste. Martine   St. Isidore   St. Édouard   St. Jean

Mississippi   Ashton   Metcalfe   Russell   Embrun   Moose Creek   St. Louis-de-Gonzague   Howick   St. Urbain   St. Rémi   St. Blaise

Almonte   N.Gower   Osgoode   Crysler   Finch   Avonmore   Lancaster   Ormstown   St. Michel   Napierville

Lanark   Winchester   Chesterville   Newington   Long Sault   Lake St. Francis   St. Anicet   Huntingdon   Hemmingford   Lacolle   Noyan

Perth   Smiths Falls   Merrickville   South Nation   Morrisburg   Williamsburg   Cornwall   Athelstan   Franklin Centre   Champlain   Rouses Point   45°

Rideau Lake   Jasper   Iroquois   Waddington   Massena   St. Regis   Fort Covington   Chateaugay   Mooers Forks   Altona   Swanton

Spencerville   Cardinal   Norfolk   N.Lawrence   Burke   Malone   Ellenburg   West Chazy   St. Albans

Westport   Portland   Prescott   International   Lisbon   Madrid   Winthrop   Upper Chateaugay L.   Lyon Mountain   Dannemora   Plattsburg

Crosby   Newboro   Athens   Glen Buell   Ogdensburg   Heuvelton   Norwood   Fort Jackson   3880   Standish   Cadyville   Saranac   Lake Champlain

Elgin   Brockville   Morristown   Rensselaer Falls   Grass   Potsdam   St.Regis Falls   Duane   ADIRONDACK   Redford   Peru   Keeseville   Burlington

Charleston L.   Mallorytown   Hammond   Canton   Parishville   FOREST   RESERVE   Silver L.   3355   Ausable Forks

Seeleys Bay   Lansdowne   Rockport   Wells   Alexandria Bay   De Kalb Jct.   Colton   South Colton   Gabriels   Paul Smiths

Gananoque   Howe I.   Grindstone   Clayton   Redwood   Hermon

Kingston   Wolfe Island   Cape Vincent   Philadelphia   Theresa   Chaumont   Evans Mills   Carthage   Watertown

Pulaski   Chaumont   Adams   Salmon Res.   Altmar

Mexico   Camden   Central Square   Phoenix   Oneida L.   Sylvan Beach   Oneida   44°

Oswego   Liverpool   Syracuse   Amsterdam   43°

U   É   B   E   C   GATINEAU   PARK   Gatineau   R. du Lièvre   R. Rouge   R. du Nord   Île Jésus   Île de Montréal   R. Ottawa   R. St. Lawrence   Lac des Deux Montagnes   St. Lawrence   Thousand Islands   Rideau Canal   Rideau   Mississippi   Lake St. Francis   International Rapids   St. Lawrence   Adirondack Forest Reserve

Inset map

URBAN LAND USE

- ■ Commercial Centres
- ▨ Industrial Districts
- □ Residential & other built-up areas
- □ Parks, open spaces, etc.

73°45'   73°30'

Îles des Mille Îles   R. des Mille Îles   ÎLE-JÉSUS   R. des Prairies   Pointe-aux-Trembles   Montréal Est

VILLE DE LAVAL   MONTRÉAL NORD   ST. MICHEL   Vie de Boucherville   Boucherville

Laurentian Autoroute   Pont Viau   Laval-des-Rapides   SHERBROOKE ST.   44°

St.-Eustache   Chomedey   MONTRÉAL   Longueuil   ST-HUBERT   JACQUES CARTIER

Deux-Montagnes   ST. LAURENT   Outremont   Île Ste. Hélène   St-Lambert

Lac des Deux Montagnes   CARTIERVILLE   45°30'

Île Bizard   ÎLE DE MONTRÉAL   Pierrefonds   Westmount   AUTOROUTE DES CANTONS DE L'EST

Metropolitan Blvd.   MONTRÉAL INTERNATIONAL   VERDUN

(Trans Canada Highway 17)   Dorval   LACHINE

Pointe Claire   La Salle   Fleuve St. Laurent   Laprairie

Beaconsfield   Beaconsfield   ST. LAWRENCE SEAWAY

Ste-Anne-de-Bellevue   Lac St. Louis   Caughnawaga   73°30'

73°45'

BOUNDARIES
- – – – Metropolitan District

AIRPORTS and AIRFIELDS
- ⊕ ⊕ International and domestic

HIGHWAYS and RAILWAYS
- Limited access
- Other main highways
- Railways and transportation yards

Scale 1 inch to 6 miles
0   3   6

Copyright Oxford University Press

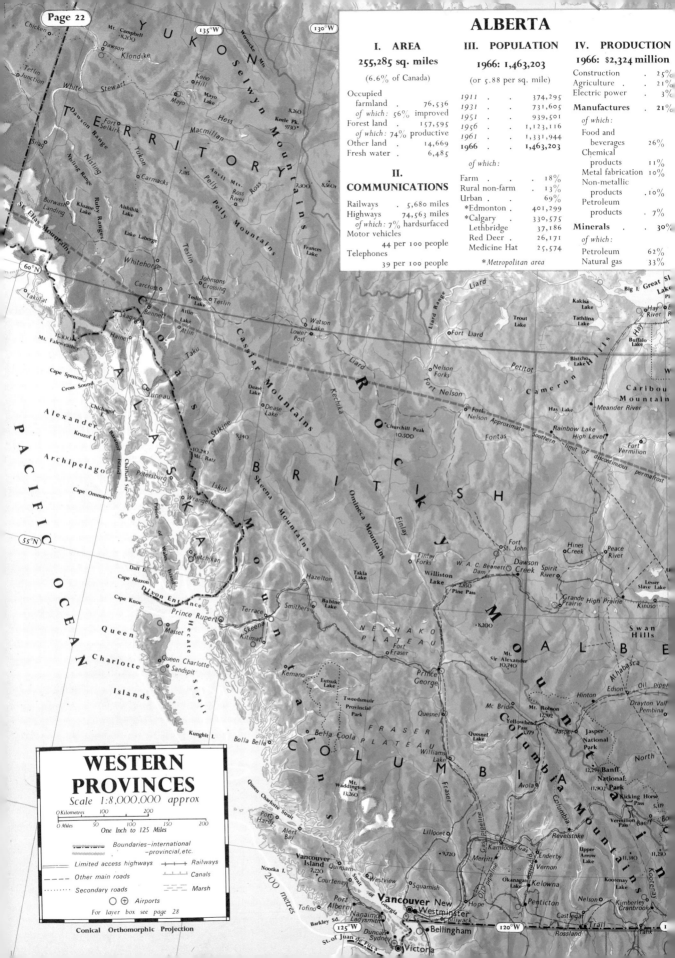

ALBERTA

I. AREA
255,285 sq. miles

(6.6% of Canada)

Occupied farmland	76,536
of which: 56% improved	
Forest land	157,595
of which: 74% productive	
Other land	14,669
Fresh water	6,485

II. COMMUNICATIONS

Railways	5,680 miles
Highways	74,563 miles
of which: 7% hardsurfaced	
Motor vehicles	
44 per 100 people	
Telephones	
39 per 100 people	

III. POPULATION

1966: 1,463,203

(or 5.88 per sq. mile)

1911	.	374,295
1931	.	731,605
1951	.	939,501
1956	.	1,123,116
1961	.	1,331,944
1966		**1,463,203**

of which:

Farm	.	18%
Rural non-farm	.	13%
Urban	.	69%
*Edmonton	.	401,299
*Calgary	.	330,575
Lethbridge	.	37,186
Red Deer	.	26,171
Medicine Hat	.	25,574

*Metropolitan area

IV. PRODUCTION

1966: $2,324 million

Construction	.	25%
Agriculture	.	21%
Electric power	.	3%
Manufactures		**21%**

of which:

Food and beverages	26%
Chemical products	11%
Metal fabrication	10%
Non-metallic products	10%
Petroleum products	7%

Minerals	.	**30%**

of which:

Petroleum	62%
Natural gas	33%

WESTERN PROVINCES

Scale 1:8,000,000 *approx*

One Inch to 125 Miles

Boundaries—international
—provincial, etc.

Limited access highways — Railways
Other main roads — Canals
Secondary roads — Marsh
Airports

For layer box see page 28

Conical Orthomorphic Projection

SASKATCHEWAN

I. AREA
251,700 sq. miles
(6.5% of Canada)

Occupied
farmland . . 101,202
of which: 70% is improved
Forest land . 116,738
of which: 36% productive
Other land . 2,342
Fresh water . 31,518

II.
COMMUNICATIONS
Railways 8,567 miles
Highways 124,615 miles
of which: 5% hardsurfaced
Motor vehicles
46 per 100 people
Telephones
34 per 100 people

III. POPULATION
1966: 955,344
(or 4.34 per sq. mile)

1911	. .	492,432
1931	. .	921,785
1951	. .	831,728
1956	. .	880,665
1961	. .	925,181
1966	. .	**955,344**

of which:

Farm	. .	29%
Rural non-farm	.	21%
Urban	. .	50%
*Regina	.	131,127
*Saskatoon	.	115,892
Moose Jaw	.	33,417
Prince Albert	.	26,269
Swift Current	.	14,485

*Metropolitan area

IV. PRODUCTION
1966: $1,488 million

Agriculture	. .	46%
Construction	.	21%
Electric power	.	4%
Manufactures		**9%**
of which:		
Food and		
beverages		41%
Petroleum		
products		13%
Printing	.	9%
Non-metallic		
products		9%
Metal		
fabrication		7%
Minerals		**20%**
of which:		
Petroleum		60%
Potash	.	18%
Copper	.	5%
Uranium	.	3%

MANITOBA

I. AREA
251,000 sq. miles
(6.5% of Canada)

Occupied
farmland . 29,818
of which: 65% is improved
Forest land . 122,820
of which: 48% productive
Other land . 59,137
Fresh water . 39,225

II.
COMMUNICATIONS
Railways 4,735 miles
Highways 43,512 miles
of which: 7% hardsurfaced
Motor vehicles
37 per 100 people
Telephones
38 per 100 people

III. POPULATION
1966: 963,066
(4.55 per sq. mile)

1871	. .	25,228
1891	. .	152,506
1911	. .	461,394
1931	. .	700,139
1951	. .	776,541
1956	. .	850,040
1961	. .	921,686
1966	. .	**963,066**

of which:

Farm	. .	16%
Rural non-farm	.	17%
Urban	. .	67%
*Winnipeg	.	508,759
Brandon		29,981
Portage la		
Prairie		13,012
Flin Flon	.	10,201

*Metropolitan area

IV. PRODUCTION
1966: $1,028 million

Agriculture	. .	27%
Construction	.	22%
Electric power	.	5%
Manufactures	.	**35%**
of which:		
Food and		
beverages		27%
Metal		
fabricating		10%
Printing	.	9%
Clothing	.	8%
Primary metals	.	8%
Minerals		**11%**
of which:		
Nickel	.	56%
Copper	.	16%
Petroleum	.	7%
Zinc	.	5%

© Copyright Oxford University Press

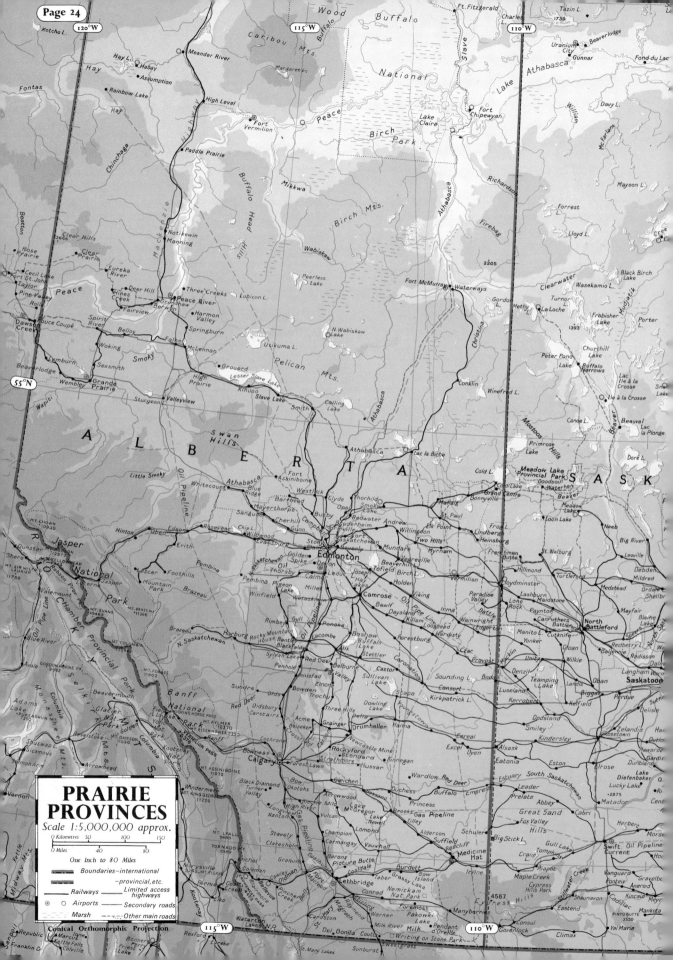

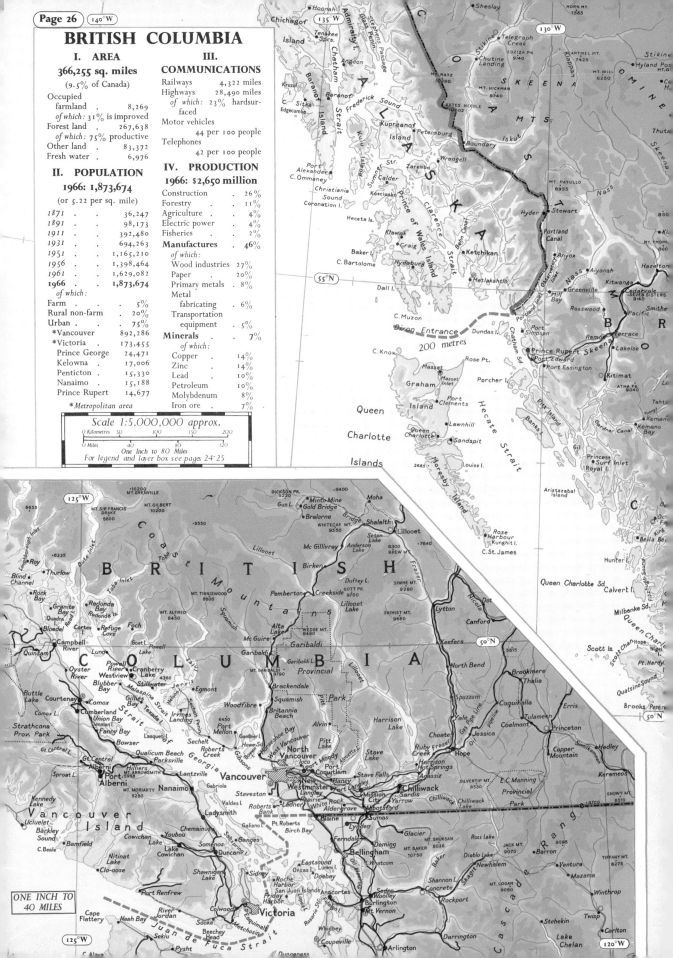

140°W

BRITISH COLUMBIA

I. AREA

366,255 sq. miles

(9.5% of Canada)

Occupied farmland	.	8,269
of which: 31% is improved		
Forest land	.	267,638
of which: 75% productive		
Other land	.	83,372
Fresh water		6,976

II. POPULATION

1966: 1,873,674

(or 5.22 per sq. mile)

1871	.	.	36,247
1891	.	.	98,173
1911	.	.	392,480
1931	.	.	694,263
1951	.	.	1,165,210
1956	.	.	1,398,464
1961	.	.	1,629,082
1966	.	**1,873,674**	

of which:

Farm	.	.	5%
Rural non-farm	.	20%	
Urban	.	.	75%
*Vancouver	892,286		
*Victoria	.	173,455	
Prince George	24,471		
Kelowna	.	17,006	
Penticton	.	15,330	
Nanaimo	.	15,188	
Prince Rupert	14,677		

*Metropolitan area

III. COMMUNICATIONS

Railways	4,322 miles	
Highways	28,490 miles	
of which: 23% hardsur-faced		
Motor vehicles		
	44 per 100 people	
Telephones		
	42 per 100 people	

IV. PRODUCTION

1966: $2,650 million

Construction	.	26%
Forestry	.	11%
Agriculture	.	4%
Electric power	.	4%
Fisheries	.	2%
Manufactures	.	**46%**

of which:

Wood industries	27%
Paper	20%
Primary metals	8%
Metal fabricating	6%
Transportation equipment	5%
Minerals	**7%**

of which:

Copper	14%
Zinc	14%
Lead	10%
Petroleum	10%
Molybdenum	8%
Iron ore	7%

Scale 1:5,000,000 approx.

Kilometres 0 50 100 150 200
Miles 0 40 80 120

One Inch to 80 Miles

For legend and layer box see pages 24-25

ONE INCH TO 40 MILES

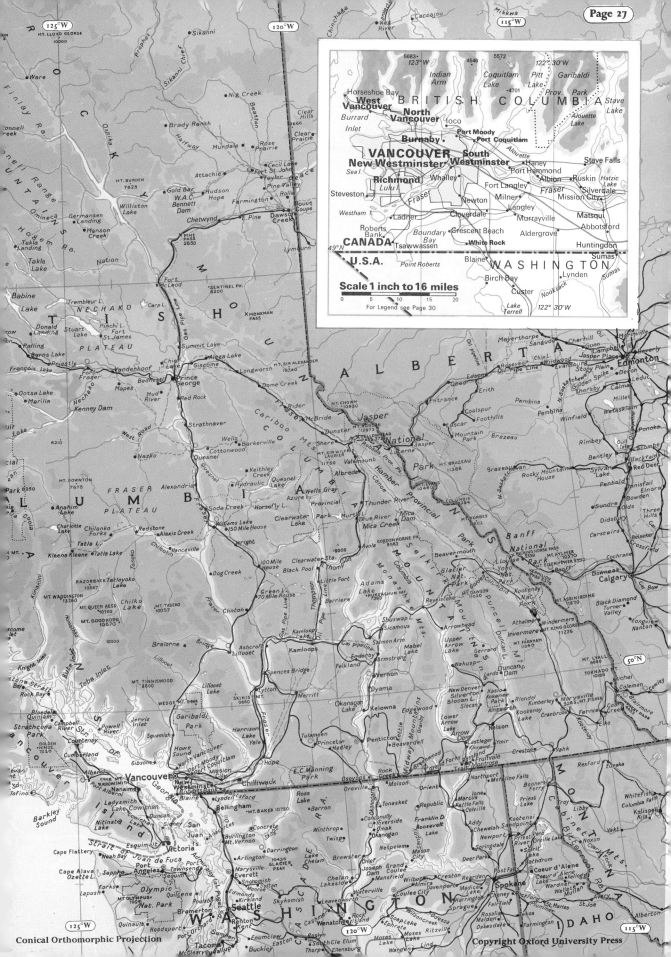

Scale 1 inch to 16 miles

For Legend see Page 30

Conical Orthomorphic Projection

Copyright Oxford University Press

THE TERRITORIES

YUKON: NORTHWEST TERRITORIES, District of Franklin (includes Arctic Archipelago), **Keewatin** (includes all islands in Hudson and James Bays) and **Mackenzie** (organized territory 1964).

I. AREA

1,511,979 sq. miles
(39.1% of Canada)

Farm land	.	9
of which: 33% improved		
Forest land	.	275,800
of which: 37% productive		
Other land	.	1,182,875
Fresh water	.	53,195

II. COMMUNICATIONS

Railways	.	58 miles
Highways	.	2,731 miles
of which: less than 1% is hardsurfaced		
Motor vehicles		
30 per 100 people		

Telephones
23 per 100 people

III. POPULATION

1966: 43,120

(0.028 persons per sq. mile)
i.e. 1 person per 35 sq. miles

1911	.	15,019
1931	.	13,546
1951	.	25,100
1956	.	31,503
1961	.	37,626
1966	.	**43,120**

of which:

Farm	. less than 1%	
Rural non-farm	.	57%

Urban	.	42%
Yellowknife	.	3,741
Fort Smith	.	2,120
Hay River	.	2,002

IV. PRODUCTION

1966: $66 million

Electric power	.	6%
Fisheries	.	2%
Trapping	.	2%
Manufacturing	.	2%
Mining	.	88%

of which:

Zinc	.	44%
Lead	.	28%
Gold	.	14%
Silver	.	7%

Scale 1:8,000,000 approx
One Inch to 125 Miles
For legend see page 22

Conical Orthomorphic Projection

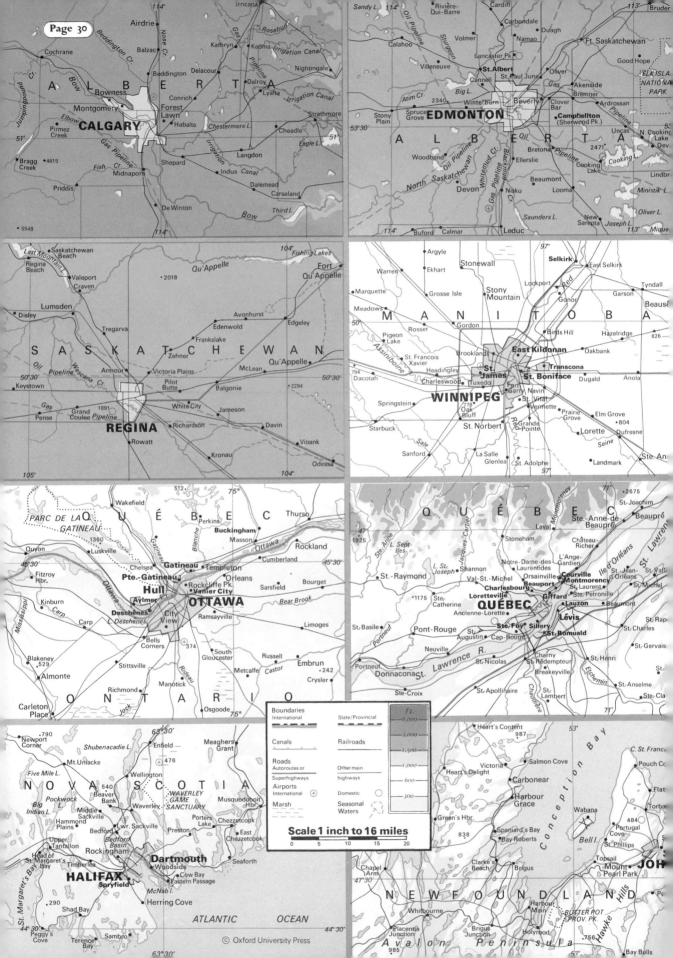

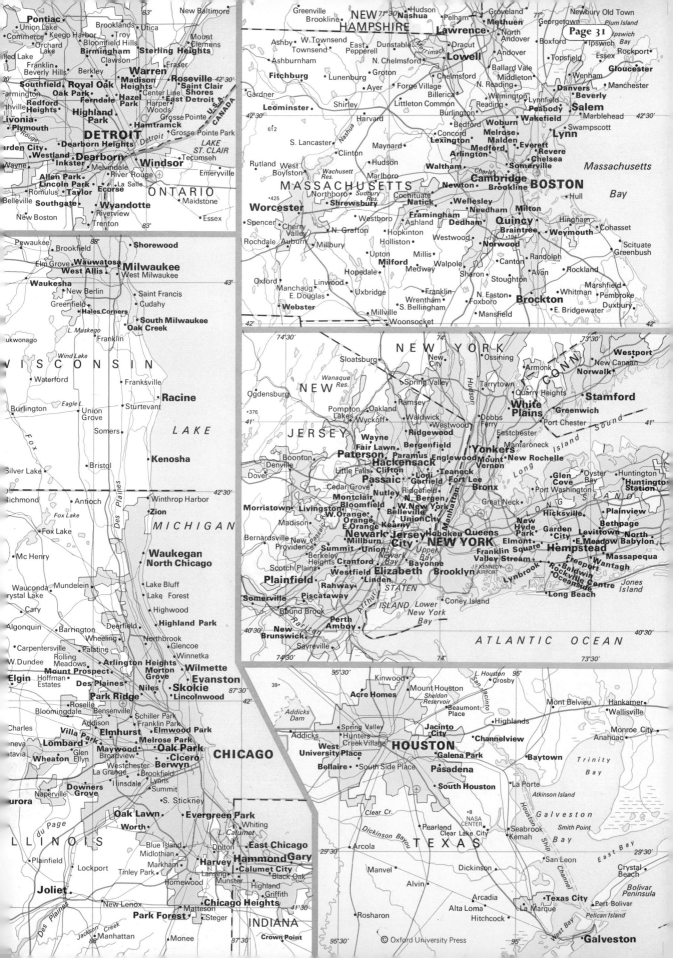

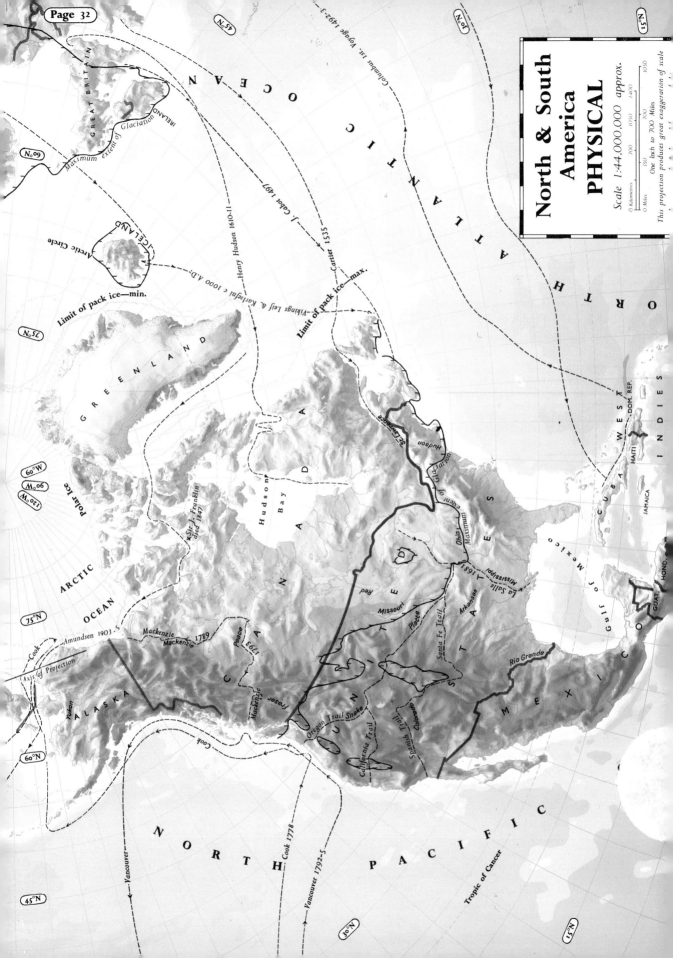

Columbus 1st. voyage 1492-3

J. Cabot 1497

Cartier 1535

GREAT BRITAIN

IRELAND

Maximum extent of Glaciation

60°N

Arctic Circle

ICELAND

Limit of pack ice—min.

Henry Hudson 1610-11

Vikings Leif & Karlsefni c 1000 A.D.

Limit of pack ice—max.

75°N

GREENLAND

60°W

90°W

120°W

Polar Ice

C A N A D A

Hudson
Bay

Sir J. Franklin
died 1847

ARCTIC

OCEAN

Amundsen 1903-5

Cook

Axis of Projection

Mackenzie 1789

Mackenzie

Peace 1793

Mackenzie

Fraser

Yukon

ALASKA

C O R D I L L E R A

Oregon Trail Snake

California Trail

Red

Missouri

Platte

Colorado

Santa Fe Trail

Spanish Trail

M O U N T A I N S

Rio Grande

R O C K Y

Mississippi

La Salle 1681

Arkansas

Maximum of Glaciation

Ohio

Hudson

St. Lawrence

NORTH ATLANTIC

OCEAN

Gulf of Mexico

M E X I C O

GUAT. HOND.

CUBA

WEST

DOM. REP.

HAITI

JAMAICA

INDIES

75°N

60°N

45°N

Cook

Vancouver

Cook 1778

Vancouver 1792-5

N O R T H   P A C I F I C

Tropic of Cancer

30°N

15°N

**North & South
America
PHYSICAL**

Scale 1:44,000,000 *approx.*

0 Kilometres 350 700 1050 1400

0 Miles 350 700 1050

One Inch to 700 Miles

This projection produces great exaggeration of scale

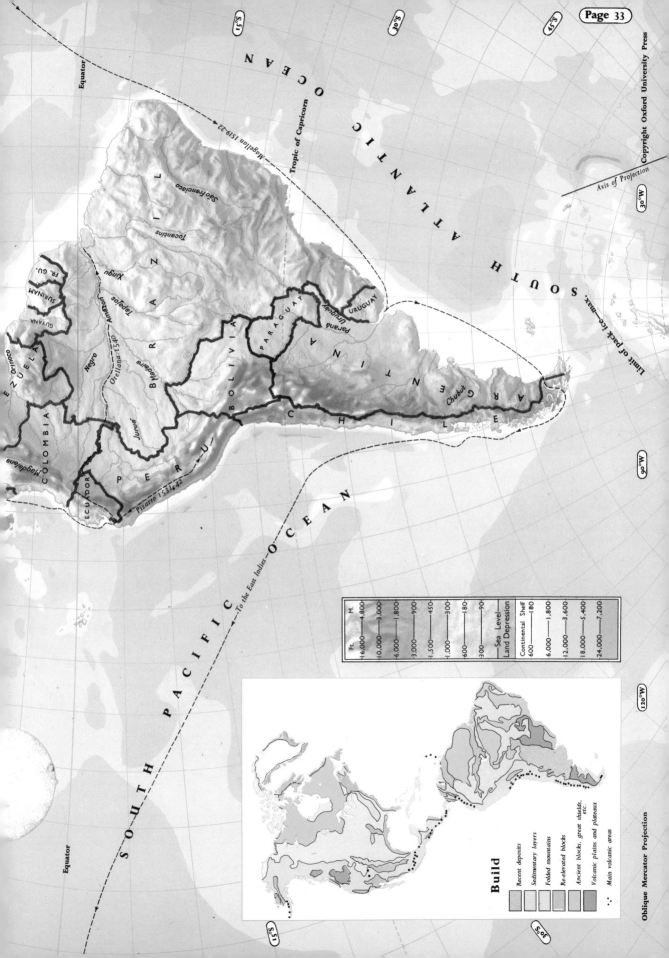

SOUTH ATLANTIC OCEAN

Equator

Tropic of Capricorn

Magellan 1519-22

15°S

30°S

45°S

Axis of Projection

30°W

90°W

120°W

Limit of pack ice—max.

São Francisco

Tocantins

Xingu

Tapejos

B R A Z I L

Orinoco

Negro

Orellana 1540

Branco

Juruá

FR. GU.

SURINAM

GUYANA

VENEZUELA

COLOMBIA

Magdalena

ECUADOR

P E R U

Pizarro 1531-42

BOLIVIA

PARAGUAY

Paraná

Uruguay

URUGUAY

A R G E N T I N A

C H I L E

Chubut

SOUTH PACIFIC OCEAN

—To the East Indies—

Equator

15°S

30°S

Ft.	M.
16,000	4,800
10,000	3,000
6,000	1,800
3,000	900
1,500	450
1,000	300
600	180
300	90
Sea Level	
Land Depression	

Continental Shelf
600 — 180
6,000 — 1,800
12,000 — 3,600
18,000 — 5,400
24,000 — 7,200

Build

Recent deposits

Sedimentary layers

Folded mountains

Re-elevated blocks

Ancient blocks, great shields, etc.

Volcanic plains and plateaux

Main volcanic areas

Oblique Mercator Projection

Copyright Oxford University Press

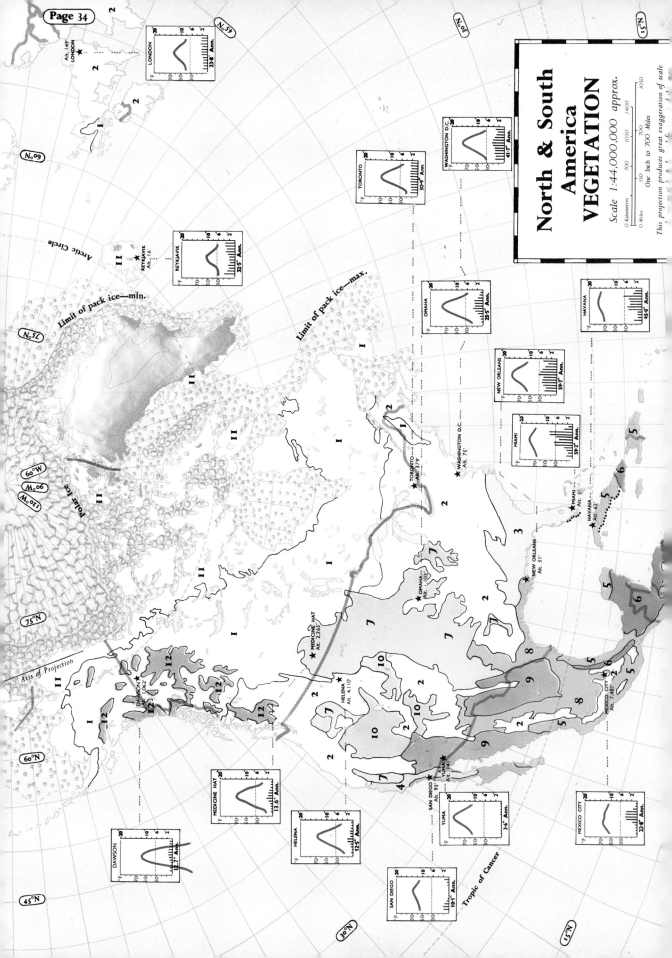

North & South America
VEGETATION

Scale 1:44,000,000 approx.

This projection produces great exaggeration of scale

Axis of Projection

Limit of pack ice—min.

Limit of pack ice—max.

Polar ice

Arctic Circle

Tropic of Cancer

DAWSON

MEDICINE HAT

HELENA

SAN DIEGO

YUMA

MEXICO CITY

NEW ORLEANS

MIAMI

HAVANA

OMAHA

WASHINGTON D.C.

TORONTO

REYKJAVIK

LONDON

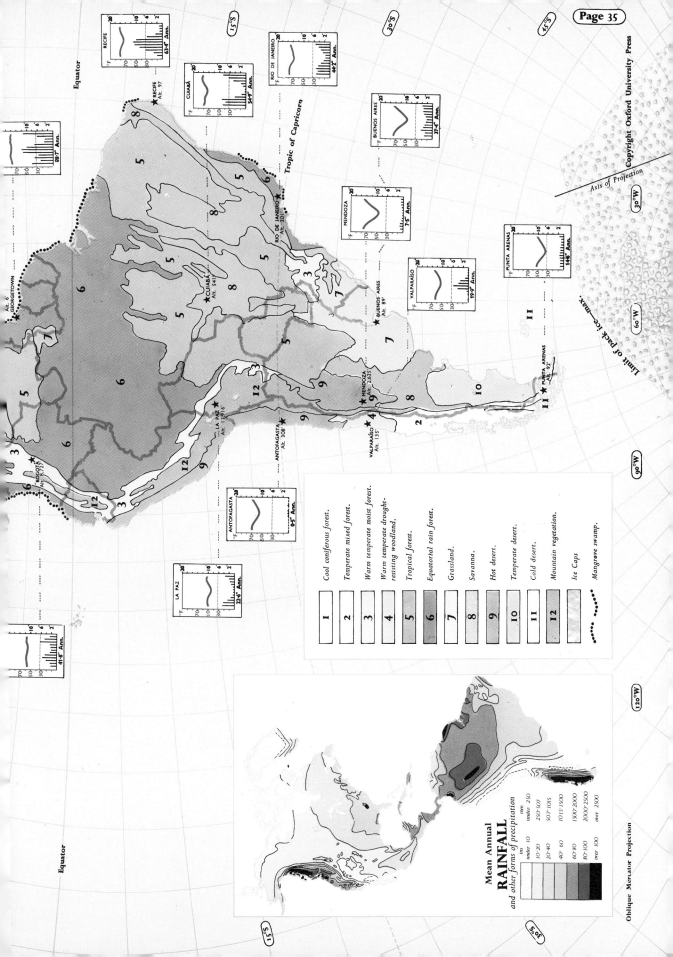

Copyright Oxford University Press

Equator

15°S

30°S

45°S

Tropic of Capricorn

Axis of Projection

Limit of pack ice—max.

30°W

60°W

90°W

120°W

30°S

15°S

Equator

RECIFE
63°F Ann.

CUIABÁ
54°F Ann.

RIO DE JANEIRO
44° Ann.

BUENOS AIRES
37·4° Ann.

MENDOZA
7·5° Ann.

VALPARAÍSO
19·9° Ann.

PUNTA ARENAS
14·6° Ann.

ANTOFAGASTA
6·5° Ann.

LA PAZ
22·6° Ann.

89·7° Ann.

41·8° Ann.

★ RECIFE
Alt. 97

★ CUIABÁ
Alt. 541

★ RIO DE JANEIRO
Alt. 201

★ BUENOS AIRES
Alt. 89'

★ MENDOZA
Alt. 2·635

★ VALPARAÍSO
Alt. 135'

★ PUNTA ARENAS
Alt. 92'

★ LA PAZ
Alt. 13·916

★ ANTOFAGASTA
Alt. 308'

★ BOGOTÁ
Alt. 8·727

★ GEORGETOWN
Alt. 6

1 | Cool coniferous forest.
2 | Temperate mixed forest.
3 | Warm temperate moist forest.
4 | Warm temperate drought-resisting woodland.
5 | Tropical forest.
6 | Equatorial rain forest.
7 | Grassland.
8 | Savanna.
9 | Hot desert.
10 | Temperate desert.
11 | Cold desert.
12 | Mountain vegetation.
| Ice Caps
| Mangrove swamp.

Mean Annual
RAINFALL
and other forms of precipitation

ins	mm
under 10	under 250
10-20	250-507
20-40	507-1015
40-60	1015-1500
60-80	1500-2000
80-100	2000-2500
over 100	over 2500

Oblique Mercator Projection

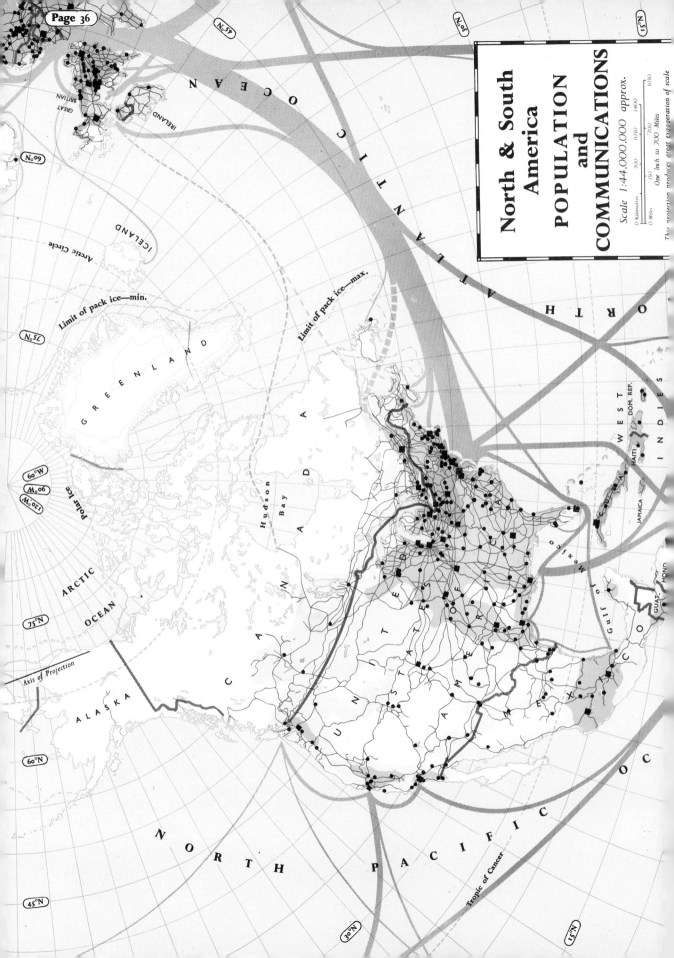

North & South America
POPULATION and
COMMUNICATIONS

Scale 1:44,000,000 *approx.*

	150	700	1050	1400	
0 Kilometres					1050

0 Miles
One Inch to 700 Miles

This projection produces great exaggeration of scale

NORTH ATLANTIC OCEAN

NORTH PACIFIC OCEAN

ARCTIC OCEAN

GREENLAND

ICELAND

GREAT BRITAIN

IRELAND

CANADA

ALASKA

UNITED STATES OF AMERICA

MEXICO

Hudson Bay

Gulf of Mexico

WEST INDIES

CUBA

JAMAICA

HAITI

DOM. REP.

GUAT.

BR. HOND.

Arctic Circle

Limit of pack ice—min.

Limit of pack ice—max.

Polar Ice

Axis of Projection

Tropic of Cancer

45°N

60°N

75°N

60°W

90°W

120°W

75°N

60°N

45°N

30°N

15°N

0°

15°N

30°N

45°N

60°N

Copyright Oxford University Press

Axis of Projection

Equator

Tropic of Capricorn

SOUTH ATLANTIC OCEAN

SOUTH PACIFIC OCEAN

Limit of pack ice—max.

30°W

60°W

90°W

120°W

15°S

30°S

45°S

15°S

30°S

VE NE ZUELA

COLOMBIA

ECUADOR

P E R U

B O L I V I A

B R A Z I L

PARAGUAY

URUGUAY

A R G E N T I N A

C H I L E

GUYANA

SURINAM

FR. GU.

PANAMA CANAL
See inset p. 39

POPULATION DENSITY

Almost uninhabited
(under 3 people per sq. mile).

Few inhabitants
(3–25 people per sq. mile).

Moderately populated
(25–125 people per sq. mile).

Thickly populated
(125–500 people per sq. mile).

Very thickly populated
(over 500 people per sq. mile).

TOWNS

● Towns with over 100,000 but
under 1 million inhabitants.

■ Towns with over 1 million
inhabitants.

25 people per sq. mile =
10 people per sq. km. approx.

RAILWAYS

SHIPPING
(by volume of traffic)

SEASONAL SHIPPING

Agriculture

1 'Western' mixed farming
(cash crops often with livestock)

2 Prairie farming—cereals

3 Irrigated areas in dry lands

4 Cattle or sheep ranching

5 Plantation agriculture

9 Native farming
(often with 'shifting cultivation')

11 Non-agricultural land

Principal areas of commercial fishing

Oblique Mercator Projection

SPOT HEIGHTS IN FEET

Ft.	M.
16,000	4,800
10,000	3,000
6,000	1,800
3,000	900
1,500	450
1,000	300
600	180
300	90
Sea Level	
Land Depression	

Gaillard Cut (Culebra)
Maximum elevation 312 feet
Minimum depth 41 feet

ATLANTIC
PACIFIC
Sea Level
Sea Level
Sea Level

0 miles   10   20   30   40   50

Gatun Locks
3 pairs
Length   1000'
Width   110'
Total Lift   85'

Pedro Miguel Locks
1 pair
Length   1000'
Width   110'
Total Lift   30½'

Miraflores Locks
2 pairs
Length   1000'
Width   110'
Total Lift   54½'

Panama Canal

1 cm. to 15 km. approx.
1" to 24 miles approx.

ATLANTIC OCEAN

PANAMÁ
CANAL
ZONE
PANAMÁ
PANAMÁ

Colón
Gatun Locks
Gatun Lake

Pedro Miguel Locks
Miraflores Locks
Balboa
Panamá

PACIFIC OCEAN

PANAMA The canal, opened 1914, is 50 miles long including approaches (actual canal 40 miles). Minimum depth 41 ft. minimum width 500 ft.(Gaillard Cut). Time of passage 8 hours. In 1969/70 15,400 ships used the canal carrying 115 million tons of cargo, over 80% of which was coming from or going to the U.S.A. or Japan.

Copyright Oxford University Press

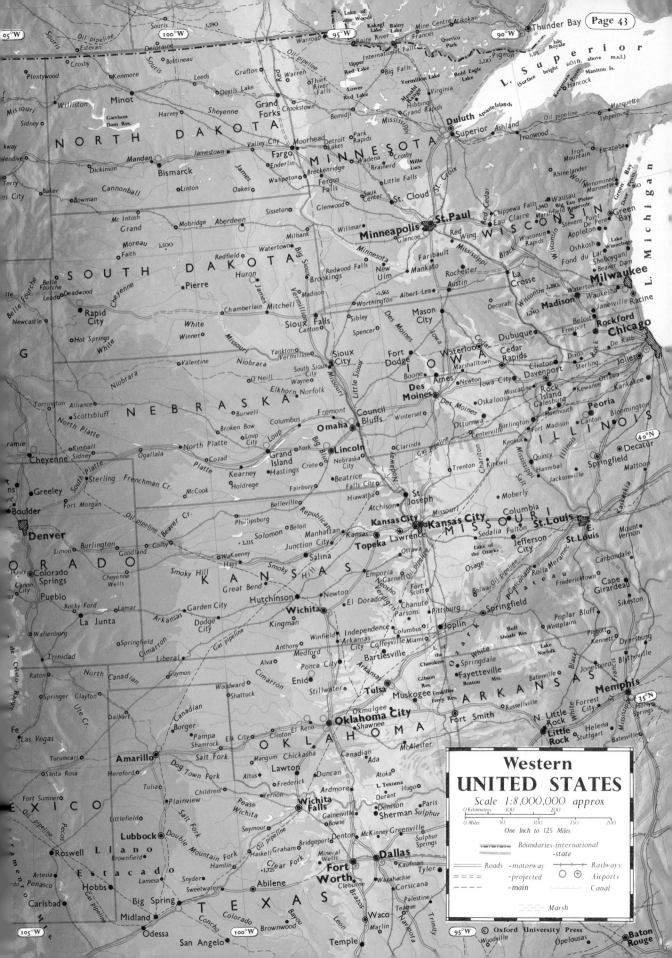

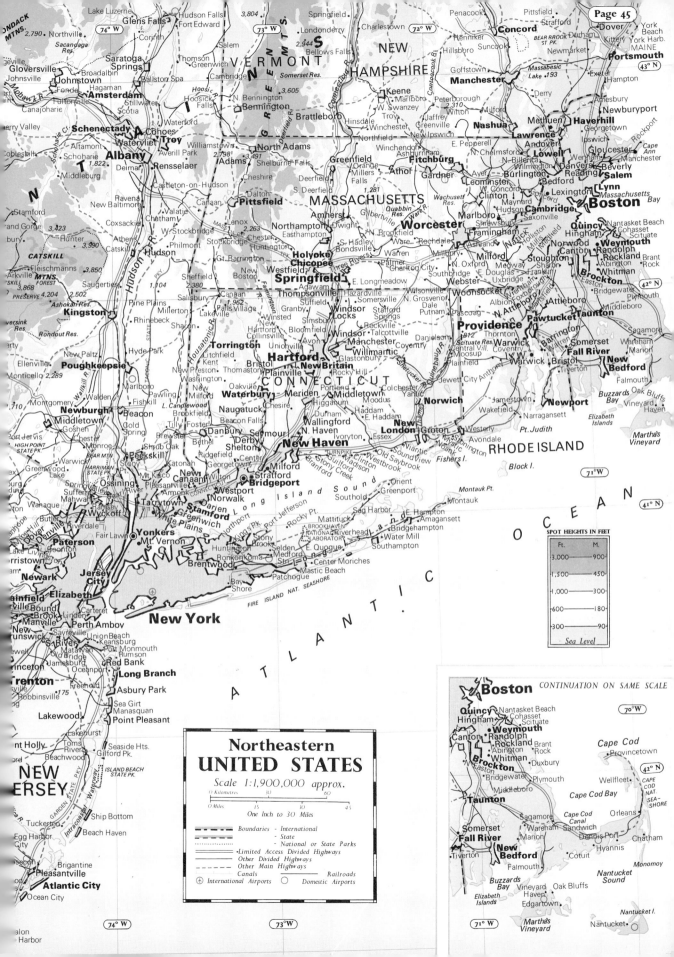

Northeastern
UNITED STATES
Scale 1:1,900,000 approx.

One Inch to 30 Miles

Boundaries - International
- State
- National or State Parks
Limited Access Divided Highways
Other Divided Highways
Other Main Highways
Canals   Railroads
International Airports   Domestic Airports

SPOT HEIGHTS IN FEET

Ft.	M.
3,000	900
1,500	450
1,000	300
600	180
300	90
Sea Level	

CONTINUATION ON SAME SCALE

CALIFORNIA

Scale 1:6,300,000 approx.

One Inch to 100 Miles

0 Miles	50	100	150

0 Kilometres	50	100	150	200	250

Boundaries:—
— — international
.... provincial etc.

Roads:—
Motorway
main
other
⊕ Airports

Railways
Sand desert
Canal
Salt pan

© Oxford University Press

Conical Orthomorphic Projection

SPOT HEIGHTS IN FEET

Ft	M
+6,000	+1,800
10,000	3,000
6,000	1,800
3,000	900
1,500	450
1,000	300
600	180
300	90
Sea Level	Sea Level
300	Land Depression

Scale 1 inch to 16 miles

0	5	10	15	20

For Legend see Page 30

GREAT BASIN

SIERRA NEVADA

CALIFORNIA

PACIFIC OCEAN

SAN GABRIEL MOUNTAINS

Angeles National Forest

DEATH VALLEY

MOJAVE DESERT

CARIBBEAN

Scale 1:12,500,000 approx.

One Inch to 200 Miles

| 0 Kilometres | 100 | 200 | 300 |
| 0 Miles | 100 | 200 | |

Towns over 1 million people
over 100,000 people
Boundaries-international
-provincial etc.
Railways
projected
Airports

Roads
track
Canal
Marsh

Ft.	M.
16,000	4,800
10,000	3,000
6,000	1,800
4,500	1,350
3,000	900
1,000	300
600	180
300	90
Sea Level	
Land Depression	

ATLANTIC

OCEAN

Cape Kennedy
Orlando
Tampa
St. Petersburg
Sarasota
Melbourne
Lake Okeechobee
Palm Beach
Miami
Everglades
Key West
Florida Keys
Straits of Florida
Tropic of Cancer

Bahama Islands
Grand Bahama
Great Abaco
Eleuthera
New Providence
Nassau
Andros
Cat I.
San Salvador (Watling)
Rum Cay
Long I.
Crooked I.
Acklins I.
Great Exuma
Mayaguana
Great Inagua
Turks Is.
Caicos Is.
Caicos Passage

HISPANIOLA
Baracoa
Cap-Haïtien
Port-de-Paix
St. Marc
HAITI
Gonâve
Port-au-Prince
Jérémie
Les Cayes
Windward Passage
Santiago
Puerto Plata
DOMINICAN REPUBLIC
Santo Domingo
Baní
Jacmel
Barahona
La Romana
San Pedro

PUERTO RICO (U.S.)
San Juan
Ponce
Aguadilla
Mayaguez
Mona Passage
Mona I.
Virgin Is.
St. Thomas (U.S.)
St. Croix (U.S.)
Anegada Passage

Sombrero (Br.)
Anguilla (Br.)
St. Martin
St. Kitts
Barbuda
Antigua (Br.)
Nevis
Montserrat (Br.)
Guadeloupe (Fr.)
Basse-Terre
Pointe-à-Pitre
Marie Galante (Fr.)
Dominica (Br.)
Roseau

Leeward Islands

Martinique (Fr.)
Fort-de-France
Castries
St. Lucia (Br.)
St. Vincent (Br.)
The Grenadines (Br.)
BARBADOS
Bridgetown
Georgetown
Grenada (Br.)
St. George
TOBAGO
Plymouth
TRINIDAD
Port of Spain

Windward Islands

Lesser Antilles

Havana
Marianao
Matanzas
C U B A
Colón
Cienfuegos
Sta. Clara
Morón
Nuevitas
Camagüey
Holguín
Santiago de Cuba
Bayamo
Guantánamo
Pinar del Río
I. de Pinos
C. San Antonio
Yucatan Channel
Jardines de la Reina
G. C. Cruz

JAMAICA
Montego Bay
Spanish Town
Port Antonio
Kingston
Pedro Cays
Cayman Is.

Greater Antilles

Caribbean Sea

Swan Is.
C. Gracias a Dios
Puerto Cabezas
Bluefields
San Andres I.
Providencia I.

Portobello
Colón
PANAMA
Panama
CANAL ZONE (U.S.)
Balboa
G. of Darién

COSTA RICA
Liberia
Puntarenas
San José
Limón
Osa Peninsula

NICARAGUA
Managua
Granada
L. Nicaragua
Ometepe I.
Bluefields

HONDURAS
Trujillo
Juticalpa
Catacamas
Matagalpa
Río Grande

200 metres

COLOMBIA
Barranquilla
Cartagena
Santa Marta
Ciénaga
Riohacha
Pt. Gallinas
Sincelejo
Cristóbal Colón
Cord. de Mérida

VENEZUELA
Maracaibo
Cabimas
Carora
Lake Maracaibo
Machiques
Coro
San Felipe
Puerto Cabello
Valencia
CARACAS
La Guaira
Maracay
Barquisimeto
San Carlos
Guanare
San Juan
San Fernando
Calabozo
Valle
El Tigre
Barcelona
Cumaná
Carúpano
Porlamar
Maturín
Bolívar
Ciudad Bolívar
Orinoco
Tucupita
Delta

Aruba (Neth.)
Curaçao (Neth.)
Willemstad
Bonaire (Neth.)
Los Roques Is.
Las Aves Is.
La Orchila
La Blanquilla (Neth.)
Margarita I.
La Tortuga
Cayo Grande
Gulf of Venezuela
Gulf of Paria
San Felix
Fernando

GUYANA

Copyright Oxford University Press

Zenithal Equidistant Projection

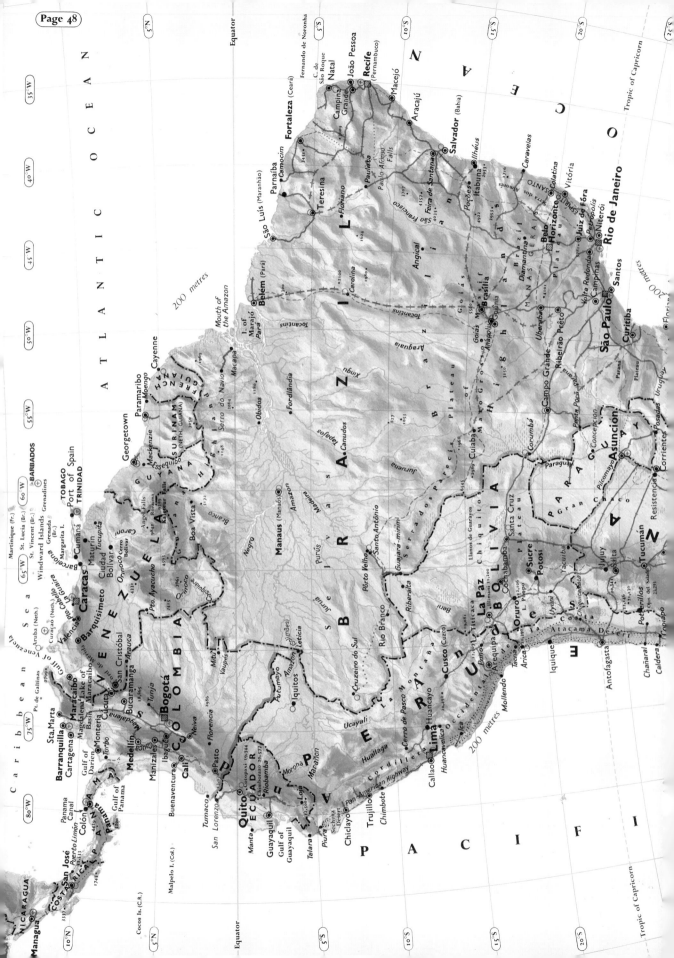

SOUTH AMERICA

Scale 1:25,000,000 approx.

0 Kilometres   200   400   600   800

0 Miles   200   400   600

Towns over 1 million people
" over 100,000 people
Boundaries - international
Railways
projected
Airports
Sand desert
Salt pan
Roads
tracks
Canal
Marsh
Ice cap

© Oxford University Press

SPOT HEIGHTS IN FEET

Ft.	M.
16,000	4,800
10,000	3,000
6,000	1,800
3,000	900
1,500	450
1,000	300
600	180
300	90
Sea Level	Sea Level
Land Depression	Land Depression

Transverse Mercator Projection

The ANTARCTIC

Scale 1:25,000,000 approx.

0 Kilometres 400 600 800 1000

0 Miles 200 400 600

One Inch to 400 Miles

Ice Cap   Shelf Ice

Glacier   Polar Ice

Permanent   Seasonal
Pack Ice   Pack Ice

⊙ Research Stations.

SOUTH AMERICA

Port Stanley

Falkland Islands (Br.)

C. Horn

Drake Passage

SOUTHERN OCEAN

Limit of icebergs - average maximum

Limit of pack ice - average maximum (Aug.-Sept.)

Antarctic Circle

GRAHAM LAND: stations divided between Chile Argentina & Britain.

South Shetland Islands

King George I. Admiralty Bay
Livingston I.
Deception
Elephant I.
Clarence I.

Anvers I. Palmer Arch.
Port Lockroy
Biscoe Is.
Trinity I. Joinville I.
Snow Hill I.
James Ross I.

South Orkney Islands
Coronation Island
Laurie

90° West

Peter I. Island (Nor.)

Adelaide I.

Stonington
Marguerite Bay

C. Agassiz
MT. WAKEFIELD
Hearst I.

Antarctic Pen.
Graham Land

Larsen Ice Shelf
Robertson I.

Thurston Pen.

Bellingshausen Sea

Alexander Island

George VI

Boggs
Dolleman I.
Steele I.
C. Knowles

Eights Coast

Eights (U.S.)

Amundsen Sea

Ellsworth Land

Sentinel Mts.

9,800

Violante Inlet
New Bedford Inlet
Nantucket Inlet

Filchner Ice Shelf

Weddell Sea

MT. SIPLE 15,000

Walgreen Coast

Wrigley Gulf

Kohler Mts.

Shepard I.

Executive Committee Ra.

Byrd Land

Hobbs Coast

Cordell Hull Glacier

MT. SIDLEY 12,000

Rockefeller Plateau

Hollick-Kenyon Plateau
6,630
6,300

8,730

Berkner Island

Gen. Belgrano (Arg.)

Alfarez de Nario-Sobral (Arg.)

Shackleton (UK)

Vahsel Bay

C. Norvegia
Maudheim

Coates Land

Caird Coast

Princess Martha Coast

Norway (Nor./S.A.)

Sanae (S. Afr.)

Cruzen I.

Emory Land Gl.

Paul Block Bay

Sulzberger Bay

Ford Ra.

Boyd Glacier

Edward VII Pen.

C. Colbeck

Okuma B.

1,460

New Byrd (U.S.)

2,810

1,840

South Ice (U.K.)

Fuchs 1957-58

80°S

Meridian of Greenwich

Ross Sea

International Date Line

Scott I.

Bay of Whales

Roosevelt Island

Discovery Inlet

Amundsen's Route

Ross Ice Shelf

Phillips Gl.
Scott Gl.
Maud Mts.

Axel Heiberg Glacier
Liv Gl.
Shackleton Gl.

South Polar Plateau

Amundsen Gl.
Devil's Gl.
South Pole Plateau

Amundsen 14.12.11.
Scott 18.1.12.

Queen Maud Land

Mühlig Hofmann Mts.
9,125

Novolazarevskaya (U.S.S.R.)
Wohlthat Massif
9875

Lazarev (U.S.S.R.)

10,825

Beardmore Gl.
3,300
Mill Gl.

MT. EREBUS
MT. TERROR
Ross Sea
Franklin I.
MT. BIRD

8,530

Queen Maud Ra.

MT. MARKHAM 15,100
MT. MC CLINTOCK 10,928

Fuchs & Hillary 1957-58

Plateau Station (U.S.)

Roi Baudouin (Belg. Neth.)

10,500

Princess Ragnhild Coast

8,200

Possession Is.
C. Adare
C. Coker
Robertson B.
Smith Inlet
C. North
MT. ELLIOT

McMurdo (U.S.)
Scott (N.Z.)

Granite Hr.
Pr. Albert Mts.
David Gl.
Ferrar Gl.

Scott's Route

Victoria Land

AFRICA

NEW ZEALAND

Sturge I.
5,000
Young I.
Williamson Head

Cook B.
C. Freshfield

King George V Coast

8,558

Oates Coast

Little Glacier
Tongue
Rennick B.
2,800

7260

South Geomagnetic Pole

Vostok (U.S.S.R.)

Sovetskaya (U.S.S.R.)

Lützow-Holm
Syowa (Jap.)

Pr. Harald Coast

TERRA INCOGNITA

Balleny Is.

2,350

8,558

Mertz Glacier
Stillwell I.
C. Denison
"Port Martin"

D'Urville Sea
Dumont d'Urville (Fr.)
C. Bickerton

South Magnetic Pole 1965

Davis B.
C. Keltie
C. Goodenough

Adélie Land

Wilkes Land

Banzare Coast

Sabrina Coast

130°
120°
110°

AUSTRALIA

Limit of pack ice - average minimum (Feb.-Mar.)

Knox Coast

Wilkes (Aust./U.S.)

MT. SANDOW 4,000

Denman Glacier

Queen Mary Coast

MT. SALUS 3,225

Helen Glacier

Mirnyy (U.S.S.R.)

West Ice Shelf

Bowman I.

Shackleton Ice Shelf

Drygalski Is.

Davis Sea

Mill I.

C. Masson I.

Princess Elizabeth Land

Ingrid Christensen Coast

Leopold & Astrid Coast

Pr. Charles Mts.
Lambert Gl.

Amery Ice Shelf

MACKENZIE BAY

C. Darnley

Mawson (Aust.)

BAILLEAU PEAK
5,215

4,000
4,085
5,200

2,060

Proclamation I.

Magnet Bay

Enderby Land

Scott Ra.

Molodezhnaya (U.S.S.R.)

Amundsen Bay

C. Ann

Douglas Is.

Zenithal Equidistant Projection

Copyright Oxford University Press

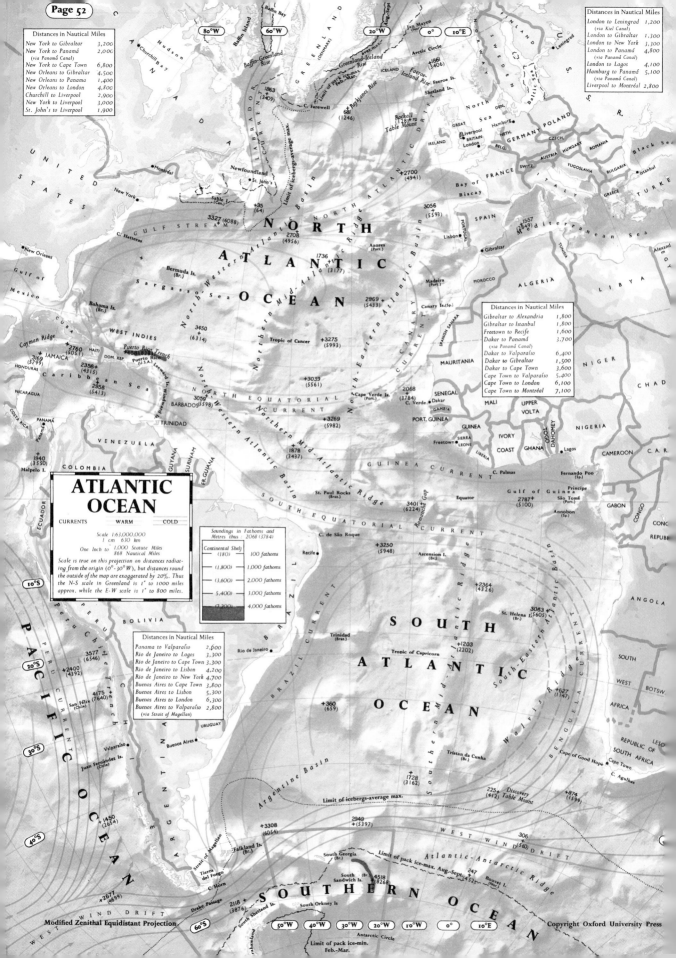

Scale 1 inch to 16 miles
0 5 10 15 20
For Legend see Page 57

North Sea

North Sea

Irish Sea

North Channel

Firth of Clyde

NORTHUMBERLAND

DURHAM

YORKSHIRE

NORTH RIDING

EAST RIDING

WEST RIDING

LANCS

CUMBERLAND

WESTMORLAND

Isle of Man

NORTHERN IRELAND

DOWN

ARMAGH

ANTRIM

INVERNESS

ARGYLL

PERTHSHIRE

ANGUS

KINCARDINE

FIFE

STIRLINGSHIRE

DUNBARTON

RENFREW

AYRSHIRE

LANARK

PEEBLES

SELKIRK

ROXBURGH

BERWICK

DUMFRIES

KIRKCUDBRIGHT

WIGTOWNSHIRE

CLACKMANNAN

WEST LOTHIAN

MIDLOTHIAN

EAST LOTHIAN

KINROSS

Aberdeen

Dundee

Perth

Stirling

Glasgow

Edinburgh

Newcastle upon Tyne

Sunderland

Middlesbrough

Teesside

Leeds

Bradford

Huddersfield

Blackburn

Belfast

Hull

Inner Hebrides

100 metres

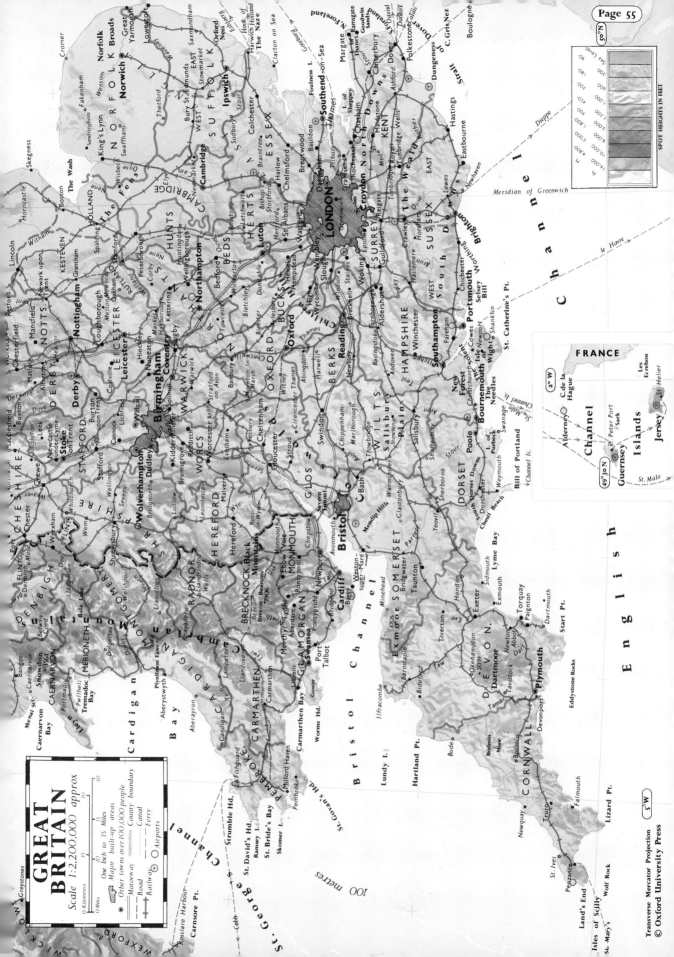

GREAT BRITAIN
Scale 1:2,200,000 approx

One inch to 35 Miles

0 Miles   35
0 Kilometres 20 40 60 80

Major built-up areas
Other towns over 100,000 people
County boundary
Motorway
Road   Canal
Railway   Ferry
Airports

SPOT HEIGHTS IN FEET

Meridian of Greenwich

Transverse Mercator Projection
© Oxford University Press

FRANCE

Channel Islands

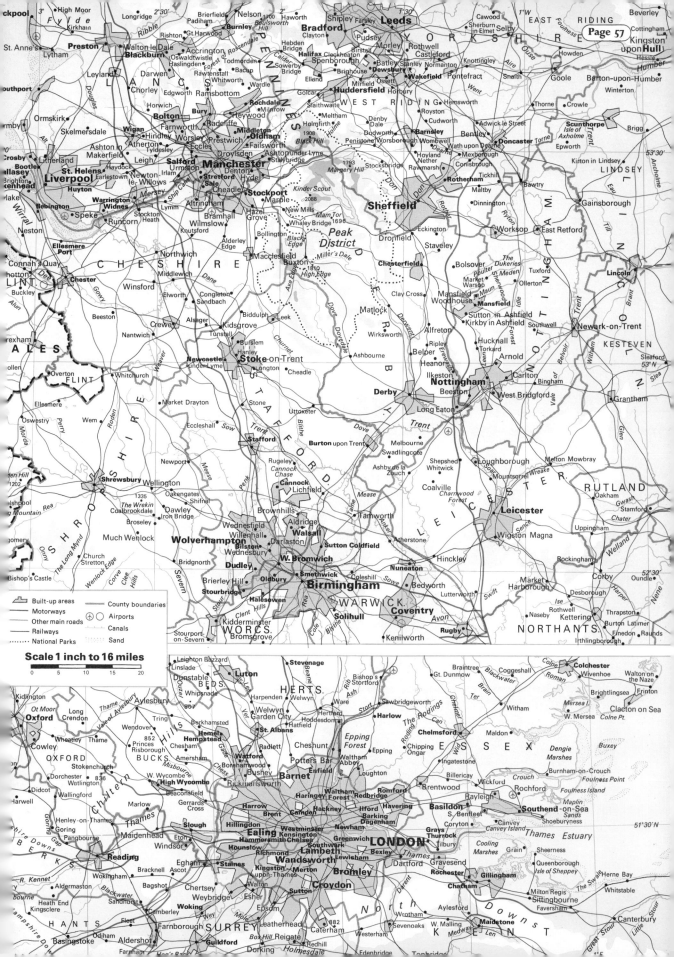

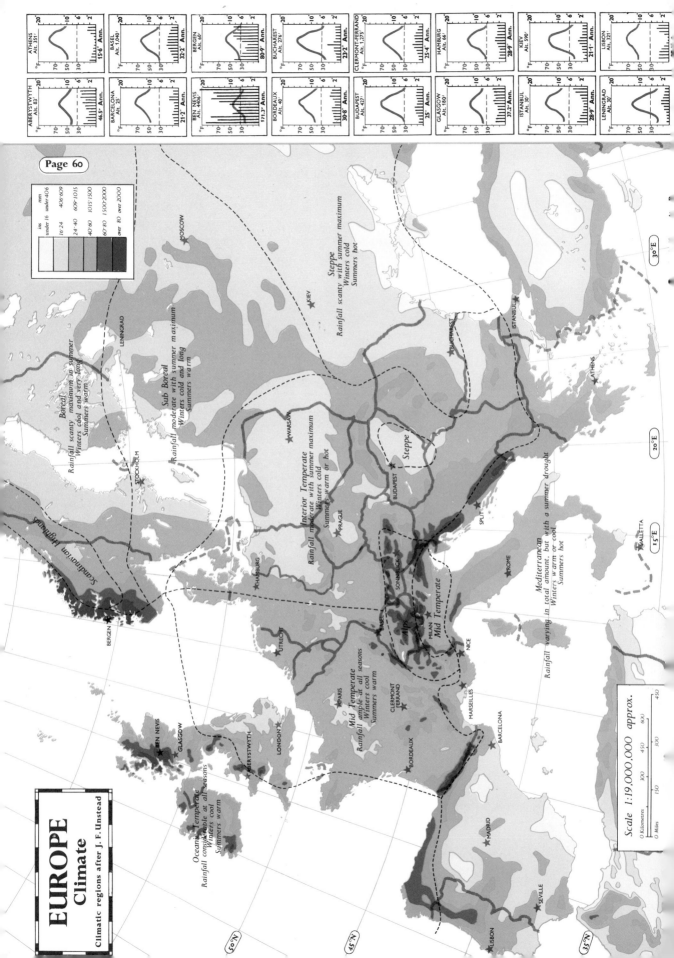

EUROPE
Climate
Climatic regions after J. F. Unstead

Scale 1:19,000,000 approx.

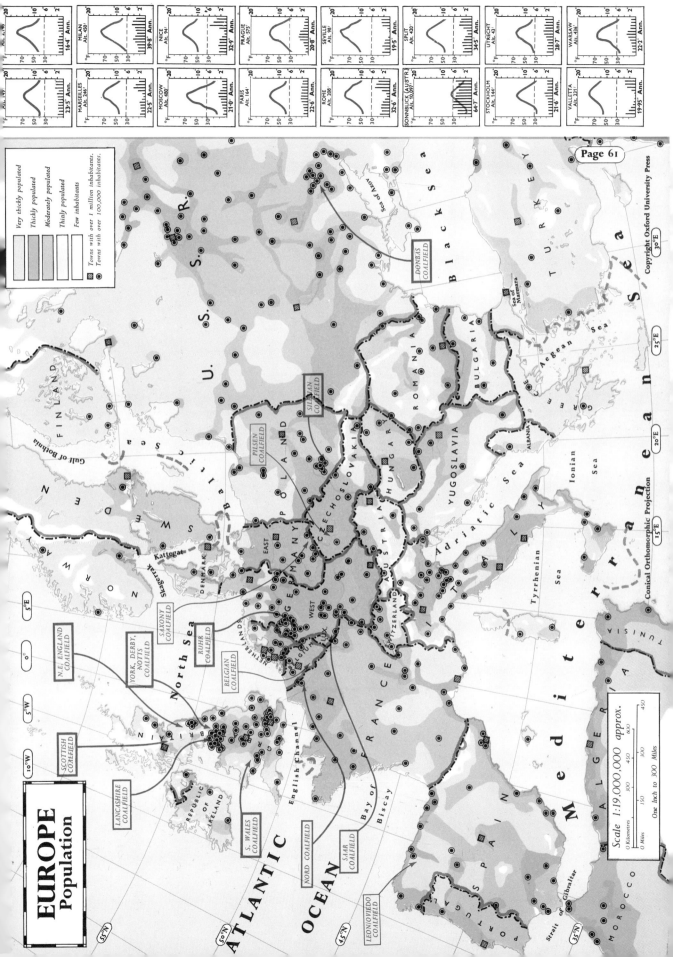

EUROPE
Population

Very thickly populated
Thickly populated
Moderately populated
Thinly populated
Few inhabitants

▨ Towns with over 1 million inhabitants.
⊚ Towns with over 100,000 inhabitants.

Scale 1:19,000,000 approx.

0 Kilometres   150   300   450   600
0 Miles   150   300   450

One Inch to 300 Miles

Conical Orthomorphic Projection

Copyright Oxford University Press

SCOTTISH COALFIELD
LANCASHIRE COALFIELD
N.E. ENGLAND COALFIELD
YORK, DERBY, NOTTS COALFIELD
SAXONY COALFIELD
RUHR COALFIELD
BELGIAN COALFIELD
S. WALES COALFIELD
NORD COALFIELD
SAAR COALFIELD
LEON/OVIEDO COALFIELD
PILSEN COALFIELD
SILESIAN COALFIELD
DONBAS COALFIELD

ATLANTIC OCEAN
North Sea
English Channel
Bay of Biscay
Mediterranean Sea
Black Sea
Baltic Sea
Gulf of Bothnia
Skagerrak
Kattegat
Adriatic Sea
Tyrrhenian Sea
Ionian Sea
Aegean Sea
Sea of Marmara
Sea of Azov
Strait of Gibraltar

NORWAY
SWEDEN
FINLAND
U.S.S.R.
DENMARK
REPUBLIC OF IRELAND
BRITAIN
NETHERLANDS
BELGIUM
LUX.
WEST GERMANY
EAST GERMANY
POLAND
CZECHOSLOVAKIA
FRANCE
SWITZERLAND
AUSTRIA
HUNGARY
ROMANIA
YUGOSLAVIA
BULGARIA
ALBANIA
GREECE
TURKEY
ITALY
SPAIN
PORTUGAL
ALGERIA
MOROCCO
TUNISIA

10°W 5°W 0° 5°E 10°E 15°E 20°E 25°E 30°E
55°N 50°N 45°N 35°N

MILAN Alt. 450' 16·4" Ann.
NICE Alt. 94' 39·8" Ann.
PRAGUE Alt. 575' 20·8" Ann.
SEVILLE Alt. 95' 19·5" Ann.
SPLIT Alt. 420' 34·5" Ann.
UTRECHT Alt. 43' 28·7" Ann.
WARSAW Alt. 436' 22·2" Ann.
MARSEILLES Alt. 246' 23·5" Ann.
MOSCOW Alt. 480' 22·5" Ann.
PARIS Alt. 164' 21·0" Ann.
ROME Alt. 208' 22·6" Ann.
SONNBLICK (AUSTRIA) Alt. 10,197' 64·7" Ann.
STOCKHOLM Alt. 144' 21·6" Ann.
VALLETTA Alt. 231' 19·95" Ann.

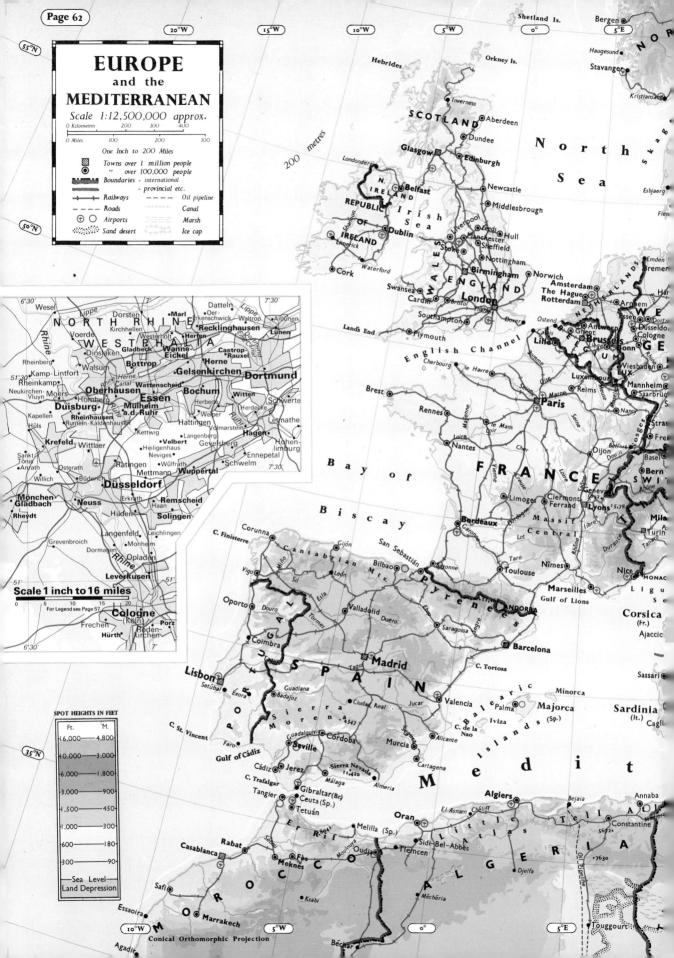

200 metres

200 metres

Copyright Oxford University Press

Western EUROPE

Scale 1:6,300,000 approx.

0 Kilometres 50 100 150 200

0 Miles 50 100 150

One inch to 100 Miles

Town over 1 million people
Town over 100,000 people
Boundaries - international
Railways
Airports
Marsh
Motorways
Canal

SPOT HEIGHTS IN FEET

Ft.	M.
16,000	4,800
10,000	3,000
6,000	1,800
3,000	900
1,500	450
1,000	300
600	180
300	90
Sea Level	
Land Depression	

Scale 1 inch to 16 miles

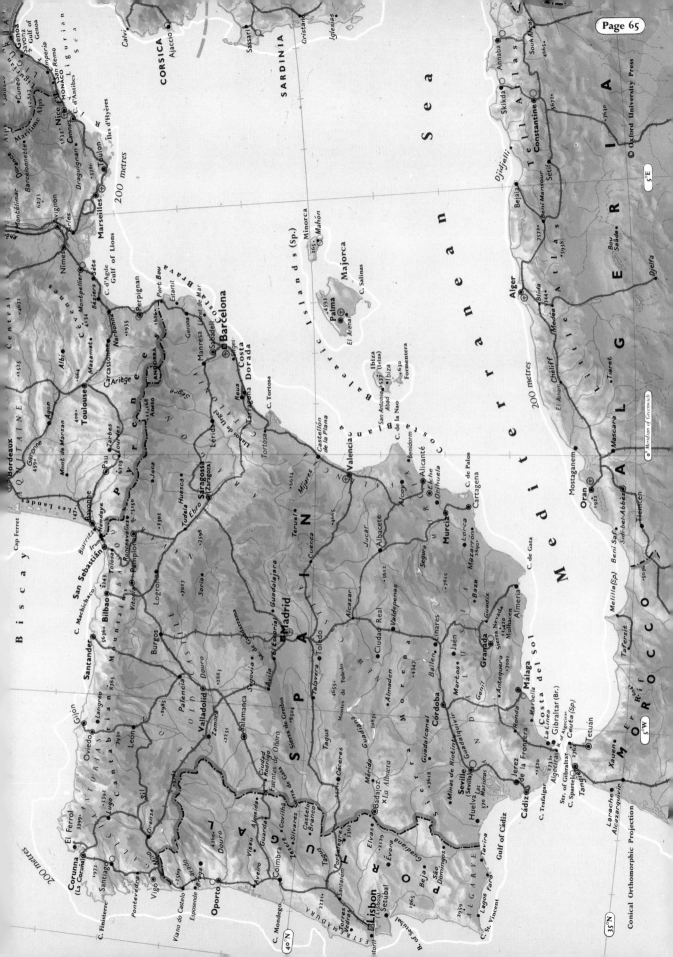

Genoa
Gulf of
Genoa
Savona
Imperia
San Remo
Cuneo
Maritime Alps
Monaco
Nice
Cannes
C. d'Antibes
Draguignan
Toulon
Îles d'Hyères
Marseilles
200 metres
Arles
Avignon
Nîmes
Montpellier
Sète
C. d'Agde
Gulf of Lions
Béziers
Narbonne
Perpignan
Port Bou
Estartit
Costa Brava
Gerona
Lloret de Mar
Manresa
Sabadell
Barcelona
Sitges
Costa Dorada
Reus
C. Tortosa
Castellón de la Plana
Valencia
C. de la Nao
Benidorm
Alicante
Elche
Orihuela
Murcia
Lorca
Mazarrón
C. de Palos
Cartagena
C. de Gata
Almería
Guadix
Baza

CORSICA
Ajaccio
Sassari
Iglesias
Cristanti

SARDINIA
Oristano

Minorca
Mahón
Majorca
Palma
El Arenal
C. Salinas
Balearic Islands (Sp.)
Ibiza (Iviza)
San Antonio Abad
Ibiza
Formentera

Mediterranean Sea

ALGERIA
Souk Ahras
Annaba
Skikda
Constantine
Djidjelli
Bejaïa
Beni Mansour
Sétif
Alger
Blida
Medéa
Cheliff
El Asnam
El Anasr
Mostaganem
Oran
Mascara
Sidi-bel-Abbès
Tlemcen
Saïda
Tiaret
Djelfa
Melilla (Sp)
Beni Saf
Tafersit

Tell Atlas
Little Atlas

0° Meridian of Greenwich
5°E

© Oxford University Press

SPAIN
Bordeaux
Cap Ferret
Bay of Biscay
Cap Ferret
Agen
Mont de Marsan
Les Landes
Bayonne
Biarritz
Hendaye
Irun
San Sebastián
Pamplona
Toulouse
Tarbes
Lourdes
Pau
Pyrenees
Aneto
ANDORRA
Ariège
Carcassonne
Mazamet
Albi
Jaca
Huesca
Lérida
Llanos de Urgel
Tortosa
Segre
Ebro
Tudela
Saragossa (Zaragoza)
Teruel
Cuenca
Mijares
Júcar
Albacete
Alcoy
Segura
Jucar
Segura

Corunna (La Coruña)
C. Finisterre
El Ferrol
Santiago
Pontevedra
Vigo
Viana do Castelo
Braga
Oporto
Aveiro
Esposende
Orense
Lugo
Oviedo
Gijón
Langreo
León
Palencia
Santander
Bilbao
Burgos
Logroño
Soria
Valladolid
Zamora
Salamanca
Ávila
Segovia
Guadalajara
Madrid
El Escorial
OLD CASTILE
Douro
Sierra de Gredos
Sierra de Guadarrama
Toledo
Talavera
Montes de Toledo
Ciudad Real
Valdepeñas
Almadén
Sierra Morena
Linares
Bailén
Jaén
Sierra Nevada
Mulhacén
Granada
Antequera
Málaga
Marbella
Costa del Sol
Ronda
Córdoba
Guadalquivir

NEW CASTILE
ANDALUSIA
EXTREMADURA

Cáceres
Mérida
La Albuera
Badajoz
Guadiana
Minas de Riotinto
Huelva
Las Marismas
Seville (Sevilla)
Jerez de la Frontera
Cádiz
C. Trafalgar
Str. of Gibraltar
C. Spartel
Tangier
Ceuta (Sp.)
Gibraltar (Br.)
La Línea
Algeciras
B. of Algeciras
Gulf of Cádiz
Tetuán
Xauen
Larache
Alcazarquivir

MOROCCO
Er Rif

PORTUGAL
Viseu
Almeida
Guarda
Serra da Estrela
Coimbra
Castelo Branco
Covilhã
Mondego
Castelo
Pombal
Santarém
Tagus
Torres Vedras
Lisbon
Setúbal
B. of Setúbal
C. Espichel
Évora
Elvas
Portalegre
Beja
São Domingos
ALENTEJO
Guadiana
Tavira
ALGARVE
Faro
Lagos
C. São Vicente
C. St. Vincent

200 metres
Conical Orthomorphic Projection
40°N
35°N
5°W
0°

Eastern EUROPE

Scale 1:6,300,000 approx.

Towns over 1 million people
" " over 100,000 people
Boundaries - international
" " - provincial etc.
Railways
" " projected
Airports

Canal
Salt pan
Motorways
Sand desert
Marsh
Ice cap

M.
4,800
3,000
1,800
900
450
300
180
90
Sea Level
Land Depression

Ft.
16,000
10,000
6,000
3,000
1,500
1,000
600
300

SPOT HEIGHTS
IN FEET

U.S.S.R.

Vitebsk
Orsha
Polotsk
Lepel
Daugavpils
West Dvina
Bobruysk
Mozyr
Minsk
Slutsk
Vileyka
Molodechno
Novogrudok
Baranovichi
Slonim
Pripet
Pinsk
David-Gorodok
Pripet Marshes
Rovno
Dubno
Lutsk
Kovel
Vladimir-Volynskiy
Zdolbunov
Zolochev
Ternopol
Berezhany
Ivano-Frankovsk
Kolomyya
Chernovtsy
Stanislav
Sambor
Borislav
Lvov
East Beskids
Uzhgorod
Mukachevo
Chop
Khust
Satu-Mare

LITHUANIAN S.S.R.

Siauliai
Klaipeda (Memel)
Vilnius
Kaunas
Grodno
Lida

BYELORUSSIA

Neman
Volkovysk
Brest Litovsky
Kobrin

Baltic Sea

Karlskrona
Bornholm
C. Arkona
Sassnitz
Rügen

DENMARK

Copenhagen
Helsingør
Helsingborg
Malmö
Lund
Hässleholm
Kristianstad
Karlshamn
Holbæk
Odense
Svendborg
Nyköbing
Lolland
Falster
Gedser
Fehmarn
Kiel
Lübeck
Flensburg
Schleswig
Neumünster
Esbjerg
Fredericia
Aabenraa
The Sound
Zealand
Funen
Great Belt
Little Belt
Kiel Bay
Grossenbrode
North Frisian Islands
Heligoland

POLAND

Warsaw (Warszawa)
Łódź
Kraków
Kalinigrad (Königsberg)
Gdańsk (Danzig)
Gdynia
Bydgoszcz
Poznań
Wrocław (Breslau)
Katowice
Częstochowa
Lublin
Radom
Kielce
Białystok
Olsztyn
Toruń
Włocławek
Kutno
Łowicz
Skierniewice
Piotrków
Sosnowiec
Gliwice
Bytom
Chorzów
Opole
Nysa
Legnica
Zielona Góra (Grünberg)
Gorzów Wielkopolski (Landsberg)
Szczecin (Stettin)
Koszalin
Słupsk
Kołobrzeg
Świnoujście
Szczecinek
Gniezno
Jelenia Góra (Hirschberg)
Wałbrzych
Kłodzko (Glatz)
Kalisz
Ostrów Wielkopolski
Łomża
Ostrów Mazowiecki
Biała Podlaska
Chełm
Zamość
Jarosław
Przemyśl
Rzeszów
Jasło
Nowy Sącz
Zakopane
Tarnów
Nowa Huta
Sanok
Cieszyn
Mława
Grudziądz
Malbork
Elbląg
Piła
Odra (Oder)
Neisse (Nysa)
Warta
Wisła (Vistula)
Inowrocław
Brzeg
Głogów
Cottbus
Frankfurt
Eberswalde

GERMANY (EAST GERMANY)

Berlin
Leipzig
Dresden
Magdeburg
Halle
Erfurt
Rostock
Schwerin
Wismar
Stralsund
Greifswald
Neubrandenburg
Brandenburg
Potsdam
Spandau
Wittenberge
Stendal
Salzgitter
Dessau
Wittenberg
Torgau
Karl-Marx-Stadt
Zwickau
Gera
Jena
Weimar
Gotha
Eisenach
Meiningen
Suhl
Plauen
Hof
Bayreuth
Nordhausen
Mühlhausen
Thüringer Wald

WEST GERMANY

Hamburg
Hanover
Bremen
Bremerhaven
Cuxhaven
Wilhelmshaven
Oldenburg
Osnabrück
Bielefeld
Kassel
Göttingen
Bielefeld
Brunswick
Wolfsburg
Celle
Lüneburg
Ulzen
Stade
Lübeck
Frankfurt am Main
Würzburg
Mannheim
Heidelberg
Stuttgart
Darmstadt
Nuremberg
Regensburg
Munich
Augsburg
Ulm
Tübingen
Reutlingen
Ingolstadt
Passau
Coburg
Schweinfurt
Main
Neckar
Donau (Danube)
Harz
Thüringer Wald
Bohemian Forest

CZECHOSLOVAKIA

Prague
Pilsen (Plzeň)
Brno
Bratislava
Ostrava
Olomouc
Moravská Ostrava
Opava
Přerov
Prostějov
Gottwaldov
Znojmo
Nymburk
Pardubice
Kolín
Mladá Boleslav
Ústí
Děčín
Liberec
Teplice
Most
Chomutov
Karlovy Vary
Cheb
Mariánské Lázně
Klatovy
Písek
České Budějovice
Tábor
Jihlava
Česká Třebová
Nitra
Košice
Lučenec
Levice
Komárno
Ružomberok
Moravian Gate
Sudeten Mts.
Krkonoše
Kamienna Góra

HUNGARY

Budapest
Debrecen
Miskolc
Szeged
Győr
Szolnok
Kecskemét
Nyíregyháza
Sopron
Szombathely
Szekszárd
Pécs
Székesfehérvár
Veszprém
Tatabánya
Salgótarján
Eger
Kaposvár
Dunaújváros
Csepel
Esztergom
Vác
Kiskunfélegyháza
Kiskunhalas
Gyula
Hódmezővásárhely
Nagykanizsa
Zalaegerszeg
Dombóvár
Balaton L.
Danube (Duna)
Drava
Mátra

AUSTRIA

Vienna (Wien)
Graz
Linz
Salzburg
Innsbruck
Klagenfurt
Villach
Wiener-Neustadt
Steyr
Wels
Leoben
Bruck
Donawitz
Semmering P.
Brenner Pass
Hohe Tauern
Niedere Tauern
Carnic Alps
Julian Alps
Tyrol
Dolomites

MOLDAVIAN S.S.R.

Kishinev
Beltsy
Tiraspol
Bendery
Tighina
Prut
Dniester

ROMANIA / TRANSYLVANIA

Cluj
Oradea
Arad
Satu-Mare
Baia-Mare
Bistrița
Târgu Mureș
Mediaș
Turda
Zalău
Alba Iulia
Dej
Botoșani
Suceava
Câmpulung
Moldovenesc
Piatra-Neamț
Roman
Bacău
Gheorghieni
Sfântu
Odorhei
Carpathian Mountains
Veretski Pass
Tatar Pass

LIECHTENSTEIN

© Oxford University Press

Conical Orthomorphic Projection

TURKEY

BULGARIA

Bucharest (Bucureşti)

Istanbul (Constantinople)

Izmir (Smyrna)

Sofia (Sofiya)

Plovdiv (Philippopolis)

Salonica (Thessaloniki)

MACEDONIA

THRACE

GREECE

THESSALY

Athens (Athínai)

Aegean Sea

Northern Sporades

Cyclades

Sea of Crete (Kríti)

Belgrade (Beograd)

YUGOSLAVIA

and

BOSNIA

HERCEGOVINA

Sarajevo

MONTENEGRO

ALBANIA

Tiranë (Tirana)

Corfu (Kérkira)

PELOPONNESE (MOREA)

Sparta

Ionian Sea

200 metres

Adriatic Sea

Rome (Roma)

LATIUM

ABRUZZI-MOLISE

Naples (Napoli)

BASILICATA

CALABRIA

Reggio di Calabria

SICILY

Palermo

Catania

Syracuse (Siracusa)

MALTA

Valletta

Tyrrhenian Sea

Mediterranean Sea

Malta Channel

Sicilian Channel

VATICAN CITY

ROME

Tivoli

Velletri

Guidonia

Marino

Albano Laziale

Monterotondo

Mentana

Scale 1 inch to 16 miles

For Legend see Page 30

SCANDINAVIA

Scale 1:6,300,000 approx.

One Inch to 100 Miles

0 Kilometres 50 100 150 200
0 Miles 50 100 150

Towns over 1 million people
" over 100,000 people
Boundaries - international
" - provincial etc
Railways ---- ----
projected ....
Airports
Canal
Salt pan
Roads
tracks
Autobahn
Marsh
Ice cap

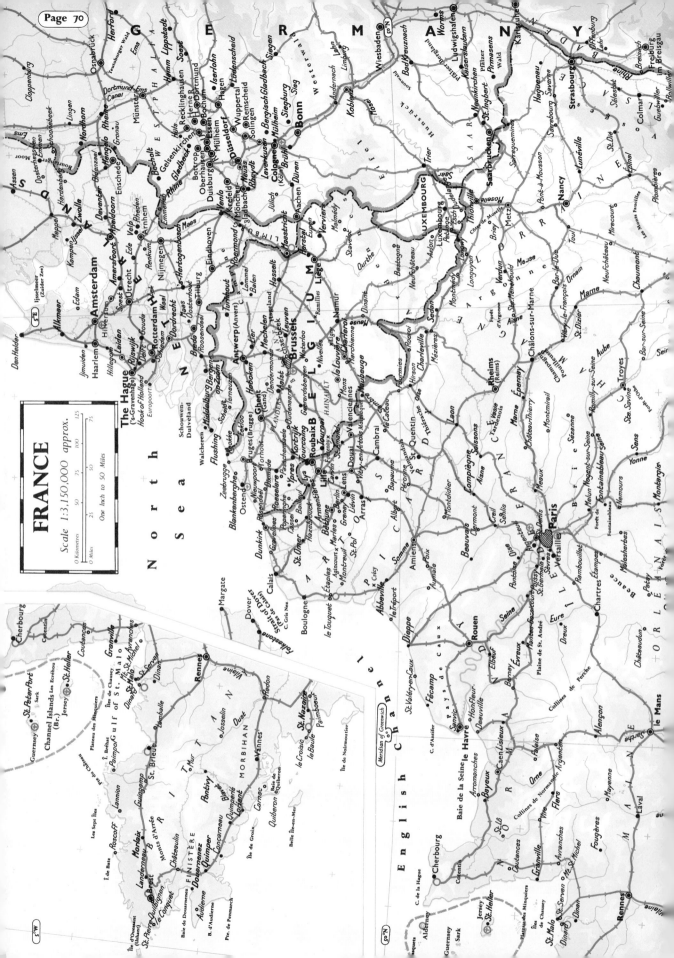

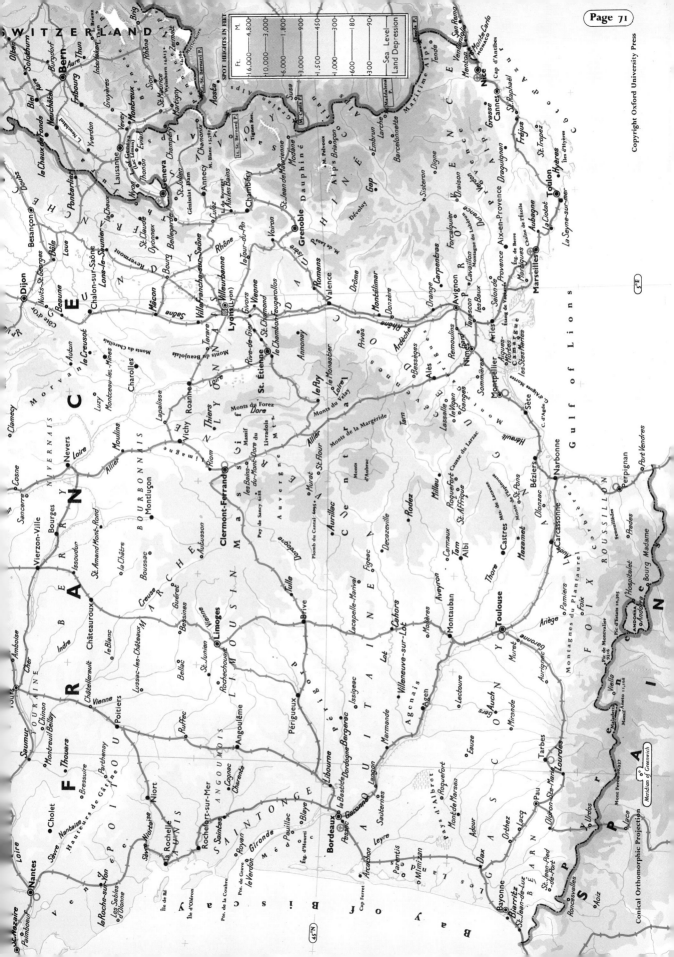

Copyright Oxford University Press

SWITZERLAND

SPOT HEIGHTS IN FEET

Ft.	M.
16,000	4,800
10,000	3,000
6,000	1,800
3,000	900
1,500	450
1,000	300
600	180
300	90
Sea Level	
Land Depression	

Bern
Fribourg
Solothurn
Burgdorf
Biel
Neuchâtel
Bâle
Besançon
Dijon
Nuits-St.-Georges
Beaune
Côte d'Or
MORVAN
Autun
le Creusot
Chalon-sur-Saône
Mâcon
Lons-le-Saunier
St. Claude
Oyonnax
Bellegarde
Bourg
NIVERNAIS
Nevers
Clamecy
Sancerre
Cosne
Bourges
Vierzon-Ville
Châteauroux
BERRY
Issoudun
St. Amand-Mont-Rond
Montluçon
BOURBONNAIS
Moulins
Lapalisse
Vichy
Thiers
Roanne
Villefranche-sur-Saône
Villeurbanne
Lyon(s)
Givors
Rive-de-Gier
St. Chamond
St. Étienne
le Chambon-Feugerolles
Monts du Forez
Dore
Monts du Lyonnais
Vienne
Annonay
Valence
Romans
Grenoble
Chambéry
Aix-les-Bains
Annecy
Geneva
Lausanne
Montreux
Vevey
Thonon
Évian
St. Julien
Chamonix
M. Blanc 15,782
Aosta
Susa
Montélimar
Die
Drôme
Gap
Digne
Sisteron
Forcalquier
Apt
Carpentras
Orange
Avignon
Nîmes
Tarascon
Arles
les Baux
Salon-de-Provence
Aix-en-Provence
Draguignan
Marseilles
la Ciotat
Aubagne
Toulon
La Seyne-sur-mer
Hyères
Fréjus
St. Raphaël
Cannes
Antibes
Cap d'Antibes
Nice
Monaco
Monte-Carlo
Menton
San Remo
Ventimiglia

FRANCE

DIJON
BURGUNDY
SAVOY
DAUPHINÉ
PROVENCE
RIVIERA
Maritime Alps

Gulf of Lions

MASSIF CENTRAL
AUVERGNE
Clermont-Ferrand
Riom
les Bains
du-Mont-Dore
Puy de Sancy 6188
Murat
St. Flour
Aurillac
Plomb du Cantal 6095
Monts d'Aubrac
Monts de la Margéride
le Puy
le Monastier
Monts du Velay
Tournon
Privas
Ardèche
Aubenas
Bessèges
Alès
Uzès
Remoulins
Pont du Gard
Aigues Mortes
les Stes Maries
CAMARGUE
Étang de Vaccarès
Étang de Berre
Martigues

Limoges
LIMOUSIN
MARCHE
Guéret
Bessines
Aubusson
la Chaize
Boussac
Bellac
St. Junien
Lussac-les-Châteaux
Châtellerault
POITOU
Poitiers
Vienne
Chinon
Montreuil-Bellay
Saumur
Thouars
Bressuire
Parthenay
Cholet
Nantes
St. Nazaire
Paimbœuf
la Roche-sur-Yon
les Sables d'Olonne
Île de Ré
la Rochelle
AUNIS
Rochefort-sur-Mer
SAINTONGE
Saintes
Royan
Pte. de Grave
Blaye
ANGOUMOIS
Angoulême
Ruffec
Niort
Cognac
Charente
Périgueux
Brive
Tulle
Figeac
Rodez
Decazeville
Villeneuve-sur-Lot
Cahors
Lot
Agen
AGENAIS
PÉRIGORD
Bergerac
Dordogne
Libourne
la Bastide
Bordeaux
Pessac
Garonne
Langon
Sauternes
Marmande
Montauban
Moissac
Toulouse
Muret
Garonne
Auch
Mirande
Lectoure
GASCOGNE
Eauze
Mont-de-Marsan
Roquefort
pays d'Albret
Dax
Adour
LANDES
Mimizan
Parentis
Arcachon
Cap Ferret
BAY OF BISCAY
Bayonne
Biarritz
St. Jean-de-Luz
St. Jean-Pied-de-Port
Roncevaux
Pau
Orthez
Oloron-Ste-Marie
Lourdes
Tarbes
BÉARN
BIGORRE
PYRENEES
Montagnes du Plantaurel
Pamiers
FOIX
Foix
Ariège
Aurignac
Montagnes de Plantaurel
Pic de Montvalier 9314
Mont Perdu 10,937
Pic d'Estats 10,305
Maladetta
Pic d'Aneto 11,168
ANDORRA
Andorra
Bourg Madame
Bagnères

CEVENNES
Mende
Millau
Causse du Larzac
Roquefort
St. Affrique
St. Pons
Olargues
Béziers
Narbonne
Sète
Montpellier
Hérault
ROUSSILLON
Perpignan
Prades
Céret
Port Vendres
CORBIÈRES
Castelnaudary
Carcassonne
Mazamet
Castres
Albi
Carmaux
Tarn
MONTAGNE NOIRE
Gaillac

Meridian of Greenwich
Conical Orthomorphic Projection

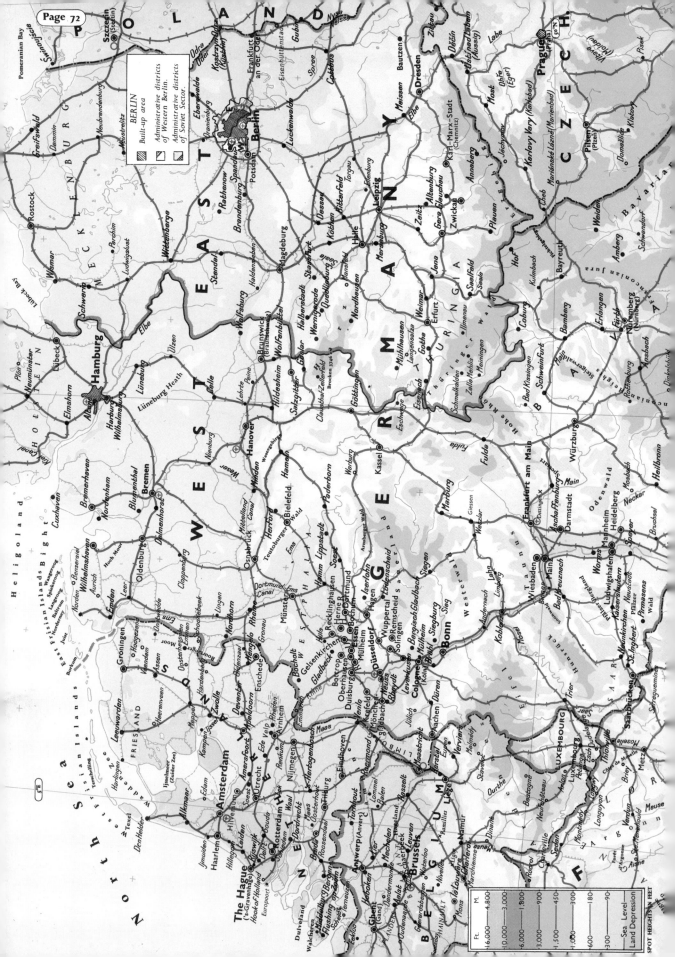

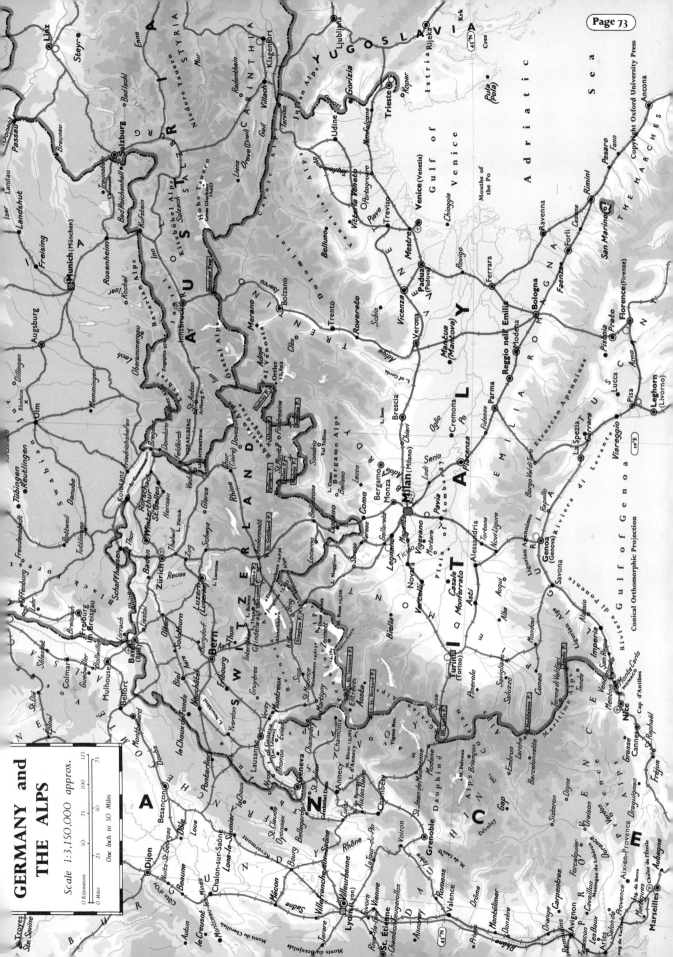

Eurasia
PHYSICAL

Scale 1:44,000,000 approx.

0 Kilometres	350	700	1050	1400
0 Miles	350	700	1050

One Inch to 700 Miles

This equal area projection (origin 40°N 95°E) produces serious distortion at the top and bottom extremities of this map i.e. farthest from the origin.

Page 74

Build

Re-elevated blocks.
Ancient blocks, great shields.
Volcanic plains & plateaux.
Recent deposits.
Sedimentary layers.
Folded mountains.
Main Volcanic areas

ARCTIC OCEAN

North Pole

Peary 1909

Limit of pack ice — max.

Polar Ice

Nordenskjöld 1878-9

Limit of pack ice — min.

Chancelor 1553

Maximum extent of Glaciation

GREENLAND

ICELAND

ALASKA

Bering Sea

Sea of Okhotsk

CANADA

Hudson Bay

UNITED STATES

Missouri

St. Lawrence

Maximum extent of Glaciation

ATLANTIC OCEAN

NORWAY

SWEDEN

FINLAND

SOVIET UNION

Lena

Yenisey

Volga

Baltic Sea

North Sea

DEN.

IREL.

G.B.

NETH.

BELG.

GERMANY

POLAND

CZECH.

AUSTRIA

HUNGARY

ROMANIA

BULG.

YUGOSLAVIA

SWITZ.

FRANCE

ITALY

ALB.

GREECE

Rhine

Danube

Black

PORTUGAL

SPAIN

Mediterranean

ALGERIA

TUNISIA

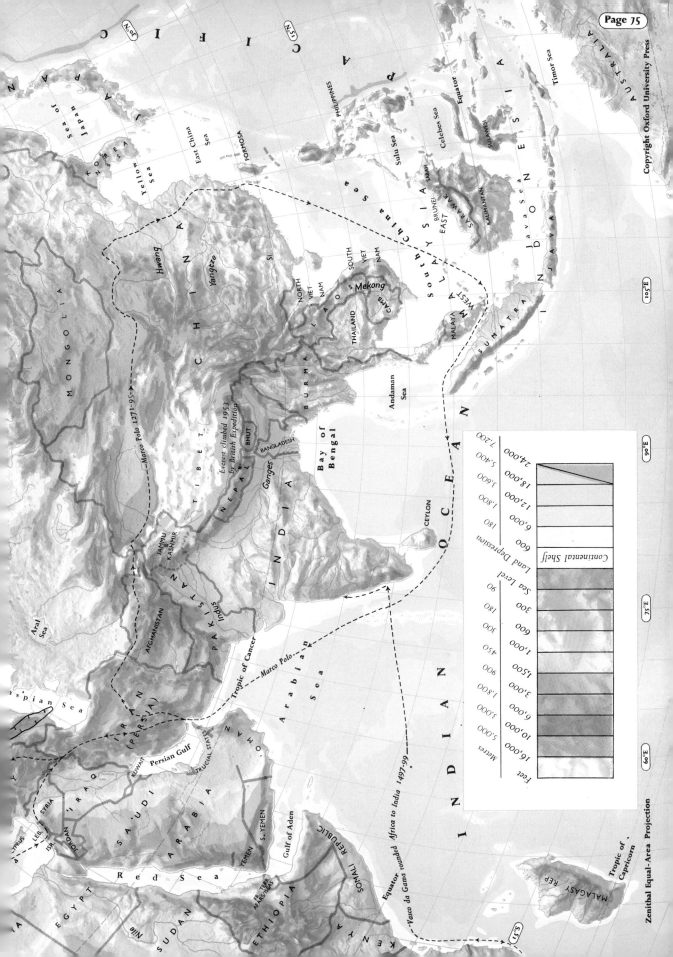

Copyright Oxford University Press

Zenithal Equal-Area Projection

Eurasia VEGETATION

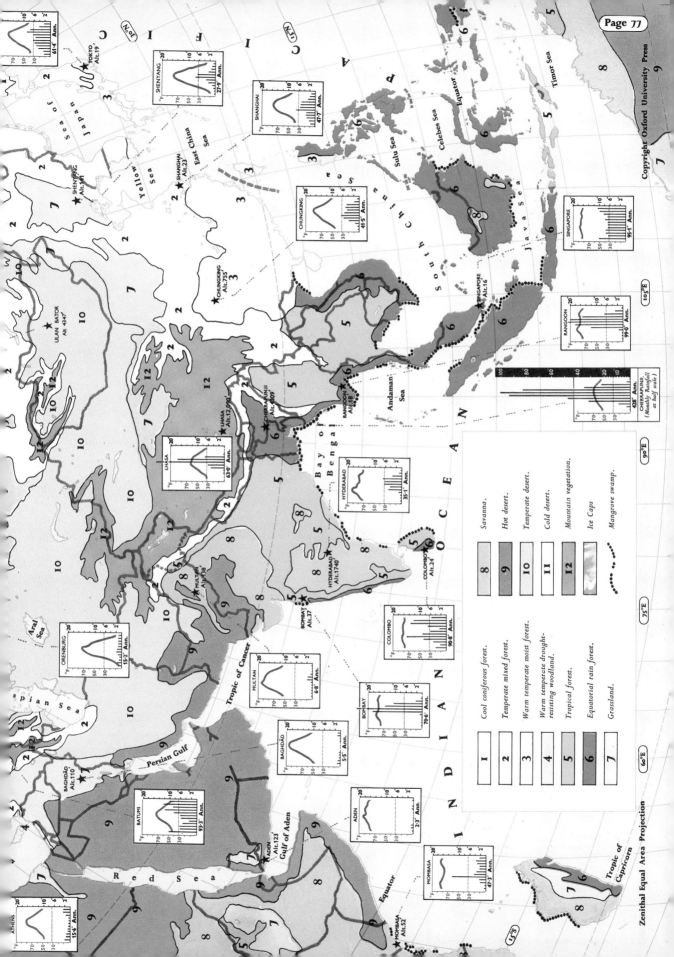

Copyright Oxford University Press

Zenithal Equal Area Projection

Legend:

1 — Cool coniferous forest.
2 — Temperate mixed forest.
3 — Warm temperate moist forest.
4 — Warm temperate drought-resisting woodland.
5 — Tropical forest.
6 — Equatorial rain forest.
7 — Grassland.
8 — Savanna.
9 — Hot desert.
10 — Temperate desert.
11 — Cold desert.
12 — Mountain vegetation.
— Ice Caps
······ Mangrove swamp.

Climate graphs:

TOKYO Alt.19′ · 61·4″ Ann.
SHENYANG Alt.141′ · 27·9″ Ann.
SHANGHAI Alt.23′ · 47·7″ Ann.
CHUNGKING Alt.755′ · 41·5″ Ann.
SINGAPORE Alt.16 · 95·1″ Ann.
RANGOON · 99·0″ Ann.
CHERRAPUNJI Alt.8 · 428″ Ann. (Monthly Rainfall at half scale)
LHASA Alt.12,090′ · 63·0″ Ann.
HYDERABAD · 35·1″ Ann.
COLOMBO Alt.24′ · 90·6″ Ann.
ORENBURG · 15·2″ Ann.
BOMBAY Alt.37′ · 70·6″ Ann.
MULTAN · 6·8″ Ann.
BAGHDĀD · 5·5″ Ann.
BATUMI · 93·3″ Ann.
ADEN · 2·3″ Ann.
MOMBASA Alt.52′ · 47·3″ Ann.
ATHENS · 15·4″ Ann.

Map labels:

PACIFIC OCEAN
30°N · 15°N
Sea of Japan
Japan
Yellow Sea
East China Sea
South China Sea
Sulu Sea
Celebes Sea
Java Sea
Timor Sea
Equator
Andaman Sea
Bay of Bengal
INDIAN OCEAN
Aral Sea
Caspian Sea
Persian Gulf
Gulf of Aden
Red Sea
Tropic of Cancer
Tropic of Capricorn
105°E · 90°E · 75°E · 60°E
15°S

TOKYO Alt.19′
SHENYANG Alt.141′
SHANGHAI Alt.23′
CHUNGKING Alt.755′
ULAN BATOR Alt.4347′
LHASA Alt.12,090′
CHERRAPUNJI Alt.8′
RANGOON Alt.8′
SINGAPORE Alt.16
HYDERABAD Alt.1740
COLOMBO Alt.24′
BOMBAY Alt.37′
MULTAN Alt.738′
ORENBURG
BAGHDĀD Alt.110′
BATUMI Alt.123′
ADEN Alt.123′
MOMBASA Alt.52′
ATHENS

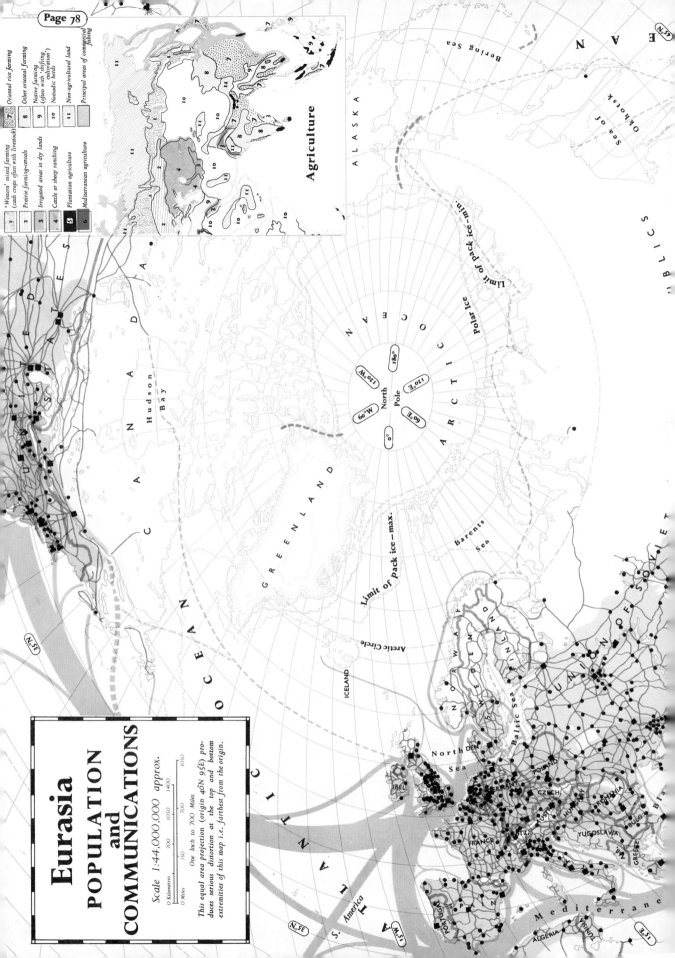

Agriculture

1	'Western' mixed farming (cash crops often with livestock)
2	Prairie farming-cereals
3	Irrigated areas in dry lands
4	Cattle or sheep ranching
5	Plantation agriculture
6	Mediterranean agriculture
7	Oriental rice farming
8	Other oriental farming
9	Native farming (often with shifting cultivation)
10	Nomadic herds
11	Non-agricultural land
	Principal areas of commercial fishing

Eurasia
POPULATION and COMMUNICATIONS

Scale 1:44,000,000 approx.

0 Kilometres	350	700	1050	1400
0 Miles		350	700	1050

One Inch to 700 Miles

This equal area projection (origin 40°N 95°E) produces serious distortion at the top and bottom
extremities of this map i.e. farthest from the origin.

North Pole

180°
150°W
120°E
90°W
60°E
0°
30°W

ARCTIC OCEAN

Limit of pack ice – min.

Limit of pack ice – max.

Polar Ice

Bering Sea

Sea of Okhotsk

ALASKA

CANADA

Hudson Bay

GREENLAND

ICELAND

Barents Sea

Arctic Circle

UNION OF SOVIET

UNITED STATES

ATLANTIC OCEAN

S. America

Baltic Sea

North Sea

NORWAY
SWEDEN
FINLAND
DEN
IRELAND
GERMANY
POLAND
CZECH
FRANCE
SWITZ
AUSTRIA
HUNGARY
ROMANIA
YUGOSLAVIA
BULG
GREECE
PORTUGAL
SPAIN
ALGERIA
TUNISIA

Mediterranean

N. 45°N
35°N
15°E
15°W

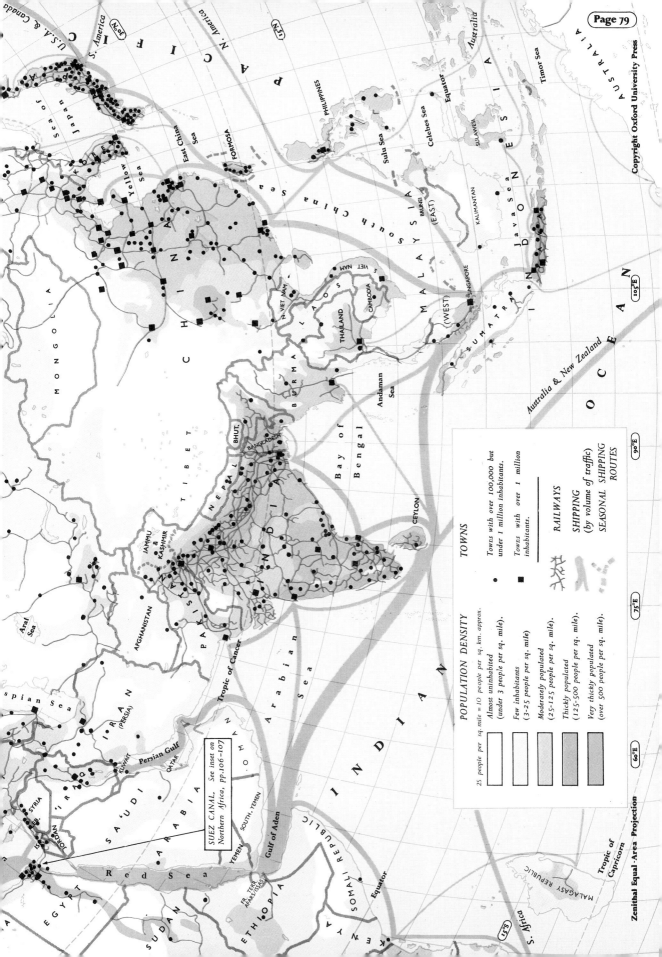

Copyright Oxford University Press

PACIFIC OCEAN

U.S.A. & Canada
S. America
N. America
PERU
Korea Strait
Japan
Yellow Sea
East China Sea
FORMOSA
PHILIPPINES
Celebes Sea
Sulu Sea
SULAWESI
Equator
Australia
Timor Sea
AUSTRALIA
Australia & New Zealand
105°E

MONGOLIA
C H I N A
South China Sea
VIET NAM
(N)
LAOS
VIET NAM (S)
THAILAND
CAMBODIA
BURMA
MALAYSIA (WEST)
Singapore
SUMATRA
BRUNEI
KALIMANTAN
(EAST)
MALAYSIA
I N D O N E S I A
Java Sea
JAVA
99°E

TIBET
NEPAL
BHUT.
BANGLADESH
I N D I A
Bay of Bengal
Andaman Sea
CEYLON
JAMMU & KASHMIR
PAKISTAN
75°E

Aral Sea
AFGHANISTAN
Tropic of Cancer
Arabian Sea
I N D I A N   O C E A N
60°E

Caspian Sea
IRAN (PERSIA)
IRAQ
KUWAIT
QATAR
Persian Gulf
SYRIA
JORDAN
ISRAEL
SAUDI   ARABIA
SOUTH YEMEN
YEMEN
Gulf of Aden
OMAN
U.A.E.

SUEZ CANAL, See inset on Northern Africa, pp.106-107

EGYPT
SUDAN
Red Sea
ETHIOPIA
FR. TERR. AFARS/ISSAS
SOMALI REPUBLIC
KENYA
Equator
S. Africa
Tropic of Capricorn
MALAGASY REPUBLIC

15°S

POPULATION DENSITY

25 people per sq. mile = 10 people per sq. km. approx.

	Almost uninhabited (under 3 people per sq. mile).
	Few inhabitants (3-25 people per sq. mile)
	Moderately populated (25-125 people per sq. mile).
	Thickly populated (125-500 people per sq. mile).
	Very thickly populated (over 500 people per sq. mile).

TOWNS

• Towns with over 100,000 but under 1 million inhabitants.

■ Towns with over 1 million inhabitants.

RAILWAYS

SHIPPING (by volume of traffic)

SEASONAL SHIPPING ROUTES

Zenithal Equal-Area Projection

U.S.S.R.

Scale 1:25,000,000 approx.

| 0 Kilometres | 400 | 600 | 800 |

| 0 Miles | 200 | 300 | 400 | 500 |

One Inch to 400 Miles

Conical Orthomorphic Projection

Copyright Oxford University Press

20°E · 25°E · 30°E · 35°E · 40°E · 45°E · 50°E · 55°E

Khiumaa

Hanko · Vyborg · Petrozavodsk ·446 · North · ·767 · Ukhta

Gotland · Saaremaa · ·167 · Helsinki · Gulf of Finland · Lake Onega · ·Dvina

Ventspils · Tallinn · ·107 · ESTONIAN · ·554 · Lake Ladoga

Baltic · Gulf of Riga · S.S.R. · Narva · Pushkin · Leningrad · Svir' · ·885 · Konosha · Vychegda · Syktyvkar

Liepāja · Riga · ·627 · Tartu · L.439 · Peipus · Novgorod · ·960 · Sukhona · Kotlas

Klaipeda · LATVIAN S.S.R. · Pskov · L. Ilmen' · ·500 · Cherepovets · Vologda · ·915 · Kama · Rudnichnyy · Solik

Kaliningrad · Siauliai · Velikiye · Luki · Vitebsk · ·1118 · Valdai Hills · Rybinsk Reservoir · Kostroma · Kirov · Glazov · Izhevsk

Gdańsk · Sovetsk · LITHUANIAN S.S.R. · Kaunas · W. Dvina · Rzhev · Volga · Kalinin · Yaroslavl' · ·965 · Ivanovo · Kineshma · ·512 · ·931 · Kazan'

POLAND · Grodno · Vilnius · Smolensk · Vyaz'ma · Moscow · Vladimir · Kovrov · Dzerzhinsk · Gor'kiy · Yoshkar-Ola · ·820 · ·839

Warsaw · Białystok · ·577 · Minsk · BYELORUSSIAN S.S.R. · Baranovichi · Mogilev · ·886 · Yel'nya · Orekhovo-Zuyevo · Kaluga · Kolomna · Oka · Murom · Arzamas · Volga · Kama

Brest Litovskiy · Pripet · Pinsk Marshes · Pripet · Bryansk · Tula · Novomoskovsk · Ryazan' · U · Saransk · ·1027 · Ul'yanovsk · S · ·833

Kovel' · ·1053 · Gomel' · Orel' · ·777 · ·964 · Penza · ·1213 · Syzran' · Kuybyshev · Sterlitam

L'vov · Rovno · Korosten' · Chernigov · Kursk · ·1089 · Chapayevsk · Samara · Buzuluk · Yermola

Ivano-Frankovsk · Zhitomir · Kiev · ·590 · Belgorod · ·774 · Voronezh · Volga · Hills · Vol'sk · ·453 · Uru

Chernovtsy · Dniester · Berdichev · UKRAINIAN · Sumy · Don · ·740 · Balashov · ·1073 · Saratov · Sol'-Ilets

Botoşani · Prut · Vinnitsa · S.S.R. · Kirovograd · Poltava · Khar'kov · Borisoglebsk · ·826 · Krasnyy Kut · Ural'sk

Bistriţa · Iaşi · MOLD. S.S.R. · Ananyev · Dnieper · Kremenchug · Dneprodzerzhinsk · Lugansk · Tsimlyansk Reservoir · Novouzensk · Aleksandrov Gay · ·55

Bacău · ·1703 · Kishinev · Bug · Krivoy Rog · Dnepropetrovsk · Yenakiyevo · ·49 · K

ROMANIA · Odessa · Nikopol' · Donetsk · Makeyevka · Krasnyy Luch · Shakhty · Volgograd · Baskunchak · Caspian Lowlands · Makat

Galaţi · ·1280 · ·223 · Nikolayev · Zaporozh'ye · ·1066 · Taganrog · Novocherkassk · Gur'yev

Sulina · Kherson · ·118 · Zhdanov · Rostov · ·52 · Astrakhan'

Bucharest · CRIMEA · Nogaysk · Yeysk · Sea of Azov · Sal'sk · ·331 · ·600

Danube · Simferopol' · Sevastopol' · Inkerman · Kerch' · Kuban' · Krasnodar · Armavir · Stavropol' · ·695 · Gur'yev

BULGARIA · Varna · Balaklava · Yalta · Novorossiysk · ·3104 · Maykop · Caspian · Fort Shevchenko

200 metres · Burgas · Black Sea · Tuapse · Sochi · Maykop · ·El'brus · Pyatigorsk · Mangyshlak Peninsula · Sea

Istanbul · Zonguldak · Sinop · Sukhumi · Caucasus · ·18,468 · Groznyy · Ordzhonikidze · Shevchenko · ·435 · UP

Adapazarı · Karabük · ·8415 · Samsun · Poti · GEORGIAN S.S.R. · Makhachkala · Caspian

Pontic · Trabzon · Batumi · Kutaisi · Tbilisi · ·13,474 · Derbent · Kara-Bogaz-Gol

TURKEY · Eskişehir · Ankara · Mountains · ·12,917 · Alaverdi · Leninakan · L. Sevan · Kirovabad · ·14,375 · Sumgait · ·11,906 · Krasnovodsk

Kütahya · Afyonkarahisar · Sivas · ·10,203 · ARMENIAN S.S.R. · AZERBAYDZHAN S.S.R. · Baku · Cheleken · Nebit-Dag

Konya · Lake Tuz · ·11,932 · Nakhichevan · Araks (Araxes) · ·14,010 · Astara · Sea

SPOT HEIGHTS IN FEET · Taurus Mts · Cilician Gates · Tabrīz · ·12,172 · Mianeh · Kara- · T

CYPRUS · Adana · Iskenderun · Antakya (Antioch) · Rasht · 200 metres · S

Nicosia · Mersin · Latakia · Baniyās · L. Reza 'īyeh (L. Urmia) · ·9510 · Qazvīn · Gorgan · Alborz Mts · Sha

Beirut · LEBANON · Tripoli · Homs · Damāvand 18,375 · Semnān

Conical Orthomorphic Projection · IRAN (PER

ISRAEL · Damascus · Tehrān

Ft.	M.
16,000	4,800
10,000	3,000
6,000	1,800
4,500	1,350
3,000	900
1,500	450
600	180
300	90

Sea Level
Land Depression

Inset map (Moscow region):

Lobn'a · 37°30'E · Pushkino · Kablukovo · 56°N

Šeremetjevskij · Pirogovskoje Res. · Trubino · 38°E

Sohodn'a · Tekstil'ščiki · Ivantejevka · Fr'azino

Dolgoprudnyj · Vinogradovo · Pervomajskij · Ščolkovo

Jurlovo · Chimki · Babuškin · Ostankino · Monino

Krasnogorsk · Novobratcevskij · Vostočnyj · ·459 · Balašicha · Staraja Kupavna

Rubl'ovo · Choroševo · ·294 · MOSCOW · Perovo · Reutov · Železnodoroznyj

Mazilovo · Kosino · Kuz'minki · Vnukovo · Ce̊r'omuski · Žuzino · L'ublino · L'ubercy · Tomlino

Odincovo · Ramenka · ·820 · ·627 · Kotel'niki · Malachovka

Oktʹabrʹskij · Lytkarino · Bykovo · Žukovskij

Scale 1 inch to 16 miles
For Legend see Page 30

RUSSIAN SOVIET FEDER

U S S

Caspian Lowlands

S. S. R.
Kazakh Uplands
Mointy
Kounradskiy
Balkhash
Lake Balkhash
Andreyevka
Ayaguz
Ulyungur Nor
MONGOLIA
Altai Range ·13,865
·12,438
·12,375
·12,590
·12,340
·9340
Gobi Desert
Yin Shan
Paotow
(Yellow)
Ordos Plateau
40°N
A

Muyun-Kum
Chu
Alma-Ata
Frunze
Rybach'ye
Issyk-Kul'
KIRGIZ S.S.R.
Osh
Fergana
Kokand
Dzungaria
Ebi Nor
·11,089
·13,307
Urumchi
(Tihwa)
·13,000
Turfan
-505
Bagrach Kol
·9217
Qomul
(Hami)
·9157
Ansi
Ala Shan
Kiuchuan
Great Wall
Yinchwan
(Ninghsia)
N A N
S h a n ·20,820
Tsing Hai
(Koko Nor)
Sining
(Kaolan)
Lanchow
35°N
Fengsiang
Wei
Tsinling Shan
Nancheng

shambe
TADZHIK S.S.R. 24,590
Faizabad
Khorog
·23,000
Pamirs
Tien Shan
Kashgar
Yarkand
Khotan
Yarkand ·24,388
Tarim
SINKIANG – UIGHUR
Takla Makan
AUTONOMOUS REGION
Khotan
Altyn Tagh
Tsaidam Swamps
Amne Machen Shan
Bayan Kara Shan
·19,680
Nan·15,170
Jyekundo
Mekong
Nanchen Japo
Chamdo
I
·22,310
H
Chengtu
Yaan
Red
Basin
30°N
Kangting
Ipin
Hsichang
Yangtze (Kinsha)
Huitse
·17,380

Hindu Kush
Chitral
·25,868
Gilgit
·26,660
Kabul
Jalalabad
Khyber Pass
·15,550
Peshawar
Islamabad
Rawalpindi
·16,221
JAMMU
KARAKORAM
KASHMIR ·28,250
·23,474
Leh
Srinagar
Kunlun Mountains
·23,890
·24,600
T I B E T
·23,290
Nyenchen Tangla Range
·21,200
Salween
·25,445
Batang
(Paan)
·21,300
Kunming
(Yunnanfu)
Chengkiang
25°N
Yuan (Red) Mengtsz

Sialkot
Jammu
Amritsar
·22,028
·23,794
Lhasa
Tsangpo
Shigatse
Gyangtse
Tsangpo/Matsang
Nyenchen
·15,100
Yuan (Red) Kinsha

Lyallpur
Lahore
Simla
Saharanpur
·25,447
·25,355
·25,393
Nepal
Everest
29,028
·26,497
·28,146
SIKKIM
Katmandu
BHUTAN
16,129
Darjeeling
ASSAM
Dibrugarh
Naga Hills 18,833
·2,553
Myitkyina
Tengchung
·10,610
Bhamo
Kunming

Multan
Sutlej
Bikaner
Thar
Patiala
Meerut
Moradabad
Delhi
Barelly
Shahjahanpur
Ganges
Lucknow
Kanpur
Patna
Bhagalpur
Rangpur
Shillong
6433
Brahmaputra
Sylhet
Kohima
·9300
Imphal
Indaw
Mawlaik
Chindwin
Shwebo
Lashio
·9040
Bawdwin

Indus
Sukkur
Jaipur
Agra
Jamuna
Gwalior
Jhansi
Allahabad
Ganges
Varanasi
Ganges
BANGLA-
Dacca
Plassey ×
B E N G A L
DESH
Chittagong
Mandalay
SHAN STATES
BURMA
Yenangyaung
Magwe

Desert
Jodhpur
Ajmer
·2154
Ahmadabad
Indore
Vindhya Range
·4429
Jabalpur
·3598
Jamshedpur
Howrah
Calcutta
Hooghly
Sundarbans
Mouths of the Ganges
Akyab
Chin Hills
909
Arakan Yoma
Pakokku
Chindwin
Irrawaddy
Thayetmyo
Prome
Toungoo
·10,018

Rajkot
Baroda
Satpura Range
Narbada
·3658
Nagpur
Mahanadi
Cuttack
Cheduba
Pegu
Rangoon
Moulmein
·3664
Surat
Tapti
·5140
(B H A R A T)
G. of Cambay

Bombay
Poona
Western Ghats
Godavari
·5513
Vishakhapatnam
Bassein
Gulf of Martaban
Ye
Pagoda Pt.
Tavoy
·6621
15°N

Sholapur
Hyderabad
Krishna
Vijayavada
Kakinada
B a y   o f
Andaman
Sea
Mergui Arch.
Chumphon
Isthmus of Kra

·3497
Eastern Ghats
Coromandel Coast
B e n g a l
Andaman Islands (India)
200 metres
Bangkok
THAILAND

Mangalore
Malabar Coast
Laccadive Sea
Bangalore
·4813
Arcot ×
Madras
O C E A N

Laccadive Islands (India)
Mysore
Nilgiri Hills
·8639
Palghat Gap
Cauvery
Tiruchirapalli
Pondicherry
Nicobar Islands (India)
Phuket I.

Kozhikode
Cochin
Palk Strait
Trincomalee
Kutaradja
Sumatra
5°N

Trivandrum
CEYLON
Kandy
·8292
Colombo
Galle
I N D I A N   O C E A N
MALDIVE ISLDS

M.
—4,800
—3,000
—1,800
—900
—450
—300
—180
—90
Level
Depression
HEIGHTS IN FEET

70°E   75°E   80°E   85°E   90°E   95°E   100°E   105°E

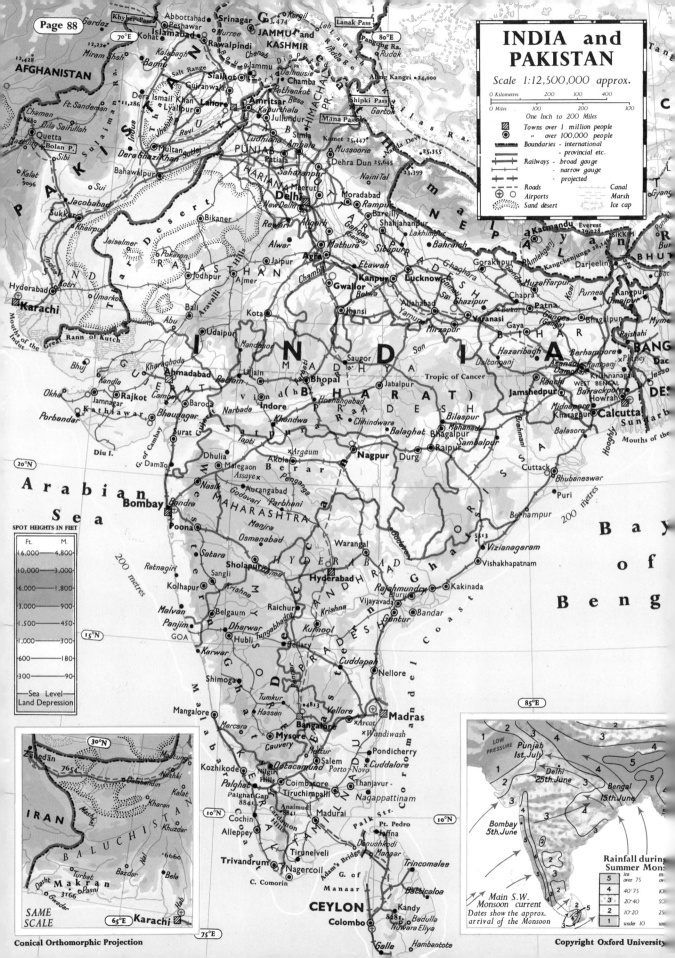

INDIA and PAKISTAN

Scale 1:12,500,000 approx.

0 Kilometres 200 300 400
0 Miles 100 200 300

One Inch to 200 Miles

Towns over 1 million people
" over 100,000 people
Boundaries - international
- provincial etc.
Railways - broad gauge
- narrow gauge
- projected
Roads   Canal
Airports   Marsh
Sand desert   Ice cap

SPOT HEIGHTS IN FEET

Ft.	M.
16,000	4,800
10,000	3,000
6,000	1,800
3,000	900
1,500	450
1,000	300
600	180
300	90

Sea Level
Land Depression

AFGHANISTAN

PAKISTAN

Arabian Sea

INDIA

Bay of Beng

NEPAL

BHUTAN

BANGLADESH

CEYLON

SAME SCALE

IRAN

BALUCHISTAN

Makran

Conical Orthomorphic Projection

Rainfall during Summer Monson

	ins	m
5	over 75	
4	40-75	10
3	20-40	50
2	10-20	25
1	under 10	

Main S.W. Monsoon current
Dates show the approx. arrival of the Monsoon

LOW PRESSURE Punjab 1st. July
Delhi 25th. June
Bengal 15th. June
Bombay 5th. June

Copyright Oxford University

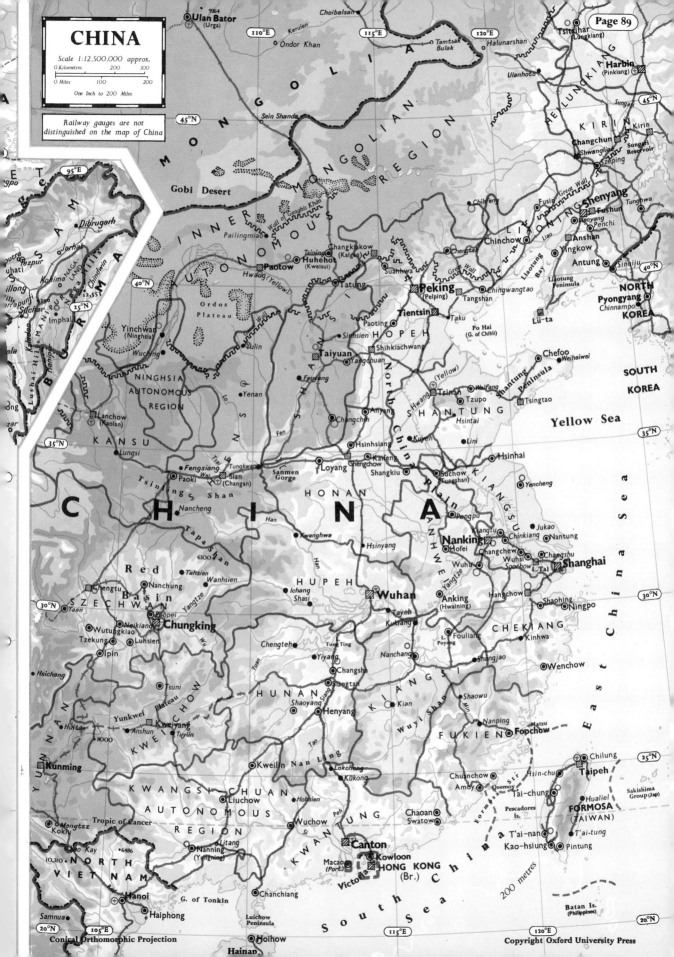

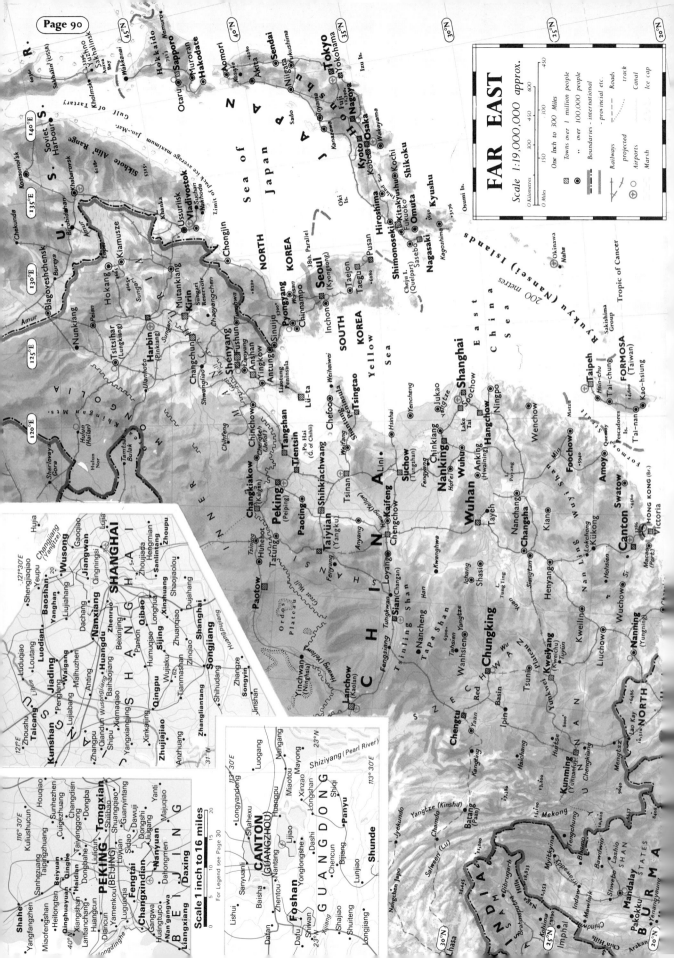

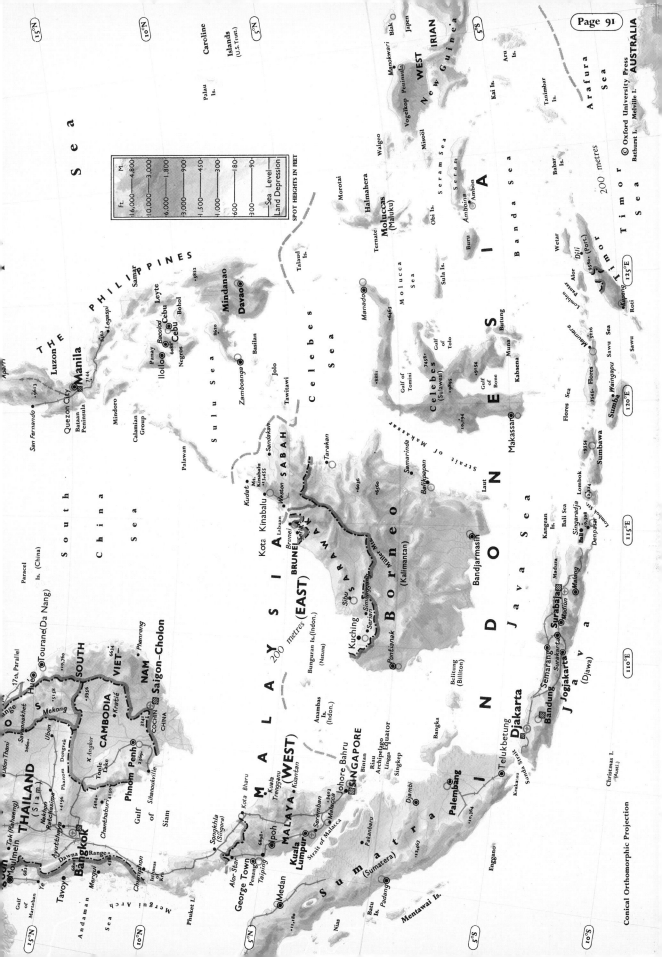

15°N   10°N   5°N

Caroline

Islands
(U.S. Trust.)

Palau
Is.

S   e   a

Biak
Japen
Manokwari

WEST   IRIAN

Vogelkop
Peninsula

New Guinea

Aru
Is.

Kai Is.

Tanimbar
Is.

Arafura
Sea

AUSTRALIA
© Oxford University Press
Bathurst I. Melville I.

5°S

SPOT HEIGHTS IN FEET

Ft.	M.
16,000	4,800
10,000	3,000
6,000	1,800
3,000	900
1,500	450
1,000	300
600	180
300	90
Sea Level	
Land Depression	

THE   PHILIPPINES

Samar

Leyte
Bacolod
Cebu   Cebu   Bohol
•8622
Iloilo   Negros
Panay   •8090
Basilan

Mindanao
Davao
•8610

Legaspi
•4463

Luzon
Manila
Quezon City
•7144
Bataan
Peninsula
San Fernando   •5613
Aparri

Mindoro

Calamian
Group

Palawan

Sulu   Sea

Jolo
Tawitawi
Zamboanga

Talaud
Is.

Morotai

Halmahera

Ternate
Moluccas
(Maluku)

Obi Is.

Seram
Seram Sea

Buru

Ambon
Amboina

Waigeo

Misool

Sula Is.

Manado

Molucca
Sea

Gulf
of
Tolo

Butung

Wetar
Alor
Pantar
Lomblen
Flores
Roti

Dili   •9580
TIMOR (Port.)

Timor   Sea

125°E

C   e   l   e   b   e   s   S   e   a

Celebes
(Sulawesi)
•6463
•7455
Gulf of
Tomini
•8881
Muna
Kabaena   •9154
•9955
•10,194

Gulf
of
Bone

Kangean
Is.

Bali Sea

Sawu Sea
Maumere   •7126
Flores
•7145
Ende
•9154

Sumba
Sumbawa   •9354
Waingapu

120°E

Makassar   •9384

Strait   of   Makassar

Samarinda
•6636
•6560

Balikpapan
Laut

Bandjarmasin

Java   Sea

Madura
Malang
Surabaja
Madiun

Bali   Denpasar   •10,308
Singaradja   Lombok
•3344
Lombok Str.

115°E

South   China   Sea

Tourane(Da Nang)
Hué
17th. Parallel

LAOS

SOUTH
VIET-
NAM
Saigon-Cholon
COCHIN
CHINA

Parcel
Is. (China)

Sandakan   SABAH
Kudat •   Mt.
Kinabalu
•13,455
Kota Kinabalu
Labuan
Weston
BRUNEI
Sibu
Simanggang
Serian
Kuching
Pontianak

Tarakan

Bunguran Is.(Indon.)
(Natuna)

Anambas
Is.
(Indon.)

Belitung
(Billiton)

MALAYSIA (EAST)
200 metres

Sarawak

K   A   L   I   M   A   N   T   A   N

B   o   r   n   e   o
(Kalimantan)

INDONESIA

THAILAND
(Siam)
Moulmein
Tavoy
Merqui
Bangkok
Ayutthaya
Nakhon
Ratchasima
Ye

Gulf
of
Martaban

Andaman
Sea

Mergui   Arch.

Phuket I.

Songkhla
(Singora)

Alor Star
Penang •
George Town
Taiping
Medan
Ipoh
Kuala Lumpur

MALAYA (WEST)
Seremban
Malacca
Johore Bahru
SINGAPORE
Bintan
Riau
Archipelago
Lingga
Singkep
Pakanbaru
Djambi

Sumatra
(Sumatera)

Palembang

Bangka

Belitung

Telukbetung
Djakarta
Bandung
Jogjakarta   Surakarta
Semarang
Java
(Djawa)

Sunda Str.
Krakatau
Christmas I.
(Aust.)

110°E

Kota Bharu
Kuala
Trengganu
Kuantan

Chumphon
Isthmus
of Kra

CAMBODIA
Phnom Penh
Angkor
Tonle
Lake
Kratié

Mekong

Kompong
Cham
Phanrang

Batu
Is.
Padang •

Mentawai Is.

Enggano

Nias

10°N   5°N   Equator   5°S   10°S

Conical Orthomorphic Projection

15°N   10°N   5°N

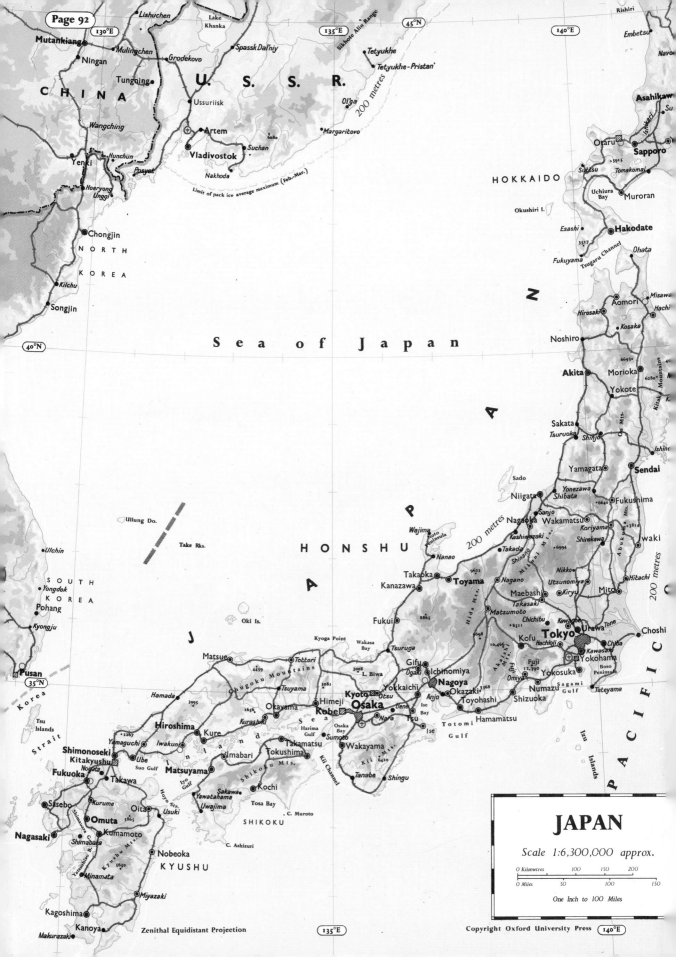

130°E

135°E

45°N

140°E

Rishiri

Embetsu

Navo

Mutankiang

Lishuchen

Lake
Khanka

Spassk Dal'niy

Sikhote Alin Range

Tetyukhe

Su

Ningan

Mulingchen

Grodekovo

Tetyukhe-Pristan'

Asahikaw

Otaru

Tungning

C H I N A

U. S. S. R.

Ol'ga

200 metres

Sapporo

Ussuriisk

Margaritovo

HOKKAIDO

Tomakomai

Wangching

Artem

6080

Suttsu

Uchiura
Bay

Muroran

Hunchun

Vladivostok

Suchan

Okushiri I.

Yenki

Posyet

Nakhoda

Esashi

Hakodate

3517

Ohata

Hoeryong

Unggi

Limit of pack ice average maximum (Feb.-Mar.)

Fukuyama

Tsugaru Channel

Chongjin

N O R T H

Misawa

Aomori

Hachi

Hirosaki

Kosaka

Akita

Z

6693

Kitakami Mountains

K.

K O R E A

Kilchu

Noshiro

Morioka

6280

Ishino

Songjin

Yokote

Oū Mts.

Sakata

Shinjo

S e a   o f   J a p a n

40°N

Tsuruoka

A

Yamagata

Sendai

Sado

Niigata

Yonezawa

Shibata

6640

Fukushima

Shinjo

P

Akita

Ullung Do.

Wajima

Noto
Peninsula

Nagaoka

Wakamatsu

Sanjo

Koriyama

1814

Take Rks.

H O N S H U

200 metres

Kashiwazaki

Shirakawa

S O U T H

Nanao

Takada

Shinano

6994

J

K O R E A

Yongdok

Takaoka

Toyama

Nagano

Nikko

Utsunomiya

Iwaki

Hitachi

Pohang

Kanazawa

9622

Hida Mts.

Maebashi

Takasaki

Mito

A

Kyongju

Fukui

8865

Matsumoto

Chichibu

Kiryu

Kawagoe

200 metres

Oki Is.

Kyoga Point

Wakasa
Bay

Tokyo

Urawa

Tone

Choshi

Kofu

Hachioji

P

Kofu

10,466

Chiba

J

Matsue

Tottori

Tsuruga

L. Biwa

Gifu

Aiz Mts.

12,390

Yokosuka

Boso
Peninsula

35°N

4459

Chugoku Mountains

3008

Ichinomiya

Fuji

Yokohama

Pusan

Hamada

Tsuyama

3081

Otsu

Nagoya

3368

Omiya

Numazu

Sagami
Gulf

Tateyama

Korea

3995

1655

Okayama

Kyoto

Yokkaichi

Anjo

Okazaki

Toyohashi

Shizuoka

Hamamatsu

Hiroshima

Kure

Kurashiki

Kobe

Osaka

Nara

Ueno

Tsu

Izu
Islands

Tsu
Islands

Himeji

Harima
Gulf

Ise
Bay

Totomi
Gulf

Strait

2267

Iwakuni

I n l a n d

S e a

Osaka
Bay

Ise

Shimonoseki

Matsuyama

Imabari

Takamatsu

Sumoto

Wakayama

PACIFIC

Kitakyushu

Iyo
Gulf

Tokushima

Kii Mts.

6420

Fukuoka

Nogata

Ube

Suo Gulf

Shikoku Mts.

Tanabe

Shingu

Takawa

Kii Channel

Sasebo

Kurume

Oita

Hoyo Str.

Sakawa

Yawatahama

Kochi

Tosa Bay

Usuki

Omuta

5865

Uwajima

. C. Muroto

Kumamoto

Nagasaki

Shimabara

SHIKOKU

Shimabara B.

C. Ashizuri

Nobeoka

Kyushu Mts.

5650

K Y U S H U

Minamata

Miyazaki

Kagoshima

Kanoya

Makurazaki

Zenithal Equidistant Projection

135°E

Copyright Oxford University Press

140°E

JAPAN

Scale 1:6,300,000 approx.

0 Kilometres	100	150	200

| 0 Miles | 50 | 100 | 150 |

One Inch to 100 Miles

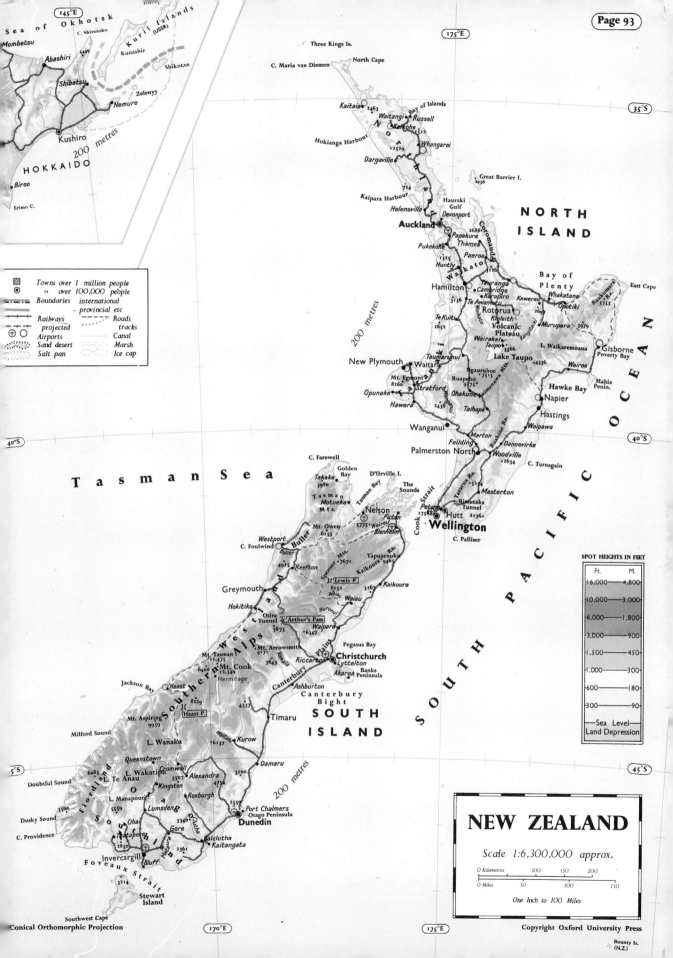

NEW ZEALAND

Scale 1:6,300,000 approx.

| 0 Kilometres | 50 | 100 | 150 | 200 |

| 0 Miles | 50 | 100 | 150 |

One Inch to 100 Miles

SPOT HEIGHTS IN FEET

Ft.	M.
16,000	4,800
10,000	3,000
6,000	1,800
3,000	900
1,500	450
1,000	300
600	180
300	90

Sea Level
Land Depression

Towns over 1 million people
" over 100,000 people
Boundaries international
- provincial etc
Railways
projected Roads
tracks
Airports
Sand desert Canal
Salt pan Marsh
Ice cap

Conical Orthomorphic Projection

Copyright Oxford University Press

Bounty Is.
(N.Z.)

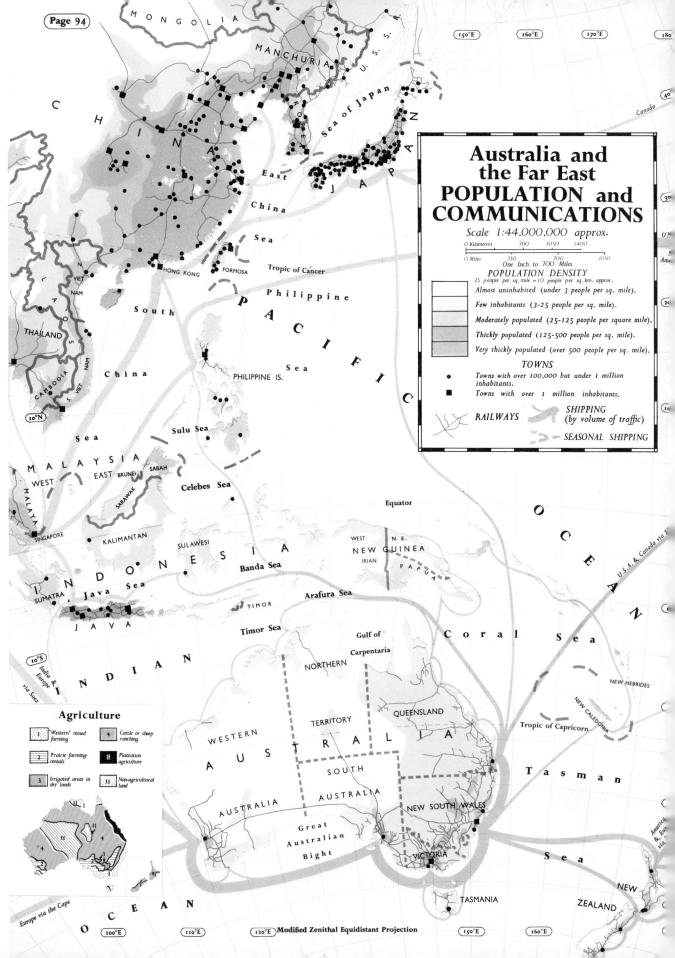

MONGOLIA

MANCHURIA

U.S.S.R.

C H I N A

Sea of Japan

J A P A N

East

China

KOREA

Sea

HONG KONG   FORMOSA   Tropic of Cancer

VIET
NAM

LAOS

THAILAND

CAMBODIA

S. VIET NAM

10°N

South

China

Sea

Philippine

Sea

P A C I F I C

O C E A N

PHILIPPINE IS.

Sulu Sea

M A L A Y S I A

WEST   EAST BRUNEI   SABAH

SARAWAK

MALAYA

SINGAPORE

KALIMANTAN

Celebes Sea

SULAWESI

I N D O N E S I A

Banda Sea

Equator

WEST   N. E.
NEW GUINEA
IRIAN   PAPUA

SUMATRA

Java Sea

J A V A

Arafura Sea

TIMOR

Timor Sea

Gulf of
Carpentaria

Coral   Sea

NEW HEBRIDES

NEW CALEDONIA

10°S

India &
Europe
via Suez

I N D I A N

NORTHERN

TERRITORY

WESTERN

QUEENSLAND

Tropic of Capricorn

A U S   R A L I A

AUSTRALIA

SOUTH

T a s m a n

U.S.A. & Canada via F

Agriculture

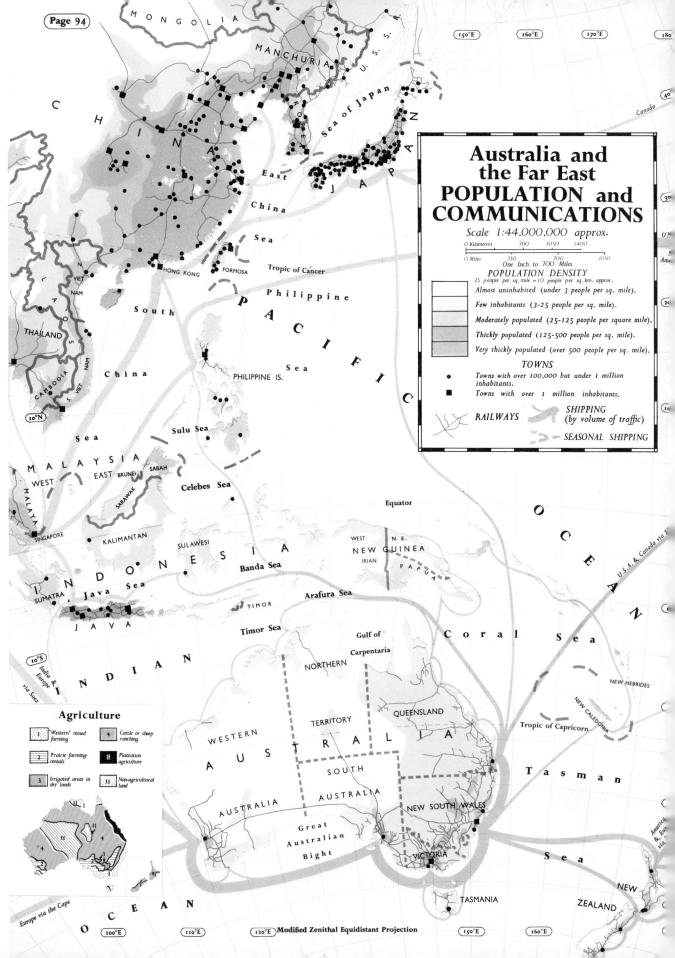

1	'Western' mixed farming	4	Cattle or sheep ranching
2	Prairie farming-cereals	5	Plantation agriculture
3	Irrigated areas in dry lands	11	Non-agricultural land

SOUTH

AUSTRALIA

NEW SOUTH WALES

VICTORIA

Great
Australian
Bight

S e a

NEW

Europe via the Cape

O C E A N   TASMANIA   ZEALAND   America
& Eur
via

100°E   110°E   120°E   150°E   160°E

150°E   160°E   170°E   180

Canada

40

30

U.!
Ame

20

10

Australia and
the Far East
POPULATION and
COMMUNICATIONS
Scale 1:44,000,000 approx.

0 Kilometres   700   1050   1400
0 Miles   350   700   1050
One Inch to 700 Miles

POPULATION DENSITY
25 people per. sq. mile = 10 people per sq. km. approx.

Almost uninhabited (under 3 people per sq. mile).

Few inhabitants (3-25 people per sq. mile).

Moderately populated (25-125 people per square mile).

Thickly populated (125-500 people per sq. mile).

Very thickly populated (over 500 people per sq. mile).

TOWNS

• Towns with over 100,000 but under 1 million inhabitants.

■ Towns with over 1 million inhabitants.

RAILWAYS   SHIPPING
(by volume of traffic)

SEASONAL SHIPPING

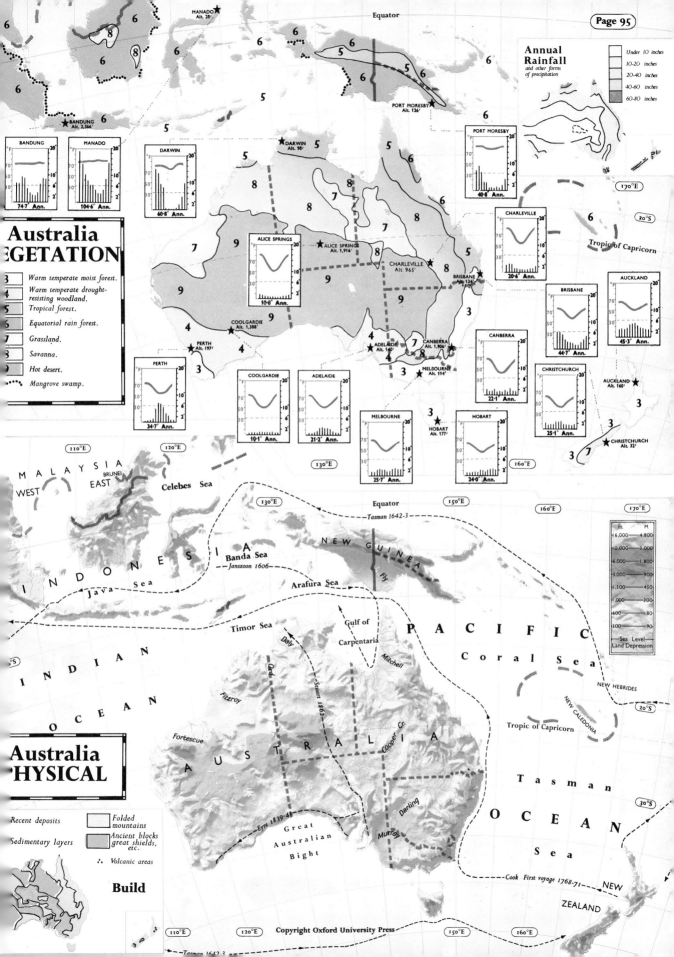

Equator

Annual Rainfall
and other forms of precipitation

	Under 10 inches
	10–20 inches
	20–40 inches
	40–60 inches
	60–80 inches

170°E

20°S

Tropic of Capricorn

MANADO Alt. 28'

BANDUNG Alt. 2,366'

MANADO

PORT MORESBY Alt. 126'

PORT MORESBY
40·8 Ann.

DARWIN Alt. 98'

DARWIN
60·8 Ann.

BANDUNG
74·7 Ann.

CHARLEVILLE
20·6 Ann.

CHARLEVILLE Alt. 965'

ALICE SPRINGS Alt. 1,916'

ALICE SPRINGS
10·8 Ann.

BRISBANE Alt. 124'

BRISBANE
44·7 Ann.

AUCKLAND
45·3 Ann.

AUCKLAND Alt. 160'

COOLGARDIE Alt. 1,388'

PERTH Alt. 197'

PERTH
34·7 Ann.

ADELAIDE Alt. 140'

CANBERRA Alt. 1,906'

CANBERRA
22·1 Ann.

CHRISTCHURCH
25·1 Ann.

CHRISTCHURCH Alt. 32'

MELBOURNE Alt. 114'

COOLGARDIE
10·1 Ann.

ADELAIDE
21·2 Ann.

MELBOURNE
25·7 Ann.

HOBART Alt. 177'

HOBART
24·0 Ann.

Australia VEGETATION

3	Warm temperate moist forest.
4	Warm temperate drought-resisting woodland.
5	Tropical forest.
6	Equatorial rain forest.
7	Grassland.
8	Savanna.
9	Hot desert.
····	Mangrove swamp.

110°E   120°E   130°E   160°E   150°E   170°E

MALAYSIA
WEST   EAST   BRUNEI

Celebes Sea

INDONESIA

Banda Sea
— Janszoon 1606 —

Java Sea

Timor Sea

Arafura Sea

NEW GUINEA
Fly

Tasman 1642-3

Gulf of Carpentaria

Daly
Ord
Stuart 1862
Mitchell

PACIFIC

Coral Sea

NEW HEBRIDES

NEW CALEDONIA

Tropic of Capricorn

20°S

Ft.	M.
16,000	4,800
10,000	3,000
6,000	1,800
3,000	900
1,500	450
600	180
300	90
Sea Level Land Depression	

Australia PHYSICAL

	Recent deposits
	Folded mountains
	Sedimentary layers
	Ancient blocks great shields, etc.
∴	Volcanic areas

Build

Fortescue
Fitzroy
Eyre 1839-41

AUSTRALIA

Great Australian Bight

Cooper Cr.
Darling
Murray

Tasman Sea

OCEAN

30°S

Tasman 1642-3

Cook First voyage 1768-71

NEW ZEALAND

Copyright Oxford University Press

110°E   120°E   130°E   150°E   160°E

AUSTRALASIA

Scale 1:22,000,000 approx.

| O Kilometres | 350 | 525 | 700 | 850 |

| O Miles | 200 | 350 | 525 |

One Inch to 350 Miles

Towns over 1 million people
" over 100,000 people
Boundaries - international
- provincial etc.
Railways -- Roads
projected .... track
Sand desert Marsh
Airports O Salt pan

Ft.	M.
16,000	4,800
10,000	3,000
6,000	1,800
3,000	900
1,500	450
1,000	300
600	180
300	90
Sea Level	
Land Depression	

SPOT HEIGHTS IN FEET

Zenithal Equidistant Projection

145°E 150°E 155°E 160°E 165°E 170°E 175°E

P

Equator

0°

Tarawa   Gilbert

A

Nauru   Ocean I.
(Br.)

Islands
(Br)

Pura   Manus
Is.   Admiralty
Is.   Kavieng
TERRITORY   OF   NEW   GUINEA

C

Aitape
Wewak
North East New Guinea
(Aust)   Madang   New
Ireland   Bismarck   Rabaul
Archipelago
New Britain   I

5°S

Central Ra.
Lae
Finschhafen   10,191   Bougainville
Bougainville
Shortland Is.   Choiseul
(Austl. Trust)   Ganongga   New   Santa   Ysabel   3900
Georgia   Vangunu   Stewart Is.
Guadalcanal
13,100
Owen Stanley Ra   11,226
Gulf of
Papua   Port
Moresby
D'Entrecasteaux Is.
Honiara   8005
Ulawa

Ellice

F

I

C

Solomon Islands
(British)

Malaita   Funafuti
Islands
(Br.)

10°S

Str.
C. York
2342
Cape
York
Peninsula   1922
1953

Louisiade Arch.
2750   San Cristobal
Rennell I.   Santa Cruz Is.   Cherry I.   Mitre I.

O

Cooktown   4552
Herberton
Cairns
Forsayth
Norman   Townsville
Hughenden
3460   Chapters
Towers
Mackay   2060

C   o   r   a   l

S   e   a

Barrier

Reef

Espiritu
Santo
Malekula
Vila Efate
Erromanga

New Hebrides
(Br.-Fr. Condominium)

F i j i I s.
Vanua Levu
Viti Levu
Suva

15°S

Lau Group

Chesterfield Is.
(Fr.)

Loyalty Is. (Fr.)

EENSLAND
Winton
Longreach
Yaraka
Barcoo
Quilpie   1293

Rockhampton   Mt.Morgan   Gladstone
Bundaberg   2420
Maryborough

New
Caledonia
(Fr.)   Nouméa

20°S

Tropic of Capricorn

O

Cunnamulla   Charleville
Darling
Toowoomba   Brisbane
Downs   Ipswich
Lismore
5100
Grafton
5300

Norfolk I.
(Austl.)

25°S

E

Bourke   Tamworth
4900
1706   Dubbo   Maitland
4180   Newcastle
Lithgow
Orange   Katoomba   Sydney
Lachlan   Wollongong
Murrumbidgee   Goulburn
Canberra
Albury
Mt. Kosciusko
7316
Cape Howe

A

30°S

Broken Hill
NEW
SOUTH
WALES
VICTORIA
Mildura
Swan Hill   Riverina
Echuca
Bendigo
3829
Ballarat   Orbost   Gippsland
Geelong
Melbourne
King I.   Bass
Strait   Furneaux
Group

T   a   s   m   a   n

S   e   a

North Cape
2529   Kaikohe
Auckland
Hamilton   2688
NORTH ISLAND
New Plymouth   5753
8260   Gisborne
9275   Napier
Cook   N

N

35°S

Z

Burnie   5160
Mt.Lyell   St.Marys
TASMANIA   Launceston
4720
Hobart

SOUTH ISLAND
Westport
Greymouth   Nelson
7671
Mt. Cook
12,349.
9959.   Southern Alps
Christchurch

3980
Palmerston N.
NEW

Wellington

ZEALAND

40°S

45°S

140°E   145°E   150°E   155°E   160°E   165°E   170°E

Invercargill   Dunedin
Stewart I.

Copyright Oxford University Press

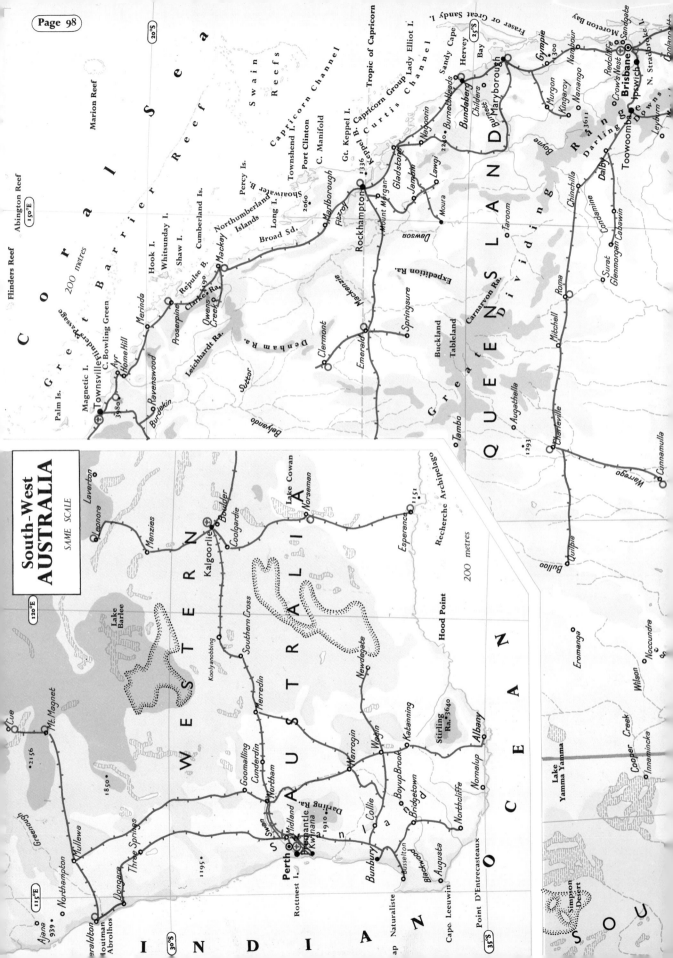

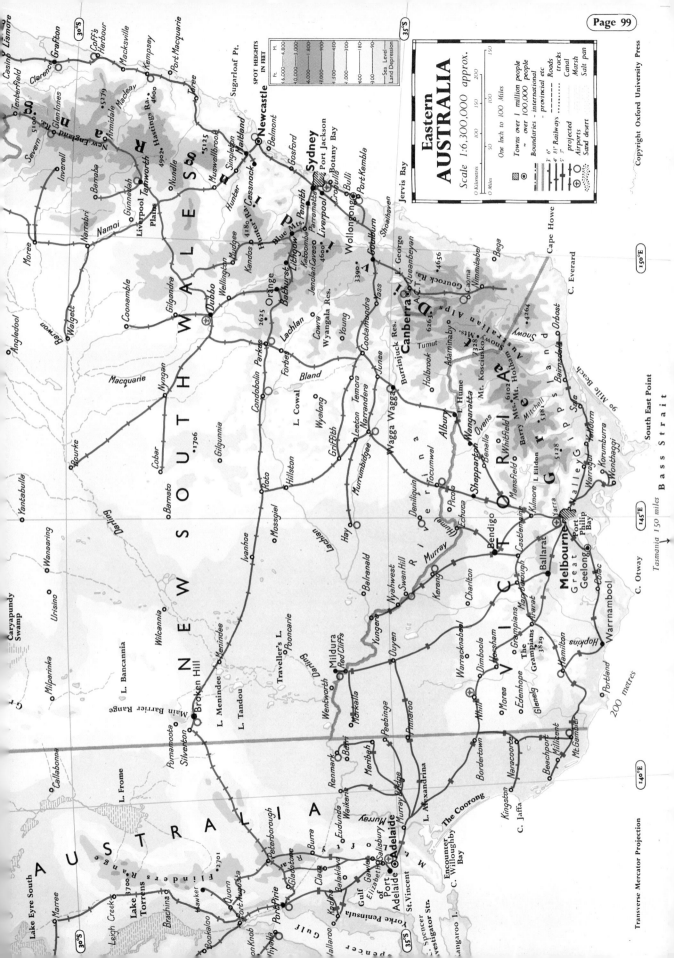

Eastern AUSTRALIA

Scale 1:6,300,000 approx.

One Inch to 100 Miles

0 Miles	50	100	150	200	
0 Kilometres	50	100	150	200	250

Towns over 1 million people
" " over 100,000 people

Boundaries - international
- provincial etc

Railways
Roads
tracks

Canal
Airports
Marsh
Sand desert
Salt pan

SPOT HEIGHTS IN FEET

Ft.	M.
16,000	4,800
10,000	3,000
6,000	1,800
3,000	900
1,500	600
1,000	300
600	180
300	90
Sea Level	
Land Depression	

Copyright Oxford University Press

Transverse Mercator Projection

South East Point

Bass Strait

Tasmania 150 miles →

200 metres

NEW SOUTH WALES

VICTORIA

AUSTRALIA

Great Dividing Range

Snowy Mts.

Australian Alps

Gippsland

Riverina

Murray

Darling

Lachlan

Macquarie

New England Ra.

Main Barrier Range

Flinders Range

Grampians

The Coorong

Lake Eyre South

Lake Torrens

L. Frome

L. Bancannia

Caryapundy Swamp

Great

Gulf

Spencer Gulf

Gulf St. Vincent

Encounter Bay

Yorke Peninsula

Investigator Str.

Kangaroo I.

Sydney
Newcastle
Wollongong
Port Kembla
Port Jackson
Botany Bay
Canberra
A.C.T.
Melbourne
Port Phillip Bay
Geelong
Adelaide
Port Adelaide

Lismore
Grafton
Coff's Harbour
Macksville
Kempsey
Port Macquarie
Taree
Armidale
Glen Innes
Inverell
Tamworth
Gunnedah
Narrabri
Moree
Walgett
Angledool
Bourke
Cobar
Dubbo
Wellington
Orange
Bathurst
Lithgow
Katoomba
Penrith
Parramatta
Liverpool
Goulburn
Yass
Cootamundra
Wagga Wagga
Albury
Wangaratta
Benalla
Shepparton
Bendigo
Ballarat
Warrnambool
Portland
Mount Gambier
Broken Hill
Mildura
Wentworth
Renmark
Port Pirie
Port Augusta
Whyalla

C. Howe
C. Everard
Orbost
Bairnsdale
Sale
90 Mile Beach
C. Otway
C. Jaffa
C. Willoughby

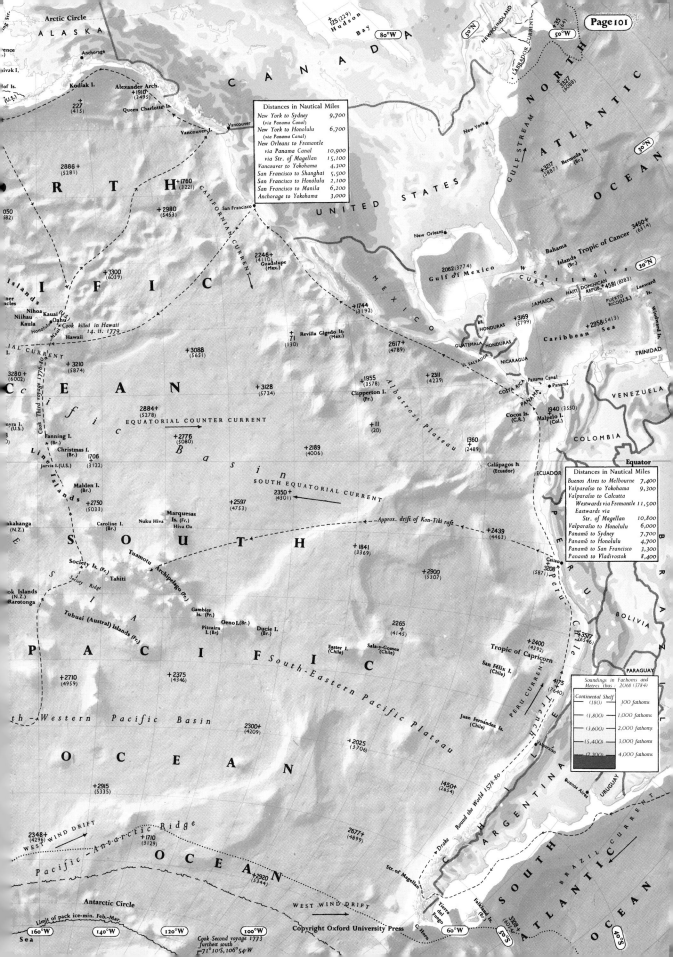

Distances in Nautical Miles

New York to Sydney	
(via Panama Canal)	9,700
New York to Honolulu	
(via Panama Canal)	6,700
New Orleans to Fremantle	
via Panama Canal	10,900
via Str. of Magellan	15,100
Vancouver to Yokohama	4,300
San Francisco to Shanghai	5,500
San Francisco to Honolulu	2,100
San Francisco to Manila	6,200
Anchorage to Yokohama	3,000

Distances in Nautical Miles

Buenos Aires to Melbourne	7,400
Valparaíso to Yokohama	9,300
Valparaíso to Calcutta	
Westwards via Fremantle	11,500
Eastwards via	
Str. of Magellan	10,800
Valparaíso to Honolulu	6,000
Panamá to Sydney	7,700
Panamá to Honolulu	4,700
Panamá to San Francisco	3,300
Panamá to Vladivostok	8,400

Soundings in Fathoms and Metres thus : 2068 (3784)

Continental Shelf (180)	100 fathoms
(1,800)	1,000 fathoms
(3,600)	2,000 fathoms
(5,400)	3,000 fathoms
(7,200)	4,000 fathoms

ARCTIC CIRCLE
ALASKA
Anchorage
Kodiak I.
Alexander Arch. +1910 (3495)
+227 (415)
Queen Charlotte Is.
Vancouver I.
Vancouver
CANADA
HUDSON BAY
+125 (229)
80°W
50°N
NEWFOUNDLAND
50°W
+35 (64)

NORTH ATLANTIC OCEAN
GULF STREAM
LABRADOR CURRENT
New York
Bermuda Is. (Br.)
+3217 (5887)
+3327 (6088)
30°N

UNITED STATES
New Orleans
Gulf of Mexico
+2062 (3774)
Bahama Islands (Br.)
Tropic of Cancer
WEST INDIES
CUBA
JAMAICA
HAITI DOMINICAN REPUB.
PUERTO RICO (U.S.)
+4581 (8383)
Leeward Is.
Windward Is.
20°N
TRINIDAD

CALIFORNIAN CURRENT
San Francisco
+1760 (3221)
+2886 (5281)
+2980 (5453)
+3300 (6039)
+2246 (4106) Guadalupe (Mex.)
+1744 (3192)
+71 (130) Revilla Gigedo Is. (Mex.)
+3088 (5651)
+3210 (5874)
+3128 (5724)
+1955 (3578) Clipperton I. (Fr.)
+2617 (4789)
+2311 (4229)
+11 (20)
+1360 (2489)
BR. HONDURAS
GUATEMALA HONDURAS
EL SALVADOR NICARAGUA
COSTA RICA
Panama Canal
Panamá
PANAMÁ
Cocos Is. (C.R.)
+1940 (3550)
Malpelo I. (Col.)
VENEZUELA
COLOMBIA
ECUADOR

PACIFIC OCEAN
NORTH PACIFIC
EQUATORIAL CURRENT
Hawaiian Islands
Nihoa Kauai Oahu
Niihau
Kaula
Honolulu Maui
Hawaii
Cook killed in Hawaii 14. ii. 1779
+3280 (6002)
Cook Third voyage 1776-80
Fanning I. (Br.)
Christmas I. (Br.)
+1706 (3122)
Jarvis I. (U.S.)
Line Islands
Malden I. (Br.)
+2750 (5033)
Palmyra I. (U.S.)
EQUATORIAL COUNTER CURRENT
+2884 (5278)
+2776 (5080)
+2189 (4006)
SOUTH EQUATORIAL CURRENT
+2350 (4301)
+2597 (4753)
Marquesas Is. (Fr.)
Nuku Hiva Hiva Oa
Caroline I. (Br.)
Albatross Plateau
Galápagos Is. (Ecuador)
Equator
+2439 (4463)
Approx. drift of Kon-Tiki raft
+1841 (3369)
+2900 (5307)
Callao
+3208 (5871)
PERU
PERU CURRENT

SOUTH PACIFIC OCEAN
Rakahanga (N.Z.)
Cook Islands (N.Z.)
Rarotonga
Society Is. (Fr.)
Tahiti
Society Ridge
Tuamotu Archipelago (Fr.)
Gambier Is. (Fr.)
Tubuai (Austral) Islands (Fr.)
Pitcairn I. (Br.)
Oeno I. (Br.)
Ducie I. (Br.)
Easter I. (Chile)
Sala-y-Gomez (Chile)
+2265 (4145)
+2710 (4959)
+2375 (4346)
South-Western Pacific Basin
+2300 (4209)
+2025 (3706)
South-Eastern Pacific Plateau
Juan Fernández Is. (Chile)
San Félix I. (Chile)
+2400 (4392)
Tropic of Capricorn
+4175 (7640)
PERU-CHILE TRENCH
Valparaíso
Round the World 1578-80
BOLIVIA
PARAGUAY
BRAZIL

+2915 (5335)
+2348 (4296)
WEST WIND DRIFT
Pacific-Antarctic Ridge
+1710 (3129)
+1450 (2654)
+2677 (4899)
Str. of Magellan
Drake
C. Horn
Tierra del Fuego
Falkland Is. (Br.)
+3208 (5868)
ARGENTINA
Buenos Aires
URUGUAY
BRAZIL CURRENT
SOUTH ATLANTIC OCEAN
50°S
40°S

OCEAN
+2920 (5344)
Antarctic Circle
Limit of pack ice-min. Feb.-Mar.
WEST WIND DRIFT
160°W 140°W 120°W 100°W
Cook Second voyage 1773 furthest south 71°10'S, 106°54'W
Copyright Oxford University Press
60°W

Marielas
60°S

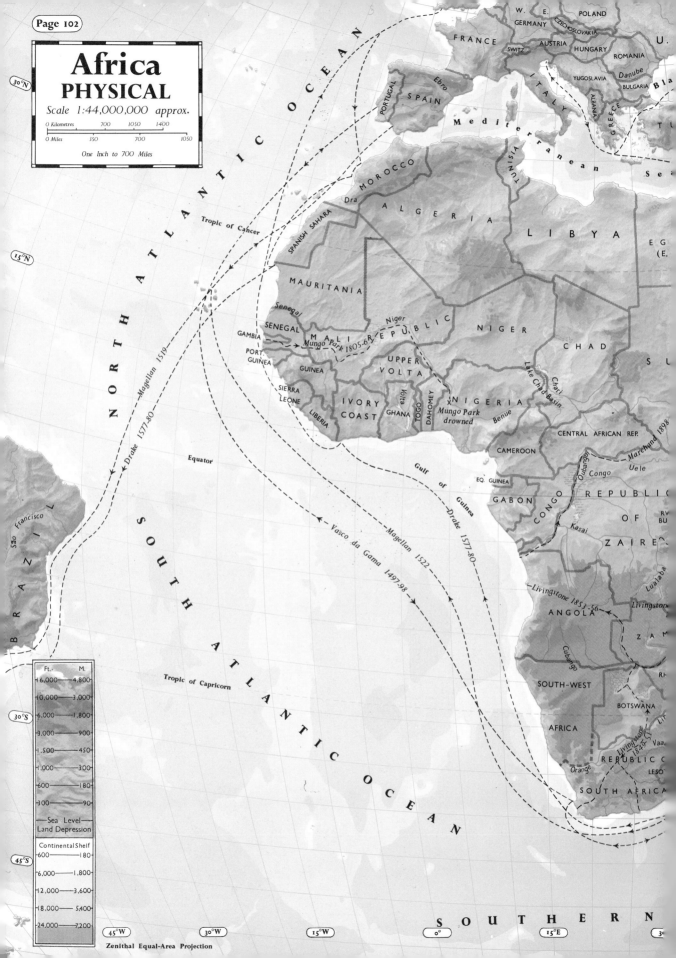

Africa
PHYSICAL
Scale 1:44,000,000 *approx.*

O Kilometres	700	1050	1400
O Miles	350	700	1050

One Inch to 700 Miles

NORTH ATLANTIC OCEAN

SOUTH ATLANTIC OCEAN

W. E. GERMANY
POLAND
CZECHOSLOVAKIA
FRANCE
SWITZ. AUSTRIA HUNGARY
ROMANIA
ITALY
YUGOSLAVIA Danube
BULGARIA Bla
ALBANIA GREECE TU

Mediterranean Sea

PORTUGAL
SPAIN
Ebro

30°N

15°N

Tropic of Cancer

MOROCCO
Dra
SPANISH SAHARA
ALGERIA
LIBYA
TUNISIA
EG (E.

MAURITANIA

Senegal
SENEGAL
GAMBIA
PORT. GUINEA
GUINEA
SIERRA LEONE
LIBERIA

MALI
Mungo Park 1805-6?
REPUBLIC
Niger
UPPER VOLTA
IVORY COAST
GHANA
Volta
TOGO DAHOMEY
NIGERIA
Mungo Park drowned
Benue

NIGER
CHAD
Lake Chad Basin
Chari
SU

CENTRAL AFRICAN REP.
Marchand 1898

Equator

Gulf of Guinea

EQ. GUINEA
CAMEROON
GABON
CONGO
Congo
Oubangui
Uele
REPUBLIC
OF
ZAIRE
Kasai
RW BU

Magellan 1519
Drake 1577-80
Vasco da Gama 1497-98
Magellan 1522
Drake 1577-80

Livingstone 1853-56
Livingston
ANGOLA
ZAM
Lualaba
Cubango

BRAZIL
São Francisco

Tropic of Capricorn

30°S

SOUTH-WEST
AFRICA
BOTSWANA
Livingstone 1849-51
Orange
Vaal
RH
REPUBLIC O
LESO
SOUTH AFRICA

45°S

Ft.	M.
6,000	4,800
10,000	3,000
6,000	1,800
3,000	900
1,500	450
1,000	300
600	180
300	90
Sea Level	
Land Depression	
Continental Shelf	
600	180
6,000	1,800
12,000	3,600
18,000	5,400
24,000	7,200

SOUTHERN

45°W   30°W   15°W   0°   15°E   3°

Zenithal Equal-Area Projection

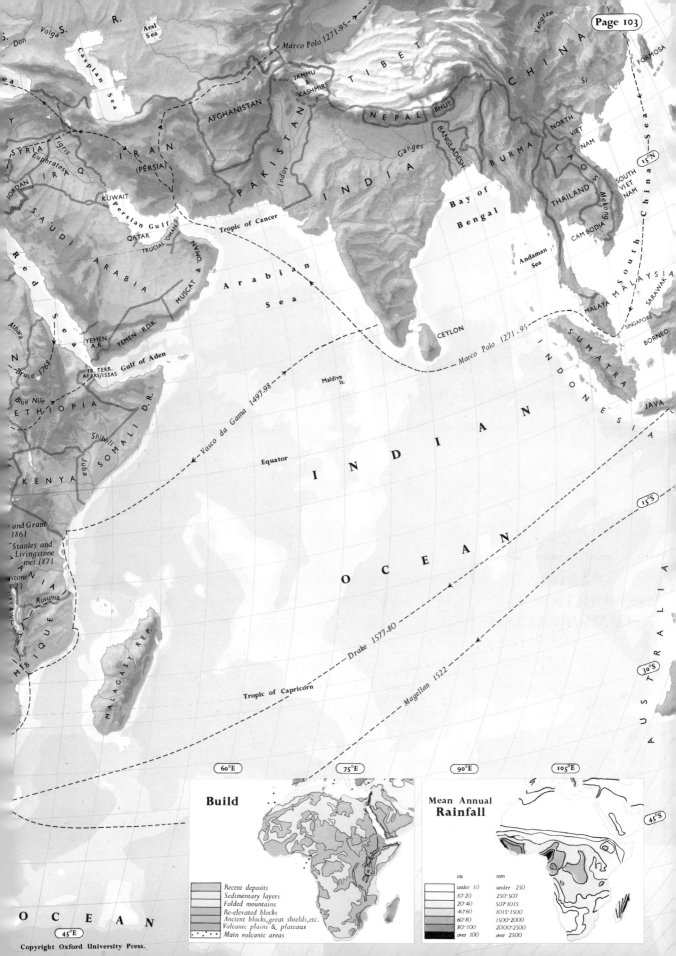

Copyright Oxford University Press.

Africa
POPULATION and COMMUNICATIONS

Scale 1:44,000,000 approx.

O Kilometres   700   1050   1400
O Miles   350   700   1050

One Inch to 700 Miles

POPULATION DENSITY

Almost uninhabited
(under 3 people per sq. mile).

Few inhabitants.
(3-25 people per sq. mile).

Moderately populated
(25-125 people per square mile).

Thickly populated
(125-500 people per sq. mile)

Very thickly populated
(over 500 people per sq. mile)

TOWNS

• Towns with over 100,000 but
under 1 million inhabitants.

■ Towns with over 1 million
inhabitants.

⊁⊀⊁ RAILWAYS

~ SHIPPING (by volume of traffic)

Zenithal Equidistant Projection

Copyright Oxford University Press

Agriculture

'Western' mixed farming
(cash crops often with livestock)

3 Irrigated areas in dry lands

4 Cattle or sheep ranching

5 Plantation agriculture

6 Mediterranean agriculture

9 Native farming
(often with 'shifting cultivation')

10 Nomadic herds

11 Non-agricultural land

Principal areas of commercial fishing

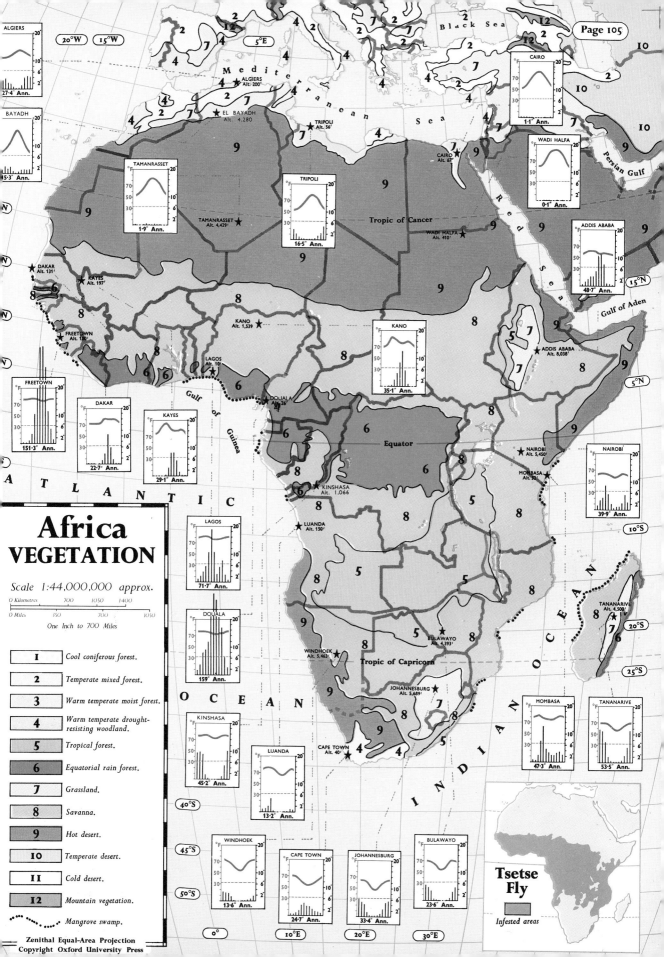

Africa
VEGETATION

Scale 1:44,000,000 approx.

O Kilometres	700	1050	1400
O Miles	350	700	1050

One Inch to 700 Miles

I	*Cool coniferous forest.*
2	*Temperate mixed forest.*
3	*Warm temperate moist forest.*
4	*Warm temperate drought-resisting woodland.*
5	*Tropical forest.*
6	*Equatorial rain forest.*
7	*Grassland.*
8	*Savanna.*
9	*Hot desert.*
IO	*Temperate desert.*
II	*Cold desert.*
I2	*Mountain vegetation.*
••••	*Mangrove swamp.*

Zenithal Equal-Area Projection
Copyright Oxford University Press

Tsetse Fly

Infested areas

Black Sea

Mediterranean Sea

Red Sea

Persian Gulf

Gulf of Aden

ATLANTIC OCEAN

INDIAN OCEAN

Gulf of Guinea

Tropic of Cancer

Equator

Tropic of Capricorn

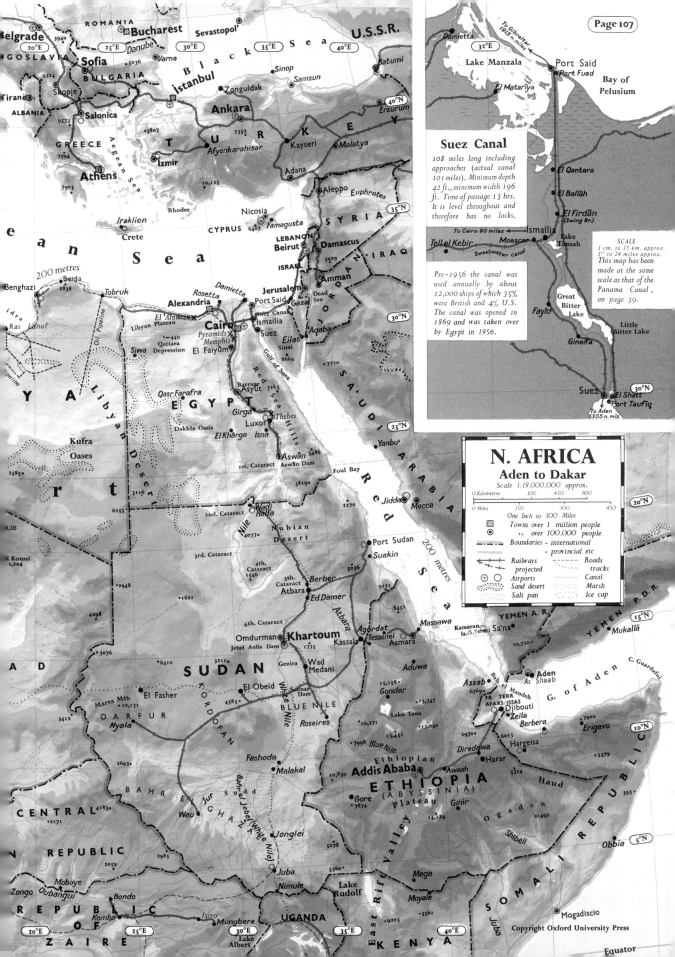

Suez Canal

108 miles long including approaches (actual canal 101 miles). Minimum depth 42 ft., minimum width 196 ft. Time of passage 13 hrs. It is level throughout and therefore has no locks.

Pre-1956 the canal was used annually by about 12,000 ships of which 35% were British and 4% U.S. The canal was opened in 1869 and was taken over by Egypt in 1956.

SCALE
1 cm. to 15 km. approx.
1'' to 24 miles approx.
This map has been made at the same scale as that of the Panama Canal, on page 39.

Lake Manzala
Damietta
Port Said
Port Fuad
To Gibraltar 1915 n. miles
El Matarîya
Bay of Pelusium
El Qantara
El Ballâh
El Firdân (Swing Br.)
Ismailia
Lake Timsah
Moascar
To Cairo 80 miles
Tell el Kebir
Sweetwater canal
Great Bitter Lake
Fayid
Little Bitter Lake
Gineifa
Suez
El Shatt
Port Taufîq
To Aden 1305 n. mls.

N. AFRICA
Aden to Dakar
Scale 1:19,000,000 approx.

0 Kilometres   300   450   600
0 Miles   150   300   450

One Inch to 300 Miles

▨ Towns over 1 million people
◉ " over 100,000 people
Boundaries - international
          - provincial etc
⊢ Railways   ⋯⋯ Roads
    projected   tracks
⊕ ⊙ Airports   ═══ Canal
    Sand desert   Marsh
    Salt pan   Ice cap

ROMANIA
Bucharest
Belgrade
3940
20°E
YUGOSLAVIA
25°E
Danube
Sevastopol
30°E
Varna
Black Sea
35°E
40°E
U.S.S.R.
Tirana
5036
Sofia
BULGARIA
9524
Sinop
Samsun
Batumi
Skopje
ALBANIA
9573
Salonica
7594
Istanbul
Zonguldak
Ankara
Erzurum
40°N
GREECE
7903
5807
Athens
Izmir
7352
Afyonkarahisar
Kayseri
Malatya
T U R K E Y
Adana
10,125
Rhodes
Aleppo
Euphrates
Nicosia
CYPRUS
6403
Famagusta
35°N
Iraklion
Crete
S Y R I A
Beirut
LEBANON
Damascus
5929
IRAQ
ISRAEL
Amman
200 metres
Benghazi
Beida
2838
Tobruk
Rosetta
Damietta
Jerusalem
Dead Sea
J O R D A N
Alexandria
Port Said
Gaza
30°N
El Alamein
Cairo
Suez Canal
Ismailia
Aqaba
Libyan Plateau
Pyramids
Memphis
Suez
Eilat
Oil Pipeline
440
Qattara Depression
El Faiyûm
Sinai
8664
Siwa
7710
Ras Lanuf
idra
Pipeline
L I B Y A
Qasr Farafra
EGYPT
Asyut
7165
S A U D I   A R A B I A
Yanbu
Kufra Oases
Girga
Thebes
Luxor
25°N
2585
Dakhla Oasis
El Khârga
Isna
3116
Aswân
5486
1st. Cataract
Aswân Dam
Foul Bay
3819
6255
Wadi Halfa
Jidda
Mecca
2nd. Cataract
2270
9335
Nile
4077
Nubian Desert
3rd. Cataract
Port Sudan
Suakin
200 metres
1204
i Koussi
4th. Cataract
1546
5036
Red Sea
5th. Cataract
Berber
9121
2948
Atbara
Ed Damer
8451
1621
6th. Cataract
Atbara
Massawa
Kamaran Is. (S.Yemen)
15°N
YEMEN A. R.
YEMEN P.D.R.
Sa'na
10,720
Mukalla
Omdurman
Khartoum
Kassala
Agordat
Tessenei
Asmara
3076
Jebel Aulia Dam
1775
S U D A N
Aduwa
15,158
C. Guardafui
6410
Gezira
Wad Medani
As Shaab
Aden
El Fasher
KORDOFAN
Gondar
13,747
Assab
Bab el Mandeb
6769
G. of Aden
3211
DARFUR
El Obeid
4583
Lake Tana
FR. TERR. AFARS/ISSAS
Zeila
Berbera
7900
Erigavo
Nyala
Marra Mts.
10,131
White Nile
Sennar Dam
2970
6013
Djibouti
Marra Mts.
BLUE NILE
10,271
13,451
Blue Nile
Diredawa
3379
3412
Roseires
7998
13,040
Harar
Hargeisa
5314
Fashoda
14,129
Diredawa
Haud
2693
Malakal
10,830
Addis Ababa
Awash
393
CENTRAL
4183
BAHR EL GHAZAL
Gore
7874
ETHIOPIA (ABYSSINIA)
Ginir
Ogaden
2171
Wau
Plateau
1492
2985
Jur
Bahr el Jebel (White Nile)
Shibeli
REPUBLIC
2059
5078
Jonglei
Mega
Obbia
5°N
Mobaye
Oubangui
Bondo
5560
Juba
Moyale
S O M A L I   R E P U B L I C
Zongo
Komba
Isiro
Mungbere
Nimule
Lake Rudolf
9203
5561
Mogadiscio
20°E
25°E
UGANDA
30°E
Lake Albert
35°E
K E N Y A
40°E
Equator
REPUBLIC OF ZAIRE

Copyright Oxford University Press

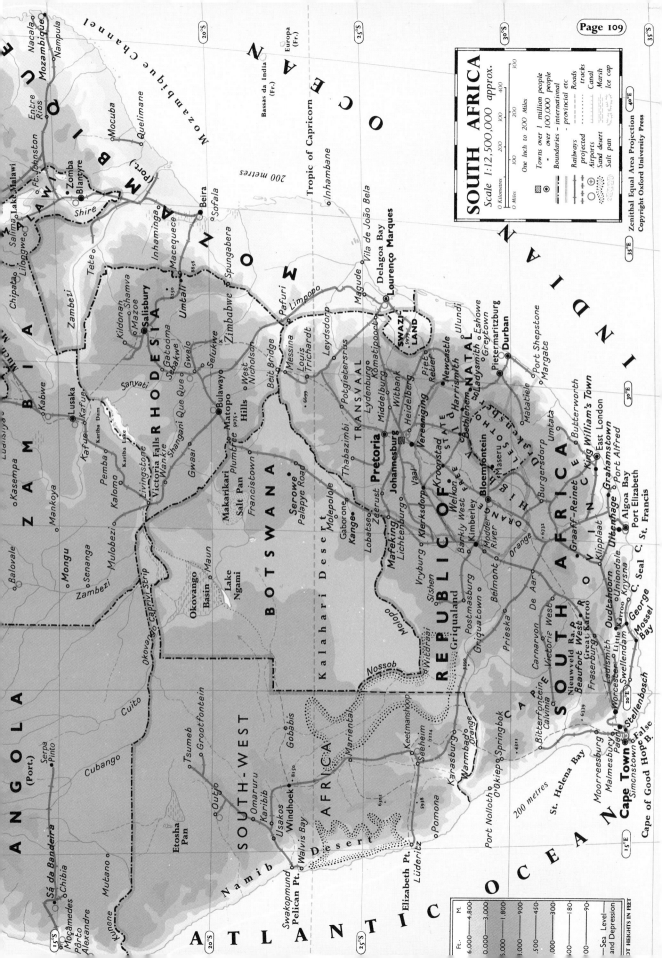

SOUTH AFRICA

Scale 1:12,500,000 approx.

One Inch to 200 Miles

0 Miles 100 200 300

0 Kilometers 100 200 300 400

- Towns over 1 million people
- ⊙ over 100,000 people
- Boundaries - international
- - provincial etc
- Railways
-   projected
- ✈ Airports
- Roads
- tracks
- Canal
- Salt pan
- Marsh
- ice cap
- Sand desert

Zenithal Equal Area Projection
Copyright Oxford University Press

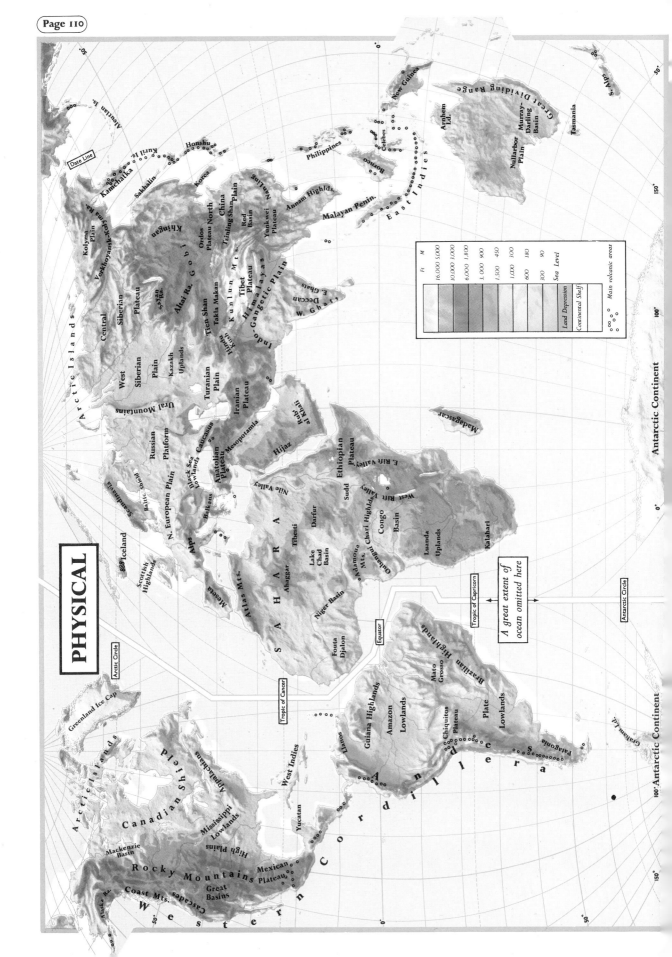

PHYSICAL

BUILD

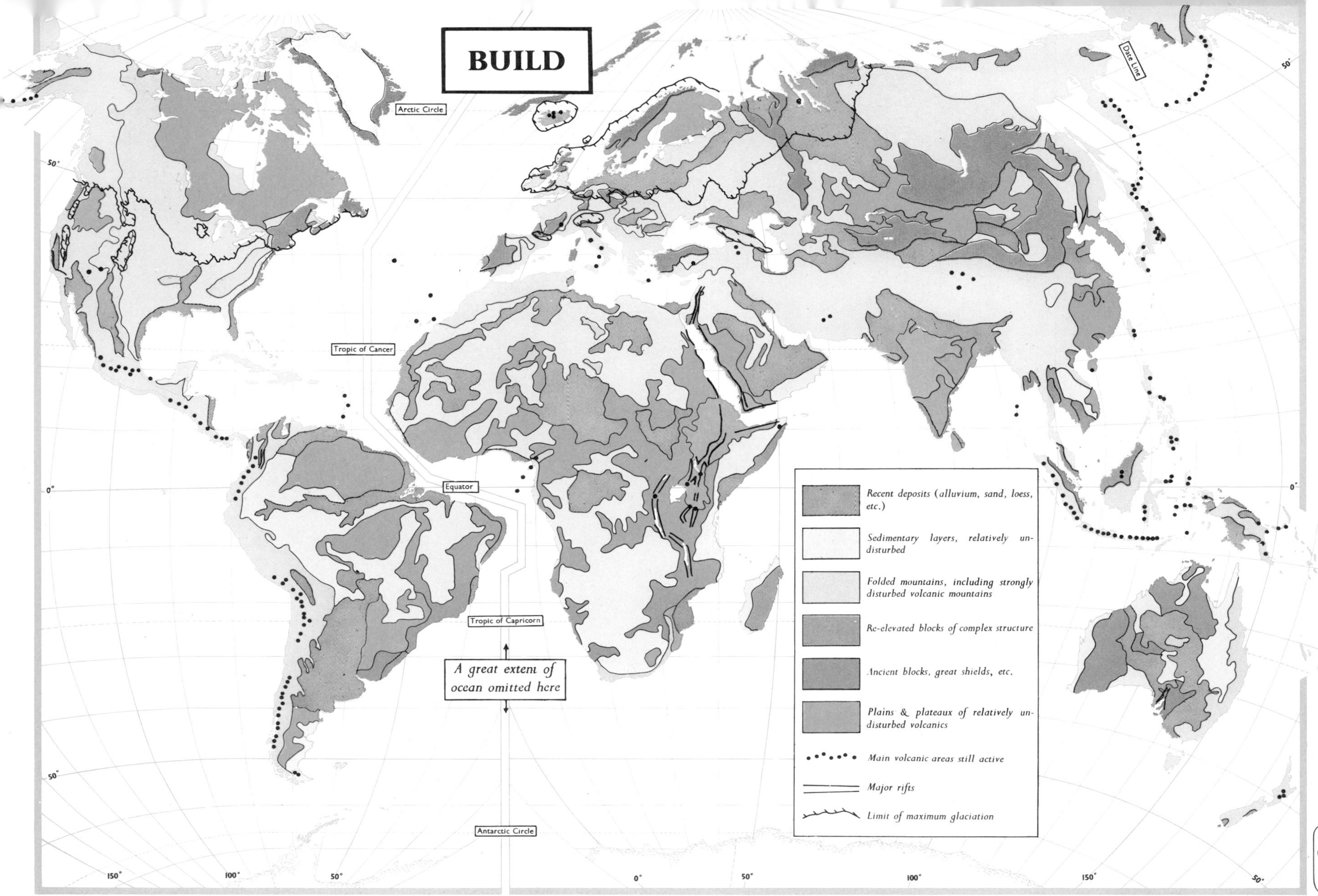
Arctic Circle
Tropic of Cancer
Equator
Tropic of Capricorn
Antarctic Circle
Date Line
A great extent of ocean omitted here
Recent deposits (alluvium, sand, loess, etc.)
Sedimentary layers, relatively undisturbed
Folded mountains, including strongly disturbed volcanic mountains
Re-elevated blocks of complex structure
Ancient blocks, great shields, etc.
Plains & plateaux of relatively undisturbed volcanics
Main volcanic areas still active
Major rifts
Limit of maximum glaciation
50°
0°
50°
150°
100°
50°
0°
50°
100°
150°
50°

Oxford Projection. Equal-Area. Scale 1 : 100 m. approx.

Copyright Oxford University Press

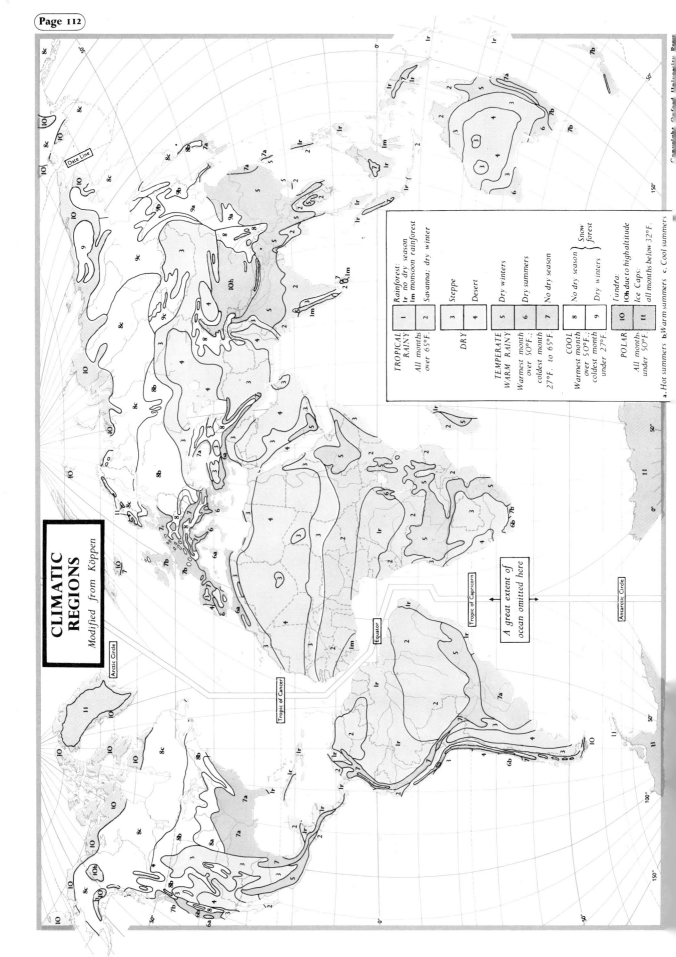

CLIMATIC REGIONS
Modified from Köppen

TROPICAL RAINY		
All months over 65°F.	1	Rainforest: 1r no dry season / 1m monsoon rainforest
	2	Savanna: dry winter

DRY		
	3	Steppe
	4	Desert

TEMPERATE WARM RAINY		
Warmest month over 50°F.; coldest month 27°F. to 65°F.	5	Dry winters
	6	Dry summers
	7	No dry season

COOL		
Warmest month over 50°F.; coldest month under 27°F.	8	No dry season }Snow forest
	9	Dry winters }Snow forest

POLAR		
All months under 50°F.	10	Tundra: 10h due to highaltitude
	11	Ice Caps: all months below 32°F.

a. Hot summers b. Warm summers c. Cool summers

A great extent of ocean omitted here

Arctic Circle

Tropic of Cancer

Equator

Tropic of Capricorn

Antarctic Circle

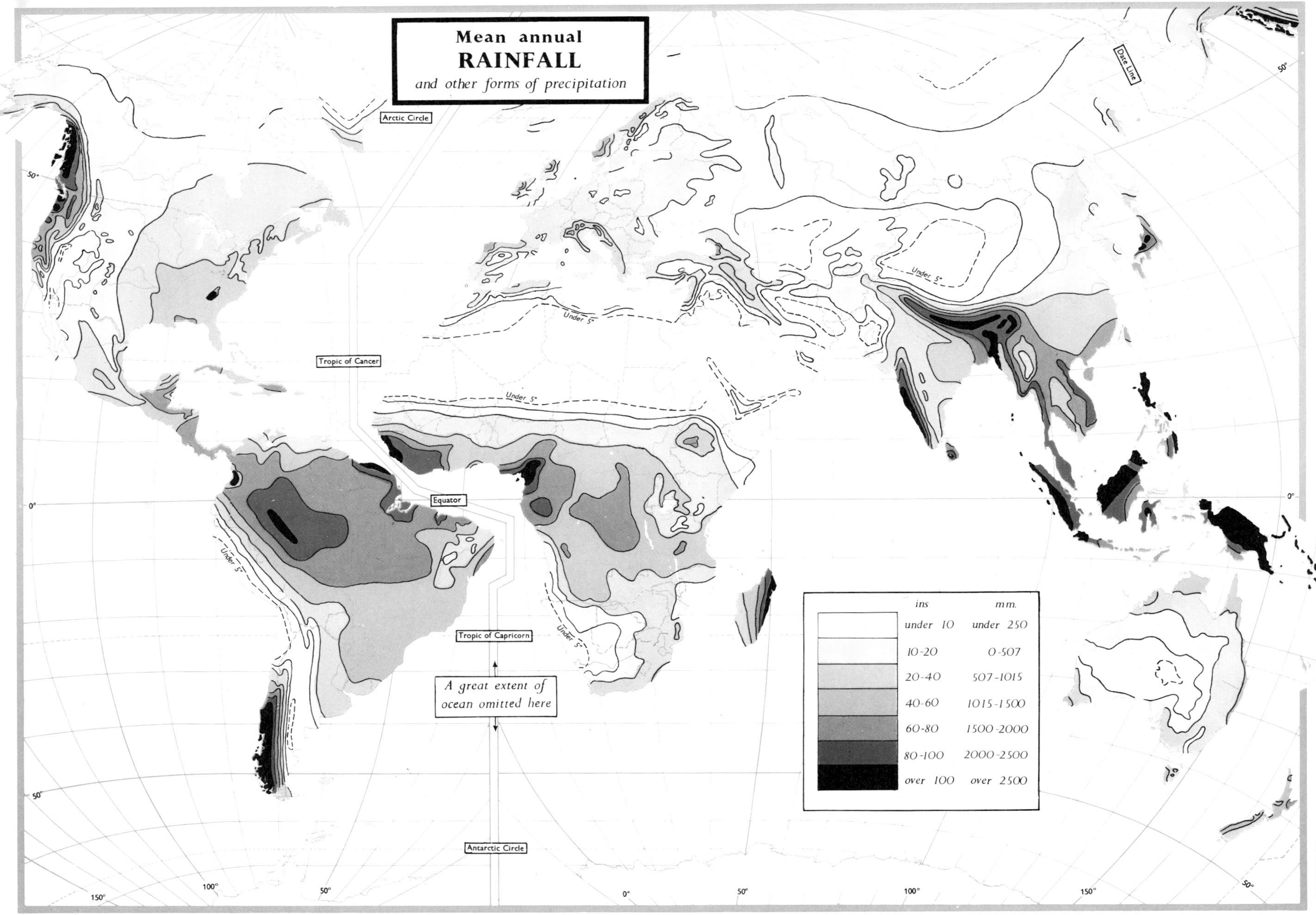

Copyright Oxford University Press.

Mean annual RAINFALL
and other forms of precipitation

ins	mm.
under 10	under 250
10-20	0-507
20-40	507-1015
40-60	1015-1500
60-80	1500-2000
80-100	2000-2500
over 100	over 2500

Date Line

Under 5"

A great extent of ocean omitted here

Tropic of Capricorn

Tropic of Cancer

Equator

Arctic Circle

Antarctic Circle

Under 5"

Under 5"

Under 5"

Oxford Projection Equal-area   Scale 1:1COm. approx.

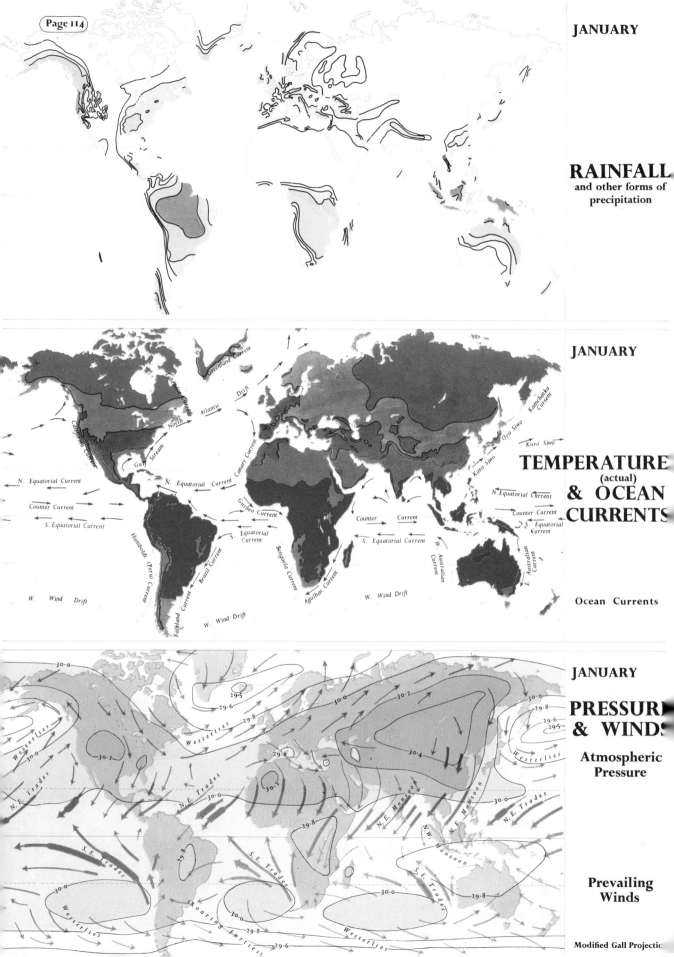

JANUARY

RAINFALL
and other forms of
precipitation

JANUARY

TEMPERATURE
(actual)
& OCEAN
CURRENTS

Ocean Currents

JANUARY

PRESSURE
& WINDS

Atmospheric
Pressure

Prevailing
Winds

Modified Gall Projection

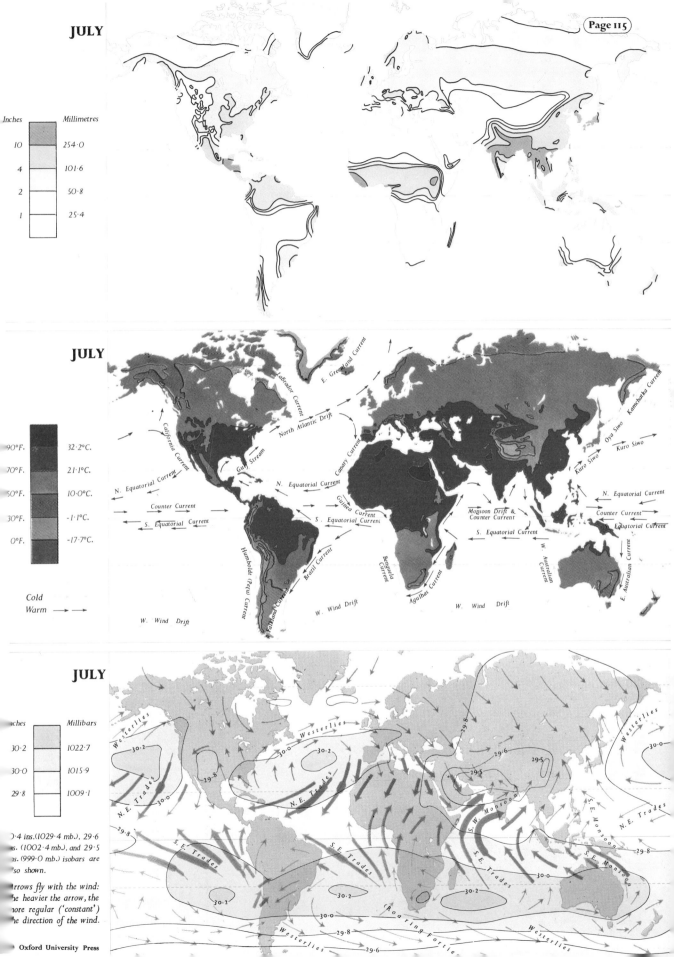

JULY

Inches	Millimetres
10	254·0
4	101·6
2	50·8
1	25·4

JULY

90°F.	32·2°C.
70°F.	21·1°C.
50°F.	10·0°C.
30°F.	-1·1°C.
0°F.	-17·7°C.

Cold
Warm ⟶ ⟶

JULY

ches	Millibars
30·2	1022·7
30·0	1015·9
29·8	1009·1

0·4 ins.(1029·4 mb.), 29·6
s. (1002·4 mb.), and 29·5
s. (999·0 mb.) isobars are
so shown.

rrows fly with the wind:
he heavier the arrow, the
nore regular ('constant')
he direction of the wind.

Oxford University Press

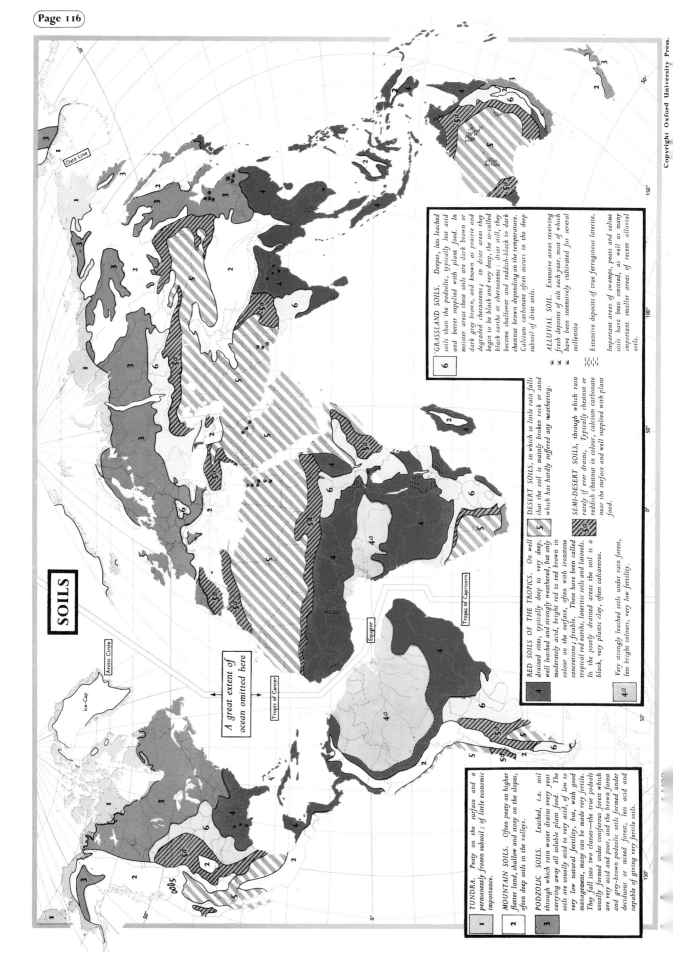

SOILS

Copyright Oxford University Press.

A great extent of ocean omitted here

Date Line

Arctic Circle

Ice-Cap

Tropic of Cancer

Equator

Tropic of Capricorn

---

1 TUNDRA. Peaty on the surface and a permanently frozen subsoil; of little economic importance.

2 MOUNTAIN SOILS. Often peaty on higher flatter land, shallow and stony on the slopes, often deep soils in the valleys.

3 PODZOLIC SOILS. Leached, i.e. soil through which rain water drains every year carrying away all soluble plant food. The soils are usually acid to very acid, of low to very low natural fertility, but, with good management, many can be made very fertile. They fall into two classes—the true podsols usually formed under coniferous forest which are very acid and poor, and the brown forest and grey-brown podzolic soils formed under deciduous or mixed forest, less acid and capable of giving very fertile soils.

4 RED SOILS OF THE TROPICS. On well drained sites, typically deep to very deep, well leached and strongly weathered, but only moderately acid, bright red to red brown in colour on the surface, often with ironstone concretions; friable. These have been called tropical red earths, lateritic soils and latosols. In the poorly drained areas the soil is a **4a** black, very plastic clay, often calcareous.

Very strongly leached soils under rain forest, less bright colours, very low fertility.

5 DESERT SOILS, in which so little rain falls that the soil is mainly broken rock or sand which has hardly suffered any weathering.

SEMI-DESERT SOILS, through which rain rarely if ever drains. Typically chestnut or reddish chestnut in colour, calcium carbonate near the surface and well supplied with plant food.

6 GRASSLAND SOILS. Deeper, less leached soils than the podzolic, typically less acid and better supplied with plant food. In moister areas these soils are dark brown or dark grey brown, and known as prairie and degraded chernozems; in drier areas they begin to be black and very deep, the so-called black earths or chernozems: drier still, they become shallower and reddish-black to dark chestnut brown depending on the temperature. Calcium carbonate often occurs in the deep subsoil of drier soils.

ALLUVIAL SOIL. Extensive areas receiving fresh deposits of silt each year, most of which have been intensively cultivated for several millennia

Extensive deposits of true ferruginous laterite.

Important areas of swamps, peats and saline soils have been omitted, as well as many important smaller areas of recent alluvial soils.

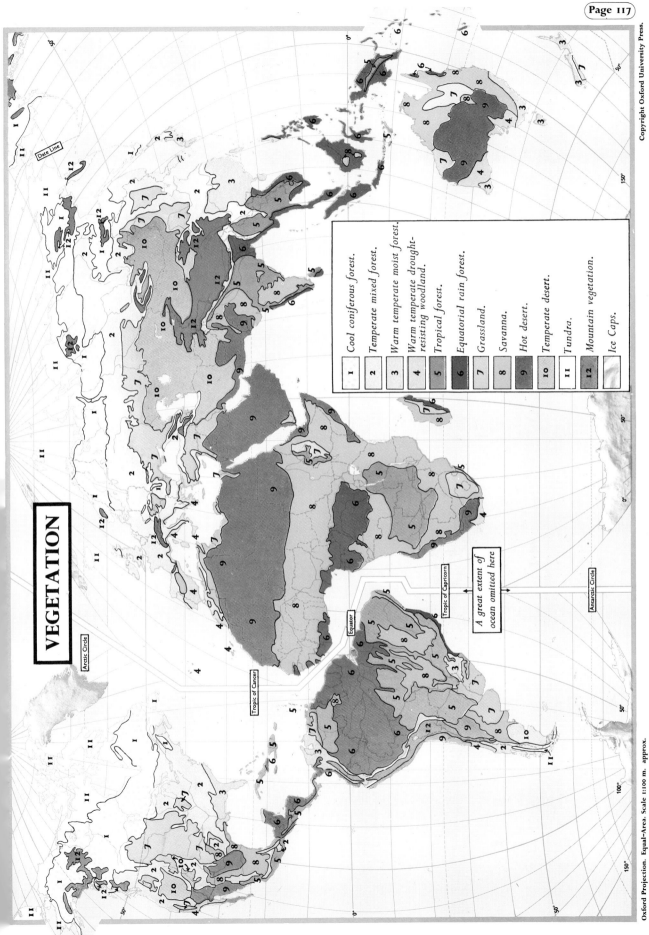

VEGETATION

1	Cool coniferous forest.
2	Temperate mixed forest.
3	Warm temperate moist forest.
4	Warm temperate drought-resisting woodland.
5	Tropical forest.
6	Equatorial rain forest.
7	Grassland.
8	Savanna.
9	Hot desert.
10	Temperate desert.
11	Tundra.
12	Mountain vegetation.
	Ice Caps.

A great extent of ocean omitted here

Arctic Circle

Tropic of Cancer

Equator

Tropic of Capricorn

Antarctic Circle

Date Line

Copyright Oxford University Press.

Oxford Projection. Equal-Area. Scale 1:100 m. approx.

AGRICULTURE

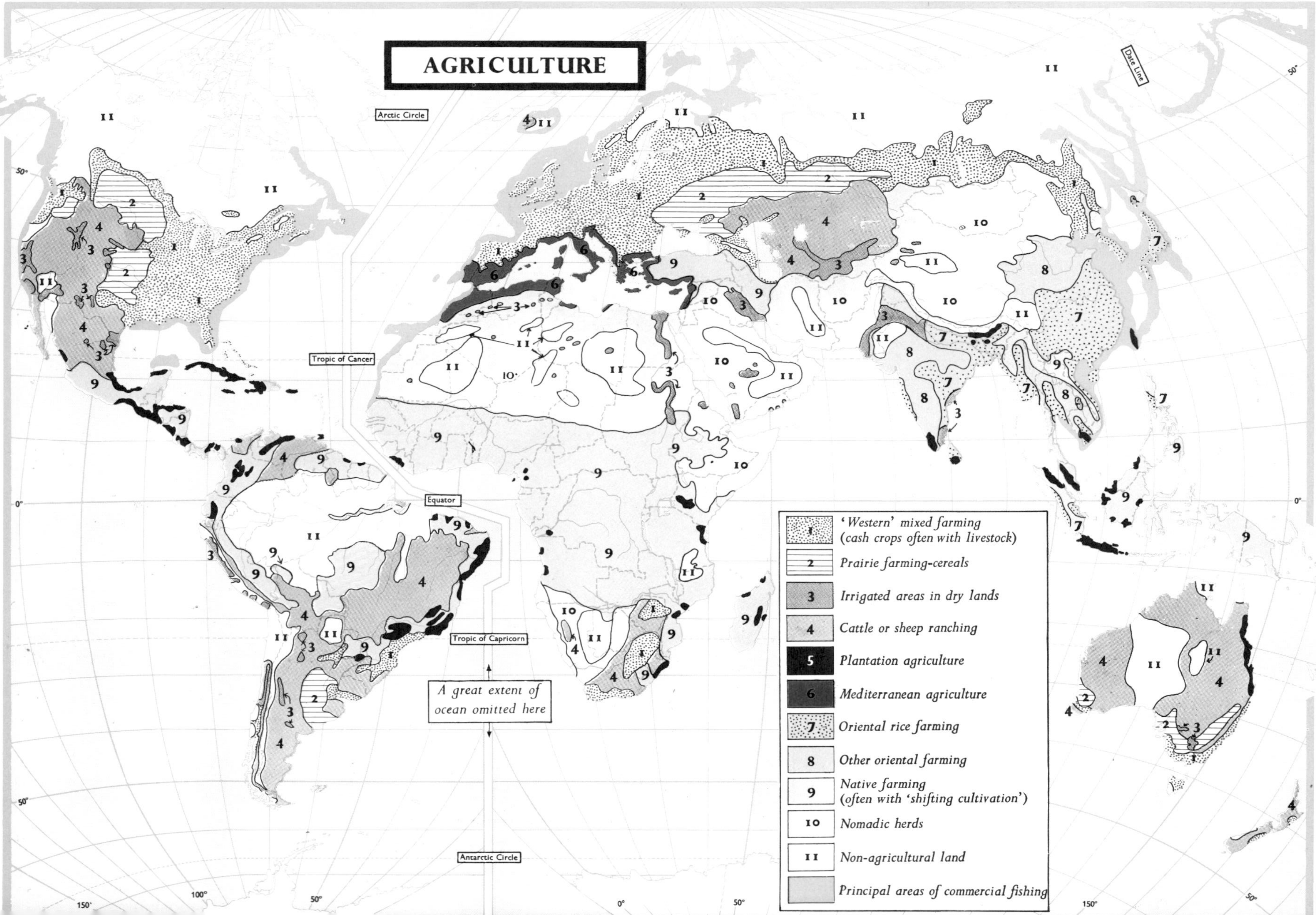

1	'Western' mixed farming (cash crops often with livestock)
2	Prairie farming–cereals
3	Irrigated areas in dry lands
4	Cattle or sheep ranching
5	Plantation agriculture
6	Mediterranean agriculture
7	Oriental rice farming
8	Other oriental farming
9	Native farming (often with 'shifting cultivation')
10	Nomadic herds
11	Non-agricultural land
	Principal areas of commercial fishing

Date Line

Arctic Circle

Tropic of Cancer

Equator

Tropic of Capricorn

A great extent of ocean omitted here

Antarctic Circle

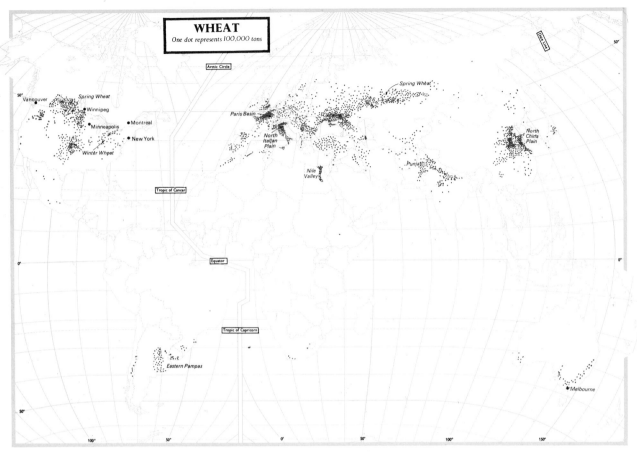

WHEAT
One dot represents 100,000 tons

Date Line

50°

Arctic Circle

Vancouver

Spring Wheat

Winnipeg

Minneapolis

Montreal

New York

Winter Wheat

Spring Wheat

Paris Basin

North Italian Plain

Nile Valley

North China Plain

Punjab

Tropic of Cancer

0°

Equator

Tropic of Capricorn

Eastern Pampas

Melbourne

50°

100°   50°   0°   50°   100°   150°

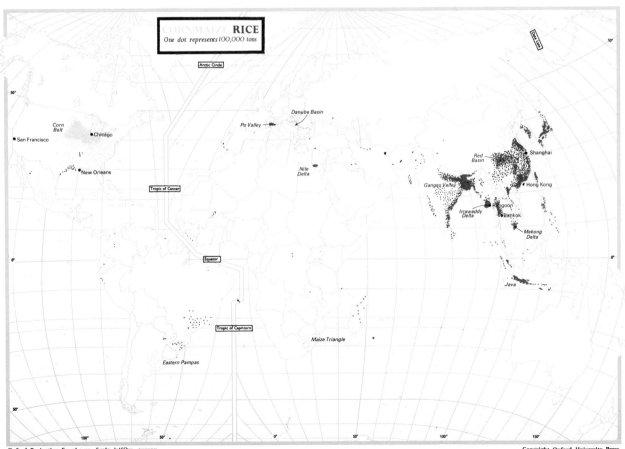

CORN/MAIZE RICE
One dot represents 100,000 tons

Date Line

50°

Arctic Circle

Corn Belt

Danube Basin

Po Valley

Chicago

San Francisco

New Orleans

Nile Delta

Red Basin

Shanghai

Ganges Valley

Hong Kong

Irrawaddy Delta

Rangoon

Bangkok

Mekong Delta

Tropic of Cancer

Equator

Java

Tropic of Capricorn

Maize Triangle

Eastern Pampas

50°

100°   50°   0°   50°   100°   150°

Oxford Projection Equal-area Scale 1:150m. approx.

Copyright Oxford University Press.

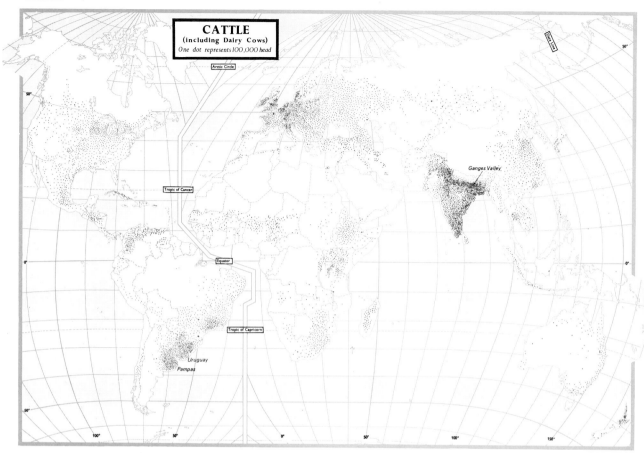

CATTLE
(including Dairy Cows)
One dot represents 100,000 head

Arctic Circle

Tropic of Cancer

Ganges Valley

Equator

Tropic of Capricorn

Uruguay

Pampas

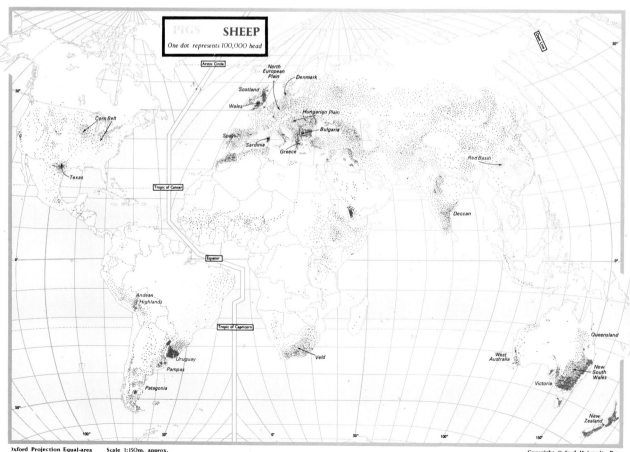

PIGS **SHEEP**
One dot represents 100,000 head

Arctic Circle

North
European
Plain
Denmark

Scotland

Wales

Corn Belt

Hungarian Plain

Spain
Sardinia

Bulgaria

Greece

Red Basin

Texas

Tropic of Cancer

Deccan

Equator

Andean
Highlands

Tropic of Capricorn

Veld

Queensland

West
Australia

Uruguay

Pampas

Patagonia

Victoria

New
South
Wales

New
Zealand

Oxford Projection Equal-area   Scale 1:150m. approx.

Copyright Oxford University Press.

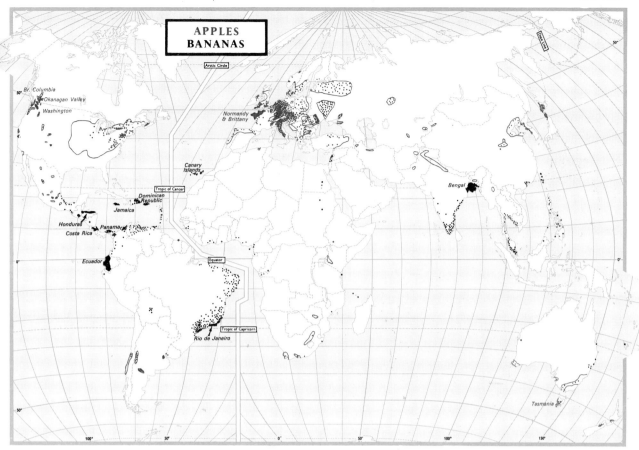

APPLES
BANANAS

Arctic Circle

Br. Columbia
Okanagan Valley
Washington

Normandy
& Brittany

Canary
Islands

Tropic of Cancer

Dominican
Republic

Jamaica

Bengal

Honduras
Costa Rica
Panama

Ecuador

Equator

Rio de Janeiro

Tropic of Capricorn

Tasmania

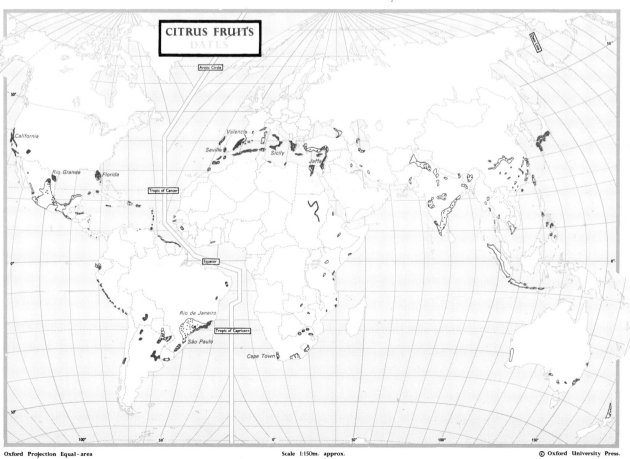

CITRUS FRUITS
DATES

Arctic Circle

California

Valencia

Seville
Sicily

Jaffa

Rio Grande
Florida

Tropic of Cancer

Sind

Equator

Rio de Janeiro

São Paulo

Tropic of Capricorn

Cape Town

Scale 1:150m. approx.

© Oxford University Press.

PETROLEUM

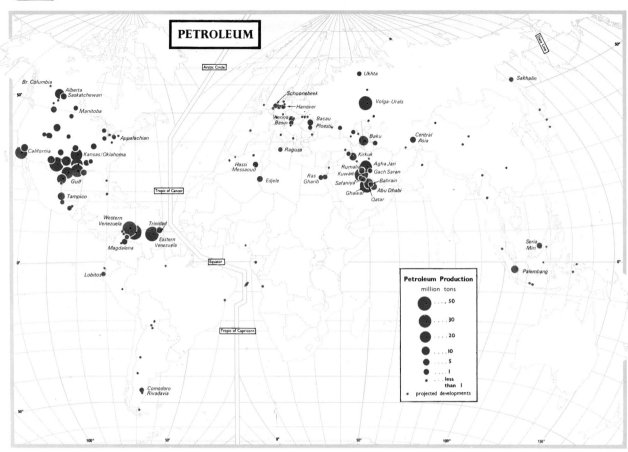

Br. Columbia *
Alberta
Saskatchewan
Manitoba
Appalachian
California
Kansas/Oklahoma
Gulf
Tampico
Western Venezuela
Trinidad
Eastern Venezuela
Magdalena
Lobitos
Comodoro Rivadavia

Ukhta
Sakhalin
Schoonebeek
Hanover
Vienna Basin
Bacau
Ploesti
Ragusa
Baku
Central Asia
Hassi Messaoud
Edjele
Kirkuk
Ras Gharib
Rumalia
Kuwait
Agha Jari
Gach Saran
Safaniya
Bahrain
Ghawar
Abu Dhabi
Qatar
Seria Miri
Palembang

Petroleum Production
million tons

- 50
- 30
- 20
- 10
- 5
- 1
- less than 1
* projected developments

Arctic Circle
Tropic of Cancer
Equator
Tropic of Capricorn
Date Line

COAL

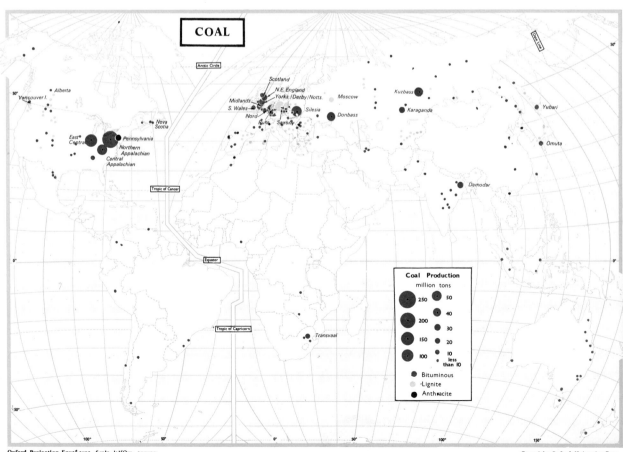

Vancouver I.
Alberta
Nova Scotia
East Central
Pennsylvania
Northern Appalachian
Central Appalachian
Scotland
N.E. England
Midlands
Yorks./Derby/Notts.
S. Wales
Nord
Ruhr
Saxony
Silesia
Moscow
Donbass
Kuzbass
Karaganda
Yubari
Omuta
Damodar
Transvaal

Coal Production
million tons

250	50
200	40
150	30
100	20
	10
	less than 10

- Bituminous
- Lignite
- Anthracite

Arctic Circle
Tropic of Cancer
Equator
Tropic of Capricorn
Date Line

Oxford Projection Equal-area Scale 1:150m. approx.
Copyright Oxford University Press.

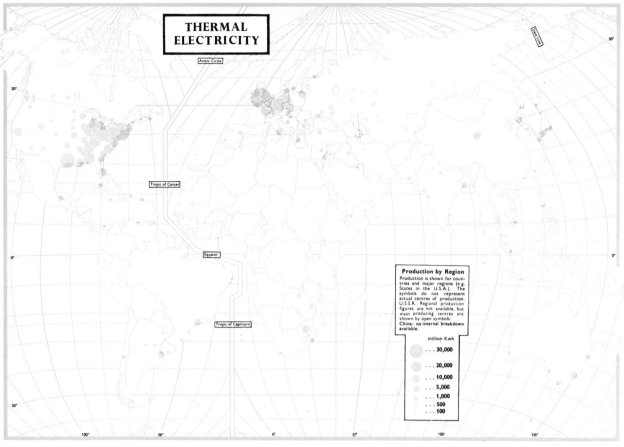

THERMAL ELECTRICITY

Arctic Circle

Tropic of Cancer

Equator

Tropic of Capricorn

Production by Region

Production is shown for countries and major regions (e.g. States in the U.S.A.). The symbols do not represent actual centres of production. U.S.S.R.: Regional production figures are not available, but main producing centres are shown by open symbols. China: no internal breakdown available.

million Kwh

. . . 30,000
. . . 20,000
. . . 10,000
. . . 5,000
. . . 1,000
. . . 500
. . . 100

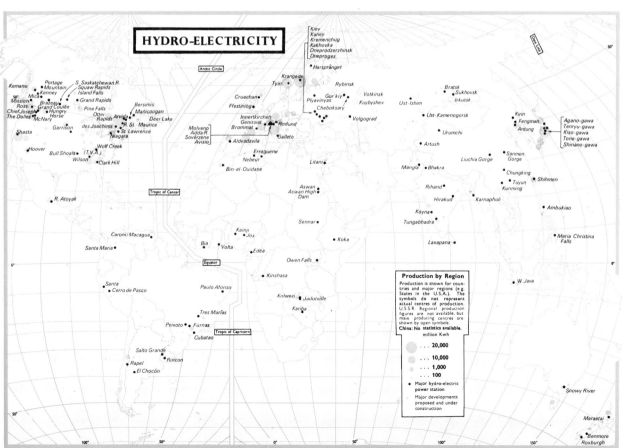

HYDRO-ELECTRICITY

Kiev
Kanev
Kremenchug
Kakhovka
Dneprodzerzhinsk
Dneproges

Harspränget

Arctic Circle

Krangede

Kemano
Portage
Mountain
Kenney
Tyin
S. Saskatchewan R.
Squaw Rapids
Island Falls
Rybinsk
Bratsk
Sukhovsk
Mica
Cruachan
Votkinsk
Mission
Braeau
Grand Rapids
 Plyavinyas
Gor'kiy
Kuybyshev
Irkutsk
Ross
Grand Coulée
Pine Falls
Ffestiniog
Cheboksary
Ust-Ishim
Chief Joseph
Hungry
Horse
Otter
Rapids
Bersimis
Manicouagan
Arvida
Volgograd
Ust-Kamenogorsk
Kirin
Fengman
Agano-gawa
The Dalles
McNary
des Joachims
Deer Lake
Innertkirchen
Genissiat
Rodund
Antung
Tenryu-gawa
Kiso-gawa
Shasta
R. St. Maurice
St. Lawrence
Molveno
Adda R.
Sovérzene
Aviso
Brommat
Galleto
Urumchi
Tone-gawa
Shinano-gawa
Niagara
Hoover
Wolf Creek
Aldeadavila
Artush
Liuchia Gorge
Sanmen
Gorge
Bull Shoals
(T.V.A.)
Erraguene
Mangla
Bhakra
Chungking
Wilson
Clark Hill
Nebeur
Litani
Rihand
Tuyun
Shihmen
Bin-el-Ouidane
Kunming
Tropic of Cancer
Hirakud
Karnaphuli
R. Atoyak
Aswan
Aswan High
Dam
Koyna
Ambukiao
Tungabhadra
Caroni Macagua
Kainji
Jos
Sennar
Laxapana
Maria Christina
Falls
Santa Maria
Bia
Volta
Edéa
Koka
Owen Falls
Equator
Kinshasa
W. Java
Santa
Cerro de Pasco
Paulo Afonso
Kolwezi
Jadotville
Tres Marías
Kariba
Peixoto
Furnas
Cubatao
Tropic of Capricorn
Salto Grande
Rincon
Rapel
El Chocón
Snowy River

Production by Region

Production is shown for countries and major regions (e.g. States in the U.S.A.). The symbols do not represent actual centres of production. U.S.S.R. Regional production figures are not available, but main producing centres are shown by open symbols. China: No statistics available.

million Kwh

. . . 20,000
. . . 10,000
. . . 1,000
. . . 100

• Major hydro-electric power station

Major developments proposed and under construction

Maraetai

Benmore
Roxburgh

Copyright Oxford University Press.

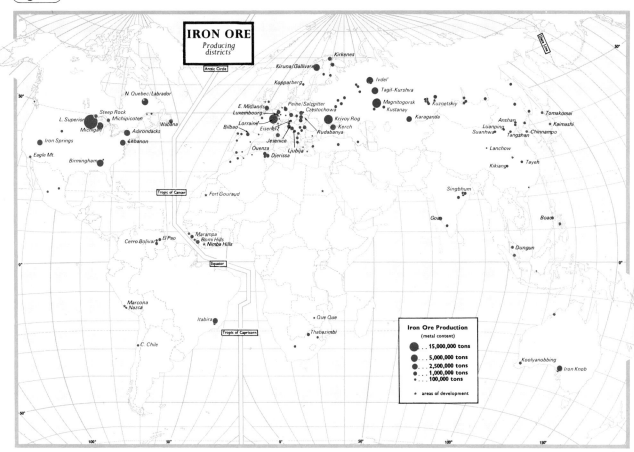

IRON ORE
Producing districts

Kirkenes
Kiruna/Gallivare
Kopparberg
N. Quebec/Labrador
Ivdel'
Tagil-Kurshva
E. Midlands
Luxembourg
Pelbe/Salzgitter
Czestochowa
Magnitogorsk
Kustanay
Kuznetskiy
Karaganda
Tomakomai
Kaimashi
Anshan
Steep Rock
Michipicoten
L. Superior
Michigan
Wabana
Lorraine
Bilbao
Eisenerz
Krivoy Rog
Kerch
Rudabanya
Luanping
Suanhwa
Tangshan
Chinnampo
Adirondacks
Jesenice
Iron Springs
Lebanon
Ljubija
Ouenza
Lanchow
Eagle Mt.
Birmingham
Djerissa
Kikiang
Tayeh
Fort Gourauâ
Singbhum
Goa
Boac
Cerro Bolivar
El Pao
Marampa
Bomi Hills
Nimba Hills
Dungun
Marcona
Nazca
Itabira
Que Que
Thabazimbi
C. Chile

Iron Ore Production
(metal content)
⬤ . . 15,000,000 tons
⬤ . . 5,000,000 tons
● . . 2,500,000 tons
• . . 1,000,000 tons
· . . 100,000 tons
✱ areas of development

Koolyanobbing
Iron Knob

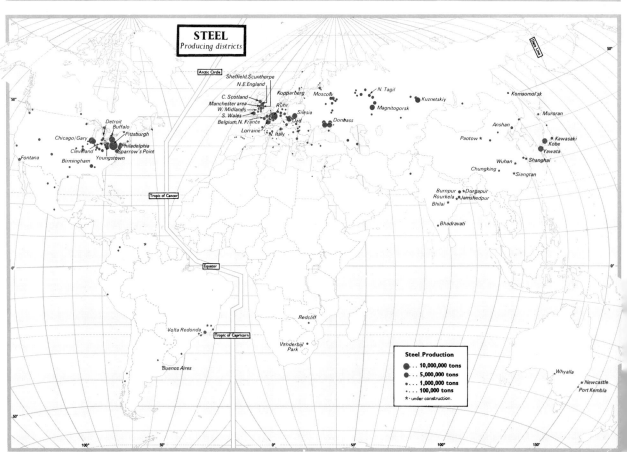

STEEL
Producing districts

Sheffield,Scunthorpe
N.E.England
C. Scotland
Manchester area
W. Midlands
S. Wales
Belgium,N. France
Kopparberg
Moscov
N. Tagil
Komsomol'sk
Ruhr
Silesia
Magnitogorsk
Kuznetskiy
Muroran
Detroit
Buffalo
Pittsburgh
Lorraine
Ozd
Donbass
Anshan
Chicago/Gary
Philadelphia
Sparrow's Point
N. Italy
Paotow ✱
Kawasaki
Kobe
Yawata
Fontana
Cleveland
Youngstown
Birmingham
Wuhan
Shanghai
Chungking
Siangtan
Burnpur
Durgapur
Rourkela
Jamshedpur
Bhilai ✱
Bhadravati
Redcliff
Volta Redonda
Vanderbijl
Park
Buenos Aires

Steel Production
● . . 10,000,000 tons
● . . 5,000,000 tons
• . . 1,000,000 tons
· . . 100,000 tons
✱ under construction.

Whyalla
Newcastle
Port Kembla

Copyright Oxford University Press.

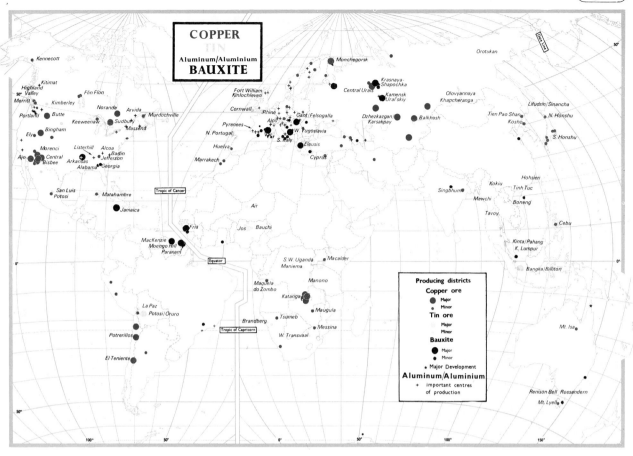

COPPER
TIN
Aluminum/Aluminium
BAUXITE

Orotukan

Kennecott

Kitimat
Highland
Valley
Merritt
Portland
Ely
Ajo
Morenci
Central
Bisbee

Flin Flón
Kimberley
Noranda
Butte
Keeweenaw
Bingham
Listerhill
Arkansas
Alabama

Arvida
Murdochville
Sudbury
Massena
Alcoa
Badin
Jefferson
Georgia

San Luis
Potosí
Matahambre
Jamaica

Fort William
Kinlochleven
Cornwall
Rhine
Pyrenees
N. Portugal
Huelva
Marrakech

Monchegorsk
Krasnaya-
Shapochka
Central Urals
Kamensk
Ural'skiy
Dzhezkazgan/
Karsakpay
Gánt/Felsogalla
Alps
W. Yugoslavia
S. Italy
Eleusis
Cyprus

Olovyannaya
Khapcheranga
Balkhash

Lifudzin/Sinancha
N. Honshu
Kosho
S. Honshu

Tien Pao Shan

Hohsien
Kokiu
Tinh Tuc
Boneng

Singbhum
Mawchi
Tavoy

Cebu

Kinta/Pahang
K. Lumpur

Bangka/Billiton

Fria
Jos
Bauchi
Air

MacKenzie
Moengo Hill
Paranam

Maquela
do Zombo
Katanga
Manono

S.W. Uganda
Maniema
Macalder

Maugula

La Paz
Potosí/Oruro

Brandberg
Tsumeb
Messina
W. Transvaal

Mt. Isa

Potrerillos

El Teniente

Renison Bell Rossandern
Mt. Lyell

Producing districts
Copper ore
● Major
· Minor
Tin ore
Major
Minor
Bauxite
● Major
● Minor
★ Major Development
Aluminum/Aluminium
+ important centres
of production

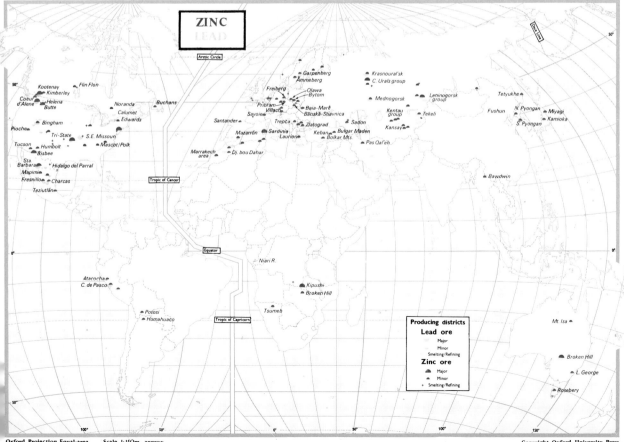

ZINC
LEAD

Arctic Circle

Kootenay
Kimberley
Coeur
d'Alene
Helena
Butte
Bingham
Pioche
Tri-State
Tucson
Humbolt
Bisbee
Sta
Barbara
Mapimí
Fresnillo
Teziutlán
Charcas

Flin Flon
Noranda
Buchans
Calumet
Edwards
S.E. Missouri
Mascot/Polk
Hidalgo del Parral

Santander
Mazarrón
Sardinia
Laurion

Garpenberg
Ammeberg
Freiberg
Olawa
Bytom
Pribram
Villach
Baia-Mare
Bánská-Stiavnica
Trepča
Zlatograd
Keban
Bolkar Mts.
Bulgar Maden
Djebou Dahar
Pas Qal'eh

Krasnoural'sk
C. Urals group
Mednogorsk
Leninogorsk
group
Kentau
group
Tekeli
Kansay

Tetyukhe

Fushun
N Pyongan
S. Pyongan

Miyagi
Kamioka

Sadon

Bawdwin

Marrakech
area

Atacocha
C. de Pasco

Potosí
Humahuaco

Niari R.

Kipushi
Broken Hill

Tsumeb

Mt. Isa
Broken Hill
L. George
Rosebery

Producing districts
Lead ore
Major
Minor
Smelting/Refining
Zinc ore
Major
Minor
Smelting/Refining

Copyright Oxford University Press.

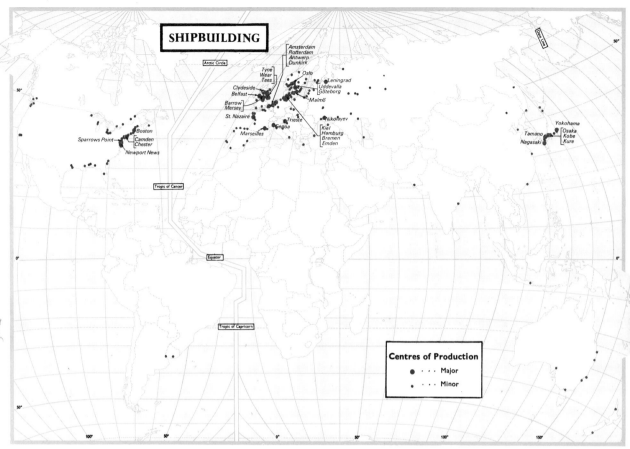

SHIPBUILDING

Arctic Circle

Amsterdam
Rotterdam
Antwerp
Dunkirk

Tyne
Wear
Tees

Oslo   Leningrad

Clydeside   Uddevalla
Belfast   Göteborg

Barrow   Malmö
Mersey

St. Nazaire   Nikolayev

Trieste
Genoa
Marseilles   Kiel
Hamburg
Bremen
Emden

Yokohama
Tamano   Osaka
Kobe
Nagasaki   Kure

Boston
Sparrows Point   Camden
Chester
Newport News

Tropic of Cancer

Equator

Tropic of Capricorn

Centres of Production
● · · · Major
• · · · Minor

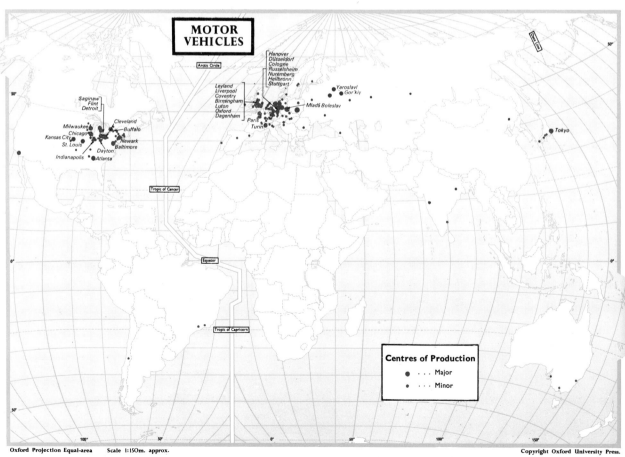

MOTOR
VEHICLES

Arctic Circle

Hanover
Düsseldorf
Cologne
Russelsheim
Nuremberg
Heilbronn
Stuttgart

Leyland   Yaroslavl
Liverpool   Gor'kiy
Coventry
Birmingham   Mladá Boleslav
Luton
Oxford
Dagenham

Saginaw   Paris
Flint   Turin
Detroit

Cleveland
Milwaukee   Buffalo
Chicago
Kansas City   Newark
St. Louis   Baltimore
Dayton
Indianapolis   Atlanta

Tokyo

Tropic of Cancer

Equator

Tropic of Capricorn

Centres of Production
● · · · Major
• · · · Minor

Oxford Projection Equal-area   Scale 1:150m. approx.

Copyright Oxford University Press.

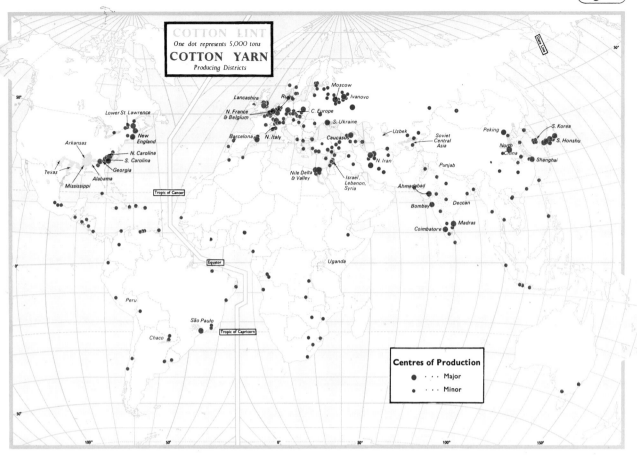

COTTON LINT

One dot represents 5,000 tons

COTTON YARN

Producing Districts

Lower St. Lawrence
New England
Arkansas
N. Carolina
S. Carolina
Texas
Georgia
Alabama
Mississippi
Lancashire
Ruhr
Moscow
Ivanovo
N. France & Belgium
C. Europe
Barcelona
N. Italy
S. Ukraine
Caucasus
Uzbek
Soviet Central Asia
Peking
S. Korea
N. Iran
North China
S. Honshu
Shanghai
Nile Delta & Valley
Israel, Lebanon, Syria
Ahmadabad
Punjab
Bombay
Deccan
Coimbatore
Madras
Peru
Uganda
São Paulo
Chaco

Tropic of Cancer
Equator
Tropic of Capricorn

Date Line
50°
50°
0°
50°
100°
50°
0°
50°
100°
150°

Centres of Production
● · · · Major
• · · · Minor

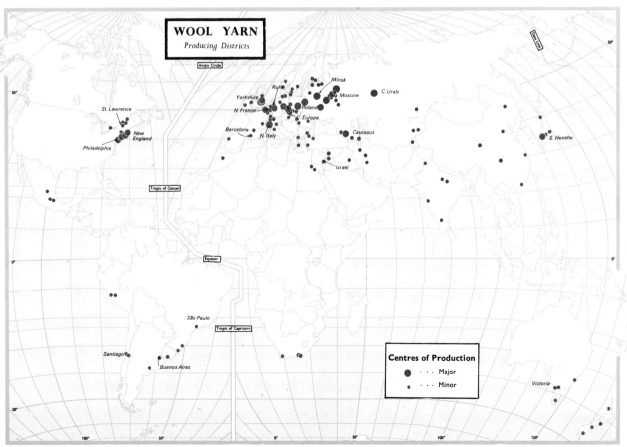

WOOL YARN

Producing Districts

Arctic Circle

St. Lawrence
New England
Philadelphia
Yorkshire
Ruhr
Minsk
N. France
Poland
Moscow
C. Urals
Barcelona
C. Europe
N. Italy
Caucasus
S. Honshu
Israel
Tropic of Cancer
Equator
São Paulo
Tropic of Capricorn
Santiago
Buenos Aires
Victoria

Date Line
50°
50°
0°
0°
50°
100°
50°
0°
50°
100°
150°

Centres of Production
● · · · Major
• · · · Minor

Oxford Projection Equal-area   Scale 1:150m. approx.

Copyright Oxford University Press.

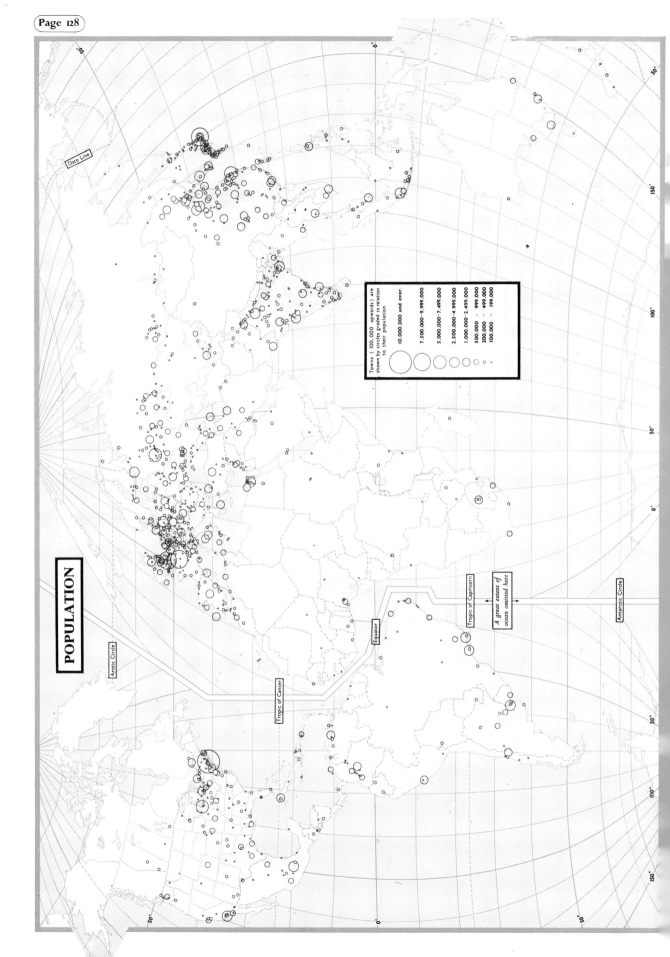

POPULATION

Towns (100,000 upwards) are
shown by circles graded in relation
to their population

10,000,000 and over.
7,500,000 - 9,999,000
5,000,000 - 7,499,000
2,500,000 - 4,999,000
1,000,000 - 2,499,000
500,000 - 999,000
200,000 - 499,000
100,000 - 199,000

Date Line

Arctic Circle

Tropic of Cancer

Equator

Tropic of Capricorn

A great extent of
ocean omitted here

Antarctic Circle

Gazetteers

Positions of places on largest scale maps (1:1,000,000 or larger) are given to nearest ¼ degree of latitude and longitude; positions of places on all other maps are given to nearest whole degree. In the Gazetteer of Canada, entries without page numbers can be located by latitude and longitude or by reference to the *Canadian Oxford Atlas*.

Abbreviations used on the maps and in the gazetteers are as follows:

A.C.T. – *Australian Capital Territory*; admin. – *administrative*; Afghan. – *Afghanistan*; Afr. – *Africa*; Ala. – *Alabama*; Alg. – *Algeria*; Alta. – *Alberta*; Antarc. – *Antarctica*; A.R. – *Autonomous Republic*; Arch. – *Archipelago*; Arg. – *Argentina*; Ariz. – *Arizona*; Ark. – *Arkansas*; Atl. O. – *Atlantic Ocean*; Austl. – *Australia*; B., b. – *Bay*; B.C. – *British Columbia*; Beds. – *Bedfordshire*; Belg. – *Belgium*; Berks. – *Berkshire*; Bol. – *Bolivia*; Bots. – *Botswana*; Br. – *British*; Braz. – *Brazil*; Bucks. – *Buckinghamshire*; Bulg. – *Bulgaria*; C., c. – *Cape*; Calif. – *California*; Can. – *Canada*; cap. – *capital*; Carib. Sea – *Caribbean Sea*; Cen. Afr. Rep. – *Central African Republic*; Chan. – *Channel*; Co. – *County*; Col. – *Colombia*; Colo. – *Colorado*; Conn. – *Connecticut*; C.R. – *Costa Rica*; Czech. – *Czechoslovakia*; D.C. – *District of Columbia*; Del. – *Delaware*; Den. – *Denmark*; dist. – *district*; Dom. Repub. – *Dominican Republic*; E. – *East, Eastern*; Ec. – *Ecuador*; Eng. – *England*; Eq. – *Equatorial*; Eth. – *Ethiopia*; Fd. – *Fiörd*; Fed. – *Federation*; Fla. – *Florida*; Fr. – *France, French*; Ft. – *Fort*; G. – *Gulf*; Ga. – *Georgia (U.S.A.)*; Ger. – *Germany*; Gl. – *Glacier*; Glos. – *Gloucestershire*; Grnld. – *Greenland*; Gt. – *Great*; Hd. – *Head*; Herts. – *Hertfordshire*; Hr., Harb. – *Harbour*; Hond. – *Honduras*; Hung. – *Hungary*; Hunts. – *Huntingdonshire*; I.(s), i.(s) – *Island(s)*; Ill. – *Illinois*; Ind. – *Indiana*; Ind. O. – *Indian Ocean*; Indon. – *Indonesia*; Int. – *International*; Irel. – *Ireland*; Kans. – *Kansas*; Ky. – *Kentucky*; L., l. – *Lake, Lac*; Labr. – *Labrador*; Lancs. – *Lancashire*; Les. – *Lesotho*; Lux. – *Luxembourg*; Malag. – *Malagasy Republic*; Man. – *Manitoba*; Mass. – *Massachussetts*; Maur. – *Mauritania*; Md. – *Maryland*; Mex. – *Mexico*; Medit. – *Mediterranean*; Mich. – *Michigan*; Minn. – *Minnesota*; Miss. – *Mississippi*; Mo. – *Missouri*; Mon. – *Monmouth*; Mong. – *Mongolia*; Mont. – *Montana*; Moz. – *Mozambique*; Mt.(n) – *Mountain*; mtns. – *Mountains*; N. – *North, Northern*; Nat. – *National*; N.B. – *New Brunswick*; N.C. – *North Carolina*; Neth. – *Netherlands*; Nebr. – *Nebraska*; Nev. – *Nevada*; Nfld. – *Newfoundland*; Nic. – *Nicaragua*; N.H. – *New Hampshire*; N.J. – *New Jersey*; N. Mex. – *New Mexico*; Nor. – *Norway*; Northants. – *Northamptonshire*; Notts. – *Nottinghamshire*; N.S. – *Nova Scotia*; N.W.T. – *Northwest Territories*; N.Y. – *New York*; N.Z. – *New Zealand*; Okla. – *Oklahoma*; Ont. – *Ontario*; Oreg. – *Oregon*; P. – *Pass*; Pa. – *Pennsylvania*; Pac. O. – *Pacific Ocean*; Pak. – *Pakistan*; P.E.I. – *Prince Edward I*; Penin. – *Peninsula*; Phil. – *Philippines*; Pk. – *Peak*; Plat. – *Plateau*; Port. – *Portugal*; Prov. – *Province*; Pt.(e) – *Point(e)*; Qué. – *Québec*; r. – *river*; R., Rep., Repub. – *Republic*; Res. – *Reservoir*; Rhod. – *Rhodesia*; R.I. – *Rhode Island*; Rom. – *Romania*; R.S.F.S.R. – *Russian Soviet Federated Socialist Republic*; S. – *South, Southern*; S. Am. – *South America*; Sask. – *Saskatchewan*; Sau. Arab. – *Sa'udi Arabia*; S.C. – *South Carolina*; Scot. – *Scotland*; Sd. – *Sound*; S. Dak. – *South Dakota*; Som. Rep. – *Somali Republic*; Sp. – *Spain, Spanish*; S.S.R. – *Soviet Socialist Republic*; St.(e) – *Saint(e)*; Str. – *Strait*; Swed. – *Sweden*; Switz. – *Switzerland*; Tanzan. – *Tanzania*; Tenn. – *Tennessee*; Territ. – *Territory*; Thai. – *Thailand*; U.S.A. – *United States of America*; U.S.S.R. – *Union of Soviet Socialist Republics*; Va. – *Virginia*; Venez. – *Venezuela*; volc. – *volcano*; Vt. – *Vermont*; W. – *West, Western*; Wash. – *Washington*; Wilts. – *Wiltshire*; Wis. – *Wisconsin*; Worcs. – *Worcestershire*; Wyo. – *Wyoming*; Yugo. – *Yugoslavia*.

Gazetteer of Canada

	Page	N	W
Abbadie, Mt. d': Yukon		62	134
Abbey: Sask.	24	51	109
Abbotsford: B.C.	27	49	122¼
Aberdeen: Sask.	24	52	106
Aberdeen Lake: N.W.T.	29	65	99
Abitibi: *riv.*, Ont.	17	50	81
Abitibi, Lake: Ont./Qué.	17	49	80
Abitibi Game Reserve: Ont.		48	80
Abloviak Fiord: Qué.	12	59	66
Abord-à-Plouffe: Qué.	21	45	74
Acland Bay: N.W.T.	29	72	101
Acme: Alta.	24	51	114
Aconi, Point: N.S.	15	46	60
Actinolite: Ont.	20	45	77
Acton: Ont.	18	44	80
Acton Vale: Qué.	19	45	72
Adams, Lake: B.C.	27	51	119
Adams Sound: N.W.T.	29	73	84
Adelaide Penin.: N.W.T.	29	68	98
Adlavik Is.: Labr.		55	59
Admiralty Inlet: N.W.T.	29	73	85
Admiralty I.: N.W.T.	29	69	101
Adolphus Reach: Ont.	20	44	77
Agassiz: B.C.	26	49	121
Agawa Bay: Ont.		47	84
Agnew Lake: Ont.	18	46	82
Aguanish: Qué.	14	50	62
Aguanus: *riv.*, Qué.	13	51	62
Agu Bay: N.W.T.	29	70	87
Ahousat: B.C.		49	126
Aigneau: *riv.*, Qué.		57	70
Aigneau, Lac: Qué.		57	70
Aillik: Labr.		55	59
Ainslie, Lake: N.S.	15	46	61
Ainsworth: B.C.	27	49	117
Airdrie: Alta.	30	51¼	114
Air Force I.: N.W.T.	12	68	75
Aishihik Lake: Yukon	28	62	138
Aiyansh: B.C.	26	55	129
Ajax: Ont.	20	44	79
Akimiski I.: N.W.T.	16	53	81
Aklavik: N.W.T.	28	68	135
Akpatok I.: Qué.	12	60	68
Alameda: Sask.	25	49	102
Alaskan Highway: Canada/U.S.A.	2	—	—
Albanel: Qué.	14	49	72
Albanel, Lac: Qué.	13	51	73
Albany, *riv.*, Ont.	17	51	85
Alberni: B.C.	26	49	125
Albert: N.B.	15	46	65
Alberta: *Prov.*, (*cap.* Edmonton)	24	—	—
Albert Edward Bay: N.W.T.	29	69	103
Alberton: P.E.I.	15	47	64
Albion: B.C.	27	49¼	122½
Albreda: B.C.	27	53	119
Aldergrove: B.C.	27	49	122½
Alderson: Alta.	24	50	111
Aldouane: N.B.	15	47	65
Alert: N.W.T.	3	83	63
Alert Bay: *town*, B.C.		50	127
Alexandra Falls: N.W.T.		60	116
Alexandria: B.C.	27	52	122
Alexandria: Ont.	21	45	75
Alexis: *riv.*, Labr.		53	57
Alexis Creek: *town*, B.C.	27	52	123
Aleza Lake: *town*, B.C.	27	54	122
Alfred: Ont.	21	46	75
Alfred, Mt.: B.C.	26	50	124
Algonquin Park: *town*, Ont.		46	79
Algonquin Prov. Park: Ont.	18	46	78
Alix: Alta.	24	52	113
Allandale: Ont.	20	44	80
Allanwater: Ont.		50	90
Allard Falls: Qué.	19	48	74
Allard, Lac: Qué.	13	51	64
Allenford: Ont.		44	81
Allison Harbour: B.C.	26	51	127
Alliston: Ont.	20	44	80
Allumettes, Ile aux: Qué.		46	77
Alma: N.B.	15	45	65
Almonte: Ont.	30	45½	76¼
Alouette Lake: *and riv.*, British Columbia	26	49	122
Alsask: Sask.	24	51	110
Alsek: *riv.*, Yukon		60	138
Alsek Range: Yukon		59	137
Alta Lake: *town*, B.C.	26	50	123
Altona: Man.	25	49	97
Alvin: B.C.	26	50	122
Amadjuak Lake: N.W.T.	12	65	71
Amaranth: Man.	25	51	99
Ameliasburgh: Ont.	20	44	77
Amery: Man.	25	56	94
Amherst: N.S.	15	46	64
Amherstburg: Ont.	18	42	83
Amherst I.: Ont.	20	44	77
Amherst I.: Qué.	14	47	62
Amherst View: Ont.	19	44	77
Amisk Lake: Sask.	25	54	102
Amitoke Penin.: N.W.T.	29	68	82
Amos: Qué.	18	48	78
Amqui: Qué.	14	48	68
Amund Ringnes I.: N.W.T.	1	78	97
Amundsen Gulf: N.W.T.	28	71	123
Amyot: Ont.		48	85
Anahim Lake: *town*, B.C.	27	52	125
Ancaster: Ont.	20	43	80
Ancienne Lorette: Qué.	30	46¾	71¼
Anderson: *riv.*, N.W.T.	28	69	128
Anderson Lake: B.C.	26	50	122
Andrew: Alta.	24	54	112
Andrew Gordon Bay: N.W.T.	12	64	75
Aneroid: Sask.	24	50	107
Angers: Qué.	21	45	75
Angijak I.: N.W.T.	12	66	62
Angikuni Lake: N.W.T.	29	62	100
Angliers: Qué.	18	47	79
Anguille, Cape: Nfld.	15	48	59
Angus: Ont.	20	44	80
Annapolis Royal: N.S.	15	45	66
Annieopsquotch Mts.: Nfld.		48	57
Anson: Ont.	20	44	78
Anstruther Lake: Ont.	20	45	78
Anticosti I.: Qué.	14	49	63
Antigonish: N.S.	15	46	62
Anuk Lake: Qué.		59	75
Anvil Mts.: Yukon	28	62	133
Anyox: B.C.	26	55	130
Apple River: *town*, N.S.	15	45	65
Apsley: Ont.	20	45	78
Arborfield: Sask.	25	53	103
Arborg: Man.	25	51	97
Arcola: Sask.	25	50	103
Arctic Red: *riv. & town*, N.W.T.	28	67	134
Ardbeg: Ont.	20	46	80
Arden: Ont.	20	45	77
Ardrossan: Alta.	30	53½	113¼
Argentia: Nfld.	15	47	54
Argyle: Man.	30	50¼	97½
Argyle: N.S.	15	44	66
Arichat: N.S.	15	45	61
Aristazabal I.: B.C.	26	53	129
Armour: Sask.	30	50¼	104¾
Armstrong: B.C.	27	50	119
Armstrong: Ont.	17	50	89
Arnold's Cove: Nfld.		48	54
Arnot: Man.	25	56	97
Arnprior: Ont.	21	45	76
Arntfield: Qué.	18	48	79
Arrowhead: B.C.	27	51	118
Arrow Dam: B.C.	27	49	118
Arrow River: *town*, Man.	25	50	101
Arrowsmith, Mt.: B.C.	26	49	124
Arrowwood: Alta.	24	51	113
Arthabaska: Qué.	19	46	72
Arthur: Ont.	18	44	80
Artillery Lake: N.W.T.	29	63	108
Arvida: Qué.	19	48	71
Asbestos: Qué.	19	46	72
Ascot Corner: Qué.	19	45	72
Ashcroft: B.C.	27	51	121
Asheweig: *riv.*, Ont.	16	54	90
Ashton: Ont.	21	45	76
Ashuanipi: Labr.		53	66
Ashuanipi Lake: Labr.	13	53	66
Ashuapmuchuan: *riv.*, Qué.	14	49	73
Ashville: Man.	25	51	100
Aspen Grove: B.C.		50	121
Aspy Bay: N.S.	15	47	60
Assiniboia: Sask.	25	49	106
Assiniboine: *riv.*, Sask./Man.	25	50	99
Assiniboine, Mt.: Alta./B.C.	27	51	116
Assinica Lake: Qué.	13	50	75
Assumption: Alta.	24	59	119
Aston Bay: N.W.T.	29	74	95
Aston Junction: Qué.		46	72
Astray Lake: Labr.		55	67
Athabasca: & *riv.*, Alta.	24	55	113
Athabasca, Lake: Alberta/Saskatchewan	24	59	109
Athalmer: B.C.	27	51	116
Athelstan: Qué.	21	45	74
Athens: Ont.	21	45	76
Atherley: Ont.	20	45	79
Athol: N.S.	15	46	64
Atikokan: Ont.	17	48	91
Atikonak Lake: Labr.	13	53	64
Atikup: Ont.	16	53	91
Atikwa Lake: Ont.	17	50	93
Atim Creek: *riv.*, Alta.	30	53¼	114
Atlin: & *lake*, B.C.	22	59	134
Atna Peak: B.C.	26	54	128
Attachie: B.C.	27	56	122
Attawapiskat: & *riv.*, Ont.	16	53	82
Attawapiskat Lake: Ont.	17	52	88
Attikamagen Lake: Labr.	13	55	66
Attikuan Point: Qué.		54	79
Aubert, Lac.: Qué.		55	71
Aubrey Falls: Ont.	18	47	83
Aubry Lake: N.W.T.	28	67	126
Aulneau Penin.: Ont.	25	49	94
Aurora: Ont.	20	44	79
Austin Channel: N.W.T.	29	75	103
Authier: Qué.		48	79
Aux Outardes: *riv.*, Qué.	13	49	68
Aux Pekans: *riv.*, Qué.		53	67
Aux Sables: *riv. & lake*, Ont.	18	46	82
Avalon, Isthmus of: Nfld.		48	54
Avalon Penin.: Nfld.	15	47	53
Aviron Bay: *town*, Nfld.		47	57
Avola: B.C.	27	52	119
Avon: *riv.*, N.S.	15	45	64
Avonhurst: Sask.	30	50¾	104¼
Avonlea: Sask.	25	50	105
Avonmore: Ont.	21	45	75
Axel Heiberg I.: N.W.T.	3	80	90
Aylen Lake: Ont.		46	78
Aylesford: N.S.	15	45	65
Aylesworth, Mt.: U.S.A./Canada		60	139
Aylmer: Ont.	18	43	81
Aylmer: Qué.	30	45½	75¾
Aylmer, Lake: N.W.T.	29	64	110
Aylmer, Lake: Qué.	19	46	71
Aylmer, Mt.: Alta.	24	51	115
Aylsham: Sask.	25	53	104
Ayton: Ont.		44	81
Azure Lake: B.C.	27	52	120
Babine Lake: B.C.	27	55	126
Bacalieu I.: Nfld.		48	53
Back: *riv.*, N.W.T.	29	65	105
Backbone Ranges: N.W.T.	28	63	129
Baddeck: N.S.	15	46	61
Baden: Ont.	18	43	81
Badger: Nfld.	15	49	56
Baffin Bay: Canada/Grnld.	3	73	70
Baffin I.: N.W.T.	3	70	75
Bagotville: Qué.	19	48	71
Baie Comeau: Qué.	14	49	68
Baie des Sables: Qué.		48	68
Baie du Poste: Qué.	13	50	74
Baie Ste. Catherine: Qué.		48	70
Baie Ste. Claire: Anticosti I.	14	50	64
Baie St. Paul: Qué.	19	47	70
Bailey: N.B.	15	45	66
Baillie: *riv.*, N.W.T.	29	65	106
Baillie Hamilton I.: N.W.T.	29	76	95
Baillie Is.: N.W.T.	28	71	128
Baine Harbour: Nfld.		47	55
Baird Penin.: N.W.T.	12	69	76
Baker Lake: & *settlement*, N.W.T.	29	64	96
Bakers Dozen Is.: N.W.T.	16	57	79
Bala: Ont.	20	45	80
Balcarres: Sask.	25	51	104
Baldock Lake: Man.	25	56	98
Balgonie: Sask.	30	50½	104¼
Baljennie: Sask.	24	53	108
Ballard, Cape: Nfld.		47	53
Balsam Lake: Ont.	20	45	79
Balzac: Alta.	30	51¼	114
Bamfield: B.C.	26	49	125
Bancroft: Ont.	18	45	78
Banff: Alta.	24	51	116
Banff National Park: Alta.	24	51	116
Banks I.: B.C.	26	53	130
Banks I.: N.W.T.	28	73	120
Bannockburn: Ont.	20	45	78
Baptiste Lake: Ont.		45	78
Baring, Cape: N.W.T.	28	70	117
Barkerville: B.C.	27	53	121
Bark Lake: Ont.		45	78
Bark Lake: Ont.	18	47	82
Bark Lake: Qué.	19	47	76
Barkley Sound: B.C.	26	49	125
Barons: Alta.	24	50	113
Barraute: Qué.	18	48	77
Barrhead: Alta.	24	54	114
Barrie: Ont.	20	44	80
Barrie I.: Ont.	18	46	82
Barriere: B.C.	27	51	120
Barrière Dam: Qué.	19	47	76
Barrington: N.S.	15	43	66
Barrington Lake: Man.	25	57	100
Barrow Head: Nfld.		49	54
Barrow Str.: N.W.T.	29	74	93

	Page	N	W
Barrys Bay: *town*, Ont.	18	45	78
Barton Lake: Ont.	25	52	94
Bashaw: Alta.	24	53	113
Basin Lake: Sask.	25	52	105
Baskatong Reservoir: Qué.	19	47	76
Bassano: Alta.	24	51	112
Basseterre Pt.: Nfld.		47	56
Basswood L.: Ont.		48	92
Batchawana: & *riv.*, Ont.	18	47	84
Batchawana, Mt.: Ont.	18	47	84
Bath: N.B.	14	46	67
Bath: Ont.	20	44	77
Bathurst: N.B.	14	47	66
Bathurst, Cape: N.W.T.	28	71	128
Bathurst Inlet: *settlement*, N.W.T.	29	67	108
Bathurst I.: N.W.T.	29	76	100
Batiscan: Qué.		46	72
Batiscan: *riv.*, Qué.	19	47	72
Batteau: Labr.		53	56
Battle: *riv.*, Alta.	24	53	110
Battleford: Sask.	24	53	108
Battle Harbour: Labr.	13	52	56
Bauld, Cape: Nfld.		51	55
Bawlf: Alta.	24	53	112
Bay Bulls: Nfld.	30	47¼	52¾
Bay de Verde: *town*, Nfld.		48	53
Bayfield: & *riv.*, Ont.	18	43	82
Bay Roberts: Nfld.	30	47½	53¼
Bays, Lake of: Ont.	18	45	79
Bazin: *riv.*, Qué.	19	48	75
Beachburg: Ont.	19	46	77
Beaconsfield: Qué.	21	45½	73¾
Beale, Cape: B.C.	26	49	125
Bear, Cape: P.E.I.	15	46	62
Bear Bay: N.W.T.	29	76	87
Bear Brook: *riv.*, Ont.	30	45¼	75¼
Bear Creek: Ont.	18	43	82
Beardmore: Ont.		50	88
Bear Head: Anticosti I.	14	49	62
Bear I.: Nfld.		47	57
Bear I.: N.W.T.	16	54	80
Bear Lake: *town*, B.C.	27	56	127
Bear Lake: Man.	25	55	96
Bear River: *town*, N.S.	15	45	66
Bearskin Lake: Ont.		54	91
Beatton: *riv.*, B.C.	27	57	121
Beauce, Lac à: Qué.	19	47	73
Beauceville: Qué.	19	46	71
Beauchêne: Qué.	18	46	79
Beaufort Sea: Arctic O.	2	73	140
Beauharnois: Qué.	21	45	74
Beauharnois Canal: Qué.	21	45	74
Beaumont: Nfld.		50	56
Beaumont: Qué.	30	46¾	71
Beauport: Qué.	30	46¾	71¼
Beaupré: Qué.	30	47	71
Beauséjour: Man.	30	50	96½
Beauval: Sask.	24	55	108
Beaver: *riv.*, Ont.	23	56	88
Beaver: *riv.*, Sask.	24	55	108
Beaver Bank: N.S.	30	44¾	63¾
Beaverdell: B.C.	27	49	119
Beaverhill Lake: Alta.	24	53	112
Beaverhill Lake: Man.	25	54	95
Beaverlodge: Alta.	24	55	119
Beaverlodge: Sask.	24	59	108
Beavermouth: B.C.	27	51	117
Beaverton: Ont.	20	44	79
Bécancour: & *riv.*, Qué.	19	46	72
Beddington: Alta.	30	51¼	114
Bedford: N.S.	30	44¾	63¾
Bedford: Qué.	19	45	73
Bednesti: B.C.	27	54	123
Beechey Head: B.C.	26	48	123
Beeton: Ont.	20	44	80
Beiseker: Alta.	24	51	114
Belcher Is.: N.W.T.	16	56	79
Belcourt: Qué.	18	48	77
Bell: *riv.*, Qué.		50	77
Bella Bella: B.C.	26	52	128
Bella Coola: & *riv.*, B.C.	27	52	127
Belle Bay: Nfld.	15	47	55
Belledune: N.B.	15	48	66
Belle Isle: Nfld.	13	52	55
Belle Isle, Str. of: Labr./Nfld.	13	51	57
Belleoram: Nfld.	15	47	55
Belle River: Ont.	18	42	83
Belleterre: Qué.	18	47	79
Belleville: Ont.	20	44	77
Bellevue: Alta.	24	50	114
Bellevue: Nfld.		47	54
Bell I.: Nfld.	30	47¾	53
Bell I.: Nfld.	13	51	55
Bellot Str.: N.W.T.	29	72	95
Belloy: Alta.	24	56	118
Bell Penin.: N.W.T.	12	64	82
Bells Corners: Ont.	30	45¼	75¾
Belly: *riv.*, Alta.	24	49	113
Belmont: N.S.	15	45	63
Beloeil: Qué.	21	46	73
Belot, Lac: N.W.T.	28	67	127
Bengough: Sask.	25	49	105
Benito: Man.	25	52	101
Bennett: B.C.	22	60	135
Bennett Lake: Yukon/B.C.		60	135
Bentley: Alta.	24	52	114
Berkley, Cape: N.W.T.	29	74	101
Berens River: *town & riv.*, Manitoba	25	52	97
Bereziuk Lake: Qué.		54	76
Berlinguet Inlet: N.W.T.	29	71	86
Bermen, Lake: Qué.	13	53	69
Bernard Lake: Ont.	20	46	79
Bernier Bay: N.W.T.	29	71	88
Bernierville: Qué.	19	46	74
Berrys Mills: N.B.	15	46	65
Berté, Lac: Qué.		51	68
Berthierville: Qué.	19	46	73
Berwick: N.S.	15	45	65
Berwyn: Alta.	24	56	118
Bethany: Ont.	20	44	79
Bethune: Sask.	15	51	105
Betsiamites: & *riv.*, Qué.	17	49	69
Beverly: Alta.	30	53½	113½
Beverly Lake: N.W.T.	29	65	100
Bewdley: Ont.	20	44	78
Bic: Qué.		48	69
Bield: Man.	25	51	101
Bienfait: Sask.	25	49	103
Bienville, Lac: Qué.	13	55	73
Big: *riv.*, Labr.		55	59
Big Bay Point: Lake Simcoe	20	44	79
Big Bear Falls: Qué.		48	73
Big Beaver Falls: Ont.		49	82
Big Beaver House: Ont.	16	53	90
Biggar: Sask.	24	52	108
Big Gull Lake: Ont.	20	45	77
Big Indian Lake: N.S.	30	44¾	64
Big I.: Labr.		58	62
Big I.: Great Slave Lake, N.W.T.	28	61	117
Big I.: N.W.T.	28	63	71
Big I.: Qué.		58	67
Big Lake: Alta.	30	53½	113¾
Big Muddy Creek: Canada/U.S.A.		48	104
Big Muddy Lake: Sask.	25	49	105
Big River: *town*, Sask.	24	54	107
Big Salmon: & *riv.*, Yukon		62	135
Big Sand Lake: Man.	25	58	99
Big Stick Lake: Sask.	24	50	109
Bigstone Lake: Man.	25	54	96
Big Trout Lake: Ont.		46	79
Big Trout Lake: Ont.	16	54	90
Big Valley: *town*, Alta	24	52	113
Bigwood: Ont.	18	46	80
Billings, Mt.: Yukon		61	129
Bilodeau: Qué.		48	72
Binscarth: Man.	25	50	101
Birch: *riv.*, Alta.	24	58	113
Birch Hills: *town*, Sask.	25	53	105
Birch Island: *town*, Ont.	18	46	82
Birch Lake: Alta.	24	53	112
Birch Lake: Labr.		54	66
Birch Mtns.: Alta.	24	57	113
Bird Creek: *town*, Ont.		45	78
Bird Rocks: *i.*, Qué.	15	48	61
Birds Hill: Man.	30	50	97
Birken: B.C.	26	50	122
Birtle: Man.	25	50	101
Biscotasing: Ont.		47	82
Bishops Falls: *town*, Nfld.	15	49	55
Biskotasi Lake: Ont.	18	47	82
Bissett: Ont.	18	46	78
Bistcho Lake: Alta.	22	60	119
Bittern Lake: *town*, Alta.		53	113
Bittern Lake: Sask.	25	54	106
Bitumount: Alta.		57	112
Bizard, I.: Qué.	21	45½	74
Black: *riv.*, Ont.	18	48	80
Black: *riv.*, Qué.	18	46	77
Black, Mt.: Yukon		61	134
Black Bay: Ont.		48	88
Black Bear Bay: *town*, Labr.		53	56
Black Bear Island Lake: Saskatchewan	25	55	105
Black Birch Lake: Sask.	24	57	108
Black Diamond: Alta.	24	51	114
Blackfalds: Alta.	24	52	114
Blackhead Bay: Nfld.		48	53
Blackie: Alta.	24	51	114
Black I.: Man.	25	51	96
Black Lake: *town*, Qué.	19	46	71
Black Lake: Sask.	25	59	105
Blackmud Creek: *riv.*, Alta.	30	53½	113½
Black Pool: B.C.	27	51	120
Black Rock Point: Labr.		60	64
Blackville: N.B.	14	47	66
Blackwater: Ont.	20	44	79
Blackwater Lake: N.W.T.	28	64	123
Blaine Lake: *town*, Sask.	24	53	107
Blairmore: Alta.	24	50	114
Blakeney: Ont.	30	45¼	76¼
Blanc Sablon: Qué.		51	57
Blanche: *riv.*, Qué.	30	45½	75¾
Blenheim: Ont.	18	42	82
Blind Channel: *town*, B.C.	26	50	125
Blind River: *town*, Ont.	18	46	83
Bloedel: B.C.	26	50	125
Bloodvein: *riv.*, Man.	25	52	96
Bloomfield: Ont.	20	44	77
Bloomfield: P.E.I.	15	47	64
Blubber Bay: *town*, B.C.	26	50	125
Blue Mt.: Nfld.	15	50	57
Blue Mt.: Ont.	18	44	80
Bluenose Lake: N.W.T.	28	68	119
Blue Ridge: *town*, Alta.	24	54	115
Blue River: *town*, B.C.	27	52	119
Bluff, Cape: Labr.		53	56
Blyth: Ont.	18	44	81
Boat Basin: *town*, B.C.		49	126
Bobcaygeon: Ont.	20	45	79
Bobs Lake: Ont.	21	45	77
Bodo: Alta.	24	52	110
Boiestown: N.B.	14	46	66
Bois, Lac des: N.W.T.	28	67	126
Boissevain: Man.	25	49	100
Boivin, Lake: Qué.		52	70
Boland: *riv.*, Ont.	18	46	82
Bolger: Qué.		48	76
Bolkow: Ont.	18	48	84
Bolton: Ont.	20	44	80
Bonar Law: Ont.	20	44	78
Bonaventure: Qué.	14	48	65
Bonaventure Head: Nfld.		48	53
Bonaventure I.: Qué.	14	48	64
Bonavista: Nfld.	15	49	53
Bonavista Bay: Nfld.	15	49	53
Bonfield: Ont.	18	46	79
Bonne Bay: Nfld.	15	49	58
Bonnechère: *riv.*, Ont.	19	45	77
Bonnet, Lac du: Man.	25	50	96
Bonnet Plume: *riv.*, Yukon	28	65	133
Bonnyville: Alta.	24	54	111
Boothia Penin.: N.W.T.	3	72	95
Boothia, G. of: N.W.T.	29	70	90
Borden: P.E.I.	15	46	64
Borden I.: N.W.T.	2	78	110
Borden Penin.: N.W.T.	29	73	82
Boston Creek: *town*, Ont.	18	48	80
Bostonnais: *riv.*, Qué.	19	47	72
Botwood: Nfld.	15	49	55
Boucherville: & *is.*, Qué.	21	46	73
Boundary: B.C.	26	57	132
Boundary Bay: B.C.	27	49	123
Boundary Ranges: U.S.A./Canada		59	134
Bourget: Ont.	30	45¼	75¼
Bourkes: Ont.	18	48	80
Bourlamaque: Qué.	13	48	78
Bourmont: Qué.		48	76
~~Bow: *riv.*, Alta.~~	~~24~~	~~51~~	~~114~~
Bowden: Alta.	24	52	114
Bowdoin Canyon: Labr.		53	64
Bowen I.: B.C.	26	49	123
Bowesville: Ont.	21	45	76
Bow Island: *town*, Alta.	24	50	111
Bowman, Lac: Qué.	21	46	76
Bowman Bay: N.W.T.	12	66	74
Bowmanville: Ont.	20	44	79
Bowness: Alta.	30	51	114½
Bowser: B.C.	26	49	125
Boxey Point: Nfld.		47	56
Boyd Lake: N.W.T.		61	103
Boyd Lake: Qué.		53	77
Boylston: N.S.	15	45	61
Bracebridge: Ont.	20	45	79
Brackendale: B.C.	26	50	123
Bradford: Ont.	20	44	80
Brady Ranch: B.C.	27	57	123
Braeburn: Yukon		61	136
Braeside: Ont.	21	45	76
Bragg Creek: Alta.	30	51	114½
Bralorne: B.C.	26	51	123
Brampton: Ont.	20	44	80
Branch: Nfld.	15	47	54
Brandon: Man.	25	50	100
Brantford: Ont.	18	43	80
Bras d'Or Lake: N.S.	15	46	61
Bray I.: N.W.T.	12	69	77
Brazeau: Alta.	24	52	116
Brazeau: *riv.*, Alta.	24	53	116
Brazeau, Mt.: Alta.	24	53	117
Brazil Lake: *town*, N.S.	15	44	66
Brazil Pond: Nfld.		48	56
Breakeyville: Qué.	30	46¾	71¼
Brechin: Ont.	20	45	79
Bredenbury: Sask.	25	51	102
Bremner: Alta.	30	53½	113¼
Brent: Ont.		46	78
Breton, Cape: N.S.	15	46	60
Bretona: Alta.	30	53½	113¼
Brew Mt.: B.C.	26	50	122
Briconnet, Lac: Qué.		51	60
Bridge: *riv.*, B.C.	26	51	122
Bridgetown: N.S.	15	45	65
Bridgewater: N.S.	15	44	64
Bridgman Mts.: Qué.		58	65
Brier I.: N.S.	15	44	66
Brig Bay: *town*, Nfld.		51	57
Brighton: Ont.	20	44	78
Brigus: Nfld.	30	47½	53¼
Brigus Junction: Nfld.	30	47½	53¼
Brion I.: Qué.	15	48	61
Brisay, Lac: Qué.		54	70
Bristol: N.B.	14	46	67
Britannia Beach: B.C.	26	50	123
British Columbia: *Prov.*, (*cap.* Victoria)	26/27	—	—
British Mts.: Can./U.S.A.	28	69	140
Britt: Ont.	18	46	80
Broadback: *riv.*, Qué.		51	78
Broadview: Sask.	25	50	102
Brochet: Man.	25	58	101
Brochet, Lac: Man.	25	59	101
Brochet, Lac: Qué.		49	69
Brochu, Lac: Qué.	19	48	75
Brock I.: N.W.T.	1	78	115
Brockville: Ont.	21	45	76
Brodeur Penin.: N.W.T.	29	73	87
Bromptonville: Qué.	19	45	72
Bronte: Ont.	20	43	80
Brookfield: N.S.	15	45	63
Brooklands: Man.	30	50	97¼
Brooklin: Ont.	20	44	79
Brookmere: B.C.	26	50	121
Brooks: Alta.	24	50	112
Brooks Penin.: B.C.	26	50	127
Broughton I.: B.C.	27	51	127
Broughton I.: N.W.T.		57	77
Brower: Ont.		49	81
Browne Bay: N.W.T.		73	98
Brown Lake: N.W.T.	29	66	92
Brownsburg: Qué.	21	46	74
Bruce Mines: Ont.	18	46	84
Bruce Peninsula: Ont.	18	45	81
Bruce Point: P.E.I.	15	46	62
Bruderheim: Alta.	30	53¾	113
Brûlé Lake: *town*, Ont.		46	79
Brunette I.: Nfld.		47	56
Bruno: Sask.	25	52	106
Brunswick Lake: Ont.		49	83
Brussels: Ont.	18	43	81
Bryde, Mt.: Yukon		60	133
Brysoné: Qué.	21	46	77
Buchans: Nfld.	15	49	57
Buchans Junction: Nfld.		49	56
Buckhorn Lake: Ont.	20	44	78
Buckingham: Qué.	30	45½	75½
Buctouche: N.B.	15	46	65
Buffalo: Alta.	24	51	111
Buffalo: *riv.*, Alta.	24	59	114
Buffalo Head Hills: Alta.	24	57	116
Buffalo Lake: Alta.	24	52	113
Buffalo Lake: N.W.T.	28	60	116
Buffalo Narrows: *town*, Saskatchewan	24	57	108
Buffalo River: *town*, N.W.T.	28	61	115
Bulkley: *riv.*, B.C.	26	55	127
Bulyea: Sask.	25	51	105
Burden, Mt.: B.C.	27	56	123
Burdett: Alta.	24	50	112
Bureau, Lac: Qué.	19	48	75
Burford: Alta.	30	53¼	114
Burgeo: Nfld.	15	48	58
Burin: & *penin.*, Nfld.	15	47	55
Burketon Station: Ont.	20	44	79
Burks Falls: *town*, Ont.	20	46	79
Burleigh Falls: Ont.	20	45	78
Burlington: Ont.	20	43	80
Burlington Beach: Ont.	20	43	80
Burnaby: B.C.	27	49¼	123
Burnside: Nfld.		49	54
Burnside: *riv.*, N.W.T.	29	66	110
Burns Lake: *town*, B.C.	27	54	126
Burnt Creek: *town*, Qué.		55	67
Burnt Lake: Qué.	13	52	64
Burnt River: *town*, Ont.	20	45	79
Burntroot Lake: Ont.		46	79
Burntwood: *riv.*, Man.	25	55	100
Burrard Inlet: B.C.	27	49¼	123¼
Burton Lake: Qué.		55	78
Burwash: Ont.	18	46	81
Burwash Landing: Yukon	28	61	139
Busby: Alta.	24	54	114
Bute Inlet: B.C.	26	50	125
Butter Pot Prov. Pk.: Nfld.	30	47½	53
Buttle Lake: B.C.	26	49	125
Button Bay: Man.	25	59	94
Button Is.: Qué.		60	65
Byam Channel: N.W.T.	29	75	105
Byam Martin I.: & *Chan.*, N.W.T.	29	75	104
Bylot I.: N.W.T.	29	73	78
Byng Inlet: *town*, Ont.	18	46	80
Byron Bay: Labr.		55	58
Cabano: Qué.	14	48	69
Cabonga Reservoir: & *dam*, Québec	19	47	76
Cabot Head: Ont.	18	45	81
Cabot Lake: Qué.		55	64
Cabot Strait: N.S./Nfld.	13	47	60
Cabri: Sask.	24	51	108
Cache Bay: *town*, Ont.	18	46	80
Cache Creek: *town*, B.C.		51	121
Cadillac: Qué.	18	48	79
Cadillac: Sask.	24	50	108
Cairns Lake: Ont.	25	52	94
Calabogie: & *lake*, Ont.	19	45	77
Calahoo: Alta.	30	53¾	114
Caledonia: N.S.	15	44	65
Caledonia: Ont.	18	43	80
Calgary: Alta.	30	51	114
Callander: Ont.	18	46	80
Calling Lake: Alta.	24	55	113
Calmar: Alta.	30	53¼	113¾
Calumet: Qué.		46	77
Calumet I.: Qué.		46	77
Calvert I.: B.C.	26	51	128
Camachigama Lake: Qué.	19	48	76
Cambrian Lake: Qué.		56	69
Cambridge Bay: *settlement*, N.W.T.	29	69	105
Cameron Falls: Ont.		49	88
Cameron Hills: N.W.T.	22	60	120
Cameron I.: N.W.T.	29	76	104
Campbell: Alta.	24	54	114
Campbell, Mt.: Yukon	28	64	139
Campbellford: Ont.	20	44	78
Campbell River: *town*, B.C.	26	50	125
Campbells Bay: Qué.	20	46	77
Campbellton (Sherwood Park): Alberta	30	53½	113¼
Campbellton: N.B.	14	48	67
Campbellton: Nfld.		49	55
Camp Borden: Ont.	18	44	80
Camperville: Man.	25	52	100
Camp Gagetown: N.B.	15	45	66
Campobello I.: N.B.	15	45	67
Camrose: Alta.	24	53	113
Camsell Range: N.W.T.	28	62	124
Canaan Station: N.B.	15	46	65
Canada Bay: Nfld.		51	56
Canairiktok: *riv.*, Labr.	13	55	61
Candle Lake: *town*, Sask.	25	54	105
Canfield: Ont.	18	43	80
Canford: B.C.	26	50	121
Canica: *i.*, Qué.		49	77
Cann: Qué.	19	48	74
Cannell: Alta.	30	53½	113¾

	Page	N	W
Canning: N.S.	**15**	45	64
Cannington: Ont.	**20**	44	79
Canoe: *riv.*, B.C.	**27**	52	119
Canoe Lake: Sask.	**24**	55	108
Canora: Sask.	**25**	52	102
Canso: & *cape*, N.S.	**15**	45	61
Canso Causeway: N.S.	**15**	45	61
Canton Bégin: Qué.		48	71
Canyon: Yukon		61	137
Canyon Ranges: N.W.T.	**28**	63	128
Caopacho Lake: Qué.		52	66
Cap à l'Aigle: Qué.	**19**	47	70
Cap Chat: Qué.	**14**	49	67
Cap de la Madeleine: Qué.	**19**	46	72
Cape Breton Highlands Nat. Park: Nova Scotia	**15**	47	61
Cape Breton I.: N.S.	**15**	46	61
Cape Broyle: Nfld.		47	53
Cape Chidley Is.: Québec/Labrador		60	65
Cape Dorset: N.W.T.	**12**	64	77
Cape Dyer: *settlement*, N.W.T.	**12**	66	62
Cape North: N.S.	**15**	47	60
Cape St. Charles: Labr.		52	56
Cape St. George: Nfld.	**15**	48	59
Cape Smith: N.W.T.	**12**	61	78
Cape Smoky: N.S.	**15**	47	60
Cape Tormentine: N.B.	**15**	46	64
Capitachouane: *riv.*, Qué.	**19**	48	76
Capitachouane, Lac: Qué.	**19**	48	76
Capreol: Ont.	**18**	47	81
Cap-Rouge: Qué.	**30**	46¾	71¼
Capstick: N.S.		47	61
Caraquet: N.B.	**14**	48	65
Carberry: Man.	**25**	50	99
Carbon: Alta.	**24**	51	113
Carbondale: Alta.	**30**	53¾	113½
Carbonear: Nfld.	**30**	47¾	53¼
Carcajou: Alta.		58	117
Carcross: Yukon	**28**	60	135
Cardiff: Alta.	**30**	53¾	113½
Cardigan: P.E.I.	**15**	46	63
Cardinal: Ont.	**21**	45	75
Cardross: Sask.	**25**	50	106
Cardston: Alta.	**24**	49	113
Cargill: Ont.		44	81
Cariboo Mtns.: B.C.	**27**	53	121
Caribou: Man.	**25**	59	98
Caribou: *riv.*, Man.	**25**	59	95
Caribou Hide: B.C.	**26**	57	127
Caribou I.: N.S.	**15**	46	63
Caribou I.: Ont.	**17**	47	86
Caribou Lake: Ont.		50	89
Caribou Mtns.: Alta.	**24**	59	115
Carillon: Qué.	**21**	46	74
Carleton: Qué.	**14**	48	66
Carleton, Mt.: N.B.	**14**	47	67
Carleton Place: Ont.	**30**	45¼	76¼
Carleton Point: Anticosti I.	**14**	50	62
Carlton: Sask.	**24**	53	106
Carlyle: Sask.	**25**	50	102
Carmacks: Yukon	**28**	62	137
Carman: Man.	**25**	49	98
Carmangay: Alta.	**24**	50	113
Carmanville: Nfld.	**15**	49	54
Carmel: Qué.		46	72
Carnduff: Sask.	**25**	49	102
Carnwath: *riv.*, N.W.T.	**28**	67	127
Carp: Ont.	**30**	45¼	76
Carp Lake: B.C.	**27**	55	123
Carrière, Lac: Qué.	**18**	48	78
Carrot: *riv.*, Man.	**25**	55	96
Carrot River: & *riv.*, Sask.	**25**	53	103
Carruthers: Sask.	**24**	53	109
Carseland: Alta.	**30**	50¾	113½
Carstairs: Alta.	**24**	52	114
Cartier: Ont.	**18**	47	81
Cartmel Mt.: B.C.	**26**	58	129
Cartwright: Labr.	**13**	53	57
Cartwright: Man.	**25**	49	99
Cascade Range: Can./U.S.A.	**26**	49	121
Casey: Qué.	**19**	48	74
Casse, Lac: Qué.		49	70
Casselman: Ont.	**21**	45	75
Cassiar: B.C.	**22**	59	130
Cassiar Mtns.: B.C.	**22**	59	130
Castel Bay: N.W.T.	**28**	74	120
Castelgar: B.C.	**27**	49	118
Castle I.: N.W.T.		56	77
Castleton: Ont.	**20**	44	78
Castor: Alta.	**24**	52	112
Castor: *riv.*, Ont.	**30**	45¼	75¼
Casummit Lake: *town*, Ont.		51	92
Catalina: Nfld.	**15**	48	53
Catchacoma Lake: Ont.	**20**	45	78
Caughnawaga: Qué.	**21**	45¼	73¾
Causapscal: Qué.	**14**	48	67
Cayuga: Ont.	**18**	43	80
Cecil Lake: *town*, B.C.	**27**	56	120
Cedar Lake: Man.	**25**	53	100
Cedar Lake: Ont.	**18**	46	78
Cedarvale: B.C.	**26**	55	128
Ceepeecee: B.C.		50	127
Central Butte: Sask.	**24**	51	107
Central Patricia: Ont.		51	90
Centreville: N.S.	**15**	44	66
Centreville: N.S.	**15**	45	65
Cereal: Alta.	**24**	51	111
Ceylon: Sask.	**25**	49	105
Chaillon, Cape: Ont.		48	85
Chakonipau Lake: Qué.		56	68
Chaleur Bay: Que./N.B.	**14**	48	65
Chalk River: *town*, Ont.	**18**	46	77
Chambly: Qué.	**21**	45	73
Chambord: Qué.	**14**	48	72

	Page	N	W
Chamcook: N.B.		45	67
Chamiss Bay: *town*, B.C.	**26**	50	128
Chamouchouane: *riv.*, Qué.	**13**	50	73
Champagne: Yukon		60	136
Champcoeur: Qué.		49	78
Champdoré, Lac: Qué.		56	66
Champion: Alta.	**24**	50	113
Champneuf: Qué.	**18**	49	78
Chandler: Qué.	**14**	48	65
Chandos Lake: Ont.	**20**	45	78
Change Island: *town*, Nfld.		50	54
Channel: Nfld.		48	59
Chantrey Inlet: N.W.T.	**29**	67	96
Chapeau: Qué.		46	77
Chapel Arm: Nfld.	**30**	47½	53¾
Chapel I.: Nfld.		48	55
Chapleau: & *riv.*, Ont.	**18**	48	83
Chapleau Game Preserve: Ontario		48	84
Chaplin Lake: Sask.	**24**	50	107
Chapman, Cape: N.W.T.	**29**	69	89
Chard: Alta.		56	111
Charlemagne: Qué.	**21**	46	73
Charlesbourg: Qué.	**30**	46¾	71¼
Charles I.: N.W.T.	**12**	63	74
Charles Lake: Alta.	**24**	60	110
Charleston Lake: Ont.	**21**	45	76
Charlotte Lake: B.C.	**27**	52	125
Charlottetown: Nfld.		48	54
CHARLOTTETOWN: Prince Edward Island	**15**	46	63
Charlton I.: N.W.T.	**17**	52	79
Charny: Qué.	**19**	47	71
Charron Lake: Man.	**25**	53	95
Chase: B.C.		51	120
Chastries, Lake: Qué.		54	68
Châteauguay: Qué.	**21**	45	74
Châteauguay: *riv.*, Qué.		56	70
Châteauguay, Lac: Qué.		56	70
Château-Richer: Qué.	**30**	47	71
Châteauvert, Lac: Qué.	**19**	48	74
Chatham: N.B.	**14**	47	65
Chatham: Ont.	**18**	42	82
Chatham Sound: B.C.	**26**	54	130
Chats, Lac des: Ont./Qué.	**21**	45	76
Chats Falls Dam: Ont./Qué.	**21**	45	76
Chatsworth: Ont.		44	81
Chaudière: *riv.*, Qué.	**30**	46	71
Cheadle: Alta.	**30**	51	113½
Chedabucto Bay: N.S.	**15**	45	61
Chelmsford: Ont.	**18**	47	81
Chelsea: Qué.	**30**	45½	75¾
Chemainus: B.C.	**26**	49	124
Cheminis: Ont.		48	79
Chemung Lake: Ont.	**20**	44	78
Chénéville: Qué.	**21**	46	75
Cherhill: Alta.	**24**	54	115
Chesley: Ont.	**18**	44	81
Chester: N.S.	**15**	45	64
Chesterfield Inlet: & *town*, N.W.T.	**29**	63	91
Chestermere Lake: Alta.	**30**	51	113¾
Chesterville: Ont.	**21**	45	75
Cheticamp: & *cape*, N.S.	**15**	47	61
Chetwynd: B.C.	**27**	56	121
Cheverie: N.S.	**15**	45	64
Chezzetcook: N.S.	**30**	44¾	63¼
Chiblow Lake: Qué.	**18**	46	83
Chibougamau: & *lake*, Qué.	**13**	50	75
Chibougamau: *riv.*, Qué.		50	75
Chicotte: Anticosti I.	**14**	49	63
Chicoutimi: & *riv.*, Qué.	**19**	48	71
Chidley, C.: Qué.	**12**	60	65
Chief Lake: *town*, B.C.	**27**	54	123
Chiefs Point: Ont.	**18**	45	81
Chignecto: *cape & bay*, New Brunswick/N.S.	**15**	45	65
Chigoubiche, Lac: Qué.		49	73
Chilanko Forks: B.C.	**27**	42	124
Chilcotin: *riv.*, B.C.	**27**	52	123
Childs Mines: Ont.		45	78
Chilko Lake: B.C.	**27**	51	124
Chilliwack: B.C.	**26**	49	122
Chilliwack Lake; & *riv.*, B.C.	**26**	49	121
Chinchaga: *riv.*, Alta.	**24**	58	119
Chinook Valley: *town*, Alta.		56	118
Chipai Lake: Ont.	**16**	53	88
Chip Lake: Alta.	**24**	54	115
Chipman: N.B.	**15**	46	66
Chippawa: Ont.	**20**	43	79
Chiputneticook Lakes: Canada/U.S.A.	**14**	45	67
Chisel Lake: Man.	**25**	55	100
Choate: B.C.	**26**	49	121
Chochocauane: *riv.*, Qué.	**19**	47	77
Choiceland: Sask.	**25**	53	104
Chomedey: Qué.	**21**	45½	73¾
Chorkbak Inlet: N.W.T.	**16**	65	74
Chown, Mt.: Alta.	**24**	53	119
Christian I.: Ont.	**18**	45	80
Christie, Mt.: Yukon/N.W.T.	**28**	63	130
Christie Bay: N.W.T.	**29**	62	111
Christina: *riv.*, Alta.	**24**	56	111
Churchill: Man.	**25**	59	94
Churchill: *riv.*, Labr.	**13**	53	64
Churchill: *riv.*, Sask./Man.	**25**	58	95
Churchill, Cape: Man.	**25**	59	93
Churchill Lake: Ont.		51	91
Churchill Lake: Sask.	**24**	56	108
Churchill Peak: B.C.	**22**	58	125
Church Point: *town*, N.S.	**15**	44	66
Chute aux Outardes: Qué.	**14**	49	68
Chutine Landing: B.C.	**26**	57	131
Cirque, Mt.: Labr.	**12**	59	64
City View: Ont.	**30**	45¼	75¾

	Page	N	W
Clair: N.B.		47	69
Clairambault, Lac: Qué.		54	69
Claire, Lake: Alta.	**24**	58	112
Clarence, Cape: N.W.T.	**29**	74	90
Clarence Creek: *town*, Ont.	**21**	45	75
Clarenville: Nfld.		48	54
Claresholm: Alta.	**24**	50	114
Clark Point: Ont.	**18**	44	82
Clarke City: Qué.	**14**	50	67
Clarke's Beach: Nfld.	**30**	47½	53¼
Clarks Harbour: N.S.	**15**	43	66
Clayoquot Sound: B.C.	**27**	49	126
Clear, Lake: Ont.	**20**	45	77
Clear Hills: Alta.	**24**	57	119
Clear Lake: Qué.	**19**	47	74
Clear Prairie: *town*, Alta.	**24**	57	119
Clearwater: *riv.*, Sask./Alta.	**24**	57	109
Clearwater Lake: B.C.	**27**	52	120
Clearwater Lake: Qué.	**13**	56	74
Clearwater Station: B.C.	**27**	51	120
Clériçy: Qué.	**18**	48	79
Clermont: Qué.	**19**	48	70
Climax: Sask.	**24**	49	108
Clinton: B.C.	**27**	51	121
Clinton: Ont.	**18**	43	82
Clinton-Colden Lake: N.W.T	**29**	64	107
Cloan: Sask.	**24**	53	109
Clo-oose: B.C.	**26**	49	125
Close Lake: Sask.	**25**	58	105
Clova: Qué.	**19**	48	75
Clover Bay: Alta.	**30**	53½	113¼
Cloverdale: B.C.	**27**	49	122¾
Clute: Ont.		49	81
Clyde: Alta.	**24**	54	114
Clyde: *riv.*, N.S.	**15**	44	65
Clyde: *riv.*, Ont.	**19**	45	76
Coal Branch: N.B.	**15**	46	65
Coal Creek: *town*, B.C.	**27**	49	115
Coaldale: Alta.	**24**	50	113
Coalhurst: Alta.	**24**	50	113
Coalmont: B.C.	**26**	49	121
Coalspur: Alta.		53	117
Coast Mtns.: B.C.	**26**	30	124
Coaticook: Qué.	**19**	45	72
Coats I.: N.W.T.	**12**	62	83
Cobalt: Ont.	**18**	47	80
Cobden: Ont.	**19**	46	77
Cobequid Bay: N.S.	**15**	45	64
Cobequid Mtns.: N.S.	**15**	45	64
Coboconk: Ont.	**20**	45	79
Cobourg: Ont.	**20**	44	78
Cochrane: Alta.	**30**	51¼	114¼
Cochrane: Ont.	**17**	49	81
Cochrane: *riv.*, Man.	**25**	58	102
Cockburn, Cape: N.W.T.	**29**	75	100
Cockburn I.: Ont.	**18**	46	83
Cockram Strait: N.W.T.	**12**	68	75
Cod I.: Labr.	**12**	58	62
Codroy: Nfld.	**15**	48	59
Codys: N.B.	**15**	46	66
Coe Hill: *town*, Ont.	**20**	45	78
Coffin I.: Magdalen Is.	**15**	47	61
Cognac, Lake: Qué.		55	70
Colborne: Ont.	**20**	44	78
Cold Lake: & *town*, Alta.	**24**	54	110
Coldspring Head: N.S.	**15**	46	64
Cold Spring Pond: Nfld.		48	56
Coldwater: Ont.	**20**	45	80
Coleman: Alta.	**24**	50	115
Coleman: P.E.I.	**15**	47	64
Colinet: Nfld.		47	54
Collingwood: Ont.	**18**	44	80
Collins Bay: Ont.	**20**	44	77
Collins Mt.: Ont.	**18**	48	81
Colombier, Cap: Qué.		49	69
Colpton: N.S.	**15**	44	65
Columbia: *riv.*, Can./U.S.A.	**27**	51	117
Columbia, Cape: N.W.T.	**3**	83	70
Columbia, Mt.: Alta.	**24**	52	117
Columbia Mtns.: B.C.	**27**	52	120
Colville Bay: N.W.T.	**29**	68	88
Colville Lake: Labr.		54	66
Colville Lake: N.W.T.	**28**	67	125
Colwell: Ont.	**20**	44	80
Colwood: B.C.	**26**	48	123
Comber: Ont.	**18**	42	82
Combermere: Ont.		45	78
Comfort, Cape: N.W.T.	**12**	65	83
Comfort Bight: Labr.		53	56
Commanda: Ont.	**20**	46	80
Commissioners Lake: Qué.	**19**	48	72
Committee Bay: N.W.T.	**29**	68	87
Como, Lake: Ont.	**18**	48	83
Comox: B.C.	**26**	50	125
Comox Lake: B.C.	**26**	50	125
Conception Bay: Nfld.	**30**	48	53
Conception Harbour: Nfld.		47	53
Conche: Nfld.		51	56
Conestogo: *riv.*, Ont.	**18**	43	81
Coniston: Ont.	**18**	46	81
Conklin: Alta.	**24**	56	111
Connors: N.B.		47	69
Conrad: Alta.	**24**	49	112
Conrad: Yukon		60	134
Conrich: Alta.	**30**	51	113¾
Consecon: Ont.	**20**	44	77
Consort: Alta.	**24**	52	111
Consul: Sask.	**24**	49	109
Contrecoeur: Qué.	**21**	46	73
Contwoyto Lake: N.W.T.	**29**	66	111
Cook, Cape: B.C.		50	128
Cook, Mt.: U.S.A./Can.		60	140
Cook Bay: Lake Simcoe	**20**	44	79
Cooking Lake: & *town*, Alta.	**30**	53½	113¼
Cookshire: Qué.	**19**	45	72

	Page	N	W
Co-op Point: Sask.	**25**	57	102
Coppell: Ont.		50	84
Copper Cliff: Ont.	**18**	46	81
Coppermine: & *riv.*, N.W.T.	**28**	67	115
Copper Mountain: *town*, British Columbia	**26**	49	120
Coquihalla: B.C.	**26**	49	121
Coquitlam Lake: B.C.	**27**	49¼	122¾
Coral Harbour: *town*, N.W.T.	**16**	64	83
Coral Rapids: *town*, Ont.		50	82
Corbeil Point: Ont.		47	85
Corbett Inlet: N.W.T.	**29**	62	92
Cordova Mines: Ont.	**20**	44	78
Cork: N.B.	**15**	46	67
Cormac: Ont.		45	77
Cormack, Mt.: Nfld.	**15**	48	56
Cormorant: & *lake*, Man.	**25**	54	101
Cornelius Grinnell Bay: N.W.T.	**12**	63	65
Corner Brook: Nfld.	**15**	49	58
Cornwall: Ont.	**21**	45	75
Cornwall I.: N.W.T.	**3**	77	95
Cornwallis I.: N.W.T.	**29**	75	95
Coronation: Alta.	**24**	52	111
Coronation Gulf: N.W.T.	**29**	68	110
Cortes I.: B.C.	**26**	50	125
Corunna: Ont.	**18**	43	82
Corvette Lake: & *riv.*, Qué.		53	74
Côteau Station: Qué.	**21**	45	74
Cottel I.: Nfld.		49	54
Cottonwood: B.C.	**27**	53	122
Couchiching, Lake: Ont.	**20**	45	79
Coulonge: *riv.*, Qué.	**18**	47	77
Coulonge Est: *riv.*, Qué.	**19**	46	76
Courcelette Camp: Qué.	**30**	47	71½
Courtenay: B.C.	**26**	49	125
Courville: Qué.	**30**	47	71¼
Coutts: Alta.	**24**	49	112
Couture, Lac: Qué.		60	75
Cove I.: Ont.	**18**	45	82
Cowansville: Qué.	**19**	45	73
Cow Bay: N.S.	**30**	44¾	63½
Cow Head Harbour: Nfld.	**15**	50	58
Cowley: Alta.	**24**	50	114
Cox's Cove: Nfld.		49	58
Crabtree: Qué.	**21**	46	73
Cracroft I.: B.C.		50	126
Cramolet, Lac: Qué.		56	68
Cranberry Lake: *town*, B.C.	**26**	50	124
Cranberry Portage: Man.	**25**	55	101
Cranbrook: B.C.	**27**	49	116
Crane Lake: Sask.	**24**	50	109
Crauford, Cape: N.W.T.	**29**	74	84
Craven: Sask.	**30**	50¾	104¾
Craven Lake: Qué.		54	77
Cree: *riv.*, Sask.	**25**	58	106
Creekside: B.C.	**26**	50	123
Crée Lake: & *town*, Sask.	**24**	57	107
Creighton: Ont.	**18**	46	81
Creighton: Sask.	**25**	55	102
Crescent Beach: B.C.	**27**	49	123
Creston: B.C.	**27**	49	116
Creston: Nfld.		47	55
Creswell Bay: N.W.T.	**29**	73	94
Croche: *riv.*, Qué.	**19**	48	73
Croix, Lac à la: Qué.		51	70
Croker, Cape: Ont.	**18**	45	81
Croker Bay: N.W.T.	**29**	75	83
Crooked Lake: Nfld.	**15**	48	56
Crooked River: *town*, Sask.	**25**	53	104
Crookston: Ont.	**20**	44	77
Crosby: Ont.		45	76
Crossfield: Alta.	**24**	51	114
Cross Lake: Ont.	**20**	45	77
Cross Lake: & *town*, Man.	**25**	55	98
Crown Prince Frederik I.: N.W.T.	**29**	70	87
Crowsnest Pass: B.C./Alta.	**27**	50	115
Crozier Chan.: N.W.T.	**28**	76	118
Crystal Falls: *town*, Ont.	**18**	46	80
Crysler: Ont.	**30**	45¼	75¼
Cudworth: Sask.	**25**	52	106
Cumberland: B.C.	**26**	50	125
Cumberland: *penin. & sound*, N.W.T.	**12**	66	65
Cumberland: Ont.	**30**	45½	75½
Cumberland Bay: *town*, N.B.	**15**	46	66
Cumberland Lake: Sask.	**25**	54	102
Cupar: Sask.	**25**	51	104
Cutknife: Sask.	**24**	53	109
Cuvillier, Lac: Qué.		49	77
Cypress Hills: & *park*, Sask.	**24**	50	109
Czar: Alta.	**24**	52	111

	Page	N	W
Dacotah: Man.	**30**	50	97¾
Dalhousie: N.B.	**14**	48	66
Dalhousie: Qué.	**13**	48	66
Dalhousie, Cape: N.W.T.	**28**	70	130
Dalmas Lake: Qué.		53	72
Dalmeny: Sask.	**24**	52	107
Dalquier: Qué.		48	78
Dalroy: Alta.	**30**	51¼	113¾
Dalton: Ont.		48	84
Dalton Mills: Ont.	**18**	48	84
Daly Bay: N.W.T.	**29**	64	90
Dana, Lac: Qué.		51	77
Dane: Ont.	**18**	48	80
Daniels Harbour: Nfld.	**15**	50	58
Danville: Qué.	**19**	46	72
Darnley Bay: N.W.T.	**28**	70	124
Dartmouth: N.S.	**30**	44¾	63½
Datemead: Alta.	**30**	50¾	113¾
Dauphin: Man.	**25**	51	100

	Page	N	W
Dauphin Lake: Man.	25	51	100
Davangus: Qué.		48	79
Davidson: Sask.	25	51	106
Davidson Mtns.: Can./U.S.A.	28	68	142
Davieau I.: N.W.T.		57	77
Davin: Sask.	30	50½	104¼
Davis Inlet: settlement, Labrador	13	56	61
Davis Str.: Can./Grnld.	3	67	58
Davy Lake: Sask.	24	59	108
Dawson: Yukon	28	64	139
Dawson, Mt.: B.C.	27	51	117
Dawson Bay: Man.	25	53	101
Dawson Creek: town, B.C.	27	56	120
Dawson Inlet: N.W.T.	29	62	93
Dawson Range: Yukon	28	62	139
Daysland: Alta.	24	53	112
Dayton: Ont.		46	83
Deadman Bay: Nfld.		49	54
Dean: riv., B.C.	27	53	126
Dean Lake: town, Ont.	18	46	83
Deans Dundas Bay: N.W.T.	28	72	119
Dease: riv., B.C.		59	129
Dease Arm: Great Bear Lake, N.W.T.	28	67	120
Dease Lake: & settlement, British Columbia	22	58	130
Dease Plateau, B.C.		60	128
Dease Str.: N.W.T.	29	69	107
Debden: Sask.	24	53	107
Deep River: town, Ont.		46	77
Deer Hill: town, Alta.	24	56	118
Deer I.: N.B.		45	67
Deer Lake: town, Ont.	25	53	94
Deer Lake: town & lake, Newfoundland	15	49	58
Deer Pond, Nfld.		48	55
Defot: B.C.		59	130
Delacourt: Alta.	30	51¼	113¾
Delamere: Ont.	18	46	81
Del Bonita: Alta.	24	49	113
Delburne: Alta.	24	52	113
Delhi: Ont.	18	43	80
Delia: Alta.	24	52	112
Delisle: Sask.	24	52	107
Deloge Hills: Qué.		49	79
Deloraine: Man.	25	49	100
Delorme, Lac: Qué.	13	54	70
Deloro: Ont.	20	44	78
Delson: Qué.	21	45	74
Denbigh: Ont.	18	45	77
Denholm: Sask.		53	108
Denman I.: B.C.	26	50	125
Denzil: Sask.	24	52	110
De Pas: riv., Qué.	13	56	65
Depot Harbour: Ont.	18	45	80
De Salis Bay: N.W.T.	28	72	122
Desbarats: Ont.	18	46	84
Desbiens: Qué.	19	48	72
Deschaillons: Qué.	19	47	72
Deschambault Lake: Sask.	25	55	103
Deschênes: lake & town, Québec	30	45½	75¾
Deseronto: Ont.	20	44	77
Desolation Lake: Labr.		55	63
Detroit: riv., Can./U.S.A.	18	42	83
Deux Montagnes: town, Québec	21	45½	74
Deux Montagnes, Lac des: Québec	21	45½	74
Deux Rivières: town, Ont.	18	46	78
Deville: Alta.	30	53¼	113
Devon: Alta.	30	53¼	113¾
Devon I.: N.W.T.	29	75	85
De Winton: Alta.	30	50¾	114
Dezadeash Lake: Yukon		60	137
Diana Lake: Qué.		58	69
D'Iberville, Lake: Qué.	13	56	73
Dickson Lake: Ont.		46	78
Dickson Peak: B.C.	26	51	123
Didsbury: Alta.	24	52	114
Didyme: Qué.		49	73
Diefenbaker, Lake: Sask.	24	51	107
Digby: N.S.	15	45	66
Digby Neck: penin., N.S.	15	44	66
Digges Is.: Qué.	12	62	68
Dihourse, Lac: Qué.		56	64
Dildo: Nfld.		47	54
Dingwall: N.S.	15	47	60
Disappointment Lake: Labradore		54	62
Disaster Rapids: Labr.		53	64
Disley: Sask.	30	50¾	105
Dismal Lakes: N.W.T.	28	67	117
Disraeli: Qué.	19	46	71
Dix: Qué.	19	48	76
Dixon Entrance: str., U.S.A./Canada	26	54	132
Doating Cove: Nfld.		49	54
Doda, Lac: Qué.		49	75
Dodge Lake: Sask.	25	60	106
Dodsland: Sask.	24	52	109
Doe Lake: Ont.	20	46	79
Dog Creek: town, B.C.	27	52	122
Dog Lake: Man.	25	51	98
Dog Lake: Ont.		49	89
Dog Lake: Ont.		48	84
Dolbeau: Qué.	19	49	72
Dolphin & Union Str.: N.W.T.	28	69	115
Dome Creek: town, B.C.	27	54	121
Dome Peak: N.W.T.		61	127
Domes, The: mtn., Labr.		58	63
Dominion, Cape: N.W.T.	12	66	74
Dominion City: Man.	25	49	97
Dominion Lake: Labr.		53	62

	Page	N	W
Don: riv., Ont.	20	43¾	79¼
Donald Lake: Ont.	25	51	95
Donald Landing: B.C.	27	54	126
Donjek: riv., Yukon	28	62	140
Donkin: N.S.	15	46	60
Donnacona: Qué.	30	46¾	71¾
Dorchester: N.B.	15	46	64
Dorchester, Cape: N.W.T.	12	65	78
Doré, Lac: Qué.	19	47	75
Doré Lake: Sask.	24	55	107
Dorion: Qué.	21	45	74
Dorset: Ont.	18	45	79
Dorset, Cape: N.W.T.	12	64	77
Dorval: Qué.	21	45½	73¾
Dosquet: Qué.	19	46	71
Dot: B.C.	26	50	121
Double Mer: inlet, Labr.		54	59
Douglas Point: Ont.	18	44	82
Douglas Station: Man.	25	50	100
Dowling Lake: Alta.	24	52	112
Downton, Mt.: B.C.	27	53	125
Doyles: Nfld.	15	48	59
Dozois Reservoir: Qué.	18	47	77
Dresden: Ont.	18	43	82
Driftwood: Ont.		49	81
Drumbo: Ont.	18	43	81
Drumheller: Alta.	24	51	113
Drummondville: Qué.	19	46	72
Dry Bay: Qué.		60	70
Dryden: Ont.	17	50	93
Duagh: Alta.	30	53¾	113½
Dubawnt: riv., N.W.T.	29	62	103
Dubawnt Lake: N.W.T.	29	63	102
Dubuisson: Qué.	18	48	78
Duchess: Alta.	24	51	112
Duck Bay: town, Man.	25	52	100
Duck I.: Ont.	20	44	77
Duck Lake: town, Sask.	24	53	106
Duck Mt.: & Prov. Pk., Manitoba	25	51	101
Duffey Lake: B.C.		50	122
Dufresne: Man.	30	49¾	96¾
Dugald: Man.	30	50	96¾
Du Gué: riv., Qué.	13	57	72
Duke of York Bay: N.W.T.	12	65	85
Du Lièvre: riv., Qué.	21	46	75
Du Loup: riv., Qué.	19	46	73
Dumoine: riv. & lake, Qué.	18	47	78
Dunblane: Sask.	24	51	107
Duncan: B.C.	26	49	124
Duncan, Cape: Akimiski I.		53	81
Duncan Dam: B.C.	27	50	117
Duncan Lake: B.C.	27	51	117
Duncan Lake: Qué.	16	53	78
Dundalk: Ont.	18	44	80
Dundas: Ont.	18	43	80
Dundas I.: B.C.	26	55	131
Dundas Penin.: N.W.T.	29	75	112
Dune Lake: Qué.		59	73
Dunkirk: Sask.	25	50	106
Dunnville: Ont.	18	43	80
Dunster: B.C.	27	53	120
Dunville: Nfld.		47	54
Duparquet: Qué.	18	49	79
Dupuy: Qué.		49	79
Durham: N.B.	15	46	67
Durham: Ont.	18	44	81
Duvernay: Alta.		54	112
Dyer, Cape: N.W.T.	12	67	61
Dyer Bay: N W.T.	28	76	122
Dyer Bay: town, Ont.		45	81
Dyke Lake: Labr.		54	66
Eabamet Lake: Ont.	17	52	88
Eagle: riv., Labr.		53	58
Eagle Lake: Alta.	30	51	113¼
Eagle Lake: Ont.	17	50	93
Earl Grey: Sask.	25	51	105
Earlton: Ont.	18	48	80
East Angus: Qué.	19	45	71
East Bay: Nfld.		47	55
East Broughton: Qué.	19	46	71
East Chezzetcook: N.S.	30	44¾	63¼
East Cub I.: N.W.T.		54	80
Eastend: Sask.	24	49	109
Eastern Passage: N.S.	30	44½	63½
East Jordan: N.S.	15	44	65
East Kildonan: Man.	30	50	97
Eastmain: & riv., Qué.	13	52	78
Eastman: Qué.	19	45	72
East Mines: N.S.	15	45	63
East Pine: B.C.	27	56	121
East Point: Anticosti I.	15	49	62
East Point: P.E.I.	15	46	62
East Point: Qué.		52	80
Eastport: Nfld.		49	54
East River St. Mary: N.S.	15	45	62
East Selkirk: Man.	30	50	96¾
East Thurlow I.: B.C.		50	125
Eastview: Ont.	30	45½	75¾
East York: Ont.	20	43¾	79¼
Eaton Canyon: Qué.		56	68
Eatonia: Sask.	24	51	110
Ebbegunbaeg Lake: Nfld.		48	56
Echo Bay: town, Ont.	18	46	84
Eclipse: riv. & chan., Labr.		60	64
Eclipse Sound: N.W.T.	29	73	79
E. C. Manning Prov. Park: British Columbia	26	49	121
Economy: N.S.	15	45	64
Ecum Secum: N.S.	15	45	62
Edehon Lake: N.W.T.	29	60	97
Edenwold: Sask.	30	50¾	104¼
Edgeley: Sask.	30	50¾	104
Edgell I.: N.W.T.	12	62	65

	Page	N	W
Edgerton: Alta.	24	53	110
Edgewood: B.C.	27	50	118
EDMONTON: Alta.	30	53½	113½
Edmund Lake: Man.	25	55	93
Edmundston: N.B.	14	47	68
Edson: Alta.	24	54	116
Eduni, Mt.: N.W.T.	28	64	128
Edziza Peak: B.C.	26	58	131
Eganville: Ont.	18	45	77
Egmont: B.C.	26	50	124
Egmont Bay: P.E.I.	16	46	64
Eileen Lake: N.W.T.	29	62	107
Eisenhower, Mt.: Alta.	24	51	116
Ekhart: Man.	30	50	97½
Ekwan Point: Ont.		53	82
Elbow: riv., Alta.	30	51	114
Eldridge Bay: N.W.T.	29	76	110
Elgin: N.B.	15	46	65
Elgin: Ont.	21	45	76
Eliot, Mt.: Labr.		59	64
Elkhorn: Man.	25	50	101
Elk Island Nat. Pk.: Alta.	30	53½	113
Elk Lake: town, Ont.	18	48	80
Elko: B.C.	27	49	115
Elk Point: town, Alta.	24	54	111
Ell Bay: N.W.T.	16	64	87
Ellef Ringnes I.: N.W.T.	1	78	103
Ellerslie: Alta.	30	53½	113½
Ellesmere I.: N.W.T.	3	80	80
Ellice: riv., N.W.T.	29	67	104
Ellice I.: N.W.T.	28	69	136
Elliot Lake: town, Ont.	17	46	83
Elliston: Nfld.		49	53
Elm Grove: Man.	30	49¾	96¾
Elmira: Ont.	18	43	80
Elmira: P.E.I.	15	46	62
Elmsdale: N.S.	15	45	63
Elmvale: Ont.	20	45	80
Elnora: Alta.	24	52	113
Elrose: Sask.	24	51	108
Elsas: Ont.		48	83
Elsie I.: N.W.T.		59	79
Elu Inlet: N.W.T.	29	68	106
Elvira, Cape: N.W.T.	29	74	107
Embarras Portage: Alta.		58	111
Embrun: Ont.	30	45¼	75¼
Emerald: P.E.I.	15	46	64
Emerald I.: N.W.T.	29	76	114
Emerson: Man.	25	49	97
Emeryville: Ont.	31	42¼	82¾
Emo: Ont.	25	49	93
Empress: Alta.	24	51	110
Emsdale: Ont.	20	46	79
Enderby: B.C.	27	50	119
Enfield: N.S.	30	45	63½
Engineer: B.C.		59	134
Englee: Nfld.	13	51	56
Englehart: Ont.	18	48	80
Englewood: B.C.		51	127
English: riv., Ont.	17	50	95
English River: town, Ont.		49	91
Ennadai: & lake, N.W.T.	29	61	101
Enterprise: Ont.		44	77
Entrance: Alta.		53	118
Entry I.: Qué.	15	47	61
Erebus Bay: N.W.T.	29	69	99
Eric Lake: Qué.		52	65
Erie, Lake: Can./U.S.A.	18	42	81
Erieau: Ont.	18	42	82
Erin: Ont.	20	44	80
Erith: Alta.	24	53	117
Erlandson Lake: Qué.	13	57	68
Erris: B.C.	26	50	120
Erskine Inlet: N.W.T.	29	76	103
Escuminac, Point: N.B.	14	47	65
Esker: Labr.	13	54	66
Eskimo Lakes: N.W.T.	28	69	131
Eskimo Point: town, N.W.T.	29	61	94
Eskwahani Lake: Qué.	19	48	76
Esnagi Lake: Ont.		49	84
Espanola: Ont.	18	46	82
Espoir, Baie d': Nfld.		48	56
Espoir, Cap d': Qué.	14	48	64
Esquimalt: B.C.	26	48	123
Essex: Ont.	31	42¼	82¾
Estaire: Ont.	18	46	81
Esterhazy: Sask.	25	50	102
Estevan: Sask.	25	49	103
Estevan Point: B.C.	27	49	126
Eston: Sask.	24	51	109
Estuary: Sask.	24	51	110
Etawney Lake: Man.	25	58	96
Etchemin: riv., Qué.	30	46¾	71
Ethelbert: Man.	24	51	100
Etobicoke: & creek, Ont.	20	43¾	79½
Eton Station: Ont.	18	47	84
Eureka River: town, Alta.	24	56	119
Eutsuk Lake: B.C.	27	53	126
Evans, Lake: Qué.	13	51	77
Evans, Mt.: Alta.	24	52	118
Evansburg: Alta.	24	54	115
Evans Strait: N.W.T.	16	63	82
Evanston: N.S.	16	45	61
Evansville: Ont.	18	46	83
Everett Mts.: N.W.T.	12	63	68
Excel: Alta.	24	51	111
Exeter: Ont.	18	43	81
Exeter Bay: N.W.T.	12	67	62
Exeter Sound: N.W.T.	12	66	62
Exploits: riv., Nfld.	15	49	56
Faber Lake: N.W.T.	28	63	117
Fabre Station: Qué.	18	47	79
Faillon, Lac: Qué.	19	48	76
Fair Ness: N.W.T.	12	63	72

	Page	N	W
Fairview: Alta.	24	56	118
Fairweather, Mt.: U.S.A./Canada	28	59	138
Falaise Lake: N.W.T.		61	116
Falconbridge: Ont.	18	47	81
Falher: Alta.	24	56	117
Falkland: B.C.	27	50	120
False: riv., Qué.		58	68
Family Lake: Man.	25	52	96
Fanny Bay: town, B.C.	26	49	125
Faribault, Lac: Qué.		59	72
Farmer I.: N.W.T.		58	81
Farmington: B.C.	27	56	120
Farnham: Qué.	19	45	73
Farnham, Mt.: B.C.	27	50	116
Fassett: Qué.	21	46	75
Father Lake: Qué.		49	75
Fatima: Qué.	13	47	62
Fauquier: Ont.		49	82
Favourable Lake: town, Ontario	25	53	94
Fawcett Lake: Ont.		51	92
Fawn: riv., Ont.	16	54	88
Felix, Cape: N.W.T.	29	70	98
Fenelon Falls: town, Ont.	20	45	79
Fergus: Ont.	18	44	80
Ferguson Lake: N.W.T.	29	70	105
Ferme Neuve: Qué.	19	47	75
Fernie: B.C.	27	49	115
Ferolle Point: Nfld.		51	57
Ferryland: Nfld.	15	47	53
Field: B.C.	24	51	116
Field: Ont.	18	47	80
Fife Lake: Sask.	25	49	106
Finch: Ont.		45	75
Fingal: Ont.		43	81
Finlay: riv., B.C.	27	56	124
Finlay Forks: B.C.	27	56	124
Finlay Range: B.C.	27	57	126
Finnegan: Alta.	24	51	112
Finnie Bay: N.W.T.	12	65	77
Firebag: riv., Alta.	24	57	110
Fire River: town, Ont.		49	83
Firth: riv., U.S.A./Can.	28	69	140
Fish Creek: riv., Alta.	30	50¾	114
Fisher: Qué.		49	78
Fisher, Mt.: B.C.	27	50	116
Fisher Strait: N.W.T.	12	63	84
Fishing Lake: Man.	25	52	95
Fishing Lakes: Sask.	30	50¾	104
Fishing Ship Harbour: Labrador		53	56
Fitzgerald Bay: N.W.T.	29	72	90
Fitzhugh Sound: B.C.	26	52	128
Fitzpatrick: Qué.		47	73
Fitzroy Harbour: Ont.	30	45½	76¼
Fitzwilliam I.: Ont.	18	45	82
Fitzwilliam Str.: N.W.T.	29	76	116
Five Mile Lake: N.S.	30	45	64
Flaherty I.: N.W.T.		56	80
Flamand Lac.: Qué.	19	48	73
Flatbush: Alta.		55	114
Flat I.: Nfld.		47	55
Flat River: town, P.E.I.	15	46	63
Flatrock: Nfld.	30	47¾	52¾
Fleming: Sask.	25	50	101
Flesherton: Ont.	18	44	81
Fleur de Lys: Nfld.		50	56
Fleur de Mai, Lac: Qué.		52	65
Flin Flon: Man.	25	55	102
Flint Lake: N.W.T.	12	69	74
Flores I.: B.C.	27	49	126
Florida: Ont.		49	81
Flower's Cove: town, Nfld.	13	52	57
Flower Station: Ont.		45	77
Foam Lake: town, Sask.	25	52	103
Foch: B.C.	26	50	124
Fogo: & i., Nfld.	15	50	54
Foleyet: Ont.	18	48	82
Foley I.: N.W.T.	12	68	75
Folly Lake: town, N.S.	15	46	64
Fond du Lac: Sask.	24	59	107
Fond du Lac: riv., Sask.	25	59	105
Fontas: riv., B.C.	22	58	121
Fonteneau, Lac: Qué.		52	61
Fonthill: Ont.	20	43	79
Foothills: Alta.	24	53	117
Forbes, Mt.: Alta.	24	52	117
Foremost: Alta.	24	49	111
Forest: Ont.	18	43	82
Forestburg: Alta.	24	53	112
Forest Lawn: Alta.	30	51	114
Forestville: Qué.	13	49	69
Forget: Qué.	19	48	77
Forget: Sask.	25	50	103
Forks: N.B.	15	46	66
Fornier, Lac: Qué.		51	65
Forrest Lake: Sask.	24	58	109
Forsythe: Qué.	19	48	76
Fort Albany: Ont.	17	52	82
Fort Assiniboine: Alta.	24	54	115
Fort Babine: B.C.	27	55	127
Fort Chimo: Qué.	12	58	68
Fort Chipewyan: Alta.	24	59	111
Fort Coulonge: Qué.	19	46	77
Forteau Bay: town, Labr.		51	57
Fort Erie: Ont.	20	43	79
Fort Fitzgerald: Alta.	24	60	112
Fort Frances: Ont.	17	49	93
Fort Fraser: B.C.	27	54	125
Fort Garry: Man.	30	49¾	97¼
Fort George: Qué.	13	54	79
Fort George (La Grande): riv., Québec	13	54	77
Fort Good Hope: N.W.T.	28	66	128
Fort Grahame: B.C.	27	57	125

	Page	N	W
Fort Hope: Ont.		51	88
Fortiérville: Qué.	19	46	72
Fortin, Lac: Qué.		51	68
Fort Langley: B.C.	27	49¼	122½
Fort Liard: N.W.T.	28	60	124
Fort McKenzie: Qué.	13	57	69
Fort Macleod: Alta.	24	50	113
Fort McLeod: B.C.	27	55	123
Fort McMurray: Alta.	24	57	111
Fort McPherson: N.W.T.	28	67	135
Fort Nelson: & *riv.*, B.C.	22	59	123
Fort Norman: N.W.T.	28	65	125
Fort Providence: N.W.T.	28	61	118
Fort Qu'Appelle: Sask.	30	50¾	103¾
Fort Reliance: N.W.T.	29	63	109
Fort Resolution: N.W.T.	28	61	114
Fort St. James: B.C.	27	54	124
Fort St. John: B.C.	27	56	121
Fort Saskatchewan: Alta.	30	53¾	113¼
Fort Selkirk: Yukon	28	63	137
Fort Severn: Ont.	16	56	88
Fort Simpson: N.W.T.	28	62	122
Fort Smith: N.W.T.	29	60	112
Fortune: & *bay*, Nfld.	15	47	56
Fortune Harbour: Nfld.		50	55
Fort Vermilion: Alta.	24	58	116
Fort William: Ont. *see* Thunder Bay			
Forty Mile: *riv.*, Canada/U.S.A.	28	64	141
Fossmill: Ont.		46	79
Foster: *riv.*, Sask.	25	56	106
Fourchu: N.S.	15	46	60
Fournière, Lac: Qué.	18	48	78
Fox Bay: *town*, Anticosti I.	14	49	62
Foxe Basin: N.W.T.	12	68	79
Foxe Channel: N.W.T.	12	65	80
Foxe Penin.: N.W.T.	12	64	77
Foxford: Sask.	25	53	105
Fox Harbour: Labr.		52	56
Fox Harbour: Nfld.		47	54
Fox Valley: *town*, Sask.	24	50	109
Frances Lake: Yukon	28	61	129
Francois: Nfld.	15	47	57
Francois Lake: B.C.	27	54	126
Frankford: Ont.	20	44	78
Franklin, District of: N.W.T.	29	—	—
Franklin Bay: N.W.T.	28	70	126
Franklin Bay: N.W.T.	29	69	85
Franklin Centre: Qué.	21	45	74
Franklin Lake: N.W.T.	29	67	96
Franklin Mts.: N.W.T.	28	64	125
Franklin Strait: N.W.T.	29	71	97
Frankslake: Sask.	30	50¼	104½
Franz: Ont.		48	84
Fraser: *riv.*, B.C.	27	50	121
Fraser: *riv.*, Labr.	13	57	64
Fraserdale: Ont.		50	82
Fraser Plateau: B.C.	27	52	124
Frater: Ont.	18	47	84
Frederick House: *lake & riv.*, Ontario		49	81
FREDERICTON New Brunswick	15	46	67
Fredericton Junc.: N.B.	15	46	67
Fredrikshald Bay: N.W.T.	29	71	105
Freels, Cape: Nfld.	15	49	53
Freeport: N.S.	15	44	66
French: *riv.*, Ont.	18	46	80
Frenchman: *riv.*, Canada/U.S.A.		49	107
Frenchman Butte: Sask.	24	54	110
Freshwater Bay: Nfld.		49	54
Frigate Lake: Qué.		53	75
Frobisher Bay: & *town*, N.W.T.	12	63	68
Frobisher Lake: Sask.	24	56	108
Frog Lake: Alta.	24	54	110
Frozen Strait: N.W.T.	12	66	85
Fruitvale: B.C.	27	49	118
Fullerton, Cape: N.W.T.	29	64	88
Fundy, Bay of: N.B./N.S.	15	45	66
Fundy Nat. Park: N.B.	15	45	65
Fury & Hecla Strait: N.W.T.	29	70	84
Gabarus: & *bay*, N.S.	15	46	60
Gabbro Lake: Labr.		54	65
Gabriel Str.: N.W.T.	12	62	65
Gabriola I.: B.C.	26	49	124
Gage, Cape: P.E.I.	15	47	64
Gagetown: N.B.	15	46	66
Gagnon: Qué.	13	52	68
Gagnon, Lac: Qué.	19	46	75
Gainsborough: Sask.	25	49	101
Galbraith: B.C.		59	132
Galiano I.: B.C.	26	49	123
Galiote: Anticosti I.	14	49	63
Galt: Ont.	18	43	80
Gambier I.: B.C.	26	49	123
Gambo: Nfld.	15	49	54
Gananoque: Ont.	21	44	76
Gander: & *lake*, Nfld.	15	49	55
Gander: *riv.*, Nfld.	15	49	55
Gander Bay: *town & bay*, Newfoundland		49	54
Ganges: B.C.	26	49	123
Garden River: & *riv.*, Ont.	18	46	84
Gardiner: Ont.		49	81
Gardiner Dam: Sask.	24	51	107
Gardner Canal: B.C.	26	53	128
Gargantua, Cape: Ont.		47	85
Garibaldi: B.C.	26	50	123
Garibaldi: *mtn. & lake*, B.C.	26	50	123
Garibaldi Prov. Park: B.C.	27	49½	122½
Garnet Bay: N.W.T.	12	65	75
Garnish: Nfld.	15	47	55
Garry Bay: N.W.T.	29	69	85
Garry Lake: N.W.T.	29	66	100
Garson: Man.	30	50	96¾
Garson: Ont.	18	46	81
Garthby: Qué.	19	46	71
Gaspé: & *cape*, Qué.	14	49	64
Gaspé Passage: *chan.*, Qué.	14	49	64
Gaspé Penin.: Qué.	14	48	66
Gaspesian Park: Qué.	14	49	66
Gataga: *riv.*, B.C.		58	129
Gate, The: *falls*, N.W.T.		61	125
Gateshead I.: N.W.T.	29	71	100
Gatineau: & *riv.*, Qué.	30	45½	75¾
Gatineau, Parc de la: Qué.	21	46	76
Gauer Lake: Man.	25	57	98
Gavot, Lac: Qué.		56	71
Geikie: *riv.*, Sask.	25	57	105
Gelert: Ont.	20	45	79
Gensart, Lake: Qué.		53	68
George, Cape: N.S.	15	46	62
George: *riv.*, Qué.	13	58	66
George, Lake: Ont.	18	46	84
George River: *town*, Qué.	12	58	66
Georges Brook: *town*, Nfld.		48	54
Georges Cove: Labr.		53	56
Georgetown: Ont.	20	44	80
Georgetown: P.E.I.	15	46	62
Georgia, Strait of: B.C.	26	49	124
Georgian Bay: Ont.	18	45	81
Georgian Bay Prov. Forest: Ontario	18	46	80
Georgina I.: Ont.	20	44	79
Geraldton: Ont.	17	50	87
Germaine, Lac: Qué.		53	68
Germansen Landing: B.C.	27	56	125
Gerrard: B.C.	27	50	117
Gethsémani: Qué.	15	50	60
Ghost River: *town*, Ont.		51	83
Giauque Lake: N.W.T.	29	63	114
Gibsons: B.C.	26	49	123
Giffard: Qué.	30	46¾	71¼
Gifford: *Fd. & riv.*, N.W.T.	20	70	83
Gilbert, Mt.: B.C.	26	51	124
Gilbert Plains: *town*, Man.	25	51	100
Gilford I.: B.C.	27	51	126
Gil I.: B.C.	26	53	129
Gillam: Man.	25	56	95
Gillian Lake: N.W.T.	12	69	75
Gillies Bay: *town*, B.C.	26	50	124
Gilmour: Ont.	20	45	78
Gimli: Man.	25	51	97
Giradrin, Lac: Qué.		58	66
Girardville Centre: Qué.		49	73
Giscome: B.C.	27	54	122
Gjoa Haven: N.W.T.	29	69	96
Glace Bay: *town*, N.S.	15	46	60
Glacier Creek: *town*, Yukon	28	64	141
Glacier Nat. Park: B.C.	27	51	117
Gladmar: Sask.		49	104
Gladstone: Man.	25	50	99
Gleichen: Alta.	24	51	113
Glenannan: Ont.		44	81
Glenboro: Man.	25	50	99
Glen Buell: Ont.		45	76
Glencoe: Ont.	18	43	82
Glenelg: N.S.	15	45	62
Glenlea: Man.	30	49¾	97¼
Glen Robertson: Ont.	21	45	75
Glenwood: Nfld.	15	49	55
Glover I.: Nfld.		49	58
Glovertown: Nfld.		49	54
Goat I.: B.C.	26	50	124
Godbout: Qué.	14	49	67
Goderich: Ont.	18	44	82
Gods: *riv.*, Man.	25	56	92
Gods Lake: *town & lake*, Manitoba	25	55	94
God's Mercy, Bay of: N.W.T.	29	64	86
Goëland, Lac au: Qué.		50	77
Gogama: Ont.	18	48	82
Gold Bar: B.C.	27	56	123
Goldboro: N.S.	15	45	62
Gold Bridge: B.C.	26	51	123
Gold Cove: Nfld.		50	57
Golden: B.C.	27	51	117
Golden Hinde: *mtn.*, B.C.	27	50	126
Golden Lake: *town*, Ont.	18	46	77
Golden Spike: Alta.	24	53	114
Goldenville: N.S.	15	45	62
Goldpines: Ont.	17	51	93
Gonor: Man.	30	50	97
Gooderham: Ont.	20	45	78
Goodeve: Sask.	25	51	103
Goodhope, Mt.: B.C.	27	51	124
Good Hope: Alta.	30	53¾	113
Goodsoil: Sask.	24	54	109
Goose: *riv.*, Labr.		53	61
Goose Bay: *town*, Labr.	13	53	60
Goose Lake: Qué.		53	75
Gordon: Man.	30	50	97¼
Gordonhorne Peak: B.C.	27	52	119
Gordon Lake: Alta.	24	56	110
Gore Bay: *town*, Ont.	18	46	82
Goshen: N.S.	15	45	62
Gott Peak: B.C.	26	50	122
Goudreau: Ont.	18	48	84
Gouin Dam: Qué.	19	48	74
Gouin Reservoir: Qué.	13	48	75
Goulais: *riv.*, Ont.	18	47	84
Goulais Point: Ont.	18	47	84
Goulais River Game Preserve: Ontario	18	47	84
Gourlay Lake: Ont.		49	85
Govenlock: Sask.	24	49	110
Gowganda: Ont.	18	48	81
Gracefield: Qué.	20	46	76
Graham: Ont.		49	91
Graham I.: B.C.	26	54	132
Graham Moore, Cape: N.W.T.	29	73	76
Grainger: Alta.	24	51	113
Granby: Qué.	19	45	73
Granby: *riv.*, B.C.	27	50	118
Grand: *riv.*, Ont.	18	43	80
Grand Bank: *town*, Nfld.	15	47	56
Grand Bay: *town*, N.B.	15	45	66
Grand Beach: *town*, Nfld.		47	55
Grand Bend: Ont.	18	43	82
Grand Coulee: Sask.	30	50½	104¾
Grande Baie: Qué.	19	48	71
Grande Pointe: Man.	30	49¾	97
Grande Prairie: *town*, Alta.	24	55	119
Grandes Bergeronnes: Qué.	14	48	69
Grandes Piles: Qué.	19	47	73
Grand Etang: *town*, N.S.	15	47	61
Grande Vallée: *town*, Qué.	14	49	65
Grand Falls: Labr.	13	54	64
Grand Falls: *town*, N.B.	14	47	67
Grand Falls: *town*, Nfld.	15	49	56
Grand Falls: Ont.	18	46	83
Grand Forks: B.C.	27	49	118
Grandin, Lac: N.W.T.	28	64	118
Grand Lac Germain: Qué.		51	67
Grand Lac Jacques Cartier: Québec	19	48	71
Grand Lac Témiscamie: Québec		51	73
Grand Lake: Labr.		54	61
Grand Lake: N.B.	15	46	66
Grand Lake: Nfld.	15	49	57
Grand Lake Victoria: Qué.	18	48	77
Grand Ligne: Qué.	21	45	73
Grand Manan I.: & *chan.*, New Brunswick	15	45	67
Grand' Mère: Qué.	19	47	73
Grand Narrows: *town*, N.S.	15	46	61
Grand Rapids: *town*, Man.	25	53	99
Grand River: *town*, N.S.	15	46	61
Grand Valley: *town*, Ont.	18	44	80
Grand View: Man.	25	51	101
Granet, Lac: Qué.	18	48	77
Granite Bay: *town*, B.C.	26	50	125
Granite Falls: Qué.		56	69
Grant Point: N.W.T.	29	68	98
Granum: Alta.	24	50	114
Granville Lake: & *falls*, Manitoba	25	56	100
Gras, Lac de: N.W.T.	29	64	111
Grass: *riv.*, Man.	25	56	97
Grass River Prov. Pk.: Man.	25	55	101
Grassy Lake: *town*, Alta.	24	50	112
Grassy Narrows: *town*, Ontario	17	50	94
Grates Cove: Nfld.	15	48	53
Grates Point: Nfld.		48	53
Gravelbourg: Sask.	24	50	107
Gravell Point: N.W.T.	12	67	77
Gravenhurst: Ont.	20	45	79
Gray Strait: Qué.		61	65
Great Bear Lake: N.W.T.	28	66	120
Great Central: B.C.	26	49	125
Great Central Lake: B.C.	26	49	125
Great Colinet I.: Nfld.		47	54
Great Duck I.: Ont.	18	46	83
Great Falls: *town*, Man.	25	50	96
Great Mecatina I.: Qué.		51	59
Great Sand Hills: Sask.	24	50	109
Great Slave Lake: N.W.T.	28	61	115
Great Village: N.S.	15	45	64
Great Whale River: & *riv.*, Québec	13	55	77
Green: *riv.*, N.B.		48	68
Green Bay: *town*, Labr.		52	56
Green Bay: Nfld.		50	56
Greening: Qué.		48	75
Green Lake: B.C.	27	51	121
Greenough Point: Ont.	18	45	81
Green Point: *town*, Ont.	20	44	77
Green Point: Nfld.		50	58
Green's Harbour: Nfld.	30	47¾	53½
Greenspond: Nfld.		49	54
Greenville: B.C.	26	55	130
Greenwater Lake Prov. Pk.: Saskatchewan	25	52	104
Greenwood: B.C.	27	49	119
Grenfell: Sask.	25	50	103
Grenville: Qué.	21	46	75
Grenville, Mt.: B.C.	26	51	124
Gretna: Man.	25	49	97
Grey: *riv.*, Nfld.	15	48	57
Grey Is.: Nfld.		51	55
Griffith I.: N.W.T.	29	75	96
Griffith I.: Ont.	18	45	81
Grimsby: Ont.	20	43	80
Grimshaw: Alta.	24	56	118
Grindstone: & *i.*, Qué.	14	47	62
Grinnell Ice Cap: N.W.T.	12	62	67
Groais I.: Nfld.	13	51	55
Gronlid: Sask.	25	53	104
Gros Morne: *mtn.*, Nfld.	15	50	58
Grosse Isle: Man.	30	50	97½
Groswater Bay: Labr.	13	54	58
Grouard: Alta.	24	56	116
Groundhog: *riv.*, Ont.	17	49	82
Gueguen, Lac: Qué.	18	48	77
Guelph: Ont.	18	43	80
Guers, Lac: Qué.		57	66
Guigues: Qué.	18	47	77
Gull Lake: Ont.	20	45	79
Gull Lake: Alta.	24	52	114
Gull Lake: Labr.		53	61
Gull Lake: *town*, Sask.	24	50	108
Gunisao: *riv.*, Man.	25	54	97
Gun Lake: B.C.	26	51	123
Gunn: Alta.	24	54	114
Gunnar: Sask.	24	59	109
Gushing, Mt.: B.C.	26	58	127
Guysborough: N.S.	15	45	62
Gypsum Point: N.W.T.	28	62	115
Gypsumville: Man.	25	52	99
Gyrfalcon Is.: Qué.	12	59	69
Habalta: Alta.	30	51	114
Habay: Alta.	24	59	119
Hades Hill: Qué.		57	65
Hadley Bay: N.W.T.	29	72	109
Hagersville: Ont.	20	43	80
Haileybury: Ont.	18	47	80
Haines Junction: Yukon		61	137
Hale: Ont.		49	84
Halfway: *riv.*, B.C.	27	56	122
Halfway Point: Ont.		52	81
Haliburton: & *lake*, Ont.	18	45	78
HALIFAX: Nova Scotia	30	44¾	63½
Hall Harbour: N.S.	15	45	65
Hall Lake: & *settlement*, N.W.T.	29	69	81
Hall Penin.: N.W.T.	12	63	66
Halls Bay: Nfld.		50	56
Hamber Prov. Park: B.C.	27	52	118
Hamilton: Ont.	20	43	80
Hamilton Inlet: Labr.	13	54	58
Hamilton Sound: Nfld.	15	49	54
Hamiota: Man.	25	50	100
Hammond Plains: N.S.	30	44¾	63¾
Ham Mt.: Qué.	19	46	71
Hampden: Nfld.	15	50	57
Hampstead: N.B.	15	46	66
Hampton: N.B.	15	46	66
Hanceville: B.C.	27	52	123
Haney: B.C.	27	49¼	122½
Hanley: Sask.	24	51	106
Hanmer: Ont.	18	47	81
Hanna: Alta.	24	52	112
Hannah Bay: Ont.	17	51	80
Hanover: Ont.	18	44	81
Hantsport: N.S.	15	45	64
Happy Valley: *town*, Labr.	13	53	60
Harbour Breton: Nfld.	15	47	56
Harbour Grace: Nfld.	30	47¾	53¼
Harbour Main: Nfld.	30	47½	53¼
Harbour Mille: Nfld.		48	55
Harcourt: N.B.	15	46	65
Hardisty: Alta.	24	53	111
Hardisty Lake: N.W.T.	28	65	118
Hardwicke I.: B.C.		50	126
Hare Bay: Nfld.	13	51	56
Hare Bay: *town*, Nfld.		49	54
Hare Indian: *riv.*, N.W.T.	28	66	127
Hare Lake: Labr.		55	62
Hares: *riv.*, N.W.T.	29	67	93
Harkin Bay: N.W.T.	12	65	78
Harmon Valley: *town*, Alta.	24	56	117
Harmony Junction: P.E.I.	15	46	62
Harricanaw: *riv.*, Qué.	13	51	79
Harricanaw Ouest: Qué.		48	78
Harrigan, Cape: Labr.		56	60
Harrington Harbour: Qué.	13	50	59
Harrison, Cape: Labr.	13	55	58
Harrison Hot Springs: B.C.	26	49	122
Harrison Lake: B.C.	26	49	122
Harriston: Ont.	18	44	81
Hart: *riv.*, Yukon	28	65	137
Hartland: N.B.	14	46	67
Hartney: Man.	25	49	100
Harty: Ont.		50	83
Harvey: N.B.		46	67
Harvey: N.B.	15	46	65
Harwood: Ont.	20	44	78
Hastings: Ont.	20	44	78
Hatzie Lake: B.C.	27	49¼	122¼
Hauterive: Qué.	13	49	68
Havelock: N.B.	15	46	65
Havelock: Ont.	20	44	78
Havre Aubert: Qué.	14	47	62
Havre Boucher: N.S.	15	46	61
Havre St. Pierre: Qué.	14	50	64
Hawarden: Sask.	24	51	107
Hawke Harbour: Labr.		53	65
Hawke Hills: Nfld.	30	47¼	52¾
Hawke I.: Labr.		53	56
Hawke Mt.: Nfld.		47	53
Hawkesbury: Ont.	21	46	75
Hawkestone: Ont.	20	45	79
Hawk Junction: Ont.	18	48	84
Hay: *riv.*, Alta./N.W.T.	28	60	116
Hay, Cape: N.W.T.	29	74	80
Hay, Cape: N.W.T.	29	74	112
Hayes: *riv.*, Man.	25	56	93
Hayes: *riv.*, N.W.T.	29	67	94
Hay I.: Ont.	18	45	81
Hay Lake: Alta.	24	59	119
Hay Lake: Ont.		45	78
Hay Lakes: *town*, Alta.	24	53	113
Hay River: *town*, N.W.T.	28	61	116
Hazelridge: Man.	30	50	96¾
Hazelton: B.C.	26	55	128
Hazen Strait: N.W.T.	1	77	110
Head Lake: Ont.	20	45	79
Headingley: Man.	30	50	97½
Head of St. Margaret's Bay: Nova Scotia	30	44¾	64
Hearst: Ont.	17	50	84

Place	Page	N	W
Hearts Content: Nfld.	30	47¾	53¼
Hearts Delight: Nfld.	30	47¾	53½
Heaslip: Ont.	18	48	80
Heath Point: Anticosti I.	15	49	61
Hébert, Lac: Qué.		49	75
Hébertville: Qué.	14	48	72
Hebron: Labr.	12	58	63
Hebron: N.S.	15	44	66
Hecate: B.C.		50	127
Hecate Strait: B.C.	26	53	131
Hecla & Griper Bay: N.W.T.	29	76	112
Hecla I.: Man.	25	51	97
Hectanooga: N.S.	15	44	66
Hedge Hills: Qué.		49	78
Hedley: B.C.	26	49	120
Heinsburg: Alta.	24	54	110
Helena I.: N.W.T.	29	76	101
Helen Falls: Qué.		58	66
Helen Mine: Ont.		48	85
Hemmingford: Qué.	21	45	74
Henley Harbour: Labr.		52	56
Henribourg: Sask.	25	53	106
Henrietta Maria, C.: Ont.	16	55	82
Henry Kater, Cape: N.W.T.	12	69	66
Henryville: Qué.	21	45	73
Hensall: Ont.	18	43	81
Herbert: Sask.	24	50	107
Hermitage: & *bay*, Nfld.	15	47	56
Hérodier, Lac: Qué.		57	69
Heron Bay: *town*, Ont.		49	86
Herring Cove: N.S.	30	44½	63½
Herschel: & *i.*, Yukon	28	69	139
Hervey: Qué.	19	47	72
Hess: *riv.*, Yukon	28	63	133
Hess Mts.: Yukon	28	63	132
Hickman, Mt.: B.C.	26	57	131
Hickman's Harbour: Nfld.		48	54
Hicks Lake: N.W.T.		61	100
High Falls: Qué.		56	68
High I.: Labr.		57	61
Highland Creek: Ont.	20	43¾	79¼
Highland Grove: Ont.	18	45	78
High Level: Alta.	24	58	117
High Prairie: *town*, Alta.	24	55	116
High River: *town*, Alta.	24	50	114
Highrock: & *lake*, Man.	25	56	100
Hilda: Ont.		49	84
Hilliers: B.C.	26	49	124
Hill Island Lake: N.W.T.		60	110
Hillmond: Sask.	24	53	110
Hillsborough: N.B.	15	46	65
Hillsborough Bay: P.E.I.	15	46	63
Hillsdale: Ont.	20	45	80
Hinds Lake: Nfld.		49	57
Hines Creek: *town*, Alta.	24	56	119
Hinton: Alta.	24	53	118
Hjalmar Lake: N.W.T.		61	109
Hoare Bay: N.W.T.	12	65	66
Hodges Hill: Nfld.		49	56
Hodgeville: Sask.	24	50	107
Hodgson: Man.	25	51	98
Hogem Range: B.C.	27	55	125
Holden: Alta.	24	53	112
Holdfast: Sask.	25	51	105
Holman Island: *settlement*, N.W.T.	28	71	117
Holton: Labr.		54	57
Holyrood: Nfld.	30	47¼	53¼
Holyrood Pond: Nfld.		47	54
Homathko: *riv.*, B.C.	27	51	125
Home Bay: N.W.T.	12	68	67
Home I.: Labr.		60	64
Honfleur: Qué.		49	72
Hood: *riv.*, N.W.T.	29	67	110
Hootalinqua: Yukon		62	135
Hope: B.C.	26	49	121
Hopedale: Labr.	13	55	60
Hope I.: B.C.	26	50	128
Hopes Advance, Cape: Qué.	12	61	70
Hopes Advance Bay: Qué.	12	59	70
Hopewell: N.S.	15	45	63
Hopewell Cape: *town*, N.B.	15	46	65
Hopewell Is.: N.W.T.		58	78
Horburg: Alta.	24	52	115
Hornell Lake: N.W.T.		62	119
Hornepayne: Ont.	17	49	85
Horn Mt.: B.C.	26	58	129
Horn Mts.: N.W.T.	28	62	120
Horsefly, Lake: B.C.	27	52	121
Horseshoe Bay: *town*, B.C.	27	49¼	123¼
Horton: *riv.*, N.W.T.	28	69	124
Horwood Lake: Ont.	18	48	82
Hotchkiss: Alta.		57	118
Hottah Lake: N.W.T.	28	65	118
Houston: B.C.	27	54	126
Houston Point: Akimiski I.		53	81
Howe I.: Ont.	21	44	76
Howe Point: P.E.I.	15	46	62
Howe Sound: B.C.	26	49	123
Howick: Qué.		45	74
Howley: Nfld.		49	57
Huard, Pte. au: Qué.		53	79
Hubbard, Mt.: U.S.A./Canada		60	139
Hubbards: N.S.	15	45	64
Hubbart Point: Man.	25	59	95
Huberdeau: Qué.	21	46	75
Hudson: Ont.	17	50	92
Hudson: Qué.	21	45	74
Hudson Bay	16	60	85
Hudson Bay: *town*, Sask.	25	53	102
Hudson Hope: B.C.	27	56	122
Hudson Strait: N.W.T./Québec	12	63	73
Hull: Qué.	30	45½	75¾

Place	Page	N	W
Humber: *riv.*, Nfld.	15	49	57
Humber: *riv.*, Ont.	20	43¾	79½
Humber Bay: Ont.	20	43½	79½
Humbermouth: Nfld.	15	49	58
Humboldt: Sask.	25	52	105
Hundred & Fifty Mile House: B.C.	27	52	122
Hundred Mile House: B.C.	27	52	121
Hundred Mile Landing: Yukon		61	134
Hunter I.: B.C.	26	52	128
Hunter I.: Ont.		48	91
Hunter River: *town*, P.E.I.	15	46	63
Huntingdon: B.C.	27	49	122¼
Huntingdon: Qué.	21	45	74
Huntingdon I.: Labr.	13	54	57
Huntsville: Ont.	20	45	79
Hurd, Cape: Ont.	18	45	82
Huron, Lake: Canada/U.S.A.	18	45	82
Hussar: Alta.	24	51	113
Hyde Lake: N.W.T.		61	95
Hydraulic: B.C.	27	52	121
Hyland: *riv.*, Yukon		61	128
Hyland Post: B.C.	26	57	128
Iberville: Qué.	21	45	73
Icefield Range: Yukon		61	140
Igloolik: N.W.T.	29	69	82
Ignace: Ont.		49	91
Ile à la Crosse: & *lake*, Sask.	24	55	108
Ile d'Orléans: Qué.	30	47	71
Ilford: Man.	25	56	96
Indian Arm: *lake*, B.C.	27	49¼	123
Indian Bay: Nfld.		49	54
Indian Brook: *town*, N.S.	15	46	61
Indian Harbour: Labr.		54	57
Indian Harbour: Labr.		55	57
Indian Head: Sask.	25	50	104
Indian House, Lake: Qué.	13	56	65
Indus: Alta.	30	51	113¾
Ingersoll: Ont.	18	43	81
Ingleside: Ont.	21	45	75
Inglewood: Ont.	20	44	80
Ingonish: N.S.	15	47	60
Inklin: B.C.		59	133
Innisfail: Alta.	24	52	114
Innuksuak: *riv.*, Qué.		58	77
Inoucdjouac: Qué.	12	58	78
International Peace Garden: Canada/U.S.A.	25	49	100
International Rapids: Canada/U.S.A.	21	45	75
Inugsuin Fiord: N.W.T.	12	70	69
Inuvik: N.W.T.	28	68	133
Invermere: B.C.	27	50	116
Inverness: N.S.	15	46	61
Ioco: B.C.	27	49¼	123
Irma: Alta.	24	53	111
Irondale: & *riv.*, Ont.	20	45	78
Iroquois: Ont.	21	45	75
Iroquois Falls: *town*, Ont.	17	48	81
Irricana: Alta.	30	51¼	113¼
Irvine: Alta.	24	50	110
Irvines Landing: B.C.	26	50	124
Isabella Bay: N.W.T.	12	69	67
Isabella Falls: Labr.		54	63
Iskut: *riv.*, B.C.	26	57	131
Island Cove: *town*, Nfld.		48	53
Island Falls: *town*, Ont.	17	50	81
Island Falls: *town*, Sask.	25	56	102
Island Falls Junc.: Ont.		50	81
Island Lake: & *town*, Man.	25	54	95
Island Rapids: Qué.		60	71
Islands, Bay of: Nfld.	15	49	58
Islands, Bay of: Ont.	18	46	82
Isle aux Coudres: Qué.	19	47	70
Isle aux Lièvres: Qué.	19	48	70
Isle Madame: N.S.	15	45	61
Isle St. Ignace: Ont.	17	48	80
Isle Verte: *town*, Qué.	14	48	69
Italy Cross: N.S.	15	44	65
Itchen Lake: N.W.T.	29	65	113
Ivanhoe: *lake*, Ont.	18	48	83
Ivujivik: Qué.	12	62	78
Jack Lake: Ont.	20	45	78
Jack Lane Bay: Labr.		56	61
Jacob I.: N.W.T.		52	79
Jacopie Lake: Labr.		54	64
Jacques Cartier: Qué.	21	45½	73½
Jacques Cartier: *riv.*, Qué.	19	47	71
Jacques Cartier, Mt.: Qué.	14	49	66
Jacques Cartier Passage: *chan.*, Québec	14	50	64
Jacquet River: *town*, N.B.	14	48	66
James Bay: Ont./Qué.	16	53	80
Jameson: Sask.	30	50½	104½
James Ross, Cape: N.W.T.	29	75	114
James Ross Strait: N.W.T.	29	70	97
Jamestown: Nfld.		48	54
Jamestown: Ont. see Wawa		48	85
Janeville: N.B.	14	48	65
Jarvis: Ont.	18	43	80
Jasper: Alta.	24	53	118
Jasper: Ont.	21	45	76
Jasper Nat. Park: Alta.	24	53	118
Jasper Place: Alta.	24	54	114
Jeannin, Lac: Qué.		56	66
Jellicoe: Ont.		50	88
Jennings: *riv.*, B.C.		59	131
Jenny Lind I.: N.W.T.	29	69	102
Jens Munk I.: N.W.T.	29	70	80
Jervis Inlet: B.C.	26	50	124

Place	Page	N	W
Jessica: B.C.	26	49	122
Jésus, Ile: Qué.	21	45¾	73¾
Jock: *riv.*, Ont.	30	45¼	75¾
Joe Batts Arm: Nfld.		50	54
Joggins: N.S.	15	46	64
Johnsons Crossing: Yukon	28	60	133
Johnstone Strait: B.C.	27	50	126
Joliette: Qué.	21	46	73
Jones, C.: Qué.	13	55	80
Jones Sound: N.W.T.	3	76	85
Jonquière: Qué.	18	48	71
Joseph, Lac.: Labr.	13	53	65
Joseph Lake: Alta.	30	53¼	113
Joseph, Lake: Ont.	20	45	80
Juan de Fuca, Str. of: Canada/U.S.A.	26	48	124
Jubilee Lake: Nfld.		48	55
Jude I.: Nfld.		47	55
Judique: N.S.	15	46	61
Julian Lake: Qué.		54	78
Jupiter: *riv.*, Qué.		49	63
Kabinakagami: *lake & riv.*, Ontario		49	84
Kaegudeck Lake: Nfld.		48	55
Kagawong: Ont.		46	82
Kaipokok Bay: Labr.		55	59
Kakagi Lake: Ont.	17	49	94
Kakisa Lake: N.W.T.	28	61	118
Kaladar: Ont.	20	45	77
Kamaniskeg Lake: Ont.	18	45	78
Kamilukuak Lake: N.W.T.	29	62	102
Kaminak Lake: N.W.T.	29	62	95
Kaministikwia: Ont.		48	89
Kaminuriak Lake: N.W.T.	29	63	96
Kamiskotia: *riv.*, Ont.		48	82
Kamloops: & *lake*, B.C.	27	51	120
Kamsack: Sask.	25	52	102
Kanaaupscow: Qué.	13	54	76
Kanaaupscow: *riv.*, Qué.	13	55	74
Kane Basin: Can./Grnld.	3	79	70
Kaniapiskau: *riv.*, Qué.	12	57	69
Kaniapiskau Lake: Qué.	13	54	70
Kapiskau: *riv.*, Ont.	17	52	84
Kapuskasing: & *riv.*, Ont.	17	49	83
Kapuskasing Lake: Ont.		48	83
Kasba Lake: N.W.T.	29	60	102
Kasheshibaw Lake: Labr.		54	63
Kaskattama: *riv.*, Man.	23	56	91
Kaslo: B.C.	27	50	117
Kasshabog Lake: Ont.	20	45	78
Kates Needle: *mtn.*, Canada/U.S.A.	26	57	132
Kathryn: Alta.	30	51¼	113¾
Kawagama Lake: Ont.	18	45	79
Kawartha Lakes: Ont.	20	45	78
Kazabazua: Qué.	21	46	76
Kazan: *riv.*, N.W.T.	29	62	100
Kearney: Ont.	20	46	79
Kechika: *riv.*, B.C.	22	58	127
Kechika Range: B.C.		58	127
Kedgwick: N.B.	14	48	67
Kedgwick: *riv.*, N.B.		48	68
Keefers: B.C.	26	50	121
Keele: *riv.*, N.W.T.	28	64	127
Keele Peak: Yukon/N.W.T.	28	63	130
Keels: Nfld.		49	53
Keene: Ont.	20	44	78
Keewatin: Ont.	17	50	95
Keewatin, District of: N.W.T.	29	—	—
Kegaska: Qué.	15	50	61
Keglo Bay: Qué.		59	66
Keg River: *town*, Alta.	24	58	118
Keith Arm: Gt. Bear Lake, N.W.T.	28	65	122
Keithley Creek: *town*, B.C.	27	53	121
Kejimkujik Nat. Pk.: N.S.	15	44	65
Kekertaluk I.: N.W.T.	12	68	67
Kelfield: Sask.	24	52	109
Keller Lake: N.W.T.	28	64	122
Kellet Str.: N.W.T.	28	76	117
Kellett, Cape: N.W.T.	28	72	126
Kelliher: Sask.	25	51	104
Kelowna: B.C.	27	50	119
Kelsey Bay: *town*, B.C.	27	50	126
Kelvington: Sask.	25	52	103
Kemano: B.C.	26	54	128
Kemano Bay: *town*, B.C.	26	53	128
Kempt Lake: Qué.	19	47	74
Kemptville: Ont.	21	45	76
Kenabeek: Ont.	18	48	80
Kenamu: *riv.*, Labr.		53	60
Kendall, Cape: N.W.T.	16	63	87
Kennebecasis: *riv.*, N.B.	15	46	65
Kennedy: Sask.	25	50	102
Kennedy Chan.: Can./Grnld.	1	81	66
Kennedy Lake: B.C.	26	49	125
Kennetcook: N.S.	15	45	64
Kenney Dam: B.C.	27	54	125
Kennisis Lake: Ont.		45	79
Kenogami: & *lake*, Qué.	19	48	71
Kenogami: *riv.*, Ont.	17	50	85
Kenogamissi: *lake & falls*, Ontario	18	48	81
Keno Hill: *town*, Yukon	28	64	135
Kenora: Ont.	17	50	94
Kensington: P.E.I.	15	46	64
Kent Junction: N.B.	15	47	65
Kent Penin.: N.W.T.	29	68	107
Kentville: N.S.	15	45	64
Keoma: Alta.	30	51¼	113¾
Keremeos: B.C.	26	49	120
Kerrobert: Sask.	24	52	109
Kesagami Lake: Ont.		50	80

Place	Page	N	W
Keswick: N.B.		46	67
Keswick: Ont.	20	44	79
Kettle: *riv.*, B.C.	27	49	118
Kettle Point: Ont.	18	43	82
Kettle Rapids, see Gillam			
Kettlestone Bay: Qué.	12	62	78
Key Harbour: Ont.		46	81
Key Junction: Ont.	18	46	81
Kiamika: Qué.	19	46	75
Kicking Horse Pass: B.C./Alberta	27	51	116
Kiglapait, Cape: Labr.	12	57	62
Kiglapait Mts.: Labr.		57	62
Kikerk Lake: N.W.T.	29	67	113
Kikkertavak I.: Labr.		56	61
Kikkertorsoak I.: Qué.	12	59	66
Kildare, Cape: P.E.I.	15	47	64
Killaloe Station: Ont.	18	46	77
Killam: Alta.	24	53	112
Killarney: Man.	25	49	100
Killinek I.: Qué.		60	64
Kilmar: Qué.	21	46	75
Kimakto Penin.: N.W.T.	29	70	88
Kimberley: B.C.	27	49	116
Kinburn: Ont.	30	45¼	76¼
Kincaid: Sask.	24	50	107
Kincardine: Ont.	18	44	82
Kindersley: Sask.	24	51	109
King Christian I.: N.W.T.	1	78	103
Kingcome Inlet: & *town*, British Columbia	27	51	126
King Cove: Nfld.		49	53
King George, Mt.: B.C.	27	51	115
King George IV Lake: Newfoundland		48	58
King George Is.: N.W.T.	16	57	79
King I.: B.C.	26	52	127
King Kirkland: Ont.	18	48	80
Kings Point: *town*, Nfld.	15	50	56
Kingsport: N.S.	15	45	64
Kingston: Ont.	21	44	76
Kingsville: Ont.	18	42	83
Kingurutik Lake: Labr.		57	63
King William I.: N.W.T.	29	69	97
Kinistino: Sask.	25	53	105
Kinmount: Ont.	20	45	79
Kinnaird: B.C.	27	49	118
Kinojevis, Lake: Qué.	18	48	79
Kinosis: Alta.		56	111
Kinsella: Alta.		53	112
Kinuso: Alta.	24	55	115
Kiosk: Ont.	18	46	79
Kipahigan Lake: Saskatchewan/Manitoba	25	55	102
Kipawa: *town & lake*, Qué.	18	47	79
Kipawa Reserve: Qué.	18	47	79
Kipling: Sask.	25	50	102
Kirkfield: Ont.	20	45	79
Kirkland Lake: *town*, Ont.	18	48	80
Kirkpatrick Lake: Alta.	24	52	111
Kirkpatrick Lake: Ont.	18	47	83
Kirton: B.C.		50	120
Kisbey: Sask.	25	50	103
Kisgegas: B.C.	26	56	128
Kississing Lake: Man.	25	55	101
Kistigan Lake: Man.	25	55	92
Kitchener: Ont.	18	43	80
Kitimat: B.C.	26	54	129
Kittigazuit: N.W.T.	28	69	134
Kitwanga: B.C.	26	55	128
Klappan: *riv.*, B.C.	26	57	129
Kleena Kleene: B.C.	27	52	125
Kleinburg: Ont.	20	43¾	79¾
Klinaklini: *riv.*, B.C.	27	51	126
Klondike: *riv.*, Yukon	28	64	138
Kluane Lake: Yukon	28	61	138
Klukshu: Yukon		60	137
Knee Lake: Man.	25	55	95
Knight Inlet: B.C.	27	51	126
Knob Lake, see Schefferville			
Knowlton: Qué.	19	45	72
Knox, Cape: B.C.	26	54	133
Koch I.: N.W.T.	12	70	78
Kogaluk: *riv.*, Qué.	12	59	77
Kogaluk Bay: Qué.	12	59	78
Kokanee Park: B.C.	27	50	117
Koksoak: *riv.*, Qué.	12	58	69
Kootenay: *riv.*, Can./U.S.A.	27	49	115
Kootenay Lake: B.C.	27	49	117
Kootenay Nat. Park: B.C.	27	51	116
Koraluk: *riv.*, Labr.	13	56	63
Korluktok Falls: Qué.		58	65
Koruk: *riv.*, Qué.		59	66
Kotcho Lake: B.C.		59	121
Koukdjuak: *riv.*, N.W.T.	12	67	72
Kovik Bay: Qué.	12	62	78
Kowkash: Ont.		50	87
Kronau: Sask.	30	50¼	104¼
Kugmallit Bay: N.W.T.	28	70	133
Kunghit I.: B.C.	26	52	131
Kusawa Lake: Yukon		60	136
Kynocks: Yukon		61	136
Labelle: Qué.	19	46	75
Laberge, Lake: Yukon	28	61	135
Labrador: Nfld.	13	—	—
Labrador City: Labr.	13	53	67
Labrador Sea: Atl. O.	12/13	—	—
Lac aux Sables: Qué.	19	47	72
La Cave: Ont.	18	46	79
Lac Baker: N.B.		47	69
Lac Bouchette: Qué.	19	48	72
Lac Castagnier: Qué.		49	78
Lac Chat: Qué.	19	47	73

	Page	N	W
Lac Decelles Reservoir: Québec	18	48	78
Lac de l'Est: Qué.	19	47	70
Lac du Bonnet: Man.	25	50	96
Lac Edouard: Qué.	19	48	72
Lac Etchemin: Qué.	14	46	70
Lac Frontière: Qué.	14	47	70
Lachine: & *rapids*, Qué.	21	45½	73¾
Lac Humqui: Qué.		48	68
Lachute: Qué.	21	46	74
Lac la Biche: Alta.	24	55	112
Lac La Ronge Prov. Park: Saskatchewan	25	55	105
Lac Mégantic: *town*, Qué.	19	45	71
Lacolle: Qué.	21	45	73
Lacombe: Alta.	24	52	114
Lacoste: Qué.		46	75
Lac Rémi: Qué.	21	46	75
La Croche: Qué.	14	48	73
Lac St. Paul: Qué.		47	75
Ladner: B.C.	27	49	123
Lady Beatrix Lake: Qué.		50	77
Lady Evelyn Falls: N.W.T.		61	117
Lady Evelyn Lake: Ont.	18	47	80
Ladysmith: B.C.	26	49	124
Laflèche: Sask.	24	50	107
Laforest: Ont.		47	81
La Grande: *riv.*, see Fort George			
Lahave: N.S.	15	44	64
Lahave: *riv.*, N.S.	15	45	65
La Hune, Cap: Nfld.		48	57
Lake Cowichan: & *lake*, British Columbia	27	49	124
Lakefield: Ont.	20	44	78
Lake Harbour: N.W.T.	12	63	70
Lake Louise: Alta.	24	51	116
Lakelse: B.C.	26	54	128
Lake River: Ont.	16	54	82
Lake St. Peter: Ont.	20	45	78
Lake Superior Prov. Park: Ontario	18	48	85
La Loche: Sask.	24	56	109
La Malbaie: Qué.	19	48	70
Lamaline: Nfld.		47	56
Lamartine: Qué.		47	70
La Martre, Lac: N.W.T.	28	63	118
Lambeth: Ont.	18	43	81
Lambton: Qué.	14	46	71
Lambton, Cape: N.W.T.	28	71	123
La Moinerie, Lac: Qué.		57	67
Lamorandière: Qué.	18	49	77
La Motte: & *lake*, Qué.	18	48	78
Lampman: Sask.	25	49	103
Lanark: Ont.	21	45	76
Lancaster: N.B.	15	45	66
Lancaster: Ont.	21	45	75
Lancaster Park: Alta.	30	53¾	113½
Lancaster Sound: N.W.T.	29	74	85
Lance Point: Nfld.		47	54
Landis: Sask.	24	52	108
Landmark: Man.	30	49¾	96¾
Landrienne: Qué.	18	48	78
Lang: Sask.	25	50	104
Langdon: Alta.	30	51	113¾
Langenburg: Sask.	25	51	101
Langham: Sask.	24	52	107
Langlade: Qué.	19	48	76
Langley: *town*, B.C.	27	49	122¾
Laniel: Qué.	18	47	79
Lanigan: Sask.	25	52	105
Lanoraie: Qué.	21	46	73
Lansdowne: Ont.	21	44	76
Lansdowne House: Ont.		52	88
L'Ange-Gardien: Qué.	30	47	71
L'Anse au Loup: Labr.		51	57
L'Anse St. Jean: Qué.	19	48	70
Lantzville: B.C.	26	49	124
Lapêche, Lake: Qué.	21	46	76
La Perade: Qué.	19	46	72
La Plonge, Lac: Sask.	24	55	107
La Pocatière: Qué.	19	47	70
La Poile Bay: Nfld.	15	48	58
Lapointe, Lac: Qué.		53	69
La Potherie, Lac: Qué.	12	59	72
Laprairie: Qué.	21	45½	73½
La Providence: Qué.	19	46	73
Larch: *riv.*, Qué.	12	57	70
Larder Lake: *town*, Ont.	18	48	80
Lardo: B.C.	27	50	117
L'Ardoise: N.S.	15	46	61
La Reine: Qué.		49	79
Larive, Lac: Qué.	18	47	77
Lark Harbour: Nfld.	15	49	58
La Ronge: & *lake*, Sask.	25	55	105
Larry River: *town*, N.S.	15	45	61
Larus Lake: Ont.	25	51	95
La Salle: Man.	30	49¾	97¼
La Salle: Ont.	31	42¼	83
La Salle: Qué.	21	45½	73¾
La Sarre: Qué.	13	49	79
L'Ascension: Qué.		49	72
La Scie: Nfld.	15	50	55
Lashburn: Sask.	24	53	110
Lasqueti I.: B.C.	26	49	124
L'Assomption: Qué.	21	46	73
L'Assomption: *riv.*, Qué.	19	46	74
Last Mountain Lake: Sask.	30	50¾	105
Latchford: Ont.	18	47	80
La Tuque: Qué.	19	47	73
Laurentides Park: Qué.	18	47	71
Lauzon: Qué.	30	46¾	71¼
Laval: Qué.	30	47	71¼
Laval-des-Rapides: Qué.	21	45½	73¾
Lavaltrie: Qué.	21	46	73
Lavant Station: Ont.		45	77

	Page	N	W
La Vérendrye Park: Qué.	18	47	77
Laverlochère: Qué.	18	47	79
Lavieille, Lac: Ont.	18	46	78
Lawn: Nfld.		47	56
Lawnhill: B.C.	26	53	132
Lawrencetown: N.S.	15	45	65
Lawrencetown: N.S.	15	45	63
Leader: Sask.	24	51	110
Leaf: *riv.*, Qué.	12	58	73
Leaf Lake: & *bay*, Qué.	12	59	70
Leaf River: *trading post*, Québec		59	69
Leamington: Ont.	18	42	83
Leduc: Alta.	30	53¼	113½
Leeville: Ont.	18	48	80
Lefroy: Ont.	20	44	80
Lemieux Is.: N.W.T.	12	64	65
Lennoxville: Qué.	19	45	72
Lenore Lake: Sask.	25	52	105
Leopold I.: N.W.T.	12	65	64
Leoville: Sask.	24	54	108
L'Epiphanie: Qué.	21	46	73
Lepreau: & *cape*, N.B.	15	45	66
Léry: Qué.	21	45	74
Les Escoumains: Qué.	14	48	69
Les Etroits: Qué.		47	69
Lesser Slave Lake: Alta.	24	55	115
Lethbridge: Alta.	24	50	113
Lethbridge: Nfld.		48	54
Levack: Ont.	18	47	81
Level Mt.: B.C.		58	131
Lévis: Qué.	30	46¾	71¼
Lewisporte: Nfld.	15	49	55
Leyson Point: N.W.T.	12	63	81
Liard: *riv.*, B.C./N.W.T.	28	61	123
Liard Plain: Yukon/B.C.		60	126
Liard Range: N.W.T.	28	61	123
Liddon Gulf: N.W.T.	29	75	114
Lillooet: B.C.	26	51	122
Lillooet: *riv.*, B.C.	26	50	122
Lillooet Lake: B.C.	26	50	122
Limerick: Sask.	24	50	106
Lime Ridge: *town*, Qué.		46	72
Limestone Falls: Qué.		57	69
Limoges: Ont.	30	45¼	75¼
Lincoln: Ont.	20	43	79
Lincoln Sea: Can./Grnld.	1	83	55
Lindbergh: Alta.	24	54	111
Lindbrook: Alta.	30	53¼	112¾
Lindsay: Ont.	20	44	79
Lingman Lake: *town*, Ont.	25	54	93
Linton: Qué.	19	47	72
Linzee, Cape: N.S.	15	46	62
Liot Point: N.W.T.	28	74	125
Lipton: Sask.	25	51	104
Liscomb: N.S.	15	45	62
Lismore: N.S.	15	46	62
Listowel: Ont.	18	44	81
Little Bay I.: & *town*, Nfld.		50	56
Little Current: Ont.	18	46	82
Little Fort: B.C.	27	51	120
Little Grand Lake: Nfld.		49	58
Little Grand Rapids: *town*, Manitoba	25	52	95
Little Longlac: Ont.		50	87
Little Manicouagan Lake: Québec		52	68
Little Mecatina: *riv.*, Qué.	13	52	62
Little Mecatina I.: Labr.	13	50	59
Little Missinaibi Lake: Ont.	18	48	84
Little Narrows: N.S.	15	46	61
Little Pic: *riv.*, Ont.		49	86
Little Smoky: *riv.*, Alta.	24	54	117
Little Vermilion Lake: Ont.	25	51	94
Little Whale: *riv.*, Qué.	13	56	76
Lively: Ont.	18	46	81
Liverpool: N.S.	15	44	65
Liverpool, Cape: N.W.T.	29	74	78
Liverpool Bay: N.W.T.	28	70	130
Livingstone Cove: N.S.	15	46	62
Lizotte: Qué.		48	72
Lloyd George, Mt.: B.C.	27	58	125
Lloyd Lake: Sask.	24	57	109
Lloydminster: Alta./Sask.	24	53	110
Lobstick Lake: Labr.	13	54	65
Lochalsh: Ont.		48	84
Lock Dam: Qué.	19	48	75
Lockeport: N.S.	15	44	65
Lockport: Man.	30	50	97
Logan, Mt.: Qué.	14	49	67
Logan, Mt.: Yukon	28	60	140
Logan Mts.: Yukon/N.W.T.	28	62	128
Logan Point: N.S.	15	46	63
Loks Land: *i.*, N.W.T.	12	63	65
Lomond: Alta.	24	50	113
Lomond: Nfld.	15	49	58
London: Ont.	18	43	81
Londonderry: N.S.	15	45	64
Lonely I.: Ont.	18	45	81
Lone Rock: Sask.	24	53	110
Lone Star: Alta.		57	118
Long I.: Nfld.		48	56
Long I.: Nfld.		50	56
Long I.: Nfld.		47	54
Long I.: N.W.T.	16	55	80
Long I.: N.S.	15	44	66
Longlac: Ont.	17	50	86
Long Lake: N.B.	14	47	67
Long Lake: Ont.		50	87
Long Point: Man.	25	53	98
Long Point: & *bay*, Ont.	18	43	80
Long Pond: Nfld.		48	56
Long Range: Nfld.	15	48	59
Long Range: Nfld.	15	50	57
Long Sault: Ont.	21	45	75
Longueuil: Qué.	21	45½	73½

	Page	N	W
Longview: Alta.	24	50	114
Longworth: B.C.	27	54	121
Lookout, Cape: Ont.		55	84
Lookout Mt.: Labr.		53	64
Looma: Alta.	30	53¼	113¼
Loon Lake: *town*, Sask.	24	54	109
Lord Mayor Bay: N.W.T.	29	70	92
Lord's Cove: Nfld.		47	56
Lorette: Man.	30	49¾	96¾
Loretteville: Qué.	30	46¾	71¼
L'Orignal: Ont.	21	46	75
Lorneville: Ont.	20	44	79
Lorrainville: Qué.	18	47	79
Lotbinière: Qué.	19	47	72
Loughborough Inlet: B.C.	26	50	125
Lougheed: Alta.	24	53	111
Lougheed I.: N.W.T.	1	77	105
Louisbourg: N.S.	15	46	60
Louise I.: B.C.	26	53	132
Louiseville: Qué.	19	46	73
Low: Qué.	21	46	76
Low, Cape: N.W.T.	16	63	85
Low Bush: Ont.		49	80
Lower Arrow Lake: B.C.	27	49	118
Lower Foster Lake: Sask.	25	57	105
Lower Post: B.C.	22	60	128
Lower Sackville: N.S.	30	44¾	63¾
Lower Seal Lakes: Qué.		56	74
Low Lake: Qué.		52	76
Lowther: Ont.		50	83
Lowther I.: N.W.T.	29	75	93
Lubicon Lake: Alta.	24	56	116
Lucan: Ont.	18	43	81
Lucania, Mt.: Yukon		61	140
Lucas Channel: Ont.	18	45	82
Lucerne: B.C.	27	53	119
Luceville: Qué.	14	48	68
Lucky Lake: *town*, Sask.	24	51	07
Ludgate: Ont.		46	80
Lulu I.: B.C.	27	49¼	123
Lumière, Cap: N.B.	15	47	65
Lumsden: Nfld.		49	54
Lumsden: Sask.	30	50¾	104¾
Lund: B.C.	26	50	125
Lunenburg: N.S.	15	44	64
Luscar: Alta.	24	53	117
Luseland: Sask.	24	52	109
Luskville: Qué.	30	45½	76
Lyall, Mt.: B.C./Alta.	27	50	115
Lyalta: Alta.	30	51	113¼
Lymburn: Alta.	24	55	120
Lynn Lake: Man.	25	57	101
Lynx Lake: N.W.T.	29	62	106
Lyon, Cape: N.W.T.	28	70	123
Lyon Inlet: N.W.T.	12	66	84
Lyster Station: Qué.	19	46	72
Lytton: B.C.	26	50	122
Mabel Lake: B.C.	27	50	119
Maberly: Ont.	21	45	77
Mabou: N.S.	15	46	61
MacAlpine Lake: N.W.T.	29	67	103
Macamic: & *lake*, Qué.		49	79
Mcbeth Fiord: N.W.T.	12	69	69
McBride: B.C.	27	53	120
Maccan: N.S.	15	46	64
Maccles Pond: Nfld.		49	54
McClintock: Man.	25	58	94
McClintock Chan.: N.W.T.	29	73	104
McClure, Cape: N.W.T.	28	75	121
McClure Str.: N.W.T.	28	75	118
McConnell Creek: *town*, British Columbia	27	57	126
McConnell Range: N.W.T.	28	64	124
McCreary: Man.	25	51	99
McDame: B.C.		59	129
Macdougall Lake: N.W.T.	29	66	99
MacDowell Lake: Ont.	25	52	92
Macduff: Ont.		49	84
McFarlane: *riv.*, Sask.	24	58	108
McGillivray: B.C.	26	51	122
McGivney: N.B.	14	46	66
McGregor Lake: Alta.	24	50	113
McGuire: B.C.	26	50	123
McInnes Lake: Ont.	25	52	94
MacKay Lake: N.W.T.	29	64	112
Mackenzie: *riv.*, N.W.T.	28	67	133
Mackenzie, District of: N.W.T.	28/29	—	—
Mackenzie Bay: Yukon	28	69	138
Mackenzie Highway: Alta.	24	57	118
McKenzie Island: *town*, Ontario	25	51	94
Mackenzie King I.: N.W.T.	1	78	112
Mackenzie Mtns.: Yukon/N.W.T.	28	64	130
Mackies: Ont.		48	90
McKinnon Harbour: N.S.	15	46	61
Macklin: Sask.	24	52	110
McLean: Sask.	30	50½	104
McLellan Strait: Labr.		60	64
McLennan: Alta.	24	55	117
Macleod Bay: N.W.T.	29	63	110
McLoughlin Bay: N.W.T.	29	67	99
McMasterville: Qué.	21	46	73
Macmillan: *riv.*, Yukon	28	63	133
McNab Island: N.S.	30	44½	63½
McNamee: N.B.	14	46	66
McNutt I.: N.S.	15	44	65
Macoun Lake: Sask.	25	56	104
MacRae: Yukon		61	135
Mactaquac: N.B.	15	46	67
McTavish Arm: Great Bear Lake, N.W.T.	28	66	118

	Page	N	W
MacTier: Ont.	20	45	80
McVicar Arm: Great Bear Lake, N.W.T.	28	65	120
Madawaska: & *riv.*, Ont.	18	45	78
Madeleine, Iles de la: Qué.	13	47	61
Madoc: Ont.	20	45	77
Madsen: Ont.	17	51	94
Magaquadavic: *riv.*, N.B.		45	67
Magnet: Man.	25	51	99
Magnetawan: Ont.	20	46	80
Magog: Qué.	19	45	72
Magpie: *riv.*, Ont.	18	48	84
Magpie: Qué.	14	50	65
Magpie Lake: Que.	13	51	65
Magrath: Alta.	24	49	113
Maguse Lake: N.W.T.	29	62	95
Maguse Point: N.W.T.		61	94
Maguse River: *town*, N.W.T.	29	61	94
Maher: Ont.		49	81
Mahone Bay: & *town*, N.S.	15	44	64
Maidstone: Ont.	31	42¼	83
Maidstone: Sask.	24	53	109
Main Brook: *town*, Nfld.		51	56
Maitland: N.S.	15	45	63
Maitland: *riv.*, Ont.	18	44	81
Makkovik: Labr.	13	55	59
Makobe Lake: Ont.	18	47	80
Malagash: N.S.	15	46	63
Malartic: Qué.	18	48	78
Malaspina Strait: B.C.	26	50	124
Malbaie: *riv.*, Qué.		48	70
Malcolm I.: B.C.	26	51	127
Mallaig: Alta.	24	54	111
Mallery Lake: N.W.T.	29	64	98
Mallorytown: Ont.	21	44	76
Malpeque Bay: P.E.I.	15	47	64
Mamainse Hill: Ont.	18	47	84
Mamainse Point: Ont.		47	85
Mamette Lake: *town*, B.C.		50	121
Mammamattawa: Ont.		50	84
Manic-cinq: Qué.	13	51	69
Manicouagan: *riv.*, Qué.	13	50	68
Manicouagan: *penin.*, Qué.		49	68
Manicouagan Lake: Qué.	13	51	68
Manigotagan Lake: Man.	25	51	95
Manitoba: *Prov.* (*cap.* Winnipeg)	25	—	—
Manitoba, Lake: Man.	25	51	99
Manito Lake: Sask.	24	53	110
Manitou: Man.	25	49	98
Manitou Gorge: Qué.		58	69
Manitou Lake: Ont.	18	46	82
Manitou Lake: Qué.		51	65
Manitou Lakes: Ont.		49	93
Manitoulin I.: Ont.	18	46	82
Manitouwadge: Ont.	17	49	86
Manitowaning: & *bay*, Ont.	18	46	82
Manitowik Lake: Ont.	18	48	84
Maniwaki: Qué.	13	46	76
Mankota: Sask.	24	49	107
Manning: Alta.	24	57	118
Manning, Cape: N.W.T.	28	76	122
Manotick: Ont.	30	45¼	75¾
Manouane: *riv.* & *lake*, Qué.	13	51	70
Manseau: Qué.	19	46	72
Mansel I.: N.W.T.	12	62	80
Manson Creek: *town*, B.C.	27	56	124
Manyberries: Alta.	24	49	111
Mapes: B.C.	27	54	124
Maple: Ont.	20	43¾	79½
Maple Creek: *town*, Sask.	24	50	109
Marathon: Ont.	17	49	86
Margaree: N.S.	15	46	61
Margaree Harbour: N.S.	15	46	61
Margaret, Cape: N.W.T.	29	70	92
Margaret Bay: *town*, B.C.	26	51	127
Margaret Lake: Alta.	24	59	115
Marguerite: *riv.*, Qué.	13	51	67
Marian Lake: N.W.T.	28	63	116
Maria Portage: Man.	25	54	95
Marieville: Qué.	19	45	73
Marilla: B.C.	27	54	126
Markdale: Ont.	18	44	80
Markham: Ont.	20	44	79¼
Markham Bay: N.W.T.	12	63	72
Markstay: Ont.	18	46	80
Marmette, Lac: Qué.		49	75
Marmion Lake: Ont.		49	91
Marmora: Ont.	20	44	78
Marquette: Man.	30	50	97¾
Marsh Lake: Yukon		60	134
Marshy Hope: N.S.	15	45	62
Marsoui: Qué.		49	66
Marten: *riv.*, Qué.		51	76
Maryfield: Sask.	25	50	102
Mary Jones Bay: N.W.T.	29	70	92
Marystown: Nfld.	15	47	55
Marysville: B.C.	27	50	116
Marysville: N.B.	15	46	66
Mascouche: Qué.	21	46	74
Maskinongé: & *riv.*, Qué.	19	46	73
Massawippi Lake: Qué.	19	45	72
Masset: B.C.	26	54	132
Masset Inlet: B.C.	26	54	132
Massey: Ont.	18	46	82
Masson: Qué.	30	45½	75½
Matachewan: Ont.	18	48	81
Matador: Sask.	24	51	108
Matagami: Qué.	13	50	78
Matane: Qué.	14	49	68
Matapédia: Qué.	14	48	67
Matapédia Lake: Qué.		48	68
Matheson: Ont.	18	48	80
Matinenda Lake: Ont.	18	46	83
Matsqui: B.C.	27	49	122¼

	Page	N	W
Mattagami: *riv.*, Ont.	17	50	82
Mattagami Lake: Ont.		48	81
Mattagami Lake: Qué.		50	77
Mattawa: Ont.	18	46	79
Mattawin: *riv.*, Qué.	19	47	73
Maunoir, Lake: N.W.T.	28	67	126
Maury Channel: N.W.T.	29	76	95
Maxville: Ont.	21	45	75
Maxwell Bay: N.W.T.	29	75	89
May, Point: Nfld.		47	56
Mayerthorpe: Alta.	24	54	115
Mayfair: Sask.	24	53	108
Maynooth: Ont.	18	45	78
Mayo: Yukon	28	63	136
Mayo Lake: Yukon	28	64	135
Mayson Lake: Sask.	24	58	107
Mazinaw Lake: Ont.	20	45	77
M'Clintock: Yukon		61	134
M'Clintock Chan.: N.W.T.	3	72	102
Meadow Lake: *town*, Sask.	24	54	108
Meadow Lake Prov. Park: Saskatchewan	24	54	109
Meadows: Man.	30	50	97½
Meaford: Ont.	18	45	81
Meaghers Grant: N.S.	30	45	63¼
Mealy Mtns.: Labr.	13	53	59
Meander River: *town*, Alta.	24	59	118
Meddonegonnix Lake: Newfoundland		48	55
Medicine Hat: Alta.	24	50	111
Medstead: Sask.	24	53	108
Medway: *riv.*, N.S.	15	44	65
Meelpaeg Lake: Nfld.	15	48	57
Mégantic: *lake*, Qué.	19	45	71
Mégantic Mt.: Qué.	19	45	71
Mégiscane: Qué.	18	48	77
Mégiscane: *riv.*, Qué.	19	49	76
Mégiscane, Lac: Qué.		48	76
Meighen I.: N.W.T.	1	80	99
Mekinac Lac: Qué.	19	47	73
Melbourne I.: N.W.T.	29	68	104
Meldrum Bay: *town*, Ont.		46	83
Melfort: Sask.	25	53	105
Melita: Man.	25	49	101
Melrose: N.B.	15	46	64
Melville: Sask.	25	51	103
Melville, Lake: Labr.	13	54	59
Melville Hills: N.W.T.	28	68	120
Melville I.: N.W.T.	29	75	110
Melville Penin.: N.W.T.	12	68	84
Melville Sound: N.W.T.	29	68	108
Memphramagog, Lake: Québec	19	45	72
Memramcook: N.B.	15	46	65
Menako Lakes: Ont.		52	90
Menihek Lakes: Labr.	13	54	66
Menistouc, Lake: Qué.		53	66
Merasheen I.: Nfld.		47	54
Mercier Dam: Qué.	19	47	76
Mercy Bay: N.W.T.	28	74	119
Merigomish: N.S.	15	46	62
Merrickville: Ont.	21	45	76
Merritt: B.C.	27	50	121
Merry I.: N.W.T.		56	77
Mesgouez, Lake: Qué.	13	51	75
Métabetchouan: Qué.		48	72
Metagama: Ont.	18	47	82
Meta Pond: Nfld.		48	55
Metcalfe: Ont.	30	45¼	75½
Metchosin: B.C.	26	48	124
Meteghan: N.S.	15	44	66
Methy Lake: Sask.	24	56	110
Métis Beach: *town*, Qué.		48	68
Métis Lake: Qué.		48	68
Meyronne: Sask.	24	50	107
Mica Creek: B.C.	27	52	118
Mica Dam: B.C.	27	52	118
Michael, Lake: Labr.		55	58
Michael Point: Ont.	18	46	82
Michaud Point: N.S.	15	46	61
Michel: B.C.	27	50	115
Michel, Pte. à: Qué.	14	49	69
Michel Peak: B.C.	27	54	126
Michelson, Cape: N.W.T.	29	71	103
Michikamau Lake: Labr.	13	54	64
Michipicoten: Ont.	18	48	85
Michipicoten I.: Ont.	17	48	86
Midale: Sask.	25	49	103
Middle I.: Ont.	18	42	83
Middle Ridge: Nfld.		48	55
Middle Sackville: N.S.	30	44¾	63¾
Middleton: N.S.	15	45	65
Midhurst: Ont.	20	44	80
Midland: Ont.	20	45	80
Midnapore: Alta.	30	51	114
Midway Mts.: B.C.	27	49	119
Mikkwa: *riv.*, Alta.	24	58	115
Milbanke Sound: B.C.	26	51	128
Mildmay: Ont.	18	44	81
Mildred: Sask.	24	53	107
Milestone: Sask.	25	50	104
Milk: *riv.*, Alta.	24	49	111
Milk River: *town*, Alta.	24	49	112
Mill Bay: *town*, B.C.	26	55	130
Millbrook: Ont.	20	44	78
Mille Îles, R. des: Qué.	21	45¾	73¾
Mille Lacs, Lac des: Ont.		48	90
Millertown: Nfld.		49	57
Millertown Junction: Nfld.		49	56
Millet: Alta.	24	53	113
Mill I.: N.W.T.	12	64	78
Mills Lake: N.W.T.	28	61	118
Milltown: N.B.	14	45	67
Mill Village: N.S.	15	44	65
Milne Inlet: N.W.T.	29	72	80
Milner: B.C.	27	49¼	122¾

	Page	N	W
Milnet: Ont.	18	47	81
Milo: Alta.	24	50	113
Milton: N.S.	15	44	65
Milton: P.E.I.	15	46	63
Milton: Ont.	20	43	80
Milverton: Ont.	18	43	81
Minaki: Ont.	25	50	95
Minas Basin: & *chan.*, N.S.	15	45	64
Minden: Ont.	20	45	79
Mine Centre: Ont.	17	49	93
Mine de Mica: Qué.	21	46	76
Mingan: & *is.*, Qué.	14	50	64
Minipi: *riv. & rapids*, Labr.		53	62
Minipi Lake: Labr.		52	61
Ministik Lake: Alta.	30	53¼	113
Minitonas: Man.	25	52	101
Minnedosa: Man.	25	50	100
Minto: N.B.	15	46	66
Minto, Lake: Qué.	12	57	75
Minto Head: N.W.T.	29	73	103
Minto Inlet: N.W.T.	28	71	117
Minto Mine: B.C.	26	51	123
Minton: Sask.	25	49	105
Miquelon Lake: Alta.	30	53¼	113
Mira: & *bay*, N.S.	15	46	60
Miramichi, N.W.: *riv.*, N.B.	14	47	66
Miramichi, S.W.: *riv.*, N.B.	14	46	67
Miramichi Bay: N.B.	14	47	65
Miscou: *i. & cape*, N.B.	14	48	64
Miscouche: P.E.I.	15	46	64
Misery Point: Labr.		52	55
Missanabie: Ont.	18	48	84
Missinaibi: *riv.*, Ont.	17	50	83
Missinaibi Lake: Ont.	18	48	84
Mission City: B.C.	27	49¼	122¼
Missisa Lake: Ont.	17	52	83
Mississagi: *riv.*, Ont.	18	46	83
Mississagi Strait: Ont.	18	46	83
Mississagi Prov. Forest: Ontario	18	47	83
Mississauga: Ont.	20	44	80
Mississippi: *riv. & lake*, Ont.	21	45	76
Missouri Coteau: Sask.	24	50	106
Mistassibi: *riv.*, Qué.	13	49	72
Mistassini: & *riv.*, Qué.	14	49	72
Mistassini, Lake: Qué.	13	51	74
Mistastin Lake: Labr.		56	63
Mistinibi, Lake: Qué.		56	64
Mitchell: Ont.	18	43	81
Mitchinamekus: *riv.*, Qué.	19	47	75
Moak Lake: Man.	25	56	97
Moar Lake: Man./Ont.	25	52	95
Moha: B.C.	26	51	122
Moira: *riv.*, Ont.	20	44	77
Moisie: & *riv.*, Qué.	13	50	66
Mojikit Lake: Ont.		51	88
Molson: Man.	25	50	96
Molson Lake: Labr.		53	66
Molson Lake: Man.	25	54	97
Monarch Mt.: B.C.	27	52	126
Monashee Mts.: B.C.	27	51	118
Moncton: N.B.	15	46	65
Monet: Qué.	19	48	76
Monkman Pass: B.C.	27	55	121
Montague: P.E.I.	15	46	63
Mont Alverne: Qué.		48	72
Montauban: Qué.		47	72
Montcerf: Qué.		46	76
Montebello: Qué.	21	46	75
Monte Creek: *town*, B.C.		51	120
Monteith: Ont.		49	81
Montgomery: Alta.	30	51	114
Montigny, Lac.: Qué.	18	48	78
Mont Joli: Qué.	14	48	68
Mont Laurier: Qué.	19	47	75
Mont Louis: Qué.	14	49	66
Montmagny: Qué.	14	47	70
Montmartre: Sask.	25	50	103
Montmorency: & *riv.*, Qué.	30	46¾	71¼
Montor, Lac: Qué.		55	64
Montréal: *City & i.*, Qué.	21	45½	73½
Montreal: *riv.*, Ont.	18	47	84
Montreal: *riv.*, Ont.		48	80
Montreal: *riv.*, Sask.	25	55	106
Montréal Est: Qué.	21	45¾	73½
Montreal Lake: & *town*, Saskatchewan	25	54	106
Montréal Nord: Qué.	21	45½	73½
Montreal River: *town*, Ont.	18	47	79
Mont Rolland: Qué.	21	46	74
Montrose: B.C.	27	49	118
Monts, Pte. des: Qué.	14	49	67
Mont Tremblant Park: Qué.	19	46	74
Moonbeam: Ont.		49	82
Moor Lake: Ont.	18	46	78
Moose: *riv.*, Ont.	17	51	81
Moose Creek: *town*, Ont.	21	45	75
Moose Factory: Ont.		51	81
Moose Jaw: Sask.	25	50	106
Moose Lake: Man.	25	54	100
Moose Mtn. Park: Sask.	25	50	102
Moose River: *town*, N.S.	15	45	62
Moosonee: Ont.	17	51	81
Moosomin: Sask.	25	50	102
Morden: Man.	25	49	98
Morden: N.S.	15	45	65
Morell: P.E.I.	15	46	63
Moresby I.: B.C.	26	52	132
Morhiban, Lac de: Qué.		52	63
Moriarty, Mt.: B.C.	26	49	124
Morice Lake: B.C.	26	54	127
Moricetown: B.C.	26	55	127
Morin Heights: Qué.	21	46	74
Morinville: Alta.	24	54	114
Morris: Man.	25	49	97
Morrisburg: Ont.	21	45	75

	Page	N	W
Morse: Sask.	24	50	107
Mortlach: Sask.	25	50	106
Mosherville: N.S.	15	45	64
Mossbank: Sask.	25	50	106
Mostoos Hills: Sask.	24	55	109
Mouni Rapids: Labr.		53	62
Mountain Grove: Ont.		45	77
Mountain Park: Alta.	24	53	117
Mountain View: Ont.	20	44	77
Mount Albert: Ont.	20	44	79
Mount Forest: Ont.	18	44	81
Mount Hope: Ont.	20	43	80
Mount Pearl Park: Nfld.	30	47½	52¾
Mount Robson Prov. Park: British Columbia	27	53	119
Mount Stewart: P.E.I.	15	46	63
Mount Uniacke: N.S.	30	45	63¾
Mozhabong Lake: Ont.	18	47	82
Muddy Bay: *settlement*, Labrador		54	57
Mudjatik: *riv.*, Sask.	24	57	107
Mud River: *town*, B.C.	27	54	123
Mugford, Cape: Labr.		58	62
Mukutawa: *riv.*, Man.	25	53	97
Mulgrave: N.S.	15	46	61
Mundare: Alta.	24	54	112
Munuscong Lake: Canada/U.S.A.	18	46	84
Murdale: B.C.	27	57	121
Murdochville: Qué.	14	49	65
Murray Harbour: P.E.I.	15	46	62
Murray Maxwell Bay: N.W.T.	29	70	80
Murray River: *town*, P.E.I.	15	46	62
Murrayville: B.C.	27	49	122¾
Murtle Lake: B.C.	27	52	120
Musgrave Town: Nfld.		48	54
Mushalagan: *riv.*, Qué.		52	69
Mushalagan Lake: Qué.	13	51	69
Muskoka, Lake: Ont.	20	45	79
Muskrat Falls: Labr.		53	61
Musquaro Lake: Qué.		51	61
Musquash: N.B.	15	45	66
Musquodoboit: N.S.	15	45	63
Musquodoboit Harbour: Nova Scotia	30	44¾	63¼
Mutton Bay: *town*, Labr.		51	59
Myrnam: Alta.	24	54	111
Myrtle: Ont.	20	44	79
Mystery Lake: Man.	25	56	98
Nabisipi: *riv.*, Qué.		51	62
Nachikapau, Lake: Qué.		57	68
Nachvak Fiord: Labr.		59	63
Nagagami Lake: Ont.		49	85
Nahanni Mt.: N.W.T.		62	123
Nahanni Range: N.W.T.	28	61	123
Nahlin: B.C.		59	131
Nahma: Ont.		49	81
Naicam: Sask.	25	52	104
Nain: Labr.	13	56	62
Nakina: Ont.	17	50	87
Nakusp: B.C.	27	50	118
Namao: Alta.	30	53¾	113½
Namur: Qué.	21	46	75
Nanaimo: B.C.	26	49	124
Nansen Sd.: N.W.T.	1	82	91
Nanton: Alta.	24	50	114
Naococane Lake: Qué.	13	53	71
Napanee: Ont.	20	44	77
Napartokh Bay: Labr.		58	62
Napierville: Qué.	21	45	73
Napinka: Man.	25	49	101
Nappan: N.S.	15	46	64
Narcisse: Man.	25	51	97
Naskaupi: *riv.*, Labr.	13	54	63
Nass: *riv.*, B.C.	26	55	129
Nastapoka: *riv.*, Qué.	13	57	76
Nastapoka Is.: N.W.T.		57	77
Natashquan: Qué.	13	50	62
Natashquan: *riv.*, Qué.	13	51	62
Nation: *riv.*, B.C.	27	55	124
Native Bay: N.W.T.	16	64	83
Naughton: Ont.	18	46	81
Nauwigewauk: N.B.	15	45	66
Navin: Man.	30	49¾	97
Nazko: B.C.	27	53	124
Nechako: *riv.*, B.C.	27	54	125
Nechako Plateau: B.C.	27	54	124
Neddy Harbour: Nfld.		50	58
Nedluk Lake: Qué.		57	73
Neeb: Sask.	24	54	108
Neepawa: Man.	25	50	99
Nejanilini Lake: Man.	25	60	98
Nelson: B.C.	27	49	117
Nelson: *riv.*, Man.	25	57	93
Nelson Forks: B.C.	22	59	124
Nelson House: Man.	25	56	99
Nelson I.: B.C.	26	50	124
Nemegos: Ont.	18	48	83
Nemegosenda: *riv.*, Ont.	18	48	83
Nemiscau: Qué.	13	51	77
Nemiskam Nat. Park: Alta.	24	49	111
Neoskweskau: Qué.		52	74
Nepewassi Lake: Ont.	18	46	81
Nestawkanow: *riv.*, Qué.		50	73
Nettilling Fiord: N.W.T.	12	66	68
Nettilling Lake: N.W.T.	12	66	70
Neudorf: Sask.	25	51	103
Neustadt: Ont.	18	44	81
Neuville: Qué.	30	46¾	71½
New Albany: N.S.	15	45	65
New Bay: Nfld.		49	55
Newboro: Ont.	21	45	76

	Page	N	W
New Brunswick: *Prov.* (*cap.* Fredericton)	14	46	66
Newburgh: Ont.	20	44	77
New Carlisle: Qué.	14	48	65
Newcastle: N.B.	14	47	65
Newcastle: Ont.	20	44	79
Newcastle Bridge: N.B.	15	46	66
Newcastle Mine: Alta.	24	51	113
New Denver: B.C.	27	50	117
Newell, Lake: Alta.	24	50	112
Newfoundland: *Prov.* (*cap.* St. John's)	12/13	—	—
Newfoundland: *i.*, Canada	13	49	56
New Germany: N.S.	15	45	65
New Glasgow: N.S.	15	46	63
New Hamburg: Ont.	18	43	81
Newington: Ont.	21	45	75
New Liskeard: Ont.	18	47	80
Newmarket: Ont.	20	44	79
Newport: N.S.	15	45	64
Newport: Qué.	14	48	65
Newport Corner: N.S.	30	45	64
New Richmond: Qué.	14	48	66
New Ross: N.S.	15	45	64
New Sarepta: Alta.	30	53¼	113¼
Newton: B.C.	27	49¼	122¾
Newville: N.S.	15	46	64
New Waterford: N.S.	15	46	60
New Westminster: B.C.	27	49¼	123
New World I.: Nfld.		50	55
Niagara: *riv.*, Can./U.S.A.	20	43	79
Niagara Escarpment: Ont.	20	43	79
Niagara Falls: *town*, Ont.	20	43	79
Niagara-on-the-Lake: Ont.	20	43	79
Nichicun, Lake: Qué.		53	71
Nicholson: & *dam*, Ont.	18	48	84
Nicobi Lake: Qué.		49	76
Nicola: & *lake*, B.C.		50	121
Nicola: *riv.*, B.C.	26	50	121
Nicolet: & *riv.*, Qué.	19	46	73
Nictau: N.B.	14	47	67
Nig Creek: *town*, B.C.	27	57	121
Nigei I.: B.C.	26	50	127
Night Hawk Lake: Ont.	18	48	81
Nightingale: Alta.	30	51¼	113¼
Nimpkish Lake: B.C.	26	50	127
Nipawin: Sask.	25	53	104
Nipawin Prov. Park: Sask.	25	54	105
Nipigon: Ont.	17	48	88
Nipigon, Lake: Ont.	17	50	88
Nipigon Bay: Ont.		49	88
Nipigon-Onaman Game Preserve: Ontario		50	87
Nipigon Prov. Forest: Ont.	17	50	88
Nipishish Lake: Labr.		54	60
Nipisiquit: *riv.*, N.B.	14	47	66
Nipissi, Lake: Qué.		50	72
Nipissing, Lake: Ont.	18	46	80
Nipissing Game Preserve: Ontario	18	47	80
Nisku: Alta.	30	53¼	113½
Nisling: *riv. & range*, Yukon	28	62	139
Nisutlin: *riv.*, Yukon		61	133
Nitchequon: Qué.	13	53	71
Nith: *riv.*, Ont.	18	43	81
Nitinat Lake: B.C.	26	49	125
Nobel: Ont.	18	45	80
Nobleton: Ont.	20	44	80
Noelville: Ont.	18	46	80
Nokomis: Sask.	25	51	105
Nokomis Lake: Sask.	25	57	103
Nomansland Point: Ont.		52	81
Nominingue: Qué.	19	46	75
Nonacho Lake: N.W.T.	29	62	109
Nootka: B.C.		50	127
Nootka: *i. & sound*, B.C.	27	50	127
Noralee: B.C.	27	54	126
Noranda: Qué.	18	48	79
Norembega: Ont.		49	81
Norman, Cape: Nfld.		52	56
Normandin: Qué.	14	49	72
Norman Wells: N.W.T.	28	65	126
Normetal: Qué.	13	49	79
Norris Arm: Nfld.		49	55
North: *riv.*, Labr.	12	57	63
North: *riv.*, Qué.	19	46	74
North, Cape: N.S.	15	47	60
North Aulatsivik I.: Labr.	12	60	64
North Battleford: Sask.	24	53	108
North Bay: *riv.*, Nfld.		48	55
North Bay: *town*, Ont.	18	46	79
North Bend: B.C.	26	50	121
North Cape: P.E.I.	15	47	64
North Caribou Lake: Ont.	16	53	90
North Channel: Ont.	18	46	83
North Cooking Lake: Alta.	30	53½	113
Northern Bay: Nfld.		48	53
Northern Indian Lake: Manitoba	25	57	97
North Gower: Ont.	21	45	7[illegible]
North Head: Nfld.		49	[illegible]
North Head: *town*, Great Manan I.		45	[illegible]
North Henik Lake: N.W.T.	29	62	[illegible]
North Knife: *riv.*, Man.	25	59	96
North Knife Lake: Man.	25	58	97
North Magnetic Pole: N.W.T.	29	76	101
North Payne: *riv.*, Qué.	12	60	73
North River: *settlement*, Labrador		54	57
North River: *town*, Man.	25	59	95
North River Bridge: N.S.	15	46	61
North Saskatchewan: *riv.*, Alberta/Saskatchewan	24	53	107
North Saugeen: *riv.*, Ont.		44	81

	Page	N	W
North Seal: *riv.*, Man.	**25**	59	100
North Sydney: N.S.	**15**	46	60
North Thames: *riv.*, Ont.	**18**	43	81
North Thompson: *riv.*, British Columbia	**27**	52	120
Northumberland Strait: Canada	**15**	46	64
North Vancouver: B.C.	**27**	49¼	123
North Wabiskaw Lake: Alberta	**24**	56	114
North West River: *settlement*, Labrador	**13**	53	60
North West St. Augustin: *riv.*, Québec		51	59
Northwest Territories: (*seat of Govt.* Yellowknife)	**28/29**	—	—
North York: Ont.	**20**	43¾	79½
Norton: N.B.	**15**	46	66
Norway Bay: N.W.T.	**29**	71	105
Norway House: Man.	**25**	54	98
Norway I.: N.W.T.	**28**	74	125
Norwegian Bay: N.W.T.	**1**	78	90
Norwich: Ont.	**18**	43	81
Norwood: Ont.	**20**	44	78
Notikewin: Alta.	**24**	57	118
Notre Dame: N.B.	**15**	46	65
Notre Dame Bay: Nfld.	**15**	50	55
Notre-Dame-de-la-Paix: Québec	**21**	46	75
Notre-Dame-de-la-Salette: Québec		46	76
Notre-Dame-des-Laurentides: Québec	**30**	47	71¼
Notre Dame du Lac: Qué.		48	69
Notre-Dame-du-Laus: Québec.	**19**	46	76
Notre Dame-du-Nord: Québec	**18**	48	80
Notre Dame Junction: Nfld.		49	55
Notre Dame Mtns.: Qué.	**14**	48	67
Notta: *riv.*, Ont.	**20**	44	80
Nottawasaga Bay: Ont.	**18**	45	80
Nottaway: *riv.*, Qué.		51	79
Nottingham I.: & *town*, N.W.T.	**12**	63	78
Nova Scotia: *Prov.* (*cap.* Halifax)	**15**	—	—
Novar: Ont.	**20**	45	79
Noyan: Qué.	**21**	45	73
Nueltin Lake: N.W.T.	**29**	60	100
Nunaksaluk: *i.*, Labr.		56	60
Nungesser Lake: Ont.	**25**	51	93
Nutak: Labr.	**12**	58	62
Nut Mountain: *town & mt.*, Saskatchewan	**25**	52	103
Oakbank: Man.	**30**	50	96¾
Oak Bluff: Man.	**30**	49¾	97¼
Oak Lake: & *town*, Man.	**25**	50	101
Oak Point: *town*, Man.	**25**	50	98
Oakville: Ont.	**20**	43	80
Obalski Lake: Qué.		49	78
Oban: Sask.	**24**	52	108
Obatogamau Lake: Qué.	**14**	50	74
Obed: Alta.	**24**	54	117
O'Brien: Ont.	**18**	48	81
Observatory Inlet: B.C.	**26**	55	130
Ocean Falls: *town*, B.C.	**26**	52	128
Odessa: Ont.	**20**	44	77
Odessa: Sask.	**30**	50¼	103¾
O'Donnell Point: Ont.	**18**	45	80
Ogahalla: Ont.		50	86
Ogema: Sask.	**25**	50	105
Ogilvie Mtns.: Yukon	**28**	65	138
Ogoki: Ont.		52	86
Ogoki: *riv.*, Ont.	**17**	51	88
Ogoki Reservoir: Ont.		51	88
Oka: Qué.	**21**	45	74
Okak Is.: Labr.		58	62
Okanagan Lake: B.C.	**27**	50	120
Okotoks: Alta.	**24**	51	114
Old Crow: & *riv.*, Yukon	**28**	68	140
Old Factory: Qué.		52	79
Old Factory Lake: Qué.		53	77
Old Fort Bay: *town*, Qué.		51	58
Oldman: *riv.*, Alta.	**24**	50	114
Old Perlican: Nfld.		48	53
Old Post Point: Qué.	**14**	50	62
Olds: Alta.	**24**	52	114
Old Wives Lake: Sask.	**25**	50	106
Oliver: Alta.	**30**	53¾	113¼
Oliver Lake: Alta.	**30**	53¼	113
Olomanc: *riv.*, Qué.		51	61
Omemee: Ont.	**20**	44	79
Omineca: *riv.*, B.C.	**27**	56	125
Omineca Mtns.: B.C.	**26**	57	127
Ommanney Bay: N.W.T.	**29**	73	101
Onaman Lake: Ont.		50	87
Onaping Lake: & *riv.*, Ont.	**18**	47	81
Onistagan, Lake: Qué.		51	71
Ontario: *Prov.* (*cap.* Toronto)	**16/17**	—	—
Ontario, Lake: Can./U.S.A.	**18**	44	78
Ootsa Lake: *town*, B.C.	**27**	54	126
Opal: Alta.	**24**	54	113
Opasatica Lake: Qué.	**18**	48	79
Opasatika: Ont.		50	83
Opasquia: Ont.	**16**	53	94
Opataca Lake: Qué.		50	75
Opawica: *lake & riv.*, Qué.		50	76
Opeongo Lake: Ont.	**18**	46	78
Opinaca: *riv.*, Qué.		53	77
Opinnagau Lake: Ont.		54	84
Opiscoteo Lake: Qué.	**13**	53	68

	Page	N	W
Orange Bay: Nfld.		50	56
Orangedale: N.S.	**15**	46	61
Orangeville: Ont.	**18**	44	80
Ordale: Sask.	**24**	53	107
Orillia: Ont.	**20**	45	79
Orleans: Ont.	**30**	45½	75½
Orleans, Île d': Qué.	**19**	47	71
Ormiston: Sask.	**25**	50	105
Ormstown: Qué.	**21**	45	74
Oromocto: N.B.	**15**	46	66
Orono: Ont.	**20**	44	79
Osgoode: Ont.	**30**	45¼	75½
Oshawa: Ont.	**20**	44	79
Oskelaneo: Qué.	**19**	48	75
Osnaburgh House: Ont.		51	90
Osoyoos: B.C.	**27**	49	120
Ospika: *riv.*, B.C.	**27**	57	124
Osprey Lake: *town*, B.C.		50	120
Ossokmanuan Lake: Labr.	**13**	53	65
Otelnuk Lake: Qué.		56	68
Otish Mtns.: Qué.	**13**	52	70
Otoskwin: *riv.*, Ont.	**17**	51	89
OTTAWA: Ontario	**30**	45½	75¾
Ottawa: *riv.*, Qué./Ont.	**21**	46	75
Ottawa Is.: N.W.T.	**16**	59	80
Otter: Anticosti I.	**14**	50	64
Otter Head: Ont.		48	86
Otter Lake: Ont.	**20**	45	80
Otter Lake: Sask.	**25**	55	104
Ouimet: Ont.		49	89
Oureau: *riv.*, Qué.	**19**	46	74
Outer I.: Qué.	**13**	51	58
Outlook: Sask.	**24**	51	107
Outremont: Qué.	**21**	45½	73½
Owen Sound: & *town*, Ont.	**18**	45	81
Owl: *riv.*, Man.	**25**	58	93
Oxbow: Sask.	**25**	49	102
Oxford: N.S.	**15**	46	64
Oxford House: Man.	**25**	55	95
Oxford Junction: N.S.	**15**	46	64
Oxford Lake: Man.	**25**	55	95
Oyama: B.C.	**27**	50	119
Oyen: Alta.	**24**	51	110
Oyster River: *town*, B.C.	**26**	50	125
Ozhiska Lake: Ont.		52	88
Pacific: B.C.	**26**	55	128
Packenham: Ont.	**21**	45	76
Pack's Harbour: Labr.		54	57
Paddle Prairie: *town*, Alta.	**24**	58	117
Paddockwood: Sask.	**25**	53	105
Padlei: N.W.T.	**29**	62	97
Pagwa River: *town*, Ont.	**17**	50	85
Pakenham: Ont.	**30**	45¼	76¼
Pakowki Lake: Alta.	**24**	49	111
Pakwash Lake: Ont.	**25**	51	93
Palling: B.C.	**27**	54	126
Palmarolle: Qué.		48	79
Palmer Point: N.W.T.	**29**	75	108
Palmerston: Ont.	**18**	44	81
Panache, Lake: Ont.	**18**	46	81
Pancake Point: Ont.		47	85
Pangnirtung: N.W.T.	**12**	66	66
Papineau, Lac: Qué.	**21**	46	75
Papineauville: Qué.	**21**	46	75
Paquet: Nfld.	**15**	50	56
Paradis: Qué.	**19**	48	77
Paradise: *riv.*, Labr.		53	58
Paradise Sound: Nfld.		47	55
Paradise Valley: *town*, Alta.	**24**	53	110
Parc, Lac du: Qué.		57	67
Parent: Qué.	**19**	48	75
Parent, Lac: Qué.	**18**	48	77
Parham: Ont.		45	77
Paris: Ont.	**18**	43	80
Parisienne, I.: Ont.		46	84
Park Head: *town*, Ont.		45	81
Park Hill: *town*, Ont.	**18**	43	82
Parksville: B.C.	**26**	49	124
Parrsboro: N.S.	**15**	45	64
Parry, Cape: N.W.T.	**28**	70	125
Parry Bay: N.W.T.	**12**	68	82
Parry Is.: N.W.T.	**29**	76	110
Parry Sound: *town*, Ont.	**20**	45	80
Parsnip: *riv.*, B.C.	**27**	55	123
Partridgeberry Hills: Nfld.		48	56
Pascalis: *lake*, Qué.	**18**	48	77
Pasfield Lake: Sask.	**25**	58	105
Pashkokogan Lake: Ont.		51	90
Pasley Bay: N.W.T.	**29**	71	97
Pasqua: Sask.	**25**	50	105
Pasquia Hills: Sask.	**25**	53	103
Passamaquoddy Bay: N.B.	**15**	45	67
Pattullo, Mt.: B.C.	**26**	56	130
Paulatuk: N.W.T.	**28**	69	123
Paul I.: Labr.	**13**	56	62
Pavilion: B.C.		51	122
Payne: *riv.*, Qué.	**12**	60	72
Payne Bay: & *settlement*, Québec	**12**	60	70
Payne Lake: Qué.	**12**	59	74
Paynton: Sask.	**24**	53	109
Peace: *riv.*, B.C./Alta.	**24**	58	114
Peace River: *town*, Alta.	**24**	56	117
Peachland: B.C.		50	120
Peakes: P.E.I.	**15**	46	63
Pearl I.: Nfld.		49	58
Peary Chan.: N.W.T.	**3**	79	100
Peel: *plat. & riv.*, Yukon	**28**	67	134
Peel Point: N.W.T.	**29**	73	115
Peel Sound: N.W.T.	**29**	73	97
Peerless Lake: Alta.	**24**	57	114
Pefferlaw: Ont.	**20**	44	79
Peggy's Cove: *town*, N.S.	**30**	44½	64
Pelee Island: *town & i.*, Ont.	**18**	42	83

	Page	N	W
Pelee Passage: *chan.*, Ont.	**18**	42	83
Pelee Point: Ont.	**18**	42	83
Pelican Bay: Man.	**25**	53	100
Pelican Lake: Man.	**25**	52	100
Pelican Lake: Qué.		60	74
Pelican Mtns.: Alta.	**24**	56	114
Pelican Narrows: *town*, Saskatchewan	**25**	55	103
Pelletier Station: Qué.		47	69
Pelly: *riv.*, Yukon	**28**	62	133
Pelly Bay: & *settlement*, N.W.T.	**29**	69	90
Pelly Lake: N.W.T.	**29**	66	102
Pelly Mtns.: Yukon	**28**	62	133
Pemberton: B.C.	**26**	50	123
Pembina: Alta.	**24**	53	115
Pembina: *riv.*, Alta.	**24**	53	116
Pembroke: Ont.	**18**	46	77
Pendant d'Oreille: Alta.	**24**	49	111
Penetanguishene: Ont.	**20**	45	80
Penguin Is.: Nfld.		45	57
Penhold: Alta.	**24**	52	114
Pennant Point: N.S.	**15**	44	64
Pennask Lake: B.C.		50	120
Pennfield: N.B.	**15**	45	67
Penny Highland: N.W.T.	**12**	67	66
Pense: Sask.	**30**	50½	105
Penticton: B.C.	**27**	49	120
Penzance: Sask.	**25**	51	105
Percé: Qué.	**14**	49	64
Perdu, Lac: Qué.		51	70
Perdue: Sask.	**24**	52	108
Péribonca: Qué.		49	72
Péribonca: *riv.*, Qué.	**13**	49	71
Péribonca Lake: Qué.		50	71
Perkins: Qué.	**30**	45½	75½
Perow: B.C.	**27**	54	126
Perrault Lake: Ont.	**25**	50	93
Perron: Qué.	**18**	48	78
Perrot, Île: Qué.	**21**	45	74
Perry River: *town*, N.W.T.	**29**	67	103
Perth: N.B.	**14**	47	68
Perth: Ont.	**21**	45	76
Petawawa: Ont.	**18**	46	78
Peterbell: Ont.		48	83
Peterborough: Ont.	**20**	44	78
Peter Pond Lake: Sask.	**24**	56	109
Peters Arm: Nfld.		49	55
Petitcodiac: N.B.	**15**	46	65
Petit Etang: *town*, N.S.	**15**	47	61
Petit Nord Penin.: Nfld.		51	57
Petitot: *riv.*, B.C.	**22**	60	121
Petitsikapau Lake: Labr.	**13**	54	66
Petre, Point: Ont.	**20**	44	77
Petries: Nfld.		49	58
Petrolia: Ont.	**18**	43	82
Petty Harbour: Nfld.	**30**	47½	52¾
Peyton, Mt.: Nfld.		49	55
Philomena: Alta.		55	112
Piacoudie, Lac: Qué.		51	71
Piapot: Sask.	**24**	50	109
Pickering: Ont.	**20**	44	79
Pickle Crow: Ont.	**17**	51	90
Pickle Lake: Ont.		51	90
Picton: Ont.	**20**	44	77
Pictou: & *i.*, N.S.	**15**	46	63
Picture Butte: Alta.	**24**	50	113
Piedmont: Qué.	**21**	46	74
Pie I.: Ont.		48	89
Pierrefonds: Qué.	**21**	45½	73¾
Pierreville: Qué.	**19**	46	73
Pigeon: *riv.*, Can./U.S.A.		48	90
Pigeon Bay: Man.	**25**	52	97
Pigeon Bay: Ont.	**18**	42	83
Pigeon Lake: Alta.	**24**	53	114
Pigeon Lake: *town*, Man.	**30**	50	97¾
Pigeon Lake: Ont.	**20**	44	78
Pikangikum Lake: Ont.	**17**	52	94
Pike: B.C.		59	133
Pikwitonei: Man.	**25**	56	97
Pilley's I.: Nfld.		50	56
Pilot Butte: Sask.	**30**	50½	104½
Pilot Mound: Man.	**25**	49	99
Pincher Creek: *town*, Alta.	**24**	49	114
Pinchi Lake: B.C.	**27**	55	124
Pine, Cape: Nfld.	**15**	47	54
Pine Falls: *town*, Man.	**25**	51	96
Pine Mt. Lake: Qué.		54	75
Pine Pass: B.C.	**27**	55	122
Pine Point: N.W.T.	**28**	61	114
Pine River: *town*, Sask.	**24**	56	107
Pine Valley: *town*, B.C.	**27**	56	120
Pins, Pte. aux: Ont.	**18**	42	82
Pinto Butte: *mtn.*, Sask.	**24**	49	107
Pipestone: *riv.*, Ont.		52	90
Pipmuacan, Lac: Qué.	**17**	49	70
Pirmez Creek: *town*, Alta.	**30**	51	114
Piscatosin Lac: Qué.	**19**	47	75
Pistolet Bay: Nfld.		51	56
Pitt: *riv. & lake*, B.C.	**26**	49	123
Pitt I.: B.C.	**26**	53	130
Pitt Sound: Nfld.		49	54
Placentia: & *bay*, Nfld.	**15**	47	54
Placentia Junction: Nfld.	**30**	47½	53¾
Plaisance: Qué.	**21**	46	75
Plantagenet: Ont.	**21**	45	75
Plaster Rock: N.B.	**14**	47	67
Plate Cove: Nfld.		49	53
Playgreen Lake: Man.	**25**	54	98
Pledger Lake: Ont.		50	84
Plessisville: Qué.	**19**	46	72
Pletipi Lake: Qué.	**13**	51	70
Plonge, Lac la: Sask.	**24**	55	107
Plum Coulee: Man.	**25**	49	98
Pockwock Lake: N.S.	**30**	44¾	63¾
Point Claire: Qué.	**21**	45	74

	Page	N	W
Pointe au Baril Station: Ontario	**18**	45	80
Pointe-aux-Trembles: Qué.	**21**	45¾	73½
Pointe Fortune: Ont.	**21**	46	74
Pointe-Gatineau: Qué.	**30**	45½	75¾
Pointe Le Bel: Qué.		49	68
Point Lake: N.W.T.	**29**	65	113
Point Leamington: Nfld.		49	55
Poisson Blanc, Lac: Qué.	**21**	46	76
Polaris Lake: Qué.		53	73
Poltimore: Qué.	**21**	46	76
Pomquet: N.S.	**15**	46	62
Pond Inlet: & *settlement*, N.W.T.	**29**	73	78
Ponds, I. of: Labr.		53	56
Ponoka: Alta.	**24**	53	114
Pons: *riv.*, Qué.		56	69
Pontax: *riv.*, Qué.		52	77
Ponteix: Sask.	**24**	50	108
Pont Rouge: Qué.	**30**	46¾	71¾
Pontypool: Ont.	**20**	44	79
Poplar: *riv.*, Man./Ont.	**25**	53	97
Poplar Hill: *town*, Ont.	**25**	52	94
Porcher I.: B.C.	**26**	54	130
Porcupine: Ont.	**18**	48	81
Porcupine: *riv.*, U.S.A./Can.	**28**	67	138
Porcupine, Cape: Labr.		54	57
Porcupine Hills: Sask./Man.	**25**	52	101
Porcupine Plain: *town*, Sask.	**25**	53	103
Porquis Junction: Ont.		48	81
Portage: P.E.I.	**15**	47	64
Portage Bay: Man.	**25**	51	99
Portage-du-Fort: Qué.		46	77
Portage la Prairie: Man.	**25**	50	98
Port Alberni: B.C.	**26**	49	125
Port Alfred: Qué.	**19**	48	71
Port Alice: B.C.	**26**	50	127
Port Anson: Nfld.		50	56
Port Arthur: Ont. *see* Thunder Bay			
Port-au-Port: *penin. & bay*, Newfoundland	**15**	49	59
Port-aux-Basques: Nfld.	**15**	47	59
Port Blandford: Nfld.	**15**	48	54
Port Bolster: Ont.	**20**	44	79
Port Burwell: Ont.	**18**	42	81
Port Burwell: Qué.	**12**	60	65
Port Carling: Ont.	**20**	45	80
Port Cartier: Qué.	**13**	50	67
Port Clements: B.C.	**26**	53	132
Port Clyde: N.S.	**15**	44	65
Port Colborne: Ont.	**20**	43	79
Port Coquitlam: B.C.	**27**	49¼	122¾
Port Credit: Ont.	**20**	43½	79½
Port Dalhousie: Ont.	**20**	43	79
Port Daniel: Qué.	**14**	48	65
Port Dover: Ont.	**18**	43	80
Port Edward: B.C.	**26**	54	130
Port Edward: Ont.	**18**	43	82
Port Elgin: N.B.	**15**	46	64
Port Elgin: Ont.	**18**	44	81
Porter: B.C.		58	130
Porter Lake: Sask.	**24**	56	107
Porters Lake: N.S.	**30**	44¾	63¼
Port Essington: B.C.	**26**	54	130
Port George: N.S.	**15**	45	65
Port Greville: N.S.	**15**	45	64
Port Hammond: B.C.	**27**	49¼	122¾
Port Hardy: B.C.	**26**	51	128
Port Harrison: Qué.	**12**	58	78
Port Hawkesbury: N.S.	**15**	46	61
Port Hood: N.S.	**15**	46	62
Port Hope: Ont.	**20**	44	78
Port Hope Simpson: Labr.		53	56
Portland: Ont.	**21**	45	76
Portland Canal: B.C.	**26**	55	130
Portland Inlet: B.C.	**26**	55	130
Portland Promontory: Qué.		58	78
Port Logan: N.W.T.	**29**	72	93
Port Loring: Ont.	**18**	46	80
Port McNicoll: Ont.	**20**	45	80
Port Maitland: N.S.	**15**	44	66
Port Mellon: B.C.	**26**	49	123
Port Menier: Anticosti I.	**14**	50	64
Port Moody: B.C.	**27**	49¼	122¾
Port Morien: N.S.	**15**	46	60
Port Mouton: N.S.	**15**	44	65
Port Nelson: Man.	**25**	57	93
Portneuf: & *riv.*, Qué.	**30**	46¾	72
Portneuf sur Mer: Qué.		48	69
Port Neville: B.C.		50	126
Port Perry: Ont.	**20**	44	79
Port Radium: N.W.T.	**28**	66	118
Port Renfrew: B.C.	**26**	49	124
Port Rexton: Nfld.		48	53
Port Rowan: Ont.	**18**	43	80
Port Saunders: Nfld.	**13**	51	57
Port Severn: Ont.		45	80
Port Simpson: B.C.	**26**	55	130
Portsmouth: Ont.	**21**	44	76
Port Stanley: Ont.	**18**	43	81
Portugal Cove: Nfld.	**30**	47¾	52¾
Port Union: Nfld.	**15**	48	53
Port Viau: Qué.	**21**	45½	73¾
Port Weller: Ont.	**20**	43	79
Poste-de-la-Baleine: Qué.	**13**	55	78
Postville: Labr.		55	60
Potrincourt Lake: Qué.	**14**	49	74
Pouce Coupé: B.C.	**27**	55	120
Pouch Cove: Nfld.	**30**	47¾	52¾
Poularies: Qué.		48	79
Poulin de Courval, Lac: Québec		49	70
Povungnituk: & *riv.*, Qué.	**12**	60	76
Powassan: Ont.	**18**	46	79
Powell Lake: B.C.	**26**	50	124

	Page	N	W
Powell River: *town*, B.C.	26	50	125
Prairie Grove: Man.	30	49¾	97
Prairie River: *town*, Sask.	25	53	103
Prairies, R. des: Qué.	21	45¾	73½
Preeceville: Sask.	25	52	103
Preissac, Lac: Qué.	18	48	78
Prelate: Sask.	24	51	109
Prescott: Ont.	21	45	76
Prescott I.: N.W.T.	29	73	97
Presqu'ile Point: Ont.	20	44	78
Press: Qué.	19	48	77
Press Lake: Ont.		50	92
Preston: N.S.	30	44¾	63½
Price: Qué.		48	68
Priddis: Alta.	30	50¾	114¼
Priestly: B.C.	27	54	125
Prim Point: P.E.I.	15	46	63
Primrose Lake: Sask.	24	55	110
Prince Albert: Sask.	25	53	106
Prince Albert Hills: N.W.T.	29	67	85
Prince Albert Nat. Park: Saskatchewan	24	54	106
Prince Albert Penin.: N.W.T.	28	72	117
Prince Albert Sound: N.W.T.	28	70	115
Prince Alfred, Cape: N.W.T.	28	75	121
Prince Charles I.: N.W.T.	12	67	76
Prince Edward Bay: Ont.	20	44	77
Prince Edward I.: *Prov.* (*cap.* Charlottetown)	14	46	63
Prince Edward I. Nat. Park: P.E.I.	15	46	63
Prince George: B.C.	27	54	123
Prince Gustaf Adolf Sea: N.W.T.	1	79	110
Prince Leopold I.: N.W.T.	29	74	90
Prince of Wales, Cape: Qué.	12	62	72
Prince of Wales I.: N.W.T.	29	72	100
Prince of Wales Str.: N.W.T.	28	73	118
Prince Patrick I.: N.W.T.	28	77	120
Prince Regent Inlet: N.W.T.	29	74	90
Prince Rupert: B.C.	26	54	130
Princes Lake (Wallace): *town*, Ontario	20	45	78
Princess: Alta.	24	51	112
Princess Royal I.: B.C.	26	53	129
Princeton: B.C.	26	49	120
Princetown: P.E.I.	15	46	64
Profits Cape: P.E.I.	15	47	64
Prophet: *riv.*, B.C.	27	58	123
Prospect: N.S.	15	44	64
Providence Bay: *town*, Ont.		46	82
Provost: Alta.	24	52	110
Pubnico: N.S.	15	44	66
Pugwash: N.S.	15	46	64
Pukatawagan: Man.	25	56	101
Pukeashun Mt.: B.C.	27	51	119
Purcell Mtns.: B.C.	27	50	117
Puskitamika Lake: Qué.		49	76
Quadra I.: B.C.	26	50	125
Qualicum Beach: B.C.	26	49	124
Qu'Appelle: Sask.	30	50½	104
Qu'Appelle: *riv.*, Sask.	30	50¾	104¼
Qu'Appelle Arm Dam: Saskatchewan	24	57	107
Quatsino Sound: B.C.	26	50	128
QUÉBEC: Québec	30	46¾	71¼
Québec: *Prov.* (*cap.* Québec)	12/13	—	—
Queen Bess, Mt.: B.C.	27	51	124
Queen Charlotte: & *is.*, British Columbia	26	53	132
Queen Charlotte Sd.: B.C.	26	52	129
Queen Charlotte Str.: B.C.	26	50	128
Queen Elizabeth Is.: N.W.T.	3	78	100
Queen Maud Gulf: N.W.T.	29	67	102
Queens Channel: N.W.T.	29	76	97
Queensport: N.S.	15	45	61
Queenstown: N.B.	15	45	66
Quesnel: & *riv.*, B.C.	27	53	122
Quesnel Lake: B.C.	27	53	121
Quetico Park: Ont.	17	48	90
Quévillon, Lac: Qué.		49	77
Quibell: Ont.	17	50	93
Quiet Lake: Yukon		61	133
Quilchena: B.C.		50	120
Quill Lake: *town*, Sask.	25	52	104
Quill Lakes: Sask.	25	52	104
Quinsam: B.C.	26	50	125
Quinte, Bay of: Ont.	20	44	77
Quinze, Lac des: Qué.	18	48	79
Quirke Lake: Ont.	18	46	83
Quoich: *riv.*, N.W.T.	29	65	95
Quorn: Ont.	17	49	91
Quyon: Qué.	30	45½	76¼
Rabast, C. de: Anticosti I.	14	50	64
Race, Cape: Nfld.	15	47	53
Racine de Bouleau: *riv.*, Québec		52	69
Radisson: Sask.	24	52	107
Radville: Sask.	25	49	104
Rae: N.W.T.	28	63	116
Rae: *riv.*, N.W.T.	28	68	117
Rae Isthmus: N.W.T.	12	67	87
Rae Strait: N.W.T.	29	69	95
Rafael Point: B.C.		49	126
Ragged Lake: Ont.		45	79

	Page	N	W
Ragueneau: Qué.		49	68
Rainbow Lake: *town*, Alta.	24	58	119
Rainy Lake: Ont.	17	48	93
Rainy River: *town*, Ont.	17	49	95
Ralleau, Lac: Qué.		58	67
Ramah: & *bay*, Labr.		59	63
Rambau, Lac: Qué.		54	70
Ramea Is.: Nfld.	15	48	57
Ramore: Ont.	18	48	80
Ramsayville: Ont.	30	45¼	75½
Ramusio, Lake: Qué.		55	64
Rancheria: Yukon		60	130
Rancheria: *riv.*, Yukon		60	129
Random I.: Nfld.		48	54
Ranger Lake: Ont.	18	47	84
Rankin Inlet: N.W.T.	29	63	92
Rapid City: Man.	25	50	100
Rapide Blanc: Qué.	19	48	73
Rapides des Joachims: Qué.	20	46	78
Rat: *riv.*, Man.	25	56	99
Rathburn: Ont.	20	45	79
Rat Rapids: *town*, Ont.		51	90
Rat River: *town*, N.W.T.	29	61	112
Ratz, Mt.: B.C.	26	57	132
Ravensworth: Ont.		46	79
Rawdon: Qué.	21	46	74
Ray, Cape: Nfld.	15	48	59
Raymond: Alta.	24	49	113
Razorback: *mt.*, B.C.	27	51	124
Read I.: B.C.	26	50	125
Read Island: *settlement*, N.W.T.	29	69	114
Red: *riv.*, Can./U.S.A.	3	48	97
Red Bay: *settlement*, Labr.		52	57
Redberry Lake: Sask.	24	53	107
Red Cedar Lake: Ont.	18	47	80
Redcliff: Alta.	24	50	111
Red Deer: Alta.	24	52	114
Red Deer: *riv.*, Alta.	24	51	111
Red Deer: *riv.*, Sask.	25	53	102
Red Deer Lake: Man.	25	53	101
Redditt: Ont.	25	50	94
Red Indian Lake: Nfld.	15	49	57
Red I.: Nfld.		47	54
Red Lake: *town*, B.C.		51	121
Red Lake: & *town*, Ont.	25	51	94
Redonda Bay: *town*, B.C.	26	50	125
Redonda Is.: B.C.	26	50	125
Red Rock: B.C.	27	54	123
Redstone: B.C.	27	52	124
Redstone: *riv.*, N.W.T.	28	63	126
Redstone Lake: Ont.		45	78
Red Sucker Lake: Man.	25	54	94
Redwater: Alta.	24	54	113
Redwater: Ont.		47	80
Red Wine: *riv.*, Labr.		54	62
Refuge Cove: *town*, B.C.	26	50	125
REGINA: Saskatchewan	30	50¼	104½
Regina Beach: Sask.	30	50¾	105
Reindeer: *riv.*, Sask.	25	56	103
Reindeer Depot: N.W.T.	28	69	134
Reindeer I.: Man.	25	52	98
Reindeer Lake: Sask./Man.	25	57	102
Remo: B.C.	26	54	129
Renews: Nfld.	15	47	53
Renfrew: Ont.	19	45	77
Renison: Ont.		51	81
Rennie Lake: N.W.T.		61	105
Renouard Point: N.B.	15	46	65
Repulse Bay: *settlement*, N.W.T.	12	67	86
Reserve: Sask.	25	52	102
Resolution I.: N.W.T.	12	61	65
Resolution Lake: Qué.		55	65
Revelstoke: B.C.	27	51	118
Rexton: N.B.	15	47	65
Reynaud: Sask.	25	53	105
Rice Lake: Ont.	20	44	78
Rich, Cape: Ont.	18	45	81
Richan: Ont.	25	50	93
Richard Collinson Inlet: N.W.T.	29	72	114
Richards I.: N.W.T.	28	69	135
Richardson: *riv.*, Alta.	24	58	110
Richardson: Sask.	30	50½	104½
Richardson Is.: N.W.T.	29	68	110
Richardson Mtns.: Yukon	28	67	136
Richelieu: *riv.*, Qué.	21	46	73
Riche Pt.: Nfld.	13	51	57
Richibucto: N.B.	15	47	65
Richmond: B.C.	27	49¼	123
Richmond: Ont.	30	45¼	75¾
Richmond: Qué.	19	46	72
Richmond Gulf: Qué.	13	56	76
Richmond Hill: Ont.	20	44	79½
Rideau: *riv.*, Ont.	30	45¼	75¾
Rideau Canal: Ont.	21	44	76
Rideau Lakes: Ont.	21	45	76
Rider: B.C.	27	53	121
Ridgetown: Ont.	18	42	82
Riding Mt.: & *Nat. Park*, Manitoba	25	51	100
Rigaud: Qué.	21	45	74
Rigolet: Labr.	13	54	58
Rimbey: Alta.	24	53	114
Rimouski: & *riv.*, Qué.	14	48	68
Riondel: B.C.	27	50	117
Riou Lake: Sask.	24	59	106
Ripley: Ont.		44	82
Ripon: Qué.	21	46	75
Ripples: N.B.	15	46	66
Riverbend: Qué.		49	72
River Hébert: N.S.	15	46	64
Riverhurst: Sask.	24	51	107
River John: N.S.	15	46	63
River Jordan: B.C.	26	48	124

	Page	N	W
Rivers: Man.	25	50	100
Rivers, Lake of the: Sask.	25	50	106
Riversdale: N.S.	15	45	63
Riverside: Ont.	18	42	83
Rivers Inlet: & *town*, B.C.	26	52	127
Riverton: Man.	25	51	97
River Valley: *town*, Ont.	18	47	80
Rivière à Pierre: Qué.	19	47	72
Rivière au Doré: Qué.		49	73
Rivière aux Graines: Qué.		50	65
Rivière au Renard: Qué.	14	49	64
Rivière Blanche: Qué.		49	68
Rivière Bleue: Qué.		47	69
Rivière-des-Prairies: Qué.	21	46	74
Rivière du Loup: Qué.	14	48	70
Rivière du Moulin: Qué.	19	49	71
Rivière Pentecôte: Qué.	14	50	67
Rivière Pigou: Qué.	14	50	66
Rivière-Qui-Barre: Alta.	30	53¾	113¾
Robenoire, Lac la: Qué.		51	63
Robert, Cape: Ont.	18	46	83
Robert Brown, Cape: N.W.T.	12	67	81
Roberts Bank: B.C.	27	49	123¼
Roberts Creek: *town*, B.C.	26	49	124
Robertson Lake: Qué.		51	59
Roberval: Qué.	14	48	72
Robillard I.: N.W.T.	28	74	124
Robinson: Yukon		60	135
Robinson's: Nfld.	15	48	59
Roblin: Man.	25	51	101
Roblin: Ont.	20	44	77
Robsart: Sask.		49	109
Robson, Mt.: B.C.	27	53	119
Robson Prov. Park: B.C.	17	53	119
Rochebaucourt: Qué.		48	77
Rocher River: *town*, N.W.T.		61	113
Rock Bay: *town*, B.C.	26	50	125
Rockcliffe Park: Ont.	30	45¼	75¾
Rock Creek: *town*, B.C.	27	49	119
Rockglen: Sask.	25	49	106
Rockingham: N.S.	30	44¾	63¾
Rock Lake: *town*, Ont.		45	78
Rockland: Ont.	30	45½	75
Rockland East: Ont.	21	46	75
Rockport: Ont.	21	44	76
Rocky Bay: *town*, Qué.		51	58
Rockyford: Alta.	24	51	113
Rocky Harbour: Nfld.	15	50	58
Rocky Island Lake: Ont.	18	47	83
Rocky Mt. House: Alta.	24	52	115
Rocky Mtns.: Can./U.S.A.	2	—	—
Rocky Saugeen: *riv.*, Ont.	18	44	81
Roddickton: Nfld.		51	56
Roes Welcome Sound: N.W.T.	16	65	87
Roger, Lac: Qué.	18	48	79
Rogersville: N.B.	14	47	65
Roggan River: *town*, Qué.		54	79
Rohault Lake: Man.		49	74
Rolla: B.C.	27	56	120
Romaine: *riv.*, Qué.	13	51	63
Romanet, Lac: Qué.		56	68
Rorketon: Man.	25	51	100
Rose Blanche: Nfld.	15	48	59
Rosée Point: Nfld.		47	55
Rose Harbour: B.C.	26	52	131
Rosemere: Qué.	21	46	74
Rose Point: B.C.	26	54	131
Rose Prairie: B.C.	27	57	120
Rosetown: Sask.	24	51	108
Rose Valley: *town*, Sask.	25	52	104
Rosevear: Alta.	24	54	116
Roseway: *riv.*, N.S.		44	65
Rosseau: & *lake*, Ont.	20	45	80
Rosser: Man.	30	50	97¼
Ross Gorge: Qué.		52	74
Rossignol, Lac: Qué.		53	74
Rossignol, Lake: N.S.	15	44	65
Ross I.: Man.	25	54	98
Ross Lake: Can./U.S.A.	26	49	131
Rossland: B.C.	27	49	118
Ross River: & *river*, Yukon	28	62	132
Rosswood: B.C.	26	55	129
Rosthern: Sask.	24	53	106
Rothesay: N.B.	15	45	66
Rouge River:	20	43¾	79¼
Rouleau: Sask.	25	50	105
Round Lake: Ont.	18	46	78
Round Pond: Nfld.	15	48	56
Rouyn: Qué.	18	48	79
Rowatt: Sask.	30	50¼	104¼
Rowley I.: N.W.T.	12	69	79
Roy: B.C.	26	50	125
Ruby Creek: *town*, B.C.	26	49	122
Ruby Ranges: Yukon	28	61	138
Ruel: Ont.		47	81
Rupert: *riv.*, Qué.	13	51	77
Rupert Bay: Qué.		52	79
Rupert House: Qué.	13	52	79
Rushy Pond: *town*, Nfld.		49	56
Ruskin: B.C.	27	49¼	122¼
Russell: Man.	25	51	101
Russell: Ont.	30	45¼	75¼
Russell, Cape: N.W.T.	28	75	117
Russell I.: N.W.T.	29	74	99
Russell Point: N.W.T.	29	73	116
Rustico: P.E.I.	15	46	63
Rutherglen: Ont.		46	79
Rutter: Ont.	18	46	81
Sabine Lake: Qué.		59	73
Sabine Penin.: N.W.T.	29	76	109
Sable, Cape: N.S.	15	43	66

	Page	N	W
Sable I.: N.S.	13	44	60
Sable River: *town*, N.S.	15	44	65
Sabourin, Lac: Qué.	18	48	78
Sachigo: *riv.*, Ont.		55	91
Sachigo Lake: Ont.	25	54	92
Sachs Harbour: N.W.T.	28	72	126
Sackville: N.B.	15	46	64
Sacré Coeur: Qué.		48	70
Sacré Coeur: Qué.		48	68
Saffray, Lac: Qué.		58	67
Saganaga Lake: Ont.	17	48	90
Saglek Bay: Labr.	12	58	63
Saguenay: *riv.*, Qué.	19	48	70
Ste. Adèle: Qué.	21	46	74
St. Adolphe: Man.	30	49¾	97
St. Agapit: Qué.	19	46	71
Ste. Agathe: Qué.	21	46	74
St. Albans: Nfld.	15	48	56
St. Albert: Alta.	30	53¾	113¾
St. Alexandre: Qué.	19	48	70
St. Alexis-de-Montcalm: Québec	21	46	74
St. Alexis des Monts: Qué.	19	46	73
St. Ambroise: Qué.		48	71
St. Anaclet: Qué.		48	68
St. André: Qué.	19	48	70
St. André-Avellin: Qué.	21	46	75
St. Andrews: N.B.	14	45	67
St. Andrew's Channel: N.S.	15	46	60
St. Andrews East: Qué.	21	46	74
Ste. Angèle: Qué.		48	68
Ste. Angèle de Laval: Qué.	19	46	72
St. Anicet: Qué.	21	45	74
St. Anne: Man.	30	49¾	96¾
Ste. Anne: Qué.	21	46	74
Ste. Anne: *riv.*, Qué.	30	47	71¾
Ste. Anne, Lac: Qué.	14	50	68
Ste. Anne de Beaupré: Qué.	30	47	71
Ste. Anne de Bellevue: Qué.	21	45½	74
Ste. Anne de Chicoutimi: Québec		48	71
Ste. Anne de Portneuf: Québec	14	49	69
Ste. Anne des Monts: Qué.	14	49	66
Ste. Anne du Lac: Qué.	19	47	75
St. Anns: N.S.	15	46	61
St. Anselme: Qué.	30	46¾	71
St. Anthony: Nfld.	13	51	55
St. Antoine: Qué.	21	46	73
St. Antoine du Lac St. Jean: Québec		49	72
St. Apollinaire: Qué.	30	46¾	71¼
St. Augustin: Qué.	30	46¾	71¼
St. Augustin: Qué.	21	46	74
St. Augustin: & *riv.*, Qué.	13	51	59
St. Barbe Is.: Nfld.	15	50	56
St. Barthelemi: Qué.		46	73
St. Basile: Qué.	30	46¾	71¾
St. Blaise de Barraute: Qué.		48	78
Ste. Blandine: Qué.		48	68
St. Boniface: Man.	30	50	97
St. Brendans: Nfld.		49	54
St. Bride's: Nfld.		47	54
St. Bruno: Qué.		48	72
St. Calixte-de-Kilkenny: Québec	21	46	74
Ste. Camille: Qué.	19	46	70
St. Catharines: Ont.	20	43	79
Ste. Catherine: Qué.	30	46¾	71¾
St. Césaire: Qué.	19	45	73
St. Charles: Qué.	30	46¾	71
St. Chrysostome: Qué.	21	45	74
St. Clair: *riv.*, Can./U.S.A.	18	43	82
St. Clair, Lake: Can./U.S.A.	18	42	83
Ste. Claire: Qué.	30	46¼	70¾
St. Clément: Qué.		48	69
St. Clet: Qué.	21	45	74
St. Coeur de Marie: Qué.	14	49	72
St. Côme: Qué.	19	46	74
St. Constant: Qué.	21	45	74
St. Croix: Qué.	30	46¾	71¾
St. Croix: *riv.*, Can./U.S.A.	14	45	67
St. Croix Lake: N.S.	15	45	64
St. Cyr: *riv.*, Qué.		49	75
St. Cyr, Mt.: Yukon		61	133
St. Davids: Nfld.	15	48	59
St. Denis: Qué.	21	46	73
St. Denis: Qué.	19	47	70
St. Donat: Qué.	19	46	74
St. Edouard: Qué.	21	45	74
St. Eleuthère: Can.		47	69
St. Elias, Mt.: Can./U.S.A.	2	60	140
St. Elias Mtns.: Yukon/B.C.	28	60	140
St. Eloi: Qué.		48	69
Ste. Emilie: Qué.	19	46	74
St. Emile-de-Suffolk: Qué.	21	46	75
St. Ephrem: Qué.		49	79
St. Esprit: Qué.	21	46	74
St. Eugène: Ont.	21	45	74
St. Eusebe: Qué.		48	69
St. Eustache: Qué.	21	45½	73¾
St. Evariste Station: Qué.		46	71
St. Fabien: Qué.		48	69
Ste. Famille: Qué.	19	47	71
St. Faustin: Qué.		46	74
St. Félicien: Qué.	14	48	72
St. Félix de Valois: Qué.	19	46	73
Ste. Foy: Qué.	30	46¾	71¼
St. Francis: *riv.*, Canada/U.S.A.		47	69
St. Francis, Cape: Nfld.	30	47¾	52¾
St. Francis, Lake: Qué.	14	46	71
St. Francis, Lake: Ont./Qué.	21	45	74
St. François Xavier: Man.	30	50	97¼
St. Gabriel: Qué.	19	46	73
St. Gabriel: Qué.		48	68

	Page	N	W
St. Gédéon: Qué.	19	46	71
St. Gédéon: Qué.		48	72
Ste. Geneviève: Qué.	21	45	74
St. George: N.B.	15	45	67
St. Georges: Nfld.	15	48	58
St. Georges: Qué.	18	46	71
St. George's Bay: Nfld.	15	48	59
St. George's Bay: N.S.	15	46	62
St. Gerard: Qué.	19	46	71
St. Gervais: Qué.	30	46¾	71
St. Grégoire: Qué.	21	45	73
St. Gregory: *mt.*, Nfld.	15	49	58
St. Guillaume: Qué.	19	46	73
St. Hedwidge: Qué.	19	48	72
Ste. Hélène, I.: Qué.	21	45½	73½
St. Henri: Qué.	30	46¾	71
St. Henri de Taillon: Qué.		49	72
St. Hilaire: Qué.	21	46	73
St. Honoré: Qué.	14	48	71
St. Hubert: Qué.		48	69
St. Hyacinthe: Qué.	19	46	73
St. Ignace, Isle: Ont.		49	88
St. Irénée: Qué.		48	70
St. Isidore: Qué.	21	45	74
St. Jacques: Nfld.		47	55
St. Jacques: Qué.	21	46	74
St. James: Man.	30	50	97¼
St. James, Cape: B.C.	26	52	131
St. Janvier: Qué.	21	46	74
St. Jean: Qué.	21	45	73
St. Jean, *riv.*, Qué.		51	64
St. Jean de Dieu: Qué.		48	69
St. Jean de Matha: Qué.	19	46	74
St. Jean-d'Orléans: Qué.	30	47	71
St. Jean Port Joli: Qué.	19	47	70
St. Jérôme: Qué.	19	47	72
St. Jérôme: Qué.	21	46	74
St. Joachim: Qué.	30	47	71
Saint John: N.B.	15	45	66
Saint John: *riv.*, Canada/U.S.A.	14	46	67
St. John, Cape: Nfld.	15	50	56
St. John, Lake: Nfld.		48	55
St. John, Lake: Qué.	14	48	72
St. John, Mt.: Ont.		50	89
St. John Bay: Nfld.		51	57
ST. JOHN'S: Newfoundland	30	47½	52¾
St. Joseph: Qué.		46	73
St. Joseph: *i.*, Ont.	18	46	84
St. Joseph, Lake: Ont.	17	51	91
St. Joseph, Lake: Qué.	30	47	71½
St. Joseph d'Alma: Qué.	14	48	72
St. Joseph-du-Lac: Qué.	21	46	74
St. Josephs: Nfld.		47	55
St. Jovite: Qué.	19	46	75
St. Jude: Qué.	19	46	73
Ste. Julienne: Qué.	21	46	74
St. Kyrans: Nfld.		47	54
St. Lambert: Qué.	21	45½	73½
St. Lambert: Qué.	30	46½	71¼
St. Laurent: Qué.	30	46¾	71
St. Laurent: Qué.	21	45½	73¾
St. Lawrence: Nfld.	15	47	55
St. Lawrence: *riv.*, Canada/U.S.A.	19	—	—
St. Lawrence (Upper): *riv. & seaway*, Canada/U.S.A.	20	—	—
St. Lawrence, Cape: N.S.		47	61
St. Lawrence, Gulf of: Can.	14	48	62
St. Lawrence, Lake: Qué.	21	45	75
St. Lazare: Qué.	30	46¾	70¾
St. Léon: Qué.		48	71
St. Leonard: N.B.	14	47	68
St. Léonard: Qué.	19	46	72
St. Lewis: *riv.*, Labr.		52	57
St. Lin: Qué.	21	46	74
St. Louis, Lac: Qué.	21	45½	73¾
St. Louis-de-Gonzague: Québec	21	45	74
St. Ludger: Qué.		45	71
St. Malachie: Qué.	19	46	71
St. Marc: Qué.	21	46	73
St. Marc des Carrières: Québec	19	47	72
St. Margaret's Bay: N.S.	30	44½	64
Ste. Marguerite: *riv.*, Qué.	19	48	70
Ste. Marie: Qué.	19	46	71
Ste. Marie: Qué.	21	46	73
St. Martin, Lake: Man.	25	52	98
Ste. Martine: Qué.	21	45	74
St. Martins: N.B.	15	45	66
St. Mary: *riv.*, Alta.	24	49	113
St. Mary, Cape: N.S.	15	45	62
St. Mary, Cape: & *bay*, N.S.	15	44	66
St. Mary's: & *bay*, Nfld.	15	47	54
St. Mary's: Ont.	18	43	81
St. Mary's: *riv.*, N.S.	15	45	62
St. Mary's: *riv.*, Ont.	18	46	84
St. Mary's, Cape: Nfld.		47	54
St. Mary's Harbour: Labr.	13	52	56
St. Maurice: *riv.*, Qué.	19	47	73
St. Maxime: Qué.	19	46	71
St. Méthode: Qué.		48	72
St. Michael's Bay: Labr.		53	56
St. Michel: Qué.	21	45½	73¾
St. Michel: Qué.	30	46¾	71
St. Michel des Saintes: Qué.	19	47	74
St. Moïse: Qué.		48	68
St. Nazaire: Qué.		48	72
St. Nicolas: Qué.	30	46¾	71¼
St. Norbert: Man.	30	49¾	97¼
St. Ours: Qué.	21	46	73
St. Pacôme: Qué.	14	47	70
St. Pamphile: Qué.	19	47	70
St. Pascal: Qué.	19	48	70

	Page	N	W
St. Paul: Alta.	24	54	111
St. Paul: Qué.		52	58
St. Paul: *riv.*, Qué.	13	52	58
St. Paul du Nord: Qué.		48	69
St. Paul June: Alta.	30	53½	113½
St. Paul l'Ermite: Qué.	19	46	74
St. Peter, Lake: Qué.	19	46	73
St. Peter, Point: Qué.	14	49	64
St. Peter's: N.S.	15	46	61
St. Peters: P.E.I.	15	46	63
Ste. Petronille: Qué.	30	46¾	71¼
St. Philémon: Qué.		47	70
St. Philippe de Neri: Qué.	19	47	70
St. Phillips: Nfld.	30	47½	53
St. Pie: Qué.	19	45	73
St. Pierre Bank: Nfld.		46	56
St. Prime: Qué.	14	48	72
St. Prosper: Qué.	19	46	70
St. Quentin: N.B.	14	47	67
St. Raphaël: Qué.	30	46¾	70¾
St. Raphael Lake: Ont.		51	91
St. Raymond: Qué.	30	47	71¾
St. Rédempteur: Qué.	30	46¾	71¼
St. Rémi: Qué.	21	45	74
St. Roch: Qué.	21	46	73
St. Roch-de-l'Achigan: Qué.	21	46	74
St. Romuald: Qué.	30	46¾	71¼
Ste. Rose: Qué.	21	46	74
Ste. Rose du Dégelé: Qué.		48	69
Ste. Rose du Lac: Man.	25	51	99
Ste. Rose du Nord: Qué.	19	48	70
Ste. Scholastique: Qué.	21	46	74
St. Shotts: Nfld.		47	54
St. Siméon: Qué.	14	48	70
St. Simon: Qué.		48	69
St. Stanislas: Qué.	14	49	72
St. Stephen: N.B.	14	45	67
Ste. Thérèse: Qué.	21	46	74
St. Thomas: Ont.	18	43	81
St. Timothée: Qué.	21	45	74
St. Tite: Qué.	19	47	73
St. Urbain: Qué.	21	45	74
St. Vallier: Qué.	30	47	70¾
St. Vincent: Nfld.		47	54
St. Vincent-de-Paul: Qué.	21	46	74
St. Walburg: Sask.	24	54	109
Sakami: *riv.*, Qué.	13	53	76
Sakami Lake: Qué.	13	53	77
Sakatawi Lake: Ont.	18	48	82
Sakwaso Lake: Ont.		53	92
Sale: *riv.*, Man.	30	49¾	97¼
Salisbury: N.B.	15	46	65
Salisbury I.: N.W.T.	12	63	77
Salmon: *riv.*, N.B.	15	46	66
Salmon: *riv.*, Ont.	20	44	77
Salmon Arm: B.C.	27	51	119
Salmon Cove: Nfld.	30	47¾	53¼
Salmon River: *town*, N.S.	15	44	66
Saltcoats: Sask.	25	51	102
Saltspring I.: B.C.	26	49	123
Samaqua: *riv.*, Qué.		49	72
Sambro: N.S.	30	44½	63½
Sandgirt Lake: Labr.		54	65
Sand Lake: Ont.	25	40	94
Sand Lake Station: Ont.	18	48	84
Sandspit: B.C.	26	53	132
Sandwich Bay: Labr.	13	53	57
Sandy: *riv.*, Qué.	13	55	68
Sandy Lake: Alta.	30	53¾	114
Sandy Lake: Nfld.	15	49	57
Sandy Lake: & *town*, Ont.	25	53	93
Sandy Lake: Qué.		54	68
Sandy Narrows: *town*, Sask.	25	55	103
Sanford: Man.	30	49¾	97¼
Sangudo: Alta.	24	54	115
Sardis: B.C.	26	49	122
Sarnia: Ont.	18	43	82
Sarsfield: Ont.	30	45¼	75¼
Sasaginnigak Lake: Man.	25	52	96
Saskatchewan: *Prov. (cap. Regina)*	24/25	—	—
Saskatchewan: *riv.*, Sask./Manitoba	25	54	103
Saskatchewan Beach: Sask.	30	50¾	105
Saskatoon: Sask.	24	52	107
Saugeen: *riv.*, Ont.	18	44	81
Sauker Head: Nfld.		47	55
Saulte Ste. Marie: Ont.	18	46	84
Saunders Lake: Alta.	30	53¼	113¼
Sauvolles, Lac: Qué.		53	73
Savant Lake: *town*, Ont.	17	50	91
Sawbill: Man.	25	58	102
Sawyer Lake: Labr.		54	66
Sayabec: Qué.	14	49	68
Sayward: B.C.		50	126
Scapa: Alta.	24	52	112
Scarborough: Ont.	20	43¾	79¼
Scatari I.: N.S.	15	46	60
Schefferville (Knob Lake): Québec	13	55	66
Schomberg: Ont.	20	44	80
Schreiber: Ont.	17	49	87
Schuler: Alta.	24	50	110
Schultz Lake: N.W.T.	29	65	97
Schumacher: Ont.	18	48	81
Scoresby, Cape: N.W.T.	29	72	94
Scotia: Ont.	20	45	79
Scotsburn: N.S.	15	46	63
Scotstown: Qué.	19	45	71
Scott Chan.: B.C.	26	51	128
Scott Is.: B.C.	26	51	129
Scott Lake: N.W.T./Sask.	24	60	106
Scudder: Ont.	18	42	83
Scugog, Lake: Ont.	20	44	79
Seaforth: N.S.	30	44¾	63¼
Seaforth: Ont.	18	43	81

	Page	N	W
Seahorse Point: N.W.T.	12	64	80
Seal: *riv.*, Man.	25	59	96
Seal Cove: *town*, N.B.	15	45	67
Seal I.: B.C.	27	49¼	123¼
Seal Lake: Labr.	13	54	62
Searchmont: Ont.	18	47	84
Seattle, Mt.: U.S.A./Can.		60	139
Sechelt: B.C.	26	49	124
Sechelt Penin.: B.C.	26	49	124
Sedley: Sask.	25	50	104
Seeleys Bay: *town*, Ont.	21	44	76
Seignelay: *riv.*, Qué.		52	69
Seine: *riv.*, Man.	30	49¾	96¾
Seldom: Nfld.		50	54
Selkirk: Man.	30	50¼	97
Selkirk: P.E.I.	15	46	62
Selkirk Mtns.: B.C.	27	51	118
Sellwood: Ont.	18	47	81
Selwyn Lake: Sask./N.W.T.	29	60	104
Selwyn Mtns.: Yukon	28	63	130
Senneterre: Qué.	18	48	77
Sentinel Peak: B.C.	27	55	122
Separation Point: *settlement*, Labr.		64	58
Sept Îles, Lake: Qué.	30	47	71¾
Sept Îles: *town*, Qué.	13	50	66
Sérigny: *riv.*, Qué.	13	55	69
Seseganaga Lake: Ont.		50	90
Seton Lake: B.C.	26	51	122
Seul, Lac: Ont.	17	50	92
Seven Islands Bay: Labr.	12	59	64
Seven Sisters: *mt.*, B.C.	26	55	128
Seventy Mile House: B.C.	27	51	121
Severn Bridge: Ont.	20	45	79
Severn: *riv.*, Ont.	16	55	88
Sexsmith: Alta.	24	55	119
Seymour Inlet: B.C.	26	51	127
Shabogamo Lake: Qué.		53	67
Shabotik: *riv.*, Ont.		49	85
Shad Bay: N.S.	30	44½	63¾
Shag Harbour: N.S.	15	43	66
Shalalth: B.C.	26	51	122
Shale Falls: Qué.		57	69
Shallop: Anticosti I.	14	59	62
Shallow Lake: *town*, Ont.		45	81
Shamattawa: Man.	25	56	92
Shapio Lake: Labr.		55	61
Sharbot Lake: Ont.	20	45	77
Shaunavon: Sask.	24	50	108
Shawanaga: Ont.		45	80
Shawbridge: Qué.	21	46	74
Shawville: Qué.	21	46	76
Shawinigan: Qué.	19	46	73
Shawnigan Lake: B.C.	26	49	124
Shebandowan Lake: Ont.		48	90
Shediac: & *bay*, N.B.	15	46	65
Sheet Harbour: N.S.	15	45	63
Sheffield: N.B.	15	46	66
Sheffield Pond: Nfld.		49	57
Shelburne: N.S.	15	44	65
Shelburne: Ont.	18	44	80
Sheldrake: Qué.	14	50	65
Shellbrook: Sask.	24	53	106
Shelter Bay: *town*, Qué.	14	50	67
Shemogue: N.B.	15	46	64
Shenacadie: N.S.	15	46	61
Shepard: Alta.	30	51	114
Shepherd Bay: N.W.T.	29	68	95
Sherard, Cape: N.W.T.	29	75	81
Sherbrooke: N.S.	15	45	62
Sherbrooke: Qué.	19	45	72
Sherbrooke Lake: N.S.	15	45	65
Shere: B.C.	27	53	120
Sherman Inlet: N.W.T.	29	68	98
Sherridon: Man.	25	55	101
Sheshegwaning: Ont.	18	46	83
Sheslay: B.C.	26	58	132
Shibogama Lake: Ont.	16	54	88
Shickshock Mtns.: Qué.	14	49	66
Shikag Lake: Ont.		50	90
Ship Cove: Nfld.		48	56
Shippegan: & *i.*, N.B.	14	48	64
Shipshaw: Qué.		48	71
Shirley Lake: Ont.		46	78
Shoal Cove: Nfld.		51	57
Shoal Harbour: Nfld.		48	54
Shoal Lake: *town*, Man.	25	50	101
Shoal Lake: Man./Ont.	25	49	95
Shoal Lakes: Man.	25	50	97
Shoe Point: Nfld.		49	54
Short Point: P.E.I.	15	46	62
Shubenacadie: & *riv.*, N.S.	15	45	63
Shubenacadie Lake: N.S.	30	45	63¼
Shuswap Lake: B.C.	27	51	119
Sicamous: B.C.	27	51	119
Sidney: B.C.	26	49	123
Sidney Dobson, Mt.: N.W.T.		62	128
Sifton: Man.	25	51	100
Sifton Pass: B.C.	27	58	126
Signai: Qué.		48	77
Sikanni: B.C.	27	58	122
Sikanni Chief: *riv.*, B.C.	27	57	123
Silene, Mt.: Labr.		59	64
Sillery: Qué.	30	46¾	71¼
Silverdale: B.C.	27	49¼	122¼
Silver Mt.: Nfld.		50	57
Silvertip Mt.: B.C.	26	49	121
Silverton: B.C.	27	49	117
Simard, Lac: Qué.	18	48	79
Simcoe: Ont.	18	43	80
Simcoe, Lake: Ont.	20	44	79
Similkameen: *riv.*, B.C.	26	49	120
Simon Lake: Qué.	21	46	75
Simoom Sound: *town*, B.C.		51	126
Sims Lake: Qué.		54	66

	Page	N	W
Simpson Bay: N.W.T.	28	69	114
Simpson I.: Ont.	17	48	88
Simpson Lake: N.W.T.	29	68	91
Simpson Penin.: N.W.T.	29	68	89
Simpson Strait: N.W.T.	29	68	98
Sinclair, Mt.: Ont.	18	48	81
Sintaluta: Sask.	25	50	103
Sioux Lookout: Ont.	17	50	92
Sipiwesk: Man.	25	56	97
Sipiwesk Lake: Man.	25	55	97
Sir Alexander, Mt.: B.C.	27	54	120
Sir Francis Drake, Mt.: British Columbia	26	51	125
Sir James McBrien, Mt.: N.W.T.	28	62	127
Sir Wilfred, Mt.: Qué.	19	47	76
Sir Wilfrid Laurier: *mt.*, British Columbia	27	53	120
Sitidgi Lake: N.W.T.	28	68	132
Siwhe Mt.: B.C.	26	50	122
Skagit: *riv.*, Can./U.S.A.	27	48	121
Skead: Ont.	18	47	81
Skeena: *riv.*, B.C.	26	54	129
Skeena Mtns.: B.C.	26	57	130
Skeleton Lake: Ont.	20	45	79
Skihist Mt.: B.C.	26	50	122
Skootamatta Lake: Ont.	20	45	77
Skownan: Man.	25	52	99
Slate Is.: Ont.	17	49	87
~~Slave: *riv.*, Alta./N.W.T.~~	~~24~~	~~60~~	~~112~~
Slave Lake: *town*, Alta.	24	55	115
Slave Point: N.W.T.		61	116
Slocan: & *lake*, B.C.	27	50	117
Smiley: Sask.	24	52	109
Smith: Alta.	24	55	114
Smith, Cape: Ont.	18	46	82
Smith Arm: Great Bear Lake: N.W.T.	28	66	123
Smithers: B.C.	26	55	127
Smith Point: N.S.	15	46	63
Smiths Falls: Ont.	21	45	76
Smith Sound: Nfld.		48	54
Smithville: Ont.	20	43	80
Smoky: *riv.*, Alta.	24	55	118
Smoky, Cape: N.S.	15	47	60
Smoky Falls: Ont.	17	50	82
Smoky Lake: *town*, Alta.	24	54	112
Smooth Rock Falls: *town*, Ontario		49	82
Smoothrock Lake: Ont.		51	89
Snag: Yukon	28	62	140
Snake: *riv.*, Yukon	28	66	133
Snake Lake: Sask.	24	55	107
Snare: *riv.*, N.W.T,	28	63	115
Snegamook Lake: Labr.		55	61
Snowbird Lake: N.W.T.	29	61	103
Snow Lake: *town*, Man.	25	55	100
Snow Road Station: Ont.	20	45	77
Snowy Mt.: B.C.	26	49	120
Snug Harbour: Labr.		53	56
Soda Creek: *town*, B.C.	27	52	122
Soldier Cove: N.S.	15	46	61
Somenos: B.C.	26	49	124
Somerset I.: N.W.T.	29	73	93
Sooke: B.C.	26	48	124
Sops I.: Nfld.	15	50	57
Sorel: Qué.	19	46	73
Soscumica Lake: Qué.		50	77
Soulanges: Qué.	21	45	74
Sounding Lake: Alta.	24	52	110
Souris: Man.	25	50	100
Souris: P.E.I.	15	46	62
Souris: *riv.*, Man.	25	49	101
South: *riv.*, Ont.	18	46	79
Southampton: Ont.	18	44	81
Southampton Cape: N.W.T.	12	62	84
Southampton Island: *town & i.*, N.W.T.	16	64	83
South Aulatsivik I.: Labr.	13	57	61
South Bay: N.W.T.	12	64	83
South Baymouth: Ont.	18	46	82
South Brook: *town*, Nfld.		49	56
South Brookfield: N.S.	15	44	65
Southend: Sask.	25	56	103
Southern Indian Lake: Manitoba	25	57	99
Southey: Sask.	25	51	104
South Gloucester: Ont.	30	45¼	75½
South Henik Lake: N.W.T.	29	61	97
South Indian Lake: *town*, Manitoba	25	57	99
South Knife: *riv.*, Man.	25	58	96
South Maitland: N.S.	15	45	63
South Nahanni: N.W.T.		61	123
South Nahanni: *riv.*, N.W.T.	28	61	126
South Nation: *riv.*, Ont.	19	45	75
South Porcupine: Ont.	18	48	81
Southport: Nfld.		48	54
South River: *town*, Ont.	20	46	79
South Roxton: Qué.		45	73
South Saskatchewan: *riv.*, Saskatchewan/Alberta	24	51	109
South Seal: *riv.*, Man.	25	58	99
South Sleeper Is.: N.W.T.		58	80
South Thompson: *riv.*, B.C.		51	120
South Westminster: B.C.	27	49¼	123
Southwest Point: Anticosti I.	14	49	64
Spaniards Bay: *town*, Nfld.	30	47½	53¼
Spanish: Ont.	18	46	82
Spanish: *riv.*, Ont.	18	47	82
Spatsum: B.C.		51	121
Spear, Cape: Nfld.	15	47	53
Speers: Sask.	24	53	107

	Page	N	W
Spence Bay: *settlement*, N.W.T.	**29**	69	93
Spencer, Cape: N.B.	**15**	45	66
Spencer Island: *town*, N.S.	**15**	45	65
Spencerville: Ont.	**21**	45	76
Spences Bridge: B.C.	**27**	50	121
Spicer Is.: N.W.T.	**12**	68	78
Spirit River: *town*, Alta.	**24**	56	119
Split, Cape: N.S.	**15**	45	64
Split Lake: & *town*, Man.	**25**	56	96
Spotted I.: Labr.		54	56
Spragge: Ont.	**18**	46	83
Springburn: Alta.	**24**	56	117
Springdale: Nfld.	**15**	49	56
Springer, Mt.: Qué.		50	75
Springfield: N.S.	**15**	45	65
Springhill: N.S.	**15**	46	64
Springstein: Man.	**30**	49¾	97½
Sproat Lake: B.C.	**26**	49	125
Sproule Point: Qué.	**14**	50	67
Spruce Brook: *town*, Nfld.		49	58
Sprucedale: Ont.	**20**	45	79
Spruce Grove: Alta.	**30**	53½	114
Spryfield: N.S.	**30**	44½	63½
Spuzzum: B.C.	**26**	50	121
Squamish: B.C.	**26**	50	123
Squamish: *riv.*, B.C.	**26**	50	123
Square I.: Labr.		53	56
Squatteck: Qué.		48	69
Squaw Rapids Dam: Sask.	**25**	54	103
Stackpool: Ont.	**18**	48	82
Stallworthy, Cape: N.W.T.	**3**	81	95
Stanbridge Station: Qué.	**19**	45	73
Standard: Alta.	**24**	51	113
Stang, Cape: N.W.T.	**29**	71	105
Stanley: N.B.	**14**	46	67
Stanley Bridge: P.E.I.	**15**	46	63
Starbuck: Man.	**30**	49¾	97¾
Star City: Sask.	**25**	53	104
Stave Falls: *town*, B.C.	**27**	49¼	122¼
Stave Lake: B.C.	**27**	49¼	122¼
Stavely: Alta.	**24**	50	114
Stayner: Ont.	**18**	44	80
Steep Rock: Man.	**25**	51	99
Steep Rock Lake: Ont.		48	91
Stefansson I.: N.W.T.	**29**	73	107
Steinbach: Man.	**25**	49	97
Stellarton: N.S.	**15**	46	63
Stephenville: Nfld.	**15**	49	69
Stephenville Crossing: Newfoundland		48	58
Stettler: Alta.	**24**	52	113
Steveston: B.C.	**27**	49¼	123¼
Stewart: B.C.	**26**	56	130
Stewart: *riv.*, Yukon	**28**	63	138
Stewiacke: & *riv.*, N.S.	**15**	45	63
Stikine: *riv.*, B.C.	**26**	57	131
Stikine Ranges: B.C.		59	130
Stillwater: B.C.	**26**	50	124
Stillwater Creek: Sask.	**24**	50	108
Stimson: Ont.		49	81
Stirling: Alta.	**24**	50	113
Stirling: Ont.	**20**	44	78
Stittsville: Ont.	**30**	45¼	76
Stonecliffe: Ont.	**18**	46	78
Stoneham: Qué.	**30**	47	71½
Stonewall: Man.	**30**	50	97¼
Stoney Creek: *town*, Ont.	**20**	43	80
Stony Lake: Man.	**25**	59	99
Stony Lake: Ont.	**20**	45	78
Stony Mountain: *town*, Manitoba	**30**	50	97¼
Stony Plain: *town*, Alta.	**30**	53½	114
Stony Point: Qué.		59	68
Stony Rapids: *town*, Sask.	**25**	59	106
Storkerson Bay: N.W.T.	**28**	73	125
Stouffville: Ont.	**20**	44	79
Stoughton: Sask.	**25**	50	103
Stout Lake: Ont.	**25**	52	94
Strasbourg: Sask.	**25**	51	105
Stratford: Ont.	**18**	43	81
Strathcona Prov. Park: B.C.	**26**	50	126
Strathlorne: N.S.	**15**	46	61
Strathmore: Alta.	**30**	51	113¼
Strathnaver: B.C.	**27**	53	123
Strathroy: Ont.	**18**	43	82
Streetsville: Ont.	**20**	44	80
Strickland: Ont.		49	82
Strzelecki Harbour: N.W.T.		72	97
Stuart Lake: B.C.	**27**	55	124
Stuie: B.C.	**27**	52	126
Sturgeon: *riv.*, Alta.	**30**	53¾	113¾
Sturgeon: *riv.*, Ont.	**18**	47	81
Sturgeon: *riv.*, Sask.	**24**	53	106
Sturgeon Bay: Man.	**25**	52	98
Sturgeon Falls: Ont.	**17**	46	80
Sturgeon Falls: *town*, Ont.	**18**	46	80
Sturgeon Lake: Alta.	**24**	55	117
Sturgeon Lake: Ont.	**20**	44	79
Sturgeon Lake: Ont.		50	91
Sturgeon Landing: Man.	**25**	54	102
Sturgis: Sask.	**25**	52	102
Sudbury: Ont.	**18**	46	81
Suffield: Alta.	**24**	50	111
Sugluk: Qué.	**12**	62	75
Sullivan Bay: *town*, B.C.		51	127
Sullivan Lake: Alta.	**24**	52	112
Sully: Qué.		47	69
Sultan: Ont.	**18**	48	83
Summerside: P.E.I.	**15**	46	64
Summit Lake: *town*, B.C.	**27**	54	123
Sunderland: Ont.	**20**	44	79
Sundre: Alta.	**24**	52	115
Sundridge: Ont.	**20**	46	79
Sunnybrae: N.S.	**15**	46	63

	Page	N	W
Superior, Lake: Canada/U.S.A.	**17**	48	88
Surf Inlet: *town*, B.C.	**26**	53	129
Surprise Lake: Qué.		49	75
Surrey: P.E.I.	**15**	46	63
Sussex: N.B.	**15**	46	66
Sutherland: Sask.	**24**	52	107
Sutton: Ont.	**20**	44	79
Sutton: Qué.	**19**	45	73
Sutton: *riv.*, Ont.		55	84
Sverdrup Is.: N.W.T.	**3**	78	100
Swain Post: Ont.	**25**	51	93
Swampy Bay: *riv.*, Qué.		56	68
Swan Hills: Alta.	**24**	55	116
Swan Lake: Man.	**25**	52	101
Swannell Range: B.C.	**27**	56	126
Swan River: *town*, Man.	**25**	52	101
Swastika: Ont.	**18**	48	80
Swift Current: Nfld.		48	54
Swift Current: Sask.	**24**	50	108
Swinburne, Cape: N.W.T.	**29**	71	99
Sydenham: Ont.	**20**	44	77
Sydenham: *riv.*, Ont.	**18**	43	82
Sydney: N.S.	**15**	46	60
Sydney Lake: Ont.	**25**	51	95
Sydney Mines: N.S.	**15**	46	60
Sykes, Mt.: Nfld.		49	57
Sylvan Lake: *town*, Alta.	**24**	52	114
Sylvester, Mt.: Nfld.		48	55
Taber: Alta.	**24**	50	112
Table Bay: Labr.		54	56
Tadoule Lake: Man.	**25**	59	98
Tadoussac: Qué.	**19**	48	70
Tagish: & *lake*, Yukon		60	134
Tahaetkun Mt.: B.C.		50	120
Tahiryuak Lake: N.W.T.	**29**	71	112
Tahoe Lake: N.W.T.	**29**	70	109
Tahtsa Lake: B.C.	**26**	54	127
Taibi Lake: Qué.		49	78
Takhini: Yukon		60	135
Takiyuak Lake: N.W.T.	**29**	66	113
Takla Lake: B.C.	**27**	55	126
Takla Landing: B.C.	**27**	56	126
Taku: B.C.		60	133
Taku: *riv.*, B.C.	**22**	59	133
Taltson: *riv.*, N.W.T.	**29**	60	111
Tamworth: Ont.	**20**	44	77
Tangier: N.S.	**15**	45	63
Tapani Lac: Qué.	**19**	47	75
Taschereau: Qué.		48	79
Taseko: *riv.* & *mtn.*, B.C.	**27**	51	123
Tashota: Ont.		50	88
Tasiat Lake: Qué.		59	75
Tassialuk Lake: Qué.		59	74
Tatamagouche: & *bay*, N.S.	**15**	46	63
Tathlina Lake: N.W.T.		60	118
Tatla Lake: & *town*, B.C.	**27**	52	124
Tatlayoka Lake: B.C.	**27**	52	124
Tatnam, Cape: Man.	**16**	57	91
Tavani: N.W.T.	**29**	62	93
Taverner Bay: N.W.T.	**12**	67	73
Tavistock: Ont.	**18**	43	81
Taylor: B.C.	**27**	56	121
Taylors Head: N.S.	**15**	45	62
Tazin Lake: Sask.	**24**	60	109
Tecumseh: Ont.	**31**	42¼	83
Teeswater: Ont.	**18**	44	81
Tehek Lake: N.W.T.	**29**	65	95
Tehkummah: Ont.		46	82
Telegraph Creek: *town*, British Columbia	**26**	58	131
Temagami: Ont.	**18**	47	80
Témiscamie: *riv.*, Qué.		52	72
Témiscamingue Reserve: Québec	**18**	47	79
Témiscouata, Lac: Qué.	**14**	48	69
Témiskaming: Qué.	**18**	47	79
Templeton: Qué.	**30**	45½	75½
Tennycape: N.S.	**15**	45	64
Terence Bay: *town*, N.S.	**30**	44½	63¾
Terrace: B.C.	**26**	55	129
Terrace Bay: *town*, Ont.		49	87
Terra Nova Nat. Park: Nfld.	**15**	48	54
Terrebonne: Qué.	**21**	46	74
Terrenceville: Nfld.		48	55
Terror Point: N.W.T.	**12**	64	81
Teslin: & *lake*, Yukon	**28**	60	132
Teslin: *riv.*, Yukon	**28**	61	134
Teslin Crossing: Yukon		61	135
Tessik Lake: N.W.T.	**12**	65	75
Tessisoak Lake: Labr.		57	63
Tetu Lake: Man./Ont.	**25**	50	95
Teulon: Man.	**25**	50	97
Texada I.: B.C.	**26**	49	124
Tha-anne: *riv.*, N.W.T.	**29**	60	96
Thalia: B.C.	**26**	50	121
Thames: *riv.*, Ont.	**18**	43	81
Thamesville: Ont.	**18**	42	82
Theano Point: Ont.		47	85
Thedford: Ont.	**18**	43	82
Thekulthili Lake: N.W.T.		61	110
Thelon: *riv.* & *Game Sanctuary*, N.W.T.	**29**	64	104
The Pas: Man.	**25**	54	101
Thesiger Bay: N.W.T.	**28**	72	125
Thessalon: Ont.	**18**	46	84
Thetford Mines: Qué.	**19**	46	71
The Two Rivers: *town*, Saskatchewan	**25**	56	103
Thévenet, Lac: Qué.		58	69
Thicket Portage: Man.	**25**	55	98
Third Lake: Alta.	**30**	50¾	113¼
Thirty One Mile Lake: Qué.	**19**	46	76
Thirty Thousand Is.: Ont.	**18**	45	80

	Page	N	W
Thlewiaza: *riv.*, N.W.T.	**29**	61	97
Thoa: *riv.*, N.W.T.		61	109
Thomaston: N.B.	**14**	46	67
Thom Bay: N.W.T.	**29**	70	92
Thomlinson, Mt.: B.C.	**26**	56	128
Thompson: Man.	**25**	56	98
Thompson: *riv.*, B.C.	**27**	51	121
Thompson Landing: N.W.T.	**29**	63	110
Thomsen: *riv.*, N.W.T.	**28**	74	120
Thorburn Lake: *town*, Newfoundland		48	54
Thorhild: Alta.	24	54	113
Thornbury: Ont.	**17**	45	80
Thornhill: Ont.	**20**	43¾	79½
Thorold: Ont.	**20**	43	79
Thorsby: Alta.	**24**	53	114
Thousand Is.: Can./U.S.A.	**21**	44	76
Three Creeks: Alta.	**24**	56	117
Three Hills: *town*, Alta.	**24**	52	113
Thunder Bay: Ont.	**17**	48	89
Thunder River: *town*, B.C.	**27**	52	119
Thurlow: B.C.	**26**	50	125
Thurso: Qué.	**30**	45½	75¼
Thutade Lake: B.C.	**26**	57	127
Thwart I.: Nfld.		49	55
Tiblemont: *lake*, Qué.	**18**	48	77
Tichborne: Ont.		45	77
Tidehead: N.B.	**14**	48	67
Tignish: P.E.I.	**15**	47	64
Tilbury: Ont.	**18**	42	82
Tilley: Alta.	**24**	50	112
Tillsonburg: Ont.	**18**	43	81
Tilt Cove: Nfld.	**15**	50	56
Tilting: Nfld.		50	54
Timagami: *lake*, Ont.	**18**	47	80
Timagami Prov. Forest: Ontario	**18**	47	81
Timberlea: N.S.	**30**	44¾	63¾
Timiskaming, Lake: Ontario/Québec	**18**	47	79
Timmins: Ont.	**18**	48	81
Tingin Fiord: N.W.T.	**12**	69	68
Tinniswood, Mt.: B.C.	**26**	50	124
Tionaga: Ont.	**18**	48	82
Tisdale: Sask.	**25**	53	104
Tiverton: N.S.	**15**	44	66
Tlogotsha Range: N.W.T.		61	125
Toba: *inlet* & *riv.*, B.C.	**26**	50	124
Tobermory: Ont.	**18**	45	82
Tobin Lake: Sask.	**25**	54	103
Tobique: *riv.*, N.B.	**14**	47	67
Tod, Mt.: B.C.		51	120
Tofield: Alta.	**24**	53	113
Tofino: B.C.	**27**	49	126
Tomiko Lake: Ont.	**18**	47	80
Tompkins: Sask.	**24**	50	109
Topsail: Nfld.	**30**	47½	53
Torbay: Nfld.	**30**	47¾	52¾
Torch: *riv.*, Sask.	**25**	54	105
Tornado Mt.: B.C./Alta.	**27**	50	115
Torngat Mtns.: Labr.		60	64
Toro, Lac: Qué.	**19**	47	74
TORONTO: Ontario	**20**	43¾	79½
Toronto Islands: Ont.	**20**	43½	79½
Torquay: Sask.	**25**	49	104
Torrance: Ont.	**20**	45	80
Tor's Cove: Nfld.		47	53
Tottenham: Ont.	**20**	44	80
Totzke: Sask.	**25**	52	106
Toulnustouc: *riv.*, Qué.		50	68
Tourville: Qué.	**19**	47	70
Tracadie: N.B.	**14**	47	65
Tracadie: N.S.	**15**	46	62
Tracadie: P.E.I.	**15**	46	63
Tracy: Qué.	**21**	46	73
Traffic Mt.: Yukon		62	130
Trail: B.C.	**27**	49	118
Tramping Lake: Sask.	**24**	52	109
Tranquille: B.C.		51	120
Trans-Canada Highway	**2/3**	—	—
Transcona: Man.	**30**	50	97
Trapp Lake: *town*, B.C.		50	120
Tregarva: Sask.	**30**	50½	104¾
Treherne: Man.	**25**	50	99
Trembleur Lake: B.C.	**27**	55	125
Trenche: *riv.*, Qué.		48	73
Trent: *riv.*, Ont.	**20**	44	78
Trent Canal: Ont.	**20**	44	79
Trenton: N.S.	**15**	46	63
Trenton: Ont.	**20**	44	78
Trepassey: Nfld.	**15**	47	53
Trinity: Bonavista Bay, Newfoundland		49	54
Trinity: & *bay*, Nfld.	**15**	48	53
Trinity Bay: *town*, Qué.	**14**	49	67
Trochu: Alta.	**24**	52	113
Trodely I.: N.W.T.		52	79
Troilus, Lac: Qué.		51	75
Trois Pistoles: Qué.	**14**	48	69
Trois Rivières: Qué.	**19**	46	73
Trout: *riv.*, N.W.T.		61	120
Trout Creek: *town*, Ont.	**18**	46	79
Trout Lake: N.W.T.	**28**	60	121
Trout Lake: Ont.	**18**	46	79
Trout Lake: Ont.	**16**	51	93
Trout Lake: *town*, Alta.		56	115
Trout Lake: *town*, Ont.		54	90
Trout Mills: Ont.		46	79
Trout River: *town*, Nfld.	**15**	50	58
Troy: N.S.	**15**	46	61
Truite, Lac à la: Qué.	**18**	47	78
Truro: N.S.	**15**	45	63
Tsawwassen: B.C.	**27**	49	123
Tsu Lake: N.W.T.		61	112
Tudhope: Ont.		49	82

	Page	N	W
Tudor, Lake: Qué.	**13**	56	65
Tukarak I.: N.W.T.		56	79
Tuktoyaktuk: N.W.T.	**28**	69	133
Tulameen: B.C.	**26**	50	121
Tulsequah Creek: B.C.	**22**	59	134
Tunulik: *riv.*, Qué.		58	66
Tunungayualuk I.: Labr.	**13**	56	61
Turbine: Ont.	**18**	46	82
Turgeon Lake: & *riv.*, Qué.		49	79
Turner's Bight: *settlement*, Labrador		54	58
Turner Valley: *town*, Alta.	**24**	51	114
Turnor Lake: Sask.	**24**	57	109
Turriff: Ont.		45	78
Turtle: *riv.*, Ont.		49	92
Turtleford: Sask.	**24**	53	109
Tusket: N.S.	**15**	44	66
Tuxedo: Man.	**30**	49¾	97¼
Tuya Lake: B.C.		59	131
Tweed: Ont.	**20**	44	77
Tweedsmuir Prov. Park: British Columbia	**27**	53	126
Twenty Mile Creek: Ont.		43	80
Twillingate: Nfld.	**15**	50	55
Twin Falls: Ont.		49	80
Twin Is.: N.W.T.	**16**	53	80
Twin Ponds: Nfld.		49	56
Two Brothers: *is.*, N.W.T.		59	80
Two Rivers, Lake of: Ont.		46	78
Tyndall: Man.	**30**	50	96¼
Tyne Valley: *town*, P.E.I.	**15**	47	64
Uchi Lake: *town*, Ont.		51	93
Ucluelet: B.C.	**26**	49	126
Uivuk, Cape: Labr.		58	63
Ukasiksalik I.: Labr.		56	61
Umfreville Lake: Ont.	**25**	50	95
Uncas: Alta.	**30**	53½	113
Ungava Bay: Qué.	**12**	59	67
Ungava Penin.: Qué.	**12**	61	75
Uniacke: Qué.		48	78
Union Bay: *town*, B.C.	**26**	49	125
Unionville: Ont.	**20**	43¾	79¼
United States Range: N.W.T.	**3**	83	80
Unity: Sask.	**24**	52	109
Upper Arrow Lake: B.C.	**27**	50	118
Upper Foster Lake: Sask.	**25**	57	105
Upper Goose Lake: Ont.		52	93
Upper Island Cove: Nfld.		48	53
Upper Musquodoboit: N.S.	**15**	45	63
Upper Rockport: N.B.	**15**	46	64
Upper Seal Lake: Qué.		56	73
Upper Tantallon: N.S.	**30**	44¾	64
Upsalquitch: N.B.	**14**	48	67
Uranium City: Sask.	**24**	60	109
Utik Lake: Man.	**25**	55	96
Utikuma Lake: Alta.	**24**	56	115
Utterson: Ont.	**20**	45	79
Uxbridge: Ont.	**20**	44	79
Val Barrette: Qué.	**19**	47	75
Val Brillant: Qué.	**14**	48	68
Valcourt: Qué.	**19**	45	72
Valdes I.: B.C.	**26**	49	124
Val d'Or: Qué.	**18**	48	78
Valemount: B.C.	**27**	53	119
Valeport: Sask.	**30**	50¾	104¾
Vallée Junction: Qué.	**19**	46	71
Valleyfield: Qué.	**21**	45	74
Valleyview: Alta.	**24**	55	117
Val Marie: Sask.	**24**	49	108
Van Bruyssel: Qué.		48	72
Vancouver: B.C.	**27**	49¼	123
Vancouver, Mt.: U.S.A./Canada		60	140
Vancouver I.: B.C.	**26/27**	—	—
Vanderhoof: B.C.	**27**	54	124
Vandry: Qué.	**19**	48	74
Vanguard: Sask.	**24**	50	107
Vankleek Hill: *town*, Ont.	**21**	45	75
Vannes, Lac: Qué.		56	67
Vansittart I.: N.W.T.	**12**	66	84
Varennes: Qué.	**21**	46	73
Vars: Ont.	**21**	45	75
Vauban: Qué.		48	69
Vauxhall: Alta.	**24**	50	112
Vegreville: Alta.	**24**	53	112
Venosta: Qué.	**21**	46	76
Verchères: Qué.	**21**	46	73
Verdun: Qué.	**21**	45½	73½
Vermette: Man.	**30**	49¾	97
Vermeulle, Lac: Qué.		55	69
Vermilion: Alta.	**24**	53	111
Vermilion: *riv.*, Qué.	**19**	47	73
Vermilion Bay: *town*, Ont.	**25**	50	93
Vermilion Pass: Alta./B.C.	**24**	51	116
Verner: Ont.	**18**	46	80
Vernon: B.C.	**27**	50	119
Vernon: P.E.I.	**15**	46	63
Vernon Lake: Ont.	**20**	45	79
Vernon River: *town*, P.E.I.	**15**	46	63
Verona: Ont.	**20**	44	77
Verte, Baie: N.B./N.S.	**15**	46	64
Verte, Baie: Nfld.	**15**	50	56
Verte I.: Qué.	**19**	48	69
Vibank: Sask.	**30**	50¼	104
VICTORIA: British Columbia	**26**	48	123
Victoria: Nfld.	**30**	47¾	53¼
Victoria: P.E.I.	**15**	46	63
Victoria: *riv.*, Nfld.		48	57
Victoria Beach: Man.	**25**	51	96
Victoria Harbour: Ont.	**20**	45	80

	Page	N	W
Victoria I.: N.W.T.	29	70	110
Victoria Lake: Nfld.		48	57
Victoria Lake: Ont.		46	78
Victoria Peak: B.C.		50	126
Victoria Plains: Sask.	30	50½	104½
Victoria Road: Ont.	20	45	79
Victoria Strait: N.W.T.	29	69	100
Victoriaville: Qué.	19	46	72
Victor Lake: Qué.		51	62
Viking: Alta.	24	53	112
Villebon, Lac: Qué.	18	48	77
Ville de Laval: Qué.	21	45½	73¾
Ville-Marie: Qué.	18	47	79
Villemontel: Qué.		49	78
Villeneuve: Alta.	30	53¾	113¾
Villeroy: Qué.		46	72
Vimy Ridge: *town*, Ont.		48	80
Virden: Man.	25	50	101
Virginia Falls: N.W.T.		62	126
Virginiatown: Ont.	18	48	80
Viscount Melville Sound: N.W.T.	2	74	110
Voiseys Bay: Labr.		56	62
Volmer: Alta.	30	53¾	113¾
Vulcan: Alta.	24	50	113
Waasis: N.B.	15	46	67
Wabakimi Lake: Ont.		51	90
Wabana: Nfld.	30	47¾	53
Wabano: *riv.*, Qué.		48	74
Wabatongushi Lake: Ont.		48	84
Wabigoon Lake: Ont.		50	93
Wabiskaw: *riv.*, Alta.	24	57	114
Wabowden: Man.	25	55	99
Wabuk Point: Ont.	16	55	85
Wabun: Ont.	18	48	80
Wabush: Labr.	13	53	67
W.A.C. Bennett Dam: British Columbia	27	56	122
Wacouna: Qué.		51	66
Waddington, Mt.: B.C.	27	51	125
Wadena: Sask.	25	52	104
Wager Bay: & *settlement*, N.W.T.	29	66	90
Wainwright: Alta.	24	53	111
Wakami Lake: Ont.	18	47	83
Wakaw: Sask.	25	53	106
Wakefield: Qué.	30	45¾	76
Wakeham Bay: *town*, Qué.	12	62	72
Wakomata Lake: Ont.	18	47	83
Wakuach Lake: Qué.		56	68
Wakwekobi Lake: Ont.	18	46	83
Waldheim: Sask.	24	53	107
Wales I.: N.W.T.	29	68	87
Walhachin: B.C.		51	121
Walker Bay: N.W.T.	28	71	119
Walkerton: Ont.	18	44	81
Wallace: N.S.	15	46	63
Wallace (Princes Lake): Ontario	18	45	78
Wallaceburg: Ont.	18	43	82
Walrus Point: Qué.		54	79
Walsh, Mt.: Yukon		61	140
Walsingham, Cape: N.W.T.	12	66	62
Walter Bathurst, Cape: N.W.T.	29	73	76
Waltham: Qué.	19	46	77
Walton: N.S.	15	45	64
Wanapitei: *lake & riv.*, Ont.	18	47	81
Wanapitei Prov. Forest: Ontario	18	47	81
Wanless: Man.	25	54	101
Wanup: Ont.		46	81
Wapanikskan, Lake: Qué.		57	69
Wapawekka Hills: & *lake*, Saskatchewan	25	54	105
Wapella: Sask.	25	50	102
Wapesi Lake: Ont.		51	92
Wapiti: *riv.*, B.C./Alta.	24	55	120
Wardlow: Alta.	24	51	112
Ware: B.C.	27	58	126
Warkworth: Ont.	20	44	78
Warman: Sask.	24	52	106
Warner: Alta.	24	49	112
Warren: Man.	30	50	97½
Warren: Ont.	18	46	80

	Page	N	W
Warren Landing: Man.	25	54	98
Warwick: Qué.	19	46	72
Wascana Creek: Sask.	30	50½	104¾
Wasekamio Lake: Sask.	24	57	109
Washagami: Ont.		47	80
Washago: Ont.	20	45	79
Washburn Lake: N.W.T.	29	70	107
Washow Bay: Man.	25	51	97
Waskesiu: Sask.	24	54	106
Waskigomog Lake: Ont.		46	79
Waswanipi: & *lake*, Qué.		50	76
Watabeag Lake: & *riv.*, Ont.	18	48	80
Watcomb: Ont.		50	91
Waterbury Lake: Sask.	25	58	104
Waterdown: Ont.	20	43	80
Waterford: Ont.	18	43	80
Waterhen: *riv.*, Sask.	24	54	109
Waterhen Lake: Man.	25	52	99
Waterloo: Ont.	18	43	81
Waterloo: Qué.	19	45	73
Waterton Glacier Int. Peace Park: Can./U.S.A.	40	49	114
Waterton Lakes Nat. Park: Alberta	24	49	114
Waterways: Alta.		57	111
Watford: Ont.	18	43	82
Wathaman: *riv.*, Sask.	25	57	104
Watino: Alta.		56	118
Watrous: Sask.	25	52	105
Watson: Sask.	25	52	104
Watson Lake: *town*, Yukon	28	60	129
Waubaushene: Ont.	20	45	80
Waugh: N.B.	14	47	66
Waugh: Man.	25	50	95
Waverley: N.S.	30	44¾	63½
Waverley Game Sanctuary: Nova Scotia	30	44¾	63½
Wawa: Ont.	17	48	85
Wawaitin Falls: Ont.	18	48	81
Wawanesa: Man.	25	50	100
Wawota: Sask.	25	50	102
Weagamow Lake: Ont.		53	91
Weaver Lake: Man.	25	53	97
Webbwood: Ont.	18	46	82
Wedge Mt.: B.C.	26	50	123
Wedgeport: N.S.	15	44	66
Weedon: Qué.	19	46	71
Weggs, Cape: Qué.	12	63	74
Wekusko: & *lake*, Man.	25	55	100
Welland: & *canal*, Ont.	20	43	79
Welland: *riv.*, Ont.	20	43	80
Wellington: Nfld.		49	54
Wellington: N.S.	30	44¾	63¾
Wellington: Ont.	20	44	77
Wellington Chan.: N.W.T.	29	75	93
Wellington Station: N.S.	15	45	64
Wellington Station: P.E.I.	15	46	64
Wells: B.C.	27	53	122
Wells Gray Prov. Park: British Columbia	27	52	120
Welsford: N.B.	15	45	66
Welshpool: N.B.	15	45	67
Wembley: Alta.	24	55	119
Wenebegon: *lake & riv.*, Ontario	18	47	83
Wentworth: N.S.	15	46	64
Wernecke Mts.: Yukon	28	65	133
Weslemkoon Lake: Ont.	18	45	77
Wesleyville: Nfld.	15	49	54
West Bay Road: N.S.	15	46	61
West Cub I.: N.W.T.		54	81
Westfield: N.B.	15	45	66
West Fiord: N.W.T.	29	76	90
Westham I.: B.C.	27	49	123¼
Westlock: Alta.	24	54	114
West Lorne: Ont.	18	43	82
West Magpie: *riv.*, Qué.		51	65
Westmount: Qué.	21	45½	73½
Weston: N.S.	15	45	65
West Point: P.E.I.	15	47	64
West Point: Qué.	14	50	65
Westport: N.S.	15	44	66
Westport: Ont.	21	45	76
Westree: Ont.		47	82
West Road: *riv.*, B.C.	27	53	123
West Vancouver: B.C.	27	49¼	123¼
Westview: B.C.	26	50	124

	Page	N	W
Westville: N.S.	15	46	63
Westwold: B.C.		50	120
Wetaskiwin: Alta.	24	53	113
Weyburn: Sask.	25	50	104
Weymouth: N.S.	15	44	66
Whale: *riv.*, Qué.	13	57	67
Whalley: B.C.	27	49¼	122¾
Wharton Lake: N.W.T.	29	64	100
Wheatley: Ont.	18	42	82
Wheeler: *riv.*, Qué.	13	56	67
Wheeler: *riv.*, Sask.	25	57	105
Whipple Point: N.S.	15	44	66
Whiskey Lake: Ont.	18	46	82
Whitbourne: Nfld.	30	47½	53½
Whitby: Ont.	20	44	79
White: *riv.*, Ont.	17	48	85
White: *riv.*, Yukon	28	63	140
White Bay: Nfld.	15	50	57
White Bear: *riv.*, Nfld.		48	57
Whitecap Mt.: B.C.	26	51	123
White City: Sask.	30	50½	104½
Whiteclay Lake: Ont.		51	89
Whitecourt: Alta.	24	54	116
Whitefish: Ont.	18	46	81
Whitefish Bay: Can./U.S.A.		46	84
Whitefish Falls: *town*, Ont.	18	46	82
Whitefish Lake: N.W.T.	29	63	107
White Fox: Sask.	25	53	104
Whitegull Lake: Qué.	13	55	64
Whitehead: N.S.	15	45	61
WHITEHORSE: Yukon	28	61	135
White I.: N.W.T.	12	66	85
White Lake: Ont.	19	45	76
White Lake: Ont.		49	86
Whitemouth: Man.	25	50	96
Whitemouth Lake: Man.	25	49	96
White Otter Lake: Ont.		49	92
White Pass: *town*, B.C.		60	135
White Rock: B.C.	27	49	122¾
Whitesail Lake: B.C.	26	53	127
Whiteshell Prov. Park: Manitoba	25	50	95
Whitewater Lake: Ont.		51	89
Whitewood: Sask.	25	50	102
Whitney: Ont.	18	45	78
Whittle, Cape: Qué.	15	50	60
Whitworth: Qué.		48	69
Wholdaia Lake: N.W.T.	29	60	104
Whycocomagh: N.S.	15	46	61
Wiarton: Ont.	18	45	81
Widdifield: Ont.		46	79
Wignes Lake: N.W.T.		60	106
Wikwemikong: Ont.	18	46	82
Wilberforce: Ont.	18	45	78
Wilberforce Falls: N.W.T.	29	67	109
Wilcox: Sask.	25	50	105
Wilderness Area: *park*, Newfoundland	15	47	53
Wilderness Area: *park*, Newfoundland	15	48	57
Wildwood: Alta.	24	54	115
Wilkie: Sask.	24	52	109
Will, Mt.: B.C.	26	58	129
Willet: Ont.		50	88
William: *riv.*, Sask.	24	59	109
Williamsburg: Ont.	21	45	75
Williams Lake: *town*, B.C.	27	52	122
William Smith, Cape: Qué.		60	65
Willingdon: Alta.	24	54	112
Willis I.: Nfld.		49	54
Williston Lake: B.C.	27	56	124
Willow Bunch: & *lake*, Sask.	25	49	106
Willow Lake: N.W.T.	28	62	119
Wilson, Cape: N.W.T.	12	67	81
Wilson, Mt.: Qué.		48	74
Winchester: Ont.	21	45	75
Windermere: B.C.	27	50	116
Windermere: Ont.	20	45	80
Windermere Lake: Ont.	18	48	84
Windigo: *riv.*, Qué.		48	73
Windigo Lake: & *riv.*, Ont.	16	53	92
Wind Rapids: Qué.		60	76
Windsor: Nfld.	15	49	56
Windsor: N.S.	15	45	64
Windsor: Ont.	30	42¼	83
Windsor: Qué.	19	46	72

	Page	N	W
Windy Tickle: *str.*, Labr.		56	60
Winefred Lake: Alta.	24	55	111
Winfield: Alta.	24	53	114
Wingham: Ont.	18	44	81
Winisk: & *riv.*, Ont.	16	55	85
Winisk Lake: Ont.	16	53	87
Winkler: Man.	25	49	98
WINNIPEG: Manitoba	30	50	97¼
Winnipeg: *riv.*, Man.	25	50	95
Winnipeg, Lake: Man.	25	52	98
Winnipegosis: Man.	25	52	100
Winnipegosis, Lake: Man.	25	52	100
Winokapau Lake: Labr.		53	63
Winter Harbour: N.W.T.	29	75	110
Winter I.: N.W.T.	12	66	83
Winterton: Nfld.		48	53
Wishart Lake: Qué.		55	67
Witless Bay: *town*, Nfld.		47	53
Woburn: Qué.	19	45	71
Woking: Alta.	24	56	119
Wolfe, Cape: P.E.I.	15	47	65
Wolf Island: & *i.*, Ont.	21	44	76
Wolf I.: Magdalen Is., Qué.	14	47	62
Wolfville: N.S.	15	45	64
Wollaston, Cape: N.W.T.	28	71	118
Wollaston Lake: Sask.	25	58	103
Wollaston Penin.: N.W.T.	28	70	115
Wolseley: Sask.	25	50	103
Wolstenholme: Qué.	12	62	77
Woodbend: Alta.	30	53½	113¾
Wood Buffalo Park: N.W.T./Alberta	24	59	113
Woodbridge: Ont.	20	43¾	79½
Woodfibre: B.C.	26	50	123
Wood Mt.: Sask.	24	49	106
Woods, Lake of the: Canada/U.S.A.	17	49	94
Woods I.: Nfld.		49	58
Wood Is.: P.E.I.	15	46	63
Woods Lake: Labr.		54	65
Woodstock: N.B.	14	46	68
Woodstock: Ont.	18	43	81
Woodville: Ont.	20	44	79
Woody Island: *town*, Nfld.		48	54
Woollett Lake: Qué.		51	74
Wright: B.C.	27	52	122
Wrigley: N.W.T.	28	63	124
Writing on Stone Park: Alberta	24	49	112
Wrong Lake: Man.	25	53	96
Wrottesley Inlet: N.W.T.		72	96
Wunnummin Lake: Ont.	16	53	89
Wurtele: Ont.		49	81
Wynniatt Bay: N.W.T.		72	111
Wynyard: Sask.	25	52	104
Yahk: B.C.	27	49	116
Yale: B.C.	26	50	121
Yamaska: Qué.	19	46	73
Yarker: Ont.	20	44	77
Yarmouth: N.S.	15	44	66
Yarrow: B.C.	26	49	122
Yathkyed Lake: N.W.T.	29	63	98
Yellow Grass: Sask.	25	50	104
Yellowhead Pass: B.C./Alta.	27	53	119
YELLOWKNIFE: N.W.T.	28	62	114
Yellowknife: *riv.*, N.W.T.	29	63	114
Ymir: B.C.	27	49	117
Yoho Nat. Park: B.C.	27	51	117
Yonker: Sask.	24	53	110
York: Ont.	20	43¾	79½
York, Cape: N.W.T.	29	74	87
York Factory: Man.	25	57	92
Yorkton: Sask.	25	51	102
Youbou: B.C.	26	49	124
Young: Sask.	25	52	106
Youngston: Alta.	24	51	111
Yukon: *riv.*, U.S.A./Can.	28	62	137
Yukon: *Territ.* (*cap.* Whitehorse)	28	—	—
Zeballos: B.C.	27	50	127
Zehner: Sask.	30	50½	104½
Zelandia: Sask.	24	52	108

Gazetteer of the World

	Page	Lat.	Long.
Aabenraa: Denmark	69	55N	9E
Aachen: Germany	72	51N	6E
Aalborg: Denmark	69	57N	10E
Aalst: Belgium	70	51N	4E
Aare: *r.*, Switzerland	73	47N	7E
Aarhus: Denmark	69	56N	10E
Ābādān: Iran	85	30N	48E
Abadla: Algeria	106	31N	2W
Abakan: U.S.S.R.	83	54N	91E
Abbeville: France	70	50N	2E
Abbeville: U.S.A.	40	30N	92W
Abbottabad: W. Pak.	88	34N	73E
Abd al Kuri: *i.*, Indian O.	85	12N	52E
Abeokuta: Nigeria	106	7N	3E
Aberayron: Wales	55	52N	4W

	Page	Lat.	Long.
Abercorn *see* Mbala			
Aberdare: Wales	55	52N	4W
Aberdeen: Scotland	54	57N	2W
Aberdeen: S. Dak., U.S.A.	43	45N	99W
Aberdeen: Wash., U.S.A.	42	47N	124W
Aberfeldy: Scotland	54	57N	4W
Aberystwyth: Wales	55	52N	4W
ABIDJAN: Ivory Coast	106	5N	4W
Abilene: U.S.A.	43	32N	100W
Abingdon: England	57	51¾N	1¼W
Abington Reef: Coral Sea	98	18S	150E
Abisko: Sweden	68	68N	19E
Åbo: Finland	69	60N	22E

	Page	Lat.	Long.
Abqaiq: Sa'udi Arabia	85	26N	49E
Abruzzi-Molise: Italy	67	42N	14E
Absaroka Range: U.S.A.	42	45N	110W
Abu: India	88	25N	73E
Abu Dhabi, Trucial State	85	24N	54E
Abukuma Mts.: Japan	92	37N	141E
ABYSSINIA *see* ETHIOPIA			
Acapulco: Mexico	38	17N	100W
ACCRA: Ghana	106	5N	0
Accrington: England	57	53¾N	2¼W
Achill I.: R. of Ireland	56	54N	10W
Achinsk: U.S.S.R.	83	56N	90E

	Page	Lat.	Long.
Acklins I.: Bahama Is.	47	22N	74W
Aconcagua: *mtn.*, Argentina	49	33S	70W
Acqui: Italy	73	45N	8E
Acre *see* Akko			
Acre Homes: U.S.A.	31	30N	95½W
Ada: U.S.A.	43	35N	97W
Adaminaby: Australia	99	36S	149E
Adam's Bridge: Ceylon/India	88	9N	80E
Adana: Turkey	84	37N	35E
Adapazari: Turkey	84	41N	30E
Adda: *r.*, Italy	73	46N	10E
Addicks: U.S.A.	31	29¾N	95¾W
ADDIS ABABA: Ethiopia	107	9N	39E

	Page	Lat.	Long.
Addison: U.S.A.	31	42N	88W
Adelaide: Australia	99	35S	139E
Adelaide I.: Antarctica	51	68S	69W
Adélie Land: Antarc.	51	70S	140E
Aden: & *gulf*	85	13N	45E
Adige: *r.*, Italy	73	46N	11E
Adirondack Mts.: U.S.A.	45	44N	74W
Admiralty B.: Antarctica	51	61S	58W
Admiralty Is.: N. Guinea	97	2S	147E
Adour: *r.*, France	71	44N	1W
Adrian: U.S.A.	41	42N	84W
Adrianople: Turkey	67	42N	27E
Adriatic Sea	67	43N	15E
Aduwa: Ethiopia	107	14N	39E
Aegean Is.: & *sea*	67	38N	26E
AFGHANISTAN: *cap.* Kabul	86/7	—	—
Afyonkarahisar: Turkey	84	39N	30E
Agadir: Morocco	106	30N	10W
Agartala: India	89	24N	91E
Agde, Cap d': France	71	43N	4E
Agen, France	71	44N	1E
Agenais: France	71	44N	1E
Agincourt: France	71	51N	2E
Agordat: Ethiopia	107	16N	37E
Agra: India	88	27N	78E
Agrigento: Sicily	67	37N	14E
Agulhas, C.: S. Afr.	108	35S	20E
Ahaggar: Algeria	106	23N	6E
Ahmadabad: India	88	23N	73E
Ahváz: Iran	85	31N	49E
Ahvenanmaa: *is.*, Finland	69	60N	20E
Aigues-Mortes: & *gulf*, France	71	44N	4E
Ailsa Craig: *i.*, Scot.	54	55N	5W
Aïn Sefra: Algeria	106	33N	1W
Aïr: Niger	106	18N	8E
Airdrie: Scotland	54	55¾N	4W
Aire: *r.*, England	57	53¾N	1W
Aisne: *r.*, France	70	49N	3E
Aitape: NE. New Guinea	97	3S	142E
Aiun: Sp. Sahara	106	27N	14W
Aix-en-Provence: Fr.	71	44N	5E
Aix-les-Bains: France	71	46N	6E
Ajaccio: Corsica	65	42N	9E
Ajana: Australia	98	28S	115E
Ajedabya: Libya	84	31N	20E
Ajmer: India	88	27N	75E
Ajo: U.S.A.	42	32N	113E
Akaishi Mts.: Japan	90	36N	138E
Akaroa: N.Z.	67	44S	173E
Akhisar: Turkey	67	39N	28E
Akita: Japan	92	40N	140E
Akko: Israel	84	32N	35E
Akola: India	88	21N	77E
Akritas, C.: Greece	67	37N	22E
Akron: U.S.A.	41	41N	82W
Aksha: U.S.S.R.	81	50N	113E
Aktyubinsk: U.S.S.R.	83	50N	57E
Akureyri: Iceland	68	66N	18W
Akyab: Burma	87	20N	92E
Alabama: *r.*, U.S.A.	41	32N	88W
Alabama: *State*, U.S.A.	41	33N	87W
Alai Range: U.S.S.R.	83	39N	71E
Ala Kul': U.S.S.R.	83	46N	82E
Al Amārah: 'Iraq	85	32N	47E
Alameda: U.S.A.	42	43N	112W
Alamogordo: U.S.A.	43	33N	106W
Alamosa: U.S.A.	40	37N	106W
Åland Is.: Finland	69	60N	20E
Alapayevsk: U.S.S.R.	83	58N	62E
Ala Shan: *mtns.*, China	87	40N	103E
Alaska: *State*, U.S.A.	2	65N	150W
Alaska, Gulf of: U.S.A.	2	58N	145W
Alaska Pen.: U.S.A.	2	56N	160W
Alaska Range: U.S.A.	2	64N	147W
Alaskan Highway: Canada/U.S.A.	2	—	—
Alassio: Italy	73	44N	8E
Alaverdi: U.S.S.R.	82	41N	45E
Alba: Italy	73	45N	8E
Alba Iulia: Romania	66	46N	24E
Albacete: Spain	65	39N	2W
ALBANIA: *cap.* Tiranë	67	41N	20E
Albany: Australia	98	35S	118E
Albany: Ga., U.S.A.	41	32N	84W
Albany: N.Y., U.S.A.	45	43N	74W
Albany: Oregon, U.S.A.	42	45N	123W
Albemarle Sd.: U.S.A.	41	36N	76W
Albert: France	70	50N	3E
Albert, Lake: Uganda	108	3N	31E
Albert Lea: U.S.A.	43	44N	93W
Albi: France	71	44N	2E
Alborz Mts.: Iran	85	36N	52E
Albret, Pays d': Fr.	71	44N	1W
Albula Pass: Switz.	73	47N	10E
Albuquerque: U.S.A.	42	35N	107W
Albury: Australia	99	36S	147E
Alcazar: Spain	65	39N	3W
Alcazarquivir: Morocco	65	35N	6W
Alcoy: Spain	65	39N	1W
Aldan: U.S.S.R.	81	58N	125E
Alderley Edge: Engl.	57	53¼N	2¼W
Aldermaston: Engl.	57	51½N	1¼W
Alderney: *i.*, Channel Is.	55		Inset
Aldershot: England	57	51N	1W
Alegranza: *i.*, Canary Islands	106	29N	13W
Aleksandrov Gay: U.S.S.R.	82	50N	49E
Aleksandrovsk: U.S.S.R.	81	51N	142E
Alençon: France	70	48N	0
Aleppo: Syria	84	36N	37E
Alès: France	71	44N	4E
Alessandria: Italy	73	45N	9E
Ålesund: Norway	68	62N	6E
Aleutian Is.: Bering Sea	100	50N	170W
Aleutian Range: U.S.A.	2	60N	155W
Alexander Arch: U.S.A.	22	57N	135W
Alexander City: U.S.A.	41	33N	86W
Alexander I Island: Antarctica	51	72S	70W
Alexandra: N.Z.	93	45S	169E
Alexandra Ra.: Antarctica	51	84S	165E
Alexandria: Egypt	84	31N	30E
Alexandria: U.S.A.	40	31N	93W
Alexandrina, L.: Australia	99	35S	139E
Alexandroúpolis: Greece	67	41N	26E
Alföld: Hungary	66	47N	21E
Alfreton: England	57	53N	1W
Algarve: *Prov.*, Port.	65	37N	8W
Algeciras: & *Bay*, Sp.	65	36N	5W
ALGER: Algeria	106	37N	3E
ALGERIA: *cap.* Alger	106	—	—
Algoa Bay: S. Africa	109	34S	26E
Algonquin: U.S.A.	31	42¼N	88¼W
Al Hajara: Sau. Arab.	85	31N	42E
Alicanté: Spain	65	38N	1W
Alice: U.S.A.	40	28N	98W
Alice Springs: Austl.	96	24S	134E
Aligarh: India	88	28N	78E
Aling Kangri: *mtn.*, China	88	33N	81E
Alingsås: Sweden	69	58N	12E
Al-Jizah: Egypt	84	30N	31¼E
Alkmaar: Neth.	72	53N	5E
Al Kut: 'Iraq	85	33N	46E
Allahabad: India	88	25N	82E
Allegheny: *r.*, U.S.A.	41	42N	80W
Allegheny Mts.: U.S.A.	41	40N	79W
Allen, L.: R. of Irel.	56	54N	8W
Allen Park: U.S.A.	31	42¼N	83¼W
Allentown: U.S.A.	41	41N	76W
Alleppey: India	88	9N	76E
Allgauer Alps: Aust./Ger.	73	47N	10E
Alliance: U.S.A.	43	42N	103W
Allier: *r.*, France	71	47N	3E
Alloa: Scotland	54	56¼N	3¾W
Alma-Ata: U.S.S.R.	83	43N	77E
Almaden: Spain	65	39N	5W
Almeida: Portugal	65	41N	7W
Almeria: Spain	65	37N	2W
Alnwick: England	54	55N	2W
Alor Star: Malaya	91	6N	100E
Alpena: U.S.A.	17	45N	83W
Alps, The: *mtns.*, Europe	66	46N	11E
Alsace: *Old Prov.*, Fr.	70	48N	7E
Alsager: England	57	53N	2¼W
Alt: *r.*, England	57	53½N	3W
Alta: Norway	68	70N	23E
Alta Loma: U.S.A.	31	29½N	95W
Altai Range: Mong.	81	46N	93E
Altenburg: Germany	72	51N	12E
Altlünen: Germany	62	51¾N	7½E
Altona: Germany	72	54N	10E
Altoona: U.S.A.	41	40N	78W
Altrincham: England	57	53½N	2¼W
Alturas: U.S.A.	42	41N	121W
Altus: U.S.A.	43	35N	99W
Altyn Tagh: *mtns.*, China	87	37N	85E
Alun: *r.*, Wales	57	53½N	3W
Alva: Scotland	54	56¼N	3¾W
Alva: U.S.A.	43	47N	99W
Alvesta: Sweden	69	57N	14E
Alvin: U.S.A.	31	29½N	95¼W
Alwar: India	88	27N	77E
Al Wudyan: Sa'udi Arabia	85	32N	40E
Amarillo: U.S.A.	43	35N	102W
Amazon: *r.*, Brazil	48	3S	60W
Ambala: India	88	31N	77E
Ambarchik: U.S.S.R.	81	70N	162E
Amberg: Germany	72	50N	12E
Amboina: Indonesia	91	4S	128E
Amboise: France	71	47N	1E
Ambon: *i.*, Indon.	91	4S	128E
Americus: U.S.A.	41	32N	84W
Amersfoort: Neth.	72	52N	5E
Amersham: England	57	51¾N	½W
Ames: U.S.A.	43	42N	94W
Amiens: France	70	50N	2E
Amlekganj: India	88	27N	85E
Amlwch: Wales	54	53N	4W
'AMMAN: Jordan	84	32N	36E
Amne Machen Shan: *mts.*, China	90	35N	100E
Amoy: China	89	24N	117E
Amritsar: India	88	32N	75E
Amsterdam: Neth.	72	52N	5E
Amsterdam: U.S.A.	17	43N	74W
Amu Dar'ya: *r.*, U.S.S.R.	83	38N	64E
Amundsen B.: Antarctica	51	67S	50E
Amundsen Sea: Antarctica	51	72S	110W
Amur: *r.*, U.S.S.R./China	81	52N	138E
Anabar: *r.*, U.S.S.R.	81	72N	112E
Anaconda: U.S.A.	42	46N	113W
Anacortes: U.S.A.	42	48N	122W
Anadyr': & *gulf*, U.S.S.R.	81	65N	178W
Anaheim: U.S.A.	46	33¾N	118W
Anahuac: U.S.A.	31	29¾N	94¾W
Anaimudi: *mtn.*, India	88	10N	77E
Anaiza: Sau. Arab.	85	26N	44E
Anambas Is.: India	91	3N	106E
Anan'yev: U.S.S.R.	82	48N	30E
Anápolis: Brazil	48	16S	49W
Anatolia: Turkey	86	39N	35E
Ancenis: France	71	47N	1W
Ancholme: *r.*, Eng.	57	53½N	½W
Anchorage: U.S.A.	2	61N	150W
Ancona: Italy	73	44N	14E
Åndalsnes: Norway	68	62N	8E
Andalusia: Spain	65	37N	5W
Andalusia: U.S.A.	41	31N	86W
Andaman Is.: & *sea*, Indian Ocean	87	12N	93E
Andermatt: Switz.	73	47N	9E
Andernach: Ger.	73	50N	7E
Anderson: Indiana, U.S.A.	41	40N	86W
Anderson: S.C., U.S.A.	41	34N	83W
Andes: *range*, S.Amer.	8/9	—	—
Andhra Pradesh: *State*, India	88	17N	79E
Andizhan: U.S.S.R.	83	41N	73E
ANDORRA: *cap.* Andorra	71	43N	2E
Andover: England	55	51N	1W
Andover: U.S.A.	31	42¾N	71¼W
Andreyevka: U.S.S.R.	83	46N	81E
Andros: *i.*, Bahama Islands	47	24N	78W
Andros: *i.*, Greece	67	38N	25E
Anegada: *i.*, W. Indies	47	19N	64W
Aneto: *mtn.*, Spain	65	43N	1E
Angara: *r.*, U.S.S.R.	83	58N	94E
Angel de la Guardia: *i.*, Mexico	38	30N	113W
Angel Falls: Ven.	48	6N	62W
Angers: France	71	47N	1W
Angical: Brazil	48	12S	45W
Angkor: *ruins*, Cambodia	91	13N	104E
Angledool: Australia	99	29S	148E
Anglesey: *Co.*, Wales	55	53N	4W
ANGOLA: *cap.* Luanda	108	—	—
Angouleme: France	71	46N	0
Angoumois: France	71	46N	0
Angren: U.S.S.R.	83	41N	70E
Anguilla: *i.*, W. Indies	47	18N	63W
Angus: *Co.*, Scotland	54	57N	3W
Anhwei: *Prov.*, China	89	32N	117E
Aniak: U.S.A.	2	62N	160W
Aniva Bay: U.S.S.R.	81	46N	143E
Anjou: *Old Prov.*, Fr.	71	48N	1W
ANKARA: Turkey	84	40N	33E
Ankarata Mts.: Malagasy Rep.	108	20S	47E
Anker: *r.*, England	57	52½N	1½W
Anking: China	89	31N	117E
Annaba: Algeria	65	37N	8E
Annaberg: Germany	72	51N	13E
Annam Range: S.E. Asia	91	18N	105E
Annapolis: U.S.A.	41	39N	76W
Ann Arbor: U.S.A.	41	42N	84W
Annecy: France	71	46N	6E
Anniston: U.S.A.	41	34N	86W
Annonay: France	71	45N	5E
Anrath: Germany	62	51¼N	6½E
Ansbach: Germany	72	49N	11E
Anshan: China	89	41N	123E
Ansi: China	87	41N	96E
Antakya (Antioch): Turkey	84	37N	36E
Antalya: & *Gulf*, Tur.	81	37N	31E
ANTANANARIVO: Malagasy Rep.	108	19S	47E
Antarctic, The	51	—	—
Antequera: Spain	65	37N	4W
Anthony: U.S.A.	43	37N	98W
Anti-Atlas: *mtns.*, Morocco	106	30N	8W
Antibes, Cap d': Fr.	71	44N	7E
Antifer, Cap d': Fr.	70	50N	0
Antigua: Guatemala	38	15N	91W
ANTIGUA: *cap.* St. John's	47	17N	62W
Antioch: U.S.A.	31	42½N	88W
Antipodes Is.: Pacific Ocean	100	50S	179E
Antofagasta: Chile	48	23S	70W
Antrim: & *Co.*, N. Ireland	56	55N	6W
Antrim Mts.: N. Irel.	56	55N	6W
Antsirane: Malagasy Rep.	108	12S	49E
Antung: China	89	40N	125E
Antwerp (Anvers): Belgium	70	51N	4E
Anvers I.: Antarc.	51	65S	64W
Anyang: China	89	36N	114E
Anzhero-Sudzhensk: U.S.S.R.	83	56N	86E
Anzio: Italy	67	41N	13E
Aoiz: Spain	71	43N	1W
Aomori: Japan	92	41N	141E
Aosta: Italy	73	46N	7E
Apalachicola: *r.*, U.S.A.	41	30N	85W
Aparri: Philippines	91	18N	122E
Apeldoorn: Neth.	72	52N	6E
Apennines: *mtns.*, It.	67	43N	12E
Appalachian Mts.: U.S.A.	41	37N	80W
Appleby: England	54	55N	3W
Appleton: U.S.A.	43	44N	88W
Apulia: Italy	67	41N	16E
'Aqaba: Jordan	84	29N	35E
Aqua Prieta: Mexico	42	31N	110W
Aquila: Italy	67	42N	13E
Aquitaine: *Old Prov.*, France	71	45N	0
Arabian Sea	85	15N	55E
Aracajú: Brazil	48	11S	37W
Arad: Romania	66	46N	21E
Arafura Sea: E. Indies	96	10S	135E
Aragon: Spain	65	42N	0
Araguaia: *r.*, Brazil	48	12S	51W
Arakan Yoma: *mtns.*, Burma	90	20N	94E
Araks (Araxes): *r.*, U.S.S.R./Iran	82	39N	47E
Aral Sea: U.S.S.R.	83	45N	60E
Aral'sk: U.S.S.R.	83	47N	62E
Aran I.: R. of Ireland	56	55N	9W
Aran Is.: R. of Ireland	56	53N	10W
Ararat, Mt.: Turkey	85	40N	44E
Arauca: Colombia	48	7N	71W
Aravalli Hills: India	88	26N	74E
Arbroath: Scotland	54	57N	3W
Arcachon: France	71	45N	1W
Arcadia: U.S.A.	31	29¼N	95W
Arcata: U.S.A.	42	41N	124W
Arcola: U.S.A.	31	29½N	95½W
Arcot: India	88	13N	79E
Arctic Ocean	80/1	—	—
Ardabīl: Iran	85	38N	48E
Ardèche: *r.*, France	71	44N	4E
Ardennes: *mtns.*, Belgium	70	50N	5E
Ardmore: U.S.A.	43	34N	97W
Ardrossan: Scotland	54	56N	5W
Ardwick le Street: England	57	53½N	1¼W
Arendal: Norway	69	58N	9E
Arequipa: Peru	48	16S	72W
Arezzo: Italy	67	43N	12E
Argaum: India	88	21N	77E
Argentan: France	70	49N	0
Argenteuil: France	70	49N	2E
ARGENTINA: *cap.* Buenos Aires	49	35S	65W
Argonne, Forêt d': France	70	49N	5E
Argos: Greece	67	37N	23E
Argostolion: Cephalonia	67	38N	20E
Argyllshire: *Co.*, Scotland	54	56N	5W
Argyrokastro: Alb.	67	40N	20E
Arica: Chile	48	18S	70W
Ariège: *r.*, France	71	43N	2E
Arizona: *State*, U.S.A.	42	34N	112W
Arkansas: *r.* & *State*, U.S.A.	40	36N	93W
Arkansas City: U.S.A.	40	37N	97W
Arkhangel'sk: U.S.S.R.	80	64N	40E
Arklow: R. of Irel.	56	53N	6W
Arkona, C.: Ger.	66	55N	14E
Arlberg Pass: Austr.	73	47N	10E
Arles: France	71	44N	5E
Arlington: U.S.A.	31	42¼N	71¼W
Arlington Heights: U.S.A.	31	42N	88W
Arlon: Belgium	70	50N	6E
Armagh: & *Co.*, N. Ireland	56	54N	7W
Armavir: U.S.S.R.	82	45N	41E
Armenian S.S.R.: U.S.S.R.	82	40N	45E
Armentières: Fr.	70	51N	3E
Armidale: Australia	99	31S	152E
Armonk: U.S.A.	31	41½N	73¾E
Arnhem: Neth.	72	52N	6E
Arnhem Land: Australia	88	14S	133E
Arno: *r.*, Italy	73	44N	11E
Arnold: England	57	53N	1W
Arran: *i.*, Scotland	54	56N	5W
Arras: France	70	50N	3E
Arrée, Mts. d': Fr.	70	48N	4W
Arromanches: Fr.	70	49N	1W
Arrowrock Res.: U.S.A.	42	44N	116W

	Page	Lat.	Long.
Arrowsmith, Mt.: New Zealand	**93**	43S	171E
Arta: Greece	**67**	39N	21E
Artemovskiy: U.S.S.R.	**83**	57N	62E
Artesia: U.S.A.	**43**	33N	104W
Arthur's Pass: N.Z.	**93**	43S	172E
Artois: *Old Prov.*, Fr.	**70**	50N	2E
Artsiz: U.S.S.R.	**66**	46N	29E
Aruba: *i.*, Carib. Sea	**47**	13N	70W
Aru Is.: Indonesia	**91**	6S	134E
Arun: *r.*, England	**55**	51N	1W
Arvidsjaur: Sweden	**68**	66N	19E
Arvika: Sweden	**69**	60N	13E
Arys': U.S.S.R.	**83**	42N	69E
Arzamas: U.S.S.R.	**82**	56N	44E
Asansol: India	**88**	24N	87E
Ascension I.: Atlantic Ocean	**52**	8S	15W
Aschaffenburg: Ger.	**72**	50N	9E
Ascoli Piceno: Italy	**67**	43N	14E
Ascot: England	**57**	51½N	¾W
Åsele: Sweden	**68**	64N	17E
Asenovgrad: Bulg.	**67**	42N	25E
Ashanti: Ghana	**106**	7N	2W
Ash: *r.*, England	**57**	51¾N	0
Ashbourne: England	**57**	53N	1¾W
Ashburnham: U.S.A.	**31**	42¾N	72W
Ashburton: N.Z.	**93**	44S	172E
Ashburton: *r.*, Austl.	**96**	23S	116E
Ashby: U.S.A.	**31**	42¾N	71¾W
Ashby de la Zouch: England	**57**	52¾N	1½W
Asheville: U.S.A.	**41**	35N	83W
Ashford: England	**55**	51N	1E
Ashington: England	**54**	55N	2W
Ashkelon: Israel	**84**	31¾N	34½E
Ashkhabad: U.S.S.R.	**83**	38N	58E
Ashland: Ky., U.S.A.	**41**	38N	83W
Ashland: Mass., U.S.A.	**31**	42¼N	71½W
Ashland: Oregon, U.S.A.	**42**	42N	123W
Ashland: Wisconsin, U.S.A.	**43**	47N	91W
Ashtabula: U.S.A.	**41**	42N	81W
Ashton: U.S.A.	**42**	44N	111W
Ashton in Makerfield: England	**57**	53½N	2¾W
Ashton under Lyne: England	**57**	53½N	2W
Asino: U.S.S.R.	**83**	57N	86E
Asir: Sa'udi Arabia	**85**	20N	42E
Asmara: Ethiopia	**107**	15N	39E
Aspiring, Mt.: N.Z.	**93**	44S	169E
Assab: Ethiopia	**107**	13N	42E
Assam: India	**89**	27N	93E
Assaye: India	**88**	20N	76E
Assen: Netherlands	**72**	53N	7E
Assisi: Italy	**67**	43N	13E
Astara: U.S.S.R.	**82**	39N	49E
Asti: Italy	**73**	45N	8E
Astipalaia: *i.*, Greece	**67**	37N	26E
Astoria: U.S.A.	**42**	46N	124W
Astrakhan': U.S.S.R.	**82**	46N	48E
ASUNCIÓN: Paraguay	**50**	25S	58W
Aswân: & *dam*, Egypt	**84**	24N	33E
Asyût: Egypt	**84**	27N	31E
Atacama Desert: Chile	**48**	22S	69W
Atasuskiy: U.S.S.R.	**83**	49N	72E
Atbara: & *r.*, Sudan	**107**	18N	34E
Atbasar: U.S.S.R.	**83**	52N	68E
Atchafalaya: *r.*, U.S.A.	**40**	31N	92W
Atchison: U.S.A.	**43**	40N	95W
ATHENS (Athenai): Greece	**67**	38N	24E
Athens: Ga., U.S.A.	**41**	34N	83W
Athens: Tenn., U.S.A.	**41**	35N	85W
Atherstone: Eng.	**57**	52½N	1½W
Atherton: England	**57**	53½N	2½W
Athlone: R. of Irel.	**56**	53N	8W
Athos: *penin.*, Greece	**67**	40N	24E
Atlanta: U.S.A.	**41**	34N	84W
Atlantic City: U.S.A.	**41**	39N	75W
Atlantic Ocean	**52**	—	—
Atoka: U.S.A.	**43**	34N	96W
Atrak: *r.*, Iran	**85**	38N	57E
Atshan: Libya	**106**	27N	11E
Attamaha: *r.*, U.S.A.	**41**	32N	82W
Aubagne: France	**71**	43N	6E
Aube: *r.*, France	**70**	48N	4E
Aubrac, Mts. d': Fr.	**71**	45N	3E
Auburn: Ala., U.S.A.	**41**	33N	85W
Auburn: Maine, U.S.A.	**17**	44N	70W
Auburn: Mass., U.S.A.	**31**	42¼N	73¾W
Auburn: N.Y., U.S.A.	**44**	43N	77W
Aubusson: France	**71**	46N	2E
Auch: France	**71**	44N	1E
Auckland: N.Z.	**93**	37S	175E
Auckland Is.: Pacific Ocean	**100**	50S	166E
Aude: *r.*, France	**71**	43N	2E
Audierne: & *bay*, Fr.	**70**	48N	5W
Augathella: Austl.	**98**	26S	147E
Augsberg: Ger.	**73**	48N	11E
Augusta: Australia	**98**	34S	115E
Augusta: Ga., U.S.A.	**41**	33N	82W
Augusta: Maine, U.S.A.	**41**	44N	70W
Aumale: France	**70**	50N	2E

	Page	Lat.	Long.
Aunis: *Old Prov.*, Fr.	**71**	46N	1W
Aurangabad: India	**88**	20N	75E
Aurignac: France	**71**	43N	1E
Aurillac: France	**71**	45N	2E
Aurora: U.S.A.	**31**	41¾N	88¼W
Austin: Minnesota, U.S.A.	**43**	44N	93W
Austin: Nev., U.S.A.	**42**	40N	117W
Austin: Tex., U.S.A.	**40**	30N	98W
Austral: *is.*, Pacific Ocean	**101**	22S	150W
AUSTRALIA: *cap.* Canberra	**96/7**	—	—
Australian Alps: Australia	**99**	37S	148E
AUSTRIA: *cap.* Vienna	**66**	47N	15E
Autun: France	**71**	47N	4E
Austurias: Spain	**65**	43N	7W
Auvergne: *Old Prov. & mtns.*, France	**71**	45N	3E
Auxerre: France	**70**	48N	4E
Avallon: France	**71**	47N	4E
Aveiro: Portugal	**65**	41N	9W
Avellaneda: Arg.	**50**	34¾S	58¼W
Aveyron: *r.*, France	**71**	44N	2E
Avignon: France	**71**	44N	5E
Avila: Spain	**65**	41N	5W
Avon: Mass., U.S.A.	**31**	42¼N	71W
Avon: *r.*, Hants., Eng.	**55**	51N	2W
Avon: *r.*, War., Eng.	**55**	52N	2W
Avon: *r.*, Wilts., Eng.	**55**	51N	2W
Avonmouth: Eng.	**55**	51N	3W
Avranches: France	**70**	49N	1W
Awash: Ethiopia	**107**	9N	40E
Awe, L.: Scotland	**54**	56N	5W
Ayaguz: U.S.S.R.	**83**	48N	80E
Aydin: Turkey	**67**	38N	28E
Ayer: U.S.A.	**31**	42½N	71½W
Aylesbury: England	**57**	51¾N	¾W
Aylesford: England	**57**	51¼N	½E
Ayon I.: U.S.S.R.	**81**	70N	168E
Ayr: & *Co.*, Scotland	**54**	55N	5W
Ayr: Australia	**98**	20S	147E
Ayutthaya: Thailand	**91**	14N	101E
Ayvalik: Turkey	**67**	39N	27E
Azerbaydzhan S.S.R.: U.S.S.R.	**82**	41N	47E
Azizia: Libya	**84**	32N	13E
Azores: *is.*, Atlantic Ocean	**52**	39N	29W
Azov, Sea of: U.S.S.R.	**82**	46N	37E
Babar Is.: Indonesia	**91**	8S	130E
Bab el Mandeb: *str.*, Ethiopia/Arabia	**107**	13N	43E
Babylon: 'Iraq	**85**	33N	44E
Bacău: Romania	**66**	47N	27E
Bacolod: Philippines	**91**	11N	123E
Bacup: England	**57**	53¾N	2¼W
Badajoz: Spain	**65**	39N	7W
Baden: *Old Prov.*, Germany	**73**	49N	8E
Baden: Switzerland	**73**	49N	8E
Baden-Baden: Ger.	**73**	49N	8E
Bad Kissingen: Ger.	**72**	50N	10E
Bad Kreuznach: Ger.	**72**	50N	8E
Bad Reichenhall: Germany	**73**	48N	13E
Badulla: Ceylon	**88**	7N	81E
BAGHDĀD: 'Iraq	**85**	33N	34E
Bagheria: Sicily	**67**	38N	14E
Bagshot: England	**57**	51¼N	¾W
BAHAMAS: *cap.* Nassau	**47**	25N	75W
Bahawalpur: W. Pak.	**88**	29N	72E
Bahia: Brazil	**48**	13S	38W
Bahia Blanca: Arg.	**49**	39S	62W
Bahraich: India	**88**	28N	82E
BAHRAIN: *cap.* Manama	**85**	26N	51E
Bahr el Ghazal: *r.*, Chad	**106**	14N	17E
Bahr el Ghazal: *Prov.*, Sudan	**107**	10N	27E
Bahr el Jebel (White Nile): *r.*, Sudan	**107**	7N	31E
Baia-Mare: Rom.	**66**	48N	24E
Bailen: Spain	**65**	38N	4W
Băileşti: Romania	**67**	44N	23E
Bailleau Pk.: Antarc.	**51**	68S	60E
Bailleul: France	**70**	53E	1N
Bainbridge: U.S.A.	**41**	31N	85W
Bairnsdale: Austl.	**99**	38S	148E
Baker: Mont., U.S.A.	**43**	46N	104W
Baker: Oreg., U.S.A.	**42**	45N	118W
Bakersfield: U.S.A.	**42**	35N	119W
Bakony Forest: Hungary	**66**	47N	18E
Baku: U.S.S.R.	**82**	40N	50E
Balaghat: India	**88**	22N	80E
Balaklava: Australia	**99**	34S	138E
Balaklava: U.S.S.R.	**82**	45N	34E
Bala Lake: Wales	**55**	53N	4W
Balashov: U.S.S.R.	**82**	51N	43E
Balasore: India	**88**	21N	87E
Balaton L.: Hungary	**66**	47N	18E
Balboa: Panamá	**39**	Inset	
Balclutha: N.Z.	**93**	46S	170E
Baldwin: U.S.A.	**31**	40¾N	73½W
Bâle: Switzerland	**73**	48N	7E
Balearic Is.: Spain	**65**	39N	3E
Balen: Belgium	**70**	51N	5E
Bali: *i.*, Indonesia	**91**	8S	115E

	Page	Lat.	Long.
Balikesir: Turkey	**84**	40N	28E
Balikpapan: Borneo	**91**	1S	117E
Balkan Mts.: Bulgaria	**67**	43N	25E
Balkhash: & *l.*, U.S.S.R.	**83**	46N	75E
Ballarat: Australia	**99**	38S	144E
Ballard Vale: U.S.A.	**31**	42½N	71¼W
Ballater: Scotland	**54**	57N	3W
Balleny Is.: Antarc.	**51**	68S	164E
Ballina: Australia	**99**	29S	154E
Ballina: R. of Irel.	**56**	54N	9W
Ballinasloe: R. of Ireland	**56**	53N	8W
Ballinrobe: R. of Ireland	**56**	54N	9W
Ballycastle: N. Irel.	**56**	55N	6W
Ballymena: N. Irel.	**56**	55N	6W
Ballymoney: N. Irel.	**56**	55N	7W
Ballyshannon: R. of Ireland	**56**	55N	8W
Balmaceda: Chile	**49**	46S	72W
Balmoral: Scotland	**54**	57N	3W
Balovale: Zambia	**109**	14S	23E
Balranald: Australia	**99**	35S	144E
Balsas: *r.*, Mexico	**38**	18N	99W
Balta: U.S.S.R.	**66**	48N	30E
Baltic Sea	**69**	—	—
Baltimore: U.S.A.	**41**	39N	77W
Baltrum: *i.*, Ger.	**72**	54N	7E
Baluchistan: W. Pak.	**88**	27N	65E
BAMAKO: Mali	**106**	13N	8W
Bamba: Mali	**106**	17N	2W
Bamberg: Germany	**72**	50N	11E
Banat: Romania	**67**	45N	22E
Banbridge: N. Irel.	**56**	54N	6W
Banbury: England	**55**	52N	1W
Bancannia, L.: Austl.	**99**	31S	142E
Banchory: Scotland	**54**	57N	2W
Bandar 'Abbās: Iran	**85**	27N	56E
Bandar-e-Shāh: Iran	**85**	37N	54E
Bandar-e-Shāhpūr: Iran	**85**	30N	49E
Banda Sea: Indon.	**91**	6S	127E
Banderas Bay: Mex.	**38**	21N	106W
Bandirma: Turkey	**67**	40N	28E
Bandjarmasin: Born.	**91**	3S	115E
Bandon: R. of Irel.	**56**	52N	9W
Bandra: India	**88**	19N	73E
Bandung: Java	**91**	7S	107E
Bangalore: India	**88**	13N	78E
Bangka: *i.*, Indon.	**91**	2S	106E
BANGKOK: Thailand	**91**	14N	100E
Bangor: N. Ireland	**56**	55N	6W
Bangor: U.S.A.	**13**	45N	69W
Bangor: Wales	**55**	53N	4W
BANGUI: Central African Repub.	**107**	4N	18E
Bangweulu, L.: Zambia	**108**	11S	31E
Ban Houeisai: Laos	**90**	20N	100E
Baniâs: Syria	**84**	35N	36E
Banja Luka: Yugo.	**67**	45N	17E
Banks Penin.: N.Z.	**93**	44S	173E
Bann: *r.*, N. Ireland	**56**	55N	7W
Bannockburn: Scot.	**54**	56N	4W
Bannu: W. Pakistan	**88**	33N	71E
Bantry: & *bay*, R. of Ireland	**56**	52N	9W
Banzare Coast: Antarctica	**51**	67S	125E
Bapaume: France	**70**	50N	3E
Barahona: Dominican Republic	**47**	18N	71W
Baranof I.: U.S.A.	**22**	57N	135W
Baranovichi: U.S.S.R.	**82**	53N	26E
Barataria Bay: U.S.A.	**41**	29N	90W
BARBADOS: *cap.* Bridgetown	**47**	13N	60W
Barbuda: *i.*, W. Ind.	**47**	18N	62W
Barce: Libya	**84**	33N	21E
Barcelona: Spain	**65**	41N	2E
Barcelona: Venezuela	**48**	10N	65W
Barcelonnette: Fr.	**71**	44N	7E
Barcoo: *r.*, Australia	**97**	24S	144E
Bardawil, Lake: Egypt	**84**	31N	33E
Bardia: Libya	**84**	32N	25E
Bardsey I.: Wales	**55**	53N	5W
Bareilly: India	**88**	28N	80E
Barents Sea: U.S.S.R.	**80**	72N	40E
Bari: Italy	**67**	41N	17E
Barking: England	**57**	51½N	0
Barkly Tableland: Australia	**96**	18S	136E
Barkly West: S. Afr.	**109**	28S	25E
Bârlad: Romania	**66**	46N	28E
Bar-le-Duc: France	**70**	49N	5E
Barlee, L.: Australia	**98**	29S	119E
Barletta: Italy	**67**	41N	16E
Barlin: France	**70**	50N	3E
Barnato: Australia	**99**	32S	145E
Barnaul: U.S.S.R.	**83**	53N	84E
Barne Inlet: Antarc.	**51**	80S	160E
Barnet: England	**57**	51¾N	¼W
Barnsley: England	**57**	54N	2W
Barnstaple: England	**55**	51N	4W
Baroda: India	**88**	22N	73E
Barquisimeto: Venez.	**48**	10N	69W
Barra: *i.* & *Hd.*, Scot.	**53**	57N	7W
Barraba: Australia	**99**	30S	151E
Barrackpore: India	**88**	23N	88E
Barranquilla: Colombia	**48**	11N	75W
Barrhead: Scotland	**54**	55¾N	4½W
Barrington: U.S.A.	**31**	42¼N	88W
Barrow-in-Furness: England	**54**	54N	3W

	Page	Lat.	Long.
Barrow, Point: U.S.A.	**2**	72N	156W
Barry: Wales	**55**	51N	3W
Barry Mts.: Austl.	**99**	37S	147E
Barstow: U.S.A.	**42**	35N	117W
Bar-sur-Seine: Fr.	**70**	48N	4E
Bartlesville: U.S.A.	**43**	37N	96W
Barton-upon- Humber: England	**57**	53¾N	¼W
Bartow: U.S.A.	**41**	28N	82W
Basel: Switzerland	**73**	48N	7E
Basildon: England	**57**	51½N	½E
Basilicata: *Reg.*, Italy	**67**	40N	16E
Basingstoke: Eng.	**57**	51¼N	1W
Basra: 'Iraq	**85**	30N	48E
Bassas da India: *i.*, Indian Ocean	**109**	22S	40E
Bassein: Burma	**91**	17N	95E
Basse-Terre: Guadeloupe	**47**	16N	62W
Bass Strait: Austl.	**97**	40S	146E
Bastogne: Belgium	**70**	50N	6E
Bastrop: U.S.A.	**40**	33N	92W
Bastutrask: Sweden	**68**	65N	20E
Bataan Penin.: Phil.	**91**	15N	120E
Batang: China	**90**	30N	99E
Batan Is.: Phil.	**89**	20N	122E
Batavia: U.S.A.	**31**	41¾N	88¼W
Batesville: Arkansas, U.S.A.	**43**	36N	92W
Batesville, Miss., U.S.A.	**41**	34N	90W
Bath: England	**55**	51N	2W
Bathgate: Scotland	**54**	56N	3½W
Bathurst: Australia	**99**	33S	150E
BATHURST: Gambia	**106**	13N	17W
Bathurst I.: Austl.	**96**	12S	130E
Batley: England	**57**	53¾N	1½W
Baton Rouge: U.S.A.	**40**	31N	91W
Batticaloa: Ceylon	**88**	8N	82E
Battle Creek: *city*, U.S.A.	**41**	42N	85W
Battle Mountain: *city*, U.S.A.	**42**	41N	117W
Batu Is.: Indonesia	**91**	0	99E
Batumi: U.S.S.R.	**82**	42N	42E
Batz, Î. de: France	**70**	49N	4W
Bauchi Plateau: Nig.	**106**	10N	10E
Bautzen: Germany	**72**	51N	14E
Bavaria: *Prov.*, Ger.	**72**	49N	11E
Bavarian Forest: Germany	**72**	49N	13E
Bawdwin: Burma	**90**	23N	97E
Bawtry: England	**57**	53½N	1W
Bayamo: Cuba	**47**	20N	77W
Bayan Kara Shan: *mtns.*, China	**90**	34N	99E
Bay City: Michigan, U.S.A.	**17**	44N	84W
Bay City: Texas, U.S.A.	**40**	29N	96W
Bayeux: France	**70**	49N	1W
Baykal, L.: U.S.S.R.	**81**	53N	107E
Baykonur: U.S.S.R.	**83**	48N	66E
Baymak: U.S.S.R.	**82**	53N	58E
Bayonne: France	**71**	43N	1W
Bayonne: U.S.A.	**31**	40¾N	74W
Bayreuth: Germany	**72**	50N	12E
Baytown: U.S.A.	**31**	29¾N	95W
Baza: Spain	**65**	37N	3W
Beachport: Austl.	**99**	37S	140E
Beachy Head: Eng.	**53**	51N	0
Beaconsfield: Eng.	**57**	51½N	½W
Beardmore Glacier: Antarctica	**51**	84S	170E
Bear I.: U.S.S.R.	**80**	74N	20E
Béarn: *Old Prov.*, Fr.	**71**	43N	1W
Bearsden: Scotland	**54**	56N	4¼W
Beas: *r.*, India	**88**	32N	76E
Beatrice: U.S.A.	**43**	40N	97W
Beauce: France	**70**	48N	2E
Beaufort: U.S.A.	**41**	32N	81W
Beaufort Sea	**2**	73N	140W
Beaufort W.: S. Afr.	**109**	32S	23E
Beaujolais, Mts. du: France	**71**	46N	4E
Beaumaris: Wales	**53**	53N	4W
Beaumont: U.S.A.	**40**	30N	94W
Beaune: France	**71**	47N	5E
Beauvais: France	**70**	49N	2E
Beaver: *i.*, U.S.A.	**17**	45N	85W
Beaver Dam: *city*, U.S.A.	**43**	43N	89W
Bebington: England	**57**	53¼N	3W
Beckley: U.S.A.	**41**	38N	81W
Bedeau: Algeria	**106**	34N	1W
Bedford: & *Co.*, Eng.	**55**	52N	0
Bedford: Mass., U.S.A.	**31**	42½N	71¼W
Bedford: Ind., U.S.A.	**41**	39N	86W
Bedford: Penn., U.S.A.	**41**	40N	79W
Bedford Heights: U.S.A.	**31**	42½N	83¼W
Bedworth: England	**57**	52½N	1½W
Beersheba: Israel	**84**	31N	35E
Beeston: Ches., Eng.	**57**	53N	2¾W
Beeston: Notts., Eng.	**57**	53N	1¼W
Beeville: U.S.A.	**40**	29N	97W
Bega: Australia	**99**	37S	150E
Begovat: U.S.S.R.	**83**	40N	69E
Beira: Mozambique	**109**	20S	35E
BEIRUT: Lebanon	**84**	34N	35E
Beit Bridge: Rhod.	**109**	22S	30E
Beith: Scotland	**54**	55¾N	4½W
Beja: Portugal	**65**	38N	8W

	Page	Lat.	Long.
Bela: W. Pakistan	**88**	26N	66E
Belaya: *r.*, U.S.S.R.	**82**	54N	56E
Belém: Brazil	**48**	1S	48W
Belen: U.S.A.	**42**	35N	107W
BELFAST: N. Ireland	**56**	55N	6W
Belfast L.: N. Irel.	**53**	55N	6W
Belfort: France	**71**	48N	7E
Belgaum: India	**88**	16N	75E
BELGIUM: *cap.* Brussels	**70**	51N	4E
Belgorod: U.S.S.R.	**82**	51N	36E
BELGRADE: Yugo.	**67**	45N	20E
Belitung: *i.*, Indon.	**91**	3S	108E
BELIZE: Br. Hond.	**38**	17N	88W
Bellac: France	**71**	46N	1E
Bellaire: U.S.A.	**31**	29¾N	95¼W
Bellary: India	**88**	15N	77E
Belle Fourche: & *r.*, U.S.A.	**43**	45N	104W
Bellegarde: France	**71**	46N	6E
Belle Glade: U.S.A.	**41**	27N	81W
Belle Ile-en-Mer: Fr.	**70**	47N	3W
Belleville: Kansas, U.S.A.	**43**	40N	98W
Belleville: Mich., U.S.A.	**31**	42¼N	83¼W
Belleville: N.J., U.S.A.	**31**	40¾N	74W
Bellingham: U.S.A.	**42**	49N	122W
Bellingshausen Sea: Antarctica	**51**	71S	85W
Bellinzona: Switz.	**73**	46N	9E
Belluno: Italy	**73**	46N	12E
Belmont: Australia	**99**	33S	152E
Belmont: S. Africa	**109**	30S	24E
Belo Horizonte: Brazil	**48**	20S	44W
Beloit: Kans., U.S.A.	**43**	39N	98W
Beloit: Wisc., U.S.A.	**43**	43N	89W
Belper: England	**57**	53N	1½W
Belturbet: R. of Irel.	**56**	54N	7W
Bel'tsy: U.S.S.R.	**66**	47N	28E
Belvoir, Vale of: Eng.	**57**	53N	1W
Belyando: *r.*, Austl.	**98**	22S	146E
Belyy I.: U.S.S.R.	**80**	73N	70E
Bemidji: U.S.A.	**43**	47N	95W
Benalla: Australia	**99**	37S	146E
Bend: U.S.A.	**42**	44N	121W
Bender Cassim: Somali Republic	**86**	11N	49E
Bendery: U.S.S.R.	**66**	47N	30E
Bendigo: Australia	**99**	37S	144E
Benevento: Italy	**67**	41N	15E
Bengal, Bay of: Ind./Pak.	**88**	17N	87E
BENGHAZI: Libya	**107**	32N	20E
Benguela: Angola	**108**	13S	13E
Beni: *r.*, Bolivia	**48**	13S	67W
Beni Mansour: Alg.	**65**	36N	4E
Benin, Bight of: Afr.	**106**	4N	3E
Beni Saf: Algeria	**65**	35N	1W
Ben Lomond: *mt.*, Scotland	**54**	56¼N	4½W
Ben Macdhui: *mt.*, Scotland	**54**	57N	4W
Ben Nevis: *mt.*, Scot.	**54**	57N	5W
Bennington: U.S.A.	**17**	43N	74W
Bensenville: U.S.A.	**31**	42N	88W
Benton: U.S.A.	**40**	35N	93W
Benton Harbour: U.S.A.	**41**	43N	86W
Benue: *r.*, Africa	**106**	9N	12E
Benwee Hd.: R. of Ireland	**56**	54N	10W
Beograd: Yugoslavia	**67**	45N	20E
Berar: India	**88**	21N	77E
Berber: Sudan	**107**	18N	34E
Berbera: Somali Republic	**107**	10N	45E
Berdichev: U.S.S.R.	**82**	50N	29E
Berezhany: U.S.S.R.	**66**	49N	25E
Berezovo: U.S.S.R.	**83**	64N	65E
Bergama: Turkey	**67**	39N	27E
Bergamo: & *Alps*, It.	**73**	46N	10E
Bergen: Norway	**69**	60N	5E
Bergenfield: U.S.A.	**31**	41N	74W
Bergen-op-Zoom: Netherlands	**72**	51N	4E
Bergerac: France	**71**	45N	0
Bergisch Gladbach: Germany	**72**	51N	7E
Berhampore: India	**88**	24N	88E
Bering Sea	**2**	61N	170W
Bering Str.: U.S.S.R./U.S.A.	**2**	65N	170W
Berkeley: U.S.A.	**42**	38N	122W
Berkeley Heights: U.S.A.	**31**	40¾N	74¼W
Berkley: U.S.A.	**31**	42½N	83¼W
Berkhamsted: Eng.	**57**	51¾N	½W
Berkshire: *Co.*, Eng.	**57**	51N	1W
BERLIN: Germany	**72**	53N	13E
Berlin: U.S.A.	**17**	45N	71W
Bermuda Is.: Atlantic Ocean	**52**	32N	65W
BERN: Switzerland	**73**	47N	7E
Bernardsville: U.S.A.	**31**	40¾N	74½W
Bernay: France	**70**	49N	1E
Bernese Alps: Switz.	**73**	46N	7E
Berre, Étg. de: Fr.	**71**	43N	5E
Berri: Australia	**99**	34S	141E
Berry: *Old Prov.*, Fr.	**71**	47N	2E
Berry Is.: Bahama Is.	**41**	26N	78W
Berwick: *Co.*, Scot.	**54**	56N	2W
Berwick upon Tweed: England	**54**	56N	2W

	Page	Lat.	Long.
Berwyn: U.S.A.	**31**	41¾N	87¾W
Besançon: France	**71**	47N	6E
Bessarabia: U.S.S.R.	**66**	47N	29E
Bessèges: France	**71**	44N	4E
Bessemer: U.S.A.	**41**	33N	87W
Bessines: France	**71**	46N	1E
Bethlehem: Jordan	**84**	31N	35E
Bethlehem: S. Afr.	**109**	28S	28E
Bethlehem: U.S.A.	**41**	41N	75W
Bethpage: U.S.A.	**31**	40¾N	73½W
Béthune: France	**70**	51N	3E
Betwa: *r.*, India	**88**	26N	80E
Betws-y-Coed: Wales	**55**	53N	4W
Beuvron: *r.*, France	**71**	47N	2E
Beverley: England	**54**	54N	0
Beverly: U.S.A.	**31**	42½N	71W
Beverly Hills: Calif., U.S.A.	**46**	34N	118½W
Beverly Hills: Mich., U.S.A.	**31**	42½N	83¼W
Bexley: England	**57**	51½N	¼E
Bezhitsa: U.S.S.R.	**82**	53N	34E
Béziers: France	**71**	43N	3E
Bhagalpur: India	**88**	25N	88E
Bhamo: Burma	**90**	24N	97E
Bhaunagar: India	**88**	22N	72E
Bhima: *r.*, India	**88**	17N	76E
Bhopal: India	**88**	23N	77E
Bhubaneswar: India	**88**	20N	86E
Bhuj: India	**88**	23N	70E
BHUTAN: *cap.* Punakha	**89**	27N	90E
Biafra, Bight of: Gulf of Guinea	**106**	3N	8E
Biak: *i.*, West Irian	**88**	1S	136E
Biala Podlaska: Pol.	**66**	52N	23E
Bialystok: Poland	**66**	53N	23E
Biarritz: France	**71**	43N	1W
Bicester: England	**55**	52N	1W
Biddeford: U.S.A.	**17**	43N	70W
Biddulph: England	**57**	53N	2¼W
Bideford: England	**55**	51N	4W
Biel: Switzerland	**73**	47N	7E
Bielefeld: Germany	**72**	52N	9E
Biella: Italy	**73**	46N	8E
Big Black: *r.*, U.S.A.	**40**	33N	90W
Big Blue: *r.*, U.S.A.	**43**	41N	97W
Big Falls: *city*, U.S.A.	**43**	48N	94W
Bighorn Mts.: & *r.*, U.S.A.	**42**	45N	108W
Big Spring: U.S.A.	**43**	32N	102W
Big Wood: *r.*, U.S.A.	**42**	43N	115W
Bihać: Yugoslavia	**67**	45N	16E
Bihar: *State*, India	**88**	25N	85E
Bikaner: India	**88**	28N	73E
Bikini: *i.*, Pacific O.	**100**	12N	165E
Bilaspur: India	**88**	22N	82E
Bilbao: Spain	**65**	43N	3W
Billerica: U.S.A.	**31**	42½N	71¼W
Billericay: England	**57**	51½N	½E
Billingham: England	**54**	54½N	1¼W
Billings: U.S.A.	**42**	46N	109W
Biloxi: U.S.A.	**41**	30N	89W
Bilston: England	**57**	52½N	2W
Bimini Is.: Bahama Is.	**41**	26N	79W
Bingen: Germany	**72**	50N	8E
Bingham: England	**57**	53N	1W
Binghamton: U.S.A.	**17**	42N	76W
Birdum: Australia	**96**	16S	133E
Bīrjand: Iran	**85**	33N	59E
Birkenhead: Eng.	**57**	53½N	3W
Birmingham: Eng.	**57**	52½N	2W
Birmingham: Ala., U.S.A.	**41**	33N	87W
Birmingham: Mich., U.S.A.	**31**	42½N	83¼W
Birobidzhan: U.S.S.R.	**81**	49N	133E
Birr: R. of Ireland	**56**	53N	8W
Birstall: England	**57**	53¾N	1¾W
Bisbee: U.S.A.	**42**	31N	110W
Biscay, Bay of	**71**	45N	2W
Biscoe Is.: Antarctica	**51**	66S	67W
Bishop Auckland: England	**54**	54¾N	1¾W
Bishop's Stortford: England	**57**	51¾N	¼E
Biskra: Algeria	**106**	35N	6E
Bismarck: U.S.A.	**43**	47N	101W
Bismarck Arch.: New Guinea	**97**	5S	150E
Bismarck Sea	**100**	5S	152E
BISSAU: Port. Guinea	**106**	12N	16W
Bistrita: Romania	**66**	47N	24E
Bitola: Yugoslavia	**67**	41N	21E
Bitterfeld: Germany	**72**	52N	12E
Bitterfontein: S. Afr.	**109**	31S	18E
Bitterroot Range: U.S.A.	**42**	46N	115W
Biwa, Lake: Japan	**92**	35N	136E
Biysk: U.S.S.R.	**83**	53N	85E
Bjøllånes: Norway	**68**	66N	15E
Bjørneborg: Finland	**68**	61N	22E
Black: *r.*, Ark., U.S.A.	**43**	36N	91W
Black: *r.*, N.Y., U.S.A.	**43**	43N	75W
Black: *r.*, Wisc., U.S.A.	**43**	44N	91W
Blackburn: England	**57**	53¾N	2½W
Blackfoot: U.S.A.	**42**	43N	112W
Black Forest: Ger.	**73**	48N	8E
Black Irtysh: *r.*, U.S.S.R./China	**83**	48N	85E
Black Mtns.: Wales	**55**	52N	3W
Blackpool: England	**57**	53¾N	3W

	Page	Lat.	Long.
Black Oak: U.S.A.	**31**	41½N	87¼W
Black Sea: U.S.S.R.	**82**	43N	35E
Black Volta: *r.*, West Africa	**106**	10N	2W
Blackwater: *r.*, Berks., Eng.	**57**	51¼N	1W
Blackwater: *r.*, Essex, England	**57**	51¾N	¾E
Blackwater: *r.*, R. of Ireland	**56**	52N	8W
Blackwood: *r.*, Austl.	**98**	34S	115E
Blagoveshchensk: U.S.S.R.	**81**	50N	127E
Blanc, C.: Sp. Sahara	**106**	20N	17W
Blanc, Mt.: Fr./Italy	**71**	46N	7E
Bland: *r.*, Australia	**99**	34S	148E
Blankenberghe: Belg.	**70**	51N	3E
Blantyre: Malawi	**109**	16S	35E
Blarney: R. of Irel.	**56**	52N	9W
Blavet: *r.*, France	**70**	48N	3W
Blaye: France	**71**	45N	1W
Blenheim: Germany	**73**	49N	10E
Blenheim: N.Z.	**93**	42S	174E
Bletchley: England	**55**	52N	1W
Blida: Algeria	**65**	36N	3E
Blithe: *r.*, England	**57**	52¾N	2W
Bloemfontein: S. Afr.	**109**	29S	26E
Blois: France	**71**	48N	1E
Bloody Foreland: R. of Ireland	**56**	55N	8W
Bloomfield: U.S.A.	**31**	40¾N	74¼W
Bloomfield Hills: U.S.A.	**31**	42½N	83W
Bloomingdale: U.S.A.	**31**	42N	88W
Bloomington: Ill., U.S.A.	**43**	40N	89W
Bloomington: Ind., U.S.A.	**41**	39N	86W
Bluefield: U.S.A.	**41**	37N	81W
Bluefields: Nicaragua	**47**	12N	84W
Blue Island: U.S.A.	**31**	41½N	115W
Blue Mts.: Australia	**99**	33S	150E
Blue Mts.: U.S.A.	**42**	45N	120W
Blue Nile: *r.*, Africa	**107**	10N	35E
Blue Ridge: *mts.*, U.S.A.	**41**	36N	81W
Bluff: N.Z.	**93**	46S	168E
Blumenthal: Ger.	**72**	53N	9E
Blyth: *town* & *r.*, England	**54**	55N	1½W
Blythe: U.S.A.	**40**	34N	115W
Blythe: *r.*, England	**57**	52½N	1¾W
Blytheville: U.S.A.	**43**	36N	90W
Bo: Sierra Leone	**106**	8N	12W
Boa Vista: Brazil	**48**	3N	61W
Bobo Dioulasso: Upper Volta	**106**	12N	4W
Bocholt: Germany	**72**	52N	7E
Bochum: Germany	**62**	51½N	7¼E
Bodelé Depression: Chad	**106**	17N	17E
Boden: Sweden	**68**	66N	22E
Bodensee *see* Constance, L.			
Bodmin: & *moor*, England	**55**	50N	5W
Bodø: Norway	**68**	67N	14E
Bogalusa: U.S.A.	**41**	31N	90W
Bog of Allen: R. of Ireland	**56**	53N	7W
BOGOTÁ: Colombia	**48**	5N	74W
Bohemia: Czech.	**66**	50N	15E
Bohol: *i.*, Phil.	**91**	10N	124E
Boise: U.S.A.	**42**	44N	116W
Bojador, C.: Sp. Sahara	**106**	26N	15W
Boké: Guinea	**106**	11N	14W
Bokn Fd.: Norway	**69**	59N	6E
Bolama: Port. Guin.	**106**	12N	15W
Bolan Pass: W. Pak.	**88**	30N	68E
Bolekhov: U.S.S.R.	**66**	49N	24E
Bolgrad: U.S.S.R.	**66**	46N	29E
Boling: U.S.A.	**41**	29N	96W
Bolivar: U.S.A.	**43**	38N	93W
BOLIVIA: *cap.* Sucre	**48**	17S	65W
Bollington: England	**57**	53¼N	2W
Bollwiller: France	**70**	48N	7E
Bologna: Italy	**73**	44N	11E
Bolsena, L.: Italy	**67**	43N	12E
Bol'shevik I.: U.S.S.R.	**81**	78N	102E
Bolsover: England	**57**	53¼N	1¼W
Bolton: England	**57**	53½N	2½W
Bolzano: Italy	**73**	47N	11E
Boma: Congo Repub.	**108**	6S	13E
Bombay: India	**88**	19N	73E
Bon, C.: Tunisia	**67**	37N	11E
Bonaire: *i.*, Caribbean Sea	**47**	12N	98W
Bondo: Congo Republic	**108**	4N	24E
Bone, G. of: Indon.	**91**	4S	121E
Bo'ness: Scotland	**54**	56N	3½W
Bonin Is.: Pacific O.	**100**	27N	142E
BONN: W. Ger.	**72**	51N	7E
Bonneville Dam: U.S.A.	**40**	46N	122W
Bookaloo: Australia	**99**	32S	137E
Boonton: U.S.A.	**31**	41N	74½W
Bootle: England	**57**	53½N	3W
Bor: Yugoslavia	**67**	44N	22E
Borås: Sweden	**69**	58N	13E
Bordeaux: France	**71**	45N	1W
Bordertown: Austl.	**99**	36S	141E
Borehamwood: Eng.	**57**	51¾N	¼W
Borger: U.S.A.	**43**	36N	101W

	Page	Lat.	Long.
Borgholm: Sweden	**69**	57N	17E
Borislav: U.S.S.R.	**66**	49N	23E
Borisoglebsk: U.S.S.R.	**82**	51N	42E
Borkum: *i.*, Ger.	**72**	54N	7E
Borlänge: Sweden	**69**	60N	15E
Borneo: *i.*, Indonesia	**91**	0	115E
Bornholm: *i.*, Den.	**69**	55N	15E
Bosnia: Yugoslavia	**67**	44N	16E
Bosporus: *str.*, Tur.	**84**	41N	29E
Bossier City: U.S.A.	**43**	33N	94W
Bosso: Niger	**106**	14N	13E
Boston: England	**55**	53N	0
Boston: U.S.A.	**31**	42¼N	71W
Botany Bay: Austl.	**99**	34S	151E
Botevgrad: Bulgaria	**67**	43N	24E
Bothnia, Gulf of	**68**	63N	20E
Botoşani: Romania	**66**	47N	26E
BOTSWANA: *cap.* Gaborone	**109**	22S	24E
Bottrop: Germany	**62**	51½N	7E
Bougainville: *i.*, New Guinea	**97**	6S	155E
Bougie: Algeria	**106**	37N	5E
Boulder: Australia	**98**	31S	122E
Boulder: U.S.A.	**43**	40N	105W
Boulder City: U.S.A.	**42**	36N	115W
Boulogne: France	**70**	51N	2E
Boulogne-Billancourt: France	**64**	48¾N	2¼E
Bound Brook: U.S.A.	**31**	40½N	74½W
Bourbonnais: France	**71**	46N	3E
Bourg: France	**71**	46N	5E
Bourges: France	**71**	47N	2E
Bourget, Lac du: Fr.	**71**	46N	6E
Bourg Madame: Fr.	**71**	42N	2E
Bounty Is.: Pacific O.	**100**	48S	179E
Bourke: Australia	**99**	30S	146E
Bournemouth: Eng.	**55**	51N	2W
Bourtanger Moor: Neth./Ger.	**72**	53N	7E
Bou Saâda: Algeria	**65**	35N	4E
Boussac: France	**71**	46N	2E
Bowling Green: U.S.A.	**41**	37N	86W
Bowling Green C.: Australia	**98**	19S	147E
Bowman: U.S.A.	**43**	46N	103W
Bowman I.: Antarc.	**51**	65S	104E
Boxford: U.S.A.	**31**	42¾N	71W
Box Hill: England	**57**	51¼N	¼W
Boyle: R. of Ireland	**56**	54N	8W
Boyne: *r.*, Australia	**98**	26S	152E
Boyne: *r.*, R. of Irel.	**56**	54N	6W
Boyup Brook: Austl.	**98**	34S	116E
Bozeman: U.S.A.	**42**	46N	111W
Brabant: Belgium	**70**	51N	4E
Brač: *i.*, Yugoslavia	**67**	43N	16E
Brachina: Australia	**99**	32S	138E
Bracknell: England	**57**	51½N	¾W
Bradenton: U.S.A.	**41**	28N	83W
Bradford: England	**57**	53¾N	1¾W
Braga: Portugal	**65**	42N	8W
Brahmani: *r.*, India	**88**	22N	85E
Brahmaputra: *r.*, India/Pakistan	**89**	26N	93E
Brăila: Romania	**67**	45N	28E
Brain: *r.*, England	**57**	51¾N	½E
Brainerd: U.S.A.	**43**	46N	94W
Braintree: England	**57**	52N	½E
Braintree: U.S.A.	**31**	42¼N	71W
Bramhall: England	**57**	53¼N	2¼W
Branco: *r.*, Brazil	**48**	1N	62W
Brandenburg: Ger.	**72**	52N	13E
Brant: *r.*, England	**57**	53¼N	½W
BRASÍLIA: Brazil	**48**	16S	48W
Bransfield Str.: Antarctica	**51**	63S	60W
Braşov: Romania	**66**	46N	26E
Brasstown Bald: *mtn.*, U.S.A.	**41**	35N	84W
Bratislava: Czech.	**66**	48N	17E
Bratsk: U.S.S.R.	**81**	56N	102E
Braunau: Austria	**73**	48N	13E
Brawley: U.S.A.	**42**	33N	115W
Bray: R. of Ireland	**56**	53N	6W
BRAZZAVILLE: Congo	**108**	4S	15E
BRAZIL: *cap.* Brasília	**48/9**	—	—
Brazilian Highlands: Brazil	**48**	15S	50W
Brazoria: U.S.A.	**41**	29N	96W
Brazos: *r.*, U.S.A.	**40**	29N	95W
BRAZZAVILLE: Congo	**108**	4S	15E
Breckenridge: U.S.A.	**43**	46N	97W
Brecknock: *Co.*, Wales	**55**	52N	3W
Brecon: Wales	**55**	52N	3W
Brecon Beacons: *mtns.*, Wales	**55**	52N	3W
Breda: Netherlands	**72**	52N	5E
Bregenz: Austria	**73**	47N	10E
Bréhat, I.: France	**70**	49N	3W
Breisach: Germany	**73**	48N	8E
Bremen: Germany	**72**	53N	9E
Bremerhaven-Wesermünde: Germany	**72**	54N	9E
Bremerton: U.S.A.	**42**	47N	123W
Brenner Pass: Austria/Italy	**73**	47N	12E
Brent: England	**57**	51½N	¼W
Brentwood: England	**57**	51½N	¼E
Brescia: Italy	**73**	46N	10E
Breslau: Poland	**66**	51N	17E
Bressuire: France	**71**	47N	0
Brest: France	**70**	48N	4W

	Page	Lat.	Long.
Brest Litovskiy: U.S.S.R.	82	52N	24E
Breton Sound: U.S.A.	41	30N	90W
Briançon: France	71	45N	7E
Bridgend: Wales	55	52N	4W
Bridge of Weir: Scot.	54	55¾N	4½W
Bridgeport: N.Y., U.S.A.	41	41N	73W
Bridgeport: Texas, U.S.A.	43	33N	99W
Bridgetown: Austl.	98	34S	116E
BRIDGETOWN: Barb.	47	13N	60W
Bridgnorth: England	57	52½N	2½W
Bridgwater: England	55	51N	3W
Bridlington: England	54	54N	0
Brie: France	70	49N	3E
Brienz, Lake: Switz.	73	47N	8E
Brierfield: England	57	53¾N	2¼W
Brierley Hill: Eng.	57	52½N	2¼W
Briey: France	70	49N	6E
Brig: Switzerland	73	46N	8E
Brigg: England	57	53½N	½W
Brigham: U.S.A.	42	42N	112W
Brightlingsea: Eng.	57	51¾N	1E
Brighouse: England	57	53¾N	1¾W
Brighton: England	55	51N	0
Brindisi: Italy	67	41N	18E
Brisbane: Australia	98	27S	153E
Bristol: England	55	51N	3W
Bristol: Tennessee, U.S.A.	41	37N	82W
Bristol: Wis., U.S.A.	31	42½N	88W
Bristol Bay: U.S.A.	2	58N	160W
Bristol Channel: Eng.	55	51N	4W
BRITISH HONDURAS: *cap.* Belize	38	17N	88W
British Isles: Europe	53	—	—
British Mts.: U.S.A./Canada	28	69N	140W
Brittany: *Old Prov.*, France	70	48N	3W
Brive: France	71	45N	2E
Brno: Czech.	66	49N	17E
Broadview: U.S.A.	31	41¾N	87¾W
Brockton: U.S.A.	31	42N	71W
Brockway: U.S.A.	43	47N	106W
Brod: Yugoslavia	67	45N	18E
Broken Bow: U.S.A.	43	41N	100W
Broken Hill: Austl.	99	32S	141E
Bromley: England	57	51½N	0
Bromsgrove: Eng.	57	52½N	2W
Bronx: U.S.A.	31	40¾N	74W
Brookfield: Mich., U.S.A.	31	42¾N	83W
Brookfield: Wis., U.S.A.	31	43N	88¼W
Brookings: U.S.A.	43	44N	97W
Brooklands: U.S.A.	31	42¾N	83W
Brookline: U.S.A.	31	42¼N	71¾W
Brooklyn: U.S.A.	31	40¾N	74W
Brooks Range: U.S.A.	2	68N	150W
Brooksville: U.S.A.	41	29N	82W
Broome: Australia	96	18S	122E
Broseley: England	57	52½N	2½W
Brough Head: Scot.	51	59N	3W
Brownhills: England	57	52¾N	2W
Brownsville: U.S.A.	40	26N	97W
Brownwood: U.S.A.	43	32N	99W
Broxburn: Scotland	54	56N	3½W
Bruchsal: Germany	72	49N	9E
Bruges (Brugge): Belgium	70	51N	3E
Brühl: Germany	72	51N	7E
BRUNEI: *cap.* Brunei	91	5N	115E
Brunswick: Ger.	72	52N	10E
Brunswick: U.S.A.	41	31N	81W
BRUSSELS: Belgium	70	51N	4E
Bryan: U.S.A.	40	30N	96W
Bryansk: U.S.S.R.	82	53N	34E
Brzeg: Poland	66	51N	17E
Bucaramanga: Colombia	48	7N	73W
Buchan Ness: Scot.	53	57N	2W
BUCHAREST (Bucureşti): Romania	67	44N	26E
Buckhaven: Scotland	54	56N	3W
Buckingham: *Co.*, England	57	51¾N	¾W
Buckland Tableland: Australia	98	25S	148E
Buckley: Wales	57	53¼N	3W
BUDAPEST: Hungary	66	48N	19E
Bude: England	55	51N	5W
Büderich: Germany	62	51¼N	6¾E
Buenaventura: Colombia	48	4N	77W
BUENOS AIRES: Arg.	50	35S	58W
Buffalo: N.Y., U.S.A.	41	43N	79W
Buffalo: Wyo., U.S.A.	42	44N	107W
Bug: *r.*, Pol./U.S.S.R.	66	51N	24E
Bug: *r.*, U.S.S.R.	82	48N	31E
Bukachacha: U.S.S.R.	81	53N	117E
Bukama: Congo Republic	108	9S	26E
Bukavu: Congo Republic	108	2S	29E
Bukhara: U.S.S.R.	83	40N	65E
Bukoba: Tanzania	108	1S	32E
Bulagan: Mongolia	81	49N	103E
Bulawayo: Rhodesia	109	20S	29E
BULGARIA: *cap.* Sofia	67	42N	25E
Buller: *mt.*, N.Z.	93	42S	172E
Bulli: Australia	99	34S	151E
Bulloo: *r.*, Australia	98	26S	143E

	Page	Lat.	Long.
Bulloo, L.: Australia	99	28S	142E
Bulloo Downs: *town*, Australia	98	28S	143E
Bull Shoals Res.: U.S.A.	43	37N	93W
Bumtang: Bhutan	89	27N	91E
Bunbury: Australia	98	33S	116E
Buncrana: R. of Irel.	56	55N	7W
Bundaberg: Austl.	98	25S	152E
Bundoran: R. of Irel.	56	54N	8W
Bunguran Is.: Indon.	91	4N	108E
Buraida: Sa'udi Arabia	85	27N	44E
Buraimi: Trucial 'Oman	85	24N	56E
Burbank: U.S.A.	46	34¼N	118¼W
Burdekin: *r.*, Austl.	98	20S	147E
Burdur: Turkey	84	38N	30E
Bureya: U.S.S.R.	81	50N	130E
Burgas: & *gulf*, Bulg.	67	42N	27E
Burgdorf: Switz.	73	47N	8E
Burgersdorp: S. Afr.	109	31S	26E
Burgos: Spain	65	42N	4W
Burgundy: *Old Prov.*, France	71	47N	5E
Burley: U.S.A.	42	42N	114W
Burlington: Colo., U.S.A.	43	39N	103W
Burlington: Iowa, U.S.A.	43	41N	91W
Burlington: Mass., U.S.A.	31	42½N	71¼W
Burlington: N.C., U.S.A.	41	36N	80W
Burlington: Vt., U.S.A.	17	44N	73W
Burlington: Wis., U.S.A.	31	42¾N	88¼W
BURMA: *cap.* Rangoon	90/1	—	—
Burnett: *r.*, Austl.	98	25S	152E
Burnett Heads: Australia	98	25S	152E
Burnham-on-Crouch: England	57	51¾N	¾E
Burnie: Tasmania	97	41S	146E
Burnley: England	57	53¾N	2¼W
Burns: U.S.A.	42	44N	119W
Burra: Australia	99	34S	139E
Burrinjuck Res.: Australia	99	35S	149E
Bursa: Turkey	84	40N	29E
Burslem: England	57	53N	2¼W
Burton Latimer: Eng.	57	52½N	¾W
Burton upon Trent: England	57	52¾N	1¾W
BURUNDI	108	3S	30E
Bury: England	57	53½N	2¼W
Bury St. Edmunds: England	55	52N	1E
Bushehr: Iran	85	29N	51E
Bushey: England	57	51¾N	½W
Busselton: Australia	98	34S	115E
Bute: *i.*, Scotland	54	56N	5W
Buteshire: *Co.*, Scot.	54	56N	5W
Butler: U.S.A.	41	41N	80W
Butte: U.S.A.	42	46N	113W
Butterworth: S. Afr.	109	32S	28E
Butt of Lewis: Scot.	53	58N	6W
Butung: *i.*, Indon.	91	5S	123E
Buxar: India	88	25N	85E
Buxton: England	57	53¼N	2W
Buyaga: U.S.S.R.	81	60N	127E
Buzău: Romania	67	45N	27E
Buzuluk: U.S.S.R.	82	53N	52E
Bydgoszcz: Poland	66	53N	18E
Byelorussian S.S.R.: U.S.S.R.	82	53N	27E
Bytom: Poland	66	50N	19E
Caballo Res.: U.S.A.	42	33N	107W
Cabawin: Australia	98	27S	150E
Cabimas: Venezuela	47	10N	71W
Cabinda: Angola	108	5S	12E
Cáceres: Spain	65	39N	6W
Cadillac: U.S.A.	17	44N	85W
Cádiz: & *Gulf*, Spain	65	37N	6W
Caen: France	70	49N	0
Caernarvon: & *Co.*, Wales	55	53N	4W
Caher: R. of Ireland	56	52N	8W
Cahersiveen: R. of Ireland	56	52N	10W
Cahors: France	71	44N	1E
Caicos Is.: Bahama Is.	47	22N	72W
Caird Coast: Antarc.	51	76S	25W
Cairngorm Mts.: Scotland	54	57N	4W
Cairns: Australia	97	17S	146E
CAIRO: Egypt	84	30N	31E
Calabozo: Venezuela	48	9N	67W
Calabria: *Reg.*, Italy	67	39N	16E
Calafat: Romania	67	44N	23E
Calais: France	70	51N	2E
Calais: U.S.A.	13	45N	67W
Calamian Group: Philippines	91	12N	120E
Călăraşi: Romania	67	44N	27E
Calcutta: India	88	22N	88E
Calder: *r.*, England	57	53¾N	2W
Caldera: Chile	48	27S	71W
Caldwell: U.S.A.	42	44N	117W
Calexico: U.S.A.	42	33N	115W
Calf of Man: I. of Man	54	54N	5W
Cali: Colombia	48	3N	77W

	Page	Lat.	Long.
Caliente: U.S.A.	42	38N	115W
California: *State*, U.S.A.	46	—	—
California, Gulf of: Mexico	38	27N	112W
Calipatria: U.S.A.	42	33N	115W
Callabonna: Austl.	99	30S	140E
Callan: R. of Ireland	56	53N	7W
Callao: Peru	48	12S	77W
Caltanissetta: Sicily	67	37N	14E
Calumet City: U.S.A.	31	41½N	87½W
Calvi: Corsica	65	43N	9E
Calvinia: S. Africa	109	32S	20E
Cam: *r.*, England	55	52N	0
Camagüey: Cuba	47	21N	78W
Camargue: France	71	44N	4E
Cambay: & *Gulf*, India	88	22N	73E
Camberley: England	57	51¼N	¾W
CAMBODIA: *cap.* Phnom Penh	91	13N	105E
Cambrai: France	70	50N	3E
Cambrian Mts.: Wales	55	52N	4W
Cambridge: & *Co.*, England	55	32N	0
Cambridge: N.Z.	93	38S	176E
Cambridge: Del., U.S.A.	41	39N	76W
Cambridge: Mass., U.S.A.	31	42½N	71W
Camden: England	57	51½N	¼W
Camden: U.S.A.	40	34N	93W
Camerón, C.: Hond.	47	16N	85W
Cameron: U.S.A.	40	31N	97W
CAMEROON: *cap.* Yaoundé	106	5N	12E
Camocim: Brazil	48	3S	41W
Camooweal: Austl.	96	20S	138E
Campania: *Reg.*, Italy	67	41N	15E
Campbeltown: Scot.	54	55N	6W
Campeche, Bay of: Mexico	38	20N	93W
Campinas: Brazil	50	23S	47W
Campine: Belgium	70	51N	5E
Campobasso: Italy	67	41N	15E
Campo Grande: Brazil	48	20S	55W
Campsie Fells: Scot.	54	56N	4¼W
Câmpulung: Rom.	67	45N	25E
Câmpulung Moldovenesc: Rom.	66	48N	26E
Can: *r.*, England	57	51¾N	½E
Canadian: *r.*, U.S.A.	43	35N	97W
Canakkale: Turkey	67	40N	26E
Canary Islands: Atlantic Ocean	106	28N	15W
CANBERRA: Australia	99	35S	149E
Candia: Crete	67	35N	25E
Canea: Crete	67	35N	24E
Canna: *i.*, Scotland	54	57N	7W
Cannes: France	71	44N	7E
Cannock: England	57	52¾N	2W
Cannock Chase: Eng.	57	52¾N	2W
Cannonball: *r.*, U.S.A.	43	46N	102W
Canon City: U.S.A.	43	38N	105W
Cantabrian Mts.: Sp.	65	43N	5W
Canterbury: England	57	51¼N	1E
Canterbury Bight: New Zealand	93	44S	172E
Canterbury Plains: New Zealand	93	43S	172E
Canton: China	90	*Inset*	
Canton: Ill., U.S.A.	43	41N	90W
Canton: Mass., U.S.A.	31	42¼N	71¼W
Canton: Ohio, U.S.A.	41	41N	81W
Canton: S. Dakota, U.S.A.	43	43N	97W
Canton I.: Pacific O.	100	3S	171W
Canudos: Brazil	48	7S	57W
Canvey: & *is.*, Eng.	57	51½N	½E
Cape Girardeaux: *city*, U.S.A.	43	37N	90W
Cape Province: South Africa	109	32S	23E
Cape Town: S. Afr.	109	34S	18E
Cape Verde Is.: Atlantic Ocean	52	18N	25W
Cape York Penin.: Australia	97	13S	143E
Cap Haitien: *town*, Haiti	47	20N	72W
Capri: *i.*, Italy	67	40N	14E
Capricorn Channel: Australia	98	23S	152E
Capricorn Group: Australia	98	23S	153E
Caprivi Strip: S. Afr.	109	18S	23E
Capua: Italy	67	41N	14F
Caqak: Yugoslavia	67	44N	20E
CARACAS: Venezuela	48	10N	67W
Caransebes: Rom.	67	45N	22E
Caratasca: Hond.	47	15N	84W
Caravelas: Brazil	48	18S	39W
Carbondale: U.S.A.	43	38N	89W
Carcassonne: Fr.	71	43N	2E
Cardamon Hills: India	88	10N	77E
CARDIFF: Wales	55	51N	3W
Cardigan: & *Co.*, Wales	55	52N	5W
Cardigan Bay: Wales	55	52N	4W
Caribbean Sea	47	15N	75W
Carinthia: *Prov.*, Austria	73	47N	14E
Carlisle: England	54	55N	3W

	Page	Lat.	Long.
Carlow: & *Co.*, R. of Ireland	56	53N	7W
Carlsbad: U.S.A.	43	32N	104W
Carlton: England	57	53N	1W
Carluke: Scotland	54	55¾N	3¾W
Carmarthen: & *Co.*, Wales	55	52N	4W
Carmaux: France	71	44N	2E
Carnac: France	70	48N	3W
Carnarvon: Australia	97	25S	114E
Carnarvon: S. Africa	109	31S	22E
Carnarvon Range: Australia	98	25S	148E
Carnic Alps: Austria/Italy	73	47N	13E
Carnsore Pt.: R. of Ireland	56	52N	6W
Carolina: Brazil	48	7S	47W
Caroline I.: Pacific O.	101	10S	150W
Caroline Is.: Pac. O.	100	2N	145W
Caroni: *r.*, Venezuela	48	6N	63W
Carora: Venezuela	47	10N	70W
Carpathian Mts.: U.S.S.R./Rom.	66	47N	25E
Carpentaria, Gulf of: Australia	96	15S	138E
Carpentersville: U.S.A.	31	42¼N	88¼W
Carpentras: France	71	44N	5E
Carrara: Italy	73	44N	10E
Carrauntuohil: *mtn.*, R. of Ireland	56	52N	10W
Carrickfergus: N. Ireland	56	55N	6W
Carrickmacross: R. of Ireland	56	54N	7W
Carrick on Shannon: R. of Ireland	56	54N	8W
Carrick-on-Suir: R. of Ireland	56	52N	7W
Carson City: U.S.A.	42	39N	120W
Carson Sink: U.S.A.	42	40N	118W
Cartagena: Colom.	48	10N	75W
Cartagena: Spain	65	38N	1W
Cartago: Costa Rica	47	10N	84W
Carthage: U.S.A.	40	32N	94W
Carúpano: Venezuela	47	10N	63W
Carvin: France	70	50N	3E
Cary: U.S.A.	31	42¼N	88¼W
Caryapundy Swamp: Australia	99	29S	143E
Casablanca: Morocco	106	34N	8W
Casale Monferrato: Italy	73	45N	8E
Cascade Range: Canada/U.S.A.	42	46N	121W
Cascavel: Brazil	48	4S	38W
Caserta: Italy	67	41N	14E
Casino: Australia	99	29S	153E
Casiquiare: *r.*, Venezuela	48	2N	66W
Casper: U.S.A.	42	43N	106W
Caspian Lowlands: U.S.S.R.	82	47N	51E
Caspian Sea: U.S.S.R./Iran	82	42N	51E
Cassel: France	70	51N	2E
Cassino: Italy	67	41N	14E
Castellón de la Plana: Spain	65	40N	0
Castelo Branco: Portugal	65	40N	7W
Castile *see* Old & New			
Castlebar: R. of Irel.	56	54N	9W
Castlederg: N. Irel.	56	55N	8W
Castleford: England	57	53¾N	1¼W
Castlemaine: Austl.	99	37S	144E
Castlerea: R. of Irel.	56	54N	8W
Castletown: England	54	54N	5W
Castres: France	71	44N	2E
Castries: St. Vincent	47	14N	61W
Castrop-Rauxel: Ger.	62	51½N	7¼E
Catalca: Turkey	67	41N	28E
Catalonia: Spain	65	41N	1E
Catamarca: Arg.	48	28S	66W
Catania: Sicily	67	37N	15E
Catanzaro: Italy	67	39N	17E
Catastrophe, C.: Australia	96	35S	136E
Caterham: England	57	51¼N	0
Cat I.: Bahama Is.	47	24N	76W
Catoche, Cape: Mex.	39	21N	87W
Catskill Mts.: U.S.A.	41	42N	75W
Cattaro: Yugoslavia	67	42N	19E
Cauca: *r.*, Colombia	48	7N	76W
Caucasus Mts.: U.S.S.R.	82	43N	45E
Cauvery: *r.*, India	88	12N	77E
Caux, Pays de: Fr.	70	50N	1E
Cavado: *r.*, Portugal	65	42N	9W
Cavaillon: France	71	44N	5E
Cavan: & *Co.*, R. of Ireland	56	54N	7W
Cawood: England	57	53¾N	1¼W
CAYENNE: Fr. Guiana	48	5N	52W
Cayman Is.: Carib. Sea	47	19N	81W
Cayo Grande: *i.*, Carib. Sea	47	12N	67W
Cayuga L.: U.S.A.	17	43N	77W
Ceará: Brazil	48	4S	38W
Cebu: & *i.*, Phil.	91	10N	124E
Cedar City: U.S.A.	42	38N	114W
Cedar Grove: U.S.A.	31	40¾N	74¼W
Cedar Rapids: U.S.A.	43	42N	92W

	Page	Lat.	Long.
Ceduna: Australia	**96**	32S	134E
Celebes: *i. & sea*, Indonesia	**91**	3S	120E
Celje: Yugoslavia	**66**	46N	15E
Celle: Germany	**72**	53N	10E
Center Line: U.S.A.	**31**	42½N	83W
Centerville: U.S.A.	**43**	41N	93W
CENTRAL AFRICAN REPUBLIC: *cap.* Bangui	**107**	7N	20E
Centralia: Ill., U.S.A.	**41**	39N	89W
Centralia: Wash., U.S.A.	**42**	47N	123W
Central Siberian Plat.: U.S.S.R.	**81**	65N	110E
Cephalonia: *i.*, Greece	**67**	38N	21E
Cerignola: Italy	**67**	41N	16E
Cerigo: *i.*, Greece	**67**	36N	23E
Cerro Bolivar: *mt.*, Venezuela	**48**	7N	63W
Cerro de Pasco: Peru	**48**	11S	76W
Cesena: Italy	**73**	44N	12E
Ceské Budejovice: Czechoslovakia	**66**	49N	14E
Česky Těšín: Czech.	**66**	50N	18E
Cessnock: Australia	**99**	33S	151E
Cetinje: Yugoslavia	**67**	42N	19E
Ceuta: Morocco	**65**	36N	5W
Céyennes: *mtns.*, Fr.	**71**	44N	4E
CEYLON: *cap.* Colombo	**88**	7N	81E
Chablis: France	**70**	48N	4E
CHAD: *cap.* Fort Lamy	**106/7**	—	—
Chad, Lake: Africa	**106**	13N	14E
Chalcis: Greece	**67**	38N	24E
Chalon-sur-Saône: France	**71**	47N	3E
Châlons-sur-Marne: France	**70**	49N	4E
Chaman: W. Pak.	**88**	31N	66E
Chamba: India	**88**	32N	76E
Chambal: *r.*, India	**88**	26N	77E
Chamberlain, L.: U.S.A.	**13**	46N	69W
Chambersburg: U.S.A.	**41**	40N	78W
Chambéry: France	**71**	46N	6E
Chamdo: China	**90**	31N	97E
Chamonix: France	**71**	46N	7E
Champagne: *Old Prov.*, France	**70**	49N	4E
Champagne-Pouilleuse: France	**70**	49N	4E
Champaign: U.S.A.	**41**	40N	88W
Champéry: Switz.	**73**	46N	7E
Champlain, L.: U.S.A.	**17**	45N	74W
Chañaral: Chile	**49**	26S	71W
Chanchiang: China	**89**	21N	110E
Chandalar: U.S.A.	**28**	68N	146W
Changan: China	**89**	34N	109E
Changchew: China	**89**	32N	120E
Changchun: China	**89**	44N	125E
Changkiakow: China	**89**	41N	115E
Changsha: China	**89**	28N	113E
Changshu: China	**89**	32N	121E
Changzindian: China	**90**	39¾N	116¼E
Channel Is.: U.K.	**55**	*Inset*	
Channelview: U.S.A.	**31**	29¾N	95W
Chanthaburi: Thai.	**91**	13N	102E
Chanute: U.S.A.	**43**	38N	95W
Chany, L.: U.S.S.R.	**83**	55N	77E
Chaoan: China	**89**	24N	116E
Chaoyangchen: China	**90**	43N	126E
Chapala, Lake: Mex.	**38**	20N	103W
Chapayevsk: U.S.S.R.	**82**	53N	50E
Chapra: India	**88**	26N	85E
Charcot I.: Antarc.	**51**	70S	75W
Chardzhou: U.S.S.R.	**83**	39N	64E
Charente: *r.*, France	**71**	46N	0
Chari: *r.*, Chad	**106**	11N	16E
Charleroi: Belgium	**70**	50N	4E
Charleston: Indiana, U.S.A.	**41**	39N	88W
Charleston: S.C., U.S.A.	**41**	33N	80W
Charleston: W. Va., U.S.A.	**41**	38N	81W
Charleville: Australia	**98**	26S	146E
Charleville: France	**70**	50N	5E
Charlotte: U.S.A.	**41**	35N	81W
Charlotte Harbour: U.S.A.	**43**	27N	82W
Charlottesville: U.S.A.	**41**	38N	79W
Charlton: Australia	**99**	36S	143E
Charnwood Forest: England	**57**	52¾N	1¼W
Charollais, Mts. du: France	**71**	46N	4E
Charolles: France	**71**	46N	4E
Charters Towers: Australia	**97**	20S	146E
Chartres: France	**70**	48N	1E
Château, Pte. du: Fr.	**70**	49N	3W
Châteaubriant: Fr.	**70**	48N	1W
Châteaudun: France	**70**	48N	1E
Châteaulin: France	**70**	48N	4W
Château Renault: Fr.	**71**	48N	1E
Châteauroux: Fr.	**71**	47N	2E
Château-Thierry: Fr.	**70**	49N	3E
Châtellerault: Fr.	**71**	47N	1E
Chater: *r.*, England	**57**	52¾N	½W

	Page	Lat.	Long.
Chatham: England	**57**	51½N	½E
Chatham I.: Pac. O.	**42**	1S	89W
Chatham Is.: Pac. O.	**100**	44S	177W
Châtillon-sur-Seine: France	**70**	48N	5E
Chatrapur: India	**88**	19N	85E
Chattahoochee: & *r.*, U.S.A.	**41**	31N	85W
Chattanooga: U.S.A.	**41**	35N	85W
Chaumont: France	**70**	48N	5E
Chausey, Iles de: Fr.	**70**	49N	2W
Chaves I.: Pacific O.	**42**	1S	90W
Cheadle: Ches., Eng.	**57**	53½N	2¼W
Cheadle: Staffs., Eng.	**57**	53N	2W
Cheb: Czech.	**66**	50N	12E
Cheduba: *i.*, Burma	**87**	18N	93E
Chefoo: China	**89**	38N	121E
Cheju: *i.*, Korea	**90**	33N	126E
Chekiang: *Prov.*, China	**89**	29N	120E
Chekunda: U.S.S.R.	**81**	51N	132E
Cheleken: U.S.S.R.	**82**	39N	54E
Chéliff: *r.*, Algeria	**65**	36N	1E
Chelkar-Tengiz, L.: U.S.S.R.	**83**	48N	63E
Chelm: Poland	**66**	51N	24E
Chelmer: *r.*, England	**57**	51¾N	½E
Chelmsford: Eng.	**55**	52N	0
Chelmsford: U.S.A.	**31**	42½N	71¼W
Chelsea: England	**57**	51½N	¼W
Chelsea: U.S.A.	**31**	42½N	71W
Cheltenham: Eng.	**55**	52N	2W
Chelyabinsk: U.S.S.R.	**83**	55N	61E
Chelyuskin, Cape: U.S.S.R.	**81**	77N	105E
Chenab: *r.*, India/W. Pak.	**88**	33N	75E
Chengchow: China	**89**	35N	113E
Chengkiang: China	**90**	25N	103E
Chengteh: China	**89**	41N	118E
Chengtu: China	**89**	31N	104E
Chepo: Panama	**47**	9N	79W
Chepstow: England	**55**	52N	3W
Cher: *r.*, France	**71**	47N	1E
Cheraw: U.S.A.	**41**	35N	80W
Cherbourg: France	**70**	50N	2W
Cheremkhovo: U.S.S.R.	**81**	53N	103E
Cherepovets: U.S.S.R.	**82**	59N	38E
Chernigov: U.S.S.R.	**82**	52N	31E
Chernogorsk: U.S.S.R.	**83**	54N	91E
Chernovtsy: U.S.S.R.	**82**	48N	26E
Chernyakhovsk: U.S.S.R.	**66**	55N	22E
Cherokees, Lake of the: U.S.A.	**43**	37N	95W
Cherrapunji: India	**89**	25N	92E
Cherry Val.: U.S.A.	**31**	42½N	71¾W
Cherskiy Range: U.S.S.R.	**81**	65N	145E
Chertsey: England	**57**	51½N	½W
Cherwell: *r.*, Eng.	**55**	52N	1W
Chesapeake Bay: U.S.A.	**41**	38N	76W
Chesham: England	**57**	51¾N	½W
Cheshire: *Co.*, Eng.	**55**	53N	3W
Cheshunt: England	**57**	51¾N	0
Chesil Beach: Eng.	**55**	51N	3W
Chess: *r.*, England	**57**	51¾N	½W
Chester: England	**57**	53¼N	3W
Chester: U.S.A.	**41**	40N	76W
Chesterfield: Eng.	**57**	53¼N	1½W
Chester le Street: England	**54**	54¾N	1½W
Chesuncook L.: U.S.A.	**13**	46N	70W
Cheviot Hills: Eng./Scot.	**54**	55N	2W
Cheyenne: U.S.A.	**43**	41N	105W
Cheyenne: *r.*, U.S.A.	**43**	44N	102W
Chhindwara: India	**88**	22N	79E
Chiang Mai: Thai.	**90**	19N	99E
Chiang Rai: Thai.	**90**	20N	100E
Chiba: Japan	**92**	36N	140E
Chibia: Angola	**109**	15S	14E
Chicago: U.S.A.	**31**	41¾N	87½W
Chicago Heights: U.S.A.	**31**	41½N	87½W
Chicagof I.: U.S.A.	**22**	58N	136W
Chichén Itzá: Mexico	**38**	21N	89W
Chichester: England	**55**	51N	1W
Chickasha: U.S.A.	**43**	35N	98W
Chicken: U.S.A.	**28**	64N	141W
Chiclayo: Peru	**48**	7S	80W
Chico: U.S.A.	**42**	40N	122W
Chico: *r.*, Arg.	**49**	45S	67W
Chief Joseph Dam: U.S.A.	**40**	48N	120W
Chiemsee I.: Ger.	**73**	48N	12E
Chieti: Italy	**67**	42N	14E
Chihli, G. of: China	**89**	38N	120E
Chihuahua: Mexico	**38**	29N	106W
Chihuahua: *Prov.*, Mexico	**40**	29N	105W
Childers: Australia	**98**	25S	153E
CHILE: *cap.* Santiago	**49**	35S	72W
Chillán: Chile	**49**	36S	72W
Chillicothe: U.S.A.	**41**	39N	83W
Chiloé I.: Chile	**49**	43S	64W
Chiltern Hills: Eng.	**57**	51¾N	¾W
Chimborazo: *volc.*, Ecuador	**48**	1S	79W
Chimbote: Peru	**48**	9S	79W

	Page	Lat.	Long.
Chimkent: U.S.S.R.	**83**	42N	70E
CHINA: *cap.* Peking	**89**	—	—
Chinchilla: Australia	**98**	27S	151E
Chinchow: China	**89**	41N	121E
Chindwin: *r.*, Burma	**90**	23N	94E
Chingwangtao: China	**89**	40N	119E
Chin Hills: Burma	**90**	22N	93E
Chinkiang: China	**89**	32N	120E
Chinnampo: N. Korea	**90**	39N	125E
Chinon: France	**71**	47N	0
Chinook: U.S.A.	**40**	49N	109W
Chioggia: Italy	**73**	45N	12E
Chios: *i. & town*, Greece	**67**	38N	26E
Chipata: Zambia	**109**	14S	33E
Chippenham: Eng.	**55**	51N	2W
Chippeya Falls: *city*, U.S.A.	**43**	45N	91W
Chipping Ongar: Eng.	**57**	51¾N	¼E
Chiquitos Plat.: Bol.	**48**	17S	62W
Chita: & *Prov.*, U.S.S.R.	**81**	52N	113E
Chitral: W. Pak.	**87**	36N	72E
Chittagong: E. Pak.	**89**	22N	92E
Choctawhatchee: *r.*, U.S.A.	**41**	31N	86W
Choibalsan: Mong.	**81**	48N	114E
Chojnice: Poland	**66**	54N	18E
Cholet: France	**71**	47N	1W
Cholon: S. Viet Nam	**91**	10N	107E
Chongjin: N. Korea	**90**	42N	130E
Chonos Arch.: Chile	**49**	45S	74W
Chop: U.S.S.R.	**66**	48N	22E
Chorley: England	**57**	53¾N	2½W
Chorzów: Poland	**66**	50N	19E
Choshi: Japan	**90**	36N	141E
Chott Djerid: *salt lake*, Tunisia	**106**	34N	8E
Christchurch: Eng.	**55**	51N	2W
Christchurch: N.Z.	**93**	43S	173E
Christmas I.: Indian Ocean	**91**	11S	106E
Christmas I.: Pac. O.	**100**	2N	157W
Chu: & *r.*, U.S.S.R.	**83**	44N	74E
Chuanchow: China	**89**	25N	119E
Chubut: *r.*, Arg.	**49**	43S	66W
Chugoku Mts.: Japan	**92**	35N	133E
Chuguchak: China	**83**	47N	83E
Chuho: China	**81**	45N	128E
Chukchi Sea: U.S.S.R.	**81**	70N	170W
Chulym: *r.*, U.S.S.R.	**83**	57N	87E
Chumphon: Thai.	**91**	10N	99E
Chungking: China	**89**	30N	107E
Chuquicamata: Chile	**48**	22S	69W
Chur (Coire): Switz.	**73**	47N	9E
Church Stretton: England	**57**	52½N	2¾W
Churnet: *r.*, England	**57**	53N	2W
Ciampino: Italy	**67**	41¾N	12½E
Cicero: U.S.A.	**31**	41¾N	87¾W
Ciénaga: Venezuela	**47**	11N	74W
Cienfuegos: Cuba	**47**	22N	80W
Cieszyn: Poland	**66**	50N	18E
Cilician Gates: Turkey	**84**	37N	35E
Cimarron: *r.*, U.S.A.	**43**	37N	99W
Cincinnati: U.S.A.	**41**	39N	84W
Circeo, C.: Italy	**67**	41N	13E
Circle: U.S.A.	**28**	66N	145W
Circle Springs: U.S.A.	**28**	66N	145W
Cirencester: Eng.	**55**	52N	2W
Ciudad Acuña: Mex.	**40**	29N	101W
Ciudad Bolivar: Venezuela	**48**	8N	64W
Ciudad Juarez: Mex.	**43**	2N	107W
Ciudad Real: Spain	**65**	39N	4W
Ciudad Rodrigo: Sp.	**65**	41N	7W
Civitavecchia: Italy	**67**	42N	12E
Clackmannan: *Co.*, Scotland	**54**	56N	4W
Clacton on Sea: Eng.	**57**	51¾N	1¼E
Clamecy: France	**71**	47N	3E
Clare: Australia	**99**	34S	139E
Clare: *Co.*, R. of Irel.	**56**	53N	9W
Clare: R. of Ireland	**56**	53N	8W
Clare: *r.*, R. of Ireland	**56**	53N	9W
Clare I.: R. of Ireland	**56**	54N	10W
Claremont: U.S.A.	**17**	43N	73W
Clarence: *r.*, Austl.	**99**	29S	153E
Clarence I.: Antarc.	**51**	61S	54W
Clarinda: U.S.A.	**43**	41N	95W
Clark Hill Res.: U.S.A.	**41**	34N	82W
Clark Range: Austl.	**98**	21S	148E
Clarksburg: U.S.A.	**41**	39N	80W
Clarksdale: U.S.A.	**40**	34N	90W
Clarksville: U.S.A.	**41**	36N	87W
Clausthal-Zellerfeld: Germany	**72**	52N	10E
Clay Cross: England	**57**	53¼N	1½W
Clayton: England	**57**	53¾N	1¾W
Clayton: U.S.A.	**43**	36N	103W
Clear, C.: R. of Irel.	**56**	51N	9W
Clear L.: U.S.A.	**42**	39N	123W
Clearwater: U.S.A.	**41**	28N	83W
Cleburne: U.S.A.	**43**	32N	97W
Cleckheaton: Eng.	**57**	53¾N	1¾W
Clee Hills: England	**57**	52½N	2¾W
Clent Hills: England	**57**	52½N	2¼W
Clermont: Australia	**98**	23S	148E
Clermont: France	**70**	49N	2E
Clermont-Ferrand: France	**71**	46N	3E

	Page	Lat.	Long.
Cleveland: Ark., U.S.A.	**40**	34N	91W
Cleveland: Ohio, U.S.A.	**41**	42N	82W
Cleveland: Tenn., U.S.A.	**41**	35N	85W
Cleveland: Texas, U.S.A.	**40**	30N	95W
Clew Bay: R. of Irel.	**56**	54N	9W
Clifton: U.S.A.	**31**	41N	74¼W
Clingmans Dome: *mtn.*, U.S.A.	**41**	36N	84W
Clinton: Iowa, U.S.A.	**43**	42N	90W
Clinton: Mass., U.S.A.	**31**	42½N	71¾W
Clipperton I.: Pacific O.	**101**	10N	110W
Clogher Hd.: R. of Ireland	**56**	54N	6W
Clonakilty: R. of Ireland	**56**	52N	9W
Cloncurry: Austl.	**97**	21S	140E
Clones: R. of Irel.	**56**	54N	7W
Clonmel: R. of Irel.	**56**	52N	8W
Cloppenburg: Ger.	**72**	53N	8E
Clovis: U.S.A.	**43**	34N	103W
Cluj: Romania	**66**	47N	24E
Clutha: *r.*, N.Z.	**93**	46S	169E
Clyde: *r.*, Scotland	**54**	55N	4W
Clyde, Firth of: Scot.	**54**	56N	5W
Clydebank: Scotland	**54**	55¾N	4¼W
Coalbrookdale: Eng.	**57**	52¾N	2½W
Coalville: England	**57**	52¾N	1¼W
Coast Ranges: U.S.A.	**42**	45N	124W
Coatbridge: Scotland	**54**	56N	4W
Coats Land: Antarc.	**51**	78S	30W
Cobar: Australia	**99**	31S	146E
Cobh: R. of Ireland	**56**	52N	8W
Coburg: Germany	**72**	50N	11E
Cochabamba: Bolivia	**48**	17S	66W
Cochin: India	**88**	10N	76E
Cochin China:, S. Viet Nam	**91**	10N	106E
Cochituate: U.S.A.	**31**	42¼N	71¼W
Cochrane, L.: Chile/Argentina	**49**	47S	72W
Cocoa: U.S.A.	**41**	28N	81W
Cocos Is.: Indian O.	**100**	11S	97E
Cocos Is.: Pacific O.	**101**	6N	87W
Cod, Cape: U.S.A.	**45**	42N	70W
Cody: U.S.A.	**42**	45N	109W
Coeur d'Alene: U.S.A.	**42**	48N	117W
Coffeyville: U.S.A.	**43**	37N	96W
Coff's Harbour: Australia	**99**	30S	153E
Coggeshall: England	**57**	51¾N	¾E
Cognac: France	**71**	46N	0
Cohasset: U.S.A.	**31**	42¼N	70¾W
Coimbatore: India	**88**	11N	77E
Coimbra: Portugal	**65**	40N	8W
Colac: Australia	**99**	38S	144E
Colatina: Brazil	**48**	20S	40W
Colby: U.S.A.	**43**	39N	101W
Colchester: England	**57**	52N	1E
Cole: *r.*, England	**57**	52¼N	1¾W
Coleraine: N. Irel.	**56**	55N	7W
Coleshill: England	**57**	52½N	1¾W
Colfax: U.S.A.	**42**	47N	117W
Coll: *i.*, Scotland	**54**	57N	7W
Colleman I.: Antarc.	**51**	71S	60W
Collie: Australia	**98**	33S	116E
Colmar: France	**70**	48N	7E
Colne: *r.*, England	**57**	52N	¾E
Colne Point: England	**57**	51¾N	1E
Cologne: Germany	**62**	51N	7E
Colomb Béchar: Alg.	**106**	32N	2W
COLOMBIA: *cap.* Bogotá	**48**	5N	72W
COLOMBO: Ceylon	**88**	7N	80E
Colón: Cuba	**47**	23N	81W
Colón: Panamá	**39**	*Inset*	
Colonsay: *i.*, Scot.	**54**	56N	6W
Colorado: *r.*, Arg.	**49**	39S	65W
Colorado: *r.*, Texas, U.S.A.	**40**	29N	96W
Colorado: *r.*, U.S.A./Mexico	**42**	33N	114W
Colorado: *State*, U.S.A.	**42**	39N	106W
Colorado Plateaux: U.S.A.	**42**	37N	111W
Colorado Springs: U.S.A.	**43**	39N	105W
Columbia: Mo., U.S.A.	**43**	39N	92W
Columbia: S.C., U.S.A.	**41**	34N	81W
Columbia: *r.*, U.S.A.	**42**	46N	120W
Columbia: Tenn., U.S.A.	**41**	36N	87W
Columbus: Ga., U.S.A.	**41**	32N	85W
Columbus: Ind., U.S.A.	**41**	39N	86W
Columbus: Miss., U.S.A.	**41**	33N	89W
Columbus: Nebr., U.S.A.	**43**	41N	97W
Columbus: Ohio, U.S.A.	**41**	40N	83W
Colville: U.S.A.	**42**	49N	118W
Comacchio, L., Italy	**73**	45N	12E
Comilla: E. Pakistan	**89**	23N	91E
Commerce: U.S.A.	**31**	42½N	83½W

	Page	Lat.	Long.
Commonwealth Range: Antarc.	**51**	86S	175W
Communism, Mt.: U.S.S.R.	**83**	39N	72E
Como: & *lake*, Italy	**73**	46N	9E
Comodoro Rivadavia: Argentina	**49**	46S	67W
Comorin, C.: India	**88**	8N	77E
Compiègne: France	**70**	49N	3E
CONAKRY: Guinea	**106**	10N	14W
Concarneau: France	**70**	48N	4W
Concepción: Chile	**49**	37S	73W
Conchos: *r.*, Mexico	**40**	29N	105W
Concord: Mass., U.S.A.	**31**	42½N	71½W
Concord: N.C., U.S.A.	**41**	35N	80W
Concord: N.H., U.S.A.	**45**	43N	71W
Condamine: *r.*, Australia	**98**	27S	150E
Condobolin: Austl.	**99**	33S	147E
Conecuh: *r.*, U.S.A.	**41**	31N	87W
Coney Island: U.S.A.	**31**	40½N	74W
Congleton: England	**57**	53¼N	2¼W
CONGO (formerly Belgian): *cap.* Kinshasa	**108**	—	—
CONGO (formerly French): *cap.* Brazzaville	**108**	0	15E
Congo: *r.*, Africa	**108**	2N	21E
Conisborough: Eng.	**57**	53½N	1¼W
Conn, L.: R. of Irel.	**56**	54N	9W
Connah's Quay: Wales	**57**	53¼N	3W
Connaught: *Old Prov.*, Ireland	**56**	54N	9W
Connecticut: *r.*, U.S.A.	**45**	43N	73W
Connecticut: *State*, U.S.A.	**45**	41N	72W
Connemara: R. of Ireland	**56**	54N	10W
Connersville: U.S.A.	**41**	40N	85W
Conrad: U.S.A.	**42**	48N	112W
Consett: England	**54**	55N	2W
Constance, Lake: Switz./Ger.	**73**	48N	9E
Constanța: Rom.	**67**	44N	29E
Constantine: Algeria	**106**	37N	7E
Constantinople: Turkey	**67**	41N	29E
Conway: U.S.A.	**41**	34N	79W
Cooch Behar: India	**88**	26N	90E
Cook Is.: Pacific O.	**100**	20S	160W
Cook, Mt.: N.Z.	**93**	44S	170E
Cookstown: N. Irel.	**56**	55N	7W
Cook Strait: N.Z.	**93**	41S	174E
Cooktown: Australia	**97**	15S	145E
Coolangatta: Austl.	**98**	28S	153E
Coolgardie: Austl.	**98**	31S	121E
Cooling Marshes: Eng.	**57**	51½N	½E
Coonamble: Austl.	**99**	31S	148E
Cooper Creek: Austl.	**98**	27S	140E
Coorong, The: Austl.	**99**	36S	139E
Cootamundra: Austl.	**99**	35S	148E
COPENHAGEN: Den.	**69**	56N	13E
Copiapó: Chile	**48**	27S	70W
Coquimbo: Chile	**49**	30S	71W
Coral Gables: U.S.A.	**41**	26N	80W
Coral Sea	**97**	15S	152E
Corbeil-Essonnes: France	**64**	48½N	2½E
Corbières: *mtns.*, Fr.	**70**	43N	2E
Corby: England	**57**	52½N	¾W
Cordele: U.S.A.	**41**	32N	84W
Cordillera de Mérida: Venezuela	**48**	9N	71W
Cordillera Isabelia: Nicaragua	**47**	13N	85W
Cordillera Occidental de la Costa: Peru/Chile	**48**	15S	75W
Córdoba: Argentina	**49**	31S	64W
Córdoba: Spain	**65**	38N	5W
Cordova: U.S.A.	**2**	61N	145W
Corfu: *i. & town*, Greece	**67**	40N	20E
Corinth: & *gulf*, Greece	**67**	38N	23E
Corinth: U.S.A.	**41**	35N	89W
Cork: & *Co.*, R. of Ireland	**56**	52N	8W
Corlu: Turkey	**67**	41N	28E
Cornwall: *Co.*, Eng.	**55**	50N	5W
Coro: Venezuela	**47**	11N	70W
Coromandel: N.Z.	**93**	37S	176E
Coromandel Coast: India	**88**	13N	81E
Coronation I.: Antarctica	**51**	61S	46W
Coronel: Chile	**49**	37S	73W
Corpus Christi: & *bay*, U.S.A.	**40**	28N	79W
Corrib, L.: R. of Ireland	**56**	53N	9W
Corrientes: Arg.	**50**	27S	59W
Corsica: *i.*, Medit. Sea	**65**	42N	9E
Corsicana: U.S.A.	**43**	32N	96W
Corumbá: Brazil	**48**	19S	57W
Corunna: Spain	**65**	43N	8W
Corvallis: U.S.A.	**42**	45N	123W
Corve: *r.*, England	**57**	52½N	2¾W
Coryton: England	**57**	51½N	½E
Cos: *i.*, Greece	**67**	37N	27E
Cosenza: Italy	**67**	39N	16E
Cosne: France	**71**	47N	3E
COSTA RICA: *cap.* San José	**47**	10N	84W
Côte d'Azur: Fr.	**71**	43N	7E
Côte d'Or: *mts.*, Fr.	**71**	47N	5E
Cotentin: France	**70**	49N	2W
Côtes de Moselle: Fr.	**70**	49N	6E
COTONOU: Dahomey	**106**	6N	2E
Cotopaxi: *volc.*, Ec.	**48**	1S	78W
Cotswolds: *hills*, Eng.	**55**	52N	2W
Cottbus: Germany	**72**	52N	14E
Cottian Alps: Fr./It.	**73**	45N	7E
Cottingham: Eng.	**57**	53¾N	½W
Coubre, Pte. de la: Fr.	**71**	46N	1W
Coulman I: Antarc.	**51**	73S	170E
Council Bluffs: U.S.A.	**43**	41N	96W
Courtrai *see* Kortrijk			
Coutances: France	**70**	49N	1W
Coventry: England	**57**	52½N	1½W
Covilhã: Portugal	**65**	40N	7W
Covington: U.S.A.	**41**	37N	80W
Cowal, Lake: Austl.	**99**	33S	147E
Cowan, Lake: Austl.	**98**	32S	122E
Cowdenbeath: Scot.	**54**	56N	3¼W
Cowes: England	**55**	51N	1W
Cowley: England	**57**	51¾N	1¼W
Cowra: Australia	**99**	34S	149E
Cox's Bazar: E. Pak.	**89**	21N	92E
Cozumel, I. of: Caribbean Sea	**47**	20N	87W
Craiova: Romania	**67**	44N	24E
Cranard: R. of Irel.	**56**	54N	7W
Cranford: U.S.A.	**31**	40¾N	74¼W
Crater L.: & *Nat. Park*, U.S.A.	**42**	43N	122W
Crawfordsville: U.S.A.	**41**	40N	88W
Crawley: England	**55**	51N	0
Crécy: France	**70**	50N	2E
Creil: France	**70**	49N	2E
Cremona: Italy	**73**	45N	10E
Cres: *i.*, Yugoslavia	**67**	45N	14E
Crescent City: U.S.A.	**42**	42N	124W
Crestview: U.S.A.	**41**	31N	87W
Crete: *i. & sea*, Greece	**67**	35N	25E
Crete: U.S.A.	**43**	41N	97W
Creuse: *r.*, France	**71**	46N	2E
Crewe: England	**57**	53N	2½W
Crieff: Scotland	**54**	56N	4W
Crimea: U.S.S.R.	**82**	45N	34E
Croatia: Yugoslavia	**67**	45N	17E
Cromer: England	**55**	53N	1E
Cromwell: N.Z.	**93**	45S	169E
Cronulla: Australia	**99**	34S	151E
Crook: England	**54**	54¾N	1¾W
Crooked I.: Bahamas	**47**	23N	75W
Crosby: England	**57**	53½N	3W
Crosby: Minn., U.S.A.	**43**	46N	94W
Crosby: N. Dakota, U.S.A.	**43**	49N	103W
Cross Sound: U.S.A.	**22**	58N	137W
Crotone: Italy	**67**	39N	17E
Crouch: *r.*, England	**57**	51¾N	¾E
Crowle: England	**57**	53¾N	¾W
Crown Point: U.S.A.	**31**	41½N	87¼W
Crow's Nest: Austl.	**98**	27S	152E
Croydon: England	**57**	51½N	0
Cruz, C.: Cuba	**47**	20N	78W
Cruzeiro do Sul: Brazil	**48**	8S	73W
Cruzen I.: Antarctica	**51**	75S	141W
Crystal Beach: U.S.A.	**31**	29½N	94¾W
Crystal Lake: U.S.A.	**31**	42¼N	88¼W
Csepel: Hungary	**66**	47N	19E
CUBA: *cap.* Havana	**47**	22N	80W
Cubango: *r.*, Angola	**109**	17S	18E
Cúcuta: Colombia	**48**	8N	73W
Cudahy: U.S.A.	**31**	43N	87¾W
Cuddalore: India	**88**	12N	80E
Cuddapah: India	**88**	15N	79E
Cudworth: England	**57**	53½N	1¼W
Cue: Australia	**98**	27S	118E
Cuenca: Spain	**65**	40N	2W
Cuiabá: Brazil	**48**	16S	56W
Cuito: *r.*, Angola	**109**	17S	19E
Cullman: U.S.A.	**41**	34N	87W
Culoz: France	**71**	46N	6E
Cumaná: Venezuela	**48**	10N	64W
Cumberland: *Co.*, England	**54**	55N	3W
Cumberland: U.S.A.	**41**	40N	79W
Cumberland Is.: Australia	**98**	21S	149E
Cumberland, L.: U.S.A.	**41**	37N	85W
Cumbernauld: Scotland	**54**	56N	4W
Cumnock: Scotland	**54**	55N	4W
Cunderdin: Austl.	**98**	31S	117E
Cuneo: Italy	**73**	44N	8E
Cunnamulla: Austl.	**98**	28S	146E
Cupar: Scotland	**54**	56N	3W
Curaçao: *i.*, Carib. Sea	**47**	12N	69W
Curicó: Chile	**49**	35S	71W
Curitiba: Brazil	**50**	25S	49W
Curtis Channel: Australia	**98**	24S	152E
Cusco (Cuzco): Peru	**48**	14S	72W
Cuttack: India	**88**	20N	86E
Cuxhaven: Germany	**72**	54N	9E
Cyclades: *is.*, Greece	**67**	37N	25E
CYPRUS: *cap.* Nicosia	**84**	35N	33E
CZECHOSLOVAKIA: *cap.* Prague	**66**	49N	17E
Częstochowa: Pol.	**66**	51N	19E
Dacca: E. Pakistan	**89**	24N	90E
Dagenham: England	**57**	51½N	¼E
Dahlak Arch: Red Sea	**85**	16N	40w
DAHOMEY: *cap.* Cotonou	**106**	10N	3E
Dairen (Dal'niy): China	**89**	39N	122E
Dajarra: Australia	**97**	22S	140E
DAKAR: Senegal	**106**	15N	17W
Dakhla Oasis: Egypt	**107**	25N	29E
Dakovica: Yugo.	**67**	42N	20E
Dalabandin: W. Pak.	**88**	29N	64E
Dalby: Australia	**98**	27S	151E
Dalhousie: India	**88**	33N	76E
Dallas: U.S.A.	**43**	33N	97W
Dall I.: U.S.A.	**22**	55N	133W
Dalmatia: Yugo.	**67**	44N	16E
Dalry: Scotland	**54**	55¾N	4¾W
Dalton: U.S.A.	**41**	35N	85W
Daltonganj: India	**88**	24N	84E
Daly: *r.*, Australia	**96**	14S	132E
Daly Waters: *town*, Australia	**96**	16S	133E
Dam: Surinam	**48**	5N	55W
Damão: India	**88**	20N	73E
DAMASCUS: Syria	**84**	34N	36E
Damietta: Egypt	**84**	31N	32E
Damodar: *r.*, India	**88**	24N	86E
Dampier Land: Australia	**96**	17S	123E
Dane: *r.*, England	**57**	53¼N	2¼W
Danilovka: U.S.S.R.	**83**	53N	71E
Dannemora: Sweden	**69**	60N	18E
Dannevirke: N.Z.	**93**	40S	176E
Danube: *r.*, Europe	**66/7**	—	—
Danushkodi: India	**88**	9N	80E
Danville: Ill., U.S.A.	**41**	40N	88W
Danville: Va., U.S.A.	**41**	37N	79W
Danzig: & *gulf*, Poland	**66**	54N	19E
Darasun: U.S.S.R.	**81**	53N	116E
Dardanelles: *str.*, Turkey	**84**	40N	26E
Darent: *r.*, England	**57**	51½N	¼E
DAR ES SALAAM: Tanzania	**108**	7S	40E
Darfur: *Prov.*, Sudan	**107**	13N	25E
Dargaville: N.Z.	**93**	36S	174E
Darien, Gulf of: Colombia	**48**	9N	77W
Darjeeling: India	**88**	27N	88E
Darlaston: England	**57**	52½N	2W
Darling: *r.*, Austl.	**99**	31S	145E
Darling Downs: Australia	**98**	27S	151E
Darling Range: Australia	**98**	32S	116E
Darlington: England	**54**	54½N	1½W
Darmstadt: Ger.	**72**	50N	9E
Dart: *r.*, England	**55**	50N	4W
Dartford: England	**57**	51½N	¼E
Dartmoor: England	**55**	51N	4W
Dartmouth: England	**55**	50N	4W
Darwen: England	**57**	53¾N	2½W
Darwin: Australia	**96**	12S	131E
Dasht-e Kavīr: *desert*, Iran	**85**	34N	55E
Dasht-e Lūt: *desert*, Iran	**85**	32N	57E
Datteln: Germany	**62**	51¾N	7¼E
Daugavpils: U.S.S.R.	**66**	56N	26E
DAUHA: Qatar	**85**	26N	51E
Dauphiné: *Old Prov.*, France	**71**	45N	6E
Dauphiné Alps: Fr.	**71**	45N	6E
Davao: Philippines	**91**	7N	126E
Davenport: U.S.A.	**43**	41N	90W
Davis Sea: Antarc.	**51**	64S	92E
Davos: Switzerland	**73**	47N	10E
Dawley: England	**57**	52¾N	2½W
Dawna Range: Burma/Thailand	**91**	13N	99E
Dawson: *r.*, Austl.	**98**	24S	150E
Dax: France	**71**	44N	1W
Dayton: U.S.A.	**41**	40N	84W
Daytona Beach: U.S.A.	**41**	29N	81W
De Aar: S. Africa	**109**	31S	24E
Dead Sea: Israel/Jordan	**84**	32N	35E
Deadwood: U.S.A.	**43**	44N	104W
Dearborn: & *Heights*, U.S.A.	**31**	42¼N	83¼
Death Valley: U.S.A.	**42**	37N	117W
Deauville: France	**70**	49N	0
Debrecen: Hungary	**66**	48N	22E
Decatur: Alabama, U.S.A.	**41**	35N	87W
Decatur: Ill., U.S.A.	**43**	40N	89W
Decazeville: France	**71**	45N	2E
Deccan: India	**88**	17N	77E
Deception I.: Antarc.	**51**	63S	60W
Děčín: Czech.	**72**	51N	14E
Dedeagach: Greece	**67**	41N	26E
Dedham: U.S.A.	**31**	42¼N	71¼W
Dee: *r.*, Eng./Wales	**55**	53N	3W
Dee: *r.*, Aber., Scot.	**54**	57N	3W
Dee: *r.*, Kirkc., Scot.	**54**	55N	4W
Deerfield: U.S.A.	**31**	42¼N	87¾W
Deer Lodge: U.S.A.	**42**	46N	113W
Dehra Dun: India	**88**	30N	78E
Deir ez Zor: Syria	**85**	35N	40E
De Kalb: U.S.A.	**43**	42N	89W
Delagoa Bay: Moz.	**109**	25S	33E
Delano: U.S.A.	**42**	36N	119W
Delano Peak: U.S.A.	**42**	38N	114W
Delaware: *State*, & *bay*, U.S.A.	**41**	39N	75W
Delft: Netherlands	**72**	52N	4E
Delmenhorst: Ger.	**72**	53N	9E
Delray Beach: *city*, U.S.A.	**41**	26N	80W
Del Rio: U.S.A.	**40**	29N	101W
DELHI: India	**88**	29N	77E
Demarcation Pt.: U.S.A.	**1**	70N	141W
Demavand: *mtn.*, Iran	**85**	36N	52E
Deming: U.S.A.	**42**	32N	108W
Demmin: Germany	**72**	54N	13E
Denbigh: & *Co.*, Wales	**55**	53N	3W
Dendermonde: Belg.	**70**	51N	4E
Denham Range: Australia	**98**	22S	148E
Den Helder: Neth.	**72**	53N	5E
Deniliquin: Austl.	**99**	36S	145E
Denison: U.S.A.	**43**	34N	97W
Denison, C.: Antarc.	**51**	67S	144E
Denizli: Turkey	**84**	38N	29E
DENMARK: *cap.* Copenhagen	**69**	56N	10E
Denny: Scotland	**54**	56N	4W
Denton: England	**57**	53½N	2W
Denton: U.S.A.	**43**	33N	98W
D'Entrecasteaux Is.: Papua	**97**	10S	151E
D'Entrecasteaux, Pt.: Australia	**98**	35S	116E
Denver: U.S.A.	**43**	40N	105W
Denville: U.S.A.	**31**	41N	74½W
De Pere: U.S.A.	**43**	44N	88W
Dera'a: Syria	**84**	32N	36E
Dera Ghazi Khan: West Pakistan	**88**	30N	70E
Dera Ismail Khan: West Pakistan	**88**	32N	71E
Derbent: U.S.S.R.	**82**	42N	48E
Derby: Australia	**96**	17S	123E
Derby: & *Co.*, Eng.	**57**	53N	1½W
Derg, L.: R. of Irel.	**56**	53N	8W
Derna: Libya	**84**	33N	22E
Derwent: *r.*, Cumb., England	**54**	55N	4W
Derwent: *r.*, Derby, England	**55**	53N	2W
Derwent: *r.*, Yorks., England	**54**	—	—
Desborough: Eng.	**57**	52½N	¾W
Des Moines: & *r.*, U.S.A.	**43**	42N	94W
Des Plaines: U.S.A.	**31**	42N	88W
Dessau: Germany	**72**	52N	12E
Dessye: Ethiopia	**86**	11N	40E
Detroit: U.S.A.	**31**	—	—
Dettingen: Ger.	**72**	50N	9E
Deva: Romania	**66**	46N	23E
Deventer: Neth.	**72**	52N	6E
Dévoluy: *mtns.*, Fr.	**71**	45N	6E
Devon: *r.*, Scotland	**54**	56¼N	3¾W
Devonport: England	**55**	50N	4W
Devonport: N.Z.	**93**	37S	175E
Devonshire: *Co.*, England	**55**	51N	4W
Dewsbury: England	**57**	53¾N	1¾W
Dexter: U.S.A.	**13**	45N	69W
Dhahran: Sa'udi Arabia	**85**	26N	50E
Dharwar: India	**88**	15N	75E
Dhulia: India	**88**	21N	75E
Diamantina: Brazil	**48**	18S	44W
Dibrugarh: India	**89**	28N	95E
Dickinson: U.S.A.	**31**	29½N	95W
Didcot: England	**57**	51½N	1¼W
Dieciocho de Marzo: Mexico	**40**	26N	98W
Diego Suarez: Malagasy Rep.	**108**	12S	49E
Dieppe: France	**70**	50N	1E
Digne: France	**71**	44N	6E
Dijon: France	**71**	47N	5E
Dili: Port. Timor	**90**	8S	126E
Dimboola: Austl.	**99**	36S	142E
Dimitrovgrad: Bulg.	**67**	42N	26E
Dimitrovgrad: Yugo.	**67**	43N	23E
Dimitrovo: Bulgaria	**67**	43N	23E
Dinajpur: E. Pak.	**88**	26N	89E
Dinan: France	**70**	48N	2W
Dinant: Belgium	**70**	50N	5E
Dinard: France	**70**	49N	2W
Dinaric Alps: Yugo.	**67**	44N	16E
Dingle: & *Bay*, R. of Ireland	**56**	52N	10W
Dingwall: Scotland	**53**	58N	4W
Dinslaken: Germany	**62**	51½N	6¾E
Diomede Is.: Bering Strait	**2**	66N	169W
Diredawa: Ethiopia	**107**	10N	42E
Dirk Hartog I.: Australia	**96**	26S	113E
Dirranbandi: Austl.	**98**	28S	148E
Disappointment, L.: Australia	**96**	23S	123E

	Page	Lat.	Long.
Discovery Inlet: Antarctica	**51**	78S	170W
Disko: *i.*, Greenland	**3**	69N	54W
Diu I.: India	**88**	21N	71E
Divriği: Turkey	**84**	40N	38E
Dixmude: Belgium	**70**	51N	3E
Dixon: U.S.A.	**43**	42N	90W
Dixon Entrance: *chan.*, U.S.A.	**22**	55N	132W
Diyarbakir: Turkey	**85**	38N	40E
DJAKARTA: Indonesia	**91**	6S	107E
Djelfa: Algeria	**106**	35N	3E
Djerba I.: Tunisia	**106**	34N	11E
DJIBOUTI: Fr. Terr. Afars/Issas.	**107**	12N	43E
Dneprodzerzhinsk: U.S.S.R.	**82**	48N	34E
Dnepropetrovsk: U.S.S.R.	**82**	48N	35E
Dnieper: *r.*, U.S.S.R.	**82**	50N	31E
Dniester: *r.*, U.S.S.R.	**82**	48N	27E
Dobb's Ferry: U.S.A.	**31**	41N	74¾W
Dobreşti: Romania	**66**	47N	22E
Dobruja: Romania	**67**	44N	28E
Dodecanese: *is.*, Greece	**67**	37N	27E
Dodge City: U.S.A.	**40**	38N	100W
Dodoma: Tanzania	**108**	6S	36E
Dodworth: England	**57**	53½N	1½W
Dôle: France	**71**	47N	5E
Dolgellau: Wales	**55**	53N	4W
Dollar: Scotland	**54**	56¼N	3¾W
Dolomites: *mtns.*, It.	**73**	46N	12E
Dolton: U.S.A.	**31**	41¾N	87½W
Dombås: Norway	**68**	62N	9E
DOMINICA: *cap.* Roseau	**47**	15N	61W
DOMINICAN REPUBLIC: *cap.* Santo Domingo	**47**	19N	70W
Don: *r.*, England	**54**	54N	1W
Don: *r.*, Scotland	**53**	57N	2W
Don: *r.*, U.S.S.R.	**82**	50N	40E
Donawitz: Austria	**66**	47N	15E
Donbass: U.S.S.R.	**82**	48N	38E
Doncaster: England	**57**	53½N	1W
Dondra Head: Ceylon	**88**	6N	81E
Donegal: & *Co.*, R. of Ireland	**56**	55N	8W
Donegal Bay: R. of Ireland	**56**	55N	8W
Donerak, Mt.: U.S.A.	**2**	68N	152W
Donets: *r.*, U.S.S.R.	**82**	49N	38E
Donetsk: U.S.S.R.	**82**	48N	37E
Dongara: Australia	**98**	29S	115E
Donzère: France	**71**	44N	5E
Dorchester: Dorset, England	**55**	51N	2W
Dorchester: Oxon., England	**57**	51¾N	1¼W
Dordogne: *r.*, Fr.	**71**	45N	0
Dordrecht: Neth.	**72**	52N	5E
Dore: *r.*, France	**71**	46N	4E
Dorking: England	**57**	51¼N	¼W
Dormagen: Germany	**62**	51N	6¾E
Dornbirn: Austria	**73**	47N	10E
Dornoch: Scotland	**53**	58N	4W
Dorset: *Co.*, England	**55**	51N	2W
Dorsten: Germany	**62**	51¾N	7E
Dortmund: Germany	**62**	51½N	7½E
Dortmund-Ems Canal: Germany	**72**	52N	7E
Dothan: U.S.A.	**41**	31N	85W
Douai: France	**70**	50N	3E
Douala: Cameroon	**106**	4N	10E
Douarnenez: & *bay*, France	**70**	48N	4W
Doubs: *r.*, France	**71**	47N	6E
Doubtful Sound: New Zealand	**93**	45S	167E
DOUGLAS: I. of Man	**54**	54N	4W
Douglas: U.S.A.	**43**	43N	105W
Douglas Is.: Antarc.	**51**	68S	65E
Douglas: *r.*, England	**57**	53¾N	2¾W
Dounreay: Scotland	**53**	59N	4W
Douro: *r.*, Sp./Port.	**65**	41N	8W
Dove: *r.*, England	**57**	53¼N	1¾W
Dovedale: England	**57**	53N	1¾W
Dover: England	**55**	51N	1E
Dover: U.S.A.	**41**	39N	76W
Dover, Strait of: England/France	**55**	51N	1E
Dovey: *r.*, Wales	**55**	53N	4W
Dovrefjell: *mtns.*, Norway	**68**	62N	10E
Down: *Co.*, N. Irel.	**56**	54N	6W
Downpatrick: N. Ireland	**56**	54N	6W
Dra: *r.*, Mor./Alg.	**106**	29N	8W
Dracut: U.S.A.	**31**	42¾N	71¼W
Draguignan: France	**71**	44N	6E
Drakensberg: *mtns.*, S. Africa	**109**	31S	28E
Drake Passage: S. America	**49**	57S	65W
Drama: Greece	**67**	41N	24E
Drammen: Norway	**69**	60N	10E
Drava (Drau or Drave): *r.*, Eur.	**66**	56N	16E
Dravograd: Yugo.	**66**	47N	15E
Dresden: Germany	**72**	51N	14E
Dreux: France	**70**	49N	1E
Drogheda: R. of Irel.	**56**	54N	6W
Drôme: *r.*, France	**71**	45N	5E
Dromore: N. Ireland	**56**	54N	6W
Dronfield: England	**57**	53¼N	1½W

	Page	Lat.	Long.
Droylsden: England	**57**	53½N	2¼W
Drygalski I.: Antarc.	**51**	65S	92E
Dubai, Trucial State	**85**	25N	55E
Dubbo: Australia	**99**	32S	149E
DUBLIN: *and Co.*, Republic of Ireland	**56**	53N	6W
Dublin: U.S.A.	**41**	32N	83W
Dubno: U.S.S.R.	**66**	50N	26E
Dubrovnik: Yugo.	**67**	43N	18E
Dubuque: U.S.A.	**43**	42N	91W
Ducie I.: Pacific O.	**101**	25S	124W
Ducktown: U.S.A.	**41**	35N	84W
Dudelange: Lux.	**70**	50N	6E
Dudinka: U.S.S.R.	**81**	70N	86E
Dudley: England	**57**	52½N	2W
Duisburg: Germany	**62**	51½N	6¾E
Dukeries, The: Eng.	**57**	53¼N	1W
Dulce: *r.*, Arg.	**49**	29S	64W
Duluth: U.S.A.	**43**	47N	92W
Dumbarton: Scot.	**54**	56N	5W
Dumfries: & *Co.*, Scotland	**54**	55N	4W
Dunaujvaros: Hung.	**66**	47N	19E
Dunbar: Scotland	**54**	56N	3W
Dunbarton: *Co.*, Scotland	**54**	56N	5W
Duncan: U.S.A.	**43**	34N	98W
Duncansby Head: Scotland	**53**	59N	3W
Dundalk: & *bay*, R. of Ireland	**56**	54N	6W
Dundee: Scotland	**54**	56N	3W
Dunedin: N.Z.	**93**	46S	171E
Dunfermline: Scot.	**54**	56N	3W
Dungannon: N. Irel.	**56**	55N	7W
Dungarvan: R. of Irel.	**56**	52N	8W
Dungeness: England	**55**	51N	1E
Dunkirk: France	**70**	51N	2E
Dunkirk: U.S.A.	**41**	42N	79W
Dun Laoghaire: R. of Ireland	**56**	53N	6W
Dunoon: Scotland	**54**	56N	5W
Duns: Scotland	**54**	56N	2W
Dunstable: England	**57**	51¾N	½W
Duque de Caxias: Brazil	**50**	22¾S	43¼W
Durance: *r.*, France	**71**	44N	6E
Durango: Mexico	**38**	24N	105W
Durango: U.S.A.	**42**	37N	108W
Durant: U.S.A.	**43**	34N	96W
Durazzo: Albania	**67**	41N	19E
Durban: S. Africa	**109**	30S	31E
Düren: Germany	**72**	51N	6E
Durge Nor: *l.*, Mong.	**90**	49N	94E
Durham: & *Co.*, Eng.	**54**	55N	2W
Durham: U.S.A.	**41**	36N	79W
Durrës: Albania	**67**	41N	19E
D'Urville I.: N.Z.	**93**	41S	174E
D'Urville Sea: Antarctica	**51**	65S	141E
Düsseldorf: Ger.	**62**	51¼N	6¾E
Dyersburg: U.S.A.	**43**	36N	89W
Dyushambe: U.S.S.R.	**83**	39N	69E
Dza: *r.*, China	**87**	32N	97E
Dzerzhinsk: U.S.S.R.	**82**	56N	43E
Dzhambul: U.S.S.R.	**83**	43N	71E
Dzherba: U.S.S.R.	**81**	60N	116E
Dzhetgara: U.S.S.R.	**83**	52N	61E
Dzhezkazgan: U.S.S.R.	**83**	48N	68E
Dzungaria: China	**87**	45N	87E
Dzungarian Gate: *pass*, China/U.S.S.R.	**83**	45N	82E
Eagle: U.S.A.	**28**	65N	141W
Eagle Pass: *city*, U.S.A.	**40**	29N	100W
Ealing: England	**57**	51½N	¼W
Earn: *r.*, Scotland	**54**	56N	4W
East Anglia: Eng.	**55**	52N	1E
East Beskids: *mtns.*, Czech./Poland	**66**	49N	22E
Eastbourne: England	**55**	51N	0
East Cape: N.Z.	**93**	38S	178E
Eastchester: U.S.A.	**31**	41N	73¾W
East Chicago: U.S.A.	**31**	41¾N	87½W
East China Sea	**89**	30N	123E
Easter I.: Pacific O.	**101**	27S	110W
Eastern Desert: Egypt	**84**	27N	32E
Eastern Ghats: *mtns.*, India	**88**	16N	80E
Eastern Sierra Madre: *range*, Mexico	**38**	24N	100W
East Indies	**100**	1S	110E
East Kilbride: Scot.	**54**	55¾N	4¼W
East Liverpool: U.S.A.	**41**	41N	81W
East London: S. Afr.	**109**	33S	28E
East Lothian: *Co.*, Scotland	**54**	56N	3W
East Meadow: U.S.A.	**31**	40¾N	73½W
East Orange: U.S.A.	**31**	40¾N	74¼W
EAST PAKISTAN (BANGLADESH)	**89**	24N	90E
East Prussia	**66**	54N	20E
East Retford: Eng.	**57**	53N	1W
East Riding: Eng.	**54**	54N	1W
East Rift Valley: Kenya/Ethiopia	**108**	5N	37E
East Siberian Sea: U.S.S.R.	**81**	73N	160E

	Page	Lat.	Long.
Eau Claire: U.S.A.	**43**	45N	92W
Eauze: France	**71**	44N	0
Ebberswalde: Ger.	**72**	53N	14E
Ebbw Vale: Wales	**55**	51N	3W
Ebi Nor: *l.*, China	**87**	45N	83E
Ebro: *r.*, Spain	**65**	42N	1W
Eccles: England	**57**	53½N	2¼W
Echuca: Australia	**99**	36S	145E
Ecorse: U.S.A.	**31**	42¼N	83¼W
ECUADOR: *cap.* Quito	**48**	2S	77W
Edam: Netherlands	**72**	53N	5E
Ed Damer: Sudan	**107**	17N	34E
Eddystone Rocks: England	**55**	50N	4W
Ede: Netherlands	**72**	52N	6E
Eden: *r.*, England	**54**	55N	3W
Edenbridge: Eng.	**57**	51¼N	0
Edenderry: R. of Irel.	**56**	53N	7W
Edenhope: Australia	**99**	37S	141E
Edgworth: England	**57**	53¾N	2¼W
Edhessa: Greece	**67**	41N	22E
EDINBURGH: Scotland	**54**	56N	3W
Edirne: Turkey	**84**	42N	27E
Edjelé: Algeria	**106**	28N	9E
Edremit: Turkey	**67**	40N	27E
Edsel Ford Range: Antarctica	**51**	78S	140W
Edward, Lake: Afr.	**108**	0	30E
Edwards Plateau: U.S.A.	**40**	30N	100W
Eekloo: Belgium	**70**	51N	4E
Eger (Ohře): *r.*, Czechoslovakia	**72**	50N	14E
Egersund: Norway	**69**	58N	6E
Egham: England	**57**	51½N	½W
Egmont, Mt.: N.Z.	**93**	39S	174E
EGYPT: *cap.* Cairo	**84**	27N	30E
Eifel: *mtns.*, Ger.	**72**	50N	7E
Eigg: *i.*, Scotland	**54**	57N	6W
Eights Coast: Antarctica	**51**	73S	90W
Eighty Mile Beach: Australia	**96**	21S	121E
Eilat: Israel	**84**	30N	35E
Eilenburg: Germany	**72**	51N	13E
Eindhoven: Neth.	**72**	51N	5E
Eisenach: Germany	**72**	51N	10E
Eisenerz: Austria	**66**	47N	15E
El 'Alamein: Egypt	**84**	31N	29E
El Atrum Oasis: Sud.	**84**	18N	26E
Elâziğ: Turkey	**85**	39N	39E
Elba: *i.*, Italy	**67**	43N	10E
El Ballah: Egypt	**107**	*Inset*	
Elbasan: Albania	**67**	41N	20E
El Bayadh: Algeria	**106**	34N	2E
Elbe: *r.*, Germany	**72**	53N	11E
Elbert, Mt.: U.S.A.	**42**	39N	107W
Elbeuf: France	**70**	49N	1E
Elblag: Poland	**66**	54N	20E
El'brus: *mtn.*, U.S.S.R.	**82**	43N	42E
El Centro: U.S.A.	**42**	33N	116W
Elche: Spain	**65**	38N	1W
El Dorado: Ark., U.S.A.	**40**	33N	93W
El Dorado: Kans., U.S.A.	**43**	38N	97W
Elephant Butte Res.: U.S.A.	**42**	33N	107W
Elephant I.: Antarc.	**51**	61S	55W
El Escorial: Spain	**65**	41N	4W
Eleuthera: *i.*, Bahama Is.	**47**	25N	76W
El Faiyum: Egypt	**84**	29N	31E
El Fasher: Sudan	**107**	14N	25E
El Ferrol: Spain	**65**	43N	8W
El Firdân: Egypt	**107**	*Inset*	
El Gatrun: Libya	**84**	25N	15E
Elgin: Scotland	**53**	58N	3W
Elgin: U.S.A.	**31**	42N	88¼W
Elgon, Mt.: Uganda	**108**	1N	35E
El'gyay: U.S.S.R.	**81**	62N	117E
Elizabeth: Australia	**99**	35S	139E
Elizabeth: U.S.A.	**31**	40¾N	74¼W
Elizabeth City: U.S.A.	**41**	36N	76W
Elizabeth Point: S.W. Africa	**109**	27S	15E
Elizabethton: U.S.A.	**41**	36N	82W
Elizabethtown: U.S.A.	**41**	38N	86W
El Jauf: Libya	**107**	24N	24E
Elk City: U.S.A.	**43**	35N	99W
El Khârga: Egypt	**84**	25N	30E
Elkhart: U.S.A.	**41**	42N	86W
Elkins: U.S.A.	**41**	39N	80W
Elko: U.S.A.	**42**	41N	116W
Elk River: *city*, U.S.A.	**42**	47N	116W
Elland: England	**57**	53¾N	1¾W
Ellensburg: U.S.A.	**42**	47N	121W
Ellesmere Port: Eng.	**55**	53N	3W
Ellice Is.: Pacific O.	**100**	8S	180
Elliott, Mt.: Antarc.	**51**	71S	168E
Ellsworth Highland: Antarctica	**51**	77S	90W
El Mansura: Egypt	**84**	31N	32E
El Matarīya: Egypt	**107**	*Inset*	
Elmhurst: U.S.A.	**31**	42N	88W
El Minya: Egypt	**84**	28N	31E
Elmira: U.S.A.	**41**	42N	77W
Elmont: U.S.A.	**31**	40¾N	74¾W
Elmshorn: Germany	**72**	54N	10E
Elmwood Park: U.S.A.	**31**	42N	87¾W

	Page	Lat.	Long.
El Obeid: Sudan	**107**	13N	30E
El Paso: U.S.A.	**42**	32N	106W
El Qantara: Egypt	**107**	*Inset*	
El Reno: U.S.A.	**43**	36N	98W
EL SALVADOR: *cap.* San Salvador	**42**	14N	89W
El Shatt: Egypt	**107**	*Inset*	
El Tigre: Venezuela	**47**	9N	64W
Elvas: Portugal	**65**	39N	7W
Ely: England	**55**	52N	0
Ely: U.S.A.	**42**	39N	115W
Emba: & *r.*, U.S.S.R.	**83**	49N	58E
Embrun: France	**71**	45N	6E
Emden: Germany	**72**	53N	7E
Emerald: Australia	**98**	23S	148E
Em Koussi: *mtn.*, Chad	**107**	20N	19E
Emilia Romagna: *Reg.*, Italy	**73**	44N	11E
Emmaboda: Sweden	**69**	56N	16E
Emmen: Neth.	**72**	53N	7E
Emmerich: Ger.	**72**	52N	6E
Emory Peak: U.S.A.	**40**	29N	104W
Ems: *r.*, Germany	**72**	53N	7E
Encounter Bay: Australia	**99**	36S	139E
Enderby Land: Antarctica	**51**	71S	50E
Enderlin: U.S.A.	**43**	47N	98W
Enfield: England	**57**	51¾N	0
Enggano: *i.*, Indon.	**91**	5S	102E
ENGLAND: *cap.* London	**57**	—	—
Englewood: U.S.A.	**31**	41N	74W
English Channel	**53**	50N	2W
Enid: U.S.A.	**43**	36N	98W
Ennepetal: Germany	**62**	51¼N	7¼E
Ennis: R. of Ireland	**56**	53N	9W
Enniscorthy: R. of Ireland	**56**	53N	7W
Enniskillen: N. Irel.	**56**	54N	8W
Enns: *r.*, Austria	**73**	48N	14E
Enschede: Neth.	**72**	52N	7E
Ensenada: Mexico	**42**	32N	117W
ENTEBBE: Uganda	**108**	0	33E
Enterprise: U.S.A.	**41**	31N	86W
Entre Rios: Moz.	**109**	15S	38E
Enugu: Nigeria	**106**	6N	8E
Épernay: France	**70**	49N	4E
Épinal: France	**70**	48N	6E
Epirus: Greece	**67**	39N	21E
Epping: England	**57**	51½N	¼E
Epping Forest: Eng.	**57**	51¾N	0
Epsom: England	**57**	51N	0
EQUATORIAL GUINEA: *cap.* Bata	**108**	2N	10E
Erebus, Mt.: Antarc.	**51**	78S	168E
Erentsab: Mongolia	**81**	50N	115E
Erewash: *r.*, England	**57**	53N	1¼W
Erfurt: Germany	**72**	51N	11E
Erie: U.S.A.	**41**	42N	80W
Erie, Lake: U.S.A./Canada	**18**	42N	81W
Erigavo: Somali Republic	**107**	11N	47E
Eritrea: *Prov.*, Eth.	**107**	15N	40E
Erkrath: Germany	**62**	51¼N	7E
Erlangen: Germany	**72**	50N	11E
Ermoupolis: Greece	**67**	37N	25E
Eromanga: Australia	**98**	27S	143E
Er Rif: *mtns.*, Mor.	**106**	35N	5W
Errigal: *mtn.*, R. of Ireland	**56**	55N	8W
Erzgebirge: Ger./Czech.	**72**	50N	13E
Erzincan: Turkey	**85**	40N	40E
Erzurum: Turkey	**85**	40N	41E
Esbjaerg: Denmark	**69**	55N	8E
Escanaba: U.S.A.	**43**	46N	87W
Esch: Luxembourg	**70**	50N	6E
Eschwege: Germany	**72**	51N	10E
Escondido: U.S.A.	**42**	33N	117W
Escondido: *r.*, Nic.	**47**	12N	84W
Esfahān: Iran	**85**	33N	52E
Eshowe: S. Africa	**109**	29N	32E
Esk: *r.*, England	**54**	54N	1W
Eskilstuna: Sweden	**69**	59N	17E
Eskişehir: Turkey	**84**	40N	30E
Esperance: Australia	**98**	34S	122E
Espinouse, Mts. de l': France	**71**	44N	3E
Espirito Santo: *State*, Brazil	**48**	20S	40W
Essaoira: Morocco	**106**	32N	10W
Essen: Germany	**62**	51N	7E
Essequibo: *r.*, Guyana	**48**	5N	58W
Essex: *Co.*, England	**57**	52N	1E
Essex: U.S.A.	**31**	42¾N	70¾W
Esslingen: Germany	**73**	49N	9E
Estats, Pic d': France	**71**	43N	1E
Estonian S.S.R.: U.S.S.R.	**82**	59N	26E
Estremadura: *Prov.*, Portugal	**65**	39N	9W
Esztergom: Hungary	**66**	48N	19E
Etampes: France	**70**	48N	2E
Etaples: France	**70**	51N	2E
Etawah: India	**88**	27N	79E
ETHIOPIA: *cap.* Addis Ababa	**107**	—	—
Ethiopian Plat.: E. Africa	**108**	10N	37E
Etna: *volc.*, Sicily	**67**	38N	15E
Étoile, Chaîne de l': France	**71**	43N	6E

Place	Page	Lat.	Long.
Eton: England	57	51½N	½W
Etosha Pan: S.W. Africa	109	19S	16E
Etruscan Apennines: Italy	73	44N	10E
Euboea: & *gulf*, Greece	67	38N	24E
Eucla: Australia	96	32S	129E
Eudora: U.S.A.	40	33N	91W
Eudunda: Australia	99	34S	139E
Eugene: U.S.A.	42	44N	123W
Eunice: U.S.A.	43	30N	91W
Eupen: Belgium	70	51N	6E
Euphrates: *r.*, Asia	85	35N	40E
Eure: *r.*, France	70	49N	1E
Eureka: California, U.S.A.	42	41N	124W
Eureka: Montana, U.S.A.	42	49N	115W
Eureka: Nev., U.S.A.	42	40N	116W
Europa: *i.*, Indian O.	109	23S	40E
Evanston: U.S.A.	31	41N	111W
Evansville: U.S.A.	41	38N	88W
Everard, C.: Austl.	99	38S	149E
Everest: *mtn.*, Himalayas	88	28N	87E
Everett: U.S.A.	31	48N	122W
Everglades: *swamp*, U.S.A.	41	26N	81W
Evesham: England	55	52N	2W
Evian: France	71	46N	7E
Évora: Portugal	65	39N	8W
Évreux: France	70	49N	1E
Exe: *r.*, England	55	51N	4W
Executive Committee Ra.: Antarctica	51	76S	120W
Exeter: England	55	51N	4W
Exmoor: England	55	51N	4W
Exmouth: England	55	51N	3W
Exmouth Gulf: Austl.	96	22S	114E
Expedition Range: Australia	98	24S	149E
Eyemouth: Scotland	54	56N	2W
Eyre, Lake: Australia	96	28S	137E
Eyre South, L.: Austl.	99	29S	137E
Faenza: Italy	73	44N	12E
Faeroe Is.: Atl. O.	80	62N	7W
Fagersta: Sweden	69	60N	16E
Faguibine, L.: Mali	106	16N	4W
Fairbanks: U.S.A.	2	65N	148W
Fair Head: N. Ireland	56	55N	6W
Fair Isle: Scotland	53	59N	2W
Fair Lawn: U.S.A.	31	41N	74¼W
Fairmont: U.S.A.	41	40N	80W
Fairweather, Mt.: U.S.A.	22	59N	137W
Faith: U.S.A.	43	45N	102W
Faizabad: Afghan.	87	37N	71E
Falaise: France	70	49N	0
Falkirk: Scotland	54	56N	4W
Falkland Is.: Atl. O.	49	52S	60W
Falköping: Sweden	69	58N	13E
Fall River: *city*, U.S.A.	17	42N	71W
Falmouth: England	55	50N	5W
False Bay: S. Africa	109	34S	19E
Falun: Sweden	69	61N	16E
Famagusta: Cyprus	84	35N	34E
Fanning I.: Pacific O.	101	4N	159W
Fano: Italy	73	44N	13E
Farafra Oasis: Egypt	107	27N	28E
Farah: Afghanistan	86	32N	62E
Farasan Is.: Red Sea	85	17N	42E
Fareham: England	55	51N	1W
Farewell: U.S.A.	2	63N	154W
Farewell, Cape: Greenland	3	60N	44W
Farewell, Cape: N.Z.	93	40S	173E
Fargo: U.S.A.	43	47N	97W
Faribault: U.S.A.	43	44N	93W
Farmington: U.S.A.	42	37N	108W
Farnborough: Eng.	57	51N	1W
Farnham: England	57	51¼N	¾W
Faro: Portugal	65	37N	8W
Fārs: Iran	85	29N	51E
Fashoda: Sudan	107	10N	32E
Faversham: England	57	51¼N	1E
Faxa Bay: Iceland	68	64N	23W
Fayette: U.S.A.	41	34N	88W
Fayetteville: Ark., U.S.A.	43	36N	94W
Fayetteville: N.C., U.S.A.	41	35N	79W
Fayîd: Egypt	107	Inset	
Fear, C.: U.S.A.	41	34N	78W
Fécamp: France	70	50N	0
Fehmarn: *i.*, Ger.	69	54N	11E
Feilding: N.Z.	93	40S	176E
Feira de Santana: Brazil	48	12S	39W
Feldkirch: Austria	73	47N	10E
Fen: *r.*, China	89	36N	111E
Fengsiang: China	89	35N	107E
Fengtai: China	90	39¾N	116¼E
Fenouillèdes: *mtns.*, France	71	43N	2E
Fens, The: England	55	53N	0
Fenyang: China	89	37N	112E
Fergana: U.S.S.R.	83	40N	72E
Fergus Falls: *city*, U.S.A.	43	46N	96W
Fermanagh: *Co.*, N. Ireland	56	54N	8W
Fermoy: R. of Irel.	56	52N	8W
Fernando de Noronha: *i.*, Brazil	48	4S	32W
Fernando Poo: *i.*, W. Africa	106	4N	9E
Ferndale: U.S.A.	31	42½N	83¼W
Ferrara: Italy	73	45N	12E
Ferret, Cap: France	71	45N	1W
Fetesti: Romania	67	44N	28E
Fethiye: Turkey	84	36N	29E
Fez: Morocco	106	34N	5W
Fezzan: *Prov.*, Libya	84	25N	15E
Fianarantsoa: Malagasy Rep.	108	22S	47E
Fife: *Co.*, Scotland	54	56N	3W
Fife Ness: Scotland	54	56N	3W
Figeac: France	71	4N	52E
FIJI: *cap.* Suva	100	18S	178E
Filchner, C.: Antarc.	51	66S	91E
Filchner Ice Shelf: Antarctica	51	78S	50W
Findlay: U.S.A.	41	41N	84W
Finedon: England	57	52¼N	¾W
Finistère: *Dept.*, Fr.	70	48N	4W
Finisterre, Cape: Sp.	65	43N	9W
FINLAND: *cap.* Helsinki	68/9	—	—
Finschhafen: N.E. New Guinea	97	7S	148E
Finsteraarhorn: *mtn.*, Switzerland	73	47N	8E
Fiordland: N.Z.	93	45S	167E
Firenze: Italy	73	44N	11E
Fishguard: Wales	55	52N	5W
Fitchburg: U.S.A.	31	42½N	71¾W
Fitzroy: *r.*, Queens., Australia	98	23S	150E
Fitzroy: *r.*, W. Austl.	96	18S	124E
Fiume: Yugoslavia	67	45N	15E
Flagstaff: U.S.A.	42	35N	112W
Flamborough Head: England	54	54N	0
Flanders: Belgium	70	51N	4E
Flathead L.: U.S.A.	42	48N	114W
Flattery, C.: U.S.A.	42	48N	125W
Fleet: England	57	51¼N	¾W
Fleetwood: England	54	54N	3W
Flensburg: Germany	66	55N	9E
Flers: France	70	49N	1W
Flinders: *r.*, Austl.	97	20S	141E
Flinders Range: Australia	99	31S	139E
Flinders Reefs: Coral Sea	98	18S	149E
Flint: U.S.A.	17	43N	84W
Flint: *Co.*, Wales	55	53N	3W
Flint: *r.*, U.S.A.	41	31N	85W
Florence: Italy	73	44N	11E
Florence: Alabama, U.S.A.	41	35N	88W
Florence: Arizona, U.S.A.	42	33N	111W
Florence: S.C., U.S.A.	41	34N	80W
Florencia: Colombia	48	2N	76W
Flores: *i.* & *sea*, Indonesia	91	9S	121E
Floreshty: U.S.S.R.	66	48N	28E
Floriano: Brazil	48	7S	43W
Florianópolis: Brazil	50	27S	48W
Florida: *State*, U.S.A.	41	28N	82W
Florida, Straits of: U.S.A.	39	24N	81W
Florida Keys: *is.*, U.S.A.	41	25N	81W
Florina: Greece	67	41N	21E
Florø: *i.*, Norway	68	62N	5E
Flushing: Neth.	72	51N	4E
Fly: *r.*, Papua	97	8S	142E
Foggia: Italy	67	41N	16E
Foix: & *Old Prov.*, Fr.	71	43N	2E
Foligno: Italy	67	43N	13E
Folkestone: England	55	51N	1E
Fond du Lac: U.S.A.	43	44N	88W
Fontainebleau: Fr.	70	48N	3E
Fontainebleau, Forêt de: France	70	48N	3E
Fontenoy: Belgium	70	51N	3E
Foochow: China	89	26N	118E
Forbes: Australia	99	33S	148E
Forcalquier: France	71	44N	6E
Fordlândia: Brazil	48	4S	55W
Forel, Mt.: Grnld.	3	67N	37W
Forez, Monts du: France	71	45N	4E
Forfar: Scotland	54	57N	3W
Forli: Italy	73	44N	12E
Formby: England	57	53½N	3W
Formentera: *i.*, Balearic Is.	65	38N	1E
Formosa: *i.* & *str.*, China	89	24N	121E
Forrest: Australia	96	31S	128E
Forrest City: U.S.A.	43	35N	91W
Forsayth: Australia	97	19S	144E
Forsyth: U.S.A.	42	46N	107W
Fortaleza: Brazil	48	4S	38W
Fort Collins: U.S.A.	43	41N	105W
Fort Dauphin: Malagasy Rep.	108	25S	47E
Fort-de-France: Martinique	47	15N	61W
Fort Dodge: U.S.A.	43	43N	94W
Fortescue: *r.*, Austl.	96	22S	118E
Fort Gouraud: Mauritania	106	23N	13W
Forth Bridge: Scot.	54	56N	3W
Forth, Firth of: Scot.	54	56N	3W
Fort Johnston: Mal.	109	15S	35E
FORT LAMY: Chad	106	12N	15E
Fort Lauderdale: U.S.A.	41	26N	80W
Fort Lee: U.S.A.	31	40¾N	74W
Fort Madison: U.S.A.	43	41N	91W
Fort Mile: *r.*, U.S.A.	28	65N	142W
Fort Morgan: U.S.A.	43	40N	104W
Fort Myers: U.S.A.	41	27N	82W
Fort Peck Res.: U.S.A.	42	47N	107W
Fort Pierce: U.S.A.	41	27N	80W
Fort Sandeman: W. Pakistan	88	31N	70E
Fort Shevchenko: U.S.S.R.	82	45N	50E
Fort Smith: U.S.A.	43	35N	94W
Fort Sumner: U.S.A.	43	34N	104W
Fort Wayne: U.S.A.	41	41N	85W
Fort William: Scot.	54	57N	5W
Fort Worth: U.S.A.	43	33N	97W
Fort Yukon: U.S.A.	28	67N	145W
Fougères: France	70	48N	1W
Foul Bay: Red Sea	84	23N	36E
Foulness I.: England	57	52N	1E
Foulwind, C.: N.Z.	93	42S	172E
Fourmies: France	70	50N	4E
Foveaux Strait: N.Z.	93	47S	168E
Fox Lake: U.S.A.	31	42½N	88¼W
Foyle, L.: Ireland	56	55N	7W
Framingham: U.S.A.	31	42¼N	71¼W
FRANCE: *cap.* Paris	70/1	—	—
Franche Comté: *Old Prov.*, France	71	47N	6E
Francistown: Bots.	109	21S	27E
Franconian Heights: Germany	72	49N	10E
Franconian Jura: Ger.	72	49N	11E
Frankfort: Indiana, U.S.A.	41	40N	86W
Frankfort: Kentucky, U.S.A.	41	38N	85W
Frankfurt am Main: Germany	72	50N	9E
Frankfurt an der Oder: Germany	72	52N	15E
Franklin D. Roosevelt Lake: U.S.A.	42	48N	118W
Franklin I.: Antarc.	51	76S	168E
Franklin Sq.: U.S.A.	31	40¾N	73¾W
Franz Josef Land: U.S.S.R.	80	80N	55E
Frascati: Italy	67	42N	13E
Fraserburgh: S. Afr.	109	33S	22E
Fraser I.: Australia	98	25S	153E
Fray Bentos: Uruguay	50	33S	58W
Fredericia: Denmark	69	56N	10E
Frederik Hendrik I.: West Irian	96	8S	138E
Frederick: U.S.A.	43	34N	99W
Fredericksburg: U.S.A.	41	38N	78W
Frederikshavn: Den.	69	57N	11E
Frederikstad: Nor.	69	59N	11E
Freeport: U.S.A.	31	40¾N	73½W
FREETOWN: Sierra Leone	106	7N	13W
Freiburg im Breisgau: Germany	73	48N	8E
Freising: Germany	73	48N	12E
Fréjus: France	71	43N	7E
Fremantle: Australia	98	32S	116E
Fremont: U.S.A.	43	41N	97W
FRENCH GUIANA: *cap.* Cayenne	48	4N	53W
Frenchman Creek: U.S.A.	43	40N	102W
FRENCH TERR. AFARS/ISSAS: *cap.* Djibouti	86	13N	43E
Freshfield, C.: Antarctica	51	68S	151E
Fresnillo: Mexico	38	23N	103W
Fresno: U.S.A.	42	37N	120W
Fribourg: Switz.	73	47N	7E
Friedrichshafen: Ger.	73	48N	9E
Friesland: *Prov.*, Netherlands	72	53N	6E
Frinton: England	57	51¾N	1¼E
Frisian Is., East: Ger.	72	54N	7E
Frisian Is., North: Germany	69	55N	8E
Frisian Is., West: Netherlands	72	53N	5E
Frome, Lake: Austl.	99	31S	140E
Frunze: U.S.S.R.	83	43N	75E
Fuentes de Oñoro: Spain	65	41N	7W
Fuerteventura: *i.*, Canary Islands	106	29N	14W
Fuji: *mtn.*, Japan	92	35N	139E
Fukien: *Prov.*, China	89	26N	118E
Fukui: Japan	92	36N	136E
Fukuoka: Japan	92	34N	130E
Fukushima: Japan	92	38N	140E
Fulda: & *r.*, Germany	72	50N	10E
Fulton: U.S.A.	43	39N	92W
Funafuti I.: Pac. O.	100	8S	178E
Funchal: Madeira	106	33N	17W
Funen: *i.*, Denmark	69	55N	10E
Furka Pass: Switz.	73	47N	8E
Furneaux Group: Australia	97	40S	148E
Fürth: Germany	72	49N	11E
Fushun: China	89	42N	124E
Fusin: China	89	42N	122E
Fyne, L.: Scotland	54	56N	5W
Gabès: & *gulf*, Tunisia	106	34N	11E
GABON: *cap.* Libreville	108	2N	12E
GABORONE: Botswana	109	24S	26E
Gabrovo: Bulgaria	67	43N	25E
Gadames: Libya	106	30N	10E
Gade: *r.*, England	57	51¾N	½W
Gadsden: U.S.A.	41	34N	86W
Gaeta: Italy	67	41N	14E
Gaffney: U.S.A.	41	35N	81W
Gafsa: Tunisia	106	35N	8E
Gail: *r.*, Austria	73	47N	13E
Gaillard Cut: Panama Canal	39	Inset	
Gainesville: Georgia, U.S.A.	41	34N	84W
Gainesville: Texas, U.S.A.	43	34N	97W
Gainsborough: Eng.	57	53N	1W
Gainsville: Florida, U.S.A.	41	30N	82W
Gairdner, L.: Austl.	96	32S	136E
Galápagos Is.: Pacific O.	101	1S	91W
Galashiels: Scotland	54	56N	3W
Galati: Romania	66	45N	28E
Galena: U.S.A.	2	65N	157W
Galesburg: U.S.A.	43	41N	90W
Galicia: Spain	65	43N	8W
Galilee, Sea of: Israel	84	33N	36E
Gallarate: Italy	73	46N	9E
Galle: Ceylon	88	6N	80E
Gallegos: *r.*, Arg.	49	52S	71W
Gallinas, Pt.: Colombia	48	13N	72W
Gallipoli: Turkey	67	40N	27E
Gällivare: Sweden	68	67N	21E
Gallup: U.S.A.	42	36N	109W
Galtymore: *mt.*, R. of Ireland	56	52N	8W
Galveston: & *bay*, U.S.A.	31	29½N	94¾W
Galway: & *Co.* & *bay*, R. of Ireland	56	53N	9W
GAMBIA: *cap.* Bathurst	106	13N	15W
Gambier Is.: Pac. O.	101	22S	135W
Gamlakarleby: Fin.	68	64N	23E
Gand: Belgium	70	51N	4E
Gandak: *r.*, India	88	27N	85E
Ganges: France	71	44N	4E
Ganges: *r.*, India/Pak.	88	25N	86E
Gânt: Hungary	66	47N	18E
Gap: France	71	45N	6E
Gard: *r.*, France	71	44N	4E
Garda, L. of: Italy	73	46N	11E
Garden City: Mich., U.S.A.	31	42¼N	83¼W
Garden City: N.Y., U.S.A.	31	40¾N	73½W
Garden Grove: U.S.A.	46	33¾N	118W
Gardez: Afghan.	88	34N	69E
Gardner I.: Pac. O.	100	5S	175W
Gardner Pinnacles: Pacific Ocean	101	25N	168W
Garelochhead: Scot.	54	56N	4¾W
Garfield: U.S.A.	31	40¾N	74W
Gargano, C.: Italy	67	42N	16E
Garnett: U.S.A.	43	38N	95W
Garonne: *r.*, France	71	45N	0
Garoua: Cameroon	106	9N	13E
Garrigues: *mtns.*, Fr.	71	44N	4E
Garrison Dam Res.: U.S.A.	43	48N	102W
Garron Pt.: N. Irel.	56	55N	6W
Gartok: China	88	32N	80E
Gary: U.S.A.	31	41½N	87¼W
Gascony: *Old Prov.*, France	71	44N	0
Gastonia: U.S.A.	41	35N	81W
Gata, C. de: Spain	65	37N	2W
Gata, Sierra de: Sp.	65	40N	7W
Gateshead: England	54	55N	2W
Gâtine, Hauteurs de: *hills*, France	71	47N	1W
Gatooma: Rhodesia	109	18S	30E
Gatun Lake: & *locks*, Panama Canal	39	Inset	
Gauhati: India	89	26N	92E
Gauss, Mt.: Antarc.	51	65S	90E
Gävle: Sweden	69	61N	17E
Gawler: Australia	99	35S	139E
Gaya: Niger	106	12N	4E
Gaya: India	88	25N	85E
Gaza: Egypt	84	31N	34E
Gaziantep: Turkey	85	37N	37E
Gdansk: Poland	66	54N	19E
Gdov: U.S.S.R.	69	59N	28E
Gdynia: Poland	66	55N	18E
Gedser: Denmark	69	54N	12E
Geelong: Australia	99	38S	144E
Geerardsbergen: Belgium	70	51N	4E
Geissen: Germany	72	51N	9E
Gelsenkirchen: Ger.	62	51N	7E
Geneva: & *l.*, Switz.	73	46N	6E
Genil: *r.*, Spain	65	37N	4W
Génissiat Dam: Fr.	71	46N	6E

	Page	Lat.	Long.
Genoa: & *gulf*, Italy	**73**	44N	9E
Géologie, Pt.: Antarc.	**51**	66S	140E
George: S. Africa	**109**	34S	22E
George, L.: Austl.	**99**	35S	149E
GEORGETOWN: Guyana	**48**	7N	58W
George Town: Mal.	**91**	5N	100E
Georgetown: St. Vincent	**47**	13N	61W
Georgetown: U.S.A.	**41**	33N	79W
Georgia: *State*, U.S.A.	**41**	33N	84W
Georgian S.S.R.: U.S.S.R.	**82**	43N	45E
Gera: Germany	**72**	51N	12E
Geraldton: Austl.	**98**	29S	115E
GERMANY	**72/3**	—	—
East *cap.* Berlin	**72**	—	—
West *cap.* Bonn	**72/3**	—	—
Gerona: Spain	**65**	42N	3E
Gers: *r.*, France	**71**	44N	1E
Gettysburg: U.S.A.	**41**	40N	77W
Gevelsberg: Ger.	**62**	51¼N	7¼E
Gezira: Sudan	**107**	14N	33E
Ghaghra: *r.*, India	**88**	27N	82E
GHANA: *cap.* Accra	**106**	7N	0
Ghardaïa: Algeria	**106**	33N	4E
Ghazipur: India	**88**	26N	83E
Ghent: Belgium	**70**	51N	4E
Gheorgheni: Rom.	**66**	47N	26E
Gibson Desert: Austl.	**96**	24S	124E
Gien: France	**71**	47N	3E
Gifu: Japan	**92**	35N	137E
Gijon: Spain	**65**	44N	6W
Gila: *r.*, U.S.A.	**42**	33N	113W
Gila Bend: U.S.A.	**42**	33N	113W
Gilbert: *r.*, Australia	**97**	17S	142E
Gilbert Is.: Pac. O.	**100**	0	175E
Gibraltar: & *strait*	**65**	36N	5W
Gilf Kebir Plateau: Egypt	**84**	24N	26E
Gilgandra: Australia	**99**	32S	149E
Gilgit: Kashmir	**87**	36N	74E
Gilgunnia: Australia	**99**	32S	146E
Gillingham: England	**57**	51½N	½E
Gineifa: Egypt	**107**	*Inset*	
Ginir: Ethiopia	**107**	7N	41E
Gippsland: Austl.	**99**	38S	148E
Girga: Egypt	**84**	26N	32E
Gironde: *r.*, France	**71**	45N	1W
Girvan: Scotland	**54**	55N	5W
Gisborne: N.Z.	**93**	39S	178E
Giurgiu: Romania	**67**	44N	26E
Givors: France	**71**	46N	5E
Gjinokastër: Albania	**67**	40N	20E
Gladbeck: Germany	**62**	52N	7E
Gladstone: Queens., Australia	**98**	24S	151E
Gladstone: S. Austl.	**99**	34S	138E
Glamorgan: *Co.*, Wales	**55**	52N	4W
Glasgow: Ky., U.S.A.	**41**	37N	86W
Glasgow: Montana, U.S.A.	**42**	48N	107W
Glasgow: Scotland	**54**	56N	4W
Glastonbury: Eng.	**55**	51N	3W
Glauchau: Germany	**72**	51N	13E
Glazov: U.S.S.R.	**82**	58N	53E
Glencoe: U.S.A.	**43**	45N	94W
Glen Cove: U.S.A.	**31**	40¾N	73¾W
Glenelg: *r.*, Australia	**99**	37S	141E
Glen Innes: Australia	**99**	30S	152E
Glenmorgan: Austl.	**98**	27S	150E
Glenwood: U.S.A.	**43**	46N	95W
Gliwice: Poland	**66**	50N	19E
Globe: U.S.A.	**42**	33N	111W
Glogów: Poland	**66**	52N	16E
Glomma: *r.*, Norway	**69**	61N	12E
Gloucester: & *Co.*, England	**55**	52N	2W
Gloucester: U.S.A.	**31**	42½N	70¾W
Gloversville: U.S.A.	**17**	43N	74W
Gniezno: Poland	**66**	53N	18E
Goa: India	**88**	15N	74E
Gobabis: S.W. Afr.	**109**	23S	18E
Gobi Desert: Mong.	**81**	43N	105E
Godavari: *r.*, India	**88**	20N	81E
Godthaab: Grnld.	**3**	64N	52W
Goiânia: Brazil	**48**	17S	49W
Goiás: Brazil	**48**	16S	50W
Goiás Massif: Brazil	**48**	15S	48W
Gol: Norway	**69**	61N	9E
Golden Bay: N.Z.	**93**	41S	173E
Gomati: *r.*, India	**88**	26N	82E
Gomel': U.S.S.R.	**82**	53N	31E
Gonave I.: Haiti	**47**	19N	73W
Gondar: Ethiopia	**107**	13N	37E
Goodenough, C.: Antarctica	**51**	66S	130E
Good Hope, C. of: S. Africa	**109**	34S	18E
Goodland: U.S.A.	**43**	39N	103W
Goodwin Sands: Eng.	**55**	51N	1E
Goole: England	**57**	54N	1W
Goomalling: Austl.	**98**	31S	117E
Goondiwindi: Austl.	**98**	29S	150E
Goose L.: U.S.A.	**42**	42N	120W
Göppingen: Ger.	**73**	49N	10E
Gorakhpur: India	**88**	27N	83E
Gordon: U.S.A.	**28**	70N	141W
Gore: Ethiopia	**107**	8N	36E
Gore: N.Z.	**93**	46S	169E
Goree: Senegal	**107**	14N	17W
Gorey: R. of Ireland	**56**	53N	6W
Gorgān: Iran	**85**	37N	55E
Goring Gap: Eng.	**57**	51½N	1¼W

	Page	Lat.	Long.
Gorizia: Italy	**73**	46N	14E
Gor'kiy: U.S.S.R.	**82**	56N	44E
Gorno-Altaysk: U.S.S.R.	**83**	52N	86E
Gorzów Wielkopolski: Poland	**66**	53N	15E
Gosford: Australia	**99**	33S	151E
Goslar: Germany	**72**	52N	10E
Gospić: Yugoslavia	**67**	45N	15E
Göta: *r.*, Sweden	**69**	58N	12E
Göteborg: Sweden	**69**	58N	12E
Gotha: Germany	**72**	51N	11E
Gotland: *i.*, Sweden	**69**	57N	19E
Göttingen: Germany	**72**	52N	10E
Gottwaldov: Czech.	**66**	49N	18E
Gouda: Neth.	**72**	52N	5E
Goulburn: Australia	**99**	35S	150E
Gourock: Scotland	**54**	56N	4¾W
Gourock Range: Australia	**99**	36S	149E
Gouverneur: U.S.A.	**17**	44N	76W
Gower: *penin.*, Wales	**55**	52N	4W
Goyllarisquizga: Peru	**48**	11S	76W
Gozo: *i.*, Medit. Sea	**67**	36N	14E
Graaff-Reinet: S. Afr.	**109**	32S	25E
Gracias a Dios, C.: Nicaragua	**47**	15N	83W
Grafton: Australia	**99**	30S	153E
Grafton: U.S.A.	**43**	48N	98W
Graham: U.S.A.	**43**	33N	99W
Grahamland: Antarc.	**51**	67S	65W
Grahamstown: S. Africa	**109**	33S	26E
Graian Alps: Fr./Italy	**73**	45N	7E
Grain: England	**57**	51½N	¾E
Grain Cost: Liberia	**106**	5N	10W
Grampians: & *mtns.*, Australia	**99**	37S	142E
Grampian Mts.: Scot.	**54**	57N	4W
Granada: Nic.	**47**	12N	86W
Granada: Spain	**65**	37N	4W
Gran Canaria: *i.*, Canary Is.	**106**	28N	15W
Gran Chaco: Arg./Paraguay	**48**	25S	61W
Grand: *r.*, U.S.A.	**43**	46N	102W
Grand Bahama: *i.*, Bahama Is.	**47**	27N	79W
Grand Canyon: & *city*, U.S.A.	**42**	36N	112W
Grand Coulee: U.S.A.	**42**	48N	119W
Grande Ronde: *r.*, U.S.A.	**42**	46N	118W
Grand Forks: U.S.A.	**43**	48N	97W
Grand Island: *city*, U.S.A.	**43**	41N	98W
Grand Junction: U.S.A.	**42**	39N	109W
Grand Rapids: *city*, Mich., U.S.A.	**41**	43N	86W
Grand Rapids: *city*, Minn., U.S.A.	**43**	47N	94W
Grane: Norway	**68**	66N	13E
Grangemouth: Scot.	**54**	56N	3¾W
Granite Harbour: Antarctica	**51**	77S	165E
Grant, Mt.: U.S.A.	**42**	38N	119W
Grantham: England	**57**	53N	1W
Grants Pass: *city*, U.S.A.	**42**	42N	123W
Granville: France	**70**	49N	2W
Grasse: France	**71**	44N	7E
Grave, Pte. de: Fr.	**71**	46N	1W
Gravelines: France	**70**	51N	2E
Gravesend: England	**55**	51N	0
Grays Harbour: U.S.A.	**42**	47N	124W
Grays Thurrock: England	**57**	51½N	¼E
Graz: Austria	**66**	47N	15E
Great Abaco: *i.*, Bahama Is.	**47**	27N	11W
Great Australian Bight	**96**	33S	130E
Great Barrier I.: New Zealand	**93**	36S	175E
Great Barrier Reef: Australia	**97**	17S	147E
Great Belt: Den.	**69**	55N	11E
Great Bend: U.S.A.	**43**	38N	99W
Great Bitter Lake: Egypt	**107**	*Inset*	
Great Dividing Range: Australia	**98/9**	—	—
Great Driffield: Eng.	**54**	54N	0
Great Dunmow: Eng.	**57**	51¾N	¼E
Greater Antilles: W. Indies	**47**	18N	75W
Great Eastern Erg: *desert*, Algeria	**106**	30N	8E
Great Exuma: *i.*, Bahamas	**47**	24N	76W
Great Falls: *city*, U.S.A.	**42**	47N	111W
Great Himalayan Range	**88/9**	—	—
Great Inagua: *i.*, Bahama Is.	**47**	21N	74W
Great Karroo: *plat.*, S. Africa	**109**	33S	23E
Great Keppel I.: Australia	**98**	23S	151E
Great Khingan Mts.: China	**90**	47N	120E

	Page	Lat.	Long.
Great Rann of Kutch: India/Pakistan	**88**	24N	69E
Great St. Bernard Pass: Switz./It.	**73**	46N	7E
Great Salt Lake: & *Desert*, U.S.A.	**42**	41N	113W
Great Sandy Desert: Australia	**96**	21S	124E
Great Sandy I.: Australia	**98**	25S	153E
Great Stour: *r.*, Eng.	**57**	51¼N	0
Great Valley: Austl.	**99**	38S	145E
Great Victoria Desert: Australia	**88**	28S	130E
Great Wall: China	**89**	39N	110E
Great Western Erg: *desert*, Algeria	**106**	30N	0
Great Yarmouth: England	**55**	53N	2E
Gredos, Sierra de: Spain	**65**	40N	5W
GREECE: *cap.* Athens	**67**	40N	23E
Greeley: U.S.A.	**43**	40N	105W
Green: *r.*, U.S.A.	**42**	40N	110W
Greenock: Scotland	**54**	56N	4¾W
Greenough: *r.*, Australia	**98**	28S	116E
Green Bay: & *city*, U.S.A.	**43**	45N	88W
Greenland	**3**	70N	40W
Green Mts.: U.S.A.	**19**	44N	73W
Green River: *city*, U.S.A.	**42**	42N	110W
Greensboro: U.S.A.	**41**	36N	80W
Greenville: Ala., U.S.A.	**41**	32N	87W
Greenville: Miss., U.S.A.	**40**	33N	91W
Greenville: S.C., U.S.A.	**41**	35N	82W
Greenville: Tenn., U.S.A.	**41**	36N	83W
Greenville: Texas, U.S.A.	**43**	33N	96W
Greenwich: England	**57**	51N	0
Greenwich: U.S.A.	**31**	41N	73¾W
Greenwood: Miss., U.S.A.	**40**	34N	90W
Greenwood: S.C., U.S.A.	**41**	34N	82W
GRENADA: *cap.* St. George's	**47**	12N	62W
Grenadines: *is.*, W. Indies	**47**	12N	61W
Grenay: France	**70**	50N	3E
Grenoble: France	**71**	45N	6E
Gretna Green: Scot.	**54**	55N	3W
Greymouth: N.Z.	**93**	42S	171E
Grey Range: Austl.	**99**	28S	142E
Greystones: R. of Ireland	**56**	53N	6W
Greytown: S. Africa	**109**	29S	31E
Griefswald: Ger.	**72**	54N	13E
Griffin: U.S.A.	**41**	33N	84W
Griffith: Australia	**99**	34S	146E
Grimsby: England	**54**	54N	0
Grimsel Pass: Switz.	**73**	47N	8E
Grindelwald: Switz.	**73**	47N	8E
Griqualand: S. Afr.	**109**	29S	24E
Griquatown: S. Afr.	**109**	29S	25E
Gris Nez: *cape*, Fr.	**70**	51N	2E
Grodno: U.S.S.R.	**82**	54N	24E
Groix, Ile de: Fr.	**70**	48N	3W
Gronau: Germany	**72**	52N	7E
Grong: Norway	**68**	64N	12E
Groningen: Neth.	**72**	53N	7E
Groote Eylandt: *i.*, Australia	**96**	14S	137E
Grootfontein: S.W. Africa	**109**	20S	18E
Grossenbrode: Ger.	**66**	54N	11E
Grosseto: Italy	**67**	43N	11E
Groton: U.S.A.	**31**	42½N	71½W
Groznyy: U.S.S.R.	**82**	43N	46E
Grudziądz: Poland	**66**	53N	18E
Grünberg: Poland	**66**	52N	16E
Gruyères: Switz.	**73**	47N	7E
Grytviken: S. Georg.	**49**	54S	34W
Guadalajara: Mexico	**38**	21N	103W
Guadalajara: Spain	**65**	41N	3W
Guadalcanal: Spain	**65**	38N	6W
Guadalcanal: *i.*, Pacific Ocean	**100**	10S	160E
Guadalquivir: *r.*, Sp.	**65**	37N	6W
Guadalupe: *i.*, Pac. O.	**38**	29N	118W
Guadalupe: *r.*, U.S.A.	**40**	29N	97W
Guadarrama, Sierra de: Spain	**65**	41N	4W
Guadeloupe: *i.*, W. Indies	**47**	16N	61W
Guadiana: *r.*, Spain/Portugal	**65**	38N	8W
Guadix: Spain	**65**	37N	3W
Guajarà-mirim: Braz.	**48**	11S	65W
Guam: *i.*, Pacific O.	**100**	14N	145E
Guanare: Venezuela	**47**	9N	70W
Guantanamo: Cuba	**47**	20N	75W
Guarda: Portugal	**65**	41N	7W
Guardafui, C.: Somali Republic	**107**	12N	51E
GUATEMALA: *cap.* Guatemala	**38**	15N	91W
Guayaquil: & *gulf*, Ecuador	**42**	2S	80W
Guaymas: Mexico	**38**	28N	111W

	Page	Lat.	Long.
Gubakha: U.S.S.R.	**83**	58N	57E
Guebwiller: France	**70**	48N	7E
Guéret: France	**71**	46N	2E
Guernsey: *i.*, Channel Islands	**55**	*Inset*	
Guiana Highlands: S. America	**48**	3N	60W
Guildford: England	**57**	51N	1W
GUINEA: *cap.* Conakry	**106**	11N	1W
Guinea, G. of	**106**	3N	0
Guingamp: France	**70**	49N	3W
Gujarat: India	**88**	22N	74E
Gujerat: *State*, India	**88**	23N	72E
Gujranwala: W. Pak.	**88**	32N	74E
Gulfport: U.S.A.	**41**	30N	89W
Gunnedah: Australia	**99**	31S	150E
Guntersville L.: U.S.A.	**41**	34N	86W
Guntur: India	**88**	16N	80E
Gur'yev: U.S.S.R.	**82**	47N	52E
GUYANA: *cap.* Georgetown	**48**	5N	58W
Guymon: U.S.A.	**40**	37N	101W
Gwaai: Rhodesia	**109**	19S	27E
Gwadar: W. Pak.	**88**	25N	62E
Gwalia: Australia	**96**	28S	122E
Gwalior: India	**88**	26N	78E
Gwelo: Rhodesia	**109**	20S	30E
Gyangtse: China	**87**	29N	90E
Gyda Peninsula: U.S.S.R.	**81**	71N	77E
Gydan Range: U.S.S.R.	**81**	62N	160E
Gympie: Australia	**98**	26S	153E
Györ: Hungary	**66**	48N	18E
Haarlem: Neth.	**72**	52N	5E
Haast: & *Pass*, N.Z.	**93**	44S	169E
Hab: *r.*, W. Pak.	**88**	25N	67E
Habbānīyah: 'Iraq	**85**	34N	43E
Hackensack: U.S.A.	**31**	41N	74W
Haddington: Scot.	**54**	56N	3W
Hadhramaut: Yemen P.D.R.	**86**	16N	48E
Hadibu: Socotra	**85**	13N	54E
Hadithah: 'Iraq	**85**	34N	42E
Hadrian's Wall: Eng.	**54**	55N	2W
Hageland: Belgium	**70**	51N	5E
Hagen: Germany	**72**	51N	7E
Hague, Cap de la: Fr.	**70**	50N	2W
HAGUE, THE: Neth.	**72**	52N	4E
Haguenau: France	**70**	49N	8E
Haifa: Israel	**84**	33N	35E
Hail: Sa'udi Arabia	**85**	27N	42E
Hainan: *i.* & *str.*, China	**91**	19N	110E
Hainault: Belgium	**70**	51N	4E
Haines: U.S.A.	**22**	59N	135W
Haiphong: N. Viet Nam	**90**	21N	107E
HAITI: *cap.* Port-au-Prince	**47**	19N	73W
Hakodate: Japan	**92**	42N	141E
Halaib: Sudan	**84**	22N	36E
Halberstadt: Ger.	**72**	52N	11E
Haldensleben: Ger.	**72**	52N	11E
Hales Corners: U.S.A.	**31**	43N	88W
Halifax: England	**54**	54N	2W
Halle: Germany	**72**	51N	12E
Hall's Creek: *town*, Australia	**96**	18S	128E
Halmahera: *i.*, Indon.	**91**	1N	128E
Halmstad: Sweden	**69**	57N	13E
Hälsingborg: Sweden	**69**	56N	13E
Hama: Syria	**84**	35N	37E
Hamadān: Iran	**85**	35N	49E
Hamamatsu: Japan	**92**	35N	138E
Hamar: Norway	**69**	61N	11E
Hambantota: Ceylon	**88**	7N	81E
Hamburg: Ger.	**72**	54N	10E
Hameenlinna: Fin.	**68**	61N	24E
Hameln: Germany	**72**	52N	9E
Hamersley Range: Australia	**96**	22S	118E
Hami: China	**87**	43N	93E
Hamilton: Australia	**99**	38S	142E
Hamilton: N.Z.	**93**	38S	175E
Hamilton: Scotland	**54**	56N	4W
Hamilton: U.S.A.	**41**	39N	85W
Hamlin: U.S.A.	**43**	33N	100W
Hamm: Germany	**72**	52N	8E
Hammerfest: Nor.	**68**	71N	24E
Hammersmith: Eng.	**57**	51½N	¼W
Hammond: U.S.A.	**31**	41½N	87½W
Hampshire: *Co.*, Eng.	**55**	51N	1W
Hampton: U.S.A.	**41**	37N	76W
Hamtramck: U.S.A.	**31**	42½N	83W
Hamun-i-Helmand: *l.*, Iran/Afghanistan	**86**	32N	61E
Han: *r.*, China	**89**	33N	111E
Hancock: U.S.A.	**43**	47N	88W
Hanford: U.S.A.	**42**	36N	120W
Hangchow: China	**89**	30N	120E
Hangö (Hanko): Fin.	**69**	60N	23E
Hankow: China	**89**	31N	114E
Hanley: England	**57**	53N	2¼W
Hannibal: U.S.A.	**43**	40N	91W
Hanö Bay: Sweden	**69**	56N	15E
HANOI: North Viet Nam	**90**	21N	106E
Hanover: Germany	**72**	52N	10E
Hanyang: China	**89**	31N	114E

	Page	Lat.	Long.
Haogoundou, L.: Mali	106	15N	3W
Haradh: Sa'udi Arabia	85	24N	49E
Harar: Ethiopia	107	9N	42E
Harbin: China	89	46N	127E
Hardanger Fiörd: Norway	69	60N	6E
Hardangervidda: Norway	69	60N	8E
Hardenberg: Neth.	72	53N	7E
Hargeisa: Somali Republic	107	10N	44E
Haringey: England	57	51½N	0
Harlingen: Neth.	72	53N	5E
Harlingen: U.S.A.	40	26N	98W
Harlow: England	57	51¾N	¼E
Harney Basin: U.S.A.	42	43N	120W
Härnösand: Sweden	68	63N	18E
Harris: *i.*, Scotland	53	58N	7W
Harrisburg: U.S.A.	41	40N	77W
Harrismith: S. Africa	109	28S	29E
Harrisonburg: U.S.A.	41	39N	79W
Harrogate: England	54	54N	2W
Harrow: England	57	51½N	¼W
Harsprånget: Sweden	68	67N	20E
Harstad: Norway	68	69N	16E
Hartford: U.S.A.	17	42N	73W
Hartland Pt.: Eng.	55	51N	5W
Hartlepool: England	54	54¾N	1¼W
Harvey: U.S.A.	31	41½N	87¾W
Harwell: England	57	51½N	1¼W
Harwich: England	55	52N	1E
Harz: *mtns.*, Ger.	72	52N	11E
Hasa: Sa'udi Arabia	85	27N	48E
Haslemere: England	55	51N	1W
Hassan: India	88	13N	76E
Hasselt: Belgium	70	51N	5E
Hassi Messaoud: Alg.	106	32N	6E
Hässleholm: Sweden	69	56N	14E
Hastings: England	55	51N	1E
Hastings: N.Z.	93	40S	177E
Hastings: U.S.A.	43	41N	98W
Hastings Range: Australia	99	31S	152E
Hatinh: N. Viet Nam	91	18N	106E
Hatteras, C.: U.S.A.	41	35N	75W
Hattiesburg: U.S.A.	41	31N	89W
Hattingen: Germany	62	51½N	7¼E
Haugesund: Norway	69	59N	5E
Hauraki Gulf: N.Z.	93	37S	175E
Hauta: Sa'udi Arabia	85	23N	47E
HAVANA: Cuba	47	23N	82W
Havering: England	57	51½N	¼E
Havre: U.S.A.	42	48N	110W
Havre, Le: France	70	50N	0
Hawaii: *i.* & *State*, Pacific O., U.S.A	101	20N	155W
Hawera: N.Z.	93	40S	174E
Hawick: Scotland	54	55N	3W
Hawke Bay: N.Z.	93	39S	177E
Haworth: England	57	53¾N	2W
Hawthorne: U.S.A.	42	38N	119W
Hay: Australia	99	34S	145E
Hayden: U.S.A.	42	33N	111W
Haydock: England	57	53½N	2¾W
Hays: U.S.A.	43	39N	99W
Hazaribagh: India	88	24N	85E
Hazelbrouck: France	70	51N	3E
Hazel Park: U.S.A.	31	42½N	83W
Hazelton: U.S.A.	41	41N	76W
Heanor: England	55	53N	1W
Hearst I.: Antarc.	51	69S	62W
Hebburn: England	54	55N	1½W
Hebron: Jordan	84	32N	35E
Heidelberg: Ger.	72	49N	9E
Heidelberg: S. Africa	109	26S	28E
Heilbronn: Ger.	72	49N	9E
Heiligenhaus: Ger.	62	51¼N	7E
Heilungkiang: *Prov.*, China	89	45N	124E
Hekla: *mtn.*, Iceland	68	64N	19W
Helena: Ark., U.S.A.	43	35N	91W
Helena: Montana, U.S.A.	42	47N	112W
Helen Glacier: Antarctica	51	66S	95E
Helensburgh: Scot.	54	56N	4¾W
Helensville: N.Z.	93	37S	174E
Heligoland: *i.* & *bight*, Germany	69	54N	8E
Helles, C.: Turkey	67	40N	26E
Helmand: *r.*, Afghanistan	86	30N	62E
Helsingør: Denmark	69	56N	13E
HELSINKI (Helsingfors): Finland	69	60N	25E
Helvellyn: *mtn.*, Eng.	54	55N	3W
Helwan: Egypt	84	29N	31E
Hemel Hempstead: England	57	52N	1W
Hempstead: U.S.A.	31	40¾N	73½W
Hendaye: France	65	43N	2W
Henderson: Ky., U.S.A.	41	38N	88W
Henderson: Nev., U.S.A.	42	36N	115W
Henderson: N.C., U.S.A.	41	36N	78W
Hengelo: Neth.	72	52N	7E
Henley-on-Thames: England	57	51½N	1W
Henlopen, C.: U.S.A.	41	39N	75W
Henry, C.: U.S.A.	41	37N	76W
Henyang: China	89	27N	112E
Herat: Afghanistan	86	34N	62E
Hérault: *r.*, France	71	44N	3E
Herberton: Austl.	97	18S	145E
Hercegovina: Yugo.	67	44N	18E
Hereford: & Co., England	55	52N	3W
Hereford: U.S.A.	43	35N	102W
Herford: Germany	72	52N	9E
Herisau: Switzerland	73	47N	9E
Hermitage: N.Z.	93	44S	170E
Herne: Germany	62	52N	7E
Herne Bay: England	57	51¼N	1¼E
Herning: Denmark	69	56N	9E
Herstal: Belgium	70	51N	6E
Hertford: & Co., Eng.	55	52N	0
Hervey Bay: Austl.	98	25S	153E
Hexham: England	54	55N	2W
Heysham: England	54	54N	3W
Hiawatha: U.S.A.	43	40N	96W
Hibbing: U.S.A.	43	47N	93W
Hicksville: U.S.A.	31	40¾N	73½N
Hidalgo del Parral: Mexico	38	27N	106W
Hida Mts.: Japan	90	36N	137E
High Atlas: *mtns.*, Morocco	106	31N	7W
Highland Park: Ill., U.S.A.	31	42¼N	87¾W
Highland Park: Mich., U.S.A.	31	42½N	83W
Highlands, The: Scotland	53	57N	5W
High Plateaux: Alg.	106	34N	0
High Point: *city*, U.S.A.	41	36N	80W
High Veld: S. Africa	109	30S	28E
High Wycombe: Eng.	57	51½N	¾W
Hijaz: Sa'udi Arabia	86	25N	39E
Hilden: Germany	62	51¼N	7E
Hildesheim: Ger.	72	52N	10E
Hillah: 'Iraq	85	32N	44E
Hillegom: Neth.	72	52N	4E
Hillingdon: England	57	51½N	½W
Hillston: Australia	99	33S	146E
Hilversum: Neth.	72	52N	5E
Himachal Pradesh: *State*, India	88	32N	77E
Himeji: Japan	92	35N	135E
Hinckley: England	57	52½N	1¼W
Hindley: England	57	53½N	2½W
Hindu Kush: *mtns.*, Afghanistan	87	36N	70E
Hingshan: China	90	47N	130E
Hiroshima: Japan	90	34N	132E
Hirson: France	70	50N	4E
Hispaniola: W. Ind.	47	20N	70W
Hjørring: Denmark	69	57N	10E
Hobart: Tasmania	97	43S	147E
Hobbs: U.S.A.	43	32N	103W
Hobbs Coast: Antarctica	51	76S	138W
Hoboken: Belgium	70	51N	4E
Hoboken: U.S.A.	31	40¾N	74W
Hodeida: Yemen	85	15N	43E
Hódmezövásárhely: Hungary	66	46N	20E
Hof: Germany	72	50N	12E
Hofei: China	89	32N	117E
Hofsjökull: *mtn.*, Ice.	68	65N	19W
Hog's Back: England	57	51¼N	¾W
Hohenlimburg: Ger.	62	51¼N	7½E
Hohe Rhön: *mts.*, Germany	72	50N	10E
Hohe Tauern: *mtns.*, Austria	73	47N	12E
Hohsien: China	89	24N	112E
Hoihow: China	89	20N	110E
Hokianga Harbour: N.Z.	93	36S	173E
Hokitika: N.Z.	93	43S	171E
Hokkaido: *i.*, Japan	90	43N	143E
Holbaek: Denmark	69	56N	12E
Holbrook: Australia	99	36S	147E
Holderness: *penin.*, England	54	54N	0
Holdrege: U.S.A.	43	40N	99W
Holguin: Cuba	47	21N	76W
Holland: *district*, Eng.	55	53N	0
Holland: U.S.A.	41	43N	86W
Holland *see* Netherlands			
Hollick-Kenyon Plat.: Antarctica	51	78S	105W
Hollywood: Calif., U.S.A.	42	34N	118W
Hollywood: Florida, U.S.A.	41	26N	80W
Holstebro: Den.	69	56N	9E
Holyhead: Wales	55	53N	5W
Holy I.: England	54	56N	2W
Holy I.: Wales	55	53N	5W
Holywood: N. Irel.	56	55N	6W
Homberg: Germany	62	51½N	6¾W
Home Hill: Austl.	98	20S	147E
Homestead: U.S.A.	41	25N	80W
Homs: Libya	106	33N	14E
Homs: Syria	84	35N	37E
Hon: Libya	84	29N	16E
Honan: *prov.*, China	89	34N	113E
HONDURAS: *cap.* Tegucigalpa	38	15N	87W
Hønefoss: Norway	69	60N	10E
Honfleur: France	70	49N	0
Hong Kong: China	89	22N	114E
Honiton: England	55	51N	3W
Honolulu: Hawaii	101	21N	158W
Honshu: *i.*, Japan	90	36N	137E
Hood, Mt.: U.S.A.	42	45N	122W
Hood Point: Austl.	98	34S	120E
Hooghly: *r.*, India	88	22N	88E
Hook I.: Australia	98	20S	149E
Hook of Holland: Netherlands	72	52N	4E
Hopeh: *prov.*, China	89	39N	116E
Hopewell: U.S.A.	41	37N	77W
Hopkins: *r.*, Austl.	99	38S	143E
Hopkinsville: U.S.A.	41	37N	87W
Hoquiam: U.S.A.	42	47N	124W
Hormuz, Str. of: Iran	85	27N	56E
Horn, Cape: Chile	49	56S	67W
Horncastle: England	55	53N	0
Hornell: U.S.A.	41	42N	78W
Horsham: Australia	99	37S	142E
Horsham: England	55	51N	0
Horwich: England	57	53½N	2½W
Hoshangabad: India	88	23N	78E
Hotham, Mt.: Austl.	99	37S	147E
Hoting: Sweden	68	64N	16E
Hot Springs: Ark., U.S.A.	40	35N	93W
Hot Springs: S. Dak., U.S.A.	43	43N	104W
Houghton le Spring: England	54	54¾N	1½W
Houma: U.S.A.	40	30N	91W
Hounslow: England	57	51½N	½W
Hourtin, Étg. d': Fr.	71	45N	1W
Houston: U.S.A.	31	29¾N	95¼W
Houtman Abrolhos: *is.*, Australia	98	29S	114E
Howe, Cape: Austl.	99	37S	150E
Howrah: India	88	23N	88E
Hoy: *i.*, Scotland	53	59N	3W
Hoylake: England	57	53½N	3¼W
Hoyo Str.: Japan	92	33N	132E
Hsichang: China	89	28N	102E
Hsin-chu: Formosa	89	25N	121E
Hsinhai: China	89	35N	120E
Hsinhsiang: China	89	35N	114E
Hualiel: Formosa	89	24N	121E
Huallaga: *r.*, Peru	48	8S	76W
Huancavelica: Peru	48	13S	75W
Huancayo: Peru	48	12S	75W
Huánuco: Peru	48	10S	76W
Hubli: India	88	15N	75E
Hucknall: England	57	53N	1¼W
Huddersfield: Eng.	57	54N	2W
Hudson: *r.*, U.S.A.	17	42N	74W
Hué: S. Viet Nam	91	16N	107E
Huelva: Spain	65	37N	7W
Huesca: Spain	65	42N	0
Hufhuf: Sa'udi Arabia	85	25N	49E
Hughenden: Austl.	97	21S	144E
Huhehot: China	89	41N	112E
Huitse: China	89	26N	103E
Hull *see* Kingston upon Hull			
Hüls: Germany	62	51½N	6½E
Hulun: China	90	49N	120E
Hulun Nor: *l.*, China	90	49N	118E
Humber: *r.*, Eng.	57	54N	0
Humboldt: *r.*, U.S.A.	42	40N	119W
Humboldt Glacier: Greenland	3	80N	63W
Hume: *r.*, Australia	99	36S	145E
Hume Res.: Austl.	99	36S	147E
Hunan: *Prov.*, China	89	27N	111E
HUNGARY: *cap.* Budapest	66	47N	20E
Hunger Steppe: U.S.S.R.	83	47N	70E
Hunsrück: *mtns.*, Germany	72	50N	7E
Hunter: *r. & range*, Australia	99	33S	151E
Huntingdon: & Co., England	55	52N	0
Huntington: Indiana, U.S.A.	41	41N	86W
Huntington: W. Va., U.S.A.	41	38N	82W
Huntington Station: U.S.A.	31	40¾N	73½W
Huntly: N.Z.	93	37S	175E
Huntsville: Alabama, U.S.A.	41	35N	87W
Huntsville: Texas, U.S.A.	40	31N	96W
Hupeh: *Prov.*, China	89	31N	112E
Huron: U.S.A.	43	44N	98W
Huron, Lake: U.S.A./Canada	18	45N	83W
Hürth: Germany	62	51N	7E
Hurunui: *r.*, N.Z.	93	43S	172E
Huskvarna: Sweden	69	58N	14E
Hutchinson: U.S.A.	43	38N	98W
Hutt: N.Z.	93	41S	175E
Huyton: England	57	53½N	2¾W
Hvar: *i.*, Yugo.	67	43N	17E
Hwaining: China	89	31N	117E
Hwang (Yellow): *r.*, China	89	41N	110E
Hyderabad: India	88	17N	78E
Hyderabad: W. Pak.	88	25N	68E
Hyères: France	71	43N	6E
Hyères, Îles d': Fr.	71	43N	6E
Iaşi: Romania	66	47N	28E
Ibadan: Nigeria	106	7N	4E
Ibagué: Colombia	48	4N	75W
Ibiza: *i. & town*, Balearic Is.	65	39N	2E
Ica: Peru	48	14S	76W
ICELAND: *cap.* Reykjavik	68	—	—
Ichang: China	89	31N	111E
Ichinomiya: Japan	92	35N	137E
Idaho: *State*, U.S.A.	42	44N	115W
Idaho Falls: *city*, U.S.A.	42	43N	112W
Igarka: U.S.S.R.	81	67N	86E
Iglesias: Sardinia	65	39N	8E
Ijmuiden: Neth.	72	52N	4E
Ijssel: *r.*, Neth.	72	52N	6E
Ijsselmeer: Neth.	72	53N	5E
Ikaria: *i.*, Greece	67	38N	26E
Ilebo: Congo Rep.	108	4S	21E
Île de France: *Old Prov.*, France	70	49N	2E
Ilford: England	57	51½N	0
Ilfracombe: Eng.	55	51N	4W
Ilhéus: Brazil	48	15S	39W
Iliamna Lake: U.S.A.	2	59N	155W
Iliodhromia: *i.*, Greece	67	39N	24E
Ilkley: England	54	54N	2W
Illimani: *mtn.*, Bolivia	48	17S	67W
Illinois: *State*, U.S.A.	43	40N	90W
Il'men', L.: U.S.S.R.	82	58N	32E
Ilmenau: Germany	72	51N	11E
Iloilo: Philippines	91	11N	122E
Imabari: Japan	92	34N	133E
Imatra: Finland	69	61N	29E
Imbabah: Egypt	84	30N	31¼E
Imperia: Italy	73	44N	8E
Imphal: India	89	25N	94E
Imroz: *i.*, Turkey	67	40N	26E
Inari, L.: Finland	68	69N	28E
Inchon: S. Korea	90	37N	127E
Indaw: Burma	90	24N	96E
Independence: U.S.A.	43	37N	96W
INDIA (Bharat): *cap.* Delhi	88/9	—	—
Indiana: *State*, U.S.A.	41	40N	86W
Indianapolis: U.S.A.	41	40N	86W
Indian Ocean	75	—	—
Indigirka: *r.*, U.S.S.R.	81	68N	146E
INDONESIA: *cap.* Djakarta	91	5S	115E
Indore: India	88	23N	76E
Indre: *r.*, France	71	47N	1E
Indus: *r.*, W. Pak.	88	26N	68E
Ingolstadt: Germany	73	49N	11E
Ingrid Christensen Coast: Antarc.	51	69S	79E
Inhambane: Mozam.	109	24S	35E
Inhaminga: Mozam.	109	18S	35E
Inishowen Penin: R. of Ireland	56	55N	7W
Inkerman: U.S.S.R.	82	45N	34E
Inkster: U.S.A.	31	42¼N	83¼W
Inland Sea: Japan	92	34N	133E
Inn: *r.*, Ger./Austr.	73	47N	12E
Innamincka: Austl.	98	28S	141E
Inner Mongolian A.R.: China	89	42N	112E
Innsbruck: Austria	73	47N	11E
Inowroclaw: Poland	66	53N	18E
Insterburg: U.S.S.R.	66	55N	22E
Interlaken: Switz.	73	47N	8E
International Falls: *city*, U.S.A.	43	48N	93W
Inveraray: Scotland	54	56N	5W
Invercargill: N.Z.	93	46S	168E
Inverell: Australia	99	30S	151E
Inverness: Scotland	53	57N	4W
Investigator Strait: Australia	99	35S	137E
Iona: *i.*, Scotland	54	56N	6W
Ionian Is.: Greece	67	38N	20E
Ionian Sea	67	38N	18E
Ios: *i.*, Greece	67	37N	25E
Iowa: *State*, U.S.A.	43	42N	93W
Iowa City: U.S.A.	43	42N	92W
Ipin: China	89	29N	105E
Ipoh: Malaya	91	5N	101E
Ipswich: Australia	98	28S	153E
Ipswich: England	55	52N	1E
Ipswich: U.S.A.	31	42¾N	70¾W
Iquique: Chile	48	20S	70W
Iquitos: Peru	48	4S	73W
Iraklion: Crete	67	35N	25E
IRAN: *cap.* Tehrān	85	—	—
'IRAQ: *cap.* Baghdad	85	33N	44E
Irbīl: 'Iraq	85	36N	44E
IRELAND, REPUBLIC OF: *cap.* Dublin	56	—	—
Irish Sea	53	53N	5W
Irkutsk: U.S.S.R.	81	52N	105E
Irlam: England	57	53½N	2½W
Iron Bridge: England	57	52¾N	2½W
Iron Gates: Yugo./Rom.	67	45N	23E
Iron Knob: Austl.	99	33S	137E
Iron Mt.: U.S.A.	42	43N	117W
Iron Mountain: *city*, U.S.A.	43	46N	88W
Ironwood: U.S.A.	43	46N	90W
Irrawaddy: *r.*, Burma	90	24N	96E
Irtysh: *r.*, U.S.S.R.	83	57N	73E
Irun: Spain	65	43N	2W
Irvine: Scotland	54	56N	5W

Place	Page	Lat.	Long.
Irvinestown: N. Irel.	**56**	54N	8W
Isafjördhur: Iceland	**68**	66N	23W
Isalmi: Finland	**58**	64N	27E
Isar: *r.*, Germany	**73**	48N	11E
Isarco: *r.*, Italy	**73**	47N	12E
Ischia: *i.*, Italy	**67**	41N	14E
Iseo, L.: Italy	**73**	46N	10E
Isère: *r.*, France	**71**	45N	5E
Iserlohn: Germany	**72**	51N	8E
Ishim: *r.*, U.S.S.R.	**83**	54N	67E
Ishimbay: U.S.S.R.	**82**	53N	56E
Ishpeming: U.S.A.	**43**	46N	88W
Isiro: Congo Rep.	**108**	3N	28E
Iskenderun: Turkey	**84**	37N	36E
Islamabad: W. Pak.	**88**	34N	73E
Islay: *i.*, Scotland	**54**	55N	6W
Ismailia: Egypt	**84**	30N	32E
Isna: Egypt	**107**	25N	33E
Isonzo: *r.*, Yugo./It.	**73**	46N	14E
ISRAEL: *cap.* Jerusalem	**84**	32N	35E
Issigeac: France	**71**	45N	1E
Issoudun: France	**71**	47N	2E
Issyk Kul': *l.*, U.S.S.R.	**83**	42N	77E
Istanbul: Turkey	**84**	41N	29E
Istria: *penin.*, Yugo.	**67**	45N	14E
Itabuna: Brazil	**48**	15S	39W
ITALY: *cap.* Rome	**66/7**	—	—
Itchen: *r.*, England	**55**	51N	1W
Ithaca: U.S.A.	**17**	42N	77W
Ithaca (Ithaki): *i.*, Greece	**67**	38N	21E
Ivailovgrad: Bulg.	**67**	41N	26E
Ivanhoe: Australia	**99**	33S	144E
Ivanovo: U.S.S.R.	**82**	57N	41E
Ivdel': U.S.S.R.	**83**	61N	60E
Ivishak: *r.*, U.S.A.	**28**	69N	150W
Iviza *see* Ibiza	**65**	39N	2E
IVORY COAST: *cap.* Abidjan	**106**	7N	6W
Izhevsk: U.S.S.R.	**82**	57N	53E
Izmail: U.S.S.R.	**66**	45N	29E
Izmir: Turkey	**84**	38N	27E
Izmit: Turkey	**84**	41N	30E
Izu Islands: Japan	**92**	34N	139E
Jabal Akhdhar: *mt.*, 'Oman	**85**	24N	57E
Jabalpur: India	**88**	23N	80E
Jabal Shammar: Sa'udi Arabia	**85**	27N	41E
Jabal Tuwaiq: Sa'udi Arabia	**85**	25N	46E
Jaca: Spain	**65**	43N	1W
Jacinto City: U.S.A.	**31**	29¾N	95¼W
Jackson: Mich., U.S.A.	**41**	42N	84W
Jackson: Miss., U.S.A.	**40**	32N	90W
Jackson: Tenn., U.S.A.	**41**	36N	89W
Jackson Bay: N.Z.	**93**	44S	169E
Jacksonville: Fla., U.S.A.	**41**	30N	82W
Jacksonville: Ill., U.S.A.	**43**	40N	90W
Jacme: Haiti	**47**	18N	72W
Jacobabad: W. Pak.	**88**	28N	69E
Jaén: Spain	**65**	38N	4W
Jaffa-Tel Aviv: Israel	**84**	32N	35E
Jaffa, C.: Australia	**99**	37S	140E
Jaffna: Ceylon	**88**	10N	80E
Jaipur: India	**88**	27N	76E
Jaisalmer: India	**88**	27N	71E
Jakobstad: Finland	**68**	64N	23E
Jalalabad: Afghan.	**87**	34N	71E
Jalo Oasis: Libya	**84**	28N	21E
JAMAICA: *cap.* Kingston	**47**	18N	77W
Jambin: Australia	**98**	24S	150E
James: *r.*, S. Dak., U.S.A.	**43**	44N	98W
James: *r.*, Va., U.S.A.	**41**	38N	78W
James Ross I.: Antarctica	**51**	65S	57W
Jamestown: N.Y., U.S.A.	**41**	42N	79W
Jamestown: N. Dak., U.S.A.	**43**	47N	99W
Jammu & Kashmir: *disputed State*	**88**	35N	77E
Jamnagar: India	**88**	22N	70E
Jamshedpur: India	**88**	23N	86E
Janesville: U.S.A.	**43**	43N	89W
JAPAN: *cap.* Tokyo	**92**	37N	137E
Japan, Sea of	**92**	40N	135E
Japen: *i.*, West Irian	**91**	2S	136E
Jarocin: Poland	**66**	52N	18E
Jaroslaw: Poland	**66**	50N	23E
Jarrow: England	**54**	55N	1½W
Jarvis I.: Pac. O.	**101**	0	160W
Jaslo: Poland	**66**	50N	22E
Jászberény: Hungary	**66**	47N	20E
Jauf: Sa'udi Arabia	**85**	30N	40E
Java: *i. & sea*, Indon.	**91**	7S	110E
Jaxartes: *r.*, U.S.S.R.	**83**	43N	67E
Jebba: Nigeria	**106**	9N	4E
Jebel Aulia Dam: Sudan	**107**	15N	32E
Jebel el Akhdar: Libya	**84**	32N	21E
Jedburgh: Scotland	**54**	55N	3W
Jedrzejów: Poland	**66**	51N	20E
Jefferson City: U.S.A.	**43**	39N	92W
Jehol: China	**89**	41N	118E
Jena: Germany	**72**	51N	12E
Jenolan Caves: Australia	**99**	34S	150E
Jeremie: Haiti	**47**	19N	74W
Jerez de la Frontera: Spain	**65**	37N	6W
Jericho: Jordan	**84**	31N	35E
Jersey: *i.*, Chan. Is.	**55**	*Inset*	
Jersey City: U.S.A.	**31**	41N	74W
JERUSALEM: Israel	**84**	32N	35E
Jervis Bay: Australia	**99**	35S	151E
Jesselton *see* Kota Kinabalu			
Jessore: E. Pakistan	**88**	23N	89E
Jesup: U.S.A.	**41**	32N	82W
Jhansi: India	**88**	25N	79E
Jhelum: *r.*, W. Pak.	**88**	31N	72E
Jibhalanta: Mongolia	**81**	47N	85E
Jidda: Sa'udi Arabia	**85**	22N	39E
Jiménez: Mexico	**38**	27N	105W
Jirgalantu: Mongolia	**81**	48N	91E
João Pessoa: Brazil	**48**	7S	35W
Jodhpur: India	**88**	26N	73E
Joensuu: Finland	**68**	63N	30E
Jofra Oasis: Libya	**106**	30N	15E
Jogjakarta: Java	**91**	8S	110E
Johannesburg: S. Afr.	**109**	26S	28E
Johnson City: U.S.A.	**41**	36N	82W
Johnstone: Scotland	**54**	55¾N	4½W
Johnstown: U.S.A.	**41**	40N	79W
Johore Bahru: Malaya	**91**	1N	104E
Joinville I.: Antarc.	**51**	63S	56W
Joliet: U.S.A.	**47**	42N	88W
Jolo: *i.*, Philippines	**91**	6N	121E
Jonesboro: U.S.A.	**43**	36N	91W
Jonglei: Sudan	**107**	7N	31E
Jönköping: Sweden	**69**	58N	14E
Joplin: U.S.A.	**43**	37N	94W
JORDAN: *cap.* 'Amman	**84**	31N	37E
Jordan: *r.*, Jordan	**84**	32N	36E
Jorhat: India	**89**	27N	94E
Jörn: Sweden	**68**	65N	20E
Joseph Bonaparte Gulf: Australia	**96**	14S	128E
Josselin: France	**70**	48N	3W
Jostedals Bre: *mtn.*, Norway	**68**	62N	7E
Jotunheimen: *mtns.*, Norway	**69**	61N	9E
Juan de Fuca, Str. of: Canada/U.S.A.	**42**	48N	125W
Juan Fernández Is.: Pacific Ocean	**101**	34S	79W
Juba: Sudan	**107**	5N	32E
Juba: *r.*, Somali Rep.	**107**	2N	42E
Jucar: *r.*, Spain	**65**	39N	1W
Juist: *i.*, Germany	**72**	54N	7E
Juiz de Fóra: Brazil	**48**	22S	43W
Jujuy: Argentina	**48**	24S	65W
Jukao: China	**89**	33N	121E
Julian Alps: It./Yugo.	**73**	46N	13E
Julich: Germany	**72**	51N	6E
Julier Pass: Switz.	**73**	46N	9E
Jullundur: India	**88**	31N	76E
Junction City: U.S.A.	**43**	39N	97W
Juneau: U.S.A.	**22**	58N	135W
Junee: Australia	**99**	35S	148E
Jungfrau: *mt.*, Switz.	**73**	47N	8E
Jur: *r.*, Sudan	**107**	9N	28E
Jura: *mtns.*, France/Switz.	**71**	47N	6E
Jura: *i. & sound*, Scotland	**54**	56N	6W
Juruá: *r.*, Brazil	**48**	5S	67W
Jussey: France	**70**	48N	6E
Juticalpa: Honduras	**47**	15N	86W
Jutland: *penin.*, Den.	**69**	36N	9E
Jyekundo: China	**90**	33N	97E
Jyväskylä: Finland	**68**	62N	26E
K2: *mtn.*, Kashmir	**87**	36N	77E
Kabaena: *i.*, Indon.	**91**	5S	122E
Kabalo: Congo Rep.	**108**	6S	27E
KABUL: Afghanistan	**87**	35N	69E
Kabwe: Zambia	**109**	15S	29E
Kadina: Australia	**99**	34S	138E
Kaduna: Nigeria	**106**	11N	7E
Kafue: & *r.*, Zambia	**109**	16S	28E
Kagoshima: Japan	**92**	32N	131E
Kagul: U.S.S.R.	**66**	46N	28E
Kaieteur Falls: Guyana	**48**	5N	59W
Kaifeng: China	**89**	35N	115E
Kai Is.: Indonesia	**91**	6S	133E
Kaikohe: N.Z.	**93**	35S	174E
Kaikoura: & *Range*, N.Z.	**93**	42S	173E
Kailas Range: China	**88**	32N	81E
Kaimanawa Mts.: New Zealand	**93**	39S	176E
Kaipara Harbour: New Zealand	**93**	36S	174E
Kaiserslautern: Ger.	**72**	49N	8E
Kaiser Wilhelm II Land: Antarc.	**51**	70S	88E
Kaitaia: N.Z.	**93**	35S	173E
Kaitangata: N.Z.	**93**	46N	170E
Kajaani: Finland	**68**	64N	28E
Kakinada: India	**88**	17N	82E
Kalabagh: W. Pak.	**88**	33N	72E
Kalachinsk: U.S.S.R.	**83**	55N	75E
Kalahari Desert: Botswana	**109**	24S	23E
Kalamata: Greece	**67**	37N	22E
Kalamazoo: U.S.A.	**41**	42N	86W
Kalat: W. Pakistan	**88**	29N	67E
Kalemie: Congo Rep.	**108**	6S	29E
Kalgoorlie: Austl.	**98**	31S	122E
Kalimnos: *i.*, Greece	**67**	37N	27E
Kalinin: U.S.S.R.	**82**	57N	36E
Kaliningrad: U.S.S.R.	**82**	55N	20E
Kalispell: U.S.A.	**42**	48N	114W
Kalisz: Poland	**66**	52N	18E
Kalmar: Sweden	**69**	57N	16E
Kalomo: Zambia	**109**	17S	26E
Kaluga: U.S.S.R.	**82**	55N	36E
Kama: *r.*, U.S.S.R.	**82**	55N	51E
Kamaran Is.: Red Sea	**85**	15N	42E
Kamchatka: U.S.S.R.	**81**	55N	160E
Kamchatka Bay: U.S.S.R.	**81**	55N	163E
Kamenskoye: U.S.S.R.	**81**	63N	165E
Kamensk-Uralskiy: U.S.S.R.	**83**	57N	62E
Kamet: *mtn.*, India/China	**88**	31N	79E
Kamienna Góra: Poland	**66**	51N	16E
Kamina: Congo Rep.	**108**	9S	25E
Kampala: Uganda	**108**	0	33E
Kampen: Neth.	**72**	53N	6E
Kamp-Lintfort: Ger.	**62**	51½N	6½E
Kamyshlov: U.S.S.R.	**83**	57N	63E
Kananga: Congo Republic	**108**	6S	22E
Kanazawa: Japan	**92**	37N	137E
Kandagach: U.S.S.R.	**83**	49N	57E
Kandahar: Afghan.	**86**	32N	66E
Kandalaksha: U.S.S.R.	**68**	67N	32E
Kandi: Dahomey	**106**	11N	3E
Kandla: India	**88**	23N	70E
Kandos: Australia	**99**	33S	150E
Kandy: Ceylon	**88**	7N	81E
Kangaroo I.: Austl.	**99**	36S	137E
Kangchenjunga: *mtn.*, Nepal/Sikkim	**89**	27N	88E
Kangean Is.: Indon.	**91**	7S	116E
Kangting: China	**90**	30N	102E
Kanin, C.: U.S.S.R.	**80**	68N	45E
Kankakee: U.S.A.	**43**	41N	88W
Kankan: Guinea	**106**	10N	9W
Kannapolis: U.S.A.	**41**	35N	80W
Kano: Nigeria	**106**	12N	8E
Kanoya: Japan	**90**	31N	131E
Kanpur: India	**88**	26N	80E
Kansas: *State*, U.S.A.	**43**	39N	98W
Kansas City: Kansas, U.S.A.	**43**	39N	95W
Kansas City: Mo., U.S.A.	**43**	39N	95W
Kansk: U.S.S.R.	**83**	56N	95E
Kansu: *Prov.*, China	**89**	35N	105E
Kanturk: R. of Irel.	**56**	52N	9W
Kao-hsiung: Formosa	**89**	23N	120E
Kapellen: Germany	**62**	51½N	6½E
Kaposvár: Hungary	**66**	46N	18E
Kapurthala: India	**88**	31N	75E
Kara: U.S.S.R.	**80**	69N	65E
Kara-Bogaz-Gol: *l.*, U.S.S.R.	**82**	42N	54E
Karabük: Turkey	**84**	41N	32E
Karachi: W. Pak.	**88**	25N	67E
Karaganda: U.S.S.R.	**83**	50N	73E
Karakoram: *mts.*, Kashmir	**87**	35N	76E
Kara-Kum: U.S.S.R.	**82**	39N	60E
Karasberg: S.W. Afr.	**109**	28S	19E
Kara Sea: U.S.S.R.	**80**	72N	62E
Kara-Tau: U.S.S.R.	**83**	44N	68E
Karaul: U.S.S.R.	**81**	70N	83E
Karbalā: 'Iraq	**85**	33N	44E
Kargil: Kashmir	**88**	35N	76E
Karibib: S.W. Afr.	**109**	22S	16E
Karl-Marx-Stadt: Germany	**72**	51N	13E
Karlovac: Yugo.	**67**	45N	16E
Karlovy Vary (Karlsbad): Czech.	**66**	50N	13E
Karlshamn: Sweden	**69**	56N	15E
Karlskoga: Sweden	**69**	59N	15E
Karlskrona: Sweden	**69**	56N	16E
Karlsruhe: Germany	**72**	49N	8E
Karlstad: Sweden	**69**	59N	13E
Karpathos: *i.*, Greece	**67**	36N	27E
Kartaly: U.S.S.R.	**83**	53N	60E
Kārun: *r.*, Iran	**86**	32N	50E
Karwar: India	**88**	15N	74E
Kasai: *r.*, Congo Rep.	**108**	4S	19E
Kasempa: Zambia	**109**	13S	26E
Kasese: Uganda	**108**	0	30E
Kāshān: Iran	**85**	34N	51E
Kashgar: China	**87**	39N	76E
Kaskaskia: *r.*, U.S.A.	**43**	39N	89W
Kasli: U.S.S.R.	**83**	56N	61E
Kasos: *i. & str.*, Greece	**67**	35N	27E
Kassala: Sudan	**107**	15N	36E
Kassala: *Prov.*, Sudan	**84**	20N	35E
Kassel: Germany	**72**	51N	9E
Katahdin, Mt.: U.S.A.	**13**	46N	69W
Katakolon: Greece	**67**	38N	21E
Katanga: Congo Republic	**108**	12S	27E
Katanning: Austl.	**98**	34S	118E
Katherine: Austl.	**96**	14S	133E
Kathiawar: *penin.*, India	**88**	22N	71E
KATMANDU: Nepal	**88**	28N	85E
Katoomba: Australia	**99**	34S	150E
Katowice: Poland	**66***	50N	19E
Katrineholm: Swed.	**69**	59N	16E
Kattegat: *str.*, Den./Sweden	**69**	57N	11E
Kauai: *i.*, Pacific O.	**101**	22N	160W
Kaufman: U.S.A.	**43**	33N	96W
Kaula: *i.*, Pacific O.	**101**	22N	160W
Kaunas: U.S.S.R.	**82**	55N	24E
Kaura Namoda: Nigeria	**106**	13N	7E
Kautokeino: Nor.	**68**	69N	23E
Kavacha: U.S.S.R.	**81**	60N	170E
Kavalla: Greece	**67**	41N	24E
Kavieng: New Irel.	**97**	3S	151E
Kawerau: N.Z.	**97**	38S	177E
Kayes: Mali	**106**	14N	11W
Kayseri: Turkey	**84**	39N	36E
Kazach'ye: U.S.S.R.	**81**	71N	136E
Kazakh S.S.R.: U.S.S.R.	**82/3**	—	—
Kazakh Uplands: U.S.S.R.	**83**	49N	75E
Kazalinsk: U.S.S.R.	**83**	46N	62E
Kazan': U.S.S.R.	**82**	56N	49E
Kazanluk: Bulgaria	**67**	43N	25E
Kea: *i.*, Greece	**67**	38N	24E
Keady: R. of Irel.	**56**	54N	7W
Kearney: U.S.A.	**43**	41N	99W
Kearny: U.S.A.	**31**	40¾N	74¼W
Kebbi: *r.*, Nigeria	**106**	13N	4E
Kecskemét: Hungary	**66**	47N	20E
Keene: U.S.A.	**17**	43N	72W
Keeper Hill: R. of Ireland	**56**	53N	8W
Keetmanshoop: S.W. Afr.	**109**	26S	18E
Kefallinia: *i.*, Greece	**67**	38N	21E
Keflavik: Iceland	**68**	64N	22W
Keighley: England	**54**	54N	2W
Kells: R. of Ireland	**56**	54N	7W
Kelso: U.S.A.	**42**	46N	123W
Kemerovo: U.S.S.R.	**83**	55N	86E
Kemi: & *r.*, Finland	**68**	66N	25E
Kemp Land: Antarc.	**51**	71S	57E
Kempsey: Australia	**99**	31S	153E
Kendal: England	**54**	54N	3W
Kenilworth: England	**57**	52½N	1½W
Kenitra: Morocco	**106**	34N	7W
Kenmare: & *r.*, R. of Ireland	**56**	52N	10W
Kenmore: U.S.A.	**43**	49N	102W
Kennebec: *r.*, U.S.A.	**13**	45N	70W
Kennedy, Cape: U.S.A.	**41**	29N	81W
Kennet: *r.*, England	**57**	51½N	1½W
Kennett: U.S.A.	**43**	36N	90W
Kennewick: U.S.A.	**42**	46N	119W
Kennicott: U.S.A.	**2**	62N	143W
Kenosha: U.S.A.	**31**	42½N	87¾W
Kensington: England	**57**	51½N	¼W
Kent: *Co.*, England	**55**	51N	1E
Kentucky: *State*, U.S.A.	**41**	37N	85W
Kentucky L.: U.S.A.	**41**	36N	88W
KENYA: *cap.* Nairobi	**108**	0	37E
Kenya, Mt.: Kenya	**108**	0	37E
Keokuk: U.S.A.	**43**	40N	92W
Keppel Bay: Austl.	**98**	23S	151E
Kerala: *State*, India	**88**	10N	76E
Kerang: Australia	**99**	36S	144E
Kerch': U.S.S.R.	**82**	45N	36E
Kerki: U.S.S.R.	**83**	38N	65E
Kerkira: *i.*, Greece	**67**	40N	20E
Kermadec Islands: Pacific Ocean	**100**	30S	179W
Kermān: Iran	**85**	30N	57E
Kermānshāh: Iran	**85**	34N	47E
Kerme, Gulf of: Turkey	**67**	37N	28E
Kerry: *Co.*, R. of Ireland	**56**	52N	10W
Kerry Head: R. of Ireland	**56**	52N	10W
Kerulen: *r.*, Mongolia	**90**	48N	111E
Kesteven: England	**55**	53N	0
Keswick: England	**54**	55N	3W
Ketchikan: U.S.A.	**22**	55N	132W
Kettering: England	**57**	52N	1W
Kewanee: U.S.A.	**43**	41N	90W
Keweenaw Penin.: U.S.A.	**43**	47N	88W
Key West: U.S.A.	**41**	25N	82W
Khabarovsk: U.S.S.R.	**81**	48N	135E
Khairpur: W. Pak.	**88**	28N	69E
Khalkis: Greece	**67**	38N	24E
Khandwa: India	**88**	22N	76E
Khania: Crete	**67**	35N	24E
Khanka, L.: U.S.S.R.	**81**	45N	133E
Khan Tengri: *mtn.*, China	**83**	42N	80E
Khanty-Mansiysk: U.S.S.R.	**83**	61N	69E
Kharagpur: India	**88**	22N	87E
Kharan: W. Pak.	**88**	28N	65E
Khārk: *i.*, Persian G.	**85**	29N	50E
Khar'kov: U.S.S.R.	**82**	50N	36E
KHARTOUM: Sudan	**107**	16N	33E
Khasi Hills: India	**88**	26N	91E
Khaskovo: Bulgaria	**67**	42N	26E
Khatanga: U.S.S.R.	**81**	72N	102E

	Page	Lat.	Long.
Kherson: U.S.S.R.	82	47N	33E
Khiumaa: *i.*, U.S.S.R.	82	59N	23E
Khiva: U.S.S.R.	83	41N	60E
Khodzheyli: U.S.S.R.	83	42N	60E
Kholmsk: U.S.S.R.	81	47N	142E
Khorāsān: Iran	85	35N	57E
Khorog: U.S.S.R.	83	37N	72E
Khorramshahr: Iran	85	30N	48E
Khotan: & *r.*, China	87	37N	80E
Khrom-Tau: U.S.S.R.	83	50N	58E
Khust: U.S.S.R.	66	48N	23E
Khuzestān: Iran	85	31N	50E
Khyber Pass: Afghan./Pak.	88	34N	71E
Kiamusze: China	90	47N	130E
Kiangsi: *Prov.*, China	89	27N	115E
Kiangsu: *Prov.*, China	89	33N	119E
Kidderminster: Eng.	57	52N	2W
Kidlington: England	57	51¾N	1¼W
Kiel: & *bay*, Ger.	66	54N	10E
Kiel Canal: Ger.	72	54N	10E
Kielce: Poland	66	51N	21E
Kiev: U.S.S.R.	82	51N	30E
Kigoma: Tanzania	108	5S	30E
Kii Channel: Japan	92	34N	135E
Kii Mts.: Japan	92	34N	136E
Kilcreggan: Scotland	54	56N	4¾W
Kildare: & *Co.*, R. of Ireland	56	53N	7W
Kildonan: Rhodesia	109	17S	31E
Kilimanjaro: *mt.*, Tanzania	108	3S	37E
Kiliya: U.S.S.R.	66	46N	29E
Kilkee: R. of Ireland	56	53N	10W
Kilkeel: N. Ireland	56	54N	6W
Kilkenny: & *Co.*, R. of Ireland	56	53N	7W
Killarney: R. of Irel.	56	52N	9W
Killyleagh: N. Irel.	56	54N	6W
Kilmallock: R. of Irel.	56	52N	9W
Kilmarnock: Scot.	54	56N	4W
Kilmore: Australia	99	37S	145E
Kilrush: R. of Irel.	56	53N	9W
Kimberley: S. Africa	109	29S	25E
Kincardine: *Co.*, Scotland	54	57N	2W
Kinder Scout: *mt.*, England	57	53½N	2W
Kindu: Congo Rep.	108	3S	26E
Kingaroy: Austl.	98	27S	152E
King Edward VII Penin.: Antarctica	51	78S	155W
King George V Coast: Antarc.	51	72S	150E
Kinghorn: Scotland	54	56N	3¼W
King I.: Australia	97	40S	144E
King Leopold & Queen Astrid Coast: Antarc.	51	67S	84E
Kingman: Arizona, U.S.A.	42	35N	114W
Kingman: Kansas, U.S.A.	43	38N	98W
King's Lynn: Eng.	55	53N	0
Kingsport: U.S.A.	41	37N	84W
Kingston: Australia	99	37S	140E
KINGSTON: Jamaica	47	18N	77W
Kingston: N.Z.	93	45S	169E
Kingston: U.S.A.	41	42N	74W
Kingston upon Hull: England	57	53¾N	½W
Kingston-upon-Thames: Eng.	57	51½N	¼W
Kingsville: U.S.A.	40	28N	98W
King William's Town: S. Africa	109	33S	27E
Kinhwa: China	89	29N	120E
Kinleith: N.Z.	93	38S	176E
Kinross: *Co.*, Scot.	54	56N	3W
Kinsale: R. of Irel.	56	52N	8W
Kinsha: *r.*, China	90	31N	99E
KINSHASA: Congo Rep.	108	4S	15E
Kinston: U.S.A.	41	35N	78W
Kintyre: Scotland	54	55N	6W
Kiølen Mts.: Nor.	68	66N	14E
Kirchheim: Ger.	73	49N	9E
Kirgiz S.S.R.: U.S.S.R.	83	42N	75E
Kirin: & *Prov.*, China	89	44N	126E
Kirkby in Ashfield: England	57	53N	1¼W
Kirkcaldy: Scotland	54	56N	3W
Kirkcudbright: & *Co.*, Scotland	54	55N	4W
Kirkenes: Norway	68	70N	30E
Kirkintilloch: Scot.	54	56N	4¼W
Kirklareli: Turkey	67	42N	27E
Kirksville: U.S.A.	43	40N	93W
Kirkuk: 'Iraq	85	35N	44E
Kirkwall: Scotland	53	59N	3W
Kirov: U.S.S.R.	82	59N	50E
Kirovabad: U.S.S.R.	82	41N	46E
Kirovograd: U.S.S.R.	82	49N	32E
Kirovsk: U.S.S.R.	83	38N	60E
Kiruna: Sweden	68	68N	20E
Kisangani: Congo Republic	108	1N	25E
Kishinev: U.S.S.R.	82	47N	29E
Kishm: Afghanistan	83	37N	70E
Kiskunfélegyháza: Hungary	66	47N	20E
Kissimmee: *r.*, U.S.A.	41	27N	81W
Kisújszállás: Hungary	66	47N	21E
Kisumu: Kenya	108	0	35E
Kithira: *i.*, Greece	67	36N	23E
Kithirai Strait: Crete	67	36N	24E
Kithnos: *i.*, Greece	67	37N	24E
Kitzbühel Alps: Austria	73	47N	12E
Kiuchüan: China	87	40N	99E
Kivak: U.S.S.R.	81	65N	174W
Kivu, L.: Congo Rep.	108	2S	29E
Kızılırmak: *r.*, Tur.	84	41N	34E
Klagenfurt: Austria	73	47N	14E
Klaipeda: U.S.S.R.	82	56N	21E
Klamath Falls: U.S.A.	42	42N	122W
Klangtu: China	89	32N	119E
Klatovy: Czech.	66	49N	13E
Klepp: Norway	69	59N	6E
Klerksdorp: S. Afr.	109	27S	26E
Klipplaat: S. Africa	109	33S	24E
Klodzko: Poland	66	50N	17E
Knokke: Belgium	70	51N	3E
Knowles, C.: Antarc.	51	72S	60W
Knox Coast: Antarc.	51	67S	105E
Knoxville: U.S.A.	41	36N	84W
Knutsford: England	57	53¼N	2¼W
Kobe: Japan	92	35N	135E
Kobenhavn: Den.	69	56N	13E
Koblenz: Germany	72	50N	8E
Kobrin: U.S.S.R.	69	52N	24E
Kochi: Japan	92	34N	134E
Kodiak I.: U.S.A.	2	57N	154W
Kofu: Japan	92	36N	139E
Kohat: W. Pakistan	88	34N	71E
Kohima: India	89	26N	94E
Kohler Ra.: Antarc.	51	75S	110W
Kokand: U.S.S.R.	83	40N	71E
Kokchetav: U.S.S.R.	83	54N	70E
Kokiu: China	89	23N	103E
Kokkola: Finland	68	64N	23E
Kokomo: U.S.A.	41	41N	86W
Koko Nor: *l.*, China	87	37N	100E
Kokura: Japan	92	34N	131E
Kola Penin.: U.S.S.R.	80	67N	38E
Kolarovgrad: Bulg.	67	43N	27E
Kolhapur: India	88	17N	74E
Köln: Germany	62	51N	7E
Kolomna: U.S.S.R.	82	55N	39E
Kolomyya: U.S.S.R.	66	48N	25E
Kolyma Plain: U.S.S.R.	81	68N	155E
Kolyma Range: U.S.S.R.	81	63N	160E
Kolyuchin, Gulf of: U.S.S.R.	81	67N	175W
Kolyvan': U.S.S.R.	83	51N	83E
Kolyvan': U.S.S.R.	83	55N	83E
Komandor Is.: U.S.S.R.	81	55N	166E
Komárno: Czech.	66	48N	18E
Komatipoort: S. Afr.	109	25S	32E
Komba: Congo Rep.	108	3N	24E
Komsomol'sk: U.S.S.R.	81	51N	137E
Kongola: Congo Republic	108	5S	27E
Kongsvinger: Nor.	69	60N	12E
Königsberg: U.S.S.R.	66	55N	20E
Konosha: U.S.S.R.	82	61N	40E
Konotop: U.S.S.R.	82	51N	33E
Konstanz: Germany	73	48N	9E
Konya: Turkey	84	38N	32E
Kopaonik Mts.: Yugo.	67	43N	21E
Koppeh Dāgh: *range*, Iran/U.S.S.R.	83	38N	57E
Korcë: Albania	67	41N	21E
Korcula: *i.*, Yugo.	67	43N	17E
Kordofan: *Prov.*, Sudan	107	13N	30E
Korea Str.: Korea/Japan	90	35N	129E
Koritsa: Albania	67	41N	21E
Korsakov: U.S.S.R.	81	47N	143E
Kortrijk: Belgium	70	51N	3E
Korumburra: Austl.	99	38S	146E
Kos: *i.*, Greece	67	37N	27E
Kosaka: Japan	90	40N	141E
Kosciusko, Mt.: Australia	99	36N	148E
Kosh-Agach: U.S.S.R.	83	50N	89E
Kosi: *r.*, Nepal/India	88	26N	87E
Košice: Czech.	66	49N	21E
Kosovska Mitrovica: Yugoslavia	67	43N	21E
Kostamo: Finland	68	67N	27E
Kostroma: U.S.S.R.	82	57N	41E
Koszalin: Poland	66	54N	17E
Kota Bahru: Malaya	91	6N	102E
Kota Kinabalu: Sabah	91	6N	116E
Kotah: India	88	25N	76E
Kothen: Germany	72	52N	12E
Kotka: Finland	69	60N	27E
Kotlach: Austria	66	47N	15E
Kotlas: U.S.S.R.	82	61N	47E
Kotor: Yugoslavia	67	42N	19E
Kotri: W. Pakistan	88	25N	68E
Kounradskiy: U.S.S.R.	83	47N	75E
Kovel': U.S.S.R.	82	51N	25E
Kovrov: U.S.S.R.	82	56N	41E
Kowloon: Hong Kong	89	22N	114E
Kozani: Greece	67	40N	22E
Kozhikode: India	88	11N	76E
Kra, Isthmus of: Thailand	91	10N	99E
Kragujevac: Yugo.	67	44N	21E
Krakatau: *volc.*, Indonesia	91	6S	105E
Kraków: Poland	66	50N	20E
Kraljevo: Yugo.	67	44N	21E
Kramfors: Sweden	68	63N	18E
Krasnodar: U.S.S.R.	82	45N	39E
Krasnovodsk: U.S.S.R.	82	40N	53E
Krasnoyarsk: U.S.S.R.	83	56N	96E
Krasnyy Kut: U.S.S.R.	82	51N	47E
Krasnyy Luch: U.S.S.R.	82	48N	38E
Kratié: Cambodia	91	12N	106E
Krefeld: Germany	62	51N	6E
Kremenchug: U.S.S.R.	82	49N	33E
Krishna: *r.*, India	88	17N	75E
Krishnagar: India	88	23N	88E
Kristiansand: Nor.	69	58N	8E
Kristianstad: Swed.	69	56N	14E
Kristiansund: Nor.	68	63N	8E
Kristinehamn: Swed.	69	59N	14E
Krivoy Rog: U.S.S.R.	82	48N	33E
Krk: *i.*, Yugoslavia	67	45N	15E
Kronotskiy Bay: U.S.S.R.	81	54N	162E
Kron Prinsesse Märtha Coast: Antarctica	51	73S	5W
Kron Prins Olaf Coast: Antarc.	51	70S	43E
Kronshtadt: U.S.S.R.	69	60N	30E
Kroonstad: S. Afr.	109	27S	27E
Krotoszyn: Poland	66	52N	18E
Kruševac: Yugo.	67	44N	21E
KUALA LUMPUR: Malaysia and Malaya	91	3N	102E
Kuantan: Malaya	91	4N	103E
Kuban: *r.*, U.S.S.R.	82	45N	38E
Kuching: Sarawak	91	2N	110E
Kudat: Sabah	91	7N	117E
Kufra Oases: Libya	107	25N	22E
Kufstein: Austria	73	48N	12E
Kukës: Albania	67	42N	20E
Kükong: China	89	25N	113E
Kulmbach: Ger.	72	50N	11E
Kulunda Steppe: U.S.S.R.	83	53N	77E
Kulundinskoye, L.: U.S.S.R.	83	53N	80E
Kumamoto: Japan	92	33N	131E
Kumasi: Ghana	106	7N	2W
Kunene: *r.*, Angola/S.W. Africa	109	17S	13E
Kungrad: U.S.S.R.	83	43N	59E
Kunlun Mts.: China	87	36N	80E
Kunming: China	89	25N	103E
Kunshan: China	90	31½N	121E
Kuopio: Finland	68	63N	28E
Kupang: Timor	91	10S	124E
Kuparuk: *r.*, U.S.A.	28	69N	150W
Kurdistan: Tur./Iran	85	37N	45E
Kure: Japan	92	34N	133E
Kurgan: U.S.S.R.	83	55N	65E
Kuria Muria Is.: Arabian Sea	85	17N	56E
Kuril Is.: U.S.S.R.	100	45N	150E
Kurnool: India	88	16N	78E
Kurow: N.Z.	93	45S	171E
Kursk: U.S.S.R.	82	52N	36E
Kushka: U.S.S.R.	83	35N	62E
Kushva: U.S.S.R.	83	58N	60E
Kustanay: U.S.S.R.	83	53N	64E
Kütahya: Turkey	84	39N	30E
Kutaisi: U.S.S.R.	82	42N	42E
Kutaradja: Indon.	87	5N	95E
Kutno: Poland	66	52N	19E
Kutum: Sudan	84	14N	24E
Kuusjärvi: Finland	68	63N	29E
KUWAIT: *cap.* Kuwait	85	29N	48E
Kuybyshev: U.S.S.R.	83	55N	78E
Kuybyshev: U.S.S.R.	82	53N	50E
Kuzbass: U.S.S.R.	83	55N	85E
Kwangsi Chuan A.R.: China	89	24N	108E
Kwantung: *Prov.*, China	89	23N	113E
Kweichow: *Prov.*, China	89	26N	107E
Kweichu: China	90	26N	107E
Kweilin: China	89	25N	110E
Kweisui: China	89	41N	112E
Kweiyang: China	89	26N	107E
Kyle of Lochalsh: Scotland	53	57N	6W
Kynsna: S. Africa	109	34S	23E
Kyoga, L.: Uganda	108	2N	33E
Kyoga Point: Japan	92	36N	135E
Kyongju: S. Korea	90	36N	129E
Kyongsong: S. Korea	90	38N	127E
Kyoto: Japan	92	35N	136E
Kyushu: *i.*, Japan	92	33N	131E
Kyushu Mts.: Japan	92	32N	131E
Kyustendil: Bulgaria	67	42N	23E
Kyzl: U.S.S.R.	81	52N	95E
Kyzyl-Kum: U.S.S.R.	83	43N	64E
Kzyl-Orda: U.S.S.R.	83	45N	65E
La Albuera: Spain	65	39N	7W
La Bastide: France	71	45N	1W
La Baule: France	70	47N	2W
Labe: *r.*, Czech.	72	50N	14E
La Blanquilla: *i.*, Caribbean Sea	47	12N	65W
Labuan: *i.*, Sabah	91	5N	15E
Lacapelle-Marival: France	71	45N	2E
Lacaune, Mts. de: Fr.	71	44N	3E
Laccadive: *is.* & *sea*, India	87	12N	73E
La Chârtre: France	71	47N	2E
La Chaux: France	71	46N	6E
La Chaux-de-Fonds: Switzerland	73	47N	7E
Lachlan: *r.*, Australia	99	33S	148E
La Ciotat: France	77	43N	6E
Laconia: U.S.A.	17	43N	72W
Lacq: France	71	43N	1W
La Crosse: U.S.A.	43	44N	91W
Ladakh R.: Kashmir	88	34N	77E
Ladismith: S. Africa	109	34S	21E
Ladoga, L.: U.S.S.R.	82	61N	31E
Lady Elliot I.: Austl.	98	24S	153E
Ladysmith: S. Africa	109	28S	30E
Lae: N.E. New Guin.	97	7S	147E
La Fayette: U.S.A.	41	40N	87W
Lafayette: U.S.A.	40	30N	92W
La Flèche: France	70	48N	0
Laghouat: Algeria	106	34N	3E
LAGOS: Nigeria	106	6N	3E
Lagos: Portugal	65	37N	9W
La Grande: U.S.A.	42	45N	118W
La Grange: U.S.A.	41	33N	85W
La Guaira: Venez.	48	11N	67W
Laguna Madre: U.S.A.	40	26N	97W
Lahej: Yemen P.D.R.	85	13N	45E
Lahn: *r.*, Germany	72	50N	8E
Lahore: W. Pakistan	88	32N	75E
Lahr: Germany	73	48N	8E
Lahti: Finland	68	61N	26E
La Junta: U.S.A.	40	38N	104W
Lake Chad Basin: Chad	106	13N	15E
Lake Charles: *city*, U.S.A.	41	30N	93W
Lake City: U.S.A.	41	30N	83W
Lake District: Eng.	54	54N	3W
Lakeland: U.S.A.	41	28N	82W
Lakhimpur: India	88	28N	81E
La Linea: Spain	65	36N	5W
La Louvière: Belg.	70	50N	4E
Lamballe: France	70	48N	3W
Lambeth: England	57	51½N	0
Lame Deer: U.S.A.	42	46N	107W
Lamesa: U.S.A.	43	33N	102W
Lamia: Greece	67	39N	22E
La Montaña: Peru	48	11S	72W
Lampedusa: *i.*, Italy	67	36N	13E
Lampeter: Wales	55	52N	4W
Lanak Pass: China/Kashmir	88	34N	80E
Lanark: & *Co.*, Scot.	54	56N	4W
Lancashire: *Co.*, Eng.	54	54N	3W
Lancaster: England	54	54N	3W
Lancaster: Ohio, U.S.A.	41	40N	83W
Lancaster: Pa., U.S.A.	41	40N	76W
Lanchow: China	89	36N	104E
Lanciano: Italy	67	42N	14E
Landerneau: France	70	48N	4W
Landeshut: Poland	66	51N	16E
Landsberg: Poland	66	53N	15E
Land's End: Eng.	55	50N	6W
Landshut: Germany	73	49N	12E
Langenberg: Ger.	62	51¼N	7¼E
Langenfeld: Ger.	62	51N	7E
Langeoog: *i.*, Ger.	72	54N	7E
Langon: France	71	45N	0
Langreo: Spain	65	43N	6W
Langres: France	70	48N	5E
Langres, Plateau de: France	70	48N	5E
Languedoc: *Old Prov.*, France	71	44N	4E
Lannion: France	70	49N	4W
Lans, Mts. de: France	71	45N	6W
Lansing: U.S.A.	31	43N	85W
Lanzarote: *i.*, Canary Islands	106	29N	13W
Laoighis: *Co.*, R. of Ireland	56	53N	7W
Lao Kay: N. Viet Nam	90	23N	104E
Laon: France	70	50N	4E
LAOS: *cap.* Vientiane	91	18N	104E
Lapalisse: France	71	46N	4E
La Paz: Bolivia	48	16S	68E
Lapland: Scandinavia	68	68N	25E
La Plata: Argentina	50	35S	58W
Lappeenranta: Fin.	68	61N	28E
Laptev Sea: U.S.S.R.	81	75N	125E
Laptev Str.: U.S.S.R.	81	73N	142E
Larache: Morocco	65	35N	6W
Laramie: U.S.A.	43	41N	106W
Larche: France	71	44N	7E
Laredo: U.S.A.	40	28N	99W
Lārestān: Iran	85	28N	54E
Largs: Scotland	54	55¾N	4¾W
La Rioja: Argentina	49	29S	67W
Larisa: Greece	67	40N	22E
Larne: N. Ireland	56	55N	6W
La Rochelle: France	71	46N	1W
La Roche sur Yon: Fr.	71	47N	1W
La Romana: Dominican Rep.	39	19N	69W

	Page	Lat.	Long.
Larsen Ice Shelf: Antarctica	**51**	68S	64W
Larzac, Causse du: Fr.	**71**	44N	3E
Las Cruces: U.S.A.	**42**	32N	107W
La Serena: Chile	**49**	30S	71W
La Seyne-sur-mer: France	**71**	43N	6E
Lashio: Burma	**90**	23N	98E
Las Marismas: *marsh*, Spain	**65**	37N	6W
Las Palmas: Canary Islands	**106**	28N	15W
La Spezia: Italy	**73**	44N	10E
Lassalle: France	**71**	44N	4E
Lassen Peak: U.S.A.	**42**	41N	121W
Lastoursville: Gabon	**108**	1S	13E
Lastovo: *i.*, Yugo.	**67**	43N	17E
Las Vegas: Nevada, U.S.A.	**42**	36N	115W
Las Vegas: N. Mex., U.S.A.	**43**	36N	105W
Las Yungas: *mtns.*, Bolivia	**42**	16S	67W
Latakia: Syria	**84**	36N	36E
Latium: Italy	**67**	42N	12E
La Tortuga: *i.*, Venez.	**47**	11N	65W
La Tour-du-Pin: Fr.	**71**	46N	5E
Latvian S.S.R.: U.S.S.R.	**82**	57N	35E
Lauder: Scotland	**54**	56N	3W
Launceston: Tas.	**97**	41S	147E
Laurel: Miss., U.S.A.	**41**	32N	89W
Laurel: Mont., U.S.A.	**42**	46N	109W
Laurie I.: Antarc.	**51**	61S	44W
Lausanne: Switz.	**73**	46N	7E
Laut: *i.*, Indonesia	**91**	4S	116E
Laval: France	**70**	48N	1W
La Vega: Dom. Rep.	**39**	19N	70W
Laverton: Australia	**98**	29S	123E
Lawgi: Australia	**98**	25S	151E
Lawrence: U.S.A.	**31**	42½N	71¼W
Lawton: U.S.A.	**43**	35N	98W
Lead: U.S.A.	**43**	44N	104W
Leatherhead: Eng.	**57**	51¼N	¼W
LEBANON: *cap.* Beirut	**84**	34N	36E
Lebanon: U.S.A.	**41**	36N	86W
Le Blanc: France	**71**	47N	1E
Lebu: Chile	**49**	38S	74W
Le Cateau: France	**70**	50N	4E
Lecce: Italy	**67**	40N	18E
Lecco: Italy	**73**	46N	9E
Lech: *r.*, Austr./Ger.	**73**	48N	11E
Le Chambon-Feugerolles: Fr.	**71**	45N	4E
Le Conquet: France	**70**	48N	5W
Le Creusot: France	**71**	47N	4E
Le Croisic: France	**70**	47N	2W
Lectoure: France	**71**	44N	1E
Lee: *r.*, R. of Ireland	**56**	52N	9W
Leeds: England	**57**	54N	2W
Leeds: U.S.A.	**43**	48N	100W
Leek: England	**57**	53N	2W
Leer: Germany	**72**	53N	7E
Leeton: Australia	**99**	35S	146E
Leeuwarden: Neth.	**72**	53N	6E
Leeuwin, C.: Austl.	**98**	34S	115E
Leeward Is.: W. Ind.	**47**	17N	63W
Legaspi: Philippines	**91**	13N	124E
Leghorn: Italy	**73**	44N	10E
Legnano: Italy	**73**	46N	9E
Leh: Kashmir	**88**	34N	78E
Le Havre: France	**70**	50N	0
Lehrte: Germany	**72**	52N	10E
Leicester: & *Co.*, England	**57**	53N	1W
Leichhardt R.: Austl.	**98**	21S	148E
Leichlingen: Ger.	**62**	51N	7E
Leiden: Netherlands	**72**	52N	4E
Leigh: England	**57**	53½N	2½W
Leigh Creek: *town*, Australia	**99**	31S	138E
Leighton Buzzard: England	**57**	52N	¾W
Leikanger: Norway	**68**	61N	7E
Leinster: *Old Prov.*, Ireland	**56**	53N	7W
Leipzig: Germany	**72**	51N	12E
Leith: Scotland	**54**	56N	3W
Leitrim: *Co.*, R. of Ireland	**56**	54N	8W
Lek: *r.*, Netherlands	**72**	52N	5E
Léman, L.: Switz./France	**73**	46N	7E
Le Mans: France	**70**	48N	0
Lemnos: *i.*, Greece	**67**	40N	25E
Le Monastier: Fr.	**71**	45N	4E
Lena: *r.*, U.S.S.R.	**81**	64N	126E
Leninabad: U.S.S.R.	**83**	40N	70E
Leninakan: U.S.S.R.	**82**	41N	44E
Leningrad: U.S.S.R.	**82**	60N	30E
Leninogorsk: U.S.S.R.	**83**	50N	84E
Lenin Pk.: U.S.S.R.	**83**	39N	73E
Leninsk-Kuznetskiy: U.S.S.R.	**83**	55N	86E
Lennox Hills: Scot.	**54**	56N	4¼W
Lens: France	**70**	50N	3E
Leoben: Austria	**66**	47N	15E
Leominster: Eng.	**55**	52N	3W
Leominster: U.S.A.	**31**	42½N	71¾W
León: Mexico	**38**	21N	102W
León: & *Old Prov.*, Spain	**65**	43N	6W
Leonora: Australia	**98**	29S	121E
Léopold II, Lake: Congo Republic	**108**	2S	17E
Lepini Mts.: Italy	**67**	42N	13E
Lepontine Alps: Switz./Italy	**73**	46N	8E
Le Puy: France	**71**	45N	4E
Lérida: Spain	**65**	42N	1E
Leros: *i.*, Greece	**67**	37N	27E
Les Bains du Mont Dore: France	**71**	46N	3E
Les Baux: France	**71**	44N	5E
Lesbos: *i.*, Greece	**67**	39N	26E
Les Ecréhou: *is.*, Channel Islands	**55**	*Inset*	
Les Landes: France	**71**	44N	1W
Les Monts Faucilles: France	**70**	48N	6E
LESOTHO: *cap.* Maseru	**109**	29S	27E
Les Sables d'Olonne: France	**71**	47N	2W
Les Saintes Maries: France	**71**	43N	4E
Les Sept Iles: Fr.	**70**	49N	3W
Lesser Antilles: *arch.*, West Indies	**47**	15N	62W
Letchworth: Eng.	**55**	52N	0
Leticia: Colombia	**48**	4S	70W
Le Touquet: France	**70**	51N	2E
Le Tréport: France	**70**	50N	1E
Leuven: Belgium	**70**	51N	5E
Leven, L.: Scotland	**54**	56½N	3½W
Leveque, C.: Austl.	**96**	17S	123E
Le Verdon: France	**71**	46N	1W
Leverkusen: Ger.	**62**	51N	7E
Levice: Czecho.	**66**	48N	18E
Le Vigan: France	**71**	44N	4E
Levittown: U.S.A.	**31**	40¾N	73½W
Lewes: England	**55**	51N	0
Lewis: *i.*, Scotland	**53**	58N	7W
Lewisham: England	**57**	51½N	0
Lewiston: Maine, U.S.A.	**13**	44N	70W
Lewiston: Wash., U.S.A.	**42**	46N	117W
Lewistown: U.S.A.	**42**	47N	109W
Lexington: Ken., U.S.A.	**41**	38N	84W
Lexington: Mass., U.S.A.	**31**	42½N	71¼W
Leyburn: Australia	**98**	28S	152E
Leydsdorp: S. Africa	**109**	24S	31E
Leyland: England	**57**	53¾N	2¾W
Leyre: *r.*, France	**71**	45N	1W
Leyte: *i.*, Philippines	**91**	11N	125E
Lhasa: China	**87**	30N	91E
L'Hospitalet: France	**71**	43N	2E
Liao: *r.*, China	**89**	41N	122E
Liaoning: *Prov.*, China	**89**	41N	121E
Liaotung Bay: China	**89**	41N	121E
Liaotung Penin.: China	**89**	40N	123E
Liaoyang: China	**89**	42N	124E
Libby: U.S.A.	**42**	48N	116W
Liberal: U.S.A.	**43**	37N	101W
Liberec: Czecho.	**66**	51N	15E
LIBERIA: *cap.* Monrovia	**106**	7N	10W
Liberia: Costa Rica	**47**	11N	85W
Libourne: France	**71**	45N	0
LIBREVILLE: Gabon	**108**	0	10E
LIBYA: *caps.* Tripoli and Benghazi	**106/7**	—	—
Libyan Desert: Libya/Egypt	**107**	25N	25E
Libyan Plat.: Egypt	**84**	30N	27E
Licata: Sicily	**67**	37N	14E
Lichfield: England	**57**	53N	2W
Lichtenburg: S. Afr.	**109**	26S	26E
Licking: *r.*, U.S.A.	**41**	38N	84W
Lida: U.S.S.R.	**66**	54N	25E
Lidköping: Sweden	**69**	58N	13E
LIECHTENSTEIN: *cap.* Vaduz	**73**	47N	10E
Liège: Belgium	**70**	51N	6E
Lieksa: Finland	**68**	63N	30E
Lienz: Austria	**73**	47N	13E
Liepája: U.S.S.R.	**82**	57N	21E
Lier: Belgium	**70**	51N	5E
Liestal: Switzerland	**73**	47N	8E
Liévin: France	**70**	50N	3E
Liffey: *r.*, R. of Irel.	**56**	53N	6W
Ligny: Belgium	**70**	50N	5E
Liguria: *Reg.*, Italy	**73**	44N	9E
Ligurian Apennines: Italy	**73**	44N	9E
Ligurian Sea: Italy	**65**	43N	9E
Likasi: Congo Rep.	**108**	11S	27E
Lille: France	**70**	51N	3E
Lillehammer: Nor.	**69**	61N	11E
LILONGWE: Malawi	**109**	14S	34E
LIMA: Peru	**48**	12S	77W
Lima: U.S.A.	**41**	41N	84W
Limagne: France	**71**	46N	3E
Limassol: Cyprus	**84**	40N	33E
Limavady: N. Irel.	**56**	55N	7W
Limburg: Germany	**72**	50N	8E
Limburg: *Prov.*, Netherlands	**72**	51N	6E
Limerick: & *Co.*, R. of Ireland	**56**	53N	9W
Limoges: France	**71**	46N	1E
Limón: Costa Rica	**47**	10N	83W
Limousin: *Old Prov.*, France	**71**	46N	1E
Limpopo: *r.*, Mozam.	**109**	23S	33E
Linares: Mexico	**40**	25N	100W
Linares: Spain	**65**	38N	4W
Linaro, C.: Italy	**67**	42N	12E
Lincoln: & *Co.*, Eng.	**55**	53N	1W
Lincoln: Ill., U.S.A.	**43**	40N	89W
Lincoln: Nebraska, U.S.A.	**43**	41N	97W
Lincoln Park: U.S.A.	**31**	42¼N	83¼W
Lincolnwood: U.S.A.	**31**	42N	87¾W
Linden: U.S.A.	**31**	40½N	74¼W
Lindsey: England	**54**	53N	0
Line Is.: Pacific O.	**101**	0	158W
Lingen: Germany	**72**	52N	7E
Lingga: *i.*, Indonesia	**91**	0	105E
Linguéré: Senegal	**106**	15N	15W
Linköping: Sweden	**69**	58N	16E
Linlithgow: Scotland	**54**	56N	3½W
Linnhe, L.: Scotland	**54**	57N	5W
Linton: U.S.A.	**43**	46N	100W
Linz: Austria	**73**	48N	14E
Lions, G. of: France	**71**	43N	4E
Lipari Is.: Italy	**67**	38N	15E
Lipetsk: U.S.S.R.	**82**	53N	40E
Lippstadt: Germany	**72**	52N	8E
LISBON: Portugal	**65**	39N	9W
Lisburn: N. Ireland	**56**	55N	6W
Lisburne, C.: U.S.A.	**2**	69N	166W
Lisianski: *i.*, Pac. O.	**100**	27N	175W
Lisieux: France	**70**	49N	0
Lismore: Australia	**99**	29S	153E
Lismore: R. of Irel.	**56**	52N	8W
Lispeszentadorján: Hungary	**66**	47N	17E
Lister, Mt.: Antarc.	**51**	78S	164E
Listowel: R. of Irel.	**56**	52N	9W
Lithgow: Australia	**99**	33S	150E
Lithuanian S.S.R.: U.S.S.R.	**82**	55N	24E
Little Atlas: *mtns.*, Algeria	**65**	36N	3E
Little Belt: *str.*, Den.	**69**	55N	10E
Little Bitter Lake: Egypt	**107**	*Inset*	
Little Black: *r.*, U.S.A.	**28**	67N	144W
Littlefield: U.S.A.	**43**	34N	102W
Little Karroo: S. Afr.	**109**	34S	22E
Little Minch: *chan.*, Scotland	**53**	58N	7W
Little Rock: U.S.A.	**43**	35N	92W
Little St. Bernard Pass: Fr./Italy	**73**	46N	7E
Liuchow: China	**89**	24N	109E
Livermore, Mt.: U.S.A.	**40**	30N	105W
Liverpool: Australia	**99**	34S	151E
Liverpool: England	**57**	53N	3W
Liverpool Plains: Australia	**99**	31S	150E
Livingstone: Zambia	**109**	18S	26E
Livingstone Falls: Congo Republic	**108**	5S	14E
Livingstone I.: Antarctica	**51**	63S	60W
Livorno: Italy	**73**	44N	10E
Livradois, Massif du: *mtns.*, France	**71**	45N	3E
Lizard Point: Eng.	**55**	50N	5W
Ljubljana: Yugo.	**66**	46N	14E
Ljunga: *r.*, Sweden	**68**	62N	17E
Llandrindod Wells: Wales	**55**	52N	3W
Llandudno: Wales	**55**	53N	4W
Llanelli: Wales	**55**	52N	4W
Llangollen: Wales	**57**	53N	3W
Llanidloes: Wales	**55**	52N	4W
Llano Estacado: U.S.A.	**43**	33N	103W
Llanos de Guarayos: Bolivia	**48**	15S	63W
Llanos de Urgel: Sp.	**65**	41N	0
Lleyn: Wales	**55**	53N	5W
Lo: *r.*, China	**89**	37N	109E
Lobito: Angola	**108**	12S	14E
Lockerbie: Scotland	**54**	55N	3W
Lod (Lydda): Israel	**84**	32N	35E
Lodi: Italy	**73**	45N	9E
Lodi: U.S.A.	**31**	40¾N	74W
Łodź: Poland	**66**	52N	19E
Lofoten Is.: Norway	**68**	68N	13E
Logan: Utah, U.S.A.	**42**	42N	112W
Logan: W. Va., U.S.A.	**41**	38N	82W
Logansport: U.S.A.	**41**	41N	86W
Logroño: Spain	**65**	42N	2W
Loir: *r.*, France	**71**	48N	0
Loire: *r.*, France	**70**	47N	1W
Lója: Ecuador	**48**	4S	79W
Lokchong: China	**89**	25N	113E
Lolland: *i.*, Denmark	**69**	55N	11E
Lombard: U.S.A.	**31**	42N	88W
Lombardy: & *Plain*, Italy	**73**	45N	9E
Lomblen: *i.*, Indon.	**91**	8S	123E
Lombok: *i.* & *str.*, Indonesia	**91**	8S	116E
LOMÉ: Togo	**106**	6N	1E
Lommel: Belgium	**70**	51N	5E
Lomond, L.: Scot.	**54**	56N	5W
Łomża: Poland	**66**	53N	22E
LONDON: England	**57**	51N	0
Londonderry: & *Co.*, N. Ireland	**56**	55N	7W
Long Bay: U.S.A.	**41**	34N	79W
Long Beach: Calif., U.S.A.	**42**	34N	118W
Long Beach: N.Y., U.S.A.	**31**	40½N	73¾W
Longford: & *Co.*, R. of Ireland	**56**	54N	8W
Long I.: Australia	**98**	22S	150E
Long I.: Bahama Is.	**47**	23N	75W
Long I.: U.S.A.	**41**	41N	73W
Long, L.: Scotland	**54**	56N	4¾W
Longmont: U.S.A.	**43**	40N	105W
Longreach: Austl.	**97**	23S	144E
Longridge: England	**57**	53¾N	2½W
Longuyon: France	**70**	49N	6E
Longview: Oregon, U.S.A.	**42**	46N	123W
Longview: Texas, U.S.A.	**40**	33N	95W
Longwy: France	**70**	49N	6E
Lønsdal: Norway	**68**	67N	16E
Lons-le-Saunier: Fr.	**71**	47N	6E
Lookout, C.: U.S.A.	**41**	35N	77W
Lopei: China	**90**	48N	131E
Lorain: U.S.A.	**41**	41N	83W
Lorca: Spain	**65**	38N	2W
Lorestān: Iran	**85**	33N	48E
Lorient: France	**70**	48N	3W
Lorne, Firth of: Scot.	**54**	56N	6W
Lörrach: Germany	**73**	48N	8E
Lorraine: *Old Prov.*, France	**70**	49N	6E
Los Alamos: U.S.A.	**42**	36N	106W
Los Andes: Chile	**48**	33S	71W
Los Angeles: U.S.A.	**46**	34N	118W
Lossiemouth: Scot.	**53**	58N	3W
Lot: *r.*, France	**71**	44N	1E
Loue: *r.*, France	**71**	47N	6E
Loughborough: Eng.	**57**	53N	1W
Loughrea: R. of Irel.	**56**	53N	9W
Loughton: England	**57**	51¾N	0
Louisiade Archipelago: Coral Sea	**97**	11S	153E
Louisiana: *State*, U.S.A.	**43**	33N	93W
Louis Trichardt: S. Africa	**109**	23S	30E
Louisville: U.S.A.	**41**	38N	86W
Loukhi: U.S.S.R.	**68**	66N	33E
Loup City: U.S.A.	**43**	41N	99W
Lourdes: France	**71**	43N	0
LOURENÇO MARQUES: Mozambique	**109**	26S	33E
Louth: England	**55**	53N	0
Louth: *Co.*, R. of Irel.	**56**	54N	6W
Louvain *see* Leuven			
Lowell: U.S.A.	**31**	42¾N	71¼W
Lower California: *Territ.*, Mexico	**38**	27N	113W
Lower Lough Erne: N. Ireland	**56**	55N	8W
Lower Tunguska: *r.*, U.S.S.R.	**81**	64N	95E
Lowestoft: England	**55**	52N	2E
Lowicz: Poland	**66**	52N	20E
Lowville: U.S.A.	**17**	44N	75W
Loyalty Is.: Pac. O.	**100**	20S	165E
Loyang: China	**89**	35N	112E
Lu: *r.*, China	**90**	30N	97E
Lualaba: *r.*, Congo Republic	**108**	6S	26E
LUANDA: Angola	**108**	9S	13E
Luangprabang: Laos	**90**	20N	102E
Luanshya: Zambia	**109**	13S	28E
Lubbock: U.S.A.	**43**	34N	102W
Lübeck: & *bay*, Ger.	**72**	54N	11E
Lubéron, Montagne du: France	**71**	44N	5E
Lublin: Poland	**66**	51N	23E
Lubumbashi: Congo Republic	**108**	12S	27E
Lucca: Italy	**73**	44N	10E
Luce Bay: Scotland	**54**	55N	5W
Lučenec: Czech.	**66**	48N	20E
Lucerne, L.: Switz.	**73**	47N	8E
Lucin: U.S.A.	**42**	41N	114W
Luckenwalde: Ger.	**72**	52N	13E
Lucknow: India	**88**	27N	81E
Lüdenscheid: Ger.	**72**	51N	8E
Lüderitz: S.W. Afr.	**109**	27S	15E
Ludhiana: India	**88**	31N	76E
Ludlow: England	**55**	52N	3W
Ludlow: U.S.A.	**42**	35N	116W
Ludvika: Sweden	**69**	60N	15E
Ludwigsburg: Ger.	**72**	49N	9E
Ludwigshafen: Ger.	**72**	49N	8E
Ludwigslust: Ger.	**72**	53N	12E
Lufkin: U.S.A.	**40**	31N	95W
Luga: U.S.S.R.	**69**	59N	30E
Lugano: Switzerland	**73**	46N	9E
Lugansk: U.S.S.R.	**82**	48N	40E
Lugnaquilla: *mtn.*, R. of Ireland	**56**	53N	6W
Lugo: Spain	**65**	43N	8W
Lugoj: Romania	**66**	46N	22E
Luhsien: China	**89**	29N	106E
Luichow Penin.: China	**89**	21N	110E
Luitpold Coast: Antarctica	**51**	78S	30W
Luleå: Sweden	**68**	66N	22E
Lüleburgaz: Turkey	**67**	41N	27E
Lumberton: U.S.A.	**41**	34N	79W
Lumsden: N.Z.	**93**	46S	168E
Lund: Sweden	**69**	56N	13E
Lundy I.: England	**55**	51N	5W
Lune: *r.*, England	**54**	54N	3W
Lüneburg: & *Heath*, Germany	**72**	53N	10E
Lunéville: France	**70**	49N	6E
Lungkiang: China	**89**	47N	124E

	Page	Lat.	Long.
Lure: France	70	48N	6E
Lurgan: N. Ireland	56	54N	6W
Lusaka: Zambia	109	15S	28E
Lusambo: Congo Republic	108	5S	23E
Lushai Hills: India	89	23N	93E
Lussac-les-Châteaux: France	71	46N	1E
Lü-ta: China	89	39N	121E
Luton: England	57	52N	0
Lutsk: U.S.S.R.	66	51N	25E
Lutterworth: Eng.	57	52½N	1¼W
Lützow-Holm Bay: Antarctica	51	69S	36E
LUXEMBOURG: *cap.* Luxembourg	70	50N	6E
Luxor: Egypt	84	26N	33E
Luzern (Lucerne): Switzerland	73	47N	8E
Luzon: *i.*, Phil.	91	15N	121E
Luzy: France	71	47N	4E
L'vov: U.S.S.R.	82	50N	24E
Lyakhov Is.: U.S.S.R.	81	73N	142E
Lyallpur: W. Pak.	88	31N	73E
Lydda *see* Lod			
Lydenburg: S. Africa	109	25S	30E
Lyme Bay: England	55	51N	3W
Lynbrook: U.S.A.	31	40¾N	73¾W
Lynchburg: U.S.A.	41	37N	79W
Lynn: U.S.A.	31	42N	71W
Lyonnais: *Old Prov.*, France	71	46N	4E
Lyons (Lyon): Fr.	71	46N	5E
Lys: *r.*, Belgium	70	51N	3E
Lys'va: U.S.S.R.	83	58N	58E
Lytham: England	57	53¾N	3W
Lyttleton: N.Z.	93	44S	173E
Ma'an: Jordan	84	30N	36E
Maarianhamina: Fin.	69	60N	20E
Maas: *r.*, Neth.	72	52N	5E
Maastricht: Neth.	72	51N	6E
McAlester: U.S.A.	43	35N	96W
McAllen: U.S.A.	40	26N	98W
Macao: China	89	22N	113E
Macclesfield: Eng.	57	53N	2W
McClintock, Mt.: Antarctica	51	83S	160E
McComb: U.S.A.	40	31N	90W
McCook: U.S.A.	43	40N	101W
Macdonnell Ranges: Australia	96	24S	132E
Macedonia: Yugo./Greece	67	41N	22E
Maceió: Brazil	43	10S	36W
Macequece: Mozam.	109	19S	33E
Macerata: Italy	67	43N	13E
McGehee: U.S.A.	40	34N	91W
Macgillycuddy's Reeks: R. of Irel.	56	52N	10W
Machichaco, C.: Sp.	65	43N	3W
Machiques: Venez.	47	10N	73W
Machrihanish: Scot.	54	55N	6W
McIntosh: U.S.A.	43	46N	101W
Mackay: Australia	98	21S	149E
Mackay, L.: Australia	96	23S	128E
Mackenzie: Guyana	48	6N	58W
Mackenzie: *r.*, Austl.	98	23S	149E
Mackenzie Bay: Antarctica	51	69S	72E
Mackinac, Str. of: U.S.A./Canada	17	46N	85W
McKinley, Mt.: U.S.A.	2	63N	151W
McKinney: U.S.A.	43	33N	97W
Macksville: Australia	99	31S	153E
McMurdo Sound: Antarctica	51	78S	168E
Mâcon: France	71	46N	5E
Macon: U.S.A.	41	33N	84W
Macquarie: *r.*, Austl.	99	31S	148E
Macquarie I.: Pac. O.	100	55S	159E
McRae: U.S.A.	41	32N	83W
Macroom: R. of Irel.	56	52N	9W
Madagascar: *see* MALAGASY REP.			
Madang: NE. New Guinea	88	5S	146E
Maddalena Pass: France/Italy	73	44N	7E
Madeira: *i.*, Atlantic Ocean	106	33N	17W
Madeira: *r.*, Brazil	48	5S	61W
Madera: U.S.A.	42	37N	120W
Madhya Pradesh: *State*, India	88	23N	78E
MADINET AS SHAAB: Yemen D.R.	85	13N	45E
Madison: Florida, U.S.A.	41	30N	84W
Madison: Ind., U.S.A.	41	39N	85W
Madison: S. Dakota, U.S.A.	43	44N	97W
Madison: Wisc., U.S.A.	41	43N	89W
Madison Heights: U.S.A.	31	42½N	83W
Madisonville: U.S.A.	41	37N	88W
Madiun: Java	91	8S	112E
Madras: India	88	13N	80E
MADRID: Spain	65	40N	4W
Madura: *i.*, Indon.	91	7S	113E
Madurai: India	88	10N	78E
Maebashi: Japan	92	36N	139E

	Page	Lat.	Long.
Mafeking: S. Africa	109	26S	25E
Magadan: U.S.S.R.	81	60N	150E
Magallanes: *see* Punta Arenas			
Magdalena: *r.*, Colombia	48	7N	74W
Magdeburg: Ger.	72	52N	12E
Magellan, Str. of: Chile/Arg.	49	53S	70W
Maggiore, Lake: Italy/Switz.	73	46N	9E
Maghera: N. Ireland	56	55N	7W
Magherafelt: N. Irel.	56	55N	7W
Magnet B.: Antarc.	51	65S	56E
Magnetic I.: Austl.	98	19S	147E
Magnitogorsk: U.S.S.R.	83	53N	59E
Magnolia: U.S.A.	40	33N	93W
Magude: Mozam.	109	25S	33E
Magwe: Burma	90	20N	95E
Mahanadi: *r.*, India	88	22N	83E
Maharashtra: *State*, India	88	24N	76E
Mahia Penin.: N.Z.	93	39S	178E
Mahón: Minorca	65	40N	4E
Maidenhead: England	57	51½N	¾W
Maidstone: England	57	51N	1E
Maiduguri: Nigeria	106	12N	13E
Maimana: Afghan.	86	36N	65E
Main: *r.*, Germany	72	50N	10E
Main: *Old Prov.*, Fr.	70	48N	1W
Main Barrier Range: Australia	99	32S	141E
Maine: *State*, U.S.A.	13	45N	70W
Mainland: *i.*, Orkney Is.	53	59N	3W
Mainz: Germany	72	50N	8E
Maitland: Australia	99	33S	152E
Majorca: *i.*, Balearic Is.	65	39N	3E
Majunga: Malagasy Republic	103	16S	46E
Makarikari Salt Pan: Botswana	109	21S	26E
Makassar: & *str.*, Indonesia	91	5S	120E
Makeyevka: U.S.S.R.	82	48N	38E
Makhachkala: U.S.S.R.	82	43N	48E
Makran: Iran/W. Pakistan	86	26N	62E
Makushino: U.S.S.R.	83	55N	67E
Malabar Coast: India	88	12N	75E
Malacca: & *str.*, Malaya	91	2N	102E
Maladetta Massif: Sp.	71	43N	1E
Málaga: Spain	65	37N	4W
MALAGASY REP.: *cap.* Antananarivo	103	*Inset*	
Malahide: R. of Irel.	56	53N	6W
Malaita: *i.*, Solomon Is.	100	9S	161E
Malakal: Sudan	107	10N	32E
Malang: Java	91	8S	112E
Malange: Angola	108	9S	16E
Mälar, L.: Sweden	69	59N	17E
Malatya: Turkey	85	38N	38E
MALAWI: *cap.* Lilongwe	108	13S	34E
Malawi, Lake: Africa	108	13S	34E
Malaya, States of	91	4N	102E
MALAYSIA: *Fed. cap.* Kuala Lumpur	91	5N	110E
Malbork: Poland	66	54N	19E
Malden: U.S.A.	31	42½N	71W
Malden I.: Pac. O.	101	5S	155W
Maldive Is.: Ind. O.	87	7N	73E
Maldon: England	57	51¾N	¾E
Malesherbes: France	70	48N	2E
Malheur L.: U.S.A.	42	43N	119W
MALI: *cap.* Bamako	106	15N	5W
Malines *see* Mechelen			
Malin Head: R. of Ireland	56	55N	7W
Malinmore Head: R. of Ireland	56	55N	9W
Mallaig: Scotland	54	57N	6W
Mallow: R. of Ireland	56	52N	9W
Malmberget: Sweden	68	67N	21E
Malmédy: Belgium	70	50N	6E
Malmesbury: S. Afr.	109	33S	19E
Malmö: Sweden	69	56N	13E
Maloja Pass: Switz.	73	46N	10E
Malonga: Congo Republic	108	10S	23E
Malpelo I.: Pac. O.	101	4N	82W
Malplaquet: France	70	50N	4E
MALTA: *cap.* Valletta	67	36N	14E
Malta: U.S.A.	42	48N	108W
Maltby: England	57	53½N	1¼W
Malvan: India	88	16N	73E
Malvern: England	55	52N	2W
Mam Tor: *mtn.*, Eng.	57	53¼N	1¾W
Man, I. of: *cap.* Douglas	54	54N	5W
Manaar: & *gulf*, Ceylon	88	9N	80E
Manado: Celebes	91	2N	125E
MANAGUA: Nic.	47	12N	86W
MANAMA: Bahrain	85	26N	51E
Mana Pass: China	88	31N	79E
Manaus (Manáos): Brazil	48	3S	60W
Manchester: Eng.	57	54N	2W

	Page	Lat.	Long.
Manchester: U.S.A.	31	42½N	70¾W
Manchester Ship Canal: England	57	53N	3W
Mandalay: Burma	90	22N	96E
Mandan: U.S.A.	43	47N	101W
Mandasor: India	88	24N	75E
Mangalore: India	88	13N	75E
Mangyshlak Penin.: U.S.S.R.	82	44N	51E
Manhattan: Kansas, U.S.A.	43	39N	97W
Manhattan: N.Y., U.S.A.	31	40¾N	74W
Manifold, C.: Austl.	98	23S	151E
MANILA: Philippine Is.	91	15N	121E
Manipur: *State*, India	89	25N	94E
Manistee: *r.*, U.S.A.	17	44N	85W
Manitou Is.: U.S.A.	43	47N	87W
Manitowoc: U.S.A.	17	44N	88W
Manizales: Colombia	48	5N	76W
Manjra: *r.*, India	88	18N	76E
Mankato: U.S.A.	43	44N	94W
Mankoya: Zambia	109	15S	25E
Mannheim: Ger.	72	49N	8E
Manokwari: W. Irian	96	1S	134E
Manresa: Spain	65	42N	2E
Mansfield: Australia	99	37S	146E
Mansfield: England	57	53N	1W
Mansfield: U.S.A.	41	41N	83W
Manta: Ecuador	48	1S	81W
Mantes-Gassicourt: France	70	49N	2E
Mantua (Mantova): Italy	73	45N	11E
Manus: *i.*, New Guin.	97	3S	147E
Manzala, L.: Egypt	107	*Inset*	
Manzanillo: Mexico	38	19N	104W
Maplin Sands: Eng.	57	51½N	1E
Maracaibo: & *lake*, Venezuela	48	11N	72W
Maracay: Venezuela	47	10N	68W
Marada: Libya	84	29N	19E
Marajó, I. of: Brazil	48	1S	50W
Marampa: Sierra Leone	106	8N	12W
Maranhão: Brazil	48	3S	44W
Marañón: *r.*, Peru	48	5S	77W
Maraş: Turkey	82	38N	37E
Marathon: Greece	67	38N	24E
Marble Bar: Austl.	96	21S	120E
Marburg: Germany	72	51N	9E
Marche: *Old Prov.*, France	71	46N	2E
Marches, The: *Reg.*, Italy	73	44N	13E
Marchienne: Belg.	70	50N	4E
Marcus I.: Pac. O.	100	25N	154E
Marcy, Mt.: U.S.A.	17	44N	74W
Mar del Plata: Arg.	49	38S	58W
Mardin: Turkey	85	37N	41E
Marfa: U.S.A.	40	30N	104W
Marganets: U.S.S.R.	83	48N	67E
Margarita I.: Venez.	48	11N	64W
Margate: England	55	51N	1E
Margate: S. Africa	109	31S	30E
Margeride, Monts de la: France	71	45N	4E
Marguerite Bay: Antarctica	51	68S	68W
Marianas Is.: Pac. O.	100	18N	145E
Mariánské Lázně: Czechoslovakia	66	50N	13E
Maria van Diemen, C.: New Zealand	93	34S	173E
Maribor: Yugoslavia	66	47N	16E
Marie Byrd Land: Antarctica	51	80S	130W
Marie Galante: *i.*, West Indies	47	16N	61W
Marienbad *see* Marianské Lazne			
Mariental: S.W. Afr.	109	25S	18E
Mariinsk: U.S.S.R.	83	56N	88E
Marinetta: U.S.A.	43	45N	88W
Marino: Italy	67	41¾N	12½E
Marion: Ind., U.S.A.	41	41N	86W
Marion: Ohio, U.S.A.	41	41N	83W
Maritime Alps: Fr.	71	44N	7E
Maritsa: *r.*, Bulgaria	67	42N	26E
Markham, Mt.: Antarctica	51	82S	160E
Market Drayton: England	57	53N	2¼W
Market Harborough: England	57	52N	1W
Markovo: U.S.S.R.	81	65N	170E
Marlborough: Austl.	98	23S	150E
Marlborough: Eng.	55	51N	2W
Marles: France	70	51N	2E
Marlow: England	57	51½N	¾W
Marmande: France	71	44N	0
Marmara, Sea of: Turkey	84	41N	28E
Marne: *r.*, France	70	49N	4E
Marquesas Is.: Pac. O.	101	10S	140W
Marquette: U.S.A.	43	46N	87W
Marrakesh: Mor.	106	32N	8W
Marra Mts.: Sudan	107	13N	24E
Marree: Australia	99	30S	138E
Marsala: Sicily	67	38N	12E
Marseilles: France	71	43N	5E
Marshall: U.S.A.	40	33N	94W
Marshall Is.: Pac. O.	100	10N	166E
Marshalltown: U.S.A.	43	42N	93W
Marshfield: U.S.A.	43	45N	90W

	Page	Lat.	Long.
Martaban, G. of: Burma	91	16N	97E
Martha's Vineyard: *i.*, U.S.A.	17	41N	71W
Martigny: Switz.	73	46N	7E
Martigues: France	71	43N	5E
Martinique: *i.*, West Indies	47	15N	61W
Martinsville: U.S.A.	41	37N	80W
Marton: N.Z.	93	40S	175E
Martos: Spain	65	38N	4W
Mary: U.S.A.	83	38N	62E
Maryborough: Queens., Austl.	98	25S	153E
Maryborough: Vict., Australia	99	37S	144E
Maryland: *State*, U.S.A.	41	38N	75W
Maryport: England	54	55N	4W
Maryville: U.S.A.	41	36N	84W
Mascara: Algeria	65	35N	0
MASERU: Lesotho	109	29S	27E
Mashhad: Iran	85	36N	60E
Mashkel: *r.*, W. Pak.	88	27N	63E
Masira: *i.*, Muscat and 'Oman	85	20N	59E
Mask, L.: R. of Irel.	56	54N	9W
Mason City: U.S.A.	43	43N	93W
Massachusetts: *State*, U.S.A.	17	42N	73W
Massapequa: U.S.A.	31	40¾N	73½W
Massawa: Ethiopia	107	16N	39E
Massena: U.S.A.	17	45N	75W
Massif Central: Fr.	71	46N	3E
Masson I.: Antarc.	51	65S	97E
Masterton: N.Z.	93	41S	176E
Mastung: W. Pak.	88	30N	67E
Masulipatam: India	88	16N	81E
Matadi: Congo Rep.	108	6S	14E
Matagalpa: Nic.	47	13N	84W
Matagorda I.: U.S.A.	40	28N	97W
Matamoros: Mexico	40	26N	97W
Matanzas: Cuba	47	23N	82W
Matapan, C.: Greece	67	36N	22E
Matatiele: S. Africa	109	30S	28E
Mataura: *r.*, N.Z.	93	46S	169E
Mateka Falls: Congo Republic	108	5S	15E
Matera: Italy	67	41N	17E
Mathura: India	88	27N	78E
Matlock: England	57	53N	2W
Mato Grosso, Plat. of: Brazil	48	15S	54W
Matopo Hills: Rhod.	109	21S	30E
Matrah: Muscat and 'Oman	85	24N	58E
Matrûh: Egypt	84	32N	27E
Matsang: *r.*, China	87	29N	86E
Matsue: Japan	90	35N	133E
Matsuyama: Japan	90	34N	133E
Matterhorn: *mtn.*, Switzerland	73	46N	8E
Mattoon: U.S.A.	43	39N	88W
Maturín: Venezuela	48	10N	63W
Matzen: Austria	66	48N	17E
Matzu: *i.*, China	89	26N	120E
Maubeuge: France	70	50N	4E
Maui: *i.*, Pacific O.	101	20N	155W
Maudheim: Antarc.	51	71S	10W
Maumee: *r.*, U.S.A.	41	41N	84W
Maumere: Indonesia	91	8S	122E
Maun: Botswana	109	20S	23E
MAURITANIA: *cap.* Nouakchott	106	20N	10W
MAURITIUS: *cap.* Port Louis		20S	57E
Mawlaik: Burma	90	24N	94E
Mawson: Antarctica	51	68S	62E
May, C.: U.S.A.	41	39N	75W
Mayenne: & *r.*, Fr.	70	48N	1W
Mayfield: U.S.A.	41	36N	89W
Maykop: U.S.S.R.	82	45N	40E
Mayo: *Co.*, R. of Irel.	56	54N	9W
Mayoumba: Gabon	108	4S	11E
Maywood: U.S.A.	31	42N	87¾W
Mazamet: France	71	43N	2E
Mazar-i-Sharif: Afghanistan	86	37N	67E
Mazarrón: Spain	65	38N	2W
Mazatlán: Mexico	38	23N	107W
Mazoe: Rhodesia	109	17S	31E
Mbala: Zambia	108	9S	32E
Mbandaka: Congo Republic	108	0	18E
Mead, Lake: U.S.A.	42	36N	114W
Meath: *Co.*, R. of Irel.	56	54N	7W
Meaux: France	70	49N	3E
MECCA: Sa'udi Arabia	85	21N	40E
Mechelen: Belgium	70	51N	4E
Medan: Indonesia	91	4N	99E
Medéa: Algeria	65	36N	3E
Medellín: Colombia	48	6N	76W
Medford: U.S.A.	31	42½N	71W
Mediaş: Romania	66	46N	25E
Medina: Sa'udi Arabia	86	25N	40E
Mediterranean Sea	62/3	—	—
Mednogorsk: U.S.S.R.	83	51N	58E
Médoc: France	71	45N	1W
Medway: *r.*, England	55	51N	0
Meerut: India	88	29N	77E
Mega: Ethiopia	107	4N	38E
Megara: Greece	67	38N	23E
Meiningen: Ger.	72	51N	10E
Meissen: Germany	72	51N	13E

	Page	Lat.	Long.
Mekong (Dza): *r.*, S.E. Asia	87	33N	96E
Melanesia: Pac. O.	100	—	—
Melbourne: Austl.	99	38S	145E
Melbourne: U.S.A.	41	28N	81W
Melilla: Morocco	65	35N	3W
Melrose: U.S.A.	31	42½N	71W
Melrose Park: U.S.A.	31	42N	87¾W
Melton Mowbray: England	57	53N	1W
Melun: France	70	49N	3E
Melville Bay: Grnld.	3	76N	62W
Melville I.: Austl.	96	11S	131E
Memmingen: Ger.	73	48N	10E
Memphis: Egypt	84	30N	31E
Memphis: U.S.A.	41	35N	90W
Menai Strait: Wales	55	53N	4W
Menderes: *r.*, Turkey	84	37N	27E
Mendip Hills: Eng.	55	51N	3W
Mendocino, Cape: U.S.A.	2	40N	125W
Mendoza: Argentina	49	33S	69W
Mène: Congo	106	2N	16E
Menemen: Turkey	67	39N	27E
Mengtsz: China	89	23N	103E
Menindee: & *lake*, Australia	99	32S	142E
Menommee: U.S.A.	43	45N	88W
Mentawai Is.: Indon.	91	3S	100E
Menton: France	71	44N	7E
Menzies: Australia	98	30S	121E
Meppel: Neth.	72	53N	6E
Meramec: *r.*, U.S.A.	43	38N	91W
Merano: Italy	73	47N	11E
Merauke: West Irian	96	9S	140E
Mercara: India	88	12N	76E
Merced: U.S.A.	42	37N	120W
Mergui: Burma	91	12N	98E
Mergui Arch.: Burma	91	10N	97E
Meribah: Australia	99	35S	141E
Mérida: Mexico	38	21N	90W
Mérida: Spain	65	39N	6W
Meridian: U.S.A.	41	32N	89W
Merinda: Australia	98	20S	148E
Merioneth.: *Co.*, Wales	55	53N	4W
Merowe: Sudan	84	18N	32E
Merredin: Australia	98	31S	118E
Merrick: *mtn.*, Scot.	54	55N	5W
Merseburg: Ger.	72	51N	12E
Mersea I.: England	57	51¾N	1E
Mersey: *r.*, England	57	53N	3W
Mersin: Turkey	84	37N	34E
Merthyr Tydfil: Wales	55	52N	3W
Merton: England	57	51½N	¼W
Merv: U.S.S.R.	83	38N	62E
Mesa: U.S.S.R.	42	33N	112W
Mesabi R.: U.S.A.	43	48N	93W
Mesolongion: Greece	67	38N	21E
Mesopotamia: 'Iraq	86	32N	46E
Messina: & *str.*, Sicily	67	38N	16E
Messina: S. Africa	109	23S	30E
Mesta: *r.*, Bulgaria	67	41N	24E
Mestre: Italy	73	45N	12E
Methuen: U.S.A.	31	42¾N	71¼W
Mettman: Germany	62	51¼N	7E
Mettur: India	88	12N	78E
Metz: France	70	49N	6E
Meuse: *r.*, Fr./Belg.	70	50N	5E
Mexborough: Eng.	57	53½N	1¼W
Mexicali: Mexico	38	33N	115W
Mexican Plat.: Mex.	38	24N	103W
MEXICO: *cap.* Mexico City	38	25N	100W
Mexico, Gulf of	38	25N	90W
MEXICO CITY: Mexico	38	19N	99W
Mézières: France	70	50N	5E
Miami: Ariz., U.S.A.	42	33N	111W
Miami: Fla., U.S.A.	41	26N	80W
Miami: Okla., U.S.A.	43	37N	95W
Miami: *r.*, U.S.A.	41	39N	85W
Miami Beach: U.S.A.	41	26N	80W
Mianeh: Iran	85	37N	47E
Miaui: *i.*, Pacific O.	101	21N	156W
Michelson, Mt.: U.S.A.	28	69N	144W
Michigan: *State*, U.S.A.	17	45N	85W
Michigan, Lake: U.S.A./Canada	17	44N	87W
Michigan City: U.S.A.	41	42N	86W
Micronesia: Pac. O.	100	—	—
Middelburg: Neth.	72	51N	3E
Middelburg: S. Afr.	109	26S	30E
Middle Atlas: *mtns.*, Morocco	106	33N	5W
Middlesboro: U.S.A.	41	37N	84W
Middlesbrough: Eng.	54	55N	1W
Middleton: R. of Irel.	56	52N	8W
Middletown: N.Y., U.S.A.	41	41N	75W
Middletown: Ohio, U.S.A.	41	40N	84W
Midland: Australia	98	32S	116E
Midland: Michigan, U.S.A.	17	43N	85W
Midland: Texas, U.S.A.	43	32N	102W
Midlothian: *Co.*, Scotland	54	56N	3W
Midnapore: India	88	22N	87E
Midway I.: Pac. O.	100	29N	179W
Midwest: U.S.A.	42	43N	106W
Mijares: *r.*, Spain	65	40N	0
Mikkeli: Finland	68	62N	27E
Mikuni Mts.: Japan	90	37N	139E
Milan (Milano): Italy	73	45N	9E
Milbank: U.S.A.	43	45N	97W
Mildura: Australia	99	34S	142E
Miles City: U.S.A.	43	46N	106W
Milford: U.S.A.	31	42¼N	71½W
Milford Haven: Wales	55	52N	5W
Milford Sound: N.Z.	93	44S	168E
Milk: *r.*, U.S.A.	42	48N	109W
Millau: France	71	44N	3E
Milledgeville: U.S.A.	41	33N	83W
Mille Lacs: U.S.A.	43	46N	94W
Miller's Dale: Eng.	57	53¼N	1¾W
Millicent: Australia	99	38S	140E
Millinocket: U.S.A.	13	46N	69W
Mill I.: Antarctica	51	65S	101E
Millburn: U.S.A.	31	40¾N	74¼W
Millport: Scotland	54	55¾N	4¾W
Milngavie: Scotland	54	56N	4¼W
Milos: *i.*, Greece	67	37N	24E
Milparinka: Austl.	99	30S	142E
Milton: U.S.A.	31	42¼N	71W
Milwaukee: U.S.A.	31	43N	88W
Min: *r.*, China	89	27N	117E
Minas de Riotinto: Spain	67	38N	7W
Minas Gerais: *State*, Brazil	48	18S	45W
Mindanao: *i.*, Phil.	91	8N	125E
Minden: U.S.A.	40	33N	93W
Mindoro: *i.*, Phil.	91	13N	121E
Minehead: England	55	51N	3W
Mine Hd.: R. of Irel.	56	52N	8W
Mineral Wells: U.S.A.	43	33N	98W
Minho: *r.*, Spain	65	42N	8W
Minneapolis: U.S.A.	43	45N	93W
Minnesota: *State*, U.S.A.	43	47N	95W
Minorca: *i.*, Balearic Is.	65	40N	4E
Minot: U.S.A.	43	48N	101W
Minquiers, Plat. des: *is.*, France	70	49N	2W
Minsk: U.S.S.R.	82	54N	28E
Minusinsk: U.S.S.R.	83	54N	92E
Miraflores Locks: Panama Canal	39		Inset
Miram Shah: W. Pak.	88	33N	70E
Mirande: France	71	44N	0
Mirecourt: France	70	48N	6E
Mirtoon Sea: Greece	67	37N	24E
Mirzapur: India	88	25N	82E
Miskolc: Hungary	66	48N	21E
Misoöl: *i.*, W. Irian	96	2S	130E
Mississippi: *r.*, U.S.A.	40	31N	92W
Mississippi: *State*, U.S.A.	40	33N	90W
Missoula: U.S.A.	42	47N	114W
Missouri: *r.*, U.S.A.	43	39N	94W
Missouri: *State*, U.S.A.	43	39N	93W
Misurata: Libya	106	32N	15E
Mitchell: Australia	98	26S	148E
Mitchell: U.S.A.	43	44N	98W
Mitchell: *r.*, Queens., Australia	97	16S	142E
Mitchell: *r.*, Vict., Australia	99	38S	147E
Mitchelstown: R. of Ireland	56	52N	8W
Mitilini: Lesbos	67	39N	26E
Mito: Japan	90	36N	141E
Mittelland Canal: Germany	72	52N	8E
Mitú: Colombia	48	1N	70W
Mizen Hd.: R. of Irel.	56	51N	10W
Mjøsa, Lake: Norway	69	61N	11E
Mlawa: Poland	66	53N	20E
Moascar: Egypt	107		Inset
Mobaye: Cen. Afr. Republic	107	4N	22E
Moberly: U.S.A.	43	39N	92W
Mobile: U.S.A.	41	31N	88W
Mocuba: Mozam.	109	17S	37E
Modane: France	71	45N	7E
Modder River: South Africa	109	29S	25E
Modena: Italy	73	45N	11E
Modeste: U.S.A.	42	38N	121W
Moengo: Surinam	48	6N	54E
Moers: Germany	62	51½N	6¾E
Moffat: Scotland	54	55N	3W
MOGADISCIO: Somali Republic	107	2N	45E
Mogador see Essaiora			
Mogilev Podol'skiy: U.S.S.R.	66	48N	28E
Mogocha: U.S.S.R.	81	53N	120E
Mogollon Plateau: U.S.A.	42	35N	111W
Mohács: Hungary	66	46N	19E
Mointy: U.S.S.R.	83	47N	74E
Mojave Desert: U.S.A.	42	35N	117W
Moji: Japan	92	34N	131E
Mokambo: Congo Republic	109	12S	29E
Mold: Wales	57	53N	3W
Moldavia: *Old Reg.*, Romania	66	47N	27E
Moldavian S.S.R.: U.S.S.R.	82	47N	28E
Molde: Norway	68	63N	7E
Mole: *r.*, England	57	51¼N	¼W
Molfetta: Italy	67	41N	17E
Molières: France	71	44N	1E
Mollendo: Peru	48	17S	72W
Mölndal: Sweden	69	58N	12E
Molodechno: U.S.S.R.	66	54N	27E
Molopo: *r.*, S. Afr.	109	26S	23E
Moluccas: *is.*, Indon.	91	0	127E
Molucca Sea: Indon.	91	0	125E
Mombasa: Kenya	108	4S	39E
MONACO: *cap.* Monte Carlo	71	44N	7E
Monadhliath Mts.: Scotland	54	57N	4W
Monaghan: & *Co.*, R. of Ireland	56	54N	7W
Mona I.: W. Indies	47	18N	68W
Monastir: Yugo.	67	41N	21E
Monchegorsk: U.S.S.R.	68	68N	33E
Mönchen-Gladbach: Germany	62	51¼N	6½E
Mondego: C., Port.	65	40N	9W
Mondovi: Italy	73	44N	8E
Monfalcone: Italy	73	46N	13E
MONGOLIA: *cap.* Ulan Bator	81	47N	105E
Mongu: Zambia	109	15S	23E
Monheim: Germany	62	51N	7E
Monmouth: & *Co.*, England	55	52N	3W
Monmouth: U.S.A.	43	41N	91W
Monroe: La., U.S.A.	40	33N	92W
Monroe: Michigan, U.S.A.	41	42N	83W
Monroeville: U.S.A.	41	31N	87W
MONROVIA: Liberia	106	6N	11W
Mons: Belgium	70	50N	4E
Montague I.: U.S.A.	2	60N	147W
Montana: *State*, U.S.A.	42	47N	110W
Montargis: France	70	48N	3E
Montauban: France	71	44N	1E
Montauk Pt.: U.S.A.	17	41N	72W
Montbéliard: France	71	47N	7E
Montceau-les-Mines: France	71	47N	4E
Mont Cenis Pass: France/Italy	73	45N	7E
Montclair: U.S.A.	31	40¾N	74¼W
Mont de Marsan: Fr.	71	44N	1W
Montdidier: France	70	50N	3E
Monte Bello Is.: Australia	96	20S	115E
MONTE CARLO: Monaco	71	44N	7E
Monte Cristo: *i.*, It.	67	42N	10E
Montego Bay: *town*, Jamaica	47	18N	78W
Montélimar: France	71	45N	5E
Montenegro: Yugo.	67	43N	19E
Monterey: & *Bay*, U.S.A.	42	37N	122W
Monterrey: Mexico	38	26N	100W
MONTEVIDEO: Uruguay	50	35S	56W
Montgomery: U.S.A.	41	32N	86W
Montgomery: & *Co.*, Wales	57	53N	3W
Montluçon: France	71	56N	4E
Montmédy: France	70	50N	5E
Montmirail: France	70	49N	4E
Montpelier: U.S.A.	17	44N	73W
Montpellier: France	71	44N	4E
Montreuil: France	70	50N	2E
Montreuil Bellay: Fr.	71	47N	0
Montreux: Switz.	73	46N	7E
Montrose: Scotland	51	57N	2W
Montrose: U.S.A.	42	38N	108W
Mont St. Michel: Fr.	70	49N	2W
Montserrat: *i.*, West Indies	47	17N	62W
Montvalier, Pic de: Spain/France	71	43N	1E
Monza: Italy	72	46N	9E
Moorhead: U.S.A.	43	47N	97W
Moorreesburg: South Africa	109	33S	18E
Moosehead, L.: U.S.A.	13	46N	69W
Moradabad: India	88	29N	79E
Moravia: Czech.	66	59N	17E
Moravian Gate: Czechoslovakia	66	59N	17E
Moravska Ostrava: Czechoslovakia	66	50N	18E
Moray Firth: Scot.	53	58N	4W
Morayshire: *Co.*, Scotland	51	57N	3W
Morbihan: *Dept.*, Fr.	70	48N	3W
Morea: Australia	99	37S	141E
Morea: Greece	67	38N	22E
Moreau: *r.*, U.S.A.	43	45N	102W
Morecambe: England	54	54N	3W
Moree: Australia	99	29S	150E
Moreton Bay: Austl.	98	27S	153E
Moreton in Marsh: England	55	52N	2W
Morgan City: U.S.A.	40	30N	91W
Morgantown: U.S.A.	41	40N	80W
Morjärv: Sweden	68	66N	23E
Morkalla: Australia	99	34S	141E
Morlaix: France	70	49N	4W
MOROCCO: *cap.* Rabat	106	32N	5W
Moron: Argentina	50	34¾S	58½W
Moron: Cuba	47	22N	78W
Morona: *r.*, Ec./Peru	48	3S	77W
Morotai: *i.*, Indon.	91	3N	128E
Morpeth: England	54	55N	2W
Morristown: U.S.A.	31	40¾N	74½W
Morton Grove: U.S.A.	31	42N	87¾W
Morvan: France	71	47N	4E
Moscow: U.S.A.	42	47N	117W
Moscow: U.S.S.R.	82	56N	37E
Mosel: *r.*, Germany	72	50N	7E
Moselle: *r.*, France	70	49N	6E
Moses Lake: *city*, U.S.A.	42	47N	119W
Moshi: Tanzania	108	3S	37E
Moss: Norway	69	59N	11E
Mossâmedes: Angola	109	15S	12E
Mossel Bay: *town*, South Africa	109	34S	22E
Mossgiel: Australia	99	33S	145E
Most: Czech.	72	50N	14E
Mostaganem: Algeria	65	36N	0
Mostar: Yugoslavia	67	43N	18E
Mosul: 'Iraq	85	36N	43E
Motala: Sweden	69	59N	15E
Motherwell: Scot.	54	56N	3W
Motueka: N.Z.	93	41S	173E
Moulins: France	71	47N	3E
Moulmein: Burma	91	17N	97E
Moultrie: U.S.A.	41	31N	84W
Moundsville: U.S.A.	41	40N	81W
Mountain Home: U.S.A.	42	43N	116W
Mount Eba: *town*, Australia	96	30S	136E
Mount Gambier: *town*, Australia	99	38S	141E
Mount Isa: *town*, Australia	96	21S	140E
Mount Lofty Range: Australia	99	35S	138E
Mount Lyell: *town*, Tasmania	97	42S	146E
Mount Magnet: *town*, Australia	96	28S	118E
Mount Morgan: *town*, Australia	98	24S	150E
Mount Pleasant: *city*, U.S.A.	17	44N	85W
Mount Prospect: *city*, U.S.A.	31	42N	88W
Mount Vernon: *city*, Ill., U.S.A.	43	38N	89W
Mount Vernon: *city*, N.Y., U.S.A.	31	41N	73¾W
Mount Vernon, *city*, Wash., U.S.A.	42	48N	122W
Mourne Mts.: N. Irel.	56	54N	6W
Moyale: Kenya	108	4N	39E
MOZAMBIQUE: *cap.* Lourenço Marques	109	—	—
Mozambique Chan.	109	15S	41E
Mpanda: Tanzania	108	6S	31E
Mtwara: Tanzania	108	10S	40E
Muchinga Mts.: Zambia	109	13S	32E
Mudgee: Australia	99	32S	150E
Mudros: Lemnos	67	40N	25E
Muğla: Turkey	84	37N	28E
Muhammad Qol: Sudan	84	21N	37E
Mühlhausen: Ger.	72	51N	10E
Mühlig-Hofmann Mts.: Antarc.	51	73S	3E
Muirhead: Scotland	54	55¾N	4W
Mukachevo: U.S.S.R.	66	48N	23E
Mukallâ: Yemen P.D.R.	85	15N	49E
Mukden: China	90	42N	124E
Mulhacen: *mtn.*, Sp.	65	37N	3W
Mülheim: *(Cologne)*, Germany	72	51N	7E
Mülheim: *(Ruhr)*, Germany	62	51N	7E
Mulhouse: France	70	48N	7E
Mull: *i.*, Scotland	54	56N	6W
Müller Mts.: Borneo	91	1N	114E
Mullewa: Australia	98	28S	116E
Mull Hd.: Scotland	53	59N	3W
Mullinger: R. of Irel.	56	54N	7W
Mull of Oa: Scotland	54	56N	6W
Mulobezi: Zambia	109	17S	25E
Multan: W. Pak.	88	30N	71E
Muna: *i.*, Indonesia	91	5S	122E
Muncie: U.S.A.	41	40N	85W
Mungbere: Congo Republic	108	3N	28E
Munich (München): Germany	73	48N	12E
Münster: Germany	72	52N	8E
Munster: *Old Prov.*, Ireland	56	52N	9W
Muonio: *r.*, Finland	68	68N	24E
Mur: France	70	48N	3W
Mur: *r.*, Austria	73	47N	14E
Murat: France	71	45N	3E
Murchison: *r.*, Austl.	88	27S	116E
Murcia: & *Old Prov.*, Spain	65	38N	1W
Muret: France	71	43N	1E
Murfreesboro: U.S.A.	41	36N	86W
Murgon: Australia	98	26S	152E
Murmansk: U.S.S.R.	80	69N	33E
Murom: U.S.S.R.	82	56N	42E

	Page	Lat.	Long.
Muroran: Japan	92	42N	141E
Murray: r., Austl.	99	35S	139E
Murray (Hume): r., Australia	99	36S	145E
Murray Bridge: Australia	99	35S	139E
Murree: W. Pak.	88	34N	73E
Murrumbidgee: r., Australia	99	35S	146E
Murupara: N.Z.	93	38S	177E
Murwillumbah: Australia	98	28S	153E
Murzuch: Libya	84	26N	14E
MUSCAT: 'Oman	85	24N	59E
MUSCAT AND 'OMAN: see 'OMAN	85	20N	55E
Muscatine: U.S.A.	43	41N	91W
Muskegon: r., U.S.A.	17	43N	86W
Muskogee: U.S.A.	43	36N	95W
Mussoorie: India	88	30N	78E
Mustafa Kemalpaşa: Turkey	67	40N	28E
Mustang I.: U.S.A.	40	27N	97W
Muswellbrook: Austl.	99	32S	151E
Mutankiang: China	90	45N	130E
Mutano: Angola	109	17S	15E
Muyun-Kum: U.S.S.R.	83	44N	71E
Muzaffarpur: India	88	26N	85E
Mwanza: Tanzania	108	3S	33E
Mweru, L.: Zambia	108	9S	29E
Mycenae: Greece	67	38N	23E
Myitkyina: Burma	90	26N	97E
Mymensingh: E. Pak.	88	25N	90E
Mysore: & State, India	88	12N	77E
Mytisci: U.S.S.R.	82	56N	37¾E
Naas: R. of Ireland	56	53N	7W
Nacala: Mozambique	109	15S	40E
Nacogdoches: U.S.A.	40	32N	95W
Naestved: Denmark	69	55N	12E
Nafud: Sa'udi Arabia	85	28N	41E
Naga Hills: India/Burma	89	26N	95E
Nagaoka: Japan	92	37N	139E
Nagapattinam: India	88	11N	80E
Nagasaki: Japan	92	33N	130E
Nagoorin: Australia	98	24S	151E
Nagoya: Japan	92	35N	137E
Nagpur: India	88	21N	79E
Nagykanizsa: Hung.	66	46N	16E
Naha: Okinawa	92	26N	127E
Naini Tal: India	88	29N	80E
Nairn: Scotland	53	58N	4W
NAIROBI: Kenya	108	2S	37E
Najaf: 'Iraq	85	32N	44E
Najd: Sa'udi Arabia	85	26N	42E
Najran: Sau. Arab.	85	17N	44E
Nakhon Ratchasima: Thailand	91	15N	102E
Namangan: U.S.S.R.	83	41N	72E
Nambour: Australia	98	27S	153E
Namib Desert: S.W. Africa	109	23S	15E
Nampa: U.S.A.	42	44N	117W
Nampula: Mozam.	109	15S	40E
Namsos: Norway	68	64N	11E
Namur: Belgium	70	50N	5E
Nanango: Australia	98	27S	153E
Nanchang: China	89	28N	116E
Nancheng: China	89	33N	107E
Nanchung: China	89	31N	106E
Nancy: France	70	49N	6E
Nanda Devi: mtn., India	88	30N	80E
Nangchen Japo: mtn., China	90	33N	94E
Nanking: China	89	32N	119E
Nan Ling: China	89	25N	112E
Nanning: China	89	23N	108E
Nansei Is.: Japan	92	27N	127E
Nan Shan: China	87	38N	100E
Nantes: France	71	47N	2W
Nantucket Inlet: Antarctica	51	75S	62W
Nantung: China	89	32N	121E
Nantwich: England	57	53N	2½W
Nanumea: i., Pac. O.	100	5S	176E
Nanyuki: Kenya	108	0	37E
Nao, C. de la: Spain	65	39N	0
Napa: U.S.A.	42	38N	122W
Napier: N.Z.	93	39S	177E
Naples (Napoli): It.	67	41N	14E
Naracoorte: Austl.	99	37S	141E
Narbada: r., India	88	22N	75E
Narbonne: France	71	43N	3E
Narrabri: Australia	99	30S	150E
Narrandera: Austl.	99	35S	147E
Narrogin: Australia	98	33S	117E
Narva: U.S.S.R.	82	59N	28E
Narvik: Norway	68	68N	17E
Nar'yan-Mar: U.S.S.R.	80	67N	53E
Naseby: England	57	52½N	1W
Nashua: U.S.A.	31	43N	72W
Nashville: U.S.A.	41	36N	87W
Nasik: India	88	20N	74E
Nasiriya: 'Iraq	85	31N	46E
NASSAU: Bahama Is.	47	25N	77W
Nassau Mts.: West Irian	96	4S	136E
Nässjö: Sweden	69	58N	15E
Natal: Brazil	48	6S	35W
Natal: Prov., S. Afr.	109	28S	31E
Natchez: U.S.A.	40	32N	91W
Natchitoches: U.S.A.	40	33N	93W
Natick: U.S.A.	31	42½N	71¼W
Natuna Is.: Indon.	91	4N	108E
Naturaliste, Cape: Australia	98	34S	115E
Nauplia: Greece	67	38N	23E
Nauru: i., Pac. O.	100	1S	167E
Navan: R. of Irel.	56	54N	7W
Navarin, C.: U.S.S.R.	81	62N	179E
Navarino, Bay of: Greece	67	37N	22E
Navarra: Old Prov., Spain	65	42N	2W
Navasota: r., U.S.A.	40	31N	96W
Naxos: i., Greece	67	37N	26E
Nazareth: Israel	84	33N	35E
Naze, The: England	55	52N	1E
Ndola: Zambia	109	13S	29E
Neagh, L.: N. Irel.	56	55N	6W
Nebit-Dag: U.S.S.R.	82	40N	55E
Nebraska: State, U.S.A.	43	42N	100W
Nebraska City: U.S.A.	43	41N	96W
Neches: r., U.S.A.	43	31N	95W
Neckar: r., Germany	72	49N	9E
Needham: U.S.A.	31	42½N	71¼W
Needles, The: Eng.	55	51N	2W
Negro: r., Argentina	49	40S	64W
Negro: r., Brazil	48	1S	64W
Negros: i., Phil.	91	10N	123E
Nehbandān: Iran	85	32N	60E
Neikiang: China	89	30N	105E
Neisse: r., Pol./Ger.	66	52N	15E
Neiva: Colombia	48	3N	75W
Nellore: India	88	14N	80E
Nelson: England	57	53¾N	2¼W
Nelson: N.Z.	93	41S	173E
Neman: r., U.S.S.R.	66	53N	25E
Nemours: France	70	48N	3E
Nemuro: Japan	90	43N	145E
Nenagh: R. of Irel.	56	53N	8W
Nenana: U.S.A.	2	64N	149W
Nene: r., England	57	53N	0
Neosho: r., U.S.A.	43	38N	96W
NEPAL: cap. Katmandu	88	28N	85E
Nerchinsk: U.S.S.R.	81	52N	116E
Neskaupstadhur: Ice.	68	65N	14W
Ness, L.: Scotland	53	57N	4W
Nestos: r., Greece	67	41N	24E
NETHERLANDS: cap. The Hague	72	52N	5E
Neubrandenburg: Germany	72	53N	13E
Neuchâtel: & lake, Switzerland	73	47N	7E
Neufchâteau: Belg.	70	50N	5E
Neufchâteau: France	70	48N	6E
Neukirchen-Vluyn: Germany	62	51½N	6½E
Neumünster: Ger.	72	54N	10E
Neunkirchen: Saar	72	49N	7E
Neuquén: Argentina	49	39S	68W
Neuse: r., U.S.A.	41	35N	78W
Neuss: Germany	62	51N	7E
Neustrelitz: Ger.	72	53N	13E
Nevada: State, U.S.A.	42	39N	117W
Nevada City: U.S.A.	42	39N	121W
Never: U.S.S.R.	81	54N	124E
Nevers: France	71	47N	3E
Neves: Brazil	50	22¾S	43W
Nevis: i., W. Indies	47	17N	63W
New Amsterdam: i., Indian Ocean	100	38S	78E
Newark: N.J., U.S.A.	31	41N	74W
Newark: Ohio, U.S.A.	41	40N	82W
Newark upon Trent: England	55	53N	1W
New Bedford: U.S.A.	17	42N	71W
New Bedford Inlet: Antarctica	51	74S	61W
New Bern: U.S.A.	41	35N	77W
Newberry: U.S.A.	17	46N	85W
New Braunfels: U.S.A.	40	30N	98W
Newbridge: R. of Ireland	56	53N	7W
New Britain: i., New Guinea	97	6S	150E
New Brunswick: U.S.A.	31	40½N	74½W
Newbury: England	57	51N	1W
New Caledonia: i., Pacific Ocean	100	21S	165E
New Castile: Spain	65	39N	4W
Newcastle: Australia	99	33S	152E
Newcastle: Down, N. Ireland	56	54N	6W
Newcastle: Limerick, R. of Ireland	56	52N	9W
New Castle: Pa., U.S.A.	41	41N	80W
Newcastle: S. Africa	109	28S	30E
Newcastle: Wyo., U.S.A.	43	44N	104W
Newcastle under Lyme: England	55	53N	2W
Newcastle upon Tyne: England	54	55N	2W
Newdegate: Austl.	98	33S	119E
New Delhi: India	88	28N	77E
New England Range: Australia	99	30S	152E
Newenham, Cape: U.S.A.	2	59N	162W
New Forest: England	55	51N	2W
New Guinea: i., East Indies	96	5S	140E
New Guinea, Territ. of: cap., with Papua, Port Moresby	97	5S	147E
Newham: England	57	51½N	0
New Hampshire: State, U.S.A.	17	44N	72W
Newhaven: England	55	51N	0
New Haven: U.S.A.	41	41N	73W
New Hebrides: is., Pacific Ocean	100	15S	168E
New Hyde Park: U.S.A.	31	40¾N	73¾W
New Iberia: U.S.A.	40	30N	92W
New Ireland: i., New Guinea	97	3S	152E
New Jersey: State, U.S.A.	41	40N	75W
Newmarket: Eng.	55	52N	0
New Mexico: State, U.S.A.	42	34N	107W
Newnan: U.S.A.	41	33N	85W
New Orleans: U.S.A.	40	30N	90W
New Plymouth: N.Z.	93	39S	174E
Newport: England	55	52N	3W
Newport: I. of Wight	55	51N	1W
Newport: Rhode Island, U.S.A.	17	41N	71W
Newport: Vt., U.S.A.	17	45N	72W
Newport News: U.S.A.	41	37N	76W
New Providence: i., Bahama Is.	47	25N	77W
Newquay: England	55	50N	5W
New Rochelle: U.S.A.	31	41N	73¾W
New Ross: R. of Ireland	56	52N	7W
Newry: N. Ireland	56	54N	6W
New South Wales: State, Australia	99	32S	146E
Newton: Iowa, U.S.A.	43	42N	93W
Newton: Kansas, U.S.A.	43	38N	97W
Newton Abbot: England	55	51N	4W
Newton-le-Willows: England	57	53½N	2½W
Newton Stewart: Scotland	54	55N	5W
Newtownabbey: N. Ireland	56	55N	6W
Newtownards: N. Ireland	56	55N	6W
New Ulm: U.S.A.	43	44N	95W
New York: U.S.A.	31	41N	74W
New York: State, U.S.A.	44/5		
NEW ZEALAND: cap. Wellington	93	—	—
Ngami, Lake: Bots.	109	21S	23E
Ngauruhoe: mtn., N.Z.	93	39S	175E
Nguru: Nigeria	106	13N	10E
Nhill: Australia	99	36S	142E
Niagara Falls: Canada/U.S.A.	17	43N	79W
NIAMEY: Niger	106	14N	2E
Nias: i., Indonesia	91	1N	98E
NICARAGUA: cap. Managua	47	13N	85W
Nicaragua, Lake: Nic.	47	11N	85W
Nice: France	71	44N	7E
Nicobar Is.: Ind. O.	87	7N	93E
NICOSIA: Cyprus	84	35N	33E
Niedere Tauern: mtns., Austria	73	47N	14E
Nienburg: Ger.	72	53N	9E
Nieuwpoort: Belg.	70	51N	3E
Nieuwveld Range: S. Africa	109	32S	21E
NIGER: cap. Niamey	106	17N	10E
Niger: r., W. Afr.	106	8N	6E
NIGERIA: cap. Lagos	106	—	—
Nihau: i., Pacific O.	101	22N	162W
Nihoa: i., Pacific O.	101	22N	162W
Niigata: Japan	93	38N	139E
Nijmegen: Neth.	72	52N	6E
Nikolayev: U.S.S.R.	82	47N	32E
Nikolayevsk: U.S.S.R.	81	53N	142E
Nikopol': U.S.S.R.	82	48N	34E
Nile: r., Egypt/Sudan	107	21N	31E
Niles: U.S.A.	31	42N	86W
Nilgiri Hills: India	88	11N	77E
Nîmes: France	71	44N	4E
Nimmitabel: Austl.	99	36S	149E
Nimule: Sudan	107	4N	32E
Ninety Mile Beach: Australia	99	38S	147E
Nineveh: 'Iraq	85	37N	43E
Ninghsia: China	89	39N	106E
Ninghsia A. R.: China	89	37N	106E
Ningpo: China	89	30N	122E
Niobrara: r., U.S.A.	43	43N	99W
Niort: France	71	46N	0
Niš: Yugoslavia	67	43N	22E
Nisiros: i., Greece	67	37N	27E
Niterói: Brazil	50	23S	43W
Nith: r., Scotland	54	55N	4W
Nivelles: Belgium	70	51N	4E
Nivernais: Old Prov., France	71	47N	3E
Nizhniy-Tagil: U.S.S.R.	83	58N	60E
Nkana: Zambia	109	13S	28E
Nobeoka: Japan	92	33N	132E
Noccundra: Austl.	98	28S	142E
Nogent-sur-Seine: France	70	48N	3E
Noirmoutier, Île de: France	70	47N	2W
Nome: U.S.A.	2	65N	165W
Norden: Germany	72	54N	7E
Nordenham: Ger.	72	53N	8E
Norderney: i., Ger.	72	54N	7E
Nordhausen: Ger.	72	52N	11E
Nordhorn: Germany	72	52N	7E
Nördlingen: Ger.	73	49N	10E
Nordvik: U.S.S.R.	81	74N	110E
Norfolk: Co., Eng.	55	53N	1E
Norfolk: Nebraska, U.S.A.	43	42N	97W
Norfolk: Va., U.S.A.	41	37N	76W
Norfolk, L., U.S.A.	43	36N	92W
Norfolk Broads: Eng.	55	53N	1E
Norfolk I.: Pac. O.	100	29S	168E
Noril'sk: U.S.S.R.	81	69N	90E
Norman: r., Austl.	97	19S	142E
Normandy: Old Prov., France	70	49N	0
Normanton: Austl.	97	18S	141E
Nornalup: Australia	98	35S	117E
Norrköping: Sweden	69	59N	16E
Norseman: Austl.	98	32S	122E
North, C.: Antarc.	51	71S	167E
Northallerton: Eng.	54	54N	1W
Northam: Australia	98	32S	117E
Northampton: Austl.	98	28S	115E
Northampton: & Co., England	57	52N	1W
Northampton: U.S.A.	17	42N	73W
North Babylon: U.S.A.	31	40¾N	73¼W
North Bend: U.S.A.	42	43N	124W
North Bergen: U.S.A.	31	40¾N	74W
North Cape: N.Z.	93	34S	173E
North Canadian: r., U.S.A.	43	37N	103W
North Cape: Nor.	68	71N	26E
North Carolina: State, U.S.A.	41	35N	80W
North Channel: Scot./N. Irel.	56	55N	6W
North Chicago: U.S.A.	31	42½N	87¾W
Northcliffe: Austl.	98	35S	116E
North Dakota: State, U.S.A.	43	47N	100W
North Downs: Eng.	57	51N	1E
North Dvina: r., U.S.S.R.	82	63N	43E
North East New Guinea	97	5S	145E
NORTHERN IRELAND: cap. Belfast	56	—	—
Northern Sporades: is., Greece	67	39N	24E
Northern Territory: State, Austl.	96	20S	135E
North Foreland: England	55	51N	1E
North Island: N.Z.	93	—	—
NORTH KOREA: cap. Pyongyang	90	40N	127E
Northland: N.Z.	93	36S	174E
North Minch: chan., Scotland	53	58N	6W
North Platte: & r., U.S.A.	43	41N	100W
North Riding: Eng.	54	54N	1W
North Sea	53	—	—
North Stradbroke I.: Australia	98	28S	154E
North Uist: i., Scot.	53	58N	7W
Northumberland: Co., England	54	55N	2W
Northumberland Is.: Australia	98	22S	150E
NORTH VIET NAM: cap. Hanoi	90	20N	105E
Northway: U.S.A.	28	63N	142W
North West Highlands: Scotland	53	57N	5W
Northwich: England	55	53N	3W
North York Moors: England	54	54N	1W
Norton Sound: U.S.A.	2	64N	163W
Norvegia, C.: Antarctica	51	72S	10W
Norwalk: U.S.A.	31	41¼N	73¼W
NORWAY: cap. Oslo	68/9	—	—
Norwich: England	55	53N	1E
Norwood: U.S.A.	31	42¼N	71¼W
Nossob: r., S. Africa	109	26S	21E
Nosy Bé: i., Malagasy Republic	108	13S	48E

	Page	Lat.	Long.
Noto Penin.: Japan	92	37N	137E
Nottingham: & Co., England	57	53N	1W
NOUAKCHOTT: Mauritania	106	18N	17W
Nova Iguaçu: Brazil	50	22¾S	43½W
Nova Lisboa: Angola	108	13S	16E
Novara: Italy	73	45N	9E
Novaya Zemlya: is., U.S.S.R.	80	75N	60E
Novgorod: U.S.S.R.	82	58N	31E
Novi Ligure: Italy	73	45N	9E
Novi Pazar: Yugo.	67	43N	20E
Novi Sad: Yugo.	67	45N	20E
Novocherkassk: U.S.S.R.	82	47N	40E
Novograd Volynskiy: U.S.S.R.	69	51N	28E
Novogrudok: U.S.S.R.	66	54N	26E
Novokuznetsk: U.S.S.R.	83	54N	87E
Novomoskovsk: U.S.S.R.	82	54N	38E
Novonazyvayevka: U.S.S.R.	83	56N	72E
Novorossiysk: U.S.S.R.	82	45N	38E
Novosibirsk: U.S.S.R.	83	55N	83E
Novosibirskiye Ostrova: is., U.S.S.R.	81	76N	140E
Novouzensk: U.S.S.R.	82	50N	48E
Novyy Port: U.S.S.R.	80	67N	74E
Nowa Huta: Poland	66	50N	20E
Nowy Sacz: Poland	66	50N	21E
Nubian Desert: Sud.	107	21N	33E
Nučice: Czech.	66	50N	14E
Nueces: r., U.S.A.	40	28N	98W
Nuevitas: Cuba	47	22N	77W
Nuevo Laredo: Mex.	40	27N	100W
Nuits St. Georges: France	71	47N	5E
Nuku Hiva: i., Pacific Ocean	101	9S	140W
Nullarbor Plain: Australia	96	30S	128E
Numazu: Japan	92	35N	139E
Nundle: Australia	99	32S	151E
Nuneaton: England	57	53N	1W
Nunivak: i., U.S.A.	2	60N	166W
Nunkiang: China	90	49N	125E
Nuremberg (Nürnberg): Germany	72	49N	11E
Nuseybin: Turkey	85	37N	41E
Nushki: W. Pak.	88	29N	66E
Nutley: U.S.A.	31	40¾N	74¼W
Nuwara Eliya: Cey.	88	7N	81E
Nyahwest: Austl.	99	35S	143E
Nyala: Sudan	107	12N	25E
Nyenchen Tanglha Range: China	87	30N	90E
Nyíregyháza: Hung.	66	48N	22E
Nykøbing: Denmark	69	55N	12E
Nykøping: Sweden	69	59N	17E
Nymburk: Czech.	66	50N	15E
Nyngan: Australia	99	32S	147E
Nysa: Poland	66	51N	18E
Nysa: r., Pol./Ger.	66	50N	15E
Oahu: i., Pacific O.	101	21N	158W
Oak Creek: U.S.A.	31	43N	88W
Oakdale: U.S.A.	42	38N	121W
Oakham: England	57	53N	1W
Oakland: U.S.A.	46	38N	122W
Oak Lawn: U.S.A.	31	41¾N	87¾W
Oak Park: Illinois, U.S.A.	31	42N	87¾W
Oak Park: Michigan, U.S.A.	31	42½N	83¼W
Oak Ridge: U.S.A.	41	36N	84W
Oamaru: N.Z.	93	45N	171E
Oates Land: Antarc.	51	71S	160E
Ob': r., U.S.S.R.	83	63N	65E
Ob', Gulf of: U.S.S.R.	81	67N	76E
Oban: Scotland	54	56N	5W
Obbia: Somali Rep.	107	5N	48E
Oberammergau: Germany	73	48N	11E
Oberhausen: Ger.	62	51N	7E
Obidos: Brazil	48	2S	56W
Obi Is.: Indonesia	91	2S	128E
Ocala: U.S.A.	41	29N	82W
Ocean I.: Pacific O.	100	1S	170E
Oceanside: U.S.A.	31	40¾N	73¾W
Ochil Hills: Scotland	54	56¼N	3¾W
Odda: Norway	69	60N	7E
Odemis: Turkey	67	38N	28E
Odense: Denmark	69	55N	10E
Odenwald: mts., Germany	72	50N	9E
Oder (Odra): r., Germany/Poland	66	53N	14E
Odessa: U.S.A.	43	32N	102W
Odessa: U.S.S.R.	82	46N	31E
Odorhei: Romania	66	46N	25E
Oeno I.: Pacific O.	101	24S	130W
Oer-Erkenschwick: Germany	62	51¾N	7¼E
Offaly: Co., R. of Ireland	56	53N	8W
Offenburg: Germany	73	48N	8E
Ofot Fiord: Norway	68	68N	17E
Ogaden: Ethiopia	107	7N	43E
Ogden: U.S.A.	42	41N	112W
Ogdensburg: U.S.A.	31	41N	74½W
Oglio: r., Italy	73	45N	10E
Ohai: N.Z.	93	46S	168E
Ohakune: N.Z.	93	39S	175E
Ohio: r., U.S.A.	41	37N	89W
Ohio: State, U.S.A.	41	40N	83W
Ohře: r., Czech.	72	50N	14E
Oise: r., France	70	49N	2E
Oita: Japan	90	33N	132E
Oka: r., U.S.S.R.	82	55N	40E
Okanogan: r., U.S.A.	42	49N	120W
Okayama: Japan	90	35N	134E
Okeechobee, L.: U.S.A.	41	27N	81W
Okehampton: Eng.	55	51N	4W
Okhotsk: U.S.S.R.	81	59N	143E
Okhotsk, Sea of	81	55N	150E
Oki Is.: Japan	92	36N	133E
Okinawa: i., Japan	92	27N	128E
Oklahoma: State, U.S.A.	43	35N	97W
Oklahoma City: U.S.A.	43	35N	98W
Oklawaha: r., U.S.A.	41	29N	82W
Okmulgee: U.S.A.	40	36N	96W
Okovango: r., Angola/S.W. Africa	109	18S	21E
Okovango Basin: Botswana	109	19S	23E
Okuma B.: Antarc.	51	78S	158W
Olaf Coast: Antarc.	51	69S	42E
Oland: i., Sweden	69	57N	17E
Old Castile: Old Prov., Spain	65	42N	5W
Oldenburg: Ger.	72	53N	8E
Oldenzaal: Neth.	72	52N	7E
Oldham: England	57	54N	2W
Old Heads of Kinsale: R. of Ireland	56	52N	9W
Olean: U.S.A.	41	42N	78W
Olekminsk: U.S.S.R.	81	60N	120E
Olenëk: r., U.S.S.R.	81	71N	120E
Oléron, Île d': Fr.	71	46N	1W
Olomouc: Czech.	66	50N	17E
Olonzac: France	71	43N	3E
Oloron-Ste.-Marie: France	71	43N	1W
Olsztyn: Poland	66	54N	20E
Olten: Switzerland	73	47N	8E
Olympia: Greece	67	38N	22E
Olympia: U.S.A.	42	47N	123W
Olympic Nat. Park: U.S.A.	42	48N	124W
Olympus: mtn., Greece	67	40N	22E
Omagh: N. Ireland	56	55N	7W
Omaha: U.S.A.	43	41N	96W
'OMAN: & Gulf	85	25N	57E
Omaruru: S.W. Afr.	109	21S	16E
Omdurman: Sudan	107	16N	32E
Ometepe I.: Nic.	47	12N	86W
Ommaney, C.: U.S.A.	22	56N	135W
Omsk: U.S.S.R.	83	55N	73E
Omuta: Japan	92	33N	131E
Omutinskoye: U.S.S.R.	83	56N	68E
Ondor Khan: Mong.	89	47N	111E
Onega, L.: U.S.S.R.	82	63N	35E
O'Neill: U.S.A.	43	42N	99W
Onekotan: i., U.S.S.R.	81	50N	155E
Oneonta: U.S.A.	17	42N	75W
Onslow Bay: U.S.A.	41	34N	77W
Onstwedde: Neth.	72	53N	7E
Ontario, Lake: Canada/U.S.A.	17	44N	78W
Oodnadatta: Austl.	96	27S	135E
O'Okiep: S. Africa	109	30S	18E
Ooldea: Australia	96	30S	132E
Oosterhesselen: Netherlands	72	53N	7E
Oosterhout: Neth.	72	52N	5E
Ootacamund: India	88	11N	77E
Opava: Czech.	66	50N	18E
Opelika: U.S.A.	41	33N	85W
Opelousas: U.S.A.	43	31N	92W
Opladen: Germany	62	51N	7E
Opole: Poland	66	51N	18E
Oporto: Portugal	65	41N	9W
Opotiki: N.Z.	93	38S	177E
Opunake: N.Z.	93	39S	174E
Oradea: Romania	66	47N	22E
Oraison: France	71	44N	6E
Oran: Algeria	106	36N	1W
Orange: Australia	99	33S	149E
Orange: France	71	44N	5E
Orange: N.J., U.S.A.	31	40¾N	74¼W
Orange: Texas, U.S.A.	40	30N	94W
Orange: r., S. Africa	109	28S	18E
Orangeburg: U.S.A.	41	33N	81W
Orange Free State: Prov., S. Africa	109	29S	27E
Oranienburg: Ger.	72	53N	13E
Orbost: Australia	99	28S	149E
Ord: r., Australia	96	16S	128E
Ordos Plat.: China	89	39N	108E
Ordzhonikidze: U.S.S.R.	82	43N	45E
Orebro: Sweden	69	59N	15E
Oregon: State, U.S.A.	42	44N	120W
Oregon City: U.S.A.	42	45N	123W
Orekhovo-Zuyevo: U.S.S.R.	82	55N	39E
Orel: U.S.S.R.	82	53N	36E
Orem: U.S.A.	42	40N	112W
Orenburg: U.S.S.R.	82	52N	55E
Orense: Spain	65	42N	8W
Orford Ness: Eng.	55	52N	1E
Orgeyev: U.S.S.R.	73	48N	29E
Orihuela: Spain	65	38N	1W
Orinoco: r., Venez.	48	8N	64W
Orinoco Delta: Venezuela	47	9N	61W
Orissa: State, India	88	20N	84E
Oristano: Sardinia	65	40N	9E
Orizaba: & mt., Mex.	38	19N	97W
Orkney Is.: Scotland	53	59N	3W
Orlando: U.S.A.	41	29N	81W
Orléanais: Old Prov., France	71	48N	2E
Orléans: France	70	48N	2E
Orléansville: Algeria	65	36N	1E
Ormskirk: England	57	53½N	3W
Ornain: r., France	70	49N	5E
Orne: r., France	70	49N	0
Orsk: U.S.S.R.	83	51N	59E
Orthez: France	71	43N	1W
Ortler: mt., Italy	73	47N	10E
Oruro: Bolivia	42	18S	67W
Oryakhovo: Bulgaria	67	44N	24E
Osage: r., U.S.A.	43	38N	96W
Osaka: Japan	92	35N	135E
Osa Penin.: C.R.	47	8N	84W
Osh: U.S.S.R.	83	41N	73E
Oshkosh: U.S.A.	43	44N	88W
Osijek: Yugoslavia	67	46N	19E
Oskaloosa: U.S.A.	43	41N	93W
Oskarshamn: Swed.	69	57N	16E
OSLO: Norway	69	60N	11E
Oslo Fiord: Norway	69	59N	11E
Osmanabad: India	88	18N	76E
Osnabruck: Ger.	72	52N	8E
Ossett: England	57	53¾N	1½W
Ostend: Belgium	70	51N	3E
Osterath: Germany	62	51¼N	6½E
Ostersund: Sweden	68	63N	15E
Ostia: Italy	67	42N	12E
Ostrovnoye: U.S.S.R.	81	68N	164E
Ostrów Mazowiecka: Poland	66	53N	22E
Ostrów Wielkopolski: Poland	66	52N	18E
Osumi Is.: Japan	92	31N	131E
Oswaldtwistle: Eng.	57	53¾N	2¼W
Oswego: U.S.A.	17	43N	76W
Oswestry: England	57	52¾N	3W
Otago: N.Z.	93	46S	169E
Otago Penin.: N.Z.	93	46S	171E
Otaru: Japan	92	43N	141E
Othe, Forêt d': Fr.	70	48N	4E
Otranto: & str., Italy	67	40N	18E
Ottawa: Ill., U.S.A.	43	41N	89W
Ottawa: Kansas, U.S.A.	43	39N	95W
Otway Cape: Austl.	99	39S	144E
Ötztal Alps: Austria	73	47N	11E
Ouachita: r., U.S.A.	40	33N	92W
OUAGADOUGOU: Upper Volta	106	12N	2W
Ouargla: Algeria	106	32N	5E
Oubangui: r., Africa	107	4N	21E
Oudenaarde: Belg.	70	51N	4E
Oudtshoorn: S. Afr.	109	34S	22E
Ouessant, Î. d': Fr.	70	48N	5W
Oughter, L.: R. of Ireland	56	54N	7W
Oujda: Morocco	65	35N	2W
Oulu: & lake, Fin.	68	65N	25E
Ou Mts.: Japan	92	39N	141E
Oundle: England	57	52½N	½W
Ourthe: r., Belgium	70	50N	6E
Ouse: r., East Anglia, England	55	53N	0
Ouse: r., Sussex, England	55	51N	0
Oust: r., France	70	48N	2W
Outer Hebrides: is., Scotland	53	58N	7W
Outjo: S.W. Africa	109	20S	17E
Ouyen: Australia	99	35S	142E
Ovens: r., Australia	99	36S	147E
Oviedo: Spain	65	43N	6W
Owen, Mt.: N.Z.	93	42S	172E
Owen Falls: Uganda	108	0	33E
Owens: l., U.S.A.	42	36N	118W
Owensboro: U.S.A.	41	38N	87W
Owens Creek: town, Australia	98	21S	149E
Owen Stanley Range: New Guinea	97	9S	147E
Owyhee Res.: U.S.A.	42	43N	118W
Oxford: & Co., Eng.	57	52N	1W
Oxnar: U.S.A.	42	34N	119W
Oxus: r., U.S.S.R.	83	37N	65E
Oyonnax: France	71	46N	6E
Ozark Plat.: U.S.A.	43	37N	93W
Ozarks, L. of the: U.S.A.	43	38N	93W
Ozd: Hungary	66	48N	20E
Paarl: S. Africa	109	34S	19E
Pacific Grove: U.S.A.	42	37N	122W
Pacific Ocean	100/1	—	—
Padang: Sumatra	91	1S	100E
Paderborn: Ger.	72	52N	9E
Padre I.: U.S.A.	40	27N	97W
Padua (Padova): It.	73	45N	12E
Paducah: U.S.A.	41	37N	89W
Paeroa: N.Z.	93	37S	176E
Pafuri: Mozam.	109	22S	33E
Pagoda Pt.: Burma	87	16N	94E
Paignton: England	55	50N	4W
Paimboeuf: France	71	47N	2W
Paimpol: France	70	49N	3W
Paisley: Scotland	54	56N	4W
Pakanbaru: Sumatra	91	1N	102E
Pakenham: England	55	53N	1E
PAKISTAN: cap. Rawalpindi	88	—	—
Pakokku: Burma	90	21N	95E
Palapye Road: Botswana	109	22S	26E
Palatka: U.S.A.	41	30N	82W
Palau Is.: Caroline Is.	91	7N	135E
Palawan: i., Phil.	91	10N	119E
Palembang: Sumatra	91	3S	105E
Palencia: Spain	65	42N	5W
Palermo: Sicily	67	38N	13E
Palestine: U.S.A.	43	32N	96W
Palghat: India	88	11N	76E
Palghat Gap: pass, India	88	11N	77E
Palisade: U.S.A.	42	41N	116W
Palk Strait: Ind./Cey.	88	10N	80E
Palliser, C.: N.Z.	93	42S	175E
Palma: Majorca	65	40N	3E
Palmas, C.: Liberia	106	4N	8W
Palm Beach: U.S.A.	41	27N	80W
Palmer Land: Antarctica	51	64S	63W
Palmerston North: New Zealand	93	40S	176E
Palm Is.: Australia	98	19S	147E
Palmyra: Syria	86	35N	38E
Palmyra I.: Pac. O.	101	6N	162W
Palo Alto: U.S.A.	46	37½N	122W
Palos, C. de: Spain	65	38N	1W
Paltamo: Finland	68	64N	28E
Pamiers: France	71	43N	2E
Pamirs: mts., U.S.S.R./Afghanistan	83	37N	73E
Pamlico Sd.: U.S.A.	41	35N	76W
Pampa: U.S.A.	43	35N	101W
Pampas: Argentina	49	33S	64W
Pamplona: Spain	65	43N	2W
PANAMA: cap. Panamá	48	8N	80W
Panama Canal	39	Inset	
Panama City: U.S.A.	41	30N	86W
Panay: i., Phil.	91	11N	122E
Pangbourne: Eng.	57	51½N	1W
Pangong R.: China	88	34N	80E
Panjim: India	88	15N	74E
Pantar: i., Indonesia	91	8S	124E
Pantellaria: i., Italy	67	37N	12E
Paoki: China	89	34N	107E
Paoting: China	89	39N	115E
Paotow: China	89	41N	110E
Papakura: N.Z.	93	37S	175E
Papua: & gulf, New Guinea	97	7S	145E
Pará: & r., Brazil	48	1S	48W
Paracel Is.: S. China S.	91	16N	112E
PARAGUAY: cap. Asunción	49	23S	58W
Paraguay: r., S. Amer.	49	26S	58W
Parakou: Dahomey	106	9N	3E
PARAMARIBO: Surinam	96	6N	55W
Paramus: U.S.A.	31	41N	74W
Paramushir: i., U.S.S.R.	81	51N	155E
Paraná: Argentina	50	32S	60W
Paraná: r., S. Amer.	50	25S	53W
Parbati: r., India	88	23N	77E
Parbhani: India	88	19N	77E
Parchim: Germany	72	53N	12E
Pardubice: Czech.	66	50N	16E
Parece Vela: i., Pacific Ocean	100	20N	135E
Paria, G. of: Venez.	47	10N	62W
PARIS: France	70	49N	2E
Paris: U.S.A.	43	34N	96W
Parkersburg: U.S.A.	41	39N	82W
Parkes: Australia	99	33S	148E
Park Forest: U.S.A.	31	41½N	87¾W
Park Range: U.S.A.	42	40N	107W
Park Rapids: U.S.A.	43	47N	95W
Parma: Italy	73	45N	10E
Parma: U.S.A.	41	41N	82W
Parnaíba: Brazil	48	3S	42W
Parnassus: mtn., Greece	67	38N	22E
Paros: i., Greece	67	37N	25E
Parramatta: Austl.	99	34S	151E
Parsons: U.S.A.	43	37N	95W
Parthenay: France	71	47N	0
Pasadena: Calif., U.S.A.	46	34N	118W
Pasadena: Texas, U.S.A.	31	29¾N	95¼W
Pascagoula: & r., U.S.A.	41	30N	89W
Pasco: U.S.A.	42	46N	119W
Passaic: U.S.A.	31	40¾N	74W
Passau: Germany	73	49N	13E
Passchendaele: Belg.	70	51N	3E

	Page	Lat.	Long.
Passero, C.: Sicily	67	37N	15E
Pasto: Colombia	48	1N	77W
Patagonia: Arg.	49	45S	70W
Patay: France	70	48N	2E
Paterson: U.S.A.	31	41N	74¼W
Pathankot: India	88	32N	76E
Pathfinder Res.: U.S.A.	42	42N	107W
Patiala: India	88	30N	76E
Patmos: *i.*, Greece	67	37N	26E
Patna: India	88	26N	85E
Patras: & *gulf*, Greece	67	38N	22E
Patuca: *riv.*, Hond.	47	15N	85W
Pau: France	71	43N	0
Paul Block Bay: Antarctica	51	76S	146W
Paulista: Brazil	48	8S	41W
Paulo Afonso Falls: Brazil	48	9S	38W
Pavia: Italy	73	45N	9E
Pavlodar: U.S.S.R.	83	52N	77E
Payette: U.S.A.	42	44N	117W
Paysandú: Uruguay	50	32S	58W
Pays d'Albret: Fr.	71	44N	1W
Pazardzhik: Bulgaria	67	42N	24E
Peabody: U.S.A.	31	42½N	71W
Peak District: Eng.	57	53N	2W
Pearl: *r.*, U.S.A.	40	32N	90W
Pease: *r.*, U.S.A.	43	34N	100W
Pechenga: U.S.S.R.	69	70N	31E
Pechora: *r.*, U.S.S.R.	82	63N	56E
Pecos: & *r.*, U.S.A.	40	31N	104W
Pécs: Hungary	66	46N	18E
Pedro, Pt.: Ceylon	88	10N	80E
Pedro Miguel Locks: Panama Canal	39	*Inset*	
Peebinga: Australia	99	35S	141E
Peebles: & Co., Scot.	54	56N	3W
Pee Dee: *r.*, U.S.A.	41	34N	79W
Peel: I. of Man	54	54N	5W
Pegasus Bay: N.Z.	93	43S	173E
Pegu: Burma	91	17N	96E
Peh: *r.*, China	89	24N	113E
Pehpei: China	89	30N	106E
Peian: China	90	48N	127E
Peine: Germany	72	52N	10E
Peipus, L.: U.S.S.R.	82	58N	27E
PEKING (Peiping): China	90	40N	116E
Pelee: *i.*, U.S.A.	41	42N	83W
Pelican Point: S.W. Africa	109	23S	14E
Peloponnese: Greece	67	38N	22E
Pelotas: Brazil	50	32S	52W
Pelusium, Bay of: Egypt	107	*Inset*	
Pelvoux, Mont: Fr.	71	45N	6E
Pemba: Zambia	109	17S	27E
Pemba: *i.*, Tanzan.	108	5S	40E
Pembroke: & Co., Wales	55	52N	5W
Penang: *i.*, Malaya	91	5N	100E
Penchi: China	89	42N	124E
Pendembu: Sierra Leone	106	8N	11W
Pendleton: U.S.A.	42	46N	119W
Pend Oreille L.: U.S.A.	42	48N	116W
Penganga: *r.*, India	88	20N	77E
Pengpu: China	89	33N	117E
Penmarch, Pte. de: France	70	48N	4W
Pennar: *r.*, India	88	14N	77E
Pennine Alps: Switzerland/It.	73	46N	7E
Pennines: *mtns.*, Eng.	57	54N	2W
Pennsylvania: *State*, U.S.A.	41	41N	77W
Penobscot: *r.*, U.S.A.	13	45N	68W
Penrith: Australia	99	34S	151E
Penrith: England	54	55N	3W
Pensacola: U.S.A.	41	30N	87W
Pentland Firth: Scot.	53	59N	3W
Pentland Hills: Scot.	54	55¾N	3¼W
Penza: U.S.S.R.	82	53N	45E
Penzance: England	55	50N	6W
Peoria: U.S.A.	43	41N	90W
Perche, Collines du: France	70	49N	1E
Percy Is.: Australia	98	22S	150E
Perdu, Mont: Fr./Sp.	71	43N	0
Pergamino: Arg.	49	34S	61W
Périgord: France	71	45N	1E
Périgueux: France	71	45N	1E
Perim I.: Yemen P.D.R.	85	13N	43E
Perm: U.S.S.R.	82	57N	55E
Pernambuco: Brazil	48	8S	35W
Pèrnik: Bulgaria	67	43N	23E
Péronne: France	70	50N	3E
Perpignan: France	71	43N	3E
PERSIA: *see* IRAN			
Persian Gulf	85	27N	52E
Perth: Australia	98	32S	116E
Perth: & Co., Scot.	54	56N	3W
Perth Amboy: U.S.A.	31	40½N	74¼W
PERU: *cap.* Lima	48	10S	75W
Perugia: Italy	67	43N	12E
Pervomaysk: U.S.S.R.	73	48N	31E
Pesaro: Italy	73	44N	13E
Pescadores Is.: Formosa	89	24N	120E

	Page	Lat.	Long.
Pescara: Italy	67	42N	14E
Peshawar: W. Pak.	88	34N	71E
Pessac: France	71	45N	1W
Petaloma: U.S.A.	42	38N	123W
Petange: Lux.	70	50N	6E
Peterborough: Austl.	99	33S	139E
Peterborough: Eng.	57	53N	0
Peterhead: Scotland	53	57N	2W
Peter I.: *i.*, Antarc.	51	69S	90W
Peterlee: England	54	54¾N	1¼W
Petersburg: Alaska, U.S.A.	22	57N	133W
Petersburg: Va., U.S.A.	41	37N	78W
Petone: N.Z.	93	41S	175E
Petoskey: U.S.A.	17	45N	85W
Petrich: Bulgaria	67	41N	23E
Petropavlovsk: U.S.S.R.	83	55N	69E
Petropavlovsk-Kamchatski: U.S.S.R.	81	53N	159E
Petrópolis: Brazil	50	23S	43W
Petroşani: Romania	67	45N	23E
Petrovgrad: Yugo.	67	45N	20E
Petrozavodsk: U.S.S.R.	82	62N	35E
Petsamo: U.S.S.R.	68	70N	31E
Petukhovo: U.S.S.R.	83	55N	68E
Pfälzer Bergland: Germany	72	49N	8E
Pforzheim: Ger.	72	49N	9E
Phanom Dongrak: Thailand	91	14N	103E
Phanrang: S. Viet Nam	91	12N	109E
Phenix City: U.S.A.	41	32N	85W
Philadelphia: U.S.A.	41	40N	75W
Philippeville: Algeria	65	37N	7E
PHILIPPINES: *cap.* Manila	91	10N	123E
Philippine Sea	91	18N	130E
Philippopolis: Bulg.	67	42N	25E
Philip Smith Mts.: U.S.A.	28	68N	147W
PHNOM PENH: Cambodia	91	11N	105E
Phoenix: U.S.A.	42	34N	112W
Phoenix Is.: Pac. O.	100	3S	175W
Phuket I.: Thailand	91	8N	98E
Piacenza: Italy	73	45N	10E
Piatra-Neamt: Rom.	66	47N	26E
Piave: *r.*, Italy	73	46N	12E
Picardy: *Old Prov.*, France	70	50N	2E
Picola: Australia	99	36S	145E
Picton: N.Z.	93	41S	174E
Piedmont: *Reg.*, It.	73	45N	8E
Piedras Negras: Mex.	40	29N	101W
Pierre: U.S.A.	43	44N	100W
Pietarsaari: Finland	68	64N	23E
Pietermaritzburg: South Africa	109	30S	30E
Piet Retief: S. Africa	109	27S	31E
Pigeon: *r.*, U.S.A./Canada	43	48N	90W
Pikeville: U.S.A.	41	37N	83W
Pilcomayo: *r.*, S. Am.	48	23S	62W
Pilsen: Czech.	66	50N	13E
Pinar del Río: Cuba	47	22N	84W
Pindus Mts.: Greece	67	40N	21E
Pine Bluff: U.S.A.	40	34N	92W
Pine Island Sound: U.S.A.	41	27N	82W
Pinerolo: Italy	73	45N	7E
Pinkiang: China	89	46N	127E
Pinnaroo: Australia	99	35S	141E
Pinos, I. de: Cuba	47	22N	83W
Pinsk: U.S.S.R.	82	52N	26E
Piotrków: Poland	66	51N	20E
Piraeus: Greece	67	38N	24E
Pirgos: Greece	67	38N	22E
Pirin Mts.: Bulgaria	67	42N	23E
Pirmasens: Germany	72	49N	8E
Pisa: Italy	73	44N	10E
Piscataway: U.S.A.	31	40½N	74½W
Pisek: Czech.	66	49N	15E
Pistoia: Italy	73	44N	11E
Pit: *r.*, U.S.A.	42	41N	121W
Pitcairn I.: Pac. O.	101	25S	130W
Piteşti: Romania	67	45N	25E
Pittsburg: Kansas, U.S.A.	43	37N	95W
Pittsburg: Texas, U.S.A.	40	33N	95W
Pittsburgh: Penn., U.S.A.	41	40N	80W
Piura: Peru	48	5S	81W
Plainfield: U.S.A.	31	40½N	74½W
Plainview: U.S.A.	31	40¾N	73½W
Plantaurel, Mts. du: France	71	43N	1E
Plassey: India	88	24N	88E
Plate, R.: S. America	50	35S	57W
Platte: *r.*, U.S.A.	43	41N	100W
Plattsburg: U.S.A.	17	45N	74W
Plauen: Germany	72	50N	12E
Plenty, Bay of: N.Z.	93	38S	177E
Plentywood: U.S.A.	43	49N	105W
Pleven: Bulgaria	67	43N	25E
Ploeşti: Romania	67	45N	26E
Plomb du Cantal: *mtn.*, France	71	45N	3E
Plombières: France	70	48N	6E
Plovdiv: Bulgaria	67	42N	25E

	Page	Lat.	Long.
Plumtree: Rhodesia	109	20S	28E
Plymouth: England	55	50N	4W
Plymouth: Tobago	47	11N	61W
Plymouth: U.S.A.	31	42½N	83½W
Plzeň *see* Pilsen			
Po: *r.*, Italy	73	45N	10E
Pocatello: U.S.A.	42	43N	112W
Poçoes: Brazil	48	15S	40W
Po Hai: *gulf*, China	89	38N	120E
Pohang: S. Korea	90	36N	129E
Pointe-à-Pitre: Guadeloupe	47	16N	61W
Pointe Noire: Congo	108	5S	12E
Poissy: France	70	49N	2E
Poitiers: France	71	47N	0
Poitou: *Old Prov.*, Fr.	71	47N	1W
Poix: France	70	50N	2E
Pola: Yugoslavia	67	45N	14E
POLAND: *cap.* Warsaw	66	52N	20E
Poliyiros: Greece	67	40N	23E
Polotsk: U.S.S.R.	66	55N	29E
Poltava: U.S.S.R.	82	50N	35E
Polunochnoye: U.S.S.R.	83	62N	60E
Polynesia: Pac. O.	100	—	—
Pomeranian Bay: Germany	72	54N	14E
Pomona: S.W. Africa	109	27S	15E
Pompeii: Italy	67	41N	14E
Ponapé: *i.*, Pacific O.	100	8N	159E
Ponca City: U.S.A.	43	37N	97W
Ponce: Puerto Rico	47	18N	67W
Pondicherry: India	88	12N	80E
Pont-à-Mousson: Fr.	70	49N	6E
Ponta Porã: Brazil	48	22S	56W
Pontarlier: France	71	47N	6E
Pontchartrain, L.: U.S.A.	40	30N	90W
Pontefract: England	57	53¾N	1¼W
Pontevedra: Spain	65	42N	9W
Pontiac: U.S.A.	31	42¾N	83¼W
Pontianak: Borneo	91	0	109E
Pontic Mts.: Turkey	84	42N	35E
Pontivy: France	70	48N	3W
Pontoise: France	70	49N	2E
Pontresina: Switz.	73	46N	10E
Pontypool: Wales	55	52N	3W
Pontypridd: Wales	55	52N	3W
Poole: England	55	51N	2W
Poona: India	88	18N	74E
Pooncarie: Austl.	99	33S	143E
Poopo, L.: Bolivia	48	18S	67W
Poperinghe: Belg.	70	51N	3E
Poplar Bluff: U.S.A.	43	37N	90W
Popocatepetl: *volc.*, Mexico	38	19N	99W
Porbandar: India	88	22N	70E
Porcupine: *r.*, U.S.A.	28	67N	142W
Pori: Finland	68	61N	22E
Porkkala: Finland	69	60N	24E
Porlamar: Venez.	47	11N	64W
Port Adelaide: Austl.	99	35S	139E
Portadown: N. Irel.	56	54N	6W
Portaferry: N. Irel.	56	54N	6W
Portalegre: Portugal	65	39N	7W
Port Alfred: S. Afr.	109	34S	27E
Port Angeles: U.S.A.	42	48N	123W
Port Antonio: Jam.	47	18N	76W
Portarlington: R. of Ireland	56	53N	7W
Port Arthur: U.S.A.	40	30N	94W
Port Augusta: Austl.	99	32S	138E
PORT-AU-PRINCE: Haiti	47	19N	72W
Port Bou: Spain	65	42N	3E
Port Chalmers: N.Z.	93	46S	171E
Port Clinton: Austl.	98	22S	151E
Port Elizabeth: South Africa	109	34S	26E
Port Ellen: Scotland	54	56N	6W
Port Étienne: Maur.	108	21N	17W
Port Fuad: Egypt	107	*Inset*	
Port Glasgow: Scot.	54	56N	4¾W
Port Harcourt: Nig.	108	5N	7E
Port Hedland: Austl.	96	20S	119E
Port Huron: U.S.A.	17	43N	82W
Port Jackson: Austl.	99	34S	151E
Port Kembla: Austl.	99	34S	151E
Portland: Australia	99	38S	142E
Portland: Maine, U.S.A.	17	44N	70W
Portland: Oregon, U.S.A.	42	46N	123W
Portland, Bill of: England	55	51N	2W
Portlaoighise: R. of Ireland	56	53N	7W
Port Lincoln: Austl.	96	35S	136E
Port Lockroy: Antarctica	51	65S	64W
Port Macquarie: Australia	99	31S	153E
Portmadoc: Wales	55	53N	4W
Port Martin: Antarc.	51	67S	141E
PORT MORESBY: Papua (*and Territory of New Guinea*)	97	9S	147E
Port Nolloth: S. Afr.	109	29S	17E
Pôrto Alegre: Brazil	48	30S	51W
Pôrto Alexandre: Angola	109	16S	12E
Pôrto Amélia: Moz.	109	13S	40E
Portobello: Panamá	47	10N	80W
PORT OF SPAIN: Trinidad	47	11N	61W

	Page	Lat.	Long.
Porto Novo: Dahomey	108	6N	3E
Porto Novo: India	88	12N	80E
Pôrto Velho: Brazil	48	9S	64W
Port Phillip Bay: Australia	99	38S	145E
Port Pirie: Australia	99	33S	138E
Portree: Scotland	54	57N	6W
Portrush: N. Ireland	56	55N	7W
Port Safaga: Egypt	84	27N	34E
Port St. Joe: U.S.A.	41	30N	85W
Port Said: Egypt	84	31N	32E
Port Shepstone: South Africa	109	31S	31E
Portsmouth: England	55	51N	1W
Portsmouth: N.H., U.S.A.	17	43N	71W
Portsmouth: Ohio, U.S.A.	41	39N	83W
Portsmouth: Va., U.S.A.	41	37N	76W
Port Stanley: Falkland Is.	49	52S	58W
Port Sudan: Sudan	107	20N	37E
Port Sulphur: U.S.A.	41	29N	90W
Port Talbot: Wales	55	52N	4W
Port Taufîq: Egypt	107	*Inset*	
PORTUGAL: *cap.* Lisbon	65	—	—
PORTUGUESE GUINEA: *cap.* Bissau	106	12N	15W
Port Vendres: Fr.	71	43N	3E
Porz: Germany	62	51N	7E
Posadas: Argentina	48	27S	56W
Possession Island: Antarctica	51	72S	171E
Postmasburg: S. Afr.	109	28S	23E
Poteet: U.S.A.	40	29N	99W
Potenza: Italy	67	41N	16E
Potgietersrus: S. Afr.	109	24S	29E
Poti: U.S.S.R.	82	42N	42E
Potomac: *r.*, U.S.A.	41	38N	77W
Potosí: Bolivia	48	20S	66W
Potrerillos: Chile	48	26S	69W
Potsdam: Germany	72	52N	13E
Potsdam: U.S.A.	17	45N	75W
Potters Bar: England	57	51¾N	¼W
Pottstown: U.S.A.	41	40N	76W
Poughkeepsie: U.S.A.	41	42N	74W
Poverty Bay: N.Z.	93	39S	178E
Powder: *r.*, U.S.A.	43	45N	106W
Poyang, L.: China	89	29N	116E
Požarevac: Yugo.	67	45N	21E
Poznań: Poland	66	52N	17E
Prades: France	71	43N	2E
PRAGUE (Praha): Czechoslovakia	66	50N	14E
Prato: Italy	73	44N	11E
Prescott: U.S.A.	42	35N	112W
Presque Isle: *city*, U.S.A.	13	47N	68W
Preston: England	57	54N	3W
Prestwick: Scotland	54	55N	5W
PRETORIA: Republic of South Africa	109	26S	28E
Preveza: Greece	67	39N	21E
Pribilof Is.: Bering Sea	101	57N	170W
Prichard: U.S.A.	41	31N	88W
Prieska: S. Africa	109	30S	22E
Prilep: Yugoslavia	67	41N	22E
Prince Albert Mts.: Antarctica	51	76S	161E
Prince of Wales I.: U.S.A.	22	56N	133W
Princes Risborough: England	57	51¾N	¾W
Princess Elizabeth Land: Antarc.	51	71S	80E
Princeton: U.S.A.	41	40N	75W
Principe: *i.*, Gulf of Guinea	106	2N	7E
Prinsesse Astrid Coast: Antarc.	51	71S	12E
Prinsesse Ragnhild Coast: Antarc.	51	73S	27E
Prins Harald Coast: Antarctica	51	70S	37E
Pripet: *r. & marshes*, U.S.S.R.	82	52N	29E
Priština: Yugoslavia	67	43N	21E
Privas: France	71	45N	5E
Prizren: Yugoslavia	67	42N	21E
Proclamation I.: Antarctica	51	65S	54E
Progreso: Mexico	38	21N	90W
Prokop'yevsk: U.S.S.R.	83	54N	86E
Prome: Burma	90	19N	95E
Proserpine: Austl.	98	20S	149E
Prostějov: Czech.	66	50N	17E
Provence: *Old Prov.*, France	71	44N	6E
Provence Alps: Fr.	71	44N	6E
Providence: U.S.A.	17	42N	71W
Providence, C.: N.Z.	93	46S	166E
Providencia I.: Carib. Sea	47	13N	80W
Provo: U.S.A.	42	40N	112W
Prut: *r.*, U.S.S.R./Romania	66	48N	27E
Prydze Bay: Antarc.	51	69S	75E
Przemyśl: Poland	66	50N	23E

	Page	Lat.	Long.
Pskov: U.S.S.R.	82	58N	28E
Ptolemais: Greece	67	41N	22E
Pudsey: England	57	53¾N	1¾W
Puebla: Mexico	38	19N	98W
Pueblo: U.S.A.	43	38N	105W
Puerto Ayacucho: Venezuela	48	6N	66W
Puerto Cabello: Venezuela	48	10N	68W
Puerto Cabezas: Nic.	47	14N	83W
Puerto Deseado: Arg.	49	48S	66W
Puerto Montt: Chile	49	41S	73W
Puerto Peñasco: Mex.	42	31N	114W
Puerto Plata: Dom. Republic	47	20N	71W
PUERTO RICO: cap. San Juan	47	18N	66W
Pukekohe: N.Z.	93	37S	175E
Pula: Yugoslavia	67	45N	14E
Pulaski: U.S.A.	41	37N	81W
Pullman: U.S.A.	42	47N	117W
PUNAKHA: Bhutan	89	28N	90E
Punjab: State, India	88	30N	75E
Puno: Peru	48	16S	70W
Punta Arenas: Chile	49	53S	71W
Puntarenas: Costa Rica	47	10N	85W
Purbeck, I. of: Eng.	55	51N	2W
Puri: India	88	20N	86E
Purnamoota: Austl.	99	31S	141E
Purnea: India	88	26N	88E
Purús: r., Brazil	48	5S	64W
Pusan: S. Korea	90	35N	129E
Pushkin: U.S.S.R.	82	59N	30E
Putoran Mts.: U.S.S.R.	81	69N	95E
Putumayo: r., S. Am.	48	2S	72W
Puy de Sancy: mtn., France	71	45N	3E
Pwllheli: Wales	55	53N	4W
Pyatigorsk: U.S.S.R.	82	44N	43E
PYONGYANG: N.Korea	90	39N	126E
Pyramid Lake: U.S.A.	42	40N	120W
Pyramids: Egypt	84	30N	31E
Pyrenees: mtns., Spain/France	65	43N	0
Qasr Farafra: Egypt	107	27N	28E
QATAR: cap. Dauha	85	25N	51E
Qattara Depression: Egypt	84	29N	28E
Qazvin: Iran	85	36N	50E
Qena: Egypt	84	26N	33E
Qila Saifullah: West Pakistan	88	31N	69E
Qom: Iran	85	35N	50E
Qomul (Hami): China	87	43N	93E
Queanbeyan: Austl.	99	35S	149E
Quedlinburg: Ger.	72	52N	11E
Queen Adelaide Arch.: Chile	49	52S	75W
Queen Mary Land: Antarctica	51	71S	97E
Queen Maud Land: Antarctica	51	75S	10E
Queen Maud Range: Antarctica	51	87S	80W
Queens: U.S.A.	31	40¾N	74W
Queensferry: Scot.	54	56N	3¼W
Queensland: State, Australia	97	23S	145E
Queenstown: N.Z.	93	45S	169E
Quelimane: Mozam.	109	18S	37E
Quelpart I. (Cheju I.): S. Korea	90	33N	126E
Quemoy: i., China	89	24N	118E
Que Que: Rhodesia	109	19S	30E
Quetta: W. Pak.	88	30N	67E
Quiberon: & bay, Fr.	70	47N	3W
Quilmes: Argentina	50	34¾S	58¼W
Quilpie: Australia	98	27S	144E
Quimper: France	70	48N	4W
Quimperlé: France	70	48N	4W
Quincy: U.S.A.	31	42¼N	71W
QUITO: Ecuador	48	0	78W
Qunfidha: Sau. Arab.	85	19N	41E
Quorn: Australia	99	32S	138E
Quwaiiya: Sau. Arab.	85	24N	45E
Rabat: Malta	67	36N	14E
RABAT: Morocco	98	34N	7W
Rabaul: New Britain	97	4S	152E
Racine: U.S.A.	31	42¾N	87¾W
Radnorshire: Co., Wales	55	52N	3W
Radom: Poland	66	51N	21E
Ragusa: Sicily	67	37N	15E
Rahway: U.S.A.	31	40½N	74¼W
Raichur: India	88	16N	77E
Rainier, Mt.: U.S.A.	42	47N	122W
Raipur: India	88	21N	82E
Rajahmundry: India	88	17N	82E
Rajasthan: State, India	88	27N	74E
Rajkot: India	88	22N	71E
Rajshahi: E. Pakistan	88	24N	88E
Rakahanga: i., Pacific Ocean	101	10S	161W
Rakaia: r., N.Z.	93	44S	172E
Raleigh: U.S.A.	41	36N	79W
Rambouillet: France	70	49N	2E
Ramillies: Belgium	70	51N	5E

	Page	Lat.	Long.
Râmnicu Sărat: Rom.	67	45N	27E
Râmnicu Vâlcea: Romania	67	45N	24E
Rampur: India	88	29N	79E
Ramsbottom: Eng.	57	53¾N	2¼W
Ramsey: I. of Man	54	54N	4W
Ramsey, I.: Wales	55	52N	5W
Ramsgate: England	55	51N	1E
Rancagua: Chile	49	34S	71W
Ranchi: India	88	23N	85E
Randers: Denmark	69	56N	10E
Rangitaiki: r., N.Z.	93	38S	177E
RANGOON: Burma	91	17N	96E
Rangpur: E. Pak.	88	26N	89E
Raniganj: India	88	24N	87E
Rankovićevo: Yugo.	67	44N	21E
Rapallo: Italy	73	44N	9E
Rapid City: U.S.A.	43	44N	103W
Rapolano: Italy	67	43N	12E
Raratonga: i., Pacific Ocean	101	20S	160W
Ras al Hadd: c., 'Oman	85	23N	60E
Rasht: Iran	85	37N	50E
Rastatt: Germany	72	49N	8E
Rathenow: Germany	72	53N	13E
Rathkeale: R. of Irel.	56	53N	9W
Rathlin I.: N. Irel.	56	55N	6W
Rathluirc: R. of Irel.	56	52N	9W
Ratingen: Germany	62	51¼N	6¾E
Ratisbon see Regensburg			
Ratlam: India	88	23N	75E
Ratnagiri: India	88	17N	73E
Raton: U.S.A.	43	37N	105W
Raukumara R.: N.Z.	93	38S	178E
Raunds: England	57	52¼N	½W
Ravenna: Italy	73	44N	12E
Ravenswood: Austl.	98	20S	147E
Ravi: r., W. Pak.	88	31N	72E
RAWALPINDI: Pakistan	88	34N	73E
Rawson: Argentina	45	43S	65W
Rawtenstall: Eng.	57	53¾N	2¼W
Rayleigh: England	57	51½N	½E
Rayleigh Bay: U.S.A.	41	35N	76W
Raymond: U.S.A.	42	47N	124W
Razdel'naya: U.S.S.R.	66	47N	30E
Ré, Île de: France	71	46N	1W
Rea: r., England	57	52½N	2W
Reading: England	57	51N	1W
Reading: U.S.A.	41	40N	76W
Recherche Arch.: Australia	98	34S	122E
Recife: Brazil	48	8S	35W
Recklinghausen: Ger.	62	52N	7E
Red: r., Can./U.S.A.	43	48N	97W
Red: r., China/N. Viet Nam	89	22N	105E
Red: r., U.S.A.	40	31N	92W
Red Basin: China	90	30N	105E
Red Bluff: U.S.A.	42	40N	122W
Redbridge: England	57	51½N	0
Redcar: England	54	54½N	1W
Red Cedar: r., U.S.A.	43	45N	92W
Redcliffe: Australia	98	27S	153E
Red Cliffs: Australia	99	34S	142E
Redding: U.S.A.	42	41N	122W
Redditch: England	57	52N	2W
Redfield: U.S.A.	43	45N	99W
Redford Heights: U.S.A.	31	42½N	83¼W
Redhill: England	57	51¼N	¼W
Red L.: U.S.A.	43	48N	95W
Redon: France	70	48N	2W
Red Sea	84/5	—	—
Red Sea Hills: Egypt	84	27N	33E
Red Wing: U.S.A.	43	45N	93W
Regensburg: Ger.	72	49N	12E
Reggio di Calabria: Italy	67	38N	16E
Reggio nell'Emilia: Italy	73	45N	11E
Reidsville: U.S.A.	41	36N	80W
Reigate: England	57	51N	0
Reims: France	70	49N	4E
Remoulins: France	71	44N	5E
Remscheid: Germany	62	51N	7E
Renfrew: Scotland	54	55¾N	4½W
Renkum: Neth.	72	52N	6E
Renmark: Australia	99	34S	141E
Rennes: France	70	48N	2W
Rennick B.: Antarc.	51	70S	162E
Reno: U.S.A.	42	39N	120W
Republican: r., U.S.A.	43	40N	97W
REPUBLIC OF SOUTH AFRICA: cap. Pretoria	109	—	—
Repulse Bay: Austl.	98	21S	149E
Resistencia: Arg.	48	27S	59W
Reşiţa: Romania	67	45N	22E
Rethimnon: Crete	67	35N	25E
Reus: Spain	65	41N	1E
Reuss: r., Switz.	73	47N	8E
Reutlingen: Ger.	73	48N	9E
Revere: U.S.A.	31	42½N	71W
Revermont: France	71	46N	5E
Revilla Gigedo Is.: Pacific Ocean	101	19N	112W
Rewari: India	88	28N	76E
Rexburg: U.S.A.	42	44N	112W
REYKJAVIK: Iceland	68	64N	22W
Reynosa: Mexico	40	26N	98W
Rezā'īyeh: Iran	85	38N	45E

	Page	Lat.	Long.
Rezekne: U.S.S.R.	69	56N	28E
Rhaetian Alps: Switzerland	73	47N	10E
Rhayader: Wales	55	52N	4W
Rheden: Neth.	72	52N	6E
Rheims: France	70	49N	4E
Rheinberg: Germany	62	51½N	6½E
Rheine: Germany	72	52N	7E
Rheinhausen: Ger.	62	51½N	6¾E
Rheinkamp: Ger.	62	51½N	6¾E
Rheydt: Germany	62	51N	6E
Rhine: r., Europe	72	52N	6E
Rhode Island: State, U.S.A.	17	42N	72W
Rhodes: i. & town, Greece	67	36N	28E
RHODESIA: cap. Salisbury	109	20S	30E
Rhodope Mts.: Bulg.	67	42N	24E
Rhône: r., Europe	71	45N	5E
Rhum: i., Scotland	54	57N	6W
Rhyl: Wales	55	53N	4W
Riau Arch.: Indon.	91	0	105E
Ribble: r., England	57	53¾N	2½W
Ribeirão Prêto: Brazil	48	21S	48W
Riberalta: Bolivia	48	11S	66W
Riccarton: N.Z.	93	44S	173E
Richfield: U.S.A.	42	39N	112W
Richland Prosser: U.S.A.	42	46N	119W
Richmond: England	57	51½N	¼W
Richmond: Illinois, U.S.A.	31	42½N	88¼W
Richmond: Indiana, U.S.A.	41	40N	85W
Richmond: Ky., U.S.A.	41	38N	84W
Richmond: Virginia, U.S.A.	41	38N	77W
Richwood: U.S.A.	41	38N	81W
Rickmansworth: Eng.	57	51¾N	½W
Ridgewood: U.S.A.	31	41N	74W
Riga: & gulf, U.S.S.R.	82	57N	24E
Rijeka: Yugoslavia	67	45N	15E
Rijswijk: Neth.	72	52N	4E
Rimini: Italy	73	44N	13E
Ringsted: Denmark	69	55N	12E
Riobamba: Ecuador	48	2S	79W
Rio Branco: Brazil	48	10S	68W
Rio de Janeiro: Brazil	50	23S	43W
Rio de Oro: Prov., Spanish Sahara	106	24N	14W
Rio Gallegos: Arg.	49	52S	69W
Rio Grande: Brazil	49	32S	52W
Rio Grande: r., Nic.	47	13N	84W
Rio Grande: r., U.S.A./Mexico	40	27N	99W
Río Grande do Sul: State, Brazil	49	30S	53W
Riom: France	71	46N	3E
Rio Muni: Equatorial Guinea	108	2N	10E
Ripon: England	54	54N	2W
Ritter, Mt.: U.S.A.	42	38N	120W
Rive-de-Gier: France	71	46N	5E
Rivera: Uruguay	50	31S	56W
Riverina: Australia	99	36S	145E
Riverside: U.S.A.	42	34N	117W
RIYADH: Sa'udi Arabia	85	25N	47E
Roanne: France	71	46N	4E
Roanoke: U.S.A.	41	37N	80W
Roanoke Rapids: U.S.A.	41	37N	78W
Robertson Bay: Antarctica	51	72S	170E
Robertson I.: Antarctica	51	65S	60W
Robstown: U.S.A.	40	28N	97W
Rochdale: England	57	54N	2W
Rochechouart: Fr.	71	46N	1E
Rochefort-sur-Mer: France	71	46N	1W
Rochester: England	57	51N	0
Rochester: Minn., U.S.A.	43	44N	92W
Rochester: N.H., U.S.A.	17	43N	71W
Rochester: N.Y., U.S.A.	17	43N	78W
Rock: r., U.S.A.	43	42N	89W
Rockall: i., Atl. O.	52	58N	14W
Rockford: U.S.A.	43	42N	89W
Rockhampton: Austl.	98	23S	151E
Rock Hill: U.S.A.	41	35N	81W
Rockingham: Eng.	57	52½N	¾W
Rock Island: city, U.S.A.	43	41N	91W
Rock Springs: U.S.A.	42	42N	109W
Rockville Centre: U.S.A.	31	40¾N	73¾W
Rockwood: U.S.A.	13	46N	70W
Rocky Ford: U.S.A.	43	38N	104W
Rocky Mount: city, U.S.A.	41	36N	78W
Rocky Mts.: Canada/U.S.A.	2	55N	117W
Rocroi: France	70	50N	5E
Rødberg: Norway	69	60N	9E
Rodenkirchen: Ger.	62	51N	7E
Rodez: France	71	44N	3E
Rodings, The: Eng.	57	51¾N	¼E
Roermond: Neth.	72	51N	6E
Roeselare: Belgium	70	51N	3E

	Page	Lat.	Long.
Rogers, Mt.: U.S.A.	41	37N	82W
Rogers City: U.S.A.	17	45N	84W
Rolla: U.S.A.	43	38N	92W
Roma: Australia	98	27S	149E
Roman: Romania	66	47N	26E
ROMANIA: cap. Bucharest	66/7	—	—
Romans: France	71	45N	5E
ROME: Italy	67	42N	12E
Rome: U.S.A.	41	34N	85W
Romford: England	57	51½N	¼E
Romilly-sur-Seine: France	70	49N	4E
Romulus: U.S.A.	31	42¼N	83½W
Rona: i., Scotland	53	59N	6W
Roncesvalles: Spain	65	43N	1W
Ronda: Spain	65	37N	5W
Rønne: Denmark	69	55N	15E
Roosendaal: Neth.	72	52N	4E
Roosevelt I.: Antarc.	51	80S	161W
Roquefort: France	71	44N	0
Roraima: mtn., Venezuela	48	5N	61W
Rorschach: Switz.	73	48N	9E
Rørvik: Norway	68	65N	11E
Rosa, Monte: Switz./Italy	73	46N	8E
Rosario: Argentina	50	33S	61W
Roscoff: France	70	49N	4W
Roscommon: & Co., R. of Ireland	56	54N	8W
Roscrea: R. of Irel.	56	53N	8W
Roseburg: U.S.A.	42	43N	123W
Roseires: Sudan	107	12N	34E
Rosendaël: France	70	51N	2E
Rosenheim: Ger.	73	48N	12E
Rosetta: Egypt	84	32N	30E
Roseville: U.S.A.	31	42½N	83W
Ross Ice Shelf: Antarctica	51	80S	180
Ross I.: Antarctica	51	76S	169E
Rosslare Harbour: R. of Ireland	56	52N	6W
Ross-on-Wye: Eng.	55	52N	3W
Ross Sea: Antarctica	51	76S	175W
Rostock: Germany	72	54N	12E
Rostov: U.S.S.R.	82	47N	40E
Roswell: U.S.A.	43	33N	105W
Rosyth: Scotland	54	56N	3¼W
Rothbury: England	54	55N	2W
Rothenburg: Ger.	72	49N	10E
Rother: r., England	57	53¼N	1¼W
Rotherham: England	57	53N	1W
Rothesay: Scotland	54	56N	5W
Roti: i., Indonesia	91	10S	124E
Roto: Australia	99	33S	146E
Rotorua: N.Z.	93	38S	176E
Rotterdam: Neth.	72	52N	4E
Rottnest I.: Austl.	98	32S	115E
Rottweil: Germany	73	48N	9E
Roubaix: France	70	51N	3E
Rouen: France	70	49N	1E
Roundup: U.S.A.	42	46N	109W
Roussillon: Old Prov., France	71	43N	3E
Rovaniemi: Finland	68	66N	26E
Rovereto: Italy	73	46N	11E
Rovigo: Italy	73	45N	12E
Rovno: U.S.S.R.	82	51N	26E
Roxburgh: Co., Scot.	54	55N	3W
Roxburgh: N.Z.	93	46S	169E
Roxo, C.: Port. Guinea	106	12N	17W
Royale, Isle: U.S.A.	43	48N	89W
Royal Oak: U.S.A.	31	42½N	83¼W
Royal Tunbridge Wells: England	55	51	0
Royan: France	71	46N	1W
Royston: England	57	52N	0
Ruahine Range: N.Z.	93	40S	176E
Ruapehu: mtn., N.Z.	93	39S	176E
Rub' al Khali: Sa'udi Arabia	85	20N	50E
Rubtsovsk: U.S.S.R.	83	52N	81E
Rudok: China	88	34N	80E
Rudolf, L.: Kenya	108	4N	36E
Ruffec: France	71	46N	0
Rugby: England	55	52N	1W
Rugeley: England	57	52 N	2W
Rügen: i., Germany	66	54N	13E
Ruhr: district, Ger.	62	Inset	
Rukwa, L.: Tanzania	108	8S	32E
Ruma: Yugoslavia	67	45N	20E
Rum Cay: i., Bahama Is.	47	24N	75W
Rum Jungle: Austl.	96	13S	131E
Runcorn: England	57	53¼N	2¾W
Rupert Coast: Antarctica	51	76S	142W
Ruschuk (Ruse): Bulgaria	67	44N	26E
Rush: R. of Ireland	56	54N	6W
Russell: N.Z.	93	35S	174E
Russian Soviet Fed. Socialist Rep.: U.S.S.R.	82/3	—	—
Rutherglen: Scot.	54	55¾N	4¼W
Rutland: Co., Eng.	55	53N	1W
Rutland: U.S.A.	17	44N	73W
Ruvuma: r., Africa	108	11S	37E
Ruwenzori, Mt.: Uganda	108	1N	30E
RWANDA	108	2S	30E
Ryazn': U.S.S.R.	82	55N	40E
Rybach'ye: U.S.S.R.	83	43N	76E

	Page	Lat.	Long.
Rybinski: & res., U.S.S.R.	82	58N	38E
Rybnitsa: U.S.S.R.	66	48N	29E
Ryukyu Is.: Japan	92	27N	127E
Rzeszów: Poland	66	50N	22E
Rzhev: U.S.S.R.	82	56N	35E
Saale: *r.*, Germany	72	50N	12E
Saalfeld: Germany	72	51N	11E
Saar: *Länd*, Germany	72	49N	7E
Saar: *r.*, Germany	72	50N	7E
Saarbrücken: Ger.	72	49N	7E
Saaremaa: *i.*, U.S.S.R.	82	58N	23E
Sabadell: Spain	65	42N	2E
Sabah: Malaysia	91	5N	118E
Sabinas: Mexico	40	28N	101W
Sabine: *r.*, U.S.A.	43	31N	94W
Sabine, Mt.: Antarc.	51	72S	170E
Sabkhat Minjora: Sa'udi Arabia	85	20N	53E
Sable, Cape: U.S.A.	41	25N	81W
Sabrina Coast: Antarctica	51	67S	115E
Saco: U.S.A.	17	43N	70W
Sacramento: & *r.*, U.S.A.	42	39N	121W
Sacramento Mts.: U.S.A.	43	34N	105W
Sá da Bandeira: Angola	109	15S	14E
Sado: *i.*, Japan	90	38N	138E
Safford: U.S.A.	42	32N	110W
Safi: Morocco	106	32N	9W
Saginaw: U.S.A.	17	44N	84W
Sahara Desert: North Africa	106/7	—	—
Saharan Atlas: *mts.*, Algeria	106	33N	3E
Saharanpur: India	88	30N	78E
Sai: *r.*, India	88	26N	82E
SAIGON: S. Viet Nam	91	11N	107E
Sain Shanda: Mong.	81	45N	110E
St. Affrique: France	71	44N	3E
St. Albans: England	57	52N	0
St. Amand: France	70	50N	3E
St. Amand-Mont-Rond: France	71	47N	2E
St. André, Plaine de: France	70	49N	1E
St. Andrews: Scot.	54	56N	3W
St. Anne's: England	57	54N	3W
St. Augustine: U.S.A.	41	30N	81W
St. Bernard Pass, Gt.: Switz./Italy	73	46N	7E
St. Bernard Pass, Little: Fr./It.	73	46N	7E
St. Bride's Bay: Wales	55	52N	5W
St. Brieuc: France	70	49N	3W
St. Catherine's Pt.: England	55	51N	1W
St. Chamond: Fr.	71	45N	5E
St. Christopher: *see* St. Kitts	47	17N	63W
St. Clair, L.: U.S.A.	17	43N	83W
Saint Clair Shores: U.S.A.	31	42½N	83W
St. Claude: France	71	46N	6E
St. Cloud: U.S.A.	43	46N	94W
St. Croix: *i.*, W. Ind.	47	18N	65E
St. David's Head: Wales	55	52N	5W
St. Denis: France	64	49N	2¼E
St. Dié: France	70	48N	7E
St. Dizier: France	70	49N	5E
St. Elias, Mt.: & *mtns.*, U.S.A./Canada	2	60N	140W
Saintes: France	71	46N	1W
Saintes, Les: *is.*, West Indies	39	16N	62W
St. Étienne: France	71	45N	4E
St. Flour: France	71	45N	3E
St. Francis: *r.*, U.S.A.	43	35N	90W
St. Francis, C.: South Africa	109	34S	25E
St. Gallen: Switz.	73	47N	9E
St. George: U.S.A.	42	37N	114W
St. George, C.: U.S.A.	41	30N	85W
St. George's: Grenada	47	12N	62W
St. George's Chan.: Wales/R. of Irel.	53	52N	6W
St. Germain: France	64	49N	2E
St. Gothard Pass: Switzerland	73	47N	9E
St. Govan's Head: Wales	55	52N	5W
St. Helena: *i.*, Atl. O.	52	16S	8W
St. Helena Bay: South Africa	108	32S	18E
St. Helens: England	57	53N	3W
Saint Helens: U.S.A.	42	46N	123W
St. Helier: Chan. Is.	55	*Inset*	
St. Ingbert: Germany	72	49N	7E
St. Ives: England	55	50N	5W
St. Jean-de-Luz: Fr.	71	43N	2W
St. Jean de Maurienne: Fr.	71	45N	6E
St. Jean Pied-de-Port: France	71	43N	1W
St. John: *r.*, U.S.A.	13	47N	69W
St. Johns: *r.*, U.S.A.	41	30N	82W
St. Joseph: Mo., U.S.A.	43	40N	95W
St. Joseph: & *r.*, Mich., U.S.A.	41	42N	87W
St. Julien: France	71	46N	6E
St. Junien: France	71	46N	1E
St. Kitts: *i.*, W. Indies	47	17N	63W
St. Lawrence: *i.*, Bering Sea	2	63N	170W
St. Lô: France	70	49N	1W
St. Louis: U.S.A.	43	39N	90W
St. Louis: Senegal	106	16N	16W
St. Lucia: *i.*, W. Ind.	47	14N	61W
St. Malo: & *gulf*, Fr.	70	49N	2W
St. Marc: Haiti	47	19N	73W
Sainte Marie, C.: Malagasy Rep.	108	25S	45E
St. Martin: *i.*, West Indies	47	18N	63W
St. Mary's: England	55	50N	6W
St. Mary's: Tasmania	97	42S	148E
St. Marys: U.S.A.	41	41N	79W
St. Matthew: *i.*, Bering Sea	2	60N	172W
St. Maurice: Switz.	73	46N	7E
Ste. Menehould: Fr.	70	49N	5E
St. Moritz: Switz.	73	46N	10E
St. Nazaire: France	70	47N	2W
St. Omer: France	70	51N	2E
Saintonge: *Old Prov.*, France	71	45N	1W
St. Paul: *i.*, Indian O.	100	39S	78E
St. Paul: U.S.A.	43	45N	93W
St. Paul, C.: Ghana	106	6N	1E
St. Paul Rocks: Atlantic Ocean	52	0	30W
St. Peter Port: Channel Islands	55	*Inset*	
St. Petersburg: U.S.A.	41	28N	83W
St. Pierre-Quilbignon: France	70	48N	5W
St. Pol: France	70	50N	2E
St. Pons: France	71	43N	3E
St. Quentin: France	70	50N	3E
St. Raphaël: France	71	43N	7E
Ste. Savine: France	70	48N	4E
St. Servan: France	70	49N	2W
St. Thomas: *i.*, West Indies	47	18N	65W
St. Tropez: France	71	43N	7E
St. Valéry en Caux: France	70	50N	1E
St. Vincent, C.: Portugal	65	37N	9W
St. Vincent, Gulf of: Australia	99	35S	138E
St. Vincent: *i.*, West Indies	47	13N	61W
Saipan: *i.*, Pac. O.	100	15N	145E
Saiwūn: Aden	85	16N	49E
Sakaka: Sau. Arab.	85	30N	40E
Sakania: Congo Rep.	109	12S	28E
Sakata: Japan	92	39N	140E
Sakhalin: *i.*, U.S.S.R.	81	50N	143E
Sakhalin Bay: U.S.S.R.	81	54N	141E
Sakishima Group: Japan	92	24N	124E
Salado: *r.*, Argentina	50	30S	61W
Salala: Muscat and 'Oman	85	17N	54E
Salamanca: Spain	65	41N	6W
Sala-y-Gomez: *i.*, Pacific Ocean	101	26S	105W
Sale: Australia	99	38S	147E
Sale: England	57	53½N	2¼W
Salekhard: U.S.S.R.	80	66N	66E
Salem: India	88	12N	78E
Salem: Mass., U.S.A.	31	42½N	71W
Salem: Oregon, U.S.A.	42	45N	123W
Salem: Va., U.S.A.	41	37N	80W
Salerno: Italy	67	41N	15E
Salford: England	57	53½N	2¼W
Salida: U.S.A.	42	38N	106W
Salima: Malawi	109	14S	35E
Salina: U.S.A.	43	39N	98W
Salinas: U.S.A.	42	37N	122W
Salinas, C.: Majorca	65	39N	3E
Saline: *r.*, U.S.A.	40	34N	92W
Salisbury: Australia	99	35S	139E
Salisbury: & *Plain*, England	55	51N	2W
SALISBURY: Rhodesia	109	18S	31E
Salmon: *r.*, U.S.A.	42	45N	116W
Salmon River Mts.: U.S.A.	42	45N	115W
Salon de Provence: France	71	44N	5E
Salonica: Greece	67	41N	23E
Salonta: Romania	66	47N	22E
Salpausselka: *mtns.*, Finland	69	61N	25E
Salt: *r.*, U.S.A.	43	40N	92W
Salta: Argentina	48	25S	65W
Saltillo: Mexico	38	25N	101W
Salt Lake City: U.S.A.	42	41N	112W
Salt Range: W. Pak.	88	33N	73E
Salto: Uruguay	50	31S	58W
Saluzzo: Italy	73	45N	7E
Salvador: Brazil	48	13S	38W
Salween: *r.*, Burma	90	20N	98E
Salzach: *r.*, Austria	73	47N	12E
Salzbitter: Germany	72	52N	10E
Salzburg: & *Prov.*, Austria	73	48N	13E
Samah: China	91	18N	110E
Samar: *i.*, Phil.	91	12N	125E
Samarinda: Borneo	91	0	117E
Samarkand: U.S.S.R.	83	40N	67E
Samarra: 'Iraq	85	34N	44E
Sambalpur: India	88	22N	84E
Sambor: U.S.S.R.	69	50N	23E
Sambre: *r.*, France/Belgium	70	50N	4E
Samoa Is.: Pac. O.	100	12S	172W
Samos: *i.*, Greece	67	38N	27E
Samothrace: *i.*, Greece	67	40N	26E
Samsun: Turkey	84	41N	36E
SAN'A: Yemen	85	15N	44E
Sanandaj: Iran	85	35N	47E
San Andres I.: Carib. Sea	47	13N	81W
San Angelo: U.S.A.	43	31N	100W
San Antonio: U.S.A.	40	29N	99W
San Antonio: *r.*, U.S.A.	40	29N	97W
San Antonio, C.: Cuba	47	22N	85W
San Benito Is.: Mex.	38	28N	115W
San Bernardino: U.S.A.	42	34N	117W
San Blas, C.: U.S.A.	41	30N	85W
San Carlos: Venez.	47	9N	72W
Sancerre: France	71	47N	3E
San Clemente: *i.*, U.S.A.	42	33N	118W
San Cristóbal: Venez.	48	8N	72W
Sandakan: Sabah	91	6N	118E
Sandane: Norway	68	62N	6E
Sandgate: Australia	98	27S	153E
San Diego: U.S.A.	42	33N	117W
Sandbach: England	57	53½N	2¼W
Sandhurst: England	57	51¼N	¾W
Sandow, Mt.: Antarc.	51	66S	100E
Sandpoint: U.S.A.	42	48N	117W
Sandringham: Eng.	55	53N	1E
Sandusky: U.S.A.	41	41N	83W
San Félix: Venez.	47	8N	63W
San Félix I.: Pac. O.	101	26S	80W
San Fernando: Chile	49	34S	71W
San Fernando: & *r.*, Mexico	40	25N	98W
San Fernando: Phil.	91	17N	120E
San Fernando: Trinidad	47	10N	61W
San Fernando: Venezuela	47	8N	67W
Sanford: Fla., U.S.A.	41	29N	80W
Sanford: Maine, U.S.A.	17	43N	71W
Sanford: N.C., U.S.A.	41	35N	79W
San Francisco: *r.*, U.S.A.	42	33N	109W
San Francisco: U.S.A.	46	38N	122W
Sangar: U.S.S.R.	81	64N	127E
Sangre de Cristo Range: U.S.A.	43	37N	105W
San Isidro: Arg.	50	34½S	58½W
San Joaquin: *r.*, U.S.A.	42	37N	120W
SAN JOSÉ: Costa Rica	42	10N	84W
San Jose: U.S.A.	42	37N	122W
San Jose: *r.*, U.S.A.	42	35N	108W
San Juan: Argentina	49	32S	69W
SAN JUAN: Puerto Rico	47	18N	66W
San Juan: Venezuela	47	10N	67W
San Juan Mts.: U.S.A.	42	37N	107W
San Luis: Argentina	49	33S	66W
San Luis Obispo: U.S.A.	42	35N	121W
San Luis Potosi: Mex.	38	22N	101W
San Marcos: U.S.A.	40	30N	98W
SAN MARINO: *cap.* San Marino	73	44N	12E
San Mateo: U.S.A.	46	37½N	122¼W
Sanmen Gorge: China	89	35N	111E
Sanok: Poland	66	50N	22E
San Pedro: *r.*, U.S.A.	42	33N	111W
Sanquhar: Scotland	54	55N	4W
San Rafael: Arg.	49	35S	68W
San Rafael: U.S.A.	46	38N	122½W
San Remo: Italy	73	44N	8E
SAN SALVADOR: El Salvador	38	14N	89W
San Salvador: *i.*, Bahama Is.	47	24N	75W
San Sebastian: Spain	65	43N	2W
San Severo: Italy	67	42N	15E
Santa Ana: U.S.A.	42	34N	118W
Santa Barbara: & *chan.*, U.S.A.	42	34N	120W
Santa Barbara Is.: U.S.A.	42	34N	120W
Santa Catalina: *i.* & *gulf*, U.S.A.	42	33N	118W
Santa Clara: Cuba	47	22N	80W
Santa Clara: U.S.A.	42	37N	122W
Santa Cruz: Bolivia	48	18S	63W
Santa Cruz: U.S.A.	42	37N	122W
Santa Cruz: *i.*, U.S.A.	42	34N	120W
Santa Cruz de Tenerife: Canary Islands	108	28N	16W
Santa Fé: Argentina	49	32S	61W
Santa Fe: U.S.A.	42	36N	106W
Santa Maria: Brazil	50	30S	54W
Santa Maria: U.S.A.	42	35N	120W
Santa Marta: Col.	48	11N	74W
Santa Monica: U.S.A.	46	34N	118½W
Santander: Spain	65	43N	4W
Santa Paula: U.S.A.	42	34N	119W
Santarém: Portugal	65	39N	9W
Santa Rosa: Arg.	49	37S	64W
Santa Rosa: Calif., U.S.A.	42	38N	123W
Santa Rosa: N.Mex., U.S.A.	43	35N	105W
Santa Rosa: *i.*, U.S.A.	42	34N	120W
SANTIAGO: Chile	49	33S	71W
Santiago: Dom. Rep.	47	20N	71W
Santiago: Spain	65	43N	9W
Santiago: *r.*, Mexico	38	21N	104W
Santiago de Cuba: Cuba	47	20N	76W
Santiago del Estero: Argentina	48	28S	64W
Santo Antônio: Brazil	48	9S	64W
SANTO DOMINGO: Dom. Repub.	47	19N	70W
Santos: Brazil	48	24S	46W
Sanvic: France	70	49N	0
Sanyate: *r.*, Rhod.	109	17S	29E
São Domingos: Port.	65	38N	7W
São Francisco: *r.*, Brazil	48	12S	43W
São Leopoldo: Brazil	50	30S	51W
São Luis: Brazil	48	3S	44W
Saône: *r.*, France	70	46N	5E
São Paulo: Brazil	48	24S	46W
São Roque, C. de: Brazil	48	5S	35W
São Romé: *i.*, Atl. O.	52	0	6E
Sapporo: Japan	92	43N	141E
Saragossa: Spain	65	42N	1W
Sarajevo: Yugo.	67	44N	18E
Saranac Lake: *city*, U.S.A.	17	44N	74W
Saransk: U.S.S.R.	82	54N	45E
Sarasota: U.S.A.	41	27N	83W
Saratov: U.S.S.R.	82	52N	46E
Sarawak: Malaysia	91	3N	113E
Sardinia: *i.*, Medit. Sea	65	40N	9E
Sargasso Sea	52	30N	60W
Sarişu: *r.*, U.S.S.R.	80	47N	67E
Sark: *i.*, Chan. Is.	55	*Inset*	
Sarny: U.S.S.R.	82	51N	27E
Sarpsborg: Norway	69	59N	11E
Sarrebourg: France	70	49N	7E
Sarreguemines: Fr.	70	49N	7E
Sarthe: *r.*, France	70	48N	0
Sasebo: Japan	92	33N	130E
Sassari: Sardinia	65	41N	9E
Sassnitz: Germany	66	54N	14E
Satara: India	88	17N	74E
Satpura Range: India	88	22N	77E
Satu-Mare: Romania	66	48N	23E
SA'UDI ARABIA: *caps.* Mecca & Riyadh	85	—	—
Sauerland: Germany	72	51N	8E
Saugor: India	88	24N	79E
Sauk Center: U.S.A.	43	46N	95W
Sault Ste. Marie: U.S.A.	17	46N	84W
Saumur: France	71	47N	0
Sauternes: France	71	45N	0
Sava: *r.*, Yugoslavia	87	45N	17E
Savannah: & *r.*, Ga., U.S.A.	41	32N	81W
Savannah: Tenn., U.S.A.	41	35N	88W
Savannakhet: Laos	91	17N	105E
Savaştepe: Turkey	67	39N	28E
Saverne: France	70	49N	7E
Savigliano: Italy	73	45N	8E
Savona: Italy	73	44N	8E
Savonlinna: Finland	68	62N	29E
Savoy: *Old Prov.*, Fr.	71	46N	6E.
Savoy Alps: France	71	46N	7E
Sawu: *i.* & *sea*, Indon.	91	10S	122E
Saxmundham: Eng.	55	52N	1E
Saxony: *Prov.*, Ger.	66	51N	13E
Sca Fell: *mtn.*, Eng.	54	54N	3W
Scania: Sweden	69	56N	14E
Scapa Flow: Scotland	53	59N	3W
Scarborough: Eng.	54	54N	0
Schaerbeek: Belgium	70	51N	4E
Schaffhausen: Switz.	73	48N	8E
Scheldt: *r.*, Belgium/Netherlands	70	51N	4E
Schenectady: U.S.A.	17	43N	74W
Schiedam: Neth.	72	52N	4E
Schio: Italy	73	46N	11E
Schleswig: Germany	66	54N	10E
Schmalkalden: Ger.	72	51N	10E
Schoonebeek: Neth.	72	53N	7E
Schouwen-Duiveland: *i.*, Netherlands	70	52N	4E
Schwäbisch-Gmünd: Germany	73	49N	10E
Schwandorf: Ger.	72	49N	12E
Schweinfurt: Ger.	72	50N	10E
Schwelm: Germany	62	51¼N	7¼E
Schwerin: Germany	72	54N	11E
Schwerte: Germany	62	51½N	7½E
Schwyz: Switz.	73	47N	9E

	Page	Lat.	Long.
Scilly, Is. of: Eng.	**55**	50N	6W
Scolkovo: U.S.S.R.	**82**	56N	38E
Scoresby Sound: Greenland	**3**	71N	23W
Scotia Sea	**49**	57S	50W
SCOTLAND: *cap.* Edinburgh	**53**	—	—
Scott Glacier: Antarctica	**51**	87S	150W
Scott I.: Antarctica	**51**	68S	180
Scott Ra.: Antarc.	**51**	68S	50E
Scottsbluff: U.S.A.	**43**	42N	104W
Scranton: U.S.A.	**41**	41N	76W
Scunthorpe: England	**57**	54N	1W
Scutari: Albania	**67**	42N	19E
Seaham: England	**54**	54½N	1¼W
Seal, C.: S. Africa	**109**	34S	24E
Seattle: U.S.A.	**42**	48N	123W
Sebakwe: *r.*, Rhod.	**109**	18S	30E
Sebcha di Tauorga: Libya	**84**	32N	15E
Sebes: Romania	**66**	46N	24E
Sebha Oasis: Libya	**106**	27N	15E
Sechura Desert: Peru	**48**	6S	80W
Sedalia: U.S.A.	**43**	39N	93W
Sedan: France	**70**	50N	5E
Sedbergh: England	**54**	54N	3W
Seeheim: S.W. Afr.	**109**	27S	18E
Segovia: Spain	**65**	42N	4W
Segovia: *r.*, Hond./Nicaragua	**47**	15N	84W
Segre: *r.*, Spain	**65**	42N	1E
Segura: *r.*, Spain	**65**	38N	2W
Seine: *r.*, France	**70**	49N	1E
Seine, Baie de la: Fr.	**70**	49N	1W
Selby: England	**57**	54N	1W
Selenga: *r.*, Mongolia	**81**	49N	101E
Sélestat: France	**70**	48N	7E
Selety-Tengiz, L.: U.S.S.R.	**83**	53N	73E
Selima Oasis: Sudan	**84**	22N	30E
Selkirk: & *Co.*, Scot.	**54**	56N	3W
Selma: U.S.A.	**41**	32N	87W
Selsey Bill: England	**55**	51N	1W
Selukwe: Rhodesia	**109**	20S	30E
Selvas: Brazil	**48**	6S	65W
Semarang: Java	**91**	7S	110E
Seminoe Res.: U.S.A.	**42**	42N	107W
Semiozernoye: U.S.S.R.	**83**	52N	64E
Semipalatinsk: U.S.S.R.	**83**	50N	80E
Semmering Pass: Austria	**66**	47N	16E
Semnān: Iran	**85**	35N	53E
Senanga: Zambia	**109**	16S	23E
Sendai: Japan	**92**	38N	141E
Seneca L.: U.S.A.	**17**	43N	77W
SENEGAL: *cap.* Dakar	**106**	15N	15W
Senja: *i.*, Norway	**68**	69N	18E
Senlis: France	**70**	49N	3E
Sennar: & *dam*, Sudan	**84**	13N	34E
Sens: France	**70**	48N	3E
Sentinel Range: Antarctica	**51**	77S	85W
SEOUL: S. Korea	**90**	38N	127E
Seram: *i. & sea*, Indonesia	**91**	3S	130E
Serbia: Yugoslavia	**67**	43N	21E
Seremban: Malaya	**91**	3N	102E
Seria: Sarawak	**91**	4N	114E
Serian: Sarawak	**91**	1N	111E
Serio: *r.*, Italy	**73**	45N	10E
Serir of Kalanshu: Libya	**84**	28N	21E
Serov: U.S.S.R.	**83**	60N	60E
Serowe: Botswana	**109**	23S	27E
Serra dos Aimorés: *mtns.*, Brazil	**48**	18S	41W
Serra dos Parecis: Brazil	**48**	12S	60W
Serraí: Greece	**67**	41N	23E
Sète: France	**71**	43N	4E
Sétif: Algeria	**65**	36N	5E
Setúbal: & *bay*, Port.	**65**	38N	9W
Sevan, L.: U.S.S.R.	**82**	41N	46E
Sevastopol': U.S.S.R.	**82**	45N	34E
Sevenoaks: England	**57**	51¼N	¼E
Severn: *r.*, Australia	**99**	29S	152E
Severn: *r.*, England	**55**	52N	2W
Severnaya Zemlya: *is.*, U.S.S.R.	**81**	79N	95E
Severn Tunnel: Eng.	**55**	52N	3W
Severoural'sk: U.S.S.R.	**83**	60N	60E
Seville (Sevilla): Sp.	**65**	37N	6W
Sèvre Nantaise: *r.*, France	**71**	47N	1W
Sèvre Niortaise: *r.*, France	**71**	46N	1W
Sèvres: France	**70**	49N	2E
Seward: U.S.A.	**2**	60N	150W
Seward Peninsula: U.S.A.	**2**	66N	165W
Seydhisfjördhur: Ice.	**68**	65N	14W
Seymour: U.S.A.	**43**	33N	99W
Sézanne: France	**70**	49N	4E
Sfântu Gheorghe: Romania	**66**	46N	26E
Sfax: Tunisia	**106**	35N	11E
's-Gravenhage: Neth.	**72**	52N	4E
Shabwah: Yemen	**85**	16N	47E
Shackleton Inlet: Antarctica	**51**	82S	160E

	Page	Lat.	Long.
Shaftesbury: England	**55**	51N	2W
Shahjahanpur: India	**88**	28N	80E
Shahrezā: Iran	**85**	32N	52E
Shahrūd: Iran	**85**	36N	55E
Shakhty: U.S.S.R.	**82**	48N	40E
Shalym: U.S.S.R.	**83**	53N	88E
Shamrock: U.S.A.	**43**	35N	100W
Shamva: Rhodesia	**109**	17S	32E
Shangani: *r.*, Rhod.	**109**	19S	28E
Shanghai: China	**90**	31N	121E
Shangkiu: China	**89**	34N	116E
Shanklin: England	**55**	51N	1W
Shannon: *r.*, R. of Ireland	**56**	53N	9W
Shansi: *Prov.*, China	**89**	37N	112E
Shan States: Burma	**90**	22N	98E
Shantung: *Prov.*, China	**89**	36N	117E
Shantung Peninsula: China	**89**	37N	120E
Shaohing: China	**89**	30N	121E
Shaoyang: China	**89**	27N	111E
Sharjah: Trucial State	**85**	25N	55E
Sharon: U.S.A.	**41**	41N	81W
Shasta, Lake: U.S.A.	**42**	41N	122W
Shasta, Mt.: U.S.A.	**42**	41N	122W
Shaw I.: Australia	**98**	20S	149E
Shawnee: U.S.A.	**43**	35N	97W
Sheboygan: U.S.A.	**43**	44N	88W
Sheeniek: *r.*, U.S.A.	**28**	68N	144W
Sheerness: England	**57**	51½N	¾E
Sheffield: England	**57**	53N	1W
Sheffield: U.S.A.	**41**	35N	88W
Shelby: U.S.A.	**42**	48N	112W
Shelbyville: U.S.A.	**41**	35N	86W
Shelekhov Bay: U.S.S.R.	**81**	60N	157E
Shenandoah: *r.*, U.S.A.	**41**	38N	79W
Shensi: *Prov.*, China	**89**	35N	109E
Shenyang: China	**89**	42N	123E
Shepard I.: Antarc.	**51**	74S	131W
Shepparton: Austl.	**99**	36S	145E
Sheppey, I. of: Eng.	**57**	51N	1E
Sherborne: England	**55**	51N	3W
Sheridan: U.S.A.	**42**	45N	107W
Sherlovaya Gora: U.S.S.R.	**81**	51N	116E
Sherman: U.S.A.	**43**	34N	97W
's-Hertogenbosch: Netherlands	**72**	52N	5E
Sherwood Forest: England	**57**	53¼N	1W
Shetland Is.: Scot.	**62**	60N	2W
Sheyenne: *r.*, U.S.A.	**43**	48N	99W
Shibeli: *r.*, Ethiopia/Somali Republic	**107**	6N	43E
Shibin al-Qanatir: Egypt	**84**	30½N	31¼E
Shigatse: China	**87**	29N	89E
Shihchan: China	**81**	51N	126E
Shihklachwang: China	**89**	38N	115E
Shikoku: *i.*, Japan	**92**	34N	134E
Shikoku Mts.: Japan	**92**	34N	134E
Shillong: India	**89**	26N	92E
Shimoga: India	**88**	14N	76E
Shimonoseki: Japan	**92**	34N	131E
Shipka Pass: Bulg.	**67**	43N	25E
Shipki Pass: India/China	**88**	32N	79E
Shīrāz: Iran	**85**	30N	53E
Shire: *r.*, Malawi	**109**	16S	35E
Shizuoka: Japan	**92**	35N	139E
Shkodër: Albania	**67**	42N	19E
Shoalhaven: *r.*, Austl.	**99**	35S	151E
Shoalwater Bay: Australia	**98**	22S	150E
Sholapur: India	**88**	18N	76E
Shorewood: U.S.A.	**31**	43N	88W
Shortland Is.: Pac. O.	**97**	7S	156E
Shotton: Wales	**57**	53¼N	3W
Shotts: Scotland	**54**	55¾N	3¾W
Shreveport: U.S.A.	**40**	32N	94W
Shrewsbury: England	**57**	53N	3W
Shrewsbury: U.S.A.	**31**	42¼N	71¾W
Shropshire: *Co.*, Eng.	**57**	53N	3W
Shubra al-Khaymah: Egypt	**84**	30N	31¼E
Shumen: Bulgaria	**67**	43N	27E
Shunde: China	**90**	22¾N	113¼E
Shwangliao: China	**89**	44N	123E
Shwebo: Burma	**90**	23N	96E
Si: *r.*, China	**89**	23N	112E
Sialkot: W. Pakistan	**88**	32N	75E
SIAM *see* THAILAND			
Siam, Gulf of	**91**	10N	102E
Sian: China	**89**	34N	109E
Siang: *r.*, China	**89**	27N	112E
Siangtan: China	**89**	28N	112E
Siauliai: U.S.S.R.	**66**	56N	23E
Sibenik: Yugoslavia	**67**	44N	16E
Sibi: W. Pakistan	**88**	30N	68E
Sibiu: Romania	**66**	46N	25E
Sibu: Sarawak	**91**	2N	112E
Sicilian Channel	**67**	37N	12E
Sicily: *i. & Reg.*, Italy	**67**	—	—
Sidi-bel-Abbès: Alg.	**65**	35N	1W
Sidley, Mt.: Antarc.	**51**	78S	130W
Sidmouth: England	**55**	51N	3W
Sidney: U.S.A.	**43**	48N	104W
Sidra, Gulf of: Libya	**107**	32N	17E
Sieg: *r.*, Germany	**72**	51N	8E
Siegburg: Germany	**72**	51N	7E

	Page	Lat.	Long.
Siegen: Germany	**72**	51N	8E
Siena: Italy	**67**	43N	11E
Siérra de Juárez: U.S.A.	**42**	32N	116W
SIERRA LEONE: *cap.* Freetown	**108**	8N	12W
Sierra Morena: *mtns.*, Spain	**65**	38N	5W
Sierra Nevada: *mtns.*, Spain	**65**	37N	3W
Sierra Nevada: *mtns.*, U.S.A.	**42**	38N	120W
Sighişoara: Romania	**66**	46N	25E
Siglufjördhur: Ice.	**68**	66N	19W
Siirt: Turkey	**85**	38N	42E
Sikeston: U.S.A.	**43**	37N	89W
Sikhote Alin' Range: U.S.S.R.	**81**	47N	137E
Sikkim: *State*, India	**88**	27N	88E
Silchar: India	**89**	25N	93E
Silesia: *Old Prov.*, Pol.	**66**	51N	17E
Silistra: Bulgaria	**67**	44N	27E
Silva Porto: Angola	**109**	13S	17E
Silvares: Portugal	**65**	40N	8W
Silverton: Australia	**99**	32S	141E
Silverton: Colorado, U.S.A.	**42**	38N	108W
Silverton: Oregon, U.S.A.	**42**	45N	123W
Simanggang: Sarawak	**91**	1N	111E
Simferopol': U.S.S.R.	**82**	45N	34E
Simla: India	**88**	31N	77E
Simonstown: S. Afr.	**109**	34S	18E
Simplon Pass: Switz.	**73**	46N	8E
Simpson Desert: Australia	**96**	25S	137E
Sinai: *penin.*, Egypt	**84**	28N	34E
Sincelejo: Colombia	**47**	9N	76W
Sind: *Prov.*, W. Pak.	**88**	26N	69E
SINGAPORE: *cap.* Singapore	**91**	1N	104E
Singaradja: Indon.	**91**	8S	115E
Singkep: *i.*, Indon.	**91**	1S	104E
Singleton: Australia	**99**	33S	151E
Singora: Thailand	**91**	7N	101E
Sining: China	**90**	36N	102E
Sin Kiang Uighur A.R.: China	**86**	40N	85E
Sinuiju: N. Korea	**90**	40N	124E
Sion: Switzerland	**73**	46N	7E
Sioux City: U.S.A.	**43**	42N	96W
Sioux Falls: *city*, U.S.A.	**43**	44N	97W
Siple, Mt.: Antarc.	**51**	74S	122W
Siret: *r.*, Romania	**66**	46N	27E
Sirte: Libya	**106**	31N	17E
Sisak: Yugoslavia	**67**	45N	16E
Sisseton: U.S.A.	**43**	46N	97W
Sistan: Iran/Afghan.	**86**	31N	61E
Sisteron: France	**71**	44N	6E
Sitapur: India	**88**	27N	81E
Sittang: *r.*, Burma	**91**	18N	97E
Sittingbourne: Eng.	**57**	51¼N	¾E
Sivas: Turkey	**84**	40N	37E
Siwa: Egypt	**84**	29N	25E
Skagerrak: *str.*, Denmark/Nor.	**69**	57N	8E
Skagway: U.S.A.	**22**	60N	135W
Skaw, The: *cape*, Denmark	**69**	58N	11E
Skegness: England	**58**	53N	0
Skellefte: *r.*, Sweden	**68**	65N	20E
Skellefteå: Sweden	**68**	65N	21E
Skerries: R. of Irel.	**58**	54N	6W
Skibbereen: R. of Ireland	**58**	52N	9W
Skien: Norway	**69**	59N	10E
Skierniewice: Poland	**66**	52N	20E
Skipton: England	**54**	54N	2W
Skiros: *i.*, Greece	**67**	39N	25E
Skive: Denmark	**69**	57N	9E
Skjold: Norway	**69**	60N	6E
Skokie: U.S.A.	**31**	42N	87¾W
Skomer I.: Wales	**55**	52N	5W
Skopelos: *i.*, Greece	**67**	39N	24E
Skopje: Yugoslavia	**67**	42N	21E
Skövde: Sweden	**69**	58N	14E
Skye: *i.*, Scotland	**54**	57N	6W
Slaney: *riv.*, R. of Ireland	**56**	53N	7W
Slatina: Romania	**67**	44N	24E
Slave Coast: Nigeria	**106**	5N	3E
Slieve Car: *mtn.*, R. of Ireland	**56**	54N	10W
Slieve Donard: *mtn.*, N. Ireland	**56**	54N	6W
Sligo: & *Co.*, & *bay*, R. of Ireland	**56**	54N	8W
Sliven: Bulgaria	**67**	43N	26E
Slonim: U.S.S.R.	**66**	53N	25E
Slough: England	**57**	52N	1W
Slovakia: Czech.	**66**	48N	18E
Slovenia: Yugo.	**66**	46N	15E
Slyne Hd.: R. of Irel.	**56**	53N	10W
Smethwick: England	**57**	52½N	2W
Smith Inlet: Antarc.	**51**	71S	168E
Smoky Hill: *r.*, U.S.A.	**43**	39N	100W
Smolensk: U.S.S.R.	**82**	55N	32E
Smyrna: Turkey	**67**	38N	27E
Snaefell: *mtn.*, I. of Man	**54**	54N	4W
Snaith: England	**57**	53¾N	1W
Snake: *r.*, U.S.A.	**42**	46N	118W

	Page	Lat.	Long.
Snowdon: *mtn.*, Wales	**55**	53N	4W
Snow Hill I.: Antarc.	**51**	65S	57W
Snowy: *mtns. & r.*, Australia	**99**	37S	148E
Snyder: U.S.A.	**43**	33N	101W
Sochi: U.S.S.R.	**82**	44N	40E
Society Is.: Pac. O.	**101**	17S	150W
Socotra: *i.*, Arab. Sea	**85**	13N	54E
Soda Mts.: Libya	**106**	29N	15E
Söderhamn: Sweden	**68**	61N	17E
Soest: Germany	**72**	52N	8E
Soest: Netherlands	**72**	52N	5E
Sofala: Mozam.	**109**	20S	35E
SOFIA (Sofiya): Bulg.	**67**	43N	23E
Sogne Fd.: Norway	**69**	61N	6E
Soissons: France	**70**	49N	3E
Sokoto: Nigeria	**106**	13N	5E
Solent, The: England	**55**	51N	1W
Solihull: England	**57**	52N	2W
Solikamsk: U.S.S.R.	**82**	60N	57E
Solimoes: *r.*, S. Amer.	**48**	4S	69W
Solingen: Germany	**62**	51N	7E
Sologne: France	**70**	48N	2E
Solomon Is.: & *Sea*, Pacific Ocean	**100**	10S	155E
Solothurn: Switz.	**73**	47N	8E
Šolta: *i.*, Yugoslavia	**67**	43N	16E
Solway Firth: Eng./Scotland	**53**	55N	4W
SOMALI REPUBLIC: *cap.* Mogadiscio	**107**	—	—
Sombor: Yugoslavia	**66**	46N	19E
Sombrero: *i.*, West Indies	**47**	18N	63W
Somerset: *Co.*, Eng.	**55**	51N	3W
Somerset: U.S.A.	**41**	37N	85W
Somerville: Mass., U.S.A.	**31**	42½N	71W
Somerville: N.J., U.S.A.	**31**	40½N	74½W
Somme: *r.*, France	**70**	50N	2E
Sommières: France	**71**	44N	4E
Son: *r.*, India	**88**	24N	81E
Sondre Stromfjörd: Greenland	**3**	67N	52W
Songea: Tanzania	**108**	11S	36E
Songjiang: China	**90**	31N	121½E
Songkhla: Thailand	**91**	7N	101E
Sonoyta: Mexico	**42**	32N	113W
Soochow: China	**89**	32N	121E
Soonwald: *mtns.*, Germany	**72**	50N	8E
Sopron: Hungary	**66**	48N	16E
Soria: Spain	**65**	42N	2W
Sosnowiec: Poland	**66**	50N	19E
Souk Ahras: Algeria	**65**	36N	8E
Souris: *r.*, U.S.A./Canada	**43**	49N	101W
Sousse: Tunisia	**106**	36N	11E
Southampton: Eng.	**55**	51N	1W
South Australia: *State*, Australia	**96**	30S	135E
South Bend: U.S.A.	**41**	42N	86W
South Carolina: *State*, U.S.A.	**41**	34N	81W
South China Sea	**91**	15N	115E
South Dakota: *State*, U.S.A.	**43**	45N	100W
South Downs: Eng.	**57**	51N	0
Southend-on-Sea: England	**57**	52N	1E
Southern Alps: N.Z.	**93**	43S	170E
Southern Cross: Australia	**98**	31S	119E
Southern Ocean	**100/1**	—	—
Southern Sierra Madre: *range*, Mexico	**38**	17N	100W
Southern Uplands: Scotland	**54**	55N	4W
Southfield: U.S.A.	**31**	42½N	83¼W
South Foreland: Eng.	**55**	51N	1E
Southgate: U.S.A.	**31**	42¼N	83¼W
South Georgia: *i.*, Atlantic Ocean	**49**	54S	37W
South Houston: U.S.A.	**31**	29¾N	95¼W
South Island: N.Z.	**93**	—	—
SOUTH KOREA: *cap.* Seoul	**90**	37N	127E
Southland: N.Z.	**93**	46S	168E
South Milwaukee: U.S.A.	**31**	43N	87¾W
South Orkney Is.: Antarctica	**51**	61S	45W
Southport: England	**57**	54N	3W
South Sandwich Is.: Southern Ocean	**52**	57S	27W
South Shetland Is.: Antarctica	**51**	62S	60W
South Shields: Eng.	**54**	55N	1W
South Sioux City: U.S.A.	**43**	42N	96W
South Uist: *i.*, Scot.	**53**	57N	7W
South Victoria Land: Antarctica	**51**	78S	169E
SOUTH VIET NAM: *cap.* Saigon	**91**	13N	108E
South West Africa: S. Africa	**109**	24S	17E
Southwark: England	**57**	51½N	0
Southwell: England	**57**	53N	1W
Southwest Cape: New Zealand	**93**	47S	168E

	Page	Lat.	Long.
Sovetsk: U.S.S.R.	**82**	55N	22E
Soviet Harbour: U.S.S.R.	**81**	49N	140E
SPAIN: *cap.* Madrid	**65**	—	—
Spalding: England	**55**	53N	0
Spandau: Germany	**72**	53N	13E
Spanish Sahara: *cap.* Villa Cisneros	**106**	25N	14W
Spanish Town: Jam.	**47**	18N	77W
Sparks: U.S.A.	**42**	40N	120W
Sparta: Greece	**67**	37N	22E
Spartanburg: U.S.A.	**41**	35N	82W
Spartel, C.: Mor.	**65**	36N	6W
Spartivento, C.: Italy	**67**	38N	16E
Spasskoye: U.S.S.R.	**83**	52N	69E
Spatha, C.: Crete	**67**	36N	24E
Speedwell, C.: U.S.S.R.	**80**	75N	55E
Speke: England	**57**	53¼N	3W
Spencer, C.: Austl.	**99**	35S	137E
Spencer Gulf: Austl.	**99**	34S	137E
Spennymoor: Eng.	**54**	55N	2W
Spenser Mts.: N.Z.	**93**	42S	173E
Sperrin Mts.: N. Irel.	**56**	55N	7W
Spessart: *mts.*, Ger.	**72**	50N	9E
Spetsai: *i.*, Greece	**67**	37N	23E
Spey: *r.*, Scotland	**53**	57N	3W
Speyer: Germany	**72**	49N	8E
Spiekeroog: *i.*, Ger.	**72**	54N	8E
Spiš: *Region*, Czech.	**66**	49N	21E
Spitsbergen: *i.*, Arctic Ocean	**80**	78N	20E
Split: Yugoslavia	**67**	44N	16E
Spokane: U.S.A.	**42**	48N	117W
Sporades: *is.*, Greece	**67**	37N	27E
Spree: *r.*, Germany	**72**	52N	14E
Springbok: S. Africa	**109**	30S	18E
Springdale: U.S.A.	**43**	36N	94W
Springfield: Col., U.S.A.	**43**	37N	103W
Springfield: Illinois, U.S.A.	**43**	40N	90W
Springfield: Mass., U.S.A.	**17**	42N	73W
Springfield: Mo., U.S.A.	**43**	37N	93W
Springfield: Ohio, U.S.A.	**41**	40N	84W
Springfield: Oregon, U.S.A.	**42**	44N	123W
Springsure: Austl.	**98**	24S	148E
Spungabera: Mozam.	**109**	20S	33E
Spurn Hd.: England	**54**	54N	0
Sretensk: U.S.S.R.	**81**	52N	118E
SRINAGAR: Kashmir	**88**	34N	75E
Stafford: & Co., Eng.	**57**	53N	2W
Staines: England	**57**	51N	1W
Stamford: England	**57**	53N	0
Stamford: U.S.A.	**31**	41N	73½W
Stanislav: U.S.S.R.	**82**	49N	25E
Stanley Falls: Congo Rep.	**108**	0	25E
Stanley Pool: *l.*, Congo/Congo Republic	**108**	4S	15E
Stanthorpe: Austl.	**99**	29S	152E
Stara Zagora: Bulg.	**67**	42N	26E
Start Pt.: England	**55**	50N	4W
Stassfurt: Germany	**72**	52N	12E
State College: *city*, U.S.A.	**41**	41N	78W
Staten I.: Argentina	**49**	55S	64W
Statesville: U.S.A.	**41**	36N	81W
Staunton: U.S.A.	**41**	38N	79W
Stavanger: Norway	**69**	59N	6E
Stavelot: Belgium	**70**	50N	6E
Stavropol': U.S.S.R.	**82**	45N	42E
Steele I.: Antarc.	**51**	71S	60W
Steigerwald: *mts.*, Germany	**72**	50N	10E
Steinkjer: Norway	**68**	64N	11E
Stellenbosch: S. Afr.	**109**	34S	19E
Stelvio Pass: Switz./Italy	**73**	47N	10E
Stendal: Germany	**72**	53N	12E
Steppes: U.S.S.R.	**83**	50N	70E
Sterling: Colorado, U.S.A.	**43**	41N	103W
Sterling: Ill., U.S.A.	**43**	42N	90W
Sterling Heights: U.S.A.	**31**	42½N	83W
Sterlitamak: U.S.S.R.	**82**	54N	56E
Stettin: Poland	**66**	53N	15E
Steubenville: U.S.A.	**41**	40N	81W
Stevenage: England	**57**	52N	¼W
Stevens Point: *City*, U.S.A.	**43**	45N	89W
Stewart I.: N.Z.	**93**	47S	168E
Steyr: Austria	**73**	48N	14E
Stillwater: U.S.A.	**43**	36N	97W
Stillwell I.: Antarc.	**51**	66S	145E
Stip: Yugoslavia	**67**	42N	22E
Stirling: & Co., Scot.	**51**	56N	4W
Stirling Range: Austl.	**98**	34S	118E
Stjernøy: *i.*, Norway	**68**	70N	23E
STOCKHOLM: Sweden	**69**	59N	18E
Stockport: England	**57**	53N	2W
Stockton: U.S.A.	**42**	38N	121W
Stockton Heath: England	**57**	53¼N	2½W
Stockton on Tees: England	**54**	55N	1W
Stockton Plateau: U.S.A.	**40**	30N	102W
Stoke on Trent: Eng.	**57**	53N	2W
Stonehaven: Scot.	**53**	57N	2W
Stonehenge: England	**55**	51N	2W
Stonington I.: Antarctica	**51**	67S	67W
Stony Tunguska: *r.*, U.S.S.R.	**81**	61N	95E
Stor L.: Sweden	**68**	63N	14E
Stornoway: Scot.	**53**	58N	6W
Storuman: Sweden	**68**	65N	17E
Stour: *r.*, Dorset, England	**55**	51N	2W
Stour: *r.*, Kent, Eng.	**55**	51N	1E
Stour: *r.*, Suff., Eng.	**55**	52N	1E
Stowmarket: Eng.	**55**	52N	1E
Strabane: N. Ireland	**56**	55N	7W
Stralsund: Germany	**66**	54N	13E
Stranca Mts.: Turkey	**67**	42N	28E
Strangford L.: N. Ireland	**56**	54N	6W
Stranraer: Scotland	**54**	55N	5W
Strasbourg: France	**70**	49N	8E
Stratford on Avon: England	**55**	52N	2W
Stratford: N.Z.	**93**	39S	174E
Strathaven: Scot.	**54**	56N	4W
Strathmore: Scot.	**54**	57N	3W
Straubing: Germany	**72**	49N	12E
Strawberry Mt.: U.S.A.	**42**	44N	119W
Stromboli: *i.*, Italy	**67**	39N	15E
Strömstad: Sweden	**69**	59N	11E
Stroud: England	**55**	52N	2W
Struma: *r.*, Bulgaria	**67**	42N	23E
Strumble Head: Wales	**55**	52N	5W
Strumica: Yugoslavia	**67**	41N	23E
Stuart Highway: Australia	**96**	20S	134E
Sturge I.: Antarc.	**51**	68S	165E
Sturt Desert: Austl.	**98**	28S	141E
Stuttgart: Germany	**73**	49N	9E
Stuttgart: U.S.A.	**40**	35N	91W
Suakin: Sudan	**107**	19N	37E
Suanhwa: China	**89**	41N	115E
Subotica: Yugoslavia	**66**	46N	20E
Suceava: Romania	**66**	48N	26E
Suchan: U.S.S.R.	**81**	43N	133E
Suchiate: Mexico	**38**	15N	92W
Suchow: China	**89**	34N	117E
Sucre: Bolivia	**48**	19S	65W
SUDAN: *cap.* Khartoum	**107**	—	—
Sudbury: England	**55**	52N	1E
Sudeten Mts.: Czech.	**66**	51N	16E
Sue Peaks: *mtn.*, U.S.A.	**40**	30N	103W
Suez: & *gulf*, Egypt	**84**	30N	32E
Suez Canal: Egypt	**107**	*Inset*	
Suffolk: *Co.*, Eng.	**55**	52N	1E
Suffolk: U.S.A.	**41**	37N	77W
Sugarloaf Pt.: Austl.	**99**	32S	153E
Suir: *r.*, R. of Ireland	**56**	52N	7W
Sukhona: *r.*, U.S.S.R.	**82**	60N	42E
Sukhumi: U.S.S.R.	**82**	43N	41E
Sukkur: W. Pakistan	**88**	28N	69E
Sula: *is.*, Indonesia	**91**	2S	125E
Sulaiman Range: W. Pakistan	**88**	30N	70E
Sulmona: Italy	**67**	42N	14E
Sulphur Springs: U.S.A.	**43**	33N	96W
Sulu Sea: Phil.	**91**	8N	120E
Sumatra: *i.*, Indon.	**91**	0	100E
Sumba: *i.*, Indonesia	**91**	10S	120E
Sumbawa: *i.*, Indon.	**91**	8S	117E
Sumgait: U.S.S.R.	**82**	40N	50E
Summan Dahna: Sa'udi Arabia	**85**	26N	47E
Summit: Alaska, U.S.A.	**2**	63N	149W
Summit: N.J., U.S.A.	**31**	40¾N	74¼W
Sumperk: Czech.	**66**	50N	17E
Sumter: U.S.A.	**41**	34N	80W
Sumy: U.S.S.R.	**82**	51N	35E
Sunbury: U.S.A.	**41**	41N	77W
Sundarbans: India/Pakistan	**88**	22N	90E
Sunda Str.: Indon.	**91**	6S	106E
Sunderland: England	**54**	55N	1W
Sundsvall: *l.*, Sweden	**68**	62N	17E
Sungari Res.: China	**89**	43N	127E
Suo Gulf: Japan	**90**	34N	132E
Superior: U.S.A.	**43**	47N	92W
Superior, L.: U.S.A./Canada	**17**	47N	90W
Sur (Tyre): Lebanon	**84**	33N	35E
Surabaja: Java	**91**	7S	113E
Surakarta: Java	**91**	7S	111E
Surat: Australia	**98**	27S	149E
Surat: India	**88**	21N	73E
SURINAM: *cap.* Paramaribo	**48**	4N	56W
Surrey: *Co.*, Eng.	**57**	51N	0
Susa: Italy	**73**	45N	7E
Susquehanna: *r.*, U.S.A.	**41**	40N	76W
Sussex: *Co.*, England	**55**	51N	0
Susuman: U.S.S.R.	**81**	63N	148E
Sutlej: *r.*, Pakistan/India	**88**	30N	73E
Sutton: England	**57**	51¼N	¼W
Sutton Coldfield: England	**57**	52½N	1¾W
Suttor: *r.*, Australia	**98**	21S	147E
Suva: Viti Levu	**100**	18S	178E
Suwannee: *r.*, U.S.A.	**41**	30N	83W
Svalbard: *i.*, Arctic O.	**82**	78N	20E
Svendborg: Den.	**69**	55N	11E
Sverdlovsk: U.S.S.R.	**83**	57N	61E
Svir': *r.*, U.S.S.R.	**82**	61N	34E
Svishtov: Bulgaria	**67**	44N	25E
Swabian Jura: *mts.*, Germany	**73**	48N	9E
Swadlincote: Eng.	**57**	52¾N	1½W
Swaffham: England	**55**	53N	1E
Swain Reefs: Austl.	**98**	22S	152E
Swakopmund: S.W. Africa	**109**	23S	14E
Swale: *r.*, England	**54**	54N	2W
Swan: *r.*, Australia	**98**	32S	116E
Swanage: England	**55**	51N	2W
Swan Hill: *town*, Australia	**98**	35S	144E
Swan Is.: Carib. Sea	**47**	17N	84W
Swanland: Australia	**98**	33S	116E
Swansea: Wales	**55**	52N	4W
Swatow: China	**89**	23N	117E
SWAZILAND: *cap.* Mbabane	**109**	27S	32E
SWEDEN: *cap.* Stockholm	**68/9**	—	—
Sweetwater: U.S.A.	**43**	32N	100W
Sweetwater Canal: Egypt	**107**	*Inset*	
Swellendam: S. Afr.	**109**	34S	20E
Swilly, L.: R. of Irel.	**56**	55N	8W
Swindon: England	**57**	52N	2W
Świnoujście: Poland	**66**	54N	14E
SWITZERLAND: *cap.* Bern	**73**	47N	8E
Swords: R. of Irel.	**56**	53N	6W
Sydney: Australia	**99**	34S	151E
Syktyvkar: U.S.S.R.	**82**	62N	51E
Sylacauga: U.S.A.	**41**	33N	86W
Sylhet: E. Pakistan	**89**	25N	92E
Syracuse: Sicily	**67**	37N	15E
Syracuse: U.S.A.	**17**	43N	76W
Syr Darya: *r.*, U.S.S.R.	**83**	43N	67E
SYRIA: *cap.* Damascus	**84/5**	—	—
Syrian Desert: Arabia	**85**	32N	40E
Syzran': U.S.S.R.	**82**	53N	48E
Szczecin: Poland	**66**	53N	15E
Szczecinek: Poland	**66**	54N	17E
Szechwan: *Prov.*, China	**89**	30N	105E
Szeged: Hungary	**66**	46N	20E
Szeping: China	**89**	43N	124E
Szolnok: Hungary	**66**	47N	20E
Szombathely: Hung.	**66**	47N	17E
Tabora: Tanzania	**108**	5S	33E
Tabríz: Iran	**85**	38N	46E
Tacna: Peru	**48**	18S	70W
Tacoma: U.S.A.	**42**	47N	122W
Tadzhik S.S.R.: U.S.S.R.	**83**	38N	72E
Taegu: S. Korea	**90**	36N	128E
Taejon: S. Korea	**90**	37N	127E
Tafersit: Morocco	**65**	35N	4W
Taff: *r.*, Wales	**55**	52N	3W
Tafilalet Oasis: Mor.	**106**	31N	4W
Taganrog: U.S.S.R.	**82**	47N	39E
Tagliamento: *r.*, Italy	**73**	46N	13E
Tagus: *r.*, Sp./Port.	**65**	40N	8W
Tahiti: *i.*, Pacific O.	**101**	18S	150W
Tahoe, Lake: U.S.A.	**42**	39N	120W
Tai, Lake: China	**89**	31N	121E
Tai-chung: Formosa	**89**	24N	121E
Taif: Sa'udi Arabia	**85**	21N	40E
Taihape: N.Z.	**93**	40S	176E
Tainan: Formosa	**89**	23N	120E
Taipeh: Formosa	**89**	25N	122E
Taiping: Malaya	**91**	5N	101E
Taitao Penin.: Chile	**49**	47S	75W
T'ai-tung: Formosa	**89**	23N	121E
TAIWAN: *see* FORMOSA			
Taiyüan: China	**89**	38N	112E
Ta'iz: Yemen	**85**	14N	44E
Tak: Thailand	**91**	17N	99E
Takamatsu: Japan	**92**	54N	134E
Takaoka: Japan	**92**	37N	137E
Takawa: Japan	**92**	34N	131E
Takla Makan: *desert*, China	**87**	39N	83E
Takoradi: Ghana	**106**	5N	2W
Talara: Peru	**48**	5S	81W
Talaud Is.: Indon.	**91**	4N	127E
Talavera: Spain	**65**	40N	5W
Talbot, C.: Austl.	**96**	14S	127E
Talladega: U.S.A.	**41**	33N	86W
Tallahassee: U.S.A.	**41**	30N	84W
Tallinn: U.S.S.R.	**82**	59N	25E
Taltal: Chile	**48**	25S	71W
Tamale: Ghana	**106**	9N	1W
Tamana: *r.*, U.S.A.	**28**	63N	143W
Tamar: *r.*, England	**55**	51N	4W
Tamatave: Malagasy Republic	**108**	18S	49E
Tambo: Australia	**98**	25S	146E
Tambov: U.S.S.R.	**82**	53N	41E
Tame: *r.*, England	**57**	52¾N	1¾W
Tamil Nadu: *State*, India	**88**	10N	78E
Tammisaari: Finland	**69**	60N	23E
Tampa: & *bay*, U.S.A.	**41**	28N	82W
Tampere: Finland	**68**	61N	24E
Tampico: Mexico	**38**	23N	98W
Tamtsak Bulak: Mongolia	**81**	47N	117E
Tamworth: Australia	**98**	31S	151E
Tamworth: England	**57**	52¾N	1¾W
Tana: & *Fd.*, Norway	**68**	70N	28E
Tana, L.: Ethiopia	**107**	12N	37E
Tanana: U.S.A.	**2**	65N	152W
Tandil: Argentina	**49**	37S	59W
Tandou, L.: Austl.	**99**	33S	142E
Tandragee: N. Irel.	**56**	54N	6W
Tanezrouft: Algeria	**106**	23N	0
Tanga: Tanzania	**108**	5S	39E
Tanganyika, L.: Afr.	**108**	8S	30E
Tangier: Morocco	**106**	36N	6W
Tanglha R.: China	**88**	34N	91E
Tangshan: China	**89**	39N	118E
Tanimbar Is.: Indon.	**91**	7S	131E
Tannenberg: Poland	**69**	53N	20E
Tanta: Egypt	**84**	31N	31E
TANZANIA: *cap.* Dar es Salaam	**108**	—	—
Tapajos: *r.*, Brazil	**48**	6S	57W
Tapa Shan: *mts.*, China	**89**	32N	108E
Tapti: *r.*, India	**88**	21N	75E
Tapuaenuku: *mtn.*, New Zealand	**93**	42S	174E
Tarakan: Borneo	**91**	3N	118E
Taranaki: N.Z.	**93**	39S	174E
Taranto: & *gulf*, Italy	**67**	40N	17E
Tarare: France	**71**	46N	4E
Tararua R.: N.Z.	**93**	41S	175E
Tarascon: France	**71**	44N	5E
Tarawa: *i.*, Pac. O.	**100**	1N	173E
Tarbes: France	**71**	43N	0
Tardenois: *hills*, Fr.	**70**	49N	4E
Taree: Australia	**99**	32S	152E
Târgu Jiu: Romania	**67**	45N	23E
Târgu Mureş: Rom.	**66**	46N	25E
Tarim: *r.*, China	**87**	41N	82E
Tarko-Sale: U.S.S.R.	**81**	65N	78E
Tarn: *r.*, France	**71**	44N	2E
Taroom: Australia	**98**	26S	150E
Tarragona: Spain	**65**	41N	1E
Tarsus: Turkey	**84**	37N	35E
Tartary, Gulf of: U.S.S.R.	**81**	50N	140E
Tartu: U.S.S.R.	**82**	58N	27E
Tashkent: U.S.S.R.	**83**	41N	69E
Tasman, Mt.: N.Z.	**93**	44S	170E
Tasman Bay: & *mts.*, New Zealand	**93**	41S	173E
Tasmania: *i.* & *State*, Australia	**97**	42S	146E
Tasman Sea: Pac. O.	**100**	35S	165E
Tassili-n-Ajjer: *plat.*, Algeria	**106**	26N	8E
Tatar Pass: U.S.S.R.	**66**	48N	25E
Tatarsk: U.S.S.R.	**83**	55N	76E
Tatry: *mtns.*, Czech.	**66**	49N	20E
Tatung: China	**89**	40N	113E
Taumarunui: N.Z.	**93**	39S	175E
Taunton: England	**55**	51N	3W
Taunton: U.S.A.	**17**	42N	71W
Taunus: *mts.*, Ger.	**72**	50N	8E
Taupo: & *lake*, N.Z.	**93**	39S	176E
Tauranga: N.Z.	**93**	38S	176E
Taurus Mts.: Turkey	**84**	37N	35E
Tavda: & *r.*, U.S.S.R.	**83**	58N	65E
Tavira: Portugal	**65**	37N	8W
Tavistock: England	**55**	51N	4W
Tavoy: Burma	**91**	14N	98E
Taw: *r.*, England	**55**	51N	4W
Tawas Pt.: U.S.A.	**17**	44N	83W
Tawitawi: *i.*, Phil.	**91**	5N	120E
Tay: *r.*, Scotland	**54**	56N	3W
Tay, L.: Scotland	**54**	56N	4W
Taylor: U.S.A.	**31**	42¼N	83¼W
Taymyr, L.: U.S.S.R.	**81**	75N	102E
Taymyr Peninsula: U.S.S.R.	**81**	75N	105E
Tayshet: U.S.S.R.	**83**	56N	97E
Tbilisi (Tiflis): U.S.S.R.	**82**	42N	45E
Teague: U.S.A.	**43**	32N	96W
Te Anau, L.: N.Z.	**93**	45S	168E
Te Awamatu: N.Z.	**93**	38S	175E
Teaneck: U.S.A.	**31**	41N	74W
Tébessa: Algeria	**65**	35N	8E
Tecuci: Romania	**66**	46N	27E
Tees: *r.*, England	**54**	55N	1W
Teesside: England	**54**	54½N	1¼W
TEGUCIGALPA: Honduras	**42**	14N	87W
TEHRĀN: Iran	**85**	35N	51E
Tehuantepec: *gulf* & *isthmus*, Mexico	**38**	17N	94W
Teifi: *r.*, Wales	**55**	52N	4W
Tekely: U.S.S.R.	**83**	45N	79E
Tekirdag: Turkey	**67**	41N	27E
Tell Atlas: *mtns.*, Algeria	**106**	37N	7E
Tell el Kebir: Egypt	**107**	*Inset*	
Teluk Betung: Sumatra	**91**	5S	105E
Temerin: Yugoslavia	**67**	45N	20E
Temir-Tau: U.S.S.R.	**83**	50N	73E
Temora: Australia	**99**	34S	148E
Temple: U.S.A.	**43**	31N	97W
Templemore: R. of Ireland	**56**	53N	8W
Temuco: Chile	**49**	39S	73W
Tenda Pass: Fr./Italy	**73**	44N	7E
Tende: France	**71**	44N	8E
Tenerife: Canary Is.	**106**	28N	16W

Name	Page	Lat.	Long.
Tengchung: China	90	25N	98E
Tengiz, L.: U.S.S.R.	83	50N	69E
Tenkiller Ferry Res.: U.S.A.	43	36N	95W
Tennant Creek: *town*, Australia	96	20S	134E
Tennessee: *r.*, & *State*, U.S.A.	41	36N	88W
Tenterfield: Austl.	99	29S	152E
Ten Thousand Is.: U.S.A.	41	26N	82W
Teramo: Italy	67	43N	14E
Teresina: Brazil	48	5S	43W
Teresópolis: Brazil	50	22½S	43W
Terme di Valdieri: Italy	73	44N	7E
Termez: U.S.S.R.	83	37N	67E
Termoli: Italy	67	42N	15E
Ternate: *i.*, Indon.	90	1N	127E
Terneuzen: Neth.	72	51N	4E
Terni: Italy	67	43N	13E
Ternopol': U.S.S.R.	66	50N	26E
Terra Nova: Antarc.	51	75S	165E
Terre Haute: U.S.A.	41	39N	87W
Terror, Mt.: Antarc.	51	78S	170E
Terschelling: *i.*, Netherlands	72	53N	5E
Teruel: Spain	65	40N	1W
Tessenel: Ethiopia	107	15N	37E
Test: *r.*, England	55	51N	1W
Tete: Mozambique	109	16S	34E
Tetlin Junction: U.S.A.	28	63N	142W
Tetuán: Morocco	106	36N	5W
Teutoburger Wald: Germany	72	52N	8E
Tewkesbury: Eng.	55	52N	2W
Texarkana: Ark., U.S.A.	43	33N	94W
Texarkana: Texas, U.S.A.	43	33N	94W
Texas: *State*, U.S.A.	43	32N	100W
Texas City: U.S.A.	31	29N	95W
Texel: *i.*, Neth.	72	53N	5E
Texoma, L.: U.S.A.	43	34N	97W
Tezpur: India	89	27N	93E
Thabazimbi: S. Afr.	109	25S	27E
THAILAND: *cap.* Bangkok	91	15N	102E
Thal: W. Pakistan	88	32N	72E
Thames: N.Z.	93	37S	176E
Thames: *r.*, England	57	52N	0
Thanet, Isle of: Eng.	55	51N	1E
Thanjavur: India	88	11N	79E
Thar Desert: India/Pakistan	88	27N	72E
Thasos: *i.*, Greece	67	41N	25E
Thebes: Egypt	84	26N	33E
The Brothers: *is.*, Indian Ocean	86	12N	53E
The Dalles: U.S.A.	42	46N	121W
The Hague *see* Hague			
Thermai, G. of: Greece	67	40N	23E
Thermia: *i.*, Greece	67	37N	24E
Thermopolis: U.S.A.	42	44N	108W
The Sound: *strait*, Den./Sweden	69	56N	13E
Thessaloniki *see* Salonica			
Thessaly: *Division*, Greece	67	39N	22E
Thetford: England	57	52N	1E
Thief River Falls: *city*, U.S.A.	43	48N	96W
Thiérache: France	70	50N	4E
Thiers: France	71	46N	4E
Thionville: France	70	49N	6E
Thira: *i*, Greece	67	36N	25E
Thirsk: England	54	54N	1W
Thomasville: Ala., U.S.A.	41	32N	88W
Thomasville: Ga., U.S.A.	41	31N	84W
Thomson's Falls: Kenya	108	0	36E
Thonon: France	71	46N	7E
Thore: *r.*, France	71	44N	2E
Thornaby on Tees: England	54	54½N	1¼W
Thouars: France	71	47N	0
Thrace: *Division*, Greece	67	41N	25E
Three Kings Is.: N.Z.	93	34S	172E
Three Points, C.: Ghana	106	5N	2W
Three Springs: Austl.	98	30S	116E
Thule: Greenland	3	76N	68W
Thun: & *l.*, Switz.	73	47N	8E
Thur: *r.*, Switz.	73	48N	9E
Thüringer Wald: *mts.*, Germany	72	50N	11E
Thurles: R. of Irel.	56	53N	8W
Thursday I.: Austl.	97	11S	142E
Thurso: Scotland	53	59N	3W
Thurston Peninsula: Antarctica	51	72S	102W
Tiaret: Algeria	65	35N	1E
Tiber: *r.*, Italy	67	43N	12E
Tiberias Lake (Sea of Galilee): Israel	84	33N	36E
Tibesti: *highlands*, Chad	106/7	—	—
Tibet: *Aut. Reg.*, China	87	33N	85E
Ticino: *r.*, Italy	73	45N	9E

Name	Page	Lat.	Long.
Tien Shan: *range*, China	87	42N	80E
Tientsin: China	89	39N	117E
Tierra del Fuego: *i.*, Argentina	49	54S	67W
Tiffin: U.S.A.	41	41N	83W
Tiflis *see* Tblisi			
Tignes Res.: France	71	45N	7E
Tigris: *r.*, Turkey/'Iraq	85	35N	44E
Tihama: Sau. Arab.	85	20N	41E
Tihwa: China	87	44N	87E
Tijuana: Mexico	42	32N	117W
Tiksi: U.S.S.R.	81	72N	129E
Tilburg: Neth.	72	52N	5E
Tilbury: England	57	51N	0
Tillabéry: Niger	106	14N	1E
Tilos: *i.*, Greece	67	36N	27E
Timaru: N.Z.	93	44S	171E
Timbuktu: Mali	106	17N	3W
Timişoara: Romania	66	46N	21E
Timor: *i.* & *sea*, S.E. Asia	91	10S	125E
Timsah, L.: Egypt	107	*Inset*	
Tipperary: & *Co.*, R. of Ireland	56	52N	8W
TIRANË (Tirana): Albania	67	41N	20E
Tiraspol': U.S.S.R.	66	47N	30E
Tire: Turkey	67	38N	28E
Tiree: *i.*, Scotland	54	56N	7W
Tirnovo: Bulgaria	67	43N	26E
Tiruchirappalli: India	88	11N	79E
Tirunelveli: India	88	9N	78E
Tista: *r.*, E. Pakistan	88	27N	89E
Tisza: *r.*, Europe	66	46N	21E
Titicaca, Lake: Peru/Bolivia	42	16S	69W
Titograd: Yugoslavia	67	42N	19E
Titovo Užice: Yugo.	67	44N	20E
Titov Veles: Yugo.	67	42N	22E
Tiverton: England	55	51N	4W
Tivoli: Italy	67	42N	13E
Tlemcen: Algeria	65	35N	1W
Tobago: *i.*, W. Ind.	47	11N	61W
Tobermory: Scot.	54	57N	6W
Tobol': *r.*, U.S.S.R.	83	56N	66E
Tobol'sk: U.S.S.R.	83	58N	68E
Tobruk: Libya	107	32N	24E
Tocantins: *r.*, Brazil	48	4S	50W
Toccoa: U.S.A.	41	35N	84W
Tocumwal: Austl.	99	36S	146E
TOGO: *cap.* Lomé	106	8N	1E
Tokaj: Hungary	66	48N	21E
Tokelau: *is.*, Pac. O.	100	9S	171W
Tokushima: Japan	92	34N	134E
TOKYO: Japan	92	36N	140E
Tolbukhin: Bulgaria	67	44N	28E
Toledo: & *mtns.*, Sp.	65	40N	4W
Toledo: Ohio, U.S.A.	41	42N	84W
Toledo: Oregon, U.S.A.	42	45N	124W
Tolo, G. of: Indon.	91	2S	122E
Tolosa: Spain	65	43N	2W
Tolstoy, C.: U.S.S.R.	81	59N	155E
Tomatlan: Mexico	38	20N	105W
Tombigbee: *r.*, U.S.A.	41	32N	88W
Tomini, Gulf of: Indonesia	91	0	121E
Tomsk: U.S.S.R.	83	56N	85E
Tonbridge: England	57	51N	0
TONGA: Pac. O.	100	20S	175W
Tongatapu: *i.*, Pacific Ocean	100	20S	175W
Tongxian: China	90	40N	116¾E
Tonkin, Gulf of: S.E. Asia	89	21N	108E
Tonle, L.: Cambodia	91	13N	104E
Tønsberg: Norway	69	59N	11E
Tooele: U.S.A.	42	41N	112W
Toowoomba: Austl.	98	28S	152E
Topeka: U.S.A.	43	39N	96W
Topozero: *l.*, U.S.S.R.	68	66N	32E
Torgau: Germany	72	52N	13E
Torne: *l.* & *r.*, Sweden/Finland	68	68N	19E
Tornio: Finland	68	66N	24E
Tororo: Uganda	108	1N	34E
Torquay: England	55	50N	4W
Torrance: U.S.A.	46	33¾N	118¼W
Torrens, L.: Austl.	99	31S	137E
Torreón: Mexico	38	26N	103W
Torres Strait: Austl.	97	10S	142E
Torres Vedras: Port.	65	39N	9W
Torridge: *r.*, England	53	51N	4W
Tortona: Italy	73	45N	9E
Tortosa: & *cape*, Sp.	65	41N	1E
Toruń: Poland	66	53N	19E
Tosa Bay: Japan	92	33N	134E
Totomi Gulf: Japan	92	34N	137E
Touba: Senegal	106	15N	16W
Touggourt: Algeria	106	33N	6E
Toul: France	70	49N	6E
Toulon: France	71	43N	6E
Toulouse: France	71	44N	1E
Toungoo: Burma	90	19N	96E
Touraine: *Old Prov.*, France	71	47N	1E
Tourane: S. Viet Nam	91	16N	108E
Tourcoing: France	70	51N	3E
Tournai: Belgium	70	51N	3E
Tours: France	71	47N	1E
Towcester: England	55	52N	1W
Townshend I.: Austl.	98	22S	151E

Name	Page	Lat.	Long.
Townsville: Austl.	98	19S	147E
Toyama: Japan	92	37N	137E
Toyohashi: Japan	92	35N	137E
Trabzon: Turkey	85	41N	40E
Trafalgar, C.: Spain	65	36N	6W
Tralee: R. of Ireland	56	52N	10W
Tramore: R. of Irel.	56	52N	7W
Tranås: Sweden	69	58N	15E
Transvaal: *Prov.*, Rep. of South Africa	109	25S	29E
Transylvania: *Prov.*, Romania	66	46N	23E
Transylvanian Alps: Romania	67	45N	24E
Trapani: Sicily	67	38N	12E
Trasimeno, L.: Italy	67	43N	12E
Traunstein: Ger.	73	48N	13E
Traveller's L.: Austl.	99	33S	142E
Traverse City: U.S.A.	17	45N	85W
Trelleborg: Sweden	69	55N	13E
Tremadoc Bay: Wales	55	53N	4W
Trent: *r.*, England	57	53N	1W
Trentino: *Reg.*, Italy	73	46N	11E
Trento: Italy	73	46N	11E
Trenton: Montana, U.S.A.	43	40N	94W
Trenton: N.J., U.S.A.	45	40N	75W
Trepča: Yugoslavia	67	43N	21E
Treviso: Italy	73	46N	12E
Trier: Germany	72	50N	7E
Trieste: Italy	73	46N	14E
Trikkala: Greece	67	40N	22E
Trincomalee: Ceylon	88	8N	81E
Trinidad: U.S.A.	43	37N	105W
TRINIDAD & TOBAGO: *cap.* Port of Spain	47	10N	61W
Trinity: *r.*, U.S.A.	43	31N	96W
Trinity I.: Antarc.	51	64S	61W
Tripoli: Lebanon	84	34N	36E
TRIPOLI: Libya	106	33N	13E
Tripolis: Greece	67	38N	22E
Tripolitania: *Prov.*, Libya	84	30N	15E
Tripura: *State*, India	89	24N	92E
Tristan da Cunha: *i.*, Atlantic Ocean	52	38S	12W
Trivandrum: India	88	8N	77E
Troitsk: U.S.S.R.	83	54N	62E
Trollhattan: Sweden	69	58N	12E
Tromsø: Norway	68	70N	19E
Trona: U.S.A.	42	36N	117W
Trondheim: & *fd.*, Norway	68	63N	11E
Trowbridge: England	55	51N	2W
Troy: Ala., U.S.A.	41	32N	86W
Troy: N.Y., U.S.A.	17	42N	74W
Troy: Turkey	84	40N	26E
Troyes: France	70	48N	4E
Trucial 'Oman *or* States: Arabia	85	24N	55E
Trujillo: Honduras	47	16N	86W
Trujillo: Peru	48	8S	79W
Trujillo: Venezuela	47	9N	71W
Truk Is.: Pac. O.	100	8N	152E
Truro: England	55	50N	5W
Truth or Consequences: U.S.A.	42	33N	107W
Tsai: *r.*, China	89	35N	108E
Tsaidam Swamps: China	87	37N	95E
Tsangpo: *r.*, China	87	29N	86E
Tselinograd: U.S.S.R.	83	51N	71E
Tsetserlig: Mong.	91	47N	102E
Tsimlyansk Res.: U.S.S.R.	82	48N	43E
Tsinan: China	89	37N	117E
Tsing Hai: *l.*, China	87	37N	100E
Tsingtao: China	89	36N	120E
Tsinling Shan: China	89	34N	108E
Tsitsihar: China	89	47N	124E
Tsu: Japan	92	35N	137E
Tsu Islands: Japan	92	34N	129E
Tsumeb: S.W. Afr.	109	19S	18E
Tuam: R. of Irel.	56	54N	9W
Tuamotu Arch.: Pacific Ocean	101	15S	140W
Tuapse: U.S.S.R.	82	44N	39E
Tuatapere: N.Z.	93	46S	168E
Tubai Is.: Pac. O.	101	25S	150W
Tübingen: Germany	73	49N	9E
Tucson: U.S.A.	42	32N	111W
Tucumán: Argentina	48	27S	65W
Tucumcari: U.S.A.	43	35N	104W
Tucupita: Venez.	48	9N	62W
Tudela: Spain	65	42N	2W
Tugssâq: Greenland	3	73N	55W
Tula: U.S.S.R.	82	54N	37E
Tulare: U.S.A.	42	36N	119W
Tul'chin: U.S.S.R.	66	49N	29E
Tulear: Malagasy Rep.	108	23S	44E
Tulia: U.S.A.	43	35N	102W
Tullahoma: U.S.A.	41	35N	86W
Tullamore: R. of Ireland	56	53N	7W
Tulle: France	71	45N	2E
Tulsa: U.S.A.	43	36N	96W
Tumaco: Colombia	48	2N	79W
Tumkur: India	88	13N	77E
Tumut: *r.*, Australia	99	36S	148E
Tungabhadra: *r.*, India	88	16N	76E
Tunghwa: China	89	42N	126E
Tungkwan: China	89	34N	110E

Name	Page	Lat.	Long.
Tung Ting, L.: China	89	29N	112E
TUNIS: Tunisia	106	37N	10E
TUNISIA: *cap.* Tunis	106	35N	10E
Tunja: Colombia	48	6N	73W
Tunstall: England	57	53N	2¼W
Tupelo: U.S.A.	41	34N	89W
Turanian Plain: U.S.S.R.	83	43N	60E
Turbat: W. Pakistan	88	26N	63E
Turbo: Colombia	48	8N	77W
Turda: Romania	66	47N	24E
Turfan: China	87	43N	89E
Turgay: & *r.*, U.S.S.R.	83	50N	64E
Turgutlu: Turkey	67	39N	28E
Turin: Italy	73	45N	8E
Turkestan: U.S.S.R.	83	43N	68E
TURKEY: *cap.* Ankara	84/5	—	—
Turkmen S.S.R.: U.S.S.R.	83	39N	57E
Turks Is.: Bahama Is.	47	22N	71W
Turku: Finland	69	60N	22E
Turlock: U.S.A.	42	37N	121W
Turnagain, C.: N.Z.	93	40S	177E
Turnhout: Belgium	70	51N	5E
Turnu Măgurele: Romania	67	44N	25E
Turnu Severin: Romania	67	45N	23E
Tuscaloosa: U.S.A.	41	33N	88W
Tuscany: *Reg.*, Italy	73	44N	11E
Tuttlingen: Germany	73	48N	9E
Tuxpan: Mexico	38	21N	97W
Tuyün: China	89	26N	107E
Tuz, L.: Turkey	84	38N	33E
Tweed: *r.*, England/Scotland	54	56N	2W
Twenty Mile House: U.S.A.	28	66N	144W
Twin Bridges: U.S.A.	42	45N	112W
Twin Falls: *city*, U.S.A.	42	43N	115W
Tygda: U.S.S.R.	81	53N	126E
Tyler: U.S.A.	43	32N	95W
Tyne, N. & S.: *rivs.*, England	54	32N	2W
Tynemouth: England	54	55N	1W
Tyre *see* Sur			
Tyrol: *Prov.*, Austria	73	47N	11E
Tyrone: *Co.*, Northern Ireland	56	55N	7W
Tyrrhenian Sea	67	40N	12E
Tywi: *r.*, Wales	55	52N	4W
Tyumen': U.S.S.R.	83	57N	65E
Tzekung: China	89	29N	105E
Tzupo: China	89	37N	118E
Ube: Japan	92	34N	131E
Uberaba: Brazil	48	20S	48W
Ubon: Thailand	91	15N	105E
Ubsa Nor.: *l.*, Mong.	90	50N	93E
Ubundu: Congo Republic	108	0	25E
Ucayali: *r.*, Peru	48	7S	74W
Udaipur: India	88	25N	74E
Uddevalla: Sweden	69	58N	12E
Udd L.: Sweden	68	66N	18E
Udine: Italy	73	46N	13E
Udon Thani: Thailand	91	17N	103E
Ufa: & *r.*, U.S.S.R.	82	55N	56E
UGANDA: *cap.* Entebbe	108	1N	32E
Uinta Mts.: U.S.A.	42	41N	111W
Uitenhage: S. Africa	109	33S	25E
Ujiji: Tanzania	108	5S	30E
Ujjain: India	88	23N	76E
Ukhta: U.S.S.R.	82	63N	54E
Ukiah: U.S.A.	42	39N	123W
Ukrainian S.S.R.: U.S.S.R.	82	50N	30E
ULAN BATOR: Mongolia	81	47N	107E
Ulangom: Mongolia	81	50N	92E
Ulanhoto: China	89	46N	122E
Ulan Ude: U.S.S.R.	81	52N	107E
Uldza: Mongolia	81	49N	112E
Uleåborg: Finland	69	65N	25E
Ullapool: Scotland	51	58N	5W
Ullswater: *l.*, Eng.	54	55N	3W
Ulm: Germany	73	48N	10E
Ulster: *Old Prov.*, Ireland	56	54N	7W
Ulundi: S. Africa	109	28S	32E
Ulu-Tau: *range*, U.S.S.R.	83	49N	67E
Ul'yanovsk: U.S.S.R.	82	54N	48E
Ulyungur Nor: *l.*, China	87	47N	87E
Ülzen: Germany	72	53N	10E
Umarkot: W. Pak.	88	25N	70E
Umbria: *Reg.*, Italy	67	43N	12E
Umeå: Sweden	68	64N	20E
Umm Samin: Muscat & 'Oman	85	22N	56E
Umtali: Rhodesia	109	19S	33E
Umtata: S. Africa	109	31S	29E
Union: U.S.A.	31	40½N	74¼W
Union City: U.S.A.	31	40¾N	74W
Uniondale: S. Africa	109	34S	23E
UNION OF SOVIET SOCIALIST REPUBLICS: *cap.* Moscow	80/1	—	—
Uniontown: U.S.A.	41	40N	80W

	Page	Lat.	Long.
UNITED KINGDOM OF GREAT BRITAIN & N. IRELAND *cap.* London	53	—	—
UNITED STATES OF AMERICA: *cap.* Washington	38/9	—	—
Upper Lough Erne: N. Ireland	56	54N	7W
UPPER VOLTA: *cap.* Ouagadougou	106	12N	1W
Uppingham: Eng.	57	52½N	¾W
Uppsala: Sweden	69	60N	18E
Ur: 'Iraq	85	31N	46E
Ural: *r.*, U.S.S.R.	82	52N	53E
Ural Mts.: U.S.S.R.	83	55N	59E
Ural'sk: U.S.S.R.	82	51N	51E
Urdos: France	71	43N	1W
Ure: *r.*, England	54	54N	2W
Urfa: Turkey	85	37N	39E
Urga: Mongolia	81	47N	107E
Urisino: Australia	99	30S	144E
Úrkút: Hungary	66	47N	17E
Uruguaiana: Brazil	50	30S	57W
URUGUAY: *cap.* Montevideo	50	32S	56W
Uruguay: *r.*, S. Am.	50	29S	56W
Urumchi: China	87	44N	87E
Usakos: S.W. Africa	109	22S	15E
Ushant: France	70	48N	5W
Uskudar: Turkey	84	41N	29E
Usol'ye: U.S.S.R.	81	53N	103E
Uspallata Pass: Chile/Arg.	49	33S	70W
Uspenskiy: U.S.S.R.	83	49N	73E
Ussurilsk: U.S.S.R.	81	44N	132E
Usti nad Labem: Czechoslovakia	72	51N	14E
Ust'-Kamenogorsk: U.S.S.R.	83	50N	83E
Ust'-Kut: U.S.S.R.	81	57N	105E
Ust'-Urt Plateau: U.S.S.R.	82	44N	57E
Ust' Uyskoye: U.S.S.R.	83	54N	65E
Utah: *State*, U.S.A.	42	39N	112W
Utah Lake: U.S.A.	42	40N	112W
Utica: U.S.A.	17	43N	75W
Utrecht: Neth.	72	52N	5E
Uttaradit: Thailand	91	17N	100E
Uttar Pradesh: *State*, India	88	27N	80E
Uttoxeter: England	57	53N	1¾W
Uvalde: U.S.A.	40	29N	100W
Uxmal: Mexico	38	20N	90W
Uyuni: Bolivia	48	20S	67W
Uzbek S.S.R.: U.S.S.R.	83	41N	62E
Uzhgorod: U.S.S.R.	66	49N	22E
Vaal: *r.*, S. Africa	109	27S	28E
Vaasa: Finland	68	63N	22E
Vaccarès: Étang de: France	71	44N	5E
VADUZ: Liechtenstein	73	47N	10E
Vahsel Bay: Antarc.	51	78S	35W
Valdai Hills: U.S.S.R.	82	57N	34E
Valdepeñas: Spain	65	39N	3W
Valdés Penin.: Arg.	49	43S	64W
Valdez: U.S.A.	2	61N	146W
Valdivia: Chile	49	40S	74W
Valdosta: U.S.A.	41	31N	83W
Valence: France	71	45N	5E
Valencia: & *Old Prov.*, Spain	65	39N	0
Valencia: & *l.*, Venez.	47	10N	68W
Valenciennes: Fr.	70	50N	4E
Valentia I.: R. of Irel.	56	52N	10W
Valga: U.S.S.R.	69	57N	25E
Valladolid: Spain	65	42N	5W
Valle: Venezuela	47	9N	66W
Vallejo: U.S.A.	42	38N	122W
VALLETTA: Malta	67	36N	14E
Valley Stream: U.S.A.	31	41¼N	73¾W
Valmiera: U.S.S.R.	69	57N	25E
Valona: Albania	67	40N	20E
Valparaiso: Chile	49	33S	72W
Valsch, Cape: West Irian	96	8S	137E
Van: & *lake*, Turkey	85	39N	43E
Vancouver: U.S.A.	42	46N	123W
Vancouver, Mt.: U.S.A./Canada	2	60N	140W
Väner, L.: Sweden	69	59N	13E
Vänersborg: Sweden	69	58N	12E
Vannes: France	70	48N	3W
Vannøy: *i.*, Norway	68	70N	20E
Vansbro: Sweden	69	60N	14E
Vanua Levu: *i.*, Pacific Ocean	100	16S	179E
Varanasi: India	88	25N	83E
Varanger Penin.: & *fd.*, Norway	68	71N	29E
Varaždin: Yugoslavia	66	46N	16E
Vardar: *r.*, Yugo./Greece	67	41N	22E
Vardo: Norway	68	70N	31E
Varese: Italy	73	46N	9E
Varna: Bulgaria	67	43N	28E
Värnamo: Sweden	69	57N	14E
Vaslui: Romania	66	47N	28E
Västerås: Sweden	69	60N	17E
Väster Dal: *r.*, Swed.	69	61N	13E
Västervik: Sweden	69	58N	17E
Vatican City: Italy	67	42N	12½E
Vatnajökull: Iceland	68	64N	17W
Vätter, L.: Sweden	69	58N	14E
Vaupés: *r.*, Col.	48	1N	71W
Växjö: Sweden	69	57N	15E
Vaygach I.: U.S.S.R.	80	70N	59E
Vega: & *i.*, Norway	68	66N	12E
Velbert: Germany	62	51¼N	7E
Velikiye Luki: U.S.S.R.	82	56N	31E
Vellore: India	88	13N	79E
Velmandois: France	70	50N	3E
Velp: Netherlands	72	52N	6E
Venado Tuerto: Argentina	49	34S	62W
Vendée: France	71	47N	1W
Vendôme: France	70	48N	1E
Venetian Alps: Italy	73	46N	13E
Venetie: U.S.A.	28	67N	146W
Venezia: & *reg.*, It.	73	46N	12E
VENEZUELA: *cap.* Caracas	48	7N	65W
Venezuela, Gulf of: Venezuela	47	11N	71W
Venice: & *gulf*, Italy	73	45N	12E
Venlo: Netherlands	72	51N	6E
Ventimiglia: Italy	73	44N	8E
Ventspils: U.S.S.R.	82	57N	22E
Veracruz: Mexico	38	19N	96W
Verde: *r.*, U.S.A.	42	34N	112W
Verde, C.: Senegal	106	15N	17W
Verdigris: *r.*, U.S.A.	43	38N	96W
Verdon: *r.*, France	71	44N	6E
Verdun: France	70	49N	5E
Vereeniging: S. Afr.	109	26S	28E
Verkhoyansk: U.S.S.R.	81	68N	134E
Verkhoyansk Range: U.S.S.R.	81	65N	130E
Vermilion L.: U.S.A.	43	48N	93W
Vermillion: *r.*, U.S.A.	43	44N	97W
Vermont: *State*, U.S.A.	17	44N	73W
Vernal: U.S.A.	42	40N	110W
Vernon: U.S.A.	43	34N	99W
Verona: Italy	73	45N	11E
Versailles: France	70	49N	2E
Verviers: Belgium	70	51N	6E
Vesle: *r.*, France	70	49N	4E
Vesoul: France	71	48N	6E
Vesterålen: *i.*, Nor.	68	69N	15E
Vest Fiord: Norway	68	68N	15E
Vesuvius: *volc.*, Italy	67	41N	15E
Veszprém: Hungary	66	47N	18E
Vevey: Switzerland	73	46N	7E
Viareggio: Italy	73	44N	10E
Viborg: Denmark	69	56N	9E
Vicenza: Italy	73	46N	11E
Vichy: France	71	46N	3E
Vicksburg: U.S.A.	40	32N	91W
Victoria: Hong Kong	89	22N	114E
Victoria: *r.*, Austl.	96	16S	130E
Victoria: *State*, Austl.	99	37S	145E
Victoria: U.S.A.	40	29N	97W
Victoria Falls: Rhod.	109	18S	26E
Victoria, L.: Africa	108	1S	33E
Victoria West: South Africa	109	31S	23E
Vidin: Bulgaria	67	44N	23E
Viella: Spain	71	43N	6E
VIENNA: Austria	66	48N	16E
Vienne: France	71	46N	5E
Vienne: *r.*, France	71	47N	1E
VIENTIANE: Laos	91	18N	103E
Viersen: Germany	62	51¼N	6½E
Vierzon-Ville: Fr.	71	47N	2E
Vigevano: Italy	73	45N	9E
Vigo: Spain	65	42N	9W
Vijarawada: India	88	16N	81E
Vikna: *i.*, Norway	68	65N	11E
Vila de João Bela: Mozambique	109	25S	34E
Vilaine: *r.*, France	70	48N	2W
Vileyka: U.S.S.R.	67	54N	27E
Villa Cabral: Mozambique	109	13S	35E
Villach: Austria	73	47N	14E
VILLA CISNEROS: Spanish Sahara	106	24N	16W
Villa Park: U.S.A.	31	42N	88W
Villefranche-sur-Saône: France	71	46N	5E
Villeneuve-sur-Lot: France	71	44N	1E
Villeurbanne: France	71	46N	5E
Vilnius: U.S.S.R.	82	55N	25E
Viña del Mar: Chile	49	33S	72W
Vincennes: U.S.A.	41	39N	88W
Vindel: *r.*, Sweden	68	65N	18E
Vindhya R.: India	88	23N	77E
Vineland: U.S.A.	41	39N	75W
Vinh: N. Viet Nam	91	19N	106E
Vinnitsa: U.S.S.R.	82	49N	28E
Vire: France	70	49N	1W
Virgin: *r.*, U.S.A.	42	37N	114W
Virginia: *State*, U.S.A.	41	37N	78W
Virginia: U.S.A.	43	48N	93W
Virgin Is.: W. Indies	47	18N	65W
Virovitica: Yugo.	66	46N	17E
Visakhapatnam: India	88	18N	83E
Visalia: U.S.A.	42	36N	119W
Visby: Sweden	69	58N	18E
Viseu: Portugal	65	41N	8W
Vistula: *r.*, Poland	66	53N	19E
Vitebsk: U.S.S.R.	82	55N	30E
Viti Levu: *i.*, Pac. O.	100	18S	178E
Vitim: & *r.*, U.S.S.R.	81	60N	113E
Vitória: Brazil	48	20S	40W
Vitoria: Spain	65	43N	3W
Vitry-en-Artois: Fr.	70	50N	3E
Vitry-le-François: Fr.	70	49N	5E
Vittoria Veneto: It.	73	46N	12E
Vizianagaram: India	88	18N	83E
Vladimir: U.S.S.R.	82	56N	40E
Vladivostok: U.S.S.R.	81	43N	132E
Vlissingen *see* Flushing			
Vlonë: Albania	67	40N	20E
Vltava: *r.*, Czech.	66	50N	14E
Voerde: Germany	62	51½N	6¾E
Vogeikop Penin.: West Irian	96	2S	132E
Voiron: France	71	45N	6E
Volga: *r.*, U.S.S.R.	82	50N	45E
Volga Hills: U.S.S.R.	82	51N	45E
Volgograd: U.S.S.R.	82	49N	45E
Volkovysk: U.S.S.R.	66	53N	24E
Volmarstein: Ger.	62	51½N	7½E
Vologda: U.S.S.R.	82	59N	40E
Volos: Greece	67	39N	23E
Vol'sk: U.S.S.R.	82	52N	47E
Volta Redonda: Braz.	50	23S	44W
Vorarlberg: *Prov.*, Austria	73	47N	10E
Vorkuta: U.S.S.R.	80	67N	64E
Voronezh: U.S.S.R.	82	52N	39E
Vosges: *mtns.*, Fr.	70	48N	7E
Voss: Norway	69	61N	6E
Vranje: Yugoslavia	67	43N	22E
Vratsa: Bulgaria	67	43N	24E
Vryburg: S. Africa	109	27S	25E
Vulcano: *i.*, Italy	67	38N	15E
Vyaz'ma: U.S.S.R.	82	55N	34E
Vyborg: U.S.S.R.	82	61N	29E
Vyshniy-Volochek: U.S.S.R.	82	58N	35E
Waal: *r.*, Neth.	72	52N	5E
Wabash: *r.*, U.S.A.	41	38N	88W
Waccasassa Bay: U.S.A.	41	29N	83W
Waco: U.S.A.	43	32N	97W
Wadden Zee: Neth.	72	53N	5E
Wadena: U.S.A.	43	46N	95W
Wadi el Milk: *r.*, Sudan	84	17N	30E
Wadi Halfa: Sudan	107	22N	31E
Wad Medani: Sudan	107	14N	34E
Wagga Wagga: Austl.	99	35S	147E
Wagin: Australia	98	33S	117E
Wahpeton: U.S.A.	43	46N	97W
Waiau: & *r.*, N.Z.	93	43S	173E
Waigeo: *i.*, W. Irian	91	0	131E
Waikaremoana, L.: N.Z.	93	39S	177E
Waikato: & *r.*, N.Z.	93	38S	176E
Waikerie: Australia	99	34S	140E
Waingapu: Indon.	91	10S	120E
Waipara: N.Z.	93	43S	173E
Waipawa: N.Z.	93	40S	177E
Wairau: *r.*, N.Z.	93	41S	174E
Wairoa: N.Z.	93	39S	177E
Waitaki: *r.*, N.Z.	93	45S	171E
Waitangi: N.Z.	93	35S	174E
Waitara: N.Z.	93	39S	174E
Wakamatsu: Japan	92	37N	140E
Wakasa Bay: Japan	92	36N	136E
Wakatipu, L.: N.Z.	93	45S	168E
Wakayama: Japan	92	34N	135E
WaKeeney: U.S.A.	43	39N	100W
Wakefield: England	54	54N	1W
Wakefield: U.S.A.	31	42½N	71W
Wakefield, Mt.: Antarctica	51	69S	64W
Wake I.: Pac. O.	100	20N	167E
Wakkanai: Japan	92	45N	142E
Walcheren: *i.*, Neth.	72	51N	4E
WALES: *cap.* Cardiff	55	—	—
Walgett: Australia	99	30S	148E
Walgreen Coast: Antarctica	51	73S	112W
Wallachia: *Old Reg.*, Romania	67	44N	25E
Wallaroo: Australia	99	34S	137E
Wallasey: England	57	53½N	3W
Walla Walla: U.S.A.	42	46N	118W
Wallingford: Eng.	57	51½N	1W
Wallis Is.: Pac. O.	100	13S	176W
Walsall: England	57	52½N	2W
Walsenburg: U.S.A.	43	38N	105W
Waltham: U.S.A.	31	42½N	71¼W
Waltham Abbey: England	57	51¾N	0
Walton: England	57	51½N	½W
Waltrop: Germany	62	51¾N	7½E
Walvis Bay: S. Afr.	109	23S	14E
Wanaaring: Australia	99	30S	144E
Wanaka, L.: N.Z.	93	44S	169E
Wandiwash: India	88	13N	80E
Wandsworth: Eng.	57	51½N	¼W
Wanganui: & *r.*, New Zealand	93	40S	175E
Wangaratta: Austl.	99	36S	146E
Wangeroog: *i.*, Ger.	72	54N	8E
Wanhsien: China	89	31N	109E
Wankie: Rhodesia	109	18S	26E
Wanne-Eickel: Ger.	62	51½N	7¼E
Wantagh: U.S.A.	31	40¾N	73½W
Warangal: India	88	18N	80E
Ware: England	57	51¾N	0
Warmbad: S.W. Afr.	109	28S	19E
Warminster: Eng.	55	51N	2W
Warracknabeal: Australia	99	36S	142E
Warragul: Australia	99	38S	146E
Warrego: *r.*, Austl.	98	28S	146E
Warren: Idaho, U.S.A.	42	45N	116W
Warren: Michigan, U.S.A.	31	42½N	83W
Warren: Minn., U.S.A.	43	48N	97W
Warren: Ohio, U.S.A.	41	41N	81W
Warren: Pa., U.S.A.	41	42N	79W
Warrenpoint: N. Ireland	56	54N	6W
Warrington: Eng.	57	53½N	2½W
Warrnambool: Australia	99	38S	143E
Warroad: U.S.A.	43	49N	95W
WARSAW (Warszawa): Poland	66	52N	21E
Warwick: Australia	98	28S	152E
Warwick: & *Co.*, England	57	52N	2W
Warwick: U.S.A.	17	42N	72W
Wash, The: *bay*, England	55	53N	0
Washington: Eng.	54	55N	1½W
Washington: Ind., U.S.A.	41	39N	87W
Washington: N.C., U.S.A.	41	36N	77W
Washington: *State*, U.S.A.	42	47N	120W
Washington, D.C.: U.S.A.	41	39N	77W
Washington, Mt.: U.S.A.	17	44N	71W
Waterbury: U.S.A.	17	42N	73W
Waterford: & *Co.*, R. of Ireland	56	52N	7W
Waterloo: Belgium	70	51N	4E
Waterloo: U.S.A.	43	42N	92W
Waterloo Glacier Int. Peace Park: Canada/U.S.A.	42	49N	114W
Watertown: N.Y., U.S.A.	17	44N	76W
Watertown: S. Dak., U.S.A.	43	45N	97W
Waterville: U.S.A.	13	45N	70W
Watford: England	57	51¾N	½W
Watling *see* San Salvador I.			
Watlington: England	57	51¾N	1W
Wattenscheid: Ger.	62	51½N	7¼E
Wattonville: U.S.A.	42	37N	122W
Wau: Sudan	107	7N	27E
Waukegan: U.S.A.	31	42¼N	87¾W
Waukesha: U.S.A.	31	43N	88W
Wausau: U.S.A.	43	45N	90W
Wauwatosa: U.S.A.	31	43N	88W
Waxahachie: U.S.A.	43	32N	97W
Waycross: U.S.A.	41	31N	83W
Wayne: U.S.A.	31	41N	74¼W
Waynesboro: U.S.A.	67	38N	79W
Weald, The: Eng.	55	51N	0
Weaverville: U.S.A.	42	41N	123W
Webster: U.S.A.	31	42N	71¾W
Weddell Sea: Antarctica	51	72S	40W
Wednesbury: Eng.	57	52½N	2W
Wednesfield: Eng.	57	52½N	2W
Weed: U.S.A.	42	41N	122W
Weiden: Germany	72	50N	12E
Weifang: China	89	37N	118E
Weihaiwei: China	89	38N	122E
Weimar: Germany	72	51N	11E
Weirton: U.S.A.	41	41N	81W
Weiser: U.S.A.	42	44N	117W
Weisshorn: *mtn.*, Switzerland	73	46N	8E
Welkon: S. Africa	109	27S	27E
Welland: *r.*, Eng.	57	52½N	¼W
Wellesley Is.: Austl.	96	17S	139E
Wellesley: U.S.A.	31	42¼N	71¼W
Wellingborough: England	55	52N	1W
Wellington: Austl.	99	32S	149E
Wellington: England	57	53N	3W
WELLINGTON: N.Z.	93	41S	175E
Wells: U.S.A.	42	41N	115W
Welper: Germany	62	51½N	7¼E
Welshpool: Wales	57	53N	3W
Welwyn: England	57	51¾N	¼W
Wem: England	55	53N	3W
Wembley: England	57	52N	0
Wenatchee: U.S.A.	42	47N	121W
Wenchow: China	89	28N	121E
Wendover: U.S.A.	42	41N	114W
Wenlock Edge: Eng.	57	52½N	2¾W
Wensum: *r.*, Eng.	55	53N	1E
Wentworth: Austl.	99	34S	141E
Wernigerode: Ger.	72	52N	11E
Wesel: Germany	62	51¾N	6½E
Weser: *r.*, Germany	72	53N	9E
Wesergebirge: *mts.*, Germany	72	52N	9E
West Allis: U.S.A.	31	43N	88W
West Bengal: *State*, India	88	23N	87E
West Bromwich: England	57	52½N	2W

	Page	Lat.	Long.
West Dvina: *r.*, U.S.S.R.	**82**	56N	28E
Westerham: Eng.	**57**	51½N	0
Westerholt: Ger.	**62**	51½N	7E
Western Australia: *State*, Australia	**96**	25S	120E
Western Desert: Egypt	**84**	27N	27E
Western Ghats: *range*, India	**88**	15N	75E
Western Sayan Mts.: U.S.S.R.	**83**	52N	91E
Western Sierra Madre: *range*, Mexico	**38**	26N	106W
Westerwald: *mts.*, Germany	**72**	51N	8E
Westfield: U.S.A.	**31**	40¾N	74¼W
West Hartlepool: England	**54**	55N	1W
West Indies	**47**	—	—
West Irian: Indonesia	**96**	5S	137E
Westland: N.Z.	**93**	43S	171E
Westland: U.S.A.	**31**	42½N	83¼W
West Lothian: *Co.*, Scotland	**54**	56N	4W
Westmeath: *Co.*, R. of Ireland	**56**	53N	8W
Westminster: Eng.	**57**	51½N	0
Westmorland: *Co.*, England	**54**	54N	3W
W. New York: U.S.A.	**31**	40¾N	74W
Weston: Sabah	**91**	5S	116E
Weston-super-Mare: England	**55**	51N	3W
West Orange: U.S.A.	**31**	40¾N	74¼W
West Pakistan:	**88**	30N	70E
West Palm Beach: U.S.A.	**41**	27N	80W
Westphalia: Ger.	**72**	52N	7E
Westport: N.Z.	**93**	42S	172E
Westport: R. of Ireland	**56**	54N	10W
Westport: U.S.A.	**31**	41½N	73¼W
West Riding: Eng.	**54**	54N	2W
West Rift Valley: Africa	**108**	0	30E
West Siberian Plain: U.S.S.R.	**83**	60N	73E
West University Place: U.S.A.	**31**	29¾N	95½W
West Virginia: *State*, U.S.A.	**41**	38N	80W
Westwood: U.S.A.	**42**	40N	121W
Wetar: *i.*, Indonesia	**91**	7S	126E
Wetzlar: Germany	**72**	51N	9E
Wexford: & *Co.*, & *bay*, R. of Irel.	**56**	52N	6W
Wey: *r.*, England	**57**	51N	1W
Weymouth: England	**57**	51N	2W
Weymouth: U.S.A.	**31**	42¼N	71W
Whakatane: N.Z.	**93**	38S	177E
Whales, Bay of: Antarctica	**51**	78S	165W
Whangarei: N.Z.	**93**	36S	174E
Wharfe: *r.*, England	**54**	54N	1W
Wheaton: U.S.A.	**31**	41¾N	88W
Wheeler L.: U.S.A.	**41**	35N	87W
Wheeling: U.S.A.	**41**	40N	81W
Whipsnade: England	**57**	51¾N	½W
Whitby: England	**54**	54N	1W
Whitchurch: Eng.	**55**	53N	3W
White: *r.*, Arkansas, U.S.A.	**43**	35N	91W
White: *r.*, Indiana, U.S.A.	**41**	39N	87W
White: *r.*, S. Dak., U.S.A.	**43**	44N	100W
Whitefield: Austl.	**99**	37S	146E
Whitefish: U.S.A.	**42**	48N	115W
Whitehead: N. Irel.	**56**	55N	6W
White Nile (Bahr el Jebel): *r.*, Sudan	**107**	7N	31E
White Plains: U.S.A.	**31**	41N	73¾W
White Sea: U.S.S.R.	**80**	65N	37E
White Volta: *r.*, West Africa	**106**	12N	2W
Whitley Bay: Eng.	**54**	55N	1½W
Whitney, Mt.: U.S.A.	**42**	37N	118W
Whitstable: England	**57**	51½N	1E
Whitsunday I.: Australia	**98**	20S	149E
Whyalla: Australia	**99**	33S	138E
Wichita: U.S.A.	**43**	38N	97W
Wichita: *r.*, U.S.A.	**43**	34N	100W
Wichita Falls: *city*, U.S.A.	**43**	34N	98W
Wick: Scotland	**53**	58N	3W
Wicklow: & *Co.*, R. of Ireland	**56**	53N	6W
Wicklow Head: R. of Ireland	**56**	53N	6W
Wicklow Mts.: R. of Ireland	**56**	53N	6W
Widnes: England	**57**	53½N	2¾W
Wiener-Neustadt: Austria	**66**	48N	16E
Wiesbaden: Ger.	**72**	50N	8E
Wigan: England	**57**	53½N	2¾W
Wight, I. of: Eng.	**55**	51N	1W
Wigtown: Scotland	**53**	55N	4W
Wigtown Bay: Scot.	**54**	54N	4W
Wilcannia: Australia	**99**	32S	143E
Wilhelmshaven: Ger.	**72**	54N	8E
Wilkes-Barre: U.S.A.	**41**	41N	76W
Wilkes Coast: Antarctica	**51**	67S	134E
Wilkes Land: Antarctica	**51**	71S	120E
Willamette: *r.*, U.S.A.	**42**	45N	123W
Willemstad: Curaçao	**47**	12N	69W
Willenhall: England	**57**	52½N	2W
Williamson: U.S.A.	**41**	37N	82W
Williamson Head: Antarctica	**51**	67S	160E
Williamsport: U.S.A.	**41**	41N	77W
Willich: Germany	**62**	51¼N	6½E
Williston: U.S.A.	**43**	48N	104W
Willmar: U.S.A.	**43**	45N	95W
Willoughby, Cape: Australia	**99**	36S	138E
Wilmette: U.S.A.	**31**	42N	87¾W
Wilmington: Del., U.S.A.	**41**	40N	75W
Wilmington: N.C., U.S.A.	**41**	34N	78W
Wilmslow: England	**57**	53½N	2¼W
Wilson: U.S.A.	**41**	36N	78W
Wiltshire: *Co.*, Eng.	**55**	51N	2W
Wiluna: Australia	**96**	27S	120E
Winchester: England	**55**	51N	1W
Winchester: Ky., U.S.A.	**41**	38N	84W
Winchester: Va., U.S.A.	**41**	39N	78W
Windermere: *l.*, England	**54**	54N	3W
Windhoek: S.W. Africa	**109**	22S	17E
Wind River Range: U.S.A.	**42**	43N	110W
Windsor: England	**57**	51N	0
Windward Is.: W. Indies	**47**	13N	62W
Windward Passage: Cuba/Haiti	**47**	20N	73W
Winfield: U.S.A.	**43**	37N	97W
Winnemucca: & *l.*, U.S.A.	**42**	41N	118W
Winner: U.S.A.	**43**	43N	100W
Winnibago, L.: U.S.A.	**43**	44N	88W
Winona: U.S.A.	**41**	33N	90W
Winslow: U.S.A.	**42**	35N	111W
Winston-Salem: U.S.A.	**41**	36N	80W
Winter Haven: U.S.A.	**41**	28N	82W
Winterthur: Switz.	**73**	48N	9E
Winton: Australia	**67**	22S	143E
Wirral: *pen.*, Eng.	**57**	53½N	3W
Wisbech: England	**57**	53N	0
Wishaw: Scotland	**54**	55¾N	4W
Wisconsin: *State*, U.S.A.	**43**	45N	90W
Wisconsin Rapids: U.S.A.	**43**	44N	90W
Wismar: Germany	**72**	54N	11E
Witbank: S. Africa	**109**	26S	29E
Witdraai: S. Africa	**109**	27S	21E
Witney: England	**55**	52N	2W
Witten: Germany	**62**	51½N	7¼E
Wittenberge: Ger.	**72**	53N	12E
Wittlaer: Germany	**62**	57¼N	6¾E
Włocławek: Poland	**66**	52N	19E
Woburn: U.S.A.	**31**	42½N	71W
Wöhlthat Massif: Antarctica	**51**	73S	12E
Woking: England	**57**	51N	1W
Wolf: *r.*, U.S.A.	**43**	45N	89W
Wolfenbüttel: Ger.	**72**	52N	10E
Wolf Rock: Eng.	**55**	50N	6W
Wolfsburg: Germany	**72**	52N	11E
Wollongong: Austl.	**99**	34S	151E
Wolverhampton: England	**57**	53N	2W
Wolverton: England	**55**	52N	1W
Wonsan: N. Korea	**90**	39N	127E
Wonthaggi: Austl.	**99**	38S	146E
Woodland: U.S.A.	**42**	39N	122W
Woodville: N.Z.	**93**	40S	176E
Woodville: U.S.A.	**43**	31N	94W
Woodward: U.S.A.	**43**	36N	99W
Woomera: Australia	**96**	31S	137E
Woonsocket: U.S.A.	**31**	42N	71½W
Worcester: & *Co.*, England	**57**	52N	2W
Worcester: S. Africa	**109**	34S	20E
Worcester: U.S.A.	**31**	42N	73W
Workington: Eng.	**54**	55N	3W
Worksop: England	**57**	53N	1W
Worms: Germany	**72**	50N	8E
Worms Hd.: Wales	**55**	52N	4W
Worth: U.S.A.	**31**	41¾N	87¾W
Worthing: England	**55**	51N	0
Wrangell: U.S.A.	**22**	56N	132W
Wrath, C.: Scotland	**53**	59N	5W
Wrekin, The: Eng.	**57**	52¾N	2½W
Wrexham: Wales	**57**	53N	3W
Wrigley G.: Antarc.	**51**	73S	129W
Wrocław: Poland	**66**	51N	17E
Wrotham: England	**57**	51½N	¼E
Wuchow: China	**89**	23N	111E
Wuhan: China	**89**	30N	115E
Wuhsi: China	**89**	32N	120E
Wuhu: China	**89**	31N	118E
Wülfrath: Germany	**62**	51¼N	7E
Wuppertal: Ger.	**62**	51¼N	7¼E
Würzburg: Ger.	**72**	50N	10E
Wusong: China	**90**	31½N	121½E
Wutungkiao: China	**89**	30N	104E
Wuyi Shan: *mtns.*, China	**89**	27N	117E
Wyalong: Australia	**99**	34S	147E
Wyandotte: U.S.A.	**31**	42¼N	83¼W
Wyangala Res.: Australia	**99**	34S	149E
Wye: *r.*, England	**57**	52N	3W
Wyndham: Austl.	**96**	15S	128E
Wyoming: *State*, U.S.A.	**42**	43N	107W
Xanthi: Greece	**67**	41N	25E
Xauen: Morocco	**65**	35N	5W
Xingu: *r.*, Brazil	**48**	7S	53W
Yaan: China	**89**	30N	103E
Yakima: & *r.*, U.S.A.	**42**	47N	120W
Yakuta: & *bay*, U.S.A.	**28**	60N	140W
Yakutsk: U.S.S.R.	**81**	62N	130E
Yallourn: Australia	**99**	38S	146E
Yalta: U.S.S.R.	**82**	45N	34E
Yamagata: Japan	**92**	38N	140E
Yamal Peninsula: U.S.S.R.	**80**	70N	70E
Yamatu: China	**83**	46N	84E
Yama Yama, L.: Australia	**98**	26S	141E
Yambol: Bulgaria	**67**	42N	27E
Yampa: *r.*, U.S.A.	**42**	40N	108W
Yampi Sound: Austl.	**96**	16S	123E
Yamuna: *r.*, India	**88**	25N	81E
Yanbu: Sa'udi Arabia	**85**	24N	38E
Yangchuan: China	**89**	38N	113E
Yangku: China	**90**	38N	113E
Yangtze: *r.*, China	**89**	31N	117E
Yannina: Greece	**67**	40N	21E
Yantabulla: Austl.	**99**	29S	145E
YAOUNDÉ: Cameroon	**106**	4N	11E
Yap: *i.*, Pac. O.	**100**	10N	138E
Yaraka: Australia	**97**	25S	144E
Yarkand: & *r.*, China	**87**	38N	77E
Yaroslavl': U.S.S.R.	**82**	58N	40E
Yarra: *r.*, Australia	**99**	38S	145E
Yass: Australia	**99**	35S	149E
Yawata: Japan	**92**	34N	131E
Yazd: Iran	**85**	32N	54E
Yazoo City: & *r.*, U.S.A.	**43**	33N	90W
Yellow Sea: China	**89**	35N	122E
Yellowstone: *l.* & *Nat. Park*, U.S.A.	**42**	45N	111W
Yellowstone: *r.*, U.S.A.	**42**	46N	108W
YEMEN A.R.: *cap.* San'a	**85**	15N	44E
YEMEN P.D.R. (S. YEMEN): *cap.* Madinet as Shaab			
Yenakiyevo: U.S.S.R.	**82**	48N	38E
Yenangyaung: Burma	**90**	20N	95E
Yencheng: China	**89**	34N	120E
Yenisey: *r.*, U.S.S.R.	**85**	59N	91E
Yenisey, Gulf of: U.S.S.R.	**81**	72N	83E
Yeniseysk: U.S.S.R.	**83**	58N	92E
Yeovil: England	**55**	51N	3W
Yerevan: U.S.S.R.	**82**	40N	44E
Yeysk: U.S.S.R.	**82**	46N	38E
Yinchwan: China	**89**	38N	106E
Yingkow: China	**89**	40N	122E
Yin Shan: China	**87**	42N	108E
Yokkaichi: Japan	**92**	35N	137E
Yokohama: Japan	**92**	35N	140E
Yokosuka: Japan	**92**	35N	140E
Yonkers: U.S.A.	**31**	41N	74W
Yonne: *r.*, France	**70**	48N	3E
York: & *Co.*, Eng.	**54**	54N	1W
York, Cape: Austl.	**96**	11S	143E
York: Nebr., U.S.A.	**43**	41N	98W
York: Pa., U.S.A.	**41**	40N	77W
Yorke Penin.: Austl.	**99**	35S	138E
Yoshkar-Ola: U.S.S.R.	**82**	57N	48E
Youghal: R. of Irel.	**56**	52N	8W
Young: Australia	**99**	34S	148E
Young I.: Antarc.	**51**	66S	163E
Youngstown: U.S.A.	**41**	41N	81W
Ypres: Belgium	**70**	51N	3E
Yreka: U.S.A.	**42**	42N	123W
Yuan: *r.*, China	**89**	29N	110E
Yuba City: U.S.A.	**42**	39N	122W
Yucatan: Mexico	**38**	20N	88W
Yucatan Channel: Mexico/Cuba	**39**	22N	86W
YUGOSLAVIA: *cap.* Belgrade	**67**	44N	20E
Yukagir Plateau: U.S.S.R.	**81**	66N	157E
Yukon: *r.*, Canada/U.S.A.	**2**	63N	159W
Yulin: China	**89**	38N	109E
Yuma: U.S.A.	**42**	33N	115W
Yungera: Australia	**99**	35S	143E
Yungning: China	**89**	23N	108E
Yunkwei Plat.: China	**89**	27N	106E
Yunnan: *Prov.*, China	**89**	25N	103E
Yverdon: Switz.	**73**	47N	7E
Zabol: Iran	**85**	31N	62E
Zabrze: Poland	**66**	50N	19E
Zacatecas: Mexico	**38**	23N	103W
Zadar: Yugoslavia	**67**	44N	15E
Zagreb: Yugoslavia	**66**	46N	16E
Zagros Mts.: Iran	**85**	32N	50E
Zāhedān: Iran	**85**	29N	61E
Zakinthos: *i.*, Greece	**67**	38N	21E
Zălău: Romania	**66**	47N	23E
Zambezi: *r.*, S. Afr.	**109**	16S	31E
ZAMBIA: *cap.* Lusaka	**109**	—	—
Zamboanga: Phil.	**91**	7N	122E
Zamora: Spain	**65**	41N	6W
Zamość: Poland	**66**	51N	23E
Zanesville: U.S.A.	**41**	40N	82W
Zante: *i.* & *town*, Greece	**67**	38N	21E
Zanthus: Australia	**96**	31S	123E
Zanzibar: E. Africa	**108**	6S	39E
Zaporozh'ye: U.S.S.R.	**82**	48N	35E
Zaragoza: Spain	**65**	42N	1W
Zaria: Nigeria	**106**	11N	8E
Zawiercie: Poland	**66**	50N	19E
Zaysan, L.: U.S.S.R.	**83**	48N	84E
Zealand: *i.*, Den.	**69**	56N	12E
Zeebrugge: Belgium	**70**	51N	3E
Zeerust: S. Africa	**109**	26S	26E
Zeila: Somali Rep.	**107**	11N	43E
Zeitz: Germany	**72**	51N	12E
Zella Mehlis: Ger.	**72**	51N	11E
Zemz: *r.*, Libya	**75**	31N	14E
Zermatt: Switz.	**73**	46N	8E
Zeya: U.S.S.R.	**81**	54N	127E
Zezere: *r.*, Portugal	**65**	40N	8W
Zhdanov: U.S.S.R.	**82**	47N	37E
Zhigalovo: U.S.S.R.	**81**	55N	105E
Zhitomir: U.S.S.R.	**82**	50N	29E
Zielona Góra: Pol.	**66**	52N	16E
Zimbabwe: Rhod.	**109**	20S	32E
Zion: U.S.A.	**31**	42½N	87¾W
Zittau: Germany	**72**	51N	15E
Zlatibor: Yugoslavia	**67**	44N	20E
Zlatograd: Bulgaria	**67**	41N	25E
Zlatoust: U.S.S.R.	**83**	55N	60E
Zliten: Libya	**84**	32N	14E
Znojmo: Czech.	**66**	49N	16E
Zomba: Malawi	**109**	15S	35E
Zongo: Congo Rep.	**107**	4N	18E
Zonguldak: Turkey	**84**	41N	32E
Zrenjanin: Yugo.	**67**	45N	20E
Zuara: Libya	**106**	33N	13E
Zug: Switzerland	**73**	47N	8E
Zuider Zee *see* IJsselmeer			
Zuni: *r.*, U.S.A.	**42**	35N	109W
Zürich: & *l.*, Switz.	**73**	47N	8E
Zwickau: Germany	**72**	51N	12E
Zwolle: Neth.	**72**	53N	6E